Studies in the Social and
Cultural Foundations of Language No. 7

Investigating obsolescence

Studies in language contraction and death

Languages die for political, economic and cultural reasons, and can
disappear remarkably quickly. Between ten and fifty per cent of all
languages currently spoken can be considered endangered, but it is only in
the past ten years or so that due importance has been given to the study of
contracting and dying languages. This volume represents the first attempt
to give a broad overview of current research in this developing field, and to
examine some of the crucial methodological and theoretical issues to which
it has given rise. It includes twenty studies by scholars who, taken together,
have worked on a range of languages currently under threat across the
globe. They occur in diverse speech communities where the expanding
languages are not only those that are very familiar – English, Spanish, or
French, for example – but also Swedish, Arabic, Thai, etc. The final part of
the volume is devoted to a consideration of the implications of research
into language obsolescence for other aspects of linguistics and anthropology – first and second language acquisition, historical linguistics, and the
study of pidgins and creoles and of language and social process. As a
whole, this collection will certainly stimulate further and better coordinated research into a topic of direct relevance to sociolinguistics and
anthropological linguistics.

Studies in the Social and Cultural Foundations of Language

The aim of this series is to develop theoretical perspectives on the essential social and cultural character of language by methodological and empirical emphasis on the occurrence of language in its communicative and interactional settings, on the socio-culturally grounded "meanings" and "functions" of linguistic forms, and on the social scientific study of language use across cultures. It will thus explicate the essentially ethnographic nature of linguistic data, whether spontaneously occurring or experi-mentally induced, whether normative or variational, whether synchronic or diachronic. Works appearing in the series will make substantive and theoretical contributions to the debate over the sociocultural–functional and structural–formal nature of language, and will represent the concerns of scholars in the sociology and anthropology of language, anthropological linguistics, sociolinguistics, and socioculturally informed psycholinguistics.

1. Charles L. Briggs: *Learning how to ask: a sociolinguistic appraisal of the role of the interview in social science research*

2. Tamar Katriel: *Talking straight: Dugri speech in Israeli Sabra culture*

3. Bambi B. Schieffelin and Elinor Ochs (eds.): *Language socialization across cultures*

4. Susan U. Philips, Susan Steele, and Christine Tanz (eds.): *Language, gender, and sex in comparative perspective*

5. Jeff Siegel: *Language contact in a plantation environment: a sociolinguistic history of Fiji*

6. Elinor Ochs: *Culture and language development: language acquisition and language socialization in a Samoan village*

7. Nancy C. Dorian (ed.): *Investigating obsolescence: studies in language contraction and death*

8. Richard Bauman and Joel Sherzer (eds.): *Explorations in the ethnography of speaking*

9. Bambi B. Schieffelin: *The give and take of everyday life: language socialization of Kaluli children*

10. Francesca Merlan and Alan Rumsey: *Ku Waru: language and segmentary politics in the western Nebilyer valley, Papua New Guinea*

11. Alessandro Duranti and Charles Goodwin (eds.): *Rethinking context: language as an interactive phenomenon*

12. John A. Lucy: *Language diversity and thought: a reformulation of the linguistic relativity hypothesis*

13. John A. Lucy: *Grammatical categories and cognition: a case study of the linguistic relativity hypothesis*

14. Don Kulick: *Language shift and cultural reproduction: socialization, self, and syncretism in a Papua New Guinean village*

15. Jane H. Hill and Judith T. Irvine (eds.): *Responsibility and evidence in oral discourse*

Investigating obsolescence

Studies in language contraction and death

Edited by
Nancy C. Dorian
Professor of Linguistics in German and Anthropology, Bryn Mawr College

CAMBRIDGE
UNIVERSITY PRESS

Published by the Press Syndicate of the University of Cambridge
The Pitt Building, Trumpington Street, Cambridge CB2 1RP
40 West 20th Street, New York, NY 10011-4211, USA
10 Stamford Road, Oakleigh, Victoria 3166, Australia

First published 1989
First paperback edition 1992

British Library cataloguing in publication data

Investigating obsolescence: studies in language contraction and death. –
(Studies in the social and cultural foundations of language; 7).
1. Languages. Contraction.
I. Dorian, Nancy C. II. Series 400

Library of Congress cataloguing in publication data

Investigating obsolescence: studies in language contraction and death
edited by Nancy C. Dorian.
    p.   cm.–(Studies in the social and cultural foundations of language; 7)
Bibliography
Includes indexes.
ISBN 0 521 32405 X (hardback).
ISBN 0 521 43757 1 (paperback).
1. Language obsolescence. I. Dorian, Nancy C. II. Series:
Studies in the social and cultural foundations of language; no. 7.
P40.5.L33I58 1989
401'.9–dc 19   88–18698   CIP

ISBN 0 521 32405 X (hardback)
ISBN 0 521 43757 1 (paperback)

Transferred to digital printing 2001

Contents

II Focus on structure

III Invited commentaries

Discussion from the perspectives of child language and aphasia; of historical linguistics; of social process; of pidgins, creoles and immigrant languages; and of second language acquisition

Contents   vii

Maps

Contributors

Prof. Roger W. Andersen TESL/Applied Linguistics, 3300 Rolfe Hall, University of California, Los Angeles 90024, USA

Dr Edith L. Bavin Division of Linguistics, La Trobe University, Bundoora, Victoria, Australia 3083.

Dr Edouard Beniak 6 Spring Mount, Toronto, Ontario M6H 2YH, Canada

Dr David Bradley Division of Linguistics, La Trobe University, Bundoora, Victoria, Australia 3083

Prof. Lyle Campbell Dept of Geography and Anthropology, Louisiana State University, Baton Rouge, Louisiana 70803-4105, USA

Dr Gerrit J. Dimmendaal Afrikaanse Taalkunde, Rijksuniversiteit te Leiden, Postbus 9515, 2300 RA Leiden, The Netherlands

Prof. Nancy C. Dorian RR 1, Box 704, South Harpswell, ME 04079, USA *or:* Dept of German, Bryn Mawr College, Bryn Mawr, PA 19010, USA

Prof. Susan Gal Dept of Anthropology, Douglass Campus, Rutgers University, New Brunswick, NJ 08903, USA

Prof. Eric P. Hamp Dept of Linguistics, University of Chicago, 1010 East 59th St., Chicago, IL 60637, USA

Dr Einar Haugen 45 Larch Circle, Belmont, MA 02178, USA

Prof. Jane H. Hill Dept of Anthropology, Bldg 30, University of Arizona, Tucson, AZ 85721, USA

Prof. Henry M. Hoenigswald Dept of Linguistics, 618 Williams Hall, University of Pennsylvania, Philadelphia, PA 19104–6305, USA

Prof. Marion Lois Huffines Dept of Modern Languages, Literature, and Linguistics, Bucknell University, Lewisburg, PA 17837, USA

Dr Ruth King Dept of Languages, Literatures, and Linguistics, York University, 4700 Keele St., North York, Ontario M3J 1P3, Canada

Dr Lois Kuter Academy of Natural Sciences, 1900 Benjamin Franklin Parkway, Philadelphia, PA 19103, USA

Ms Katrin Maandi Institutionen för Lingvistik, Stockholms Universitet, S–10691 Stockholm, Sweden

Prof. Lise Menn Dept of Linguistics, University of Colorado, Boulder, CO 80309–0295, USA

Dr Elizabeth Mertz American Bar Association, 750 No. Lake Shore Dr., Chicago, IL, 60611, USA

Prof. Marianne Mithun Dept of Linguistics, University of California, Santa Barbara, CA 93106, USA

Prof. Raymond Mougeon Dept of French Studies, York University, 4700 Keele Street, North York, Ontario M3J 1P3, Canada

Ms Martha C. Muntzel Depto de Lingüistica, INAH, Museo Nal. de Antropologia, Esq. Reforma y Ghandi, 11560 México D.F., Mexico

Prof. Suzanne Romaine Merton College, Oxford University, Oxford OX1 4JD, England

Prof. Aleya Rouchdy Dept of Near Eastern Languages and Literatures, Wayne State University, Detroit, MI 48202, USA

Prof. Allan R. Taylor Dept of Linguistics, Campus Box 295, University of Colorado, Boulder, CO 80309, USA

Dr Lukas D. Tsitsipis Dept of French, Faculty of Philosophy, Aristotle University of Thessaloniki, Thessaloniki, Greece

Dr Seosamh Watson Roinn na Nua-Ghaeilge, An Coláiste Ollscoile, Baile Átha Cliath, Eire/Ireland

Prof. Kathryn A. Woolard Dept of Sociology, University of California San Diego, La Jolla, CA 92093, USA

Preface

This volume came about in response to a need which had become time-consumingly obvious to the editor: people investigating a wide variety of precariously placed speech forms, in geographically diverse locations, were working in ignorance of each other's efforts. A kind of clearinghouse role had fallen to me, simply because I had published a book in a subfield which had no journal or other regular publication outlet, the subfield which had come to be known (for better or worse) as "language death". I was spending increasing amounts of time putting researchers in touch with colleagues whose work was likely to be of interest to them, arduously passing along information on a case-by-case basis. Very late one night I found myself considering alternative solutions to the problem; this volume represents one of those alternatives.

Because of the circumstances in which the volume was conceived, a firm, ongoing part of the enterprise has been intercommunication: dissemination of methodologies, data, ideas, analyses, implications, hypotheses. A set of focus questions (see Introduction) was circulated to all potential contributors to help stimulate thinking along various but shared lines, and a month or so after the target date for first drafts from contributors, each manuscript then in hand was circulated to those who were clearly working on matters of relevance to one another's subject. Contributors were encouraged to correspond with each other and to incorporate crossreferences to each other's papers in their own chapters. All of the internal crossreferencing in this volume arises from authors' perception of what in other papers has special relevance to their own work, not from the editor's perception.

The inclusion of invited commentaries by scholars expert in one or more areas for which the study of language obsolescence might have special value was likewise intended as a form of crossfertilization. The commentator role was intentionally kept as fluid as possible: each commentator received all 20 papers from Parts I and II, with no individual apportionment of responsibility but rather a free hand to treat any material whatever, from any paper, which seemed of interest and particular importance to the commentator's specialty.

All Part I and II contributors were originally offered the choice of writing a single longer paper or two related papers, one longer and one shorter; in case of the latter choice, material more clearly connected with social questions would be presented in one paper and material more clearly connected with questions of linguistic structure would be presented in the other. Although a number of contributors initially chose this option, various considerations eventually led to the unitary choice except in the case of Egyptian Nubian, which Professor Aleya Rouchdy has indeed treated from quite different perspectives in two papers, one in each of the first two parts.

A great deal of good will, cooperation, flexibility, and good nature went into the preparation of this volume. The chapter contributors endured, and responded to cheerfully, a high volume of editorial communication on matters great and small; the commentators tackled their large-scale assignments with seeming relish. Word processing was expertly handled by Hubbard Goodrich of West Harpswell, Maine, invaluably at home with both computers and linguistics. Penny Carter of Cambridge University Press was a model of both efficient and benevolent oversight. Over two fiscal years Bryn Mawr College provided, through its Madge Miller Fund for support of faculty research, the considerable funds which allowed multiple photocopying for circulation of papers among contributors and for whole-text circulation to commentators, as well as funds for word processing. Polly Johnsen spent a generous part of her Maine "vacation" creating the first draft of the Index of Languages. Megan Klose brought order to an untidily stitched bibliography as it approached final amalgamation. David Odell worked far beyond the bounds of simple duty in helping to subdue the copy produced by an editor-indexer with grandiose notions unmatched by her physical capacity. Suzanne Romaine unflinchingly kept to a schedule which foreseeably placed a visit to me at a deadline time in the volume's production when her ability to enter IPA symbols and various diacritics by hand would be heavily drawn upon. Since it was her interest in the project which had brought it to the attention of Cambridge University Press at the outset, her help at manuscript-delivery time was the perfect – literal *and* figurative – finishing touch.

Bryn Mawr College   Nancy C. Dorian
Bryn Mawr, Pennsylvania

South Harpswell
Maine

World map showing main languages discussed in this volume

Canada
1. Ontario Cayuga
2. Welland French
3. Cape Breton Scottish Gaelic
4. Newfoundland French

USA
5. Gros Ventre
6. Pennsylvania German
7. Oklahoma Cayuga
8. Cupeño
   (for Norwegian see p. 66)

Mexico
9. Ocuilteco

10. Malinche-region Mexicano
11. Chiapanec; Southeastern
    Tzeltal; Chicomuceltec;
    Tuxtla Chico Mam

Guatemala
12. Jumaytepeque Xinca;
    Yupiltepeque Xinca;
    Guazacapan; Chiquimulilla
    Xinca

El Salvador
13. Pipil; Cacaopera;
    Salvadoran Lenca

Hondorus
14. Honduran Lenca; Jicaque
    Yoro

British Isles
15. Irish Gaelic
16. Scottish Gaelic

Sweden
17. Swedish Estonian

France
18. Breton

Spain
19. Catalan

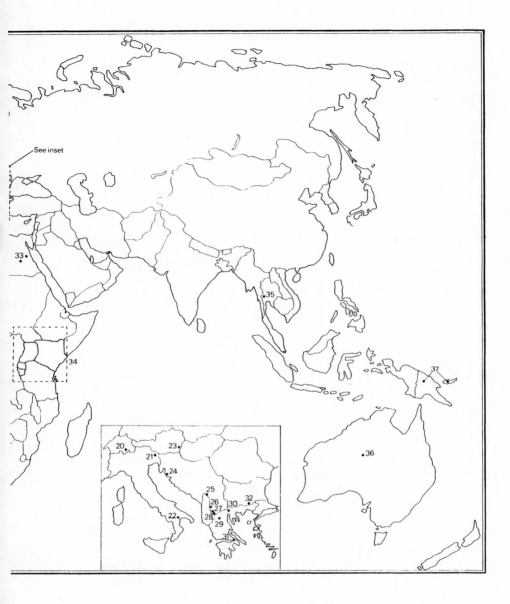

Switzerland
20 Surmeir Romauntsch
Italy
21 Resian (Slovene)
22 Arbresh (Albanian)
Austria
23 Oberwart Hungarian
Yugoslavia
24 Arbanasi Albanian
25 Gusî Albanian
26 Tetovo Albanian
27 Dibrë/Debar Albanian

28 Aromân/Vlašk
Greece
29 Aromân/Koutsovlahiká
30 Màndres Albanian
31 Arvanítika (Albanian)
Bulgaria
32 Mandrìtsa Albanian
Egypt
33 Nubian
Eastern Africa
34 Shaded areas of Sudan,
   Ethiopia, Uganda, Kenya,

Tanzania and Ruanda
Burundi: numerous Nilo-
Saharan languages, some
Afro-Asiatic, and some
Niger-Kordofanian languages
Thailand
35 Ugong
Australia
36 Warlpiri
Papua New Guinea
37 Tok Pisin

Most of us feel that we could never become extinct. The Dodo felt that way, too.

Will Cuppy, *How to become extinct*

Introduction

During the preparation of this volume, a participant suggested that the resulting collection might represent a "state of the art" milestone roughly comparable to Wanner and Gleitman's (1982) *Language acquisition* volume. Looking closely at that suggestion is perhaps a little dispiriting, but it's also revealing.

The subfield of child language is designated as foremost specialty by a fair number of linguists these days. There are at least two journals (*The Journal of Child Language, First Language*) devoted to the subject, and there are well-established annual conferences, in addition to special sessions, workshops, and so forth, at larger meetings. Researchers in child language have enough recognized outlets and enough predictably scheduled get-togethers so that they can identify one another and exchange findings and ideas with relative ease and speed. The impulse for this volume was the lack of those things (as yet) in the field of language obsolescence.

Few of the contributors to the first two parts of this book would identify themselves as specialists in some one particular area which this volume could be said to be devoted to. There is even some difficulty in locating any such area: "obsolescence", "contraction", and "death" all fall short of a precise (perhaps even an acceptable) rubric; see especially the commentaries, but various authors in Parts I and II wrestle with this problem as well. Not only is there uncertainty about the designation of the field, but in addition other terminological uncertainties hamper communication among researchers. This is not an area of inquiry in which many useful measuring devices have yet been discerned; we have no ordered measure of progression comparable, say, to the Mean Length of Utterance (to retain the analogy to the field of child language) and overall time measurement is itself entangled with the unresolved definitions of such things as "full fluency" and "extinction" (one can't establish a particular speech form as being at "extinction minus 20 years", for example). Campbell and Muntzel's chapter offers a catalog of terms sometimes applied to less-than-full capacity at the low end of the proficiency continuum in what they (helpfully) designate "gradual death"; the profusion of terms is dismaying. But lack of enough distinct terms is a problem, too. "Bilingual" describes nearly all of the populations focused on

1

in this volume: even when modified by additional phrases such as "high proficiency", "near-passive", "___-dominant", "receptively intact" (etc.), the word is inadequate to distinguish among those who can understand a language but not speak it; dredge up a few fossilized expressions and/or some lexical items; say the little they can say in socially appropriate but linguistically flawed fashion; say little in flawed linguistic fashion but socially inappropriately as well; speak readily at some length but with many and obvious deviations from the conservative norm; speak easily in a strikingly modified "young people's" version of an ancestral tongue; be conservative in lexicon but not in phonology or morphology; be conservative in phonology but not in morphology or lexicon; speak in a fashion different from their age-mates an ancestral tongue in which they were once fully fluent but which they have latterly had almost no occasion to use; and so on through the nearly limitless possibilities of combination and recombination of capacities.

Because of the immaturity of this area of investigation, comparisons are still extraordinarily difficult to make. There is good reason to suspect, as Romaine suggests in the first section of her commentary, that "researchers may fail to identify similarities among dying languages . . . [because] they are comparing entities which are not at comparable stages of development". What seemed an unmet need for sets of data which would carry a single investigator's assumptions, methodologies, and interpretive perspectives across at least two populations prompted a noticeable tilt toward the inclusion in this volume of researchers who have themselves worked with more than one population. Obvious examples are Watson, Rouchdy, Mertz, Hill, Huffines, Mithun, and the more geographically sweeping studies such as Dimmendaal's, Campbell and Muntzel's, and Hamp's. Some other papers have a less immediately obvious comparative basis: Bradley reports on four different villages; Tsitsipis draws his data from two villages, although the source-village differences are not at issue in this particular paper; Mougeon and Beniak's study of Welland French gains much resonance from the fact that they have studied a good many other Ontarian French locales as well.

Beset as it is by definitional indeterminacies and terminological non-comparabilities, the study of language obsolescence (for want of a better term) is nevertheless clearly growing in sophistication as the number of studies increases. This research area has always represented something of a refusal to leave out of account what seemed to be imperfect (i.e. to be a lesser example of something else). The earlier view that a contracting language was unworthy of study because "corrupt", "broken-down", "deviant" (all from the point of view of former norms or from that of standard-language norms) has by now almost been stood on its head. The very deviance which was off-putting at one time is what we look to now for clues to organizational principles in language and in cognition generally.

The "errors" of imperfect speakers may also be indications of an active and innovative language-processing capacity (Gal); heavy lexical borrowing from a language of wider currency may prove characteristic not just of shift-prone speakers (Haugen) but also – even especially, under some conditions – of stably bilingual speakers (Hamp, Huffines). Structural contraction does not necessarily reduce the social power or utility of a language (Mertz, Hill).

Matters which might at one time have seemed relatively straightforward prove to require considerable investigative care, nowhere more than in minority speech communities. As ethnographers a few decades ago confronted more difficult and ambiguous postmarital residence rules than they thought likely (Goodenough 1956), linguists confront "ethnoglottic" identities of challenging complexity. The intricacies of tribal identity noted by Taylor (see his discussion of the "blood quantum rule" and the arbitrariness of enrollment as Gros Ventre or Assiniboine on the Fort Belknap Indian reservation) is matched in other areas where Aboriginal populations have been settled and resettled in districts set aside for them. Donaldson (1985) traces four different locations, all within the twentieth century, for the Ngiyambaa of New South Wales, Australia; in all three of the settlement locations (that is, clustered habitation as opposed to traditional camping-ground territory) there were speakers of other Aboriginal languages present as well, with eventual intermarriage and mixed ethnicity. Scollon and Scollon (1979) give an illuminating account of how they ultimately fathomed the puzzle of oddly shifting tribal population figures for the town in which they carried out their research, Fort Chipewyan. In an area with a 150-year history of intermarriage among speakers of Cree (Algonquian), Chipewyan (Athabascan), French, and English, a Canadian commission arriving in the town of Fort Chipewyan in the summer of 1899 required discrete identity assignments of nonnative and native, and among the latter, of Chipewyan and Cree:

In the same way that people of mixed native and European ancestry were made to choose whether or not they would consider themselves to be native, people of mixed Cree and Chipewyan ancestry were made to choose a unique identity. Although in some circumstances this may not have been difficult, at that time it tended to operate at cross-purposes to an ongoing process of ethnic convergence. At a time when the distinctions between Chipewyans and Crees were rapidly dissolving into a pan-bush identity, the Treaty Commission introduced a discrete distinction between the groups that it required to be perpetuated indefinitely into the future. (1979:222; see pp. 211–31 generally)

It isn't surprising, under these circumstances, that the labels "Cree" and "Chipewyan" are deceptive in the same fashion as the ethnic labels Bradley met with in the traditional Ugong area of Thailand: like the Scollons, Bradley found many shifted identities under the contemporary labels. At the extreme of complex ethnic interaction and movement, Dimmendaal finds Tenet who seem fully to assume Lopid identity, apparently for occupational reasons, in the Sudan; and Mithun finds speakers of "pure Cayuga" in Oklahoma who "consider themselves 'Seneca' ", even though Cayuga and Seneca were originally distinct members of the Iroquoian language family in their precontact locations.

At the opposite pole are the regionally rooted speakers of Breton and Irish Gaelic (Kuter, Watson), who even under extreme pressure do not seem to feel an overarching language identity: one is not so much a Breton speaker or an Irish speaker as a speaker of a particular local dialect of Breton or Irish, with French and English respectively perhaps the preferred language for use with bilinguals from different districts. Regionally rooted minority-language speakers may resist identity shifts better than most, but they run the risk of being unable to make common cause with other scattered bilingual speech-islands and so of succumbing island-by-island (and perhaps more rapidly toward the end of the process) to language shift.

In the same way that individual contributors found themselves reconfronting seemingly elemental yet difficult questions about ethnic and linguistic identity, about language viability, and so forth, the commentators' reviews of all the papers tended to cast up very large issues (as well, of course, as area-specific ones). For example, Menn and Andersen (each invoking Slobin 1973, 1985a, b) move quickly to the properties of human cognition which seem to be at work in language contraction as also in its initial acquisition and in its expansion by deliberate second language acquisition. Menn's "four broad levels of acquisition", identified and labeled, offer a method to handle better the odd mix of capacities many imperfect speakers display, such as – simultaneously – control of elaborate traditional optative forms (in wishes, curses, prayers, and the like) and incomplete, idiosyncratically-leveled control of derivational verb morphology. Andersen's "principles" suggest likely lines along which structural change may be expected to appear in first, and especially in second, language learning, including the imperfect learning of an ancestral tongue; it remains, no doubt, for researchers working on particular languages to weight or order the still moderately large number of contributing factors recognized in his second ("Transfer to Somewhere") principle.

Among other notable parallels which she discusses, Romaine calls attention to the confounding lack of success, in the study of language shift and in the study of creolization, in locating some unique set of social conditions which can reliably be identified as causal in the death of a language or the emergence of a creole. Hoenigswald pointedly calls our attention to the preference for discussing the easy cases, where the language systems in contact are clearly and obviously different, while we pass over in silence the fact that the actual linguistic competition (and shift) is often between regional dialects of each of the languages or between a regional dialect and a form of the standard language; in either case, there may already have been a good deal of transfer (phonetic, lexical, syntactic, semantic) from the shrinking language into the expanding one.

Romaine and Woolard, in their commentaries, both recognize the problems raised by the attempt to apply the labels "internally motivated" and "externally motivated" to changes in an obsolescent language. Romaine points to the parallel problem, in pidgin and creole studies, of assessing the possible effect of internal universals of language development in the structural expansion of a pidgin. Woolard points to the possibility that externally motivated change may be *divergent* rather than convergent: overproduction of subordinate-language features which are absent in the politically dominant language is as much a sign of language contact as adoption of dominant-language features themselves in the subordinate language.

Perhaps this question of internally vs. externally motivated change (and also divergent vs. convergent change) is a useful one in connection with which to return to the note of modest expectations on which this Introduction opened. All of us tilt at this question – it's almost irresistible. But I suspect that our thinking on the subject is relatively simple-minded still. The structure of a language is layered and chambered; different configurations of features can and do appear within various systems of a single language. If a shrinking language which "has gender" is in intense contact with English, which does not, is a decline in gender-marking sure to be the result of contact with English? Suppose that the shrinking language uses gender-marking inescapably and widely in the formation of diminutives, as well as in other syntactic or morphologial environments, and the variety of English spoken in that part of the world is one which is enormously given to the use of diminutives. (There are such varieties of English.) If the strength of the diminutive in English lends even more weight to the strength of the diminutive in the shrinking language, then it is possible that gender-marking might weaken in some environments but remain relatively strong in diminutive formation. This is a deliberately exaggerated version, for argument's sake, of a minor tendency which does appear in East Sutherland Gaelic, all the speakers of which are bilingual in English as well (see Dorian 1981:125–6, 146–8.)

An actual and suitably rich problem for consideration arises in East Sutherland Gaelic (ESG) in connection with pronominal possessives. Among semi-speakers the 1st and 2nd person singular possessive forms *less* like English (prepositions conjugated for person, following the noun modified) are increasing at the expense of the possessive forms *more* like English (free-standing possessive pronouns preceding the nouns). Factors which need to be considered in the expansion of precisely the possessives so unlike anything in English include not only those acknowledged in Andersen's "Transfer to Somewhere" principle (invariance, frequency, congruence, and free-morpheme, simple-morpheme status), but also an underlying reality which is easily neglected in the profusion of surface forms: the use of the free-standing possessive pronouns in the 1st and 2nd person singular is tied to a distinction not productively necessary to any other lexical or morphological choice in the language, namely (roughly stated) alienability vs. inalienability in nouns. A distinction without any overt marker of its own, revealing itself only in one lexical/syntactic choice, may be a candidate for early loss, even when the result seems "perversely" noncongruent.

Participant-observation work with a speech form as complex as ESG over a long period (15 years) provides the advantage – and the burden – of a kind of built-in filtering machine through which propositions and generalizations automatically pass. My attempts to get generalizations (my own as well as others') about internally vs. externally motivated change through the filter have produced a great deal of clanking and rattling, but not much outspill at the far end. I take the questions still to be more complicated than the propositions which I'm tipping in.

Fortunately, the commentators, exercising their specialized perspectives over the full range of chapters in Parts I and II, offer a number of cautions and reminders of problems and complexities still abounding; and indeed a good many of the authors of Parts I and II highlight uncertainties and point to difficulties. Where the commentaries are concerned, there has been no effort to eliminate overlap. If more than one commentator raises questions in connection with the notion of "simplification", raises doubts about the utility of the "death" metaphor, or makes reference to the (1971) Gumperz and Wilson study, there is likely to be good reason for that, and the perspective is in any case slightly different with each successive commentator.

The contributors to the first two parts of this volume are generally strong, by design, in field experience with the language they write about. An impressive amount of firsthand information has been sifted, the results pondered, the insights and analyses shared. There has been an unusually high level of intercommunication among all participants in the volume (see Preface), even apart from the reviews by the commentators.

The authors represented here make reference to many others who have done related or similar work – e.g. earlier pioneers like Bloomfield (1927) and Swadesh (1948), contemporary pioneers like Hymes (especially 1964 and since), Fishman (Fishman *et al.* 1966 and since), Dressler (1972 and since) – and to outstanding work currently being done by researchers deeply engaged with like matters (Silva-Corvalán 1986b and her rapidly accumulating publications since, for one very deserving example). The references are rich, and yet not rich enough to reflect adequately the recent and current growth of the literature. One of the chapter authors in this volume has himself meanwhile edited a collection of papers devoted exclusively to Native American languages in intense contact situations

(Taylor, *Language obsolescence, shift, and death in native American communities*, an issue of *The International Journal of the Sociology of Language*). A volume dealing with *Language shift in Aboriginal Australia* in particular is well along under the editorship of Patrick McConvell of the University College of the Northern Territory. Research which shares a great many of the preoccupations to be found in the present volume appears (as McConvell's title indicates) under various established rubrics which signal a different angle of vision, e.g. "language spread", "language shift", "language maintenance", often also "language planning" and "language revival". Special note should be taken, since the angle of vision seems reversed and the similarities of focus are easily overlooked, of the work of Spicer and those who followed his lead on "persistent peoples" (see e.g. Spicer 1980: ch. 7; Castile and Kushner 1981).

Since much of the thrust of this collection has been to widen the circle of shared communication further, a set of focus questions circulated among contributors at the very outset of the project is reproduced as an addendum at the close of this Introduction. Some of the proposed lines of investigation are evident as a kind of subsurface presence here and there in the volume, and direct reference is made to them at the close of one paper (Mougeon and Beniak).

The special knowledge and hard-won expertise reflected in these papers is best discerned, perhaps, in the summarizing comment offered by one veteran researcher in a questionnaire about field methods and experience (sent to authors of Parts I and II). Here is a distillation from his long and varied experience:

Every case is special. You must deal with the idiosyncratic situation (Sunday in Scotland, keeping a bottle handy, avoiding a meddlesome ignorant [spouse], avoiding street commotions when Cyprus and Anglos [don't] mix, keeping infirm or senile people awake, concealing your identity to authorities, dealing with Marxist bureaucracies, flat tyres, impassable roads, writing between the steering wheel of a car to keep your subject trapped, living through indigestion, diarrhea and body lice, humoring your hosts in every improbable way). You simply cater to every obstacle as if there will never be another chance. Never offend if you want to go back. Wait an afternoon for 3 sentences or phrases. Assume you'll be the last linguist ever to get there.

However much the list of likely obstacles and trials might shift from fieldworker to fieldworker and from setting to setting, endorsement of the opening and closing sentences would not be likely to stray far from 100 percent.

The state of this art doesn't admit of a milestone at the moment, but on the other hand it does require some stepping stones in order to promote forward movement. To that relatively modest goal it's appropriate to aspire.

Focus Questions

1. *Problems in locating terminal speakers and assessing their skills*

Self-definition: Do the speakers claim speaker status and ethnic membership?

How does the speech community identify its members, internally and with respect to outsiders?

What approaches can investigators adopt to gain access to speakers and to assess speaker skills with some degree of reliability?

What special problems are created by negative prestige or outright stigmatization for the display of skills and the opportunity to assess them?

2. *Skewed performance in terminal speech communities*

Are there constraints operating to reduce the display of language skills, such as paucity of interlocutors, insufficiently initiated audiences for the traditional verbal events, decay of key cultural activities or traditional occupations associated with verbal activity?

Can highly valued cultural activities preserve specialized skills beyond the speakers' genuine productive capacity and even beyond the ability of either speaker or audience to comprehend the performance fully?

Can highly valued verbal activities be preserved at a minimal level with reduced linguistic means (e.g. can forms of extended discourse be continued despite loss of all but a few conjunction or subordination mechanisms)?

What are the consequences of greatly unbalanced skills which are more typically symmetrical in "healthier" languages (production and reception; writing and reading; more formal and less formal registers)?

3. *Linguistic change and reductive processes as a structured phenomenon*

Can this be demonstrated for various types of speaker in terminal speech communities, say:
(a) the formerly fluent
   i. children whose normal early skills decay?
   ii. young adults who relocate and cease to use their home language?
(b) children and grandchildren of immigrants?
(c) the impaired (the hard of hearing, the mentally retarded)?

Is variability typically higher in terminal speech communities than in healthy ones, or is variability itself variable?

Does variability carry the freight of social meaning in terminal speech communities that it does in the urban communities where it has been most intensively studied?

Is change in dying speech forms the result of interference, convergence, independent autogenetic processes, or all of these?

Can certain types of change be expected typically to show up earlier in the decline of a speech form and certain other types typically later?

Are particular types of change likely to be associated with particular language typologies, regardless of genetic affiliations?

4. *The phenomena of abrupt transmission failure or "tip", and of persistence against seemingly high odds*

Can sudden cessation of home language transmission or use be established within:
(a) individuals?   (c) particular communities?
(b) families?   (d) regions, ethnic groups, or whole countries?

Can such "tip" to the dominant language be traced to:
(a) personal trauma (experience of discrimination, perception of personal "difference", etc.)?
(b) family dynamics or size?
(c) tacit group-wide change in values and norms?
(d) external events such as war with the ancestral country of origin, sharp economic expansion or contraction, sudden development of communication with outside regions, introduction of compulsory military service or education in the dominant language?
(e) a number of these in combination?

Where persistence appears against seemingly high odds, is this:
(a) a group trait which correlates with other conservative ethnic behaviors?
(b) a boundary marker, associated with self-definition or conscious exclusion of or by others?
(c) a reflection of an unusual degree of voluntary or involuntary isolation (geographical/physical, cultural/material)?
(d) a feature of family or individual behavior which reflects such factors as:
    i. level of education and/or awareness of cultural heritage?
   ii. family or kin structure of a particular sort?
  iii. personal experience which enhances the value of ethnic identity?
  iv. political action (or reaction)?

    v. a recognizable personality type which appears sporadically among the population?

    vi. accidental isolation by distance or physical difference (hearing impairment, blindness, or other physical or mental peculiarity)?

I
Focus on context

1 On language death in eastern Africa

GERRIT J. DIMMENDAAL

1. Introduction

Eastern Africa does not constitute a unit linguistically or culturally. Instead, this area, roughly comprising the countries of Djibouti, Ethiopia, Kenya, Somalia, Sudan, Tanzania and Uganda, is characterized by a large variety of language families and groups on the one hand, and a considerable degree of cultural diversity on the other. In one sense the present geographical delimitation for the discussion of language obsolescence is therefore arbitrary. Such a regional approach, however, allows for a comparison of different circumstances relevant to the actuation problem of dying languages. One such variable concerns the social and economic structure of interacting groups, whilst a further variable relates to demographic factors.

The present contribution is directed towards disseminating general information on the causes and effects of language shift. It is not a survey of all known cases of language contraction and death in eastern Africa. Instances of partial and complete language shift are so numerous that it can be stated without exaggeration that most ethnic groups in this part of Africa, and probably elsewhere, are the result of an amalgamation of various groups which were distinct at an earlier stage. More specifically, this paper tries to provide answers, at least in part, to the following questions:

1. To what extent, and in what ways, do economic and social factors play a role as causal mechanisms in the gradual "default assignment" of certain languages?
2. How important is language as a potential symbol of ethnic identity relative to other symbols?
3. What kind of traces, linguistically or otherwise, does language shift leave behind, once the extinction of a particular language has become a fact?

Genotypes and phenotypes discussed below have been selected mainly on the basis of these three issues. Although a number of other questions are highly relevant in themselves, for example the actual assessment of skills or the social stratification of proficiency in a dying language, they are not dealt

13

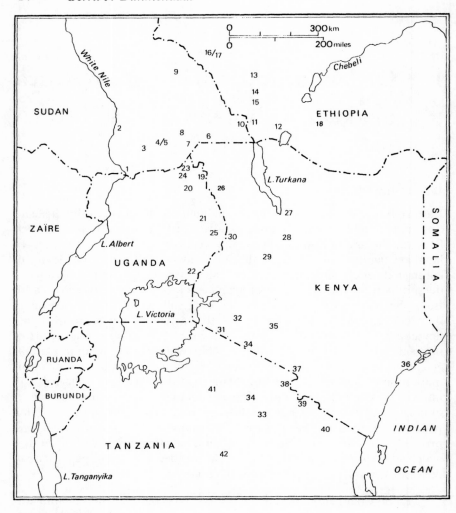

Eastern Africa

The classification on page 15, referred to in the text of this chapter, follows Greenberg (1963a). Sub-branches are given in parentheses. Numbers in parentheses correspond to numbers on the map.

with here, the main reason being lack of accurate and up-to-date information on these topics.[1] For the sake of clarity, a genetic classification for the various languages mentioned throughout the text accompanies the map. Although orthographies have been developed for many of them in more recent times, we are essentially dealing with languages without literary traditions (with notable exceptions like Swahili and Ge'ez), and more often

'Key' to Map of Eastern Africa

NIGER–KORDOFANIAN
(West Atlantic)
Peul
(Bantu)
Chagga (38)
Kikuyu (35)
Pare (39)
Shambaa (40)
Swahili

AFRO–ASIATIC
(Semitic)
Amharic
Ge'ez
(Cushitic)
Aasáx
Elmolo (27)
Konso (18)
Oromo
Somali
Weyto
(Omotic)
Hamar (12)

NILO–SAHARAN
(Central Sudanic)
Madi (1)
(Nilotic)
Akie(k) (33)
Bari (2)
Camus (29)
Dodos (19)
Jie (20)
Karimojong (21)

Kore (36)
Lopid (4)
Lotuxo (3)
Maa
Maasai (34)
Nyangatom (10)
Omotik (31)
Ongamo (37)
Pokot (30)
Samburu (28)
Sogoo (32)
Teso (22)
Toposa (6)
Turkana (26)
(Kuliak)
Dorobo
Ik (23)
Nyang'i (24)
Tepes (25)
(Surma)
Bodi (13)
Didinga (7)
Kwegu (14)
Longarim (8)
Majang (16)
Murle (9)
Mursi (15)
Omo–Murle (11)
Shabo (17)
Tenet (5)

KHOISAN
Hadza (41)
Sandawe (42)

than not there are no institutions that can dictate a norm. Many Africans are multilingual or, at least, bilingual. In various areas, lingua francas have developed (Heine 1970), giving rise to situations of rather stable bilingualism or diglossia. However, encroaching diglossia (a term suggested by Peter Unseth, pers. comm.), resulting in the gradual substitution of one language for another, can also be observed in various regions. Section 2 below examines the case of one hunter–gatherer community in southwest Ethiopia, known as the Kwegu, and their interaction with neighboring pastoralists. The Kwegu language is about to disappear; circumstances leading to the death of the Kwegu language seem to be comparable, if not identical, to those leading to the vanishing of numerous other languages spoken by hunter–gatherers in eastern Africa, as the second part of section 2 illustrates. Section 3 treats the tremendous expansion of one particular language, Maa, and the social and economic provisions which may have led to a rapid increase in the number of Maa speakers. The description includes a closer look at one group absorbed linguistically and culturally by Maa-speaking communities, namely the Aasáx, who gave up their original language in less than a century. Section 4 gives some indication of what kind of physical anthropological, cultural, or linguistic traces one may expect to find, once language replacement has been completed. It is often assumed that language and ethnicity are isomorphic. This rather widespread view does not seem to be corroborated in all cases by situations observable in eastern Africa. Section 4 shows how language and ethnicity may in fact be opposed to each other, especially in the context of language shift. The paper finishes with a number of conclusions on cause and effect in language shift in that part of the world and compares these with such other historical processes as pidginization and convergence.

2.   Absorption of hunter–gatherer populations: "Encroaching diglossia"

There are several communities in eastern Africa whose main means of subsistence consists of hunting and the gathering of wild fruits and honey; many of these societies also practice some agriculture. They often live in close contact with pastoral or agricultural peoples, with whom they have a symbiotic relationship, and whose language they also speak apart from their own language. Such a division of roles and language use puts the original mother tongue of the hunter–gatherers in an extremely weak position. The case of the Kwegu shows why this is so.

2.1.   The Kwegu of southwest Ethiopia

The Kwegu (also known as Muguji) are scattered in villages along the banks of the Omo River in the extreme southwestern corner of Ethiopia. They mainly hunt hippopotamus, but they also practice flood cultivation as well as rain cultivation along the banks of the Omo, with maize and durra as main crops. The Kwegu see themselves as "river people" in contradistinction to groups like the Mursi and Bodi (also known as Me'en), by whom they are surrounded and who think of themselves as "cattle people". Nevertheless, a large proportion of the daily diet of the Mursi and Bodi people consists of millet which they grow in the same area as the Kwegu and on the same basis of shifting cultivation. What matters is presumably how people see themselves, not what their actual behavior is like. The Kwegu also have an extensive apiculture. They sell honey to their pastoral overlord groups in exchange for utensils like axes. Honey is extremely popular in the Ethiopian Highlands and elsewhere because of its intoxicating properties when converted into mead by mixing it with water and yeast. The Kwegu, who only number about 500 these days, are dominated by the far more numerous Mursi and Bodi, whose number has been estimated at around 6,000 individuals each. Because the Kwegu eat the meat of various wild animals, they are considered to be unclean by the neighboring Mursi and Bodi, who have taboos against eating the meat of particular wild animals.

The languages of the Kwegu, Mursi, and Bodi are closely related historically. They belong to the Surma group within Nilo-Saharan, but they are no longer mutually intelligible. When the Kwegu are among themselves, they speak their own language, but they are also fluent in either Mursi or Bodi, depending on whom they are in closer contact with. Turton and Bender (1976:535) make the following interesting observation:

> The Mursi claim that Kwegu is particularly difficult to learn, a fact which is presumably related to the socially inferior position to which the Kwegu are allotted by both their Mursi and Bodi neighbors, who do not allow them to keep cattle, and who believe indeed that close contact between a Kwegu and cattle is extremely harmful to the latter.

The disparate social roles are thus reflected in a sociolinguistic situation whereby Kwegu speak both their own language and the language of the Mursi or Bodi while the latter tend not to speak Kwegu. This division of language use is typical for hunter–gatherer societies interacting with pastoral and agricultural people. Although the Kwegu are looked upon as second-class citizens inside Mursi and Bodi society, they seem to accept their social inequality. Each Kwegu home, or man in particular, has a Mursi or Bodi patron who looks after his interests. If a Kwegu man wants to get married, he asks permission from his patron who then provides some head of cattle for eating at the bridal feast. A Kwegu man is free to choose a new patron whenever he feels that his Mursi or Bodi lord falls short in his duties. The Kwegu see this client relationship as essential to their continued existence. They have a strong feeling that through this symbiotic relation with the Mursi or Bodi they are better off.

Interestingly, taboos against Kwegu among Mursi and Bodi people are fading away nowadays. Mursi and Bodi men marry Kwegu girls (who become Mursi or Bodi in this way), but the reverse match does not seem to be possible. The Kwegu are diminishing in number because of intermarriage, and they are beginning to lose their identity as a separate ethnic group, a fact of which they are very much aware. The domains in which either Kwegu or Mursi and Bodi are spoken are beginning to overlap, a situation abetted by intermarriage. The contexts in which Kwegu is used among adults are decreasing, and the acquisition of Kwegu as a first language becomes less frequent because it strongly depends on the social network of which the parents are part. Muldrow (1976:606) reports that the smallest groups of Kwegu, of sometimes ten or twenty or even single individuals, have often forgotten their own language and speak only Bodi. The Kwegu language is nearly extinct as a result of the shifting language solidarity. Numerous other hunter–gatherer bands in eastern Africa are known to have given up their language in recent times. The following section discusses some of these cases.

2.2.   The dying languages of other hunter–gatherer communities

Hunter–gatherer bands are small by necessity, although the exact size of settlements may vary with the season. Such ecological conditions do not necessarily put a strain on their linguistic situation. It is only when they start interacting with neighboring groups whose cultures are viewed as more prestigious that their own languages become particularly threatened. In the Ethiopian context, the Weyto probably gave up their earlier language this way. They are known as hippopotamus hunters of the Lake Tana region. The ethnic Weyto live in an area surrounded by speakers of Amharic which they use as their primary and first language; their former language probably belonged to Cushitic (Bender, Bowen, Cooper and Ferguson 1976:14).

The language of the Shabo of southwest Ethiopia also seems to be threatened. Subsistence activities among the Shabo consist of hunting and bee-keeping. They are scattered among the agricultural Majang, whose language they all speak, but only very few Majang speak the language of the Shabo (Unseth 1985:15). Majang belongs to the Surma group within Eastern Sudanic, as suggested by Bender (1977). Unseth (1985:17) notes that the language of the Shabo appears to be outside the scope of the standard genetic models of descent. The Shabo have become subject to, and have come to be dominated by, the Majang after having been saved by them from slave traders, according to some sources quoted in Unseth (1985). Majang people quickly distinguish between a Majang and a Shabo by physical appearance alone. The Shabo are dark-skinned and shorter than the average Majang, with rounder, wider faces (Unseth 1985:15). Stauder (1971), in his monograph on the Majang, observes that their subsistence activities consist of shifting cultivation as well as hunting and bee-keeping. The Majang do not keep cattle since they live in a heavily forested region infested by tsetse flies. There do not seem to be any significant economic relations between the Shabo and Majang people.

As noted, the Shabo are scattered among the Majang. This raises a more general problem for the discovery of minority groups and their languages. It is almost impossible to pinpoint settlements, for we are often dealing with vast areas, which makes it difficult to locate speakers, especially terminal speakers, let alone estimate their exact number. A further reason why they are hard to spot is related to the way submerged groups often identify themselves to the outside world. For example, the Ongamo language near

Mount Kilimanjaro is only spoken as dominant tongue by a few elderly individuals; the younger generations are Chagga-dominant. To neighboring people the ethnic Ongamo are known as Ngasa, but the same name is used for the larger ethnic unit, most of whom speak Chagga as a first language and who are not able to speak Ongamo. In other words, the Ongamo language is not (or is no longer) an intrinsic part of Ongamo ethnic identity. Only meticulous scanning and survey work makes it possible to discover particular minority groups. Due to the outstanding scholarship of Africanists like Heine, who discovered various virtually extinct languages, we have a fairly accurate picture of the linguistic setting of Kenya. Some of these Kenyan languages threatened by extinction are looked at more closely in the following section. They often illustrate a phenomenon which can also be observed in the interaction between Mursi or Bodi and Kwegu: a gradual fading away of group identity among the minority group, especially as a result of intermarriage, which further restricts the domain in which the minority language is used.

There are a number of groups in northeastern Uganda whose actual languages are threatened by extinction, namely the Kuliak languages of Karamoja District. The name Kuliak has been suggested by Heine (1976a) as a cover term for three genetically related languages: Ik (Teuso), Nyang'i, and Tepes. It is derived from a word meaning "poor people, people without cattle" in the Teso–Turkana languages surrounding the home area of the former three groups. These neighboring ethnic units are typical pastoralists, although they do practice agriculture to some extent. The people speaking Kuliak languages are known as hunters, but they too do some cultivating. The cover term "Kuliak" is also useful from a sociological point of view because the three groups share features of social behavior. They consider a kindred spirit to exist between them as "mountain people", whereas the pastoral groups of the plains with whom they interact are regarded with some contempt. Young boys from the Kuliak group herd cattle for the surrounding pastoralists, a phenomenon observed in various parts of eastern Africa, but also elsewhere, for example among the Peul (Fulani) of West Africa. Such services are one way of ultimately acquiring cattle oneself, clearly something envisaged and highly sought after by most of them. As a result of such contacts, speakers of the Kuliak group are often in a position where they are obliged to be able to speak Dodos, Karimojong, or Turkana, all the more because the latter do not speak a Kuliak language. Driberg (1932:608) had already observed that the Nyang'i were shifting their sense of language solidarity. At present, only elderly people still speak Nyang'i principally. The younger generations use Dodos as their first language and Nyang'i as a second language. The younger Tepes speak Karimojong as their primary language, Tepes being restricted in use mainly to people above the age of 40, although there seems to be some regional variation in the degree of proficiency in Tepes. Thanks to a wordlist containing 38 items published by Wayland (1931) we know of a fourth language historically belonging to Kuliak. This language is referred to as "Dorobo", a general name used in eastern Africa to refer to hunter–gatherers. The language of these "Dorobo" is now extinct. The sociolinguistic situation for Ik is somewhat better. Current Tepes and Nyang'i communities consist of a few hundred people, but the Ik probably number several thousands.[2]

Although the Kuliak people do not share the "cattle complex" and "bovine idiom" with the surrounding Nilotic pastoralists, they do have various terms in their language relating to pastoralism and to agriculture. Several of the terms in the three languages are cognate and thus share a reconstructible common ancestor form (Heine 1976a). This strongly suggests that we are dealing with impoverished cattle people who may have been forced to have recourse to hunting and gathering. Present-day societies living on hunting and gathering do not necessarily represent archaic cultural stages, i.e. they are not necessarily descendants of early hunter–gatherer groups. It would be wrong to suggest that there has been cultural continuity and a unidirectional evolutionary development from hunting and gathering to pastoralism and agriculture in the context of African culture history. Stock holdings may be wiped out due to ecological disasters such as a desiccating environment, thereby forcing people to resort to different means of subsistence. In terms of energy expenditure, and given such variables as the reliability of rainfall, the hunting of wild animals and gathering of wild fruits makes the most sense. This is probably what happened to several communities in eastern Africa. In their reduced circumstances such groups often seek close associations with remaining pastoral or agricultural peoples.

3.   The reverse view: Expansion of a language or language group via the probable assimilation of socially and economically weaker populations

The state of affairs presented above might give rise to the erroneous conclusion that economic transformations provide the decisive incentives in processes of language shift. The following "blow up" on the gradual linguistic expansion of Maa as a language of prestige tries to offset this claim by showing how a confrontation with new social values may also lead to the imposition and substitution of one language for another; in the case of the expansion of Maa, however, economic factors have also played a role.

3.1.   Maa as an assimilating language

The term Maa refers to a cluster consisting of the following dialects:

```
              ┌─── North Maa: Camus and Samburu
Maa ──────────┼─── Central Maa: Kore
              └─── South Maa: Maasai
```

Maa is spoken by approximately 500,000 people, inhabiting a vast area ranging from northern Kenya to central Tanzania, a stretch of almost 1,000 kilometres. The closest linguistic ties of Maa are with the language called Ongamo, spoken only by elderly people living among the Chagga of northern Tanzania (see section 2.2). The next closest link in the genetic chain is with a series of dialects known as the Lotuxo cluster, spoken in the southern Sudan. The ancestors of the present-day Maa, or at least some of them, probably expanded from that region in search of temporary grazing grounds, as is the case with most pastoral peoples. There is some disagreement as to whether this gradual migration and expansion took place in a peaceful manner or not. (For a summary of the oral history and an extensive discussion of the literature on Maa, the interested reader is referred to Vossen 1980, 1982:69–84.) Clearly the traditional pastoral Maa were well-organized and feared by neighboring ethnic groups. They have long attracted the attention of Europeans in eastern Africa, as is testified to by the enormous flow of reports by missionaries and travelers, many of whom were impressed by the personal garb and social behavior of Maa groups. The current Maa community is rather heterogeneous in composition, although the various groups do share specific cultural features such as age sets and circumcision. Pastoralism is regarded as the favored culture and the traditional ideal of Maa society. The actual means of subsistence range from pure pastoralism to agriculture, or hunting and gathering.

Maa is not a lingua franca; its expansion is probably due to the fact that it has been a dominant-culture language for some time. Such assimilating languages tend to oust others. The Maa community contains several absorbed groups who saw no advantage in transmitting their own low-prestige language in their interaction with pastoral Maa in particular.

Among the pastoral Samburu of northern Kenya, there are hunter–gatherer bands referred to as L-Torrob (again the general name for these groups in many parts of eastern Africa). Although we don't have any direct evidence of a former "Dorobo" language in this case, one does find oral traditions among the Samburu of meeting with hunter–gatherers during their migration. The Dorobo boys are employed as cattle herders in the same way and for the same reason as among other pastoral groups. Their herds are sometimes so large that they require the help of various relatives as well as non-kin in order to be able to tend them. For Dorobo people this means a way of getting away from hunting and gathering. Knowledge of the language of the stock owner facilitates acquisition of material advantages, or it may even be a prerequisite to social mobility.

Thanks to the survey work by Heine and others, we do know about the former language of fishermen who have their settlements on the southeastern shores of Lake Turkana and who are known as Elmolo. Heine (1982:173–218) gives a short sketch of this language which was recorded in the form used shortly before it was given up in favor of the Samburu dialect of Maa. The Elmolo language belonged to the Omo-Tana group of Eastern

Cushitic. The community which Heine met with consisted of approximately two hundred people at the time. Four old women and four old men were still fluent in Elmolo; they used this language as a secret code to exclude others from communication, their primary language now being Samburu.

The first contacts between the Elmolo and the Samburu seem to date from the turn of the century when some Elmolo started picking up Samburu in their initial economic and cultural contacts with the Samburu people. Intensification of contacts and subsequent gradual linguistic assimilation took place in the 1920s and 1930s. Elmolo children born in this period acquired Samburu as their mother tongue rather than Elmolo. Heine (1982:177) notes that adults really seem to have insisted on speaking Elmolo to their children, but that the children would reply in the Samburu language, presumably because this was the only language in which they were fluent. This gradually led to a situation where, only eighty years after the contacts started, the Elmolo language is on the brink of extinction.

Another Cushitic language whose speakers have been absorbed into Maa society is Yaaku, also known as Mogogodo. As suggested by Greenberg (1983b) the language probably belonged to the same subgroup of Eastern Cushitic as Konso and Oromo. The present-day Yaaku inhabit the foothills to the north of Mount Kenya. In the 1930s there seems to have been a decision to abandon Yaaku in favor of Maasai, presumably as part of an adaptive strategy in order to become pastoralists. At present, there seem to be only some fifty Yaaku speakers left, who still practice hunting and gathering. They are all over 40 years of age, according to Heine (1982:30).

The Camus (Njemps) community, situated on the southern edge of Lake Baringo (Kenya), shares with the pastoral Maasai such cultural traits as the practicing of circumcision and the division of their society into generation (age) sets, but besides animal husbandry they also practice farming and fishing. The present-day Camus are a mixture of various historically distinct groups as well as immigrants from various other ethnic groups. This is at least suggested by their current cultural heterogeneity as well as by their oral traditions which make reference to various historical events whereby immigrants became integrated into the Camus society. Among the traditional pastoral Maa as well as among other eastern African pastoralists, there is a strict taboo on fish eating. Although the Elmolo gave up their language, they did not give up fishing, even after they started acquiring cattle. The cultural behavior of the Camus also shows that groups may become integrated without necessarily giving up all their previous customs such as the eating of fish.

As striking as the fishermen communities among the Maa are the agricultural groups who live in northern Tanzania, known as L-Arusa. In physical appearance (i.e. in somatic traits) they are rather distinct from most pastoral Maasai groups. They seem to be descendants of agricultural people, probably speaking a Bantu language, who were already in the area when the first Maasai appeared on the scene. The Arusa community probably also absorbed Maasai who lost their cattle; this at least is the position taken by one of the specialists on Maa culture, Jacobs (e.g. 1965). Pastoral Maasai and, in fact, most other African pastoral groups regard agricultural activities with some contempt. What the Arusa case shows is a partial adoption and assimilation of Maa customs by a group which does not give up traditional customs such as farming. It has to be concluded therefore that changing subsistence patterns are not the only causal mechanisms of language shift; changes in social values and attitudes may lead to the same result, the ultimate disappearance of a language in favor of the one spoken by a prestigious group. Maa society has also incorporated hunter–gatherer groups speaking Nilotic languages, Omotik being one of them. This language, not to be confused with the Omotic language-group in Ethiopia, is no longer the language of an ethnic group. It is only remembered as a separate language by a few old women, all of whom have been incorporated into Maasai society. As observed by Rottland (1982:26), their personal garb and material culture is not (or is no longer) distinct from that of the traditional Massai.

We know of one variant of Maa, the Kore dialect, which is virtually extinct, although the Kore as an ethnic group are still found on Lamu Island off the Kenyan coast and on the mainland opposite Lamu Island. The first language of the Kore people is now Somali, with probably only two people left who still remember some Kore (Heine and Vossen 1980; Romero Curtin 1985; Dimmendaal 1986). One striking aspect of the phenomenon of language replacement among the Kore and other groups in eastern Africa is the speed with which this process takes place. One such rather abrupt cessation of home language transmission is that of Aasáx.

3.2.   Maasai dominance and Aasáx contraction

Aasáx, a Southern Cushitic language, used to be spoken by hunter–gatherer groups in northern Tanzania. The last speaker (in his own judgement) died in 1976. Winter (1979) was able to reconstruct the causes of the decreasing use and ultimate extinction of Aasáx on the basis of interviews with this terminal speaker, whom he interviewed during several visits between 1973 and 1975. The actual processes leading from partial to total shift started less than one hundred years ago according to Winter, who distinguishes four stages for the historical development of Aasáx contraction.

During the initial stage, local Aasáx settlements were affiliated to Maasai clans in terms which may have been comparable to the Kwegu–Mursi/Bodi client relationship discussed earlier. Intermarriage did take place to some extent: Maasai men could marry Aasáx girls, but only Aasáx youths who had acquired cattle in return for doing herdsman's service were allowed to marry Maasai girls. Adult Aasáx men, and probably women as well, had some command of Maasai at that stage, a fact which may be interpreted as part of an adaptive strategy of becoming integrated to some extent within the Maasai community.

The second stage was initiated by a Rinderpest epidemic reaching the Maasai region around 1890 and lasting about six years. Clearly the epidemic had a catalyzing effect on Aasáx language abandonment. During this period Maasai who had lost their cattle had recourse to Aasáx settlements. The Maasai lodgers would not permit the Aasáx to speak their own language (which the Maasai did not understand) in their presence. The result was that small children no longer learned Aasáx, while older children unlearned it. The proficiency of adult native speakers of Aasáx in the language of the Maasai was sufficient for their daily communicative needs. After 1895, Maasai who had been occupying Aasáx camps gradually went back to their former herding life, but several ethnic Aasáx also had become integrated into Maasai society as a result of intermarriage and clientship. Those who continued their hunter–gatherer way of life still had occasional contacts with their traditional kinsmen, but they would speak to each other in Maasai.

The use of Aasáx among those still adhering to their traditional way of life slightly expanded again because it was reintroduced in council meetings. Through the upheaval it developed from a vocational language of males into a men's language in general at this period, roughly around 1906. This is where the third stage began. The gradual decimation of wild game (due in particular to hunting by colonial officers and settlers) posed a threat to the traditional existence of the Aasáx. Many of them tried to adopt the life of cattle herders, but they still preserved at least part of their ethnic independence by continuing their favorite activities, hunting and apiculture, a practice which was incompatible with the Maasai ethos, and which distinguished the Aasáx from the latter group. The feasibility of Aasáx pastoral activities depended very much on the effectiveness of the local colonial government forces against the far more numerous Maasai, who would not have permitted the Aasáx to use grazing land otherwise.

The fourth and final stage was characterized by a rather mysterious cargo cult which swept through Maasai society, whereby hecatombs of cattle were slaughtered by the Maasai at various ceremonies. The Aasáx, as successful cattle-breeding people, presumably saw reasons for doing the same. Winter (1979:189) observes:

When the Aasáx realized their folly had lost them their livelihood, and when a desperate return to hunting and gathering proved not viable, they decided, about a year later, to disband their communities.

The majority of Aasáx decided to join neighboring Bantu communities, or local Maasai groups, and gave up their language at once, thus leaving only a few individuals who still used Aasáx as a primary language. This stage was reached around 1920. Some fifty years after the Aasáx community ceased to exist as a group, the last speaker who still had some knowledge of the Aasáx language died.

4. The arguments for shifts in language use by linguistic, cultural, or physical traces of earlier difference

Language shift must have been an important facet of the cultural history of eastern Africa. Various strata or traces are reminiscent of processes of language replacement in the recent and more distant past. These traces are of a physical anthropological, socio-anthropological, and linguistic nature. Linguistic assimilation does not necessarily imply social assimilation. Once an ethnic group has become incorporated into the dominant culture, its social status may be one of equality; alternatively, submerged groups may only be incorporated at the fringes. One such society showing caste-like features is found among the traditional Bari of the southern Sudan. Their language belongs to the Eastern Nilotic branch of Nilotic. Most likely, the linguistic Bari entered their present homeland from the east, where Bari's closest linguistic ties are to be found. The oral tradition makes reference to an encounter with hunters, fishermen, and blacksmiths when ancestors of the Bari entered the current territory. The traditional Bari society consists of free men (Lui), groups practicing fishing and smithing (Tomonok), and serfs (Dupi), who are considered to be an inferior class or caste by the Lui and Tomonok; the latter do not intermarry with Dupi. According to Spagnolo (1933:xii–xiii) the Dupi are the descendants of a submerged hunter–gatherer society which lived in the area prior to the invading Bari, whereas at least part of the Tomonok seem to be of Madi stock. Spagnolo's hunch seems to have been based primarily on the bodily appearance of Tomonok people in the Bari community.

Distinct social ascendancy does not necessarily imply the retention of a separate network of friendship and marriage or social stigmatization, as the situation of the Tenet in the southern Sudan illustrates (Dimmendaal 1983b). The Tenet language is closely related to Didinga, Longarim, and Murle. Speakers from these groups have a common oral tradition which makes reference to a quarrel after which the ancestors of the modern Tenet and Murle left the original homeland.[3] Didinga, Longarim, and Murle people are typical representatives of pastoralism. However, the present-day Tenet have very few cattle, and they no longer adhere to, or identify with, pastoralism; whether they lost their cattle as a result of severe droughts or otherwise is unknown. The ancestors of the modern Tenet found new means of subsistence by affiliating themselves with Lopid people. The Lopid are famous blacksmiths in Sudan's Eastern Equatorial Province. The iron utensils and weapons which they produce are of utmost importance to agricultural and cattle-rearing people in the area. They can be acquired by exchanging for them cattle and other useful objects. Tenet is spoken in six villages in the Lopid (Lafid) Mountains, the home area of the Lopid people. At home the Tenet speak either Tenet or Lopid; all ethnic Tenet seem to be fluent in both languages, but the Tenet language is clearly threatened because its use is tending to become more and more restricted socially. Tenet strongly identify themselves with Lopid culture; they no longer live in a Didinga–Longarim–Murle lifestyle tradition. Their shifting language allegiance is probably not due to the negative prestige of Tenet but, rather, to the importance of Lopid iron-working and, by consequence, of the Lopid language. Blacksmiths often form a stigmatized class when incorporated into an agricultural or pastoral society in eastern Africa; they are sometimes not allowed to own cattle. Because the Lopid are not a submerged group themselves, there does not seem to be any such stigmatization with regard to them. Some of the ancestors of the Murle, who migrated with the Tenet, seem to have affiliated with the Nyangatom, an Eastern Nilotic pastoral group living along the Kibish River, southwest Ethiopia. This offshoot of the Murle seems to be practically extinct, at least linguistically. The Omo-Murle language is only remembered by a few old women among the Nyangatom (Tornay 1978), whilst other former speakers of the language have already been absorbed completely by the Nyangatom, who currectly number about 5,000. The descendants of originally Murle-speaking people still exist as an ethnic group, however, on the Boma Plateau in the border area between Sudan and Ethiopia.

A language (or rather dialect, as there are only minor tonal differences) closely related to Nyangatom is Turkana, spoken by approximately 260,000 people. The Turkana have absorbed large numbers of people with different ethnic backgrounds, most often not resulting in castes or stigmatized groups. They live in the arid and semi-arid plains of northwestern Kenya, but claim to have come from an area in northeastern Uganda where closely related languages (or dialects, from a linguistic point of view) are spoken. Most of these latter languages have a much smaller number of speakers. Given the fact that the territory of the Turkana is rather marginal in economic terms, it seems highly unlikely that a massive exodus took place from Uganda into this area. Oral tradition makes mention of a confrontation with Pokot and Samburu people living in the area which Turkana people invaded. Place-names in the Turkana area are still reminiscent of this earlier presence. Also, one finds local customs and taboos probably reminiscent of the traditional culture of the absorbed Pokot and Samburu. Some of the Pokot and Samburu may in fact have been expelled from the area, Many of them, however, switched their allegiance to the Turkana and became absorbed into their society. Because the Pokot and Samburu are cattle people like the Turkana, a label shift (and language shift) would not imply any major shift in cultural identity. There is one group of Turkana speakers, living along the Turkwell River in the southwestern part of Turkana District, who are basically hunter–gatherers, although they do practice agriculture. They speak a slightly different variant of Turkana (Dimmendaal 1983a:3). Because they do not have cattle, they are not considered to be "real Turkana" by their pastoral kinsmen. There is no knowledge among these "poor people" (so called since they lack cattle) of a former language, but their distinct culture suggests a different origin from the pastoral Turkana.

The ethnogenesis of the Turkana and the expansion of their speech community seem typical for several groups in eastern Africa. Smaller groups, especially, will welcome the assimilation of other groups, in order to strengthen their position as a community. The emergence of a socially united group with internal dialect or mode-of-subsistence differentiation, and a political system characterized by gerontocracy dominated by elders and ritual leaders in each region, implies language shift and, to some extent, modification of earlier cultural norms. One striking feature of cultural identity among eastern Africa ethnic groups is similarity of material culture and personal adornment (at least superficially). The Hamar of southwest Ethiopia, who speak an Omotic language, live at a considerable geographical distance from the Nilotic Turkana and Toposa. However, the personal adornment of Hamar men and Turkana men, and of Hamar women and Toposa women, is almost identical. One reason for this may simply be that people migrate on a voluntary or compulsory basis, replace their former language by one which is spoken by a group they have contacts with subsequently (although they may, alternatively, impose their own language on others) but still perpetuate rudiments of their traditional culture (such as body adornment).

When people give up one language for another they may consciously or unconsciously also transmit part of the former language into their new mother tongue. Prominent features of their cultures are reflected in the lexicon; accordingly, one may expect to find a substratum in the newly acquired language. In the recent shift from Elmolo to Samburu, the original Elmolo lexicon pertaining to lake bio-nomenclature and fishing largely survived unscathed (Heine 1982:22). In the current Samburu dialect of the Elmolo, a few terms relating to fishing activities are also attested in other Maa dialects, but most terms are reminiscent of the former Elmolo language.[4]

There are various loan items appearing in Bantu languages whose traces go back to Southern Cushitic, but the donor languages and the communities that spoke these languages are now extinct. The Bantu languages at hand are spoken in Kenya and Tanzania and possibly elsewhere in the area around Lake Victoria (see, for example, the loanword sets in the Taita Bantu languages as described by Ehret and Nurse 1981). There is linguistic evidence that Cushitic groups penetrated into these areas, a claim which fits in with archaeological findings, such as burial sites, which are associated with Cushitic peoples.

The Tanzanian Sandawe and Hadza share at least one typological feature with the Khoisan languages of southern Africa, namely clicks. Given the fact that clicks are unique to these languages and neighboring Bantu languages into which they spread, and to one other in eastern Africa (apart maybe from one or two secret languages in Australia), and given the geographical distance between the two languages in Tanzania and those in southern Africa, there must have been geographical contiguity at one point (also because the languages are genetically related, according to Greenberg 1963a). The additional eastern African language with clicks is a Cushitic language, Dahalo, spoken on the mainland of Kenya near Lamu Island. In view of all this, the early presence of Khoisan languages in eastern Africa seems likely. Whether their speakers were actually driven out or gradually absorbed linguistically and culturally is not clear. The ultimate answer to this question should come from physical anthropology, not from any of the social sciences or linguistics. Investigation of genetic features such a blood types and lactose tolerance (which allows for extensive use of milk) help to reconstruct such patterns. For example, African pygmies are clearly distinct physically from the neighboring negroid peoples with whom they share a symbiotic relationship. The former always speak the language of surrounding nonpygmy groups (mainly Bantu and Adamawa Eastern). Since they are hunter–gatherers with an outstanding knowledge of their natural environment, one might expect to find a substratum influence from their former language. The only trace of earlier languages concerns botanic terminology common to geographically noncontiguous pygmy groups. The same terms, however, are found in genetically related Bantu and Adamawa Eastern languages. The pygmies constitute an old dispersion; what the linguistic facts (substrata) suggest is that they (as well as many other hunter–gatherer bands) shifted their language solidarity several times in their history. Language death as a result of actual genocide is extremely rare in eastern Africa. The spreading and disappearance of languages and language families seems more often than not to be due to horizontal spreading (from one group to another).[5]

5.   Some final remarks

It seems to be generally assumed that language and ethnicity are linked in a direct way, or are even isomorphic (see e.g. Fishman 1977). Giles, Bourhis and Taylor (1977:326) claim that "ethnic group members identify more closely with someone who shares their language than with someone who shares their cultural background". Such a position seems far too strong in the context of eastern Africa (see also Hohenthal and McCorkle 1955; Newman 1970; Dorian 1980a; and Rottland and Okoth Okombo 1986 for a description of cases where language and ethnicity notions are not isomorphic). Language may not be as important a potential symbol of ethnic identity as some are led to believe. The blacksmiths we met in Kapoeta and

Torit (Eastern Equatorial Province, Sudan) identified themselves as Lopid people, and they were known as such, despite the fact that several of them had Tenet as their first language (Dimmendaal 1983b). In their interaction with other groups, even far away from their home area in the Lopid Mountains, they did not claim speaker status as Tenet. It was only after we started collecting terms related to iron-working that it became clear that their actual language was not Lopid, although all of them were also fluent in this language. Pastoral Turkana do not identify themselves with the hunter–gatherers in their territory, despite the fact that the latter share the Turkana linguistic code and refer to themselves as Turkana. The former feel greater empathy and a historic bond with the Jie and Karimojong across the border in Uganda.

A common language is not an immutable part of group identity, and one culture area may comprise different languages. We only have to think of the Ma'a (Mbugu) case in northern Tanzania in order to see the kind of structural linguistic complications such strong ethnic links may give rise to. The lexicon of Ma'a is still the most salient part of the Cushitic heritage in this language. Ma'a has retained features of non-Bantu morphology, but there has been strong interference from Bantu with regard to inflectional morphemes (Ma'a has noun classes like neighboring Bantu languages), whereas derivational morphemes have their source in a Bantu, as well as in a Cushitic (or non-Bantu) language. The historical development of Ma'a probably falls outside the scope of genetic linguistics, according to Thomason (1983b), who also suggests an analogy with the historical development of Anglo-Romani. The strong interference from Bantu (more specifically Pare) is the result of interaction with their Bantu-speaking kinfolk who used to speak the same (non-Bantu) language but shifted to Pare (or Shambaa).

The Ma'a case is, admittedly, rather exceptional, but ethnic membership and identity may be seen as something flexible and negotiable. Intermarriage between members from different ethnic groups further complicates the relation between language and ethnicity. Descendants from intermarriage between patrilineal people may claim their father's ethnicity, but their primary language may be that of the mother, whereas matrilineal people's offspring may acquire both ethnicity and the language of the mother. (See also Bender *et al.* 1976 for a discussion of these matters.)

Situations of stable bilingualism may exist when the functions of particular languages are complementary, as in the case of trade languages. When there is no longer a strict social division of functions one language may expand at the expense of another. Shrinking domains for home language transmission are apparently frequent among hunter–gatherers interacting with other groups in eastern Africa. Population size in combination with significant cultural distance and sociolinguistic isolation of the hunter–gatherers are major causes here. Even hunter–gatherer groups which speak closely related languages (or dialects) may not be aware of each other's existence.

The Akiek of northern Tanzania live as hunter–gatherers among the Maasai, with whom they have close contacts, and whose language they have mastered. In Kenya's Rift Valley, there are people who refer to themselves as the Akiek of Kinare (the name of an area). Their original language, which is closely related to Tanzanian Akiek, is still remembered by a few old men married to Kikuyu women and living in Kikuyu communities. Proficiency in their earlier language does not seem to go beyond the level of a limited corpus of lexical items and phrases, as they all speak Kikuyu nowadays. The two Akiek groups are not aware of each other's existence, nor is there any oral tradition relating them to some other group, although there is at least a third group (the Sogoo) whose language is closely related to theirs (Heine 1973; Rottland 1982:24–5). Clearly these people have lost identity as a group. They have dissolved into separate groups, and ethnic solidarity is now directed towards other societies.

Economic and political conditions are changing rapidly in eastern Africa. Processes of urbanization and modern industrialization these days further act as agents for the diffusion of particular languages at the expense of others. In the case of Amharic and Oromo the expansion was also strengthened by the former imperial administration, missionary activity and mass media (Bender *et al.* 1976:576). Other processes of language contact in the area include pidginization and convergence phenomena. The nature of contact leading to pidginization may be characterized as one in which bilingualism is lacking, and further characterized by social distance and sparsity of contacts. Convergence areas have been described by Heine (1976b). One such convergence area, in this case a syntactic one, is found in Ethiopia where Cushitic and Semitic languages (or, rather, their speakers), have been in close contact with each other over a long period of time. Intrusion of Semitic languages into the area resulted in a major restructuring of the Semitic-language grammars in question, affecting word order (from verb-initial to verb-final, and inversion of other head–modifier constructions), morphology, and phonology (manifested in the rephonologization of systems). Languages were not abandoned but rather restructured as a result of longterm interference from other languages mastered to some extent by speakers (Leslau 1952).

The complexity of situations leading to shift, pidginization, or convergence forces one to refrain from rash generalizations about their causes, let alone from making predictions about when some one of these is supposed to take place. Many cases of language shift in the area are still awaiting investigation. For scholars interested in language contraction from a linguistic or social point of view, eastern Africa is an Eldorado. May the present contribution serve to spur on those in search of such treasure hoards.

Notes

Thanks are due to the following people for their comments and suggestions: Nancy Dorian, Bernd Heine, Harry Stroomer, George van Driem, Peter Unseth.

1. We know very little about the actual processes of structural decay in the dying languages at hand apart from a few case studies such as the one by Heine and Vossen (1980) on Kore. The question of whether language contraction in Kore is comparable to pidginization or, instead, to changes in natural "healthy" languages is discussed in Dimmendaal (1986).

2. According to Greenberg (1963a), the languages now referred to as Kuliak belong to the Eastern Sudanic branch within Nilo-Saharan. Greenberg may have been misled, however, by the numerous borrowings from Nilotic languages, which themselves are clearly part of Eastern Sudanic. It has also been suggested by others that the Kuliak languages belong to Afro-Asiatic. It may well be, however, that they represent the last three languages of a separate language family which has now almost disappeared.

3. The ancestors of the Murle and Tenet constituted the younger generation (age) sets at the time of the dispersal, whereas the older generation sets were formed by the ancestors of the Didinga and Longarim. Ethnogenesis on the basis of generation sets which have split up is a recurrent phenomenon in the eastern African context. When clans are exogamous they cannot form new ethnic groups by themselves. (See also Lamphear 1976 for an illustration on the basis of the ethnogenesis of Teso-Turkana groups.)

4. Such an intrusion of terms may, of course, come about through borrowing without language shift (see e.g. Dimmendaal 1982).

5. This point has also been raised by Lamb (1964:458–9), who notes that territorial expansion and its resulting diversification must ordinarily be accompanied by a roughly corresponding amount of linguistic extinction, since there is a limit to the amount of inhabited area. By implication, linguistic classifications not only shed light on the prehistory of surviving linguistic groups, but also furnish an indication of the extent to which other languages have become extinct. A comparison with the expansion of Indo-European might be enlightening in this respect. As in the case of African migrants, speakers of Indo-European languages may have reached areas which were not yet inhabited by human beings. But the presence of such languages as Basque and Etruscan suggests that in Europe non-Indo-European languages have disappeared from the scene.

2 The disappearance of the Ugong in Thailand

DAVID BRADLEY

The Ugong speech community in western Thailand has been in decline ever since it was first reported, by a surveyor (Kerr 1927); he said that the language was on its last legs in the 1920s. The anthropologist Theodore Stern encountered this group in the 1960s and found the language very moribund (pers. comm.). In a series of visits beginning in 1977, I have found several locations where the language is still regularly used, even by some second-language speakers; but indeed it is virtually dead in the two locations found by Kerr, one of which was also visited by Stern. The language is in the Burmic subgroup of the Tibeto-Burman family.

Factors contributing to language maintenance in the surviving locations are various; some or all of these factors are absent in the other former locations. The political prestige and individual dynamism of recently deceased headmen, though in decline as the Ugong area became settled by Thais, was a major factor in two cases, but failed to promote Ugong in a third where other negative factors were present. Geographical isolation and lack of schools, economic independence, and continuing in-group contacts were all also favorable to Ugong in the same two locations until very recently. Now roads, schools, cash crops, and large-scale influx of Thais have changed this. Another negative factor has been extensive marriage with other groups, partly due to a lack of suitable Ugong spouses as the community contracted. There is a strong stigma in Thailand attached to minority status; some of the effects are noted below (p. 39); Ugong are beginning to feel this stigma increasingly strongly.

To consider the political aspect first, it should be noted that the Ugong have been in contact with the Thai government for over two hundred years; they marched as subjects in parades from the beginning of the current dynasty in 1782.[1] This is hardly surprising, as they live along the major invasion route between Burma and Thailand, which the Burmese had used in the attacks that ended the preceding Thai dynasty. In particular, the Ugong village recently known as *Ban Lawa* ('Lawa village', hereafter *BL*), was next to the western branch of the *Khwɛ* or *Mɛklong* river (the River Kwai of Thailand–Burma railway fame) at the head of navigation, near the Three Pagodas Pass.

This particular village was until recently the township center (*tambol*) for a cluster of villages; it was probably under the political control of the Karen chiefs of nearby Sangkhlaburi before direct Thai administration. The township headman (*kamnan*) was Ugong; the last Ugong to hold this position is still alive, and still has some local prestige. The township was demoted to being a village (*muban*) with only a village headman (*phujajban*) when he retired quite some time ago; and the village headman is his son-in-law, who is Thai.

On the other branch of the same river was the village of *Nasuan* ('field and garden', hereafter *NS*). There the political leadership has been Thai for some time; in fact the father of the last Ugong township headman at *BL* was headman at *NS* some fifty years ago, but the current leaders did not acknowledge any Ugong ancestry. In the more vigorously Ugong village of *Kok Chiang* (hereafter *KC*[2]) to the east, the last Ugong village headman had died a couple of years before my first visit, to be replaced by his Lao son-in-law. Finally, in the village of *Khɔk Khwaj* (hereafter *KK*) to the north, the last Ugong township headman had retired some years before and died about ten years ago; since his retirement all the headmen have been Thai, and the township has been demoted to a village.

Headmen are usually selected by village consensus, but are often the sons or sons-in-law of the previous incumbent; they serve only while still vigorous, since they must settle village disputes, control who lives in the village, and act as the village's contact and spokesman with the district officer (*naj amphə*). Thus an Ugong headman both provides prestige for the group and maintains an Ugong focus for his village or township. There are no serving Ugong headmen left, but those of *KC* and *KK* are remembered with affection and respect.

In recent times, the other natural leader in a village, especially if he is a local person, has been the teacher in charge of the primary school. Education reform in the 1930s resulted in the establishment of a school at *BL*; naturally the teachers were all Thai at first, and according to still-current policy they forbade the use of any language other than Thai in school. Later there was one Ugong teacher at this school; he met Stern, but had died long before I first came to the village in 1977. At *NS* there was also a school, but it never had any Ugong teachers to my knowledge. In *KK* a school was set up a couple of kilometers away during the late 1960s; all the teachers have always been Thai. For *KC* there is no readily accessible school; a new school set up in the late 1970s is about 5 kilometers away but is not attended by any village children.

Though in theory primary education is compulsory, and has been since the 1930s, it is only the Ugong at *BL* and *NS* who have had access to schools for this long. At *KK* some Ugong have now completed primary school; but at

KC the only education has been in monasteries. There are a few monasteries around Thailand which specialize in educating members of non-Thai minorities; some individual Ugong males have gone to one in Chiangmai or one near Suphanburi, but most have no education, or only go to nearby monasteries with very modest facilities. In summary, local availability of education for about fifty years is clearly a major factor in the death of Ugong at *NS* and *BL*, with the Ugong teacher in the latter as a mitigating factor. The absence of schools until quite recently is similarly a factor in the maintenance of Ugong at *KK* and *KC*.

The geographical isolation of *KK* and *KC*, which are in hilly areas with little in the way of natural communications, is in stark contrast to the accessibility of *BL* and *NS*, both of which were on the banks of navigable rivers. Until recently, rivers were the main channels of communication in Thailand. With the development of railways in the early twentieth century and the truly massive expansion of roads over the last couple of decades this changed radically; but *BL* and *NS* were both well-favored by these developments. The Thailand–Burma Railway passed near *BL*; older individuals remember using it for travel to Bangkok in the 1940s before the British removed the tracks. *NS* had a reasonable road by the mid-1970s; *KC* and *KK* only became accessible by dry-weather road in the late 1970s.

Also in the late 1970s, the Electricity Generating Authority of Thailand built two hydro-electric dams on the two branches of the *Khwɛ* river. These dams have flooded the original sites of *BL* and *NS*; the inhabitants have been relocated elsewhere, on land allocated by lot. There was some compensation for irrigable land and fruit trees, but the new land is not similar to that flooded, and the unity of the villages has not been preserved. I have not been to one area since the inundation, but in the other case old speakers or semi-speakers of Ugong are scattered among three or more settlement sites and have no one to speak to in Ugong. Thus the final stage is almost literally language death by immersion.

Even prior to the resettlements, there had been very large migrations of Thais and others into the formerly uninhabited areas around all four Ugong villages. *BL* had a Thai village a kilometer away and a Thai district town about 4 kilometers away; *NS* had become engorged by Thais and hemmed in upslope by Karens. *KC* has had an adjacent Lao village for many years, but recent Thai arrivals have moved into the village, especially in the last eight years since roads were cut nearby and a school set up. *KK* has had Karens nearby for a long time, but latterly Thais have also come in, especially since the road was built.

The influx of Thais has led to the Ugong being a minority everywhere except within the boundaries of their own hamlets; both *KC* and *KK* villages now have a non-Ugong majority, mostly living in separate hamlets or isolated houses but some even in the Ugong hamlets. The Thais also cause severe economic dislocation because of land tenure; title to land has been given without regard to traditional Ugong fallow cycles for swiddening, and Thais now own much of the traditional Ugong territory. Ugong families have been left with no choice but to replant fields that would normally have been left fallow for years, since their other fields no longer belong to them. The Thai farmers have been growing cash crops, such as sugarcane and tapioca, which will deplete the soil much more rapidly than traditional Ugong rice, grain, and vegetable crops. A further depredation is due to timber companies which come in and remove all the trees; this leads to erosion and flooding, which the Thai authorities like to blame on swidden agriculture.

Though the economic selfreliance of the Ugong has been severely shaken by these changes, they have gained some benefits. In the traditional Ugong society there were no cash crops and the villages were almost entirely selfsufficient. Recently, the timber companies and Thai farmers at *KC* and *KK* have been employing Ugong as day-laborers, and Thai traders have set up in both villages to buy certain Ugong produce for sale elsewhere. This development has only been possible since the arrival of roads; and the produce-buyers are the only vehicular transport regularly traveling from *KC* and *KK* to the market towns and back. The markups are severe: for example, cherry tomatoes bought from the Ugong for about six cents a kilogram are sold for up to ten times that elsewhere. Fruits and vegetables are the main cash crops; soft drinks, sauces, candy, canned foods, and cigarettes are sold by the traders in their shops in the village. It is odd to see Ugong drinking warm soft drinks (no electricity, and thus no ice, is available) which cost the equivalent of three kilograms of cherry tomatoes or a tenth of a day's wage. Another Thai entrepreneur has set up a small rice mill in *KC*; unfortunately this mill removes the husks, and thus most of the protein, far more efficiently than the traditional but slow foot mortar. Ugong are pleased about this, however, both because it saves a lot of time and because it represents a sign of progress.

The Ugong villages formerly maintained some contact with each other; in fact *KC* was established within living memory from intermediate villages, since changed into Thai villages, which had been settled from *NS*; and *KK* was the result of a migration of about the same date from *BL*. As noted above, the former headman of *BL* had come from *NS* as a youth; some current residents of *KC* came from *KK* within the last couple of decades to marry. There is still very occasional visiting between *KC* and *KK*; but much more visiting goes on between *KC* and the much closer Lao villages.

Marriage has long been a negative influence for the maintenance of Ugong. The Ugong tend to marry people from an adjacent village; in the last fifty years or so, in-migration has meant that for every Ugong village the nearby villages are Karen, Thai, Lao, or almost anything but Ugong. In *BL*, the last marriage between two Ugong is said to have been about fifty years ago; there were Thai, Karen, Khmer, Khmu, and other non-Ugong in *BL* before it was relocated, and only a few people, mostly semi-speakers and all over age 50, who had some recall of Ugong. The more fluent speakers were all aged over 60, and all married to non-Ugong. In the surrounding villages a few former speakers and semi-speakers could be found, also all old; their spouses, were Mon, Karen, Thai, and so on.

As for *NS*, the community was so far gone prior to relocation that no one in *NS* itself would admit to speaking Ugong; I found two 60-year-old semi-speakers in a Thai village, and an extremely old speaker in a Khmu village; all his descendants, who had trundled him out, proclaimed that they were Thai. Paradoxically, the best speaker in this area was an old Khmu widow whose husband had been Ugong. This evidence of dispersion and intermarriage presumably suggests a further stage beyond *BL*; in fact the former headman of *BL* was very surprised to hear that Ugong was no longer spoken at *NS*, as it was more vigorous there than in *BL* when he came to *BL* from *NS* in the 1920s.

At *KC* the neighboring Lao village has long been the source of spouses: Lao males tend to come and live in *KC* with their Ugong wives; presumably the reverse also occurs, but I was not able to find anyone in the surrounding Lao villages who would admit to being Ugong. In *KC* several of the Lao males who have lived in the village for the longest time now speak fluent Ugong. Some of their children also speak Ugong fluently, despite the fact that because of their fathers they are officially Lao, not Ugong;[3] but some of the children are semi-speakers. The most recent marriage between two Ugong involved a spouse who came from *KK* some 15 years ago; after the couple had two children, a kinship connection was discovered that Thais would classify as incestuous. This has discouraged any further group-internal marriages; nearly all the Ugong in *KC* are already too closely related for marriage.

In *KK* there are quite a few marriages, even recent ones, involving two Ugong spouses; but there are also Lao, Northern Thai, and Thai husbands. The village has two hamlets; one is next to the Thai headman's new house and the other is a couple of kilometers away. The latter is perhaps the most solid Ugong community surviving. Most of the mixed couples live in the first-mentioned hamlet, and most of the Ugong who have attended school come from there. The Thai headman's son has taken an Ugong wife from this hamlet, but on the whole the non-Ugong have not learned to speak Ugong at *KK*; this may reflect the more recent onset of extensive intermarriage.

With a long past history of intermarriage, many individuals have assumed the non-Ugong ethnicity of one parent. In a couple of generations the memory of any Ugong background may disappear. It may be that this is what had already happened in *NS*, and nearly so around *BL*.

It is therefore almost impossible to enumerate the Ugong population; as noted, much of the population of the Ugong villages is officially not classified as Ugong, and many Ugong have married out and are living in nearby villages where they are difficult to find. Further, there are various villages between *NS* and *KC* which people in *KC* cite as Ugong communities but which now claim to be entirely Thai. The example of the Ugong grandfather in the Khmu resettlement village near *NS* is not unusual: people who can be shown to have been Ugong by descent are now regarded, and regard themselves, as Thai. Relatives of Ugong people in *KC* have also "passed" in the same way to create the "Thai" villages; one person will deny that he is Ugong and that he speaks Ugong and will cite an individual in another village who is, and does. But on arrival in that village the investigator finds that the named individual will deny it but will cite the original person in the first village as a speaker.

It is only in the two Ugong-solidary villages, *KC* and *KK*, that speakers are readily findable; these are the only locations where Ugong is regularly spoken, even in the presence of outsiders. And it was only when I already spoke some Ugong after work in *KC* that I was able to elicit Ugong at all successfully from former speakers at *BL* and *NS*. With Thai officials and traders all Ugong speak Thai; it is safe to say that there are no monolingual Ugong. In *KC* most Ugong also speak the local variety of Lao, known as Lao Dan (the village is in *Dan Chang* district); in *BL* those individual former speakers and semi-speakers who have intermarried with the surrounding Karen also speak Karen. Ugong spouses who go to live in other minority villages learn those languages (Mon, Khmu, Karen, and so on), all as second languages; in nearly all cases they cease to use Ugong on leaving an Ugong village.

At *BL* I found three speakers and a small number of semi-speakers in 1977, as well as a few former speakers and former semi-speakers in adjacent villages; but there are certainly many more who have "passed". In villages around *NS* there were a few former speakers or former semi-speakers, and many more who were cited by others but denied any speaking ability. In *KC* there are some eighty speakers, plus about ten Lao second-language speakers and about ten of their children who are semi-speakers; nearby villages contain a number of former speakers, nearly all of whom have "passed". AT *KK* I would estimate over a hundred speakers, and a couple of second-language speakers with very limited knowledge of Ugong. Thus the number of current speakers is around two hundred, with a substantial but indeterminable number of former speakers, a small number of semi-speakers of various ages, and a handful of second-language speakers.

The Thai official classification of minorities includes Ugong in the category *Lawa*; this category also includes various unrelated Mon–Khmer languages in northern Thailand, several hundred kilometers away. Ugong is a Tibeto-Burman language fairly closely related to Burmese, and more distantly related to Karen; it is genetically and structurally quite different from Mon–Khmer languages as well as from Thai. The Thai category *Lawa* is a sort of residual one, for small groups of people following similar cultural patterns to the Thai but in marginal areas. It is only *KC* and *KK* which are officially categorized as *Lawa* villages, despite the name of *BL*; and in view of the current linguistic situation this is quite appropriate.

Being a member of a recognized minority conveys certain privileges in Thai society, but even these are often regarded as a disability. For example, minorities are not required to register and have identity cards; they are not required to do military service. Many Ugong nevertheless register themselves as Thai, and males often wish to serve in the army because of travel and pay. The Thai government provides special welfare centres (*nikhom*) for the minorities, which are intended to assist with agricultural, animal husbandry, and educational services; *KC* is within the geographical area of one such center, but has gained no benefit from it.[4] There are also provincial centers for minorities, including one in the province where *KK* is located; but the services provided are more relief than assistance: blankets during the cool season and suchlike.

By contrast, there is a strong stigma attached by most individual Thais at the local level to minorities. Thais feel considerable pride in their history; they gradually conquered what is now Thailand from a variety of other large groups such as the Mons, Khmers, and others, finishing about five hundred years ago. Thailand has guarded its independence against other local as well as colonial powers ever since. Thai ethnicity includes various subgroups, all speaking very closely related dialects; its three pillars are the Thai race, the Thai King, and the Thai religion, Theravada Buddhism. By contrast, minorities are on the whole conquered or peripheral groups who have come into the Thai orbit. Though the government officially recognizes them as equal, in practical terms they are not.

The resulting unofficial stigma has motivated the virtually complete assimilation of the longstanding Mon and Khmer residents of central Thailand into the Thai population, though more recent arrivals or those in remoter regions have not disappeared. For the Ugong, the stigma often results in individuals rejecting and denying their ethnicity, and making substantial efforts to assimilate and disappear. Such assimilation is facilitated by the absence of any major cultural or religious differences between Thai and Ugong at the village level. The religion is the same; *KC* and *KK* both have small monasteries, and *BL* and *NS* used to have these before they were flooded out. Both follow similar agricultural practices,[5] have similar diets, wear the same clothes, have similar houses, and attend the same schools if they attend a school. Some of this similarity is not old: Ugong clothes used to be distinctive, and some crops are fairly recently introduced; but the general lack of distinctness has facilitated individual and even whole-village "passing", while the low status of minorities generally has motivated it.

Thus it seems that it is only a combination of an effective political leader, geographical and economic isolation, and lack of extensive contact with Thais and Thai education that has maintained the Ugong-speaking communities at *KC* and *KK*. However, all these factors have changed radically in the last ten years. In communities which have not had such isolation, Ugong is effectively a dead language. It is therefore possible to investigate the disappearance of an ethnicity and its language as a process, and it will be possible to observe the process as it continues.

Ugong shows profound linguistic effects from its contact with Thai; dialect diversification has been rapid, as reported in Bradley (1978, 1981). Most changes have been in the direction of convergence with Thai, as described in Bradley (1986); the causes of this are explored in Bradley (1985b). For evidence on the loss of morphological and phonological complexity in the speech of semi-speakers, see Bradley (1988).

Notes

I am pleased to acknowledge the support of the Australian Research Grants Committee under grant A76/15652 in 1977 and of the Joint Southeast Asia Programs of the American Council of Learned Societies and the Social Science Research Council, supported by the Ford Foundation, in 1979–80. I also gratefully thank the National Research Council of Thailand, colleagues and friends at Thai universities, and especially the Ugong, who welcomed me to their villages and helped me to study their language.

1. These annual parades in Bangkok were the formal expression of subject status; the Ugong (under the Thai name *Lawa*, which now also refers to other groups speaking a variety of Mon–Khmer languages) and the Karen were the only two minorities represented from the beginning. These parades are no longer held.
2. *Kok Chiang* and *Khɔk Khwaj* are placenames with no obvious meaning.
3. Children of mixed marriages usually take the ethnicity of their parent in the higher-prestige group; this is generally the father. The decision is normally made when registering for an identity card at the age of 18, though not all Ugong do register. Lao is one of the main subgroups of Thai ethnicity.
4. The center is only a couple of kilometers away in a straight line, but the only road is very circuitous; village leaders generally regard the center as useless in any case, as the Ugong are too advanced to benefit from the rudimentary assistance available there.
5. Ugong and Thai both prefer irrigated land when available, but in marginal areas swidden agriculture prevails. As the only remaining Ugong villages are in marginal areas, this type of farming is now more common for them.

3   Scottish and Irish Gaelic: The giant's bed-fellows

SEOSAMH WATSON

When a language has been in retreat for a long time and its distribution has been shrinking at the same time that its functions have been dwindling, difficulties are very likely to arise in even such basic matters as determining just who should be considered a "speaker" or a "member" of the speaker community. The "native speaker" population itself may not agree on who falls within that category: some people may claim speaker status when others would not accept them as such; some may say that they are *not* speakers when others would include them as speakers. If the speaker population cannot agree on its own membership, then the problems for the researcher are bound to be even more acute. This chapter tries to deal with each of these matters in turn, community structure and speaker self-identification on the one hand, and encounters between communities and the investigator in search of speakers on the other.

1.   The community

1.1.   Irish and Scottish Gaelic-speaking areas

The modern native Irish and Scottish Gaelic-speaking populations, now largely confined to the extreme northern and western fringes of Ireland and Scotland and having the appearance of being self-contained entities are, nonetheless, in many ways a community within a community.[1] Their members for the most part share the same racial inheritance as the general Irish and Scottish populations respectively and have religious affiliations in common with a greater or smaller section of the larger community. But above all, they must struggle for a place alongside English, that giant among the world's modern languages. And it is in English, the public language in both countries, that most official business, and especially written transactions, are negotiated, the percentage of monoglot speakers of these minority languages being now so small as to be irrelevant (Thomson 1983:11). The totality of the areas in which the modern descendants of the historical

Goedelic (or Q-Celtic) division of the Celtic branch within the Indo-European language family survive is conveniently referred to as the *Gaeltacht* in modern Irish usage and the *Gaidhealtachd* in Scottish Gaelic. The Irish usage, moreover, employs the *Gaeltacht* (pl. *Gaeltachtaí*) with reference to each individual locality where Irish has survived as the speech of at least some percentage of the community. It is my intention to make use of the Irish term in this way throughout the paper, with respect to both Irish and Scottish Gaelic-speaking areas.

The actual boundaries of the modern Gaeltachtaí (as distinct from the territorial extent ascribed to them in Ireland by act of Parliament) are usually well known, as Fennel has shown (1981:35–6), both to their inhabitants and to those of neighboring areas.

1.2.   Linguistic make-up of Gaeltacht areas

The inherent weakness of the Irish and Scottish Gaelic-speaking communities is illustrated by the fact that some individuals within the community itself frequently dissociate themselves from the language, behaving as if they were virtually monoglot English speakers, and many others use the language but rarely. The number of resident monoglot English speakers has itself increased as a result of incomers,[2] returning emigrés, and people who have grown up in homes in which the language is no longer spoken – and the majority of parents in the major Gaeltachtaí have not used Gaelic with their children since the 1970s, according to Fennel (1981; see also Ó Murchú 1985:29).[3]

This linguistically mixed composition of the Gaeltacht population means that it is not always clear to outsiders, or even to the oldest members of the community, who can speak the traditional language and who cannot. Likewise, the youngest speakers, who have ever more limited opportunities to practice the language, what with the constant reduction of the community, may not themselves always be aware of the full extent of their linguistic abilities. The inhabitants of an area where Irish or Scottish Gaelic is spoken by a smaller or greater percentage of their number recognize the local community as the total population of the village/parish/townland/island in question, and not on the basis of who can or cannot speak the traditional language. Speakers do not, on the whole, feel the need to define themselves according to language, possibly because the linguistic distinction is more incidental than essential to the basic functioning of the community. Ó Murchú sums up the situation (1985:34): "[T]he relationship is not that of national language to regional language . . . nor are distinctive subcommunities as strongly defined by language allegiance as they are, for example, by denominational allegiance."

A notable feature of relic linguistic populations in those parts of Ireland and Scotland where the number of speakers has been reduced to a relatively small group is that they often follow one or another of the traditional means

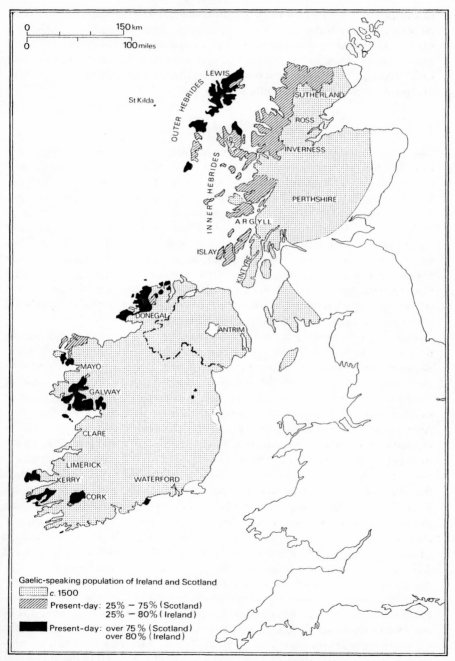

Irish and Scottish Gaelic speakers circa *1500 and at the present day*
Sources: *Census Reports (Ireland 1961, Scotland 1971), and for the Gaelic-speaking areas*
circa *1500, Ó Murchú (1985: Map 6)*

of livelihood – fishing, crofting, sheep-rearing, etc. (Dorian 1978b:11–13). Noteworthy too is the fact that surviving speakers of the language under such circumstances sometimes belong to one or another of a very small number of families. In Ireland such people are often characterized by strong loyalty to a particular political party or doctrine, as I have myself observed in Gaeltacht areas in several regions.

1.3.   Attitude of speakers towards the language

The Irish language has a specially recognized status under the Republic's Constitution as "the national language" and "the first official language" (Constitution of Ireland. Article 8). Such official recognition of the language, although in many ways theoretical, means that most speakers, who are also aware that their language was once the speech of most of Ireland, are of the opinion that it is still of some relevance to the population as a whole. They have, however, no illusions about their role and are unwilling to make inordinate sacrifices, as it seems to them, in depriving their children of a knowledge of English. A common catch-phrase used by Gaeltacht people on the subject is that they will not become "the conscience of the nation" with regard to the revival of Irish; such a revival is an avowed objective of all major political parties in the State.

The situation described contrasts in many ways with that found among Gaelic speakers in Scotland, where the language is now primarily regarded as pertaining only to the western Highlands and Western Isles as opposed to the Germanic speech of the lowland zone; this very prevalent notion disregards the true historical situation with regard to the previous extent of Gaelic throughout the whole country (see Thomson 1976:3). On the other hand, Gaelic seems to inspire large numbers of its native speakers with a degree of attachment and affection not encountered in the Irish Gaeltacht. This feeling may derive, as Withers (1985:161, 173, 203, 246) has suggested, from the connection of the language with religious observance over the past few centuries, but it may equally be connected with the Jacobite era and the proscriptions which followed the 1745 Rising in the Highlands. After "the '45" Gaelic was often perceived as being both an emblem of nationhood and a bond of brotherhood, as expressed in Mac Mhaighstir Alasdair's famous poem of the period in praise of the language (MacDonald and Macdonald 1924:2–9). Gaelic is portrayed as a badge of trust in an anecdote related to me by my main informant in east Ross-shire. It recounts how an elderly relative of hers, having traveled to Canada in her old age to be with relatives there, found no one at the quayside to meet her. On being approached with an offer of assistance by a Gaelic-speaking stranger, her reaction was: "Oh, I'll go along with you when you speak the Gaelic, though you were a tramp – though you were a robber." The same sentiment is echoed in the statement made to me by a neighbor of the above informant's, an old lady with only a passive knowledge of the language: "Because we have a side [i.e. a liking] to anyone that'll speak the Gaelic. It draws us like a magnet. Anybody that'll speak the Gaelic I've a side to them and I'll trust my life to them."

1.4. Public and private faces of the language

Insofar as the Irish-speaking element of a Gaeltacht population has a separate *public* existence this will tend to revolve around activities organized in the language, such as church services, local festivals or national festivals celebrated in a Gaeltacht venue, e.g. the annual national cultural festival of each language, the *Oireachtas* in Ireland and the *Mòd* in Scotland, or the activities of a local Summer Language College or radio station. The Colleges are often of crucial importance in Ireland in assisting the survival of traditional verbal art forms such as singing or storytelling, as well as in developing some of the more modern idioms like drama and debate, in that they provide a stimulus for local talents and a focal point for speakers of the language. The Irish Gaeltacht radio service, first introduced on Easter Monday 1972, provides the larger community with access to expert practitioners of the skills referred to and helps, in turn, to develop similar abilities in others. At the private level, the traditional forms of entertainment in Irish and Scottish Gaelic may continue in a given neighborhood in particular houses which are noted for their hospitality and good cheer. This practice of night-visiting, known in many areas as going on *céilí*, is stronger in more isolated communities and ensures the continuing survival of these prestigious verbal skills.

1.5. Speakers in an urban setting

In addition to the linguistic communities in those areas where the languages have traditionally been spoken, groups of speakers are also to be found in the regional and local capitals. These urban communities are of long standing both in Ireland (O'Rahilly 1913:156–62) and in Scotland (MacKinnon 1984:503; Withers 1985:182–208) but do not appear to have been selfperpetuating.[4] In Scotland the focus for such groups has traditionally been the Gaelic Chapel. In modern times the cultural activities of these urban speakers often appear to have been subsumed, both in Scotland and in Ireland, under their respective county associations in the city in which they happen to reside, as, for example, in the case of the *Donegalmen's Association* in Dublin which contains many native Irish speakers from that county but which, as an institution, functions in English. Attempts to set up a similar organization in Irish to cater for the people in question were made over a decade ago but came to naught. Only those individuals who are particularly motivated in support of the language will join the urban-based linguistic and cultural organizations such as *Conradh na Gaeilge* ('The

Gaelic League') in Ireland and *An Comann Gàidhealach* ('the Highland Association') in Scotland, or involve their children in the recent projects to provide them with education in the native language of the parents – very often not now the language of the home.

1.6.   The dialectal nature of the languages

As previously mentioned, the various Irish and Scottish Gaeltachtaí are largely fragmented and divided from each other – islands, as it were, in a sea of English. What was once a Gaelic continuum, extending from the extreme south of Ireland to the far north of Scotland, linked at the level of the intelligentsia by the prestigious Classical Irish norm until the dissolution of the learnèd orders in the former country in the mid-seventeenth century and the mid-eighteenth in the latter, has now developed into three separate languages (the moribund Gaelic of the Isle of Man being the third) expressed in a whole series of dialects along the way.[5] The pre-eminence of these dialects in modern Ireland is amply demonstrated by the fact that the Gaeltacht radio service divides its broadcasting time by and large among the three major dialect groupings with control residing in the central dialect region.

Speakers tend to view themselves principally as members of their own local dialect group and their allegiances are thus equally local on the linguistic level.[6] They will relate fairly well to speakers of reasonably similar dialects, say, within the same county or along the same valley or coastline, and, to a diminishing extent, to speakers of dialectal varieties which are less comprehensible to them. (The older generation in Donegal, for example, do not generally listen to radio broadcasts from the other counties.) In some instances speakers of widely dissimilar dialects resort to their respective brands of English in order to carry on a conversation together, rather than make the effort of continuing to struggle with one another's comparatively unfamiliar native speech forms. A learner who masters the dialect of a particular area will be deemed a good speaker by the local inhabitants while another who may speak a different dialect with even greater proficiency will not be reckoned as good. Unfamiliar dialects will be described as *crua*[7] (Irish 'hard'), and where a speaker has enough confidence in his own dialect he may even stigmatize others as wrong or, in Scotland, associate them with particular forms of Gaelic often spoken of with disfavour, such as *Gàidhlig nan Ceàirdean* ('Tinkers' Gaelic') or Lochaber Gaelic.[8]

Speakers of dialects which have a number of features unfamiliar to the majority of speakers from other regions, e.g. County (Co.) Donegal Irish or the Gaelic of eastern mainland Scotland, are often aware of the unusual nature of their dialect. This awareness is heightened in the case of individuals who have learned to read, as they will also perceive the gap between their own dialect and the literary form.

The situation in Ireland is additionally complicated by the fact that, apart from the traditional dialectal variations, the State has, since 1958, been promoting a synthetic standard written form of the language (generally referred to as *An Caighdeán* 'the Standard'), which is based on historical and modern regional variants (Greene 1966: 14–15; Ó Murchú 1985: 46–7). This standard is taught nationally at all levels in the educational system and employed by government agencies in official documents where an Irish version is required.

In Scotland, on the other hand, the most vigorously flourishing dialects are reasonably similar to one another and are to be encountered as a group in close proximity one to the other, i.e. in the Outer Hebrides, Skye, and the mainland opposite. The speech of this area – corresponding as it does also to the literary language of the post-classical era – is generally taken as the modern standard form, with the outlying dialects of the south and east largely ignored. (A recent BBC television series, *Can Seo* [Macleod 1979], aimed at teaching Gaelic to beginners, employed actors from Lewis and Skye, in the Outer and Inner Hebrides respectively.)

2. Researchers and the community

2.1. Gaining access

Investigators making approaches to members of an Irish or Scottish Gaelic-speaking community with a view to studying their speech generally have no difficulties at the outset, as the traditional Gaelic code of hospitality and generosity (see Ó Catháin 1985:6 for illustration from folk legend and also O'Rahilly 1921:1–4 for didactic material from literary sources), together with at least a limited amount of pride in the local language, will afford him or her a first hearing. This is all the more true should the researcher have a reasonable command of the language in question.

Much also depends on the investigator forging strong personal links with an informant; and, in the case of Irish or Scottish Gaelic communities where members follow, or have until recently followed, the traditional occupations of fishing, crofting, weaving, etc., a familiarity with such work on the part of the researcher can create a lasting bond between him or her and the informant, as vividly described by a folklore collector from Co. Donegal (Ó hEochaidh 1966:11). An awareness of local customs and habits, as, for instance, nicknaming,[9] the importance of which in one Scottish Gaelic-speaking community is described by Dorian (1970:303–19), and a sensitivity to the beliefs of the people, such as sabbatarianism (i.e. the avoidance of unnecessary work or travel on a Sunday) in the Scottish Highlands, are obviously indispensable to a fieldworker hoping to be accepted by the community he or she is intending to work among.

Another group of people who can assist a researcher gain access to a Gaeltacht community are its members who are resident in the urban areas of the country (see above). Introductions obtained from such people as well as through professional people in the Gaeltacht area itself, such as clergy, teachers, etc., can be most helpful and are often well worth seeking.

2.2.   *Local attitudes towards the local speech*

Many researchers working in communities where the numbers of speakers have been reduced to a mere handful will have had the experience of being directed by the very people whom they wished to interview to approach other individuals in the locality who spoke a dialect belonging to an area where the language still thrived. In such cases as these and also where speakers feel their dialect is "out on a limb", as it were, it is often difficult to persuade a local speaker that one wishes seriously to study his or her dialect. In the east Ross-shire village where I carried out most of my Scottish fieldwork I met with two reactions which are worthy of mention à propos of this. My chief informant announced to her neighbors initially that I was studying the local Gaelic because it was the "Inverness-shire Gaelic" and therefore the "right Gaelic", but, as years passed and she came to accept my attention to her dialect, she derived confidence from this and began to tell people that I was working with her because she had the right Gaelic which was (now) "the Ross-shire Gaelic". The other reaction which I encountered was from speakers of Lewis Gaelic (the most vigorous of all the Scottish dialects) living locally who were – as they continue to be to this day – incredulous that I could seriously have embarked on the study of what was from their point of view such a corrupt, or at best eccentric, dialect.

2.3.   *Interference from other dialects*

The fieldworker in his or her efforts to record and study a particular dialect of Irish or Scottish Gaelic felt by its speakers to be somewhat isolated or less prestigious than other dialects is liable to meet with interference from other dialects in the form of intrusive features at all levels of the language. Broadcasters from Co. Donegal, for instance, are known to adopt dialectal forms used by their colleagues from other regions, and one north Co. Donegal informant of mine regularly substitutes the negative particle *ní* for *cha* (which is the common form in his own dialect) when engaged in recording sessions with me. The effects of having been educated through the medium of Irish, increasingly apparent nowadays in the form of spelling pronunciations, are detectable even with older people who were at school before the Standard began to be introduced. I cite in this connection the abandonment of the traditional vigesimal system of counting; Lucas (1979:80) has drawn attention to this in a north Co. Donegal dialect and a septuagenarian informant of mine in the south of the same county regularly uses *nócha* 'ninety' for *ceithre fichid is a deich* 'four twenties and ten'.

While working in eastern Scotland I discovered that certain informants had a tendency to pronounce stressed final -*aigh* as /ai̯/ from time to time, rather than /ɛ/, the normal reflex in their dialect (see Watson 1986:66), in an endeavor to conform to the pronunciation of speakers of the western dialects. In one instance the only surviving speaker in a particular village had introduced standardizations like this one into his speech in the case of certain words and it was only by questioning him directly on the unusual forms that I discovered what the true situation was.

3. Weakening of the community

3.1. The effects of English

The phenomenon referred to above of native speakers completely opting out of their maternal speech community is, of course, directly related to the economic and cultural power of the majority language by which they are surrounded. MacKinnon (1984:505) puts it very graphically in the following statement: "[T]he line of bilingualism runs through every home and meeting place in Gaelic Scotland", and this is literally true of Ireland also. In more than one Gaeltacht area I have spoken to young people whose parents would communicate with them as children in English, whereas communication between the parents themselves or between the children would be largely in Irish.

At the present time pressure on young people and on school-going children to opt for English as their everyday language may have originated in the school environment where either the instruction may be given in English – in Ireland this would apply where there are not sufficient numbers of Irish-speaking children in a school catchment area within the Gaeltacht – or where the instruction may be given in the traditional language but where the presence of a handful of English-speaking children is often sufficient to induce the children generally to employ English as their language of play. Other areas in which I myself have noted a particularly strong impact from English are the various modern cosmopolitan youth cults such as pop music,[10] fashion, and football, particularly as purveyed through the omnipresent media of radio and television. The dramatic effect these have had on the linguistic behavior of the youth in the Gaeltacht has not been systematically studied, to my knowledge, but is quite evident even to the casual observer.

As regards the view which the native community as a whole has of the language, there is no doubt that both Irish and Scottish Gaelic suffer from a traditional lack of prestige as languages, e.g. they have not been the medium of important public institutions and personages, nor have they been perceived as the languages of education or as having a strong written tradition,[11] but are associated rather with an unsophisticated, nonlearnèd folk culture, particularly since the Great Famine and other events which took place in the nineteenth century, according to Wall (1969:85). In the Irish of Co. Donegal the word *Gael* itself, meaning traditionally a person of Irish speech and habits, has now come to be used to refer to a Roman Catholic, in contradistinction to *Albanach* which originally signified a Scot and now denotes a Protestant in Co. Donegal Irish, since many Protestants are descended from Scottish planters of past centuries (Ó Catháin 1985:17).

The ability to speak English is often a status marker for Gaeltacht people, as is clear not only from their eagerness to be seen to be competent to speak the language whenever the opportunity arises but also from the number and nature of English loanwords in the modern dialects. As in other cases of prolonged language contact, there is not only a modern technical element in the vocabulary, but also a number of everyday loanwords from English, such as *beautiful, done, clean, nice,* etc. (MacBain 1894:79), whose presence is more difficult to explain. One researcher (Ó Catháin 1985:xx), referring to the presence of these loans in the speech of elderly Co. Donegal *monoglots,* posits a stylistic motivation. In a personal communication to me he cites in this connection the interesting example *"bhí sé* black *dubh",* literally 'It was black black'.

3.2.   *Borrowings from English*

The dual phenomenon of such technical and colloquial loanwords has the effect of making the languages appear more like patois to nonspeakers and, at the same time, reducing the confidence of the native speakers themselves in their language.[12] The status of speakers in the eyes of their English-speaking neighbors may sometimes also be lowered by unsuccessful efforts on the part of the former to locate an appropriate English word for incorporation into an Irish phrase, as when I was once informed that petrol was *"iontach* ('very') expenses" by a Co. Donegal speaker who should have said "expensive". This practice has been so prevalent in that particular county at least that it has been effectively parodied by a modern novelist in a work by him set in his native community there (Mac Grianna 1969).

The borrowing by Irish and Scottish Gaelic of technical vocabulary has naturally increased apace since the early decades of this century and as virtually all speakers of these languages are now also English speakers there is no comprehension barrier to employing the English term for a new object or concept, this in fact being the easiest course of action. The apparent inability of their languages to deal with the ranges of thought and activity of the modern world no doubt leads to further loss of confidence on the part of speakers.[13] Efforts to introduce equivalent modern native terms via the media and the educational system in order to supply this need have not been notably successful so far. This is the more effortful course of action and is at variance with the traditionally accepted means of supplying new vocabulary;

and some coined terms are so close to the English word colloquially used as to seem something of a ludicrous distortion of this, e.g. *aspeist* 'asbestos', the use of which would make the speaker appear ridiculous in the eyes of his neighbors or at best mark him out as something of an eccentric in the community. Only young people trained in Irish in the schools could expect to introduce and employ such words among themselves with any degree of success. On the other hand, it is clear that increasing numbers of young people are opting for English altogether.

3.3.   Traditional domains of the language

Reference has already been made to those areas of community life such as public administration, justice, and education from which Irish and Scottish Gaelic have traditionally been excluded, and it is necessary now to examine areas in which the languages have traditionally been strong and note the current situation here also.

Religion. This has always played an important part in the social life of both the Irish and the Scottish Gaels. In Roman Catholic parishes throughout the Irish Gaeltacht where Irish is still the daily language of a large number of the parishioners, the language received something of a boost in the 1960s when Masses in the vernacular were introduced in place of the previous Latin services. The variety of Irish chosen for the translation, modernization, or composition of the hymns, prayers, gospels, etc. contained in the new liturgy reflects the standard language very largely, with various departures according to the provenance of the pieces' author or translator. (I have myself heard a native Irish-speaking priest adapt certain features in such items in order to make them comprehensible to his Gaeltacht congregation.) In areas where Irish is spoken by a smaller number of the inhabitants, however, and services and the ministry of the clergy generally may be in English, the traditional prayers and other devotional pieces, with their specialized religious terminology, have largely fallen into disuse and been forgotten. This deprives the language of a domain which had been particularly well developed by previous generations.

The English language orientation of the Roman Catholic Church in Ireland since the late eighteenth century – the period when the clergy ceased being educated in the Irish Colleges on the European Continent – is aptly demonstrated by the fact that even in the strongly Irish-speaking districts of Counties Donegal, Mayo, and Galway the clergy are generally referred to as, e.g. Father Gibbons, rather than *an tAthair* ('Father') or *an Sagart* ('Priest') *Mac Giobúin*, even by the oldest generation.

In Scotland, similarly, Scottish Gaelic is still employed in worship by the various denominations in those regions which remain strongly Gaelic-speaking, but in others where the language has seriously declined this is no longer the case. In my own experience in eastern Scotland not even the oldest speakers (born in the late 1880s) could remember more than a few scraps from prayers, hymns, or items of catechisms learned by heart in childhood. Wherever Scottish Gaelic has been abandoned by the Reformed Churches in their religious services, this has left a large vacuum in Gaelic cultural and intellectual life locally. The vacuum reflects the disappearance, particularly, of the active involvement of numbers of male parishioners as *eilldeirean* 'church elders' who used to assist in ministering to the spiritual and other needs of the congregation, including the composition of prayers and sermons *ex tempore* and engaging in disputations on points of doctrine, all in Gaelic. Large numbers of younger and middle-aged Gaelic speakers in these relic areas have never experienced the linguistic richness of this side of Gaelic life, and the older ones for whom it was a reality in childhood are now incapable of reproducing more than a bare outline for the benefit of a modern researcher.

Connected with matters of religion in the lives of the Roman Catholic communities of the Irish and Scottish Gaeltachtaí, and formerly of great importance in Protestant communities also, were the ancient Celtic and other pre-Christian festivals such as *Samhain* (Hallowe'en), *Bealtaine* (May-day), etc. Each of these had its own lore and observances (see MacNeill 1962 for *Samhain* and Danaher 1972 in general) which now persist only vestigially among the older generation in the various localities where the language has survived.

Traditional medicine. One exception to the general disuse into which religious matter has fallen in Irish and in Scottish Gaelic regions is the category of spells or charms (Ir. *orthaí,* SG *orthachan* < Latin *oratio*). Used, for example, in treating motes in the eye, sprained joints, excessive bleeding, and, especially, erysipelas, they are the preserve of particular individuals in the community. These people inherited them from members of the previous generation who had been their guardians. They are spoken only in secret and are often passed on to selected individuals of the opposite sex in a succeeding generation, so that the effect of their survival on the language of the community as a whole would hardly be great.

This subject is, of course, intimately linked with the use of traditional herbal medicine, a practice which entailed a knowledge of large numbers of plant names and of particular processes employed in preparing the plants for use (e.g. Beckett 1967). As the State began more and more to oversee the health care of the nation and medical practitioners became commoner in the more remote rural districts, so the practice of this herbal lore began to decline, and likewise the knowledge of plant names associated with it, to such an extent that it is now often difficult to obtain from speakers the names of any but the commonest of native flora.

Folk life. The setting of the Gaeltachtaí, as explained above, is virtually exclusively rural, so that a large percentage of the inherited vocabulary naturally relates to this setting: flora and fauna, geographical features, and the institutions of rural life such as markets, fairs, and traditional commercial and agricultural practices. The modern urban-oriented, media-entertained society of many Gaeltachtaí has obliterated much of the terminology relating to this time-honored way of life from the minds of even the older members of the group. Such individuals would also have been brought up in households where one or more of the traditional ancestral means of earning a livelihood were followed (e.g. farming, fishing, weaving, shoe-making). Each of these professions had its own specialized vocabulary, as well as songs and lore associated with it, all of which has largely been lost to the upcoming generations (for fishing, e.g., see Ó hEochaidh 1965). Since the early decades of this century great economic and social changes have taken place in these areas. In the first place, such occupations are now no longer followed by large numbers of the population – indeed in certain areas particular occupations have all but disappeared. Alternatively, where an ancestral occupation such as farming continues, new technology from English-language sources replaces old, and Irish or Scottish Gaelic terminology gives way to English, with the result that these realms of vocabulary are swept into oblivion while whole new lists of foreign words are substituted. In eastern Ross-shire, for example, as elsewhere in Scotland and, indeed, in Ireland, the traditional roofing material was a thatch of straw or bent-grass so that one normally spoke of roofing the house as *a' cur tugha air an taigh* (literally 'putting a thatch on the house'). As thatching has now become obsolete, it is the English word *roof* which appears to be most commonly used.

Needless to say, completely new occupations have been introduced into the various Irish Gaeltachtaí: factories have been erected and offices opened, and the vocabulary relating to the work carried on in these, where significant numbers of local young people are often employed, makes a strong impact on the community as a whole.

Pastimes. (a) *Storytelling*: Where community pastimes are concerned, the emphasis in Gaelic culture has always been strongly oral, partly by inherited preference and partly by having been denied through foreign domination the opportunity to develop and spread literary skills in an appropriate way throughout the community. The wealth of Irish and Scottish Gaelic folk tradition has been held to be unparalleled in Western Europe (Delargy 1945:178). Within this tradition, storytelling and singing are two major branches. Storytelling has always been a very popular and prestigious pastime in Irish and Scottish Gaelic, and to this day most regions where the languages have survived contain at least one or two individuals noted for their ability to spin a yarn.

In bygone days a storyteller's repertoire would include many and various types of tales. A favorite genre was *Fiannuigheacht,* centering on the mythical hero Fionn Mac Cumhail (Murphy 1955). Today such involved tales are preserved only occasionally, and then often under the patronage of a Summer College or national competition (see above). There is one individual of my acquaintance whose father, a celebrated storyteller, provided the Irish Folklore Commission with much material; but the son took pains to learn only one tale from his father's repertoire; a long and very impressive story, full of archaic descriptive "runs". This he recites very formally as a show-piece at competitions and other Irish-language cultural events. It is commoner, however, for the children of storytellers (or indeed for others who have had the opportunity of frequent association with such tradition bearers) to pick up shorter, less complex items from the storytellers' repertoires. Such pieces are, it seems to me, more readily appreciated nowadays principally because they *are* shorter and people are not prepared any more to devote large amounts of time to participating in these traditional forms of entertainment; other varieties channeled through the media claim their attention much more insistently. Some of the traditional oral tales have been shown to have a complex relationship to written versions in medieval manuscripts (Bruford 1969) and are known to contain obscure items of vocabulary and other archaic linguistic features (Ó Catháin 1985:87, 94).

Whenever formal sessions of storytelling are arranged nowadays, part of the audience will not be fully capable of understanding the language of the pieces. They will nonetheless remain attentive and show appreciation out of regard for the storyteller's art, an attitude inherited from the predominantly oral-based culture which once held sway among their Gaelic (and ultimately Celtic) ancestors.

(b) *Singing*: This art-form has, on the whole, survived better than storytelling. In Ireland there is a particular category of song, with very ornate style, quite often, and a particular mode of rendition, known as *sean-nós* ('old style': Ó Canainn 1978:49–80) which is held in high esteem. Preserved better in some regions than in others, it receives additional support in the form of special prizes awarded in prestigious annual competitions and through the patronage of the government-subsidized Summer Colleges. Rather predictably, many other more popular varieties have survived better in Irish. These are often learned and sung by young and old alike and are enjoying something of a revival now in modern idiom at the hands of contemporary musical groups. The same situation by and large seems to obtain in Scotland. There exists a declining number of tradition-bearers preserving a limited repertoire of examples in a variety of older genres of Scottish Gaelic song; but other, more popular songs are known by much larger numbers of the population and sometimes receive the same sort of up-dated treatment from present-day musicians (Thomson 1983:272–3).

In both countries, modern songs are being produced in small numbers and often owe a good deal to current English and American exemplars. But as noted, pop music in English is greatly in vogue among young people; and in those regions of the Irish Gaeltacht where Irish speakers are in a minority – and indeed, in many where they are in the majority – the singing of songs in Irish in local public houses and hotels is often discouraged through the disapproval of English-speaking patrons.

Finally, other simpler oral pastimes still survive[14] which can be enjoyed by virtually the whole community, as are, for example, riddling, the exchange of proverbial, weather, and placename lore, etc.; and in many areas card games are still exceedingly popular, with full use of traditional terminology throughout the game.

3.4. *"The generation gap"*

Added to the weakening of Irish and Scottish Gaelic in specific domains in which they were once strong, there is a further general dimension of weakening which extends throughout the community as a whole. This is the failure of the younger speakers to benefit, as previous generations did, from intercourse with the oldest generation of speakers – precisely those speakers who normally have the widest range of linguistic skills within the community, save in respect of literary speech and modern technical vocabulary. The reasons for this relate largely to the phenomenon known popularly as "the generation gap"; the acquired wisdom of such old folk is not generally highly regarded by modern young people whose preoccupations lie mainly outside the scope of these old people's experience and who also may lead much of their daily lives in English. Furthermore, as more and more of the older generation die off, taking with them many untransmitted items in the local store of language, the dialect of the area must become increasingly monochromatic. Even traditional greetings and blessings are often unfamiliar nowadays to younger speakers in many of the Gaeltachtaí, in my experience.

A number of factors noted above have the cumulative effect, then, of restricting the modern speakers' level of functioning in Irish or Scottish Gaelic: the constant thinning-out of the speech community, especially the oldest generation of speakers with the widest linguistic range; the tendency for increasing numbers of speakers to opt for use of English in everyday speech; and the gradual erosion of native-language vitality even in domains where traditionally it was strong. In some cases this progressive restriction can bring modern speakers to the point where only a limited selection of topics can be discussed satisfactorily by them in their own mother tongue. Thus, whenever a subject more complicated than the weather, community news, or basic farming or fishing is raised, individuals can be heard switching over into English in order to deal adequately with it.

4.   The researcher and the weakened community

4.1.   *Locating speakers*

The present condition and internal structures of Irish and Scottish Gaelic-speaking communities pose a number of difficulties for researchers. In the first place it is not always easy to gain the cooperation of local speakers in areas where the language is extinct except for a mere handful of speakers who may preserve only a minimal knowledge of their native speech form (Wagner 1958:xix), either because they have developed a sense of inferiority about the language (an attitude I experienced both in Co. Antrim and in eastern Ross-shire), or else because they recognize that the knowledge they have of the dialect in question is rather too limited. I noted above the problem of being directed to fluent but nonlocal speakers. In addition, one will sometimes be directed to approach a local semi-speaker, or even a person with a passive knowledge of the spoken form, simply because that individual happens to have some small knowledge of the *written* language. Furthermore, on account of the fundamental nature of the changes which have affected Gaeltacht society in recent decades, it will often be extremely difficult, if not downright impossible, to explore whole ranges of vocabulary relating to now defunct or obsolescent practices, observances, and beliefs.

4.2.   *English bilingualism*

The presence of English bilingualism within the communities as an every-day phenomenon, especially since the arrival of television, raises many questions for the contemporary fieldworker. Where the structure of the language itself is concerned, for example, how far are current developments here, such as loss of inflection (e.g. loss of genitive case and generalization of nominative), to be ascribed to the influence of English and how far to simplification in the morphology of the languages themselves (a development in progress since the Middle Irish period, ca. tenth century onwards; see Ó Murchú 1985:41)? Undoubtedly, the facility of some old and basically very conservative and proficient speakers has been adversely affected by the constant demands of having to speak English as well as their native tongue, with the result (as I have observed e.g. in Co. Donegal) that they fail to implement on occasions even such basic rules of the language as initial mutations.[15]

The English element in modern Irish and Scottish Gaelic speech is itself problematical in a number of ways. While, for instance, there is a tendency for many native speakers to judge the relative strength or "purity" of a dialect by their assessment of its freedom from English borrowings, such loanwords can be shown (Withers 1985:301) to have existed in the language throughout the last century, and indeed within dialects which are among the most vigorous up to the present day. Very often, too, the Gaelic in a certain locality singled out by natives of the surrounding areas as being relatively free from English loans may be found to have at least as many of these as the Gaelic of any other location in that particular region.

Some speakers tend to avoid English loanwords when talking to people they consider educated speakers of the language, so that the minimal occurrence of these loanwords in speech may, therefore, be an indicator of formality with certain speakers. An informant of mine in south central Co. Donegal, a teller of traditional tales, replaces at least the commonest loanwords such as *room* and *happen-áil* with *seomra* and *tharla* respectively, in her sessions with me. On one memorable occasion in the home of the premier storyteller of the Rosses area in west Co. Donegal I noted only one such loan from any member of the family during an entire interview which lasted more than an hour. The one loan was used by the storyteller's niece, who employed the term *umbrella*; but when recounting for a second time the incident in which the item in question occurred, she substituted a native equivalent, *sciath fearthanna*, a modern coinage meaning literally 'rain shield'. It was obviously a point of honour for her, a noted storyteller herself, to know the native term. While it may be relatively easy to spot substitutions like this one, others, such as *seomra* for *rúm* – the two words coexist in certain dialects – will not be so straightforward. The length of time English loanwords have been in use is often difficult to assess in view of the tendency of speakers to employ even colloquial English words, apparently for stylistic purposes or from motives of maintaining prestige within the community (see above). Evidence bearing on this question may be available in the form of material recorded from local speakers of preceding generations which with luck may show the presence of the loanword under investigation; or, alternatively, the word may have disappeared from the neighboring English or Scots dialect from which it was originally borrowed, as has, for example, Co. Donegal *heat*, meaning 'occasion, time', or *daunt-áil* 'fail to do' (Ó Catháin 1985:92). However, there must be many cases where only a comparative study of the frequency of particular loans in the speech of a number of selected individuals within the community will provide the necessary clues as to the true status of such borrowings within the dialect. As opportunities for such study with the oldest generation – as with all other research projects directed at these speakers – become progressively more limited the full evidence will certainly never come to light. In this respect, as in so many others, time is quickly running out.

Notes

1. The discussion contained in this paper, necessarily somewhat abbreviated owing to constraints of space, is based on a fairly intimate knowledge of a number of

Irish-speaking regions, particularly in Co. Donegal, from 1966 onwards, as well as on the opportunity to monitor the bilingual situation throughout the country as a whole. My experience in Scotland, on the other hand, has been primarily with one particular Gaelic-speaking community, reinforced by a general awareness of the situation with regard to other similar communities.

2. A phenomenon of the Irish Gaeltacht is the number of individuals from non-Gaeltacht areas who, out of allegiance to the language (which they have usually succeeded in learning reasonably well), have settled in these regions, often in key posts, such as schoolteacher, manager, etc. Though they are comparatively few in number, the presence of this band of people does help to counterbalance the prevailing movement away from Irish and restore confidence in the language to some extent.

3. Irish-using parents in the Donegal Gaeltacht have reported to me on occasion the reluctance of their children to speak Irish to them, a phenomenon also noted by Rouchdy (this volume) for Nubian.

4. Rouchdy (this volume) has noted the tendency among urban-dwelling Nubians to abandon their language more readily than those who live in the country.

5. Jackson (1951) and O'Rahilly 1932 [1972] detail the evolution of Irish and Scottish Gaelic dialects from the earlier language down to the present time.

6. Kuter (this volume) records the fact that Breton speakers likewise view their language primarily from the standpoint of their own particular dialect.

7. The reaction of a speaker of Uist Gaelic in the Outer Hebrides to the dialect of eastern Perthshire is recorded in Mac'Ill-Fhialain (1972:47–8), one of the few such references in print known to me.

8. While engaged on research among the Scottish Gaelic-speaking community in Inverness County on Cape Breton Island in Nova Scotia in the summer of 1983, I noted reference to the speech of certain individuals in the community called *Abaraich* 'Lochaber folk' who were reckoned to be more than usually difficult to understand.

9. A topic not discussed in this paper, owing to constraints of space, is the massive influence of English on the naming system in Irish and Scottish Gaeltachts which is bound to have had an adverse effect on attitudes of speakers of the Gaelic languages to their native tongue. English names have been in use, both in their original forms, e.g. John, Kit, Jimmy, or with Gaelic diminutive endings, e.g. John*dan*, Bell*ag*, Tim*lín*, for generations.

10. See p. 55 for a minor countertrend in music.

11. Rouchdy (this volume) records a similar negative attitude among Nubian speakers towards their language on account of its lack of a written tradition.

12. A similar loss of confidence in their language by speakers of Breton on account of deficiencies in vocabulary has been noted: see Kuter (this volume).

13. This phenomenon has, of course, been observed in the case of other obsolescent minority languages such as, for example, Albanian in Greece (Tsitsipis, this volume).

14. Verbal virtuosity has traditionally been much prized in Gaelic society, as in other societies where the oral tradition has been primary and much cultivated: cf. Mithun (this volume) for the case of Cayuga.

15. This involves substitutions of various kinds in the initial sound-segment(s) of words, particularly under the influence of a preceding particle (see Thomson

1983:97–8 and Watson 1983). In a number of instances where a speaker failed to produce an initial mutation, the functional load of the mutation was not great, in that its appearance was conditioned entirely by the occurrence of a preceding particle. Whether mutation in environments not controlled by such particles is also in decline in many Irish and Scottish Gaelic dialects will not become clear until analyses have been undertaken in these dialects similar to that carried out in East Sutherland by Dorian (1977a).

4 The rise and fall of an immigrant language: Norwegian in America

EINAR HAUGEN

In my study of the Norwegian language in America (Haugen 1953 [1969]) I surveyed the language usages of Norwegian immigrants in the United States from the beginnings of immigration in 1825 to the 1950s. I devoted two chapters (10 and 11) to the use and gradual disuse of the language over the more than a century in which it played a significant role in American life. I entitled the first chapter "The struggle over Norwegian" and the second "The triumph of English". In the present article I shall (1) briefly summarize my findings in the book for the benefit of readers who may not be familiar with it; (2) present some personal data gathered in my fieldwork; and (3) provide a short account of what has happened in the intervening quarter of a century.

1. Norwegian America: the rise

My point of departure is an 1898 quotation from an eminent Norwegian-American educator: "Now the question no longer is: how shall we learn English so that we may share in the social life of America and partake of her benefits; the great question is: how can we preserve the language of our ancestors here in a strange environment and pass on to our descendants the treasures it contains? (Bothne 1898:828; cit. Haugen 1953:238). It is significant that this question was posed at the turn of the century. By that time Norwegians had been pouring into America for two generations, settling for the most part in the upper Midwest, from Illinois to North Dakota.

More than a half-million Norwegians had changed countries in these years, seeking opportunity in the rural Midwest. The typical Norwegian immigrant began as a farmer, though many gradually branched out into urban occupations. For daily use they brought with them a rich variety of dialects, while for literate purposes they had usually mastered the Dano-Norwegian language that was the established medium of their schooling in Norway. For our present purposes we shall overlook the variegated brands of Norwegian and comprise them all under the label of "Norwegian", as did the immigrants themselves (though a favorite anecdote is told of a new-comer woman who heard an unfamiliar dialect and after a while exclaimed, "Ah, if only I could talk English as well as you do!")

By 1898 Norwegians had enjoyed three-fourths of a century of living in the United States. The combination of cheap land and the organizing talents of their clerical Lutheran leaders led to the rise of so-called "settlements" dotting the Midwest. Such rural settlements constituted the heartland of what was known as "Norwegian America" (*Det norske Amerika*). From the start these were culturally ambivalent. Economically and politically they were part of rural and small-town America. Socially, religiously, and linguistically they clung to traditions brought over from a traditionally rural Norway. A high degree of social and religious cohesion was crucial to the retention of the language beyond that of many other North European languages. Their ambivalence only became apparent as time went on and they were gradually acculturated into American life through the public schools, the English-language press, and the growth of communications.

Meanwhile they developed their own network of internal communication: a Norwegian-language Lutheran church (split into rival synods), a Norwegian-language press (totaling hundreds of minor journals, dominated by two or three major papers), Norwegian–American secular organizations (from temperance to socialism, choral music to revivalism), and Norwegian–American language schools (from elementary to college level). At the turn of the century these activities were still flourishing, and to some they seemed to promise a bright future for the Norwegian language in America. Unitarian pastor and poet Kristofer Janson (in America from 1881 to 1893) commented on the fact that in some areas he could walk from farm to farm and never hear any other language than Norwegian (Haugen 1953:38).

Leadership in the maintenance of the language was assumed by a number of educated men and women, often based on such urban centers as Chicago or Minneapolis, not to overlook such smaller towns as Duluth, Willmar, and Moorhead, Minnesota; LaCrosse, Eau Claire, and Madison, Wisconsin; Decorah and Sioux City, Iowa; Sioux Falls, South Dakota; Fargo and Minot, North Dakota. A major influx to the Far West, especially Washington, followed in the 1880s.

The relative isolation of the individual farms and of the Norwegian-speaking community/parish was exploited by religious as well as secular organizations. As one later pastoral observer noted, "The Norwegian language was an instrument of union and a barrier against the sects", the latter referring to the many rival English-speaking Protestant denominations. The conservative "Norwegian Synod", organized in 1853, took a firm stand in favor of the Norwegian language. Its leaders envisaged a school system modeled on that of the German Missouri Synod, with which they had friendly relations. Debate began already in the 1850s, but as late as 1900 the sole language employed in these churches was Norwegian. The 1890s were rife with change. In 1892 a Norwegian Synod pastor wrote that in his student days he had seen no need for preaching in English, but now the time had come when it was inevitable in the preaching and teaching of the church (Haugen 1953:247). In 1904 a more aggressive, younger pastor declared that "the English question is coming upon us as a mighty rushing tide. Let us be ready" (Haugen 1953:248).

The years around the turn of the century also saw the beginning of an organized movement in defense of Norwegian. In these years, as historian Chrislock has put it, perhaps too pointedly, "Norwegian America experienced an ethnic awakening" (Chrislock 1981:3). On the popular level, a Norwegian insurance fraternity, the Sons of Norway, was organized in 1900 "to encourage and maintain an interest among its members in the Norwegian language", with the significant addition: "To an extent that is not in conflict with the loyalty they owe the United States" (Haugen 1953:249). On the academic level, a society was organized in 1903 under the name of *Det norske Selskab i Amerika* (The Norwegian Society in America). Its first declared purpose was to "to work for the preservation by the Norwegian people in America of their ancestral tongue" (Haugen 1953:258). Again there was the addition: "To the extent that this can be reconciled with our obligations and position in American society." The Society was widely hailed in the press; its chief promoter was author and editor Waldemer Ager, who also became the editor of its quarterly periodical, known as *Kvartalskrift*. It also provided prizes for literary work, conducted declamatory contests, and erected monuments to Norwegian literary figures.

Its membership remained modest, and in 1925 the journal had to be abandoned, though the society lingered on until 1974, when its assets were employed to publish a collection of essays originally appearing in the journal, most of them by Ager himself. Edited by O. Lovoll, they were, ironically, translated into the English that Ager resisted (Lovoll 1977). The first decade of 1900 also saw the growth of Norwegian choral groups and of the peculiarly Norwegian native-district societies known as *bygdelag*. Newspapers prospered, and a spate of novels, short stories, essays, and poems rolled from the presses. This literary flowering was in part a response to Norway's parting from Sweden in 1905, and in part a celebration of the centennial of Norway's liberation from Danish dominion in 1814. There was a growth of Norwegian instruction in advanced schools, partly in response to the founding of a Society for the Advancement of Scandinavian Study in 1911. At about the same time, interest arose in Norway concerning the fate of their many emigrated citizens, and a society entitled *Nordmannsforbundet* (The League of Norsemen) was founded, with headquarters in Oslo, for the purpose of maintaining overseas contacts, not just with American emigrants. It published a journal of the same name, bringing articles and news relevant to its purpose.

At the same time the current of popular usage was running in the opposite direction. In 1912 the president of the United Norwegian Lutheran Church declared that the great need of the Church was for English-speaking ministers: "It is an incontrovertible fact that our young people are growing more and more unfamiliar with our mother tongue" (Haugen 1953:254). By 1915 one-fourth of the services were in English, since 1900 rising from zero to 22 percent; Sunday school and confirmations were at 27 percent. The Church was obviously not going to make language a crucial issue, in keeping with the policy of most Protestant churches.

The year 1917 was crucial in this development. In that year the three major Norwegian synods joined into a truly United Church; and the United States declared war on Germany. These unrelated events brought to the surface a trend that had been growing since 1900: new generations were assuming the leadership of the Church. An anti-foreign wave of opinion threatened to sweep away all non-English activities, primarily German, but also Norwegian, itself a "Lutheran" language. Statistical tables (displayed in Haugen 1953:262–7) show a sharp war-time dip, as well as a longterm steady decline in the Norwegian language. Services which had stood at 73 percent in 1917 fell to 6.4 by 1944 as congregation after congregation canceled or limited its Norwegian worship. By 1949 only 2.7 percent were left. A breakdown by regions shows a more rapid anglification in the Rocky Mountain district, where Norwegians were scattered and urban, than in the older settlements of the Midwest. A vote to abolish the word "Norwegian" in the name of the Church was adopted in 1918, reversed in 1936, but finalized in 1946.

A last, desperate holding action for Norwegian was organized by Professor O. E. Rølvaag in 1919. As a teacher of Norwegian at St Olaf College he felt a deep commitment to the language, not only on behalf of his students of Norwegian ancestry, but also to its use as an instrument of literature. He founded a society under the name for *For Fædrearven* (For Our Ancestral Heritage); but its only important accomplishment was the volume of essays that he published under a closely similar name in 1922: *Omkring Fædrearven*. The imposing celebration of the centennial of Norwegian immigration in the Twin Cities (Minneapolis/St Paul) in 1925 proved to be a kind of last hurrah. In that year was founded a Norwegian–American Historical Association, of which more below.

Meanwhile, the secular organs followed the lead of the Church. In 1942 the Sons of Norway changed the language of its organ to English, pleading that "A Norwegian activity in this country does not become any less Norwegian even if English is given the place of honor." This disingenuous statement set the tone for all later events. The then still flourishing newspapers in the Midwest fell by the wayside one by one: *Minneapolis Tidende* in 1935, *Skandinaven* (Chicago) in 1942, and *Decorah-Posten* (which in 1949 still had 35,436 subscribers) in 1952.

For the old guard these were sad dates.

2. Fieldwork

In 1936 I undertook my first field trips in search of American Norwegian speakers. Personal experience and research in the sources told me approximately where I should seek them. I had mapped out the Norwegian settlements of Wisconsin and Minnesota, with some attention to Iowa and the Dakotas. As it turned out, I had no difficulty in finding informants. I prepared a tentative questionnaire, later greatly revised, to some extent modeled on one devised for the *American dialect atlas* by Hans Kurath (of Brown, later Michigan) and Miles Hanley, my Wisconsin colleague (Kurath 1939). Eventually I also provided myself with recording equipment. Between 1936 and 1942 I interviewed and/or recorded 206 informants. In 1947–8 I was fortunate in getting an additional crop of interviews, altogether 44 made by Magne Oftedal, a Norwegian dialectologist (later professor of Celtic in Oslo). This made a total of 250, which I considered to be an adequate sample.

At this time I was particularly in search of second-generation speakers, i.e. of individuals whose parents were born in Norway but who were themselves born in America. Counting now only those who were interviewed and not just recorded, we found a total of 117, ranging in age from 22 to 89, averaging 61 years. Those of the first or immigrant generation whom we also chanced to include, numbered only 55, aged from 39 to 93, averaging 72 years. Those of mixed second and third or of third and even fourth generation numbered only 51, aged from 19 to 64, averaging 41 years; they were fewer and younger, for obvious reasons. All my informants, with few exceptions, were born or raised on farms or in small towns, many now retired.

My primary goal was to investigate the Norwegian used by these informants, to establish their retention of the local Norwegian dialects and the extent to which English had penetrated their Norwegian. The dialects ranged over nearly the entire spectrum of Norwegian and were often remarkably well preserved samples of the homeland varieties.

For our present purposes we shall turn to the more relevant theme of their anglification, a feature they all shared in roughly equal amounts. One could occasionally detect local differences, as when one community regularly used English numerals, e.g. "fifti-tu" instead of "to-og-femti"; elsewhere only the fourth of July turned up in English as "fort-ov-yulai". In most respects the overall drift was similar.

A few speakers actually commented on what they called their "mixing". RN (6Q3) declared, "They are all more or less the same in mixing; if they can't think of the Norwegian word, they use English." (Note that informants are here identified by initials and code-marker; readers are referred to Haugen 1969 for full names and identification.) HOS (12Q4), a pastor, said, "Interposing English words is virtually automatic." Mrs JLR (4P1) observed that those who (like her) were born in America took more care to

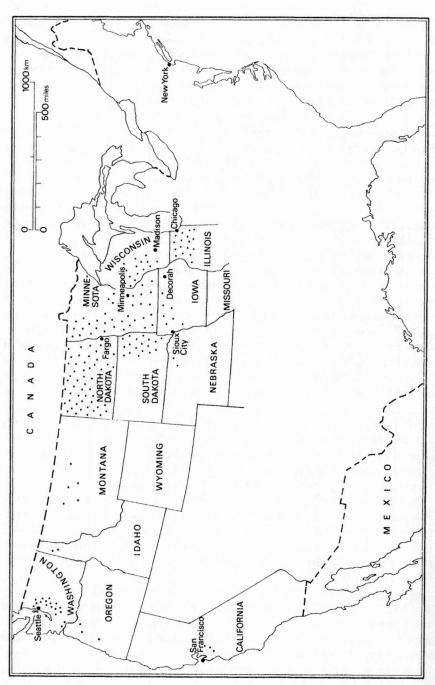

Norwegians in the United States, 1930

avoid English loans than those who came over from Norway. This view was not confirmed in my experience, except for persons who like her had a father who was strict in rejecting English mixture, or who were academically infected. She was apparently one of the aberrant type that resisted complete assimilation. Most informants did not comment and seemed to be very little aware of what they were doing in this respect.

It was clear that they and their parents had shaped their language to fit their new environment. Even phenomena which they all knew from Norway were regularly denominated by English words that were appropriately reshaped into Norwegian form, e.g. *fil* 'field' (Norwegian *åker*), *fens* 'fence' (Norwegian *gjerde* or *skigard*), *barn* or even *bare* 'barn' (Norwegian *fjøs* or *låve*), etc.

I came to the conclusion that this *American Norwegian* was in fact *their* Norwegian. This was what they meant when they responded affirmatively to my question of whether and when they spoke Norwegian, just as their often accented English was *their* English. As long as the linguistic framework, the phonology and the grammar, remained substantially Norwegian, they identified it as such. The English loans were for the most part as fully integrated as the Anglo-Norman loans in English or the Latin loans in French – or for that matter, the innumerable Low German loans in Norwegian. One first-generation immigrant (Mrs SN, 11R1) reported with some asperity on her dismay after arrival among her fellow countrymen to discover that she simply could not understand them: they asked her to go out into *pastre* 'the pasture' and remove *håltradn* 'the halters' from the horses, leaving her baffled. The adoption of English loans was my informants' first great step in the direction of English.

The second step came as new generations began learning English from scratch and became effectively bilingual. This was the price immigrant children paid for their new status, one which they paid more or less willingly. The influences were many.

First we must consider the nature of the school systems. On the one hand the Lutheran Church, which began following the immigrants in the 1840s and 1850s, organized parochial schools. Practically all my informants proved on inquiry to have attended the summer sessions of a school almost entirely conducted in Norwegian. In contrast to the German–American Lutheran community, they rarely managed to set up a full-time system to compete with the public schools. They did hire teachers to inculcate the Norwegian of the Bible stories and the Catechism (with its "Explanation"), and it is clear from my informants' testimony that even these six- or eight-week sessions were effective. Nearly all of them claimed ability to read Norwegian, though most of them had little practice beyond reading newspapers. They could also write, but admitted that they generally had no one to whom they could write Norwegian. None of them had visited Norway, and they had only occasional contact with Norwegian relatives.

Competing with the Norwegian summer school were eventually the regular winter sessions of the American district school. Several informants reported that they had first learned English at this school, after speaking only Norwegian in their home. The discipline could be traumatic: JHL (4F1) told me that "at the district school we were not allowed to speak Norwegian"; Mrs MG (4N1) said that "the teacher would punish us for not speaking English". LG (6Q4) put it that "when we were little, we couldn't talk yankee, and the teacher would keep us after school if we didn't"; OGB (7H3) "didn't know a word of English until I started school"; SWA (9G2) "spoke Norwegian until I went to school"; Mrs JO (20P2) reported that "at school we were virtually threatened to speak English"; similarly TSS (5H4).

The school was of course not alone in promoting English. Several mentioned contact with non-Norwegian neighbors, especially Irish and Germans (Mrs OK 5Q1) though there was an occasional German who learned Norwegian from his surroundings (WvR 10C14). A potent factor could be a move to town where English was dominant; or marriage to a spouse unfamiliar with Norwegian: PVP (5L4) spoke Norwegian "until a daughter-in-law came". Children who had not been taught to use Norwegian could also be influential: Mrs RN (6P1) "spoke Norwegian until my youngest boy started to learn English".

Among our informants there was a general consensus that Norwegian was on its way out. Many of them contrasted the current situation with what they had known as children. Mrs AH (2C1) spoke Norwegian only as long as her husband lived; OMH (2C4) had not spoken it since his mother died 28 years earlier; one man (3C5) spoke it at home while he was a boy; Mrs ST (4F2) spoke it until the children started school; Mrs IA (4F3) found that "Norwegian is retreating"; Mrs EE (4K1) "spoke it until she was married"; Mrs SR (4P1) "as long as my father lived"; Mrs MG (4N1) "as long as mother and father lived"; AG (5L1) "we all spoke it, but lately it's been mostly English"; Mrs CQ (6Q5) learned it while working for Norwegians and after she married a Norwegian; JQ (7H1) spoke it until twenty years earlier: "I suppose the change has to go on, there's nothing we can do", he sighed.

Many informants claimed to be still speaking Norwegian regularly, if not consistently, especially in places like Westby, Wisconsin (Coon Prairie) and the neighboring Coon Valley, i.e. the more isolated Norwegian settlements: CW (8C1) "daily"; HA (8C2) "all the time"; AH (8G1) "with parents and old people"; ETL (8L2) "with father, but not with my wife"; MF (8L4) "with wife and children, but mostly English since we came to town"; FS (8L7) "three-fourths of the time"; RLA (8L8) "generally every day"; WL (10C6) "at home all my life"; RB (10N1) "more Norwegian than English at home"; AB (11C1) "we talked Norwegian all the time, but now it's more up and down"; RS (11C4) "at home and in the neighborhood, even the children if they don't go away to school"; ABQ (12Q1) "all the time until 1921, when we moved here and got together with English and German people";

HOS (12Q4) "only when I meet one of the old folks"; Mrs JQ (12R4) "to mother, in the seven years I cared for her, until she died six years ago – our oldest child was confirmed in Norwegian sixteen years ago"; RBM (12R6) "not the last ten years – the children talk only English even if they can understand; in daily practice it turns out to be English".

We may sum up the general usage as one in which Norwegian, even in the most conservative communities, turned into a *family* language. It became a medium for in-group use, outside the family limited to like-minded neighbors. As soon as one stepped outside the home, one had to consider the preference of one's speech partner. In meeting strangers the automatic response of these bilinguals was English.

There were those who expressed regret at the change, without having been directly queried. MH (2C2) was a third–fourth generation speaker (father and mother of different generations) who was proud at age 19 to be known as the youngest remaining speaker of Norwegian in his southern Wisconsin community. Mrs GM (4H1) deplored "that they've gotten so yankeefied (*jenkisprengt*) that they can't preach in Norwegian any more, adding "I suppose it's the way the world goes." JRL (4F1) felt that "we ought to keep the language we got from our parents"; JT (4Q2) observed that "after the War Norwegian has been quite washed away", noting that his wife "was more Norwegian" than he – she "didn't like English at all"; AG (5L1) "understood a Norwegian sermon better than an English one"; TH (8F1) "would have liked it if we had kept up Norwegian. I think the pastor should preach Norwegian a little oftener than he does"; AQ (8M1) felt that "they're moving too fast".

There was a good deal of testy Norwegian stubbornness among the older informants. Mrs GG (8M4) recalled that "when they spoke English at table, father refused to answer"; Mrs MD (10C5) was "glad I learned Norwegian, it's no handicap", and she particularly enjoyed her mother's sprightly wit and pithy expressions; CJH (10C7) crustily asserted "it's changing a little too fast, and I blame that in part on our pastor"; ABQ (12Q1) "gets more out of a Norwegian sermon than an English one, when they start rattling away in yankee again"; Mrs RL (12R5) "liked Norwegian better, it's not the same as in English"; RAH (18C2) agreed that he "got more out of a Norwegian sermon and wouldn't like it if Norwegian disappeared"; CWG (20C1) felt that "they should keep Norwegian, I'm afraid that in ten or fifteen years it will all be gone". TTS (12Q2), who had been brought to America at 2 years old in 1857, told us "I've been a defender of Norwegian in America – as a delegate to the meetings of the United Norwegian Church I spoke against the resolution to eliminate Norwegian". Interestingly enough, his children, he admitted, did not use the language even though they had been confirmed in it. But in general, respect for one's elders and the intactness of family cohesion, with few non-Norwegian spouses, was a leading factor in the strong persistence of Norwegian.

Countering these regrets were some who welcomed the change. WKK (8M2) held that "a one-tongue country is preferable", but he also regretted the loss of Norwegian. MG (13N3) considered that "we talk together too much Norwegian"; VN (14C2), a third-generation speaker born in 1905, was aware of his own failure to speak "plain English", which he attributed to speaking "too much Norwegian", but "there are many who speak it worse than I". His father ON (14D4) was one of my best informants, but he too "would have wished that this area had been Norwegian from the start, for we can't move very far before we can no longer use the language". He attributed their Norwegian to his mother's opposition to English. In fact these speakers from the traditional community of Blair, Wisconsin, did speak an English strongly marked by Norwegian accent.

Most of our rural speakers, however, did not express an opinion for or against Norwegian. In these communities the second generation, mostly raised in pre-World War I days, before the coming of automobiles, radio, and TV, were fluent and natural speakers of American English as well as American Norwegian. To my query on language usage most of them replied that they spoke whatever language the situation called for. But in the then current generation they were virtually unanimous in stating that their children may have understood some Norwegian, but rarely used it. In a few cases interviews initiated with such children had to be interrupted for lack of response.

As long as there are still persons alive of the pre-1918 generation, one can count on a response in the old rural settlements. But the close allegiance to Norway and Norwegian affairs often felt by the early immigrants is rare indeed. Occasions for oral use of the language are few, and any skills they may have had in either reading or writing have atrophied.

The scenario here outlined does not seem to be very different from that which applies to most immigrant languages in the United States (and Canada). There are special profiles, e.g. for Pennsylvania German, where immigration was early and massive. In a comparison of various more modern groups, numbers and religious boundaries may lead to greater retentiveness, as with American Germans, or to less, as in the case of American Danes. English is not only the proto-American language of choice, promoted by official and private usage; it is also the lingua franca of all the earlier immigrants, who are sooner or later driven to communicate with each other. Current (1986) immigrants may face quite different conditions, at least for a time.

3.   Norwegian America: the fall

By 1986 the passing of Norwegian on the folk level may be regarded as complete, barring a trickle of later immigrants. Most of these are urban or academic in background, and they are either quickly absorbed into Anglo-

American life, or they commute back and forth between the two countries. Their status as immigrants permits many of them to live and work in the United States without even bothering to take out American citizenship.

But evidence still remains of an earlier mass immigration. This consists of three types of social activity: (a) voluntary associations; (b) academic instruction; and (c) historical research and publication.

(a) As examples of *voluntary associations* that still unite at least some Norwegian immigrants or their descendants, one may cite local societies like the Ygdrasil Society of Madison, Wisconsin, or a countrywide organization like the previously mentioned Sons of Norway, with headquarters in Minneapolis. In both cases the language is entirely English, but programs and recreational activities are focused on a Norwegian tradition. Visits to Norway are encouraged and promoted. Norwegians are also included in the programs of the American–Scandinavian Foundation, based in New York, with associates in many American cities. In the 1980s even *Nordmannsforbundet* has shifted to English and publishes its journal under the name *The Norseman* with predominantly English text.

(b) The loci of *academic instruction* in Norwegian also reflect the old immigration. The traditional church colleges of Norwegian background have offered courses in Norwegian more or less continuously since the founding of Luther College (Decorah, Iowa) in 1861. Even after the colleges turned from Norwegian to English as their everyday language, which we may date to the early 1900s, a faculty devoted to the teaching of Norwegian had been maintained as a separate department. In early years the language was required to meet the need for pastors serving a Norwegian-language laity. More recently it has become an optional subject, modestly competing with such "major" languages as German, French, or Spanish. Many thousands of Norwegian-descended students have "taken" Norwegian without necessarily becoming fluent. Fluency occurred only among those few whose interest grew to a passion, leading to specialization, and the seeking of scholarships in Norway or the United States.

In states with a considerable contingent of Norwegian descendants the teaching of Norwegian has invaded also the schools and advanced institutions of America. High school teaching was especially popular immediately before World War I, but withered on the vine in the period of anti-German hysteria, and did not do much better in the atmosphere of anti-foreign language trends that followed. State universities have been more hospitable, ever since the University of Wisconsin introduced Norwegian in 1875. At present Norwegian is also taught at such universities as Minnesota, North Dakota, Illinois, Washington, and California, plus some others. Such instruction has usually been under the aegis of a "Scandinavian" department, in which such varied courses have been offered as the medieval Old Norse–Icelandic, Modern Danish, Icelandic, Norwegian, and Swedish, as well as auxiliary studies in Scandinavian history, sociology, or folklore.

Between them, the instructors in these departments have acted as leaders on the folk level, but have also been active in the production of textbooks, dictionaries, translations, and all manner of scholarly work. A favorite umbrella organization has been the Society for the Advancement of Scandinavian Studies, founded in 1911, and still fulfilling an active and even growing function in the field.

Over the period from 1870 to 1930 there was also a fertile production of literary works, some by journalists and teachers, others by laymen. As leading exemplars one may mention, from the journalistic camp, novelist Waldemar Ager (1869–1942) and from the academic, novelist Ole Edvart Rølvaag (1876–1931). Some of their work has been translated into English, and at least one of them, Rølvaag's *Giants in the earth* (1927) has entered American literature as a significant contribution depicting Norwegian pioneering in the 1870s.

(c) The *history* of Norwegian immigration has long been a concern of far-sighted academics. Museums have sprung up in various locations, e.g. at Little Norway, west of Mount Horeb, Wisconsin. But the leading center of Norwegian museum activity is the institution now know as Vesterheim, located in Decorah, Iowa. Started in a modest way at Luther College in 1877, it gradually grew after 1925 under historian Knut Gjerset's leadership, and since 1965 has been expanded into a professional institution by art historian Marion Nelson of the University of Minnesota (and his wife Lila). Here one can find a whole "village" of buildings reflecting the material phases of Norwegian migration, supplemented each summer by an attractive folk festival. A program of genealogical research has also been instituted.

While the literate Norwegian–American community had already sprouted willing amateur historians of the group during their first century of immigration, the first concerted effort stemmed from the centennial celebrated in the Twin Cities (Minneapolis/St Paul) in 1925. At that time was founded the Norwegian-American Historical Association, with headquarters and archives at St Olaf College in Northfield, Minnesota. The spark plug in this movement was the distinguished professor Theodore C. Blegen of the University of Minnesota, whose two-volume work *Norwegian migration to America* (Blegen 1931, 1940) set a new standard for American ethnic-group history. Since its founding, the Association has published an annual volume of *Studies and Records*, and a great number of special studies and scholarly monographs. The latest is *The promise of America: A history of the Norwegian-American people* (1984) by Odd S. Lovoll, present editor of the Association. This volume appeared in Norwegian in Norway and in English in the United States, reflecting the bilingual background of the Association and the monolingual nature of present-day Norwegian America.

4.   Conclusions

After an initial migration of 1925, Norwegians emigrated to the United States in such numbers that they were able to create a Norwegian America which flourished from 1850 to 1940. During most of this period the chief medium of internal communication, oral and written, was the Norwegian language, which served as an in-group identity-marker. Research on informant usage shows that in the more conservative and isolated rural settlements the language persisted well into the second (i.e. the first American) generation. As late as the 1940s one could still find speakers who claimed to be using Norwegian regularly, at least one-half of their time. Among these bilinguals Norwegian became typically a family or neighborhood language, gradually abandoned as contacts with American institutions and individuals grew. This was not a sudden change, but one that affected individuals differentially, through the schools, change of residence, new occupations, intermarriage, improved communications, urbanization etc. The Norwegian used by the immigrants already represented a first step toward acculturation by being heavily interlarded with English, and was in fact an American Norwegian. A "drift" toward English was apparent from the start, preceding the ultimate "shift": they developed from *drift* to *shift* in the second generation, via a more or less extended bilingual phase. Norwegian identity or identification has in part persisted into the English-speaking generations thanks to the activity of social organizations, academic instruction, and historical-genealogical research. The Norwegian experience may be regarded as a typical profile for the older non-English immigration.

5.   Coda

The United States Census for 1980 found an estimated number of 184,491 speakers of Norwegian, out of 4,120,000 who claimed a wholly or partly Norwegian ancestry. But it is not clear how many of these actually used the language. I owe the reference to Dr Dorothy Waggoner, a Washington consultant on Language Minority Statistics and Bilingual Education. See US Bureau of the Census, *1980 Census of population*, vol. 1, *Characteristics of the population*, Chapter D, Detailed population characteristics, Part 1, US Summary (PC80-1-D1), Washington, DC: US Government Printing Office, 1984.

5 Breton vs. French: Language and the opposition of political, economic, social, and cultural values

LOIS KUTER

1.   Introduction

The Breton language has been and remains today a powerful symbol of identity for Bretons. Both positive and negative symbolic values attached to Breton are critical variables in this language's persistence and in its impending death. The symbolic opposition of Breton with French is the most important variable in identifying why today Bretons speak most often of language death.

Language use has never been a part of the census of France, but various estimations of Breton speakers have been made by researchers in the nineteenth and twentieth centuries.[1] In 1808 Cocquebert de Monbref estimated 967,000 native speakers, and in 1886 Paul-Yves Sébillot estimated the number to be 1,300,000. The Breton literary group Gwalarn estimated in 1927 that there were one million everyday users of Breton, and Francis Gourvil, a scholar of the Breton language and literature, estimated a figure of 1,200,000 for people who knew Breton. Figures for the 1970s and 1980s vary. Gwennole Le Menn (1975:72), a researcher on Celtic languages for the Centre National de la Recherche Scientifique (CNRS), estimated that 12 years ago there were approximately 1,200,000 people who knew Breton and 300,000 capable of using it as their everyday language, out of a total population in Brittany of approximately 3.7 million. In a 1987 survey of 999 people in Lower Brittany (of a total population of 1.7 million), Fanch Broudic, a Breton-language broadcaster for Radio-France/Bretagne Ouest (FR3), calculated that 61.1 percent understand Breton and 51.7 percent speak it 'very often', 'fairly often', or 'sometimes'. The survey showed that an estimated 240,000 Bretons in Lower Brittany use Breton every day (Kuter 1987:4). Statistics can be deceiving. Those who know Breton are different both from those capable of speaking it and from those who regularly do speak it as their everyday language. As Lenora A. Timm has pointed out in her article "Bilingualism, diglossia and language shift in

Brittany'' (1980), almost all speakers of Breton today also speak French. She estimates that those who know only Breton represent less than 10 percent of the Breton-speaking population. Most importantly, in terms of the issue of language death, this 10 percent is typically 70 years old or more. In fact, a larger percentage of those who use Breton as their first language today are older people or middle-aged people who are not passing this language on to their children.

The negative and positive values attached by Bretons to French and to Breton are the key variables in the transmission of these languages. This chapter examines the political, economic, social, and cultural factors which influence the symbolic values attached to Breton and French. Three basic oppositions of these languages are presented:

   (i) The political symbolism of French as the "national" language, opposed to Breton as a "regional" language.
  (ii) The socio-economic symbolism of French as the language of civilization, progress and the future, opposed to Breton as a language of the past, fit only for backward peasants.
 (iii) The cultural symbolism of French as an international, urban language, opposed to Breton as a marker of a uniquely local, rural identity.

In a fourth section, the connection between present-day Breton identity and the Breton language is briefly considered.

2.   Political symbolism

The attachment of strong political values to both Breton and French is a relatively new phenomenon, linked to the idea of a French nation-state. While the 1532 Edict of Union between France and Brittany symbolizes for some the end of independent Brittany, this union in fact guaranteed a significant degree of autonomy, including a Breton Assembly which had ultimate decision-making powers for taxes. French kings sometimes tried to ignore Breton independence. Efforts on the part of seventeenth- and eighteenth-century French rulers to levy taxes in Brittany without the approval of the Breton Assembly met with resistance – put down by bloody reprisals which served as occasions to gradually strip power from the Assembly. While for some Bretons, France remained a foreign country until train lines and roadways to Paris were built in the mid-nineteenth century, the real turning point in shaping people's identities came with the French Revolution of 1789. Up to this point, if being a Frenchman meant anything at all, it meant that one lived in the French State. As Eugen Weber points out in his study of nineteenth- and twentieth-century transformations of rural France (1976), cultural diversity had not bothered people in earlier centuries. It was only with the Revolution that ". . . diversity became imperfection, injustice, failure, something to be noted and remedied" (Weber 1976:9). From this period on, being a Frenchman was to mean being French. The idea of national unity meant that France was to become a unity bound together not only by a common administrative, social, and economic system, but also by a standard culture.

A common language was the key to achieving the egalitarian aims of the French Revolution. The idea of unifying language at this point in history was in the interest of insuring equal citizenship and participation in the new Republic. Speaking French meant full citizenship in the French nation. Since that period, French nationalists have viewed the persistence of non-French languages – potential agents of division and counterrevolution – as a threat to the unity of France (Falc'hun 1969:109; Calvet 1973:78–9; Giacomo 1975:19; Nicolas 1982:19–20). In the wake of the Revolution, France, and not the local region was to become the "Fatherland", and French was to replace local languages to become the "mother tongue" (Weber 1976:333–4). However, the French Revolution did not change overnight the more immediate reality that the land of one's father remained the local *pays* for most Bretons, just as the language of one's mother remained Breton.

The schools had their work cut out for them in the nineteenth century. By 1863, of a population of 7.5 million in France, an estimated one-fifth of the population knew no French (Weber 1976:313). In the late 1800s, the persistence of languages such as Breton, Alsatian, Flemish, Catalan, Corsican and Basque still worried those who linked political stability with linguistic standardization. The loss of Alsace-Lorraine in the Franco-Prussian war of 1870 reinforced perceptions that work was needed to strengthen French unity – particularly in non-French-speaking areas. During the 1880s the role of the schools in educating children throughout France was strengthened by the Jules Ferry laws which introduced obligatory and free primary school classes. During this period the schools began a campaign to strengthen French patriotism through the *bataillons scolaires*. Carrying sticks for guns, children drilled to retake Alsace-Lorraine.

Breton's role in World War I in the French army left little doubt as to their patriotism, but their linguistic foreignness continued to bother French officials in the postwar period. Despite the fact that they – like other non-French speakers – impeded the unification of a French nation-state, Bretons persisted in speaking their own language. In a report of 1922, I. Carré, the General Inspector of Schools, speaks of the need to use non-Breton teachers in schools of Brittany:

It is of first order importance that Bretons understand and speak the national language: they will only truly be French on that condition. . . . It is Frenchmen that are needed to Frenchify the Bretons; they will not Frenchify themselves by themselves.

(Quoted in Piriou 1971:30)[2]

In 1927 the Minister of National Education of France, A. de Monzie, felt threatened enough by the persistence of Breton to issue the following statement: "Pour l'unité linguistique de la France, la langue bretonne doit disparaître ('For the linguistic unity of France, the Breton language must disappear'). This has become one of the most frequently used quotes to document French attitudes and the history of Breton in the schools (cited, for example, by Piriou 1971:24; Gwegen 1975:35; Le Menn 1975:74; Deniel 1976:47; Henry 1979:17; Giordan 1982:50).

The fear that linguistic disunity will pull the French State apart persists to the present day. Even modest steps on the part of the Socialist government of François Mitterrand to give Breton a limited place in university programs have met with resistance on the part of government officials who feel that cultural concessions will inevitably lead to political separatism. The following *New York Times* report of reactions to Minister of Culture Jack Lang's announcement of the creation of an advanced teaching degree for Breton is revealing of lingering paranoia about regional diversity within France:

the move, an initiative of the Minister of Culture, Jack Lang, has aroused its share of controversy, even during the slow summer season. It got front page treatment in virtually all the newspapers and drew angry complaints that, as a former Gaullist Prime Minister, Michel Debré[,] put it, the Socialists, for the sake of winning votes among the minorities, were "undertaking an action that would weaken French unity by shattering its culture." There is no problem with maintaining languages like Breton and Basque where they have been traditionally spoken, Mr. Debré said. That is a matter of "justice and liberty." But, he went on, the government's move "to raise these languages to the ranks of official instruments of education and communication in France is to work for the end of the nation, which is to say the end of democracy."

(Bernstein 1985:6E)

The astounding aspect of such expressions of outrage is that, in fact, concessions granted for Breton and other non-French languages in France have been of such a small scale that they offer no conceivable threat to the dominance of French. The Socialist government of Mitterrand will be remembered as the first to acknowledge the persistence of "regional" languages and cultures. Yet this acknowledgement is a cautious one. In setting up the Conseil des langues et cultures régionales in January 1986, Prime Minister Laurent Fabius, its president, describes this consultative body in his inaugural speech as a manifestation of the recognition that France is a pluricultural society. However, his model of the French nation as a body whose members are the provinces clearly emphasizes the ideal of "France, one and indivisible":

It is necessary to find the right equilibrium so that France does not fly apart. Inside this true community that is the nation, we must promote the fusion of particular cultures, we must preserve the national cohesion and develop provincial identity . . . France is a body which needs all its members, each member must know its role and participate in the identity of the whole

(Fabius, in Anonymous 1986:13).

3. Socio-economic symbolism

Increased incorporation of Brittany into the centralized French administrative system has had a strong negative impact on Breton identity. Cities have historically been centers where contact with the outside world has been strongest. The development of transportation and communication lines from Paris to the outlying rural areas of France helped Bretons become all the more aware of a division between rural and urban society. Nineteenth-century city dwellers in Brittany had little love for peasants of "the brush" whom they unfavorably compared with colonized peoples within the French empire. Peasants were considered backward and savage. A popular saying of the time sums up city people's feelings about rural Bretons: "Les pommes de terre pour les cochons, les épluchures pour les Bretons" ('Potatoes for the pigs, the peelings for the Bretons').

The animosity was mutual; peasants ridiculed those who tried to imitate city ways, but at the same time "French civilization" and anything from Paris was viewed as superior to rural life. In terms of technological development, rural Brittany *was* backward, and cities were centers for industrial development. Rural areas clearly lagged behind in their access to resources from central government that contributed to a more comfortable lifestyle. Confronted by the contrast between their own and urban lifeways, rural dwellers came to view their own as inherently archaic (Elegoet 1978:219–20; Simon 1979:38–9).

Getting rid of the backward peasant world meant for rural Bretons that one got rid of the "old ways". These old ways were Breton ways, while the "new ways" of the progressive, modern, urban world were French ways, and usually Parisian ways. Becoming modern meant becoming French. As described by Pierre Simon, a Breton sociologist: "[O]n s'affirme deux fois Français tant on craint de ne pas l'être assez" ('One doubly affirms one's Frenchness to the extent that one is afraid of not being French enough') (1979:38).

Rejection of the old ways included rejection of the Breton language and of Gallo, a French dialect of rural Upper Brittany. Jettisoned also were distinctive furniture, costume, music, and dances, as well as farming practices. Technological change was motivated by a desire for economic development and a more comfortable lifestyle. Cultural changes were motivated in addition by a desire to change social status. Women, who were affected strongly by the drudgery of farm work, were the first to seek escape from a Breton identity which they felt chained them to this lifestyle (Elegoet 1978:216–17; Le Du 1980:154; Timm 1980:36). The utilization of language shift by rural women is not surprising and has been documented elsewhere, for instance by Susan Gal (1978).

The processes underlying the formation of a negative socio-economic Breton identity are most visible in the realm of the Breton language.[3] In schools, in the army, and as emigrants, Bretons have learned that their culture, and language especially, are considered inferior and backward, and ridicule has served to reinforce feelings of shame in being Breton. The exclusion of the Breton language from schools and administrative offices has been interpreted accurately by Bretons as a formal condemnation of their language and culture as a whole (Elegoet 1971–2:208–16; Person 1973:104–5; Hélias 1975:505). In a world where all social and cultural institutions are controlled and dominated by French speakers, lack of fluency in French has been considered a serious handicap, stigmatizing Bretons as less intelligent beings. Fanch Elegoet, a Breton sociologist who has done extensive oral history work among native Breton speakers in Leon, sums this up best in the title of his publication (1978) of a peasant's memoirs: "*Nous ne savions que le breton et il fallait parler français*" ('We knew only Breton and it was necessary to speak French').[4]

The school was an especially important institution in terms of its role in the formation of a negative Breton identity. Weber reports that in the 1860s and 1870s the theme of introducing civilization to children of rural France was an important element in school inspectors' reports which:

reflected the prevailing belief that areas and groups of some importance were uncivilized, that is, unintegrated into, unassimilated to French civilization: poor, backward, ignorant, savage, barbarous, wild, living like beasts with their beasts. They had to be taught manners, morals, literacy, a knowledge of French, and of France, a sense of the legal and institutional structure beyond their immediate community. The peasant had to be integrated into the national society, economy, and culture: the culture of the city and of the city par excellence, Paris.

(Weber 1976:5)

In the late nineteenth and early twentieth centuries the civilizing influence of schools was limited in Breton-speaking rural communities since children needed on farms left school by the time they were 14 years old. A solid knowledge of French was not transmitted to children, but the idea that being a Breton peasant is a negative identity *was* effectively transmitted (Elegoet 1978:192). The Breton language was viewed by rural Bretons as an old tool, no longer useful in a world where power depends on a knowledge of French. Two Breton scholars of the Breton language, François Falc'hun (1969) and Jean Le Du (1980) have emphasized that knowing French has not only been socially desirable in shedding a peasant identity, but economically necessary in a society where emigration out of Breton-speaking communities to find work is a common experience. Those most likely to resist efforts to defend or promote a language such as Breton are often the very people who best know the language. These native speakers, from the remotest and least industrialized districts, need a more widely spoken language to find work outside their home area.

Getting ahead for Bretons has meant not only learning French, but getting rid of Breton as a marker of backwardness. Pierre Simon cites Elegoet's characterization of the pejorative image given to Breton by schools as well as newspapers, books, radio, and television – an image which has been internalized by Bretons:

It is a peasant *patois*, unable to insure communication even with the neighboring village, even more incapable of expressing the modern world – the world of tractors, automobiles, airplanes, television. A language only good enough to talk to cows and pigs. From that you get the refusal to transmit this language to children – a language considered to be a burden, a handicap in social promotion, a source of humiliation and shame.

(Elegoet, in Simon 1979:39)

The army experience has also been very important in the formation of a negative Breton identity. Compulsory military service was often the first time Bretons made contact with the outside world in the early twentieth century. The lack of French which had been a problem in the schools was once again a social handicap in the army. Most Bretons entering the army learned that without French they were powerless. This army experience is described in the life history collected by Fanch Elegoet from an 80-year-old man of the Leon area: "If you cannot defend yourself in French, what can you do? You can only keep quiet and let others step all over you" (Elegoet 1978:208).

World War I is cited as an important turning point in the use of Breton. Returning soldiers tended to switch to French within their family, hoping to spare their children the humiliation and lack of power they had suffered in the non-Breton world. Military service was recognized by French officials as a "civilizing" influence well before this period:

Military service rendered "inestimable services"[,] reckoned a report from Rennes in 1880. "The young Bretons who don't know how to read, write or speak French when they get to their units are promptly civilized, . . . lose the prejudices of their *pays*, abandon native superstitions and backward opinions; and when they return to the village they are sufficiently Frenchified to Frenchify their friends by their influence."
(AN, F17 9292, Rapport sur les trois départements bretons, Octobre 1880, in

Weber 1976:299)

Bretons returning from military service had marked influence not only in the realm of language use, but also in the de-Bretonnization of costume and music (Falc'hun 1969; Deniel 1976:48; Reece 1977:34; Elegoet 1978:191).

Through the combined experiences of school, the army, and emigration, Bretons growing up in the early twentieth century learned that social advancement and power were linked to mastery of French. They also learned to reject their own Breton identity as a negative one. Getting rid of that identity meant discarding *all* markers of Bretonness. As described in the following reflections by Reun ar C'halan, a native Breton speaker now living in the United States, Bretons found it natural to escape to a new identity:

The Breton people had been so alienated that they had come to despise their own past, their own culture, their own language. The contempt with which the dominant language treated Breton peasants (one only has to read Balzac or Hugo) was internalized to such an extent that many Bretons rejected what they were, and came to despise their own parents and grandparents. . . . The most damning thing about it is that so many Breton children and their parents found it "natural" to assume another identity. Bretons . . . had been so thoroughly brainwashed that their highest ambition was to be taken for Parisians.

(ar C'halan 1983, pers. comm.)

Whether successful or not in efforts to pass for Parisians, Bretons came to deny their own existence.[5] The generations of Bretons who suffered humiliation, or a sense of inferiority and powerlessness, have not in all cases given up their Breton identity, but they have contributed greatly to the "civilization" of their children by blocking transmission of the Breton language and cultural traditions linked to rural Breton society. With a firm belief that French is the language of the future, and Breton the language of the past, older generations of Bretons have taught their children to look to a French future.

The idea that Breton is a language incapable of expressing modern ideas or technological or scientific knowledge has been commonly accepted by many Bretons (Person 1973:110–11; Henry 1979:16–17). This is reflected in efforts some Bretons have made to counter that idea and prove Breton can be modern. For example, the first student successfully to take all his Baccalaureate examinations in Breton explained: "I wanted to prove that Breton could be, in 1979, a language of modern expression, the same as French" (Gilles Quilévéré, in Anonymous 1979:3).

4.   "Big" vs. "little" languages

Bretons who view the Breton language solely as the language of their ancestors are reinforced in their thinking by non-Bretons who feel that efforts to maintain "little languages" are a waste of time. In 1975, for example, Gérard Antoine, a professor at the Université de Paris III questions, "[I]s it wise or opportune to urge little French children towards a bi- or tri-lingualism turned not towards the future of the planet, but towards the past of a little country?" (1975). In 1985 the French Minister of National Education, Jean-Pierre Chevénement, responsible for implementing bilingual programs his own government has introduced, states in reference to Corsican that: "One does no favor to youth in teaching them languages which offer no prospects" (in Anonymous 1985a). Ironically, French President Mitterrand has proposed that the interest of youth in regional languages and cultures is an effective force of resistance against the influence of North American mass culture (Anonymous 1985b).

French has long served in Brittany as the language of communication with strangers – used to show that one is fully educated and civilized, or simply because it is the only standard language learned by all people in Brittany. Standardization of Breton is discouraged by Bretons' belief that their language is fit only for limited intra-group communication and local oral traditions. Standardization has also been hindered by the fact that Breton has had only token presence in the schools and media. The peripheral place Breton has had in the schools has also discouraged the growth of a literary tradition for Breton. Breton remains a language with a relatively small written tradition.[6]

Division within the Breton language has followed oral-transmission lines related to historical and geographical divisions within Brittany. The four major dialects of Breton correspond roughly to earlier diocesan and ducal domains. The current areas in which are found these dialects – Leon (Léonais), Kernev (Cornouaillais), Treger (Trégorrois), and Gwened (Vannetais) – is shown in the map below. There is considerable linguistic diversity within these dialects in terms of vocabulary and pronunciation on the level of *pays*.

Studies of Breton history indicate that division within the Breton language is relatively modern. An examination of Breton language texts from the sixteenth through nineteenth centuries reveal that Breton was a much more uniform language in the eighteenth century than it is today. The modern dialects of Breton are not ancient, but rather the products of changes in the past few centuries (Fleuriot 1981:7–8). Successful communication among different dialect speakers can be dated well back in history with travel over relatively long distances for agricultural markets. Since 1829 Breton onion sellers have managed communication with Welsh speakers in their regular excursions across the Channel to sell their products door-to-door. One must

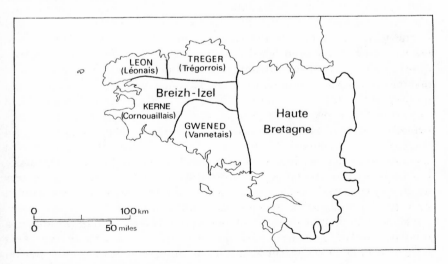

Major dialects of the Breton language

ask why, today, some Bretons can understand perfectly another dialect of Breton, while others find all dialects but their own incomprehensible.

The answer to this question is only in part linguistic. Pierre-Jakez Hélias emphasizes the *pays* level of identity within the Breton-speaking population, arguing that Breton speakers value the exclusive nature of a local dialect that expresses the "color" of a particular territory (1975:535). Most native speakers of Breton have received no formal training in their own language. Their knowledge of other Breton dialects is based on limited interactions and a local sense of what is "good" or "bad" Breton, what is "true" or "deformed" Breton.[7]

The standardization of spoken Breton is as inconceivable to native Breton speakers as the standardization of costume or dance. Most Bretons are horrified by the idea of creating or designating any one costume or dance style to serve as a common marker for *all* Bretons. These cultural markers, like the Breton language, express cultural diversity within Brittany. French has served as the language of unity within Brittany. It is a standard language for communication with all outsiders – whether they come from outside Brittany or outside one's village. French has also served as an urban language to the extent that cities and towns in Brittany have become centers for French acculturation.[8]

The idea that Breton is a "rural" language is reinforced by the fact that from roughly the tenth century on, urban Breton aristocrats and middle classes tended to shun the use of Breton and spoke French as the language of refinement and education.[9] Although records dating the earliest use of French in Brittany are scant, its presence in Breton towns by the sixteenth century is documented. In his detailed study of sixteenth- and seventeenth-century Brittany, Alain Croix found the association between elite classes and French language use already well documented (1981).

The idea that Breton is the language of "the people" – farmers and fishermen – and that French is the language of the bourgeoisie is reinforced today by Bretons with leftist leanings. It is ironic, but by no means untypical of minority language movements, that it has been members of the upper and middle classes, often learning Breton as a second language, who have had the resources, time, and interest to work most actively to promote the language, while rural native speakers have, on the whole, attempted to rid themselves of this language as part of a negative Breton identity. The social separation of language learners and militants from rural native speakers of Breton is often overemphasized. Even if many active language promoters are of an urban middle-class background, they are usually not far removed from rural grandparents, aunts, uncles, and cousins.

The perception that local Breton dialects express a different world than a standardized Breton is, however, a major factor separating native speakers from second-language learners. In the rare instance where a young person may learn Breton locally from native speakers at evening or weekend classes, his or her distance from native speakers will be relatively small. This learner may make some grammatical errors, but the Breton he or she speaks will sound comfortably familiar to local native speakers.

In most cases, young people who learn Breton as a second language do not have the opportunity to study the specific dialect of their home area. They will learn from teachers who are native speakers of another dialect or who use a standard, neutral Breton which does not bear the markings of any particular area of Brittany. These learners may acquire a "perfect" Breton, but it will be foreign to the native speakers of their home area. Those who learn a standard Breton find themselves in a no-man's land, speaking a colorless language which to many native speakers might as well be French for all the relation it bears to their own "real" Breton.

Problems caused by dialect diversity in the introduction of Breton to schools and major public media are exacerbated by the fact that the institutionalization of Breton counts on the intensive work of a small number of cultural militants. One does not have a large pool of qualified Breton teachers for different dialects who can be mobilized to meet the specific needs of schools throughout Brittany. Only exceptionally motivated Bretons have worked to become Breton teachers, since one has to train with only the slim hope of finding a job as a Breton teacher. Breton teachers have, for the most part, been educated to teach other subjects, since the French educational system has refused to create certification and examinations necessary for teachers to be hired specifically as Breton teachers. After years of petitioning and a clear expression on the part of students and parents that Breton classes are desired, some gaps in the training program have been filled, but it still takes an unusually strong commitment to become a Breton teacher.

Those who have persisted through administrative odds to train as a Breton teacher are not necessarily native speakers of Breton. Those who are native speakers do not always find jobs where their native dialect is spoken. Teachers can resort to a standard Breton which will give students a base to go on to perfect any particular dialect they want to master, or they can develop courses and materials which sample all dialects. In most cases, Breton teachers are trained to have a good ear for different dialects, but one can only become a native speaker by being or becoming a native.

While administrative obstacles still continue to block full institutionalization of Breton, changing attitudes have encouraged both learners and teachers. Today many young Bretons who live in Breton-speaking communities consider it natural to learn Breton. French and English are languages one learns to get ahead in the world. Breton is a language one learns because one lives in Brittany. Speaking Breton is no longer viewed as a marker of backwardness. While one may be considered impractical for learning Breton, it has become socially acceptable to speak Breton, and other non-French languages, in France today. For many young Bretons, learning Breton, whether they come from Breton-speaking communities or not, is a way to show one's pride in being Breton. Older native speakers, who have had a negative experience as Breton speakers, are surprised by the positive attitudes of young people, and also flattered by their new prestige as masters of "authentic" Breton. The outlook for Breton is, however, not promising.

Cases of children being raised in the home as Breton speakers are rare. While children of the 1980s find it perfectly natural to learn Breton, parents of the 1950s, 1960s, and 1970s considered it natural to speak French to their children. In areas of Brittany where Breton remains an everyday language for adults, children will understand the Breton language, but not be able to speak it, unless they have made an effort to learn it in a language class. Timm found in her research in the Carhaix area that households with monoglot Breton-speaking grandparents, bilingual parents, and monoglot French-speaking children with a passive knowledge of Breton were common. Children born after grandparents had died were likely to have no knowledge of Breton (Timm 1980:32). Jean Le Du, in his research in Plougrescant, also found a significant split according to age, attributable to the fact that, without exception, parents in the early 1950s addressed their elders in Breton and their children in French (1980:160). Young people today who master Breton in school classes or evening workshops are using Breton with Breton-speaking parents who brought them up in French, but the number of young people learning Breton and using it as an everyday language is very small. It is easier to continue to use French in a world where Breton has little public presence.

5.   Breton identity and the Breton language

The fact that young people in Brittany today view learning Breton positively is due to the fact that they view Breton identity as a positive identity. It is a geographic/cultural/social/political identity which is both ascribed and achieved.[10] "Being Breton" ultimately involves the use of cultural markers as a participant in the everyday life of a Breton community. Bretons judge authenticity of Breton identity by evaluating both social participation and cultural competence. Residence and ancestry can be used to predict cultural competence, but are not in themselves sufficient qualifications for Breton identity. The acquisition of culture, is, of course, closely tied to ancestry and residence, but geographical mobility and increasing communication with the world outside Brittany has meant that cultural borders have grown indistinct. Whether or not the borders are clear, a return to the *pays* in recent years in Brittany for an examination of one's roots shows that cultural diversity within Brittany is still important to young Bretons defining their identity. A renaissance of *pays*-level cultural expressions is based on the persistence of a significant amount of cultural diversity within Brittany, rather than on a nostalgic reintroduction of old customs.

Language is but one cultural marker of Breton identity – significant to the extent that it gives one the tools to participate in communities where Breton remains an everyday language. It is the participation that counts in defining who is and is not Breton. A well-known illustration in Brittany is the Japanese student, Makoto Naguchi, who pursued Celtic Studies at the Université de Haute-Bretagne in Rennes. Mastering Breton better than French, he now lives in a small rural town in Lower Brittany and teaches Breton to local youth. "Going native" in this case was not simply a matter of learning Breton, but of using it as a community participant. Origins are not ignored or forgotten, however. The fact that Makoto Naguchi has become an "example" indicates that people remain highly conscious of his ancestry, even if they fully accept him today as a fellow Breton.

6. Conclusion

Symbolic values attached to both French and Breton have affected the use of these languages in Brittany. Rather than being viewed as two alternative languages for varying situations, French and Breton have been perceived as oppositional languages. On a political level, French has been endowed with the status of "national" language of "France, one and indivisible". For French nationalists there is room in France for just one national language. Breton and other non-French languages are tolerated to the extent that they remain "regional" languages – part of the colorful folklore of France. To the degree that regions remain culturally distinctive, however, they are viewed by French nationalists as potential threats to the unity of the French nation-state since cultural distinctiveness can encourage a sense of cultural independence – a prerequisite for claims to political independence. The persistence of Breton thus symbolizes the fragility of French unity for those who equate political unity with cultural unity.

Of stronger symbolic impact is the promotion of French as the language of civilization and education. This has been effectively contrasted with the notion that Breton is fit only for backward peasants. To learn French is to advance socially and morally. These strong social values for French and Breton have been promoted through French institutions since the French Revolution, affecting generations of Breton speakers who have worked to spare their children the stigma of backwardness by blocking the transmission of Breton. In the past few decades a strong economic symbolism has been added, promoting French as an international language and demoting Breton as an impractical language, of use only in talking to neighboring farmers of one's own village. "Usefulness" and "practicality" have become key concepts.

The cultural exclusivity of Breton makes it attractive for those willing to work around the dominance of French in the media and public institutions of Brittany. Breton is the language of one's ancestors and a symbol of the persistence of a "small" people against all odds in a world which seems to favor "big" peoples and cultural standardization. Useful or not, Breton is a language with enough positive symbolism to justify some optimism for its survival. The future of this language will depend on its symbolic strength, the belief of young Bretons that a Breton identity can be a positive one and that the Breton language is an irreplaceable element in that identity.

Notes

I wish to thank Reun ar C'halan for comments on an earlier draft, and Nancy Dorian for probing questions and useful suggestions which helped with this chapter.

1. Figures have been drawn from Le Menn (1975:72) and Levesque (1982:286). Information on statistics can also be found in Gwegen (1975:55–8).
2. All translations of quotations are my own.
3. These processes were equally at work on the Gallo dialect of Upper Brittany. The complexity of Gallo identity is not treated in this chapter. See Kuter (1985).
4. Work by Elegoet and others collecting and analyzing oral histories has been published by an organization called Tud ha Bro – Sociétés Bretonnes. See Kuter (1984) for a review of this work.
5. The psychological impact of the suppression of the Breton language and Bretons' own selfdenial of their identity has been studied by Breton researchers who published the results of a conference on this subject in 1986: *Permanence de la langue bretonne – de la linguistique à la psychanalyse* (Collection "Anthropologie médicale", Institut culturel de Bretagne).
6. While written Breton can be dated to the end of the eighth century, it remained largely a language for a limited amount of religious writing until the end of the eighteenth century. Although the language was excluded from the schools, the churches had taught Breton speakers to read, and within families it is likely that Bretons taught themselves to read. A study of printing in Brittany indicates that significant quantities of religious and secular Breton language material was distributed in Brittany in the late eighteenth and nineteenth centuries (Le Menn 1985:239). The development of a modern Breton-language literature has grown in proportion to a growth of readers. In its switch to French, the church ceased to serve as an institution which taught Bretons to read their language. Breton classes in schools have remained limited, although their expansion in recent years accounts for a growth of readership for Breton in the 1970s and 1980s. In the 1950s, books in Breton were rarely printed in quantities of more than five to eight hundred, with four or five new titles appearing each year. Today there are a dozen Breton-language publishing houses, and it is common to have printings of 1,500 to 2,000 copies, with fifty to sixty new titles each year (Le Nail 1985:26). Standardization of written Breton has been an issue debated with great passion in Brittany, fueled by political and personal antagonisms. See Morvannou (1980:38–47) and Timm (1982:4) for an introduction to issues in the standardization of Breton orthography.

7. See Jean Le Du (1980) for an interesting discussion of perceptions of the differences within the Breton language that he found among Breton speakers in Plougrescant.
8. See Timm (1980) for a detailed discussion of the use of Breton and French in the town of Carhaix, and Le Du (1980) for the area of Plougrescant. See Levesque (1982) for a good discussion of the urban/rural linguistic split as well as other sociolinguistic factors dividing Breton speakers.
9. Many Breton writers have pointed out the abandonment of Breton by the upper classes: see Piriou (1971:6), Keineg (1973:139), Gwegen (1975:28), Le Lannou (1978:25), Morvannou (1980:36–7), and Le Menn (1985:229).
10. See Kuter (1985) for an analysis of different levels of Breton identity.

6 "Persistence" or "tip" in Egyptian Nubian

ALEYA ROUCHDY

"In terms of possible routes toward language death it would seem that a language which has been demographically highly stable for several centuries may experience a sudden 'tip' after which the demographic tide flows strongly in favor of some other language."

(Dorian 1981:51)

The picture of Nubia and Nubian history was originally drawn by historians and archaeologists; in recent times, anthropologists and modern linguists have contributed their works. Actually, the first linguists were travellers in the seventh century who discovered and recorded the Nubian dialects of the Nile Valley. But it was not until the nineteenth century that specific studies dealt with these dialects, studies such as that of Reinisch in 1879, or Lepsius in 1840–53.

In the twentieth century starting as early as 1910, there was a discovery of ancient text written in Nubian. Scholars became interested in finding out the affinity between the Nubian language and other languages, and between the different dialects of Nubian.

Nubian has historically been classified as:

1. Mixed negro by Lepsius (1880);
2. Proto-Hamitic by Reinisch (1911) ("Proto" postulates Hamitic in its earliest underdeveloped stage);
3. Sudanic by Westermann (1911) and Meinhof (1912);
4. Eastern Sudanic by Greenberg (1948), MacGaffey (1961) and Trigger (1965).

Today there is a preponderance of opinion that Nubian is an Eastern Sudanic language, a branch of Nilo-Saharan. The Eastern Sudanic people settled in the Nile Valley and brought their language, which became the Nubian of the present day. Linguistically, there are two different groups of Nubians, each represented both in Egypt and in the Sudan: the Kenuz, who speak a dialect called Matoki in Egypt and Dongolawi in the Sudan, and the Fadicca,[1] who speak a dialect called Fadicca in Egypt and Mahasi in the

Sudan. Within each group, Matoki/Dongolawi and Fadicca/Mahasi, there are dialect variations that distinguish the Egyptian Nubian speakers from the Sudanese Nubian speakers.

Linguists have long debated the meaning of the terms language and dialect, and it seems that the question is not settled. Both Matoki and Fadicca belong to the Nile Nubian language group and are closely related linguistically. Nubian is thus a dialect in the sense that it is defined in reference to the Nile Nubian language. A large number of Nubiologists use the term dialect when referring to Nubian generally. In this study Fadicca and Matoki are both referred to as dialect (*rutana* or *lahga* in Arabic), as the Nubian speakers themselves refer to their spoken language, by comparison with Arabic as a "real language".

The origin of the word Nubia has been tentatively explained by Arkell as deriving from a word in the Nubian language which meant 'slaves', but he also says that the ancient Egyptian word *nab* meant 'gold' and that Nubia had been named based on the fact that the metal came to the Egyptians from their southern neighbors, whom they considered slaves (Arkell 1961:177). Another source mentions that the word *nebed* was used in an inscription of Thotmes I (ca. 1450 BC) to designate people with curly hair who had been invaded by Thotmes (Hillelson 1930:142). Whatever the origin of the word, Nubia is now a linguistic and ethnic term applied to a new area currently occupied primarily by resettled Nubians.

The Nubian language is used by 200,000 people of whom one-quarter live in Egypt and the remainder in the Sudan (Adams 1977:2). Voegelin and Voegelin maintain that there are 1,000,000 speakers of Nubian (1977a:320).[2]

In Egypt, before the construction of the High Dam, the Nubians were located between Aswan and the Sudanese border. The Kenuz were in the northern section and had 17 villages, while the Fadicca were located in the south with 18 villages. In the middle there was an enclave of Arabs with five villages. The building of dams on the Nile starting in the late nineteenth and early twentieth centuries had a direct impact upon the Nubians. "About 60 percent of the territory of Nubia has been destroyed or rendered unfit for habitation, and about half of the surviving Nubian-speaking people have been obliged to find new homes, either within or outside their traditional homeland" (Adams 1977:653).

When the first dam was built in 1889, and enlarged in 1907 and 1934, the Egyptian government had no organized programs of resettlement (Fahim 1983). Some of the Nubians resettled independently. The Kenuz, for instance, established themselves among the Mahasi in the Sudan and the Fadicca in Egypt (Adams 1977:653). The Kenuz' early migration is reflected by the fact that the older speakers among them (but only the older speakers) can handle Matoki and Fadicca. Other Kenuz migrated to cities north of Aswan. It was an unorganized but forced migration, as opposed to the migration that has prevailed and still continues in the twentieth century: Nubian men migrating to Cairo and Alexandria looking for wage labor, while maintaining their homes and relatives in Nubia and visiting them on certain occasions.

With the construction of the High Dam in the 1960s, the inhabitants of Old Nubia had to abandon their ancestral land along the Nile, which was to be covered by the water of the artificial Lake Nasser behind the High Dam. The Egyptian government organized programs to resettle the 45,000 to 50,000 Nubians in a new geographical area, on newly reclaimed land, which became known as New Nubia. The new villages kept their old names and were grouped geographically in the same way as they were prior to the resettlement.

Old Nubia stretched along the Nile for about 350 kilometers. New Nubia is shaped like a crescent and is about 60 kilometers in length. It is not along the Nile but at some 3–10 kilometers away. One good aspect of the resettlement is the provision of amenities which were lacking in Old Nubia. For instance, each village has a primary school, a public health unit, water pump, market, mosque, and guesthouse. Junior high schools and high schools are accessible; although not found in every village, they can be easily reached by bus or train.

There are also negative aspects to the resettlement. In Old Nubia people were grouped by location of houses in terms of close kin. In New Nubia this factor was not taken into consideration and houses were based upon the size of the nuclear family. During my interviews, people expressed their dissatisfaction with the size of the houses and the fact that they were located at a distance from the Nile. Another complaint was that they were too close to the $Sa^{9}idi^{3}$ peasants whom they looked down upon. They feared the disintegration of their values, customs, and language due to the close contact. Some of the Nubians, however, hired $Sa^{9}idis$ to work in their fields while they themselves pursued wage labor in the cities. In spite of their dissatisfaction, some of the Nubians interviewed were aware that they must compromise to some extent in order to live in their new land.

The relocation of the Nubian communities brought about changes in the new, resettled Nubian villages. Women started going to the market to sell their products either in their own villages or in a neighboring city, where they also did their weekly shopping. These changes brought more Nubians into daily contact with Arabic speakers, especially the women and children, who used to be very isolated in Old Nubia.

During my most recent visit to the villages (January 1986) I observed new forms of communication among the various Nubian villages, and between the villages and cities. Telephones are accessible and found in many homes. Moreover, there are more means of transportation, such as cars, taxis, and trains. This has resulted in easy access to Arabic newspapers issued in Cairo and brought daily into the villages, a trend that did not prevail in 1979. The availability of the various means of transportation has allowed village girls to go to school and work in the nearby cities. Children and elderly people (grandparents) are sent to visit relatives in urban centers, and urban children are sent to the villages during the holidays.

In order for a minority[4] group to maintain its language, certain social factors should prevail. Some of these factors are more significant and should be considered as primary factors, for example:

1. A situation of "stable bilingualism" (Greenberg 1965:59; Fishman 1971a: 73);
2. The maintenance/rise of ethnic identity (Greenberg 1965:59; Giles 1977:308);
3. The language being used for primary socialization (Greenberg 1965:60), and its frequency of usage and function.

The secondary factors are:

1. Endogamous marriage (Greenberg 1965:59; Dorian 1981:56) and group interaction;
2. Political non-interference. (The Nubian language is ignored by the government in its language planning policy.)

First, let us examine the two secondary factors as they apply to the Nubian case. In cities, Nubians have more contact with non-Nubians. Each group visits the other's homes and attends the other's weddings. However, in spite of this interaction between Nubians and non-Nubians and between Nubians speaking different dialects, intermarriage is not favorably looked upon. In cities there are some cases of intermarriage, but mostly of Nubian men marrying non-Nubian women.[5] In the villages I visited in 1979, I met only one couple where the husband is a Fadicca and the wife is a non-Nubian Egyptian. Nubians, before their relocation, were not in a very favorable social position, a fact which explains the non-Nubian negative attitude toward intermarriage. This social disfavor was based on the following factors:

1. Skin-color differences: the range of difference in features within the Nubian population is wide. The Kenuz claim that the Fadicca have "more African features" and "darker skin" than themselves. Both, the Fadicca and the Matoki, have dark skin, a feature that they share with many southern non-Nubian Egyptians.
2. Linguistic differences, and the fact that Nubians speak "broken" Arabic.
3. Occupational and educational differences. Many Nubians prior to 1964 were working as cooks, waiters, or doormen in hotels and Egyptian homes in Cairo and Alexandria. These occupations placed Nubians in relatively low status in the overall Egyptian

society. (There is a reverse side to this however. Due to the inadequate means of transportation to Old Nubia, the Nubians working in Egyptian homes could not easily return to their villages and visit their families. They thus developed strong ties to their employers' household members, who in turn trusted them and preferred them to non-urban Arab–Egyptian helpers. This trust enhanced the Nubians' self-image and made them feel superior to non-Nubian Egyptians performing similar services, whom they described as "unclean" and "not very bright". This Nubian attitude toward their equivalent non-Nubians in the Egyptian social strata explains Nubians' own reluctance to marry non-Nubians. Thus there is also a Nubian inclination to disfavor exogamy.)

Intermarriage between the two Nubian-speaking communities, Fadicca–Matoki,[6] was also not very common in the villages. In 1986, however, I was told that the number of intermarriages of this type has increased among the educated urban Nubians, and that there were also many cases of exogamy, where a Nubian marries a non-Nubian. What is of interest is that this trend, which has developed recently (1979–86), reflects a significant change in the traditional preferred-marriage system.

As for political non-interference in relation to the Nubian language, it should be mentioned that in Egypt there is a centralization of state authority. This leads to a conformism in the educational system and to the promotion of the Arabic language, which is the medium of instruction. Nubian is an intra-group language used only among the Nubians themselves. The government language planning policy does not promote the use of Nubian. It embraces a policy position that supports Arabic as the only national language. It is true that one good aspect of the resettlement is that Nubians are able to participate in a more efficient educational system, but as a Nubian university student put it, "the Nubians have a better chance of education than they had before; however, this is affecting the Nubian language and culture".

Where the primary factors are concerned, a situation of "stable bilingualism" exists when the dominant language, although known and used by minority-group members, does not replace the subordinate language. Reserving the subordinate language for intimacy, since it is learned in the home, among people who are intimate with the speaker, and relegating the dominant language to public spheres, since it is typically learned outside the home and used principally with people who are not intimate with the speakers (Dorian 1986a:73–4), may favor the development of a "stable bilingualism". In other words, it is a case where the members of the minority group feel that the dominant language is learned for practical purposes, and not as a bond of solidarity.

Older Nubians, and those in more isolated non-urban areas, try to maintain their language in order to preserve their cultural heritage. They have more of a sense of group identity and loyalty to the traditional ways than urban Nubians; however, they do learn Arabic, since it is the official language of the country. Gardner and Lambert (1972: ch. 4) discuss the two-way learning process in which one language is preserved and the second is learned, referring to the learners as either "integrative" or "instrumental". The first type learns his/her second language to participate in the cultural heritage and merge to some extent with it, while the "instrumental" learner learns the second language to ameliorate his/her social position in society. The Nubians can be considered both "integrative" and "instrumental" learners. Urban and non-urban speakers alike learn Arabic not only because it is the official language of the country and thus important to social and economic success, but also because it is the religious language. Nubians are Muslims and Arabic is the language of the Qur'an; thus by learning it they become integrated into Egyptian Muslim society as a whole. The use of Arabic in this respect creates a certain bond of solidarity between the Nubian and non-Nubian Egyptians. Under these conditions the term "stable" cannot be applied to bilingualism among the Nubian speakers. In the writer's opinion this is a situation of unstable bilingualism, and, unless there are other strong motives for the preservation of Nubian, "tip" to the dominant language, Arabic – already underway – will proceed further.

In non-urban areas, Nubians consider themselves as either Matoki or Fadicca, thus defining their ethnic identity according to the linguistic community to which they belong. They use the language more often and there are fewer external factors opposing it than among the urbanized Nubians.

The urbanites attach less importance to their language as a symbol of ethnic-group membership than do the rural dwellers. Thus, the idea of maintaining the language as being the major symbol of ethnicity is not *de rigueur* among them. Customs and cultural traditions other than language are stressed and revived. And even under threat of their cultural loss, they use Arabic to speak to each other, and to work out programs to revive their heritage. For instance in the Nubian clubs[7] I visited in Cairo in 1981 and in 1986, the conversation among the Nubian members was always conducted in Arabic.

From the beginning of the resettlement, Nubians were disappointed with the new setting, and continued to feel as if they were going through a transitional period. After coping with the immediate practical problems of housing and cultivation during the first years, the Nubians began to realize that their culture and language were threatened by the new environment. They were nostalgic about their old land and requested the government to give them their lands which were not covered by the new Lake Nasser behind the High Dam. The dream of returning to their lands materialized in 1977 through the formation of government-aided cooperatives. Three villages were established. First, *As-Salam*, which in 1985 had 25 resettled Nubian families. It has an elementary school. Second, *As-Shuhada* with three families; and finally, *As-Sadat*, which is now deserted due to the lack of water. Non-urban Nubians were enthusiastic from the first about the establishment of these villages. They thought it was an ideal situation where Nubians could gather alone, avoiding outside interference, thus maintaining their language and customs. Moreover, they look at their return to their old land from an economic point of view. There is the notion that there is a future in the new villages in the form of a fishing industry and in the development of tourism. They would like to establish themselves in the area to reaffirm their claim to the land, especially since the *Sa⁹idis* have already put a claim on some of the lands in the area, by establishing fishing rights.

Urban Nubians have a different attitude regarding the return to the old land. During my most recent visit to a Nubian club in Cairo, I asked the members if they would like to return to the newly established villages in the recovered lands. I was told that young Nubians are not interested in starting their lives in a new and harsh environment. However, the idea of returning to the old land revived both urban and non-urban Nubian pride in their ethnic background. And in 1979, 1981, and 1986 I noticed that there was indeed a revival of Nubian ethnicity compared to what had existed in Egypt prior to 1960. In cities, such as Cairo and Alexandria, Nubian clubs were more active and better attended. Arabic, however, remained the language used to converse in these clubs.

With the rise of ethnic identity among Nubians, and since Nubian relocation into the midst of non-Nubians, Egyptians in general are more aware of the Nubians and their culture. For instance, the most important daily newspaper *Al Ahram*, had in January 1986 four articles dealing with different Nubian topics. A weekly magazine, *Al Musawwar* had, in February, 1986, a lengthy article on the establishment of the new Nubian museum in Aswan, and about the Nubians' daily activities in the villages of New Nubia.

The recent attention given by the mass media to Nubians, and the turn of events among the Nubian themselves, such as the return to the old lands, is bringing Nubianism into perspective and reviving the Nubian sense of ethnicity: "ethnicity . . . is the key variable in the maintenance of the first language" (Koenig 1980:12). Will the recent revival of ethnic identity among Nubians and the simultaneous rise in interest in Nubians among non-Nubians prevent a "tip" to Arabic, the dominant language?

If a minority language ceases to be used in homes for primary socialization, the maintenance of the language is threatened in spite of the rise of ethnic feeling. Thus the importance of home use for the persistence of a minority language can scarcely be overstated.

There is a difference in choice of language for primary socialization in urban and non-urban Nubian homes. In urban areas Nubian women are more educated. They go to school and speak Arabic fluently. They usually speak Arabic to their children. Some are monolinguals and Arabic is their only language. This situation prevails among young women whose children grow up speaking only Arabic. Women above 40 are bilinguals, but they too use Arabic when speaking to their children and reserve Nubian for addressing their husbands. The children grow up speaking Arabic and understanding and generating some Nubian, although faulty in terms of traditional Nubian grammar. They are what Dorian refers to as "semi-speakers" (Dorian 1981:155).

Prior to the resettlement of 1964, women in Old Nubia were monolinguals, speaking only Nubian. (Nubian speakers are categorized into different groups in my other chapter in this volume.) They were not educated, a factor that kept this group linguistically more conservative than other Nubians. By 1986, due to the increasing contact with Arabic speakers, bilingualism had become a widespread phenomenon among the older non-urban women. Thus their influence in maintaining the Nubian language among the young children is diminishing. The major factors linked to the decreasing use of Nubian for primary socialization in non-urban areas can be traced to:

1. The introduction of electricity which has allowed every house to acquire a radio and television. Arabic broadcast media have expanded and reach deep into Nubian villages. Television, which is the main source of entertainment, propagates Arabic culture and promotes the learning of Arabic. Nubian songs are only transmitted through the radio. Children grow up listening to and watching only Arabic programs.
2. The better system of education which was provided to the Nubians after the resettlement, and the development of new means of communication, has increased the number of educated females. As mentioned previously, educated women tend to speak Arabic to their children. "It is the change in the position of women which is of key importance in the New Nubia settlement" (Fernea 1979:46).
3. The availability of male relatives (fathers) in the house. In Old Nubia, prior to the resettlement, the majority of men were absent seeking work in cities far away from their isolated villages. In the new setting, the availability of jobs has increased. The men are employed in the area and live with their families. They tend, thus, to play an important role in the process of socialization. In general Nubian men, who already prior to the resettlement were better educated than Nubian women, tend to speak Arabic to their children.

The above three factors are causing a major decrease in the use of Nubian for primary socialization.

Finally, the religious Islamic revival observed in the past years in all of

Egypt will surely have an impact on future shift in language use, promoting the change-over from Nubian to Arabic. The number of men attending mosques has greatly increased. Sons accompany their fathers for the Friday prayers, which are always followed by a sermon presented in Classical Arabic. During my most recent visit to one of the villages, I was told that the children are taught the Qur'an after school, and that those who recite it well are given a prize. Moreover, more women are actively practicing Islam. They learn Arabic in order to recite the Qur'an and practice Islam properly. Thus this religious revival under conditions in which Arabic is the lingua sacra is an important factor to be considered when tracing the influences that lead to a "tip" toward the dominant language.

The occasions on which Arabic or Nubian are used vary according to the location and the topic of conversation. In non-urban areas, in 1979, Nubian high school students mixed with a majority of non-Nubian speakers and had to use Arabic with their friends as well as their teachers. In the elementary schools, however, Nubian children spoke both Arabic and Nubian. In their homes these children spoke Nubian to their mothers. By 1986 there was a noticeable change in the language use among the children in these villages. The children insisted on responding in Arabic when addressed in Nubian by their parents or adult family friends. The only time I heard Nubian exchanged fluently in the villages was among women themselves, or when women were speaking to older men. A recent change was observed among the non-urban speakers. Members of the group categorized in 1979 as monolinguals, spoke to me in Arabic in 1986; they greeted me in Arabic and to my surprise used only Arabic during our conversation. Moreover, their greetings to each other were in Arabic, and any fixed phrase incorporating the word 'God' (*Allah*) was uttered in Arabic, e.g.

măsa ʔ allah	'God willing'
ħamdulillah	'thank God'
allah yixallīk	'God bless you'

In cities the transition to Arabic is so complete that it is used to address the children. That specific segment of Nubian speakers, when interviewed, expressed the view that Nubian is not an important language.

Nubian is used in both urban and non-urban areas when speakers do not want outsiders (such as two non-Nubian friends of mine from Cairo and myself) to understand their conversation, especially when dealing with family affairs. For instance, at a gathering (which a friend of mine and I attended) in a village of Fadicca speakers where a marriage was arranged, only Nubian was used by the adults, despite the presence of us Arabic speakers. On the other hand, young relatives visiting from Cairo, who spoke Arabic only, used Nubian words to refer to events and traditional practices related to wedding rituals, even though such words have direct counterparts in Arabic, such as:

karray	'exchange of favors in weddings'
kofferay-dibbi	'the henna night (a celebration on the eve of the wedding)'
bali-dibbi	'actual wedding day'

However, in order to participate in the full range of daily-life activities in both urban and non-urban areas, whether it is the child at school, or the man and woman at work, Egyptian Nubians have to use Arabic. Thus, Arabic is taking over function by function, while Nubian is becoming more specialized to topics related to family occasions.

Since the Nubians recognize themselves as an ethnic group distinct from the rest of the Egyptian population, I thought it would be important to know what they themselves think of the status of the Nubian language. I asked (in Arabic) some people of Nubian ethnicity about their feelings toward the language. The following statements were chosen as revealing ones to be paraphrased in translation.

1. A Nubian in Upper Egypt was astonished to find that I, a non-Nubian, was interested in the Nubian language. He thought that Nubian is a language with no importance in society, with no advantage to learning it.
2. A young respondent from Cairo claimed that Nubian is becoming extinct, that only the elderly speak it, and with them goes the language.
3. Another maintained that Nubian is not a language since it is not written.
4. "Nubian is an ethnic language not a scientific language", said another respondent.
5. A Nubian teacher in New Nubia said that their customs and culture are changing, and this is affecting the language.
6. One respondent, who is a middle-aged singer, said that the language will always be maintained as long as new Nubian songs are composed. He further said that as long as he can express feelings of sadness or happiness, then Nubian is useful to him emotionally, and thus will remain a viable language.

In general, the Nubians attitude towards their mother tongue, coupled with the fact that they identify with the attitude of the dominant group, is another threat to the survival of their language. Respondents 1, 5, and 6 (older people) regretted the changes in the Nubian language, and the fact that Arabic is taking over. They had a fatalistic attitude, however, in that they felt powerless to change the flow of events in Egyptian society. Respondents 2, 3, and 4 (younger people) did not care whether the language was affected or not, and felt that the changes were positive since Nubian "is not an important language".

The above quotations reflect the attitude of the Nubians in general. Young Nubians, more than the older ones, come to identify with the negative attitude of the dominant group, Arab Egyptians, in that Nubian "is not a real language" and "not an important language".

The Nubian language does not have official status, nor is it used in the media or as a language of instruction in schools, nor is it the religious language even among Nubians, and although there is no official government policy of assimilation, the fundamental change in lifestyle since the resettlement is leading to assimilation. Moreover, in spite of the fact that circumstances and attitudes in the wider society have changed positively since the relocation of Nubians among non-Nubians, the early unfavorableness of the Nubian position makes the sudden-seeming shift to Arabic understandable.

In conclusion, the longer-term consequences, at which I could only guess in 1979, are becoming clearer in 1986. "Tip" to the dominant language, Arabic, is occurring. It is taking place unevenly in the two different settings, urban and non-urban, but even the temporary "persistence" of Nubian in villages is now increasingly threatened by recent linguistic, social, and economic developments.

Notes

The research reported in this paper was supported by grants from the American Research Center in Egypt and the Social Science Research Council (1979), and again by the American Research Center in Egypt in 1984.

1. The Fadicca speakers use both the terms "Nubian" and "Fadicca" to refer to their subgroup, and "Fadicca" only to refer to their dialect. In this chapter, however, the term "Nubian", will be used for all people of that ethnic group, Kenuz as well as Fadicca.

2. Egyptian census data cannot be used to determine the number of Nubian speakers since the population is divided into Muslim and Christian categories, and Nubians are all Muslims, like most other Egyptians.

3. $Sa^{9}idi$ is the term used to refer to the dialect of Southern Egyptian, and to the Southern Egyptians in general. The symbol ^{9} is a transliteration convention indicating a voiced pharyngeal.

4. I would like to support Erik Allardt's (1984) categorization of a minority language. He rejects the idea that restricts the use of the word minority to a "fixed percentage or a proportion that a linguistic minority cannot exceed. The decisive factor in making them linguistic minorities is not the size but rather the social organization and their place in society" (Allardt 1984:198). Nubian is thus a minority language on other grounds besides the relatively small numbers of speakers, since it is markedly subordinate to Arabic, the dominant language.

5. Islam allows greater freedom to men in the choice of their partners. Muslim men can marry non-Muslim women. This religious aspect is generalized beyond religion and is reflected in the ethnic pattern of more Nubian men marrying non-Nubian women, although these extra-ethnic marriages are normally between Muslims.

6. The Fadicca and the Kenuz themselves do not trace their origin to the same geographical area. The Kenuz trace their origin to the Arabian peninsula (Badr 1955; Hamid 1973; also from personal interviews). The Kenuz claim that Matoki refers to the dialect spoken by the people who came from the east, since *mato* in their dialect means 'east'. Western Nubiologists are rather doubtful about this origin (Trigger 1976; Peter Shinnie and Robin Thelwall, pers. comm.). The Fadicca, who refer to their dialect as *Nubi*, insist that they are "the real Nubians" of African origin, who speak "real Nubian". They look on the Kenuz as originally being Arabs who were nubianized.

7. Each Nubian village in New Nubia is represented by a social club in Cairo. It is a gathering place where men socialize in the evening with members of the same village. In the morning there are special programs for women where they learn how to sew, and to read and write Arabic. Moreover, these clubs provide financial help to needy Nubian students who have left their villages to attend college in the city.

7 Sociolinguistic creativity: Cape Breton Gaelic's linguistic "tip"

ELIZABETH MERTZ

1. Introduction

Sudden shifts in a community's linguistic usage patterns afford sociolinguists interested in "explaining" linguistic changes a tempting opportunity. In cases of gradual shift, it is easier to understand change as the result of myriad social and linguistic factors and pressures, each contributing incrementally to the final result. With sudden change, on the other hand, we are more tempted to look for the one cause or factor tipping the linguistic balance. But, even in cases where rapid shift is clearly a response to a particular social change – for example, Dorian's account of shift away from Gaelic as the Scottish Highlands became less isolated (1981:51), or Tabouret-Keller's of shift in response to ongoing industrialization (1972) – there is still a complicated web of social, linguistic, and ideological factors at work. Thus Dorian notes that "English seemed to have come quickly to eastern Sutherland, but the climate which led to its rapid adoption had been centuries in the making" (1981:51). Dorian's caveat is even more clearly à propos where there is no sudden social shift corresponding with a change in language use.

The Scottish Gaelic speakers of Cape Breton, Nova Scotia, experienced a rapid language shift during the 1930s and 1940s. Their case is an excellent example of linguistic "tip", as Dorian first defined it: "A language which has been demographically highly stable for several centuries may experience a sudden 'tip', after which the demographic tide flows strongly in favor of some other language" (1981:51). Unlike Dorian's Scottish case, the Cape Breton tip is not clearly traceable to any particular social change:

By the 1970s effective transmission of Gaelic had ceased . . . an interesting sociolinguistic problem, for there had evidently been little change in power relationships, cultural arrangements, values, or populations in Cape Breton.
(MacKinnon 1977:10)

This chapter examines the "tip" toward English monolingualism in two very different Cape Breton communities. Although one was an isolated Protestant fishing community and the other an accessible Catholic town with a diverse economic base, both experienced the "tip" at the same time. I will argue that in order to understand this phenomenon, it is necessary to look not only at regional (and larger) social and economic patterns, but also at the linguistic–cultural beliefs and ideologies which filtered and translated wider social change at the local level. Using this perspective, we can appreciate the creativity of local speakers even as they apparently yield to wide-scale political or economic pressures – not only in how they continue transmission of minority languages, but also in how they cease transmission, and in how they put their minority language to powerful use even after transmission has ended. The Cape Breton case, then, demonstrates the complex inter-causality (Weber 1958) involved in language shift and maintenance. This approach takes seriously Gal's (1976) warning against simplistic external correlations of change in linguistic usage with discretely cataloged social "factors", and Romaine's (1982a) insistence on a complex socially grounded epistemology for sociolinguistic explanation.

2.   Language "tip" in Cape Breton

The island of Cape Breton, located at the northernmost tip of the Canadian province of Nova Scotia, divides into two "arms". The two communities of this study are located on opposite sides of the western, more mountainous "arm", within which there is a strong religious split; Catholic communities are concentrated in the western and southern portions, while Protestant communities cluster on the eastern shoreline. Mabou, a predominantly Catholic community, is located on the western coast of Cape Breton, just 13 miles south of the coal-mining center of Inverness. The "North Shore", a Protestant community, occupies a more isolated stretch of the rough northeast coast.

The two communities present a stark contrast in many ways. Mabou, with rolling farmland and easy access to good harbors, attracted some of the earliest and better-off immigrants to Cape Breton (see MacDougall 1976:249,263,190; Mabou Pioneer Committee 1977:86). The first settlers were English-monolingual Loyalists (MacDougall 1976:290). Then, during the 1790s, Gaelic-speaking Scots, some Protestant but most Catholics, began arriving in Mabou (MacKinnon 1903:75), and soon outnumbered the Loyalist population. Throughout the early nineteenth century Mabou grew as a business center, and was among the first settlements in Cape Breton to request a school or form an Agricultural Society (Campbell and MacLean 1974:93). Its harbor made Mabou accessible to large sea-going ships, and its agricultural prosperity allowed it to export foodstuffs, including wheat. During the late nineteenth century, the town of Inverness, directly to the north of Mabou, became a coal-mining center. Mabou itself experienced a brief "boom town" era during the early twentieth century when a local coal mine was opened. The mine attracted a flood of English monolinguals to this predominantly Gaelic-speaking community. The outsiders left when the Mabou Coal Mines closed during the second decade of the twentieth century. Lobster canneries opened, providing an outlet for local fishermen. The proximity of the railroad line also brought Mabou into increased contact with the world beyond Cape Breton.

By contrast, the North Shore was always a more isolated, homogeneous community. It was settled entirely by Presbyterian Gaels during one of the last waves of emigration from the Scottish Islands, a time characterized by government-supported emigration from the most poverty-stricken areas of Scotland.[1] The first immigrant group of which there is certain evidence arrived on the "Shore" from the Isle of Harris in 1843, although there may have been settlers from Harris during the 1830s (see Mertz 1982a:60). Stretched along twenty miles of the mountainous, rocky northeastern coast, the Shore was among the last areas of Cape Breton to receive settlers, probably because its infertile rocky land made farming difficult. Although the settlers made their living by fishing, the Shore also lacked natural harbors; the northernmost end of the area is entitled "Wreck Cove" because of the frequent shipwrecks on the rocky shore there. The community remained relatively isolated throughout the nineteenth century, with no railroad line and no good harbors for sea-going ships. Indeed, until the river at the southern end of the Shore was bridged, the only contact with the outside was provided by a boat, the *Aspy*, which made a regular run between remote areas on the northeastern coast and the nearest large town of Sydney. Regular schools came late; by the end of the nineteenth century the Shore was still serviced by traveling school teachers holding school at homes in the community on an irregular basis.

The North Shore, then, affords a sharp contrast with Mabou. Where Mabou was settled early, by relatively affluent settlers, the North Shore was settled late. Mabou was always diverse in terms of language and religion, with the English-monolingual Loyalists holding many of the higher-status positions in town during the early period of settlement by Catholic Gaels. The Shore was composed entirely of Presbyterian Gaelic speakers. Mabou was also diverse in economic terms, drawing upon farming and fishing for export, coal-mining, and many businesses which served the surrounding communities. The North Shore residents were fisherfolk, eventually becoming almost completely economically dependent upon the export of lobsters and fish. Where Mabou was in constant contact with the outside English-monolingual world, the North Shore was sheltered and isolated. English-language schooling came early to Mabou, but late to the Shore. In spite of all of these differences, residents of both areas remained bilingual in Gaelic and English until the 1930s and 1940s, when transmission of Gaelic ceased in both communities. Today there are no fluent Gaelic speakers in either community under the age of 40.

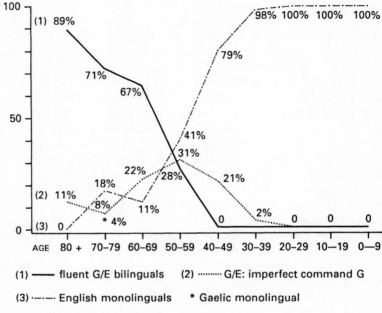

Figure 1. *The North Shore*

Evidence of this linguistic "tip" emerges from contemporaneous reports by social scientists, from informants' recollections, and from age breakdowns of current proficiency data. The use of current proficiency data alone, of course, provides only a rough guideline, but linguists and sociolinguists have used this method in assessing historical change in language (Labov 1965; Gal 1976). We can see the clear, patterned change in Cape Breton by comparing age breakdowns from Mabou and the North Shore (see Figures 1 and 2). Fluent ability in Gaelic is limited to informants aged 40+ in both communities.[2] Further, the distribution of Gaelic-speaking abilities among people in their 40s shows only a small number of fluent, or even halting, speakers, and a larger number of non-speakers, in that age category. There is no large group of younger semi-speakers such as might emerge from a process whereby Gaelic gradually disappeared from general use. It would seem, then, that during the 1930s and 1940s very few children were learning to speak Gaelic at home.[3]

This is borne out by the reports of social scientists who studied Gaelic in Cape Breton. In the late 1920s and early 1930s, we know that children were socialized in Gaelic by their parents at home (Campbell 1948). After that time, there was a shift in socialization practices, and a concurrent "tip" in

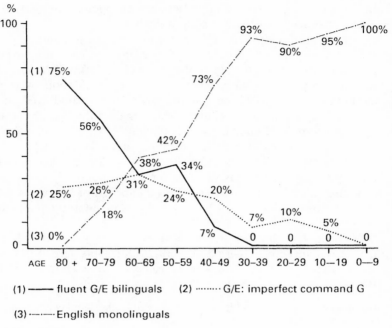

(1) —— fluent G/E bilinguals　　(2) ········ G/E: imperfect command G

(3) ·—·— English monolinguals

Figure 2. *Mabou*

patterns of language use. Children did not learn Gaelic, as it ceased to be used between parents and children at home (Dunn 1953; Campbell and MacLean 1974; MacKinnon 1977). The shift in the home was accompanied by a reluctance to use Gaelic in public as well (see Dunn 1953:149).

We can supplement this broad picture of a "tip" in Gaelic usage and transmission by using informants' recollections. Because it is obviously problematic to rely heavily on present reports of past usage (we know that even present reports of *present* usage can be dubious sources), I draw upon these data with caution, relying only on reports which have been extensively cross-checked and which are consistent with contemporaneous social science reports. As regards the timing of the "tip", informants from both communities were unanimous:

. . . and then, I don't know, it [Gaelic] kind of died out there . . . by forty years ago . . . and nobody was speaking Gaelic hardly.

[M-5][4]

. . . like I would say nineteen – at least 1935 – from there on it started slipping, and once it got to five or ten years later, well it [Gaelic] was just about finished.

[NS-12]

Informants also noted the rapidity of the change, saying that "it [Gaelic] died out so fast", or that it "went quickly here".

In Mabou, descriptions of usage patterns in the community prior to the 1930s paint a picture of Gaelic as a private language used more in homes and private conversations than in public places (see Mertz 1982a:101–18). Many of the shopkeepers and business people of Mabou were English-monolingual Loyalists; the schools were always conducted in English, including those run by the church (MacDonald n.d.: 50). Thus the Scots in Mabou maintained Gaelic–English bilingualism for more than 130 years primarily by virtue of Gaelic socialization "in the home". Children in small schools within the Gaelic-speaking sub-areas of Mabou also spoke Gaelic in the school yards; if adults working on farms, boats, or at the mines and canneries found themselves in groups composed of bilinguals they would feel free to codeswitch. But English predominated in the public life of the town of Mabou.

This was less the case in the more homogeneous North Shore, where Gaelic was more widely used in public. Informants agreed, however, that codeswitching to English was more common while shopping in the small stores:

I probably would speak a bit of Gaelic with him [the shopkeeper]. But when I went going to buy, I'd always speak English.

[NS-6]

When we were buying, there's things we can't say in Gaelic, we'd have to say that in English.

[NS-23]

Conversely, the prevailing ethic dictated exclusive use of Gaelic at home with one's grandparents: "If you didn't speak Gaelic to them, they'd say 'He's too stuck up to speak Gaelic' " [NS-23]. Although members of the grandparents' generation were bilingual, they felt that a proper feeling of community solidarity dictated use of Gaelic at home. Similarly, many North Shore residents became literate in Gaelic because home worship, involving the reading of Gaelic Bibles and religious materials, was almost exclusively in Gaelic.

Informants from both communities who were born during the 1930s recall a change in their parents' linguistic behavior: "Well, I guess when I got near school age they started talking English" [NS-18]. Gaelic became a language for adult and/or secret conversations: "[My mother and father] was always speaking Gaelic to each other and when people was coming to visit and that, it was all Gaelic they spoke. But they never spoke Gaelic to me – English, that's all" [NS-4]. Another informant similarly notes: "We didn't speak that much [Gaelic] at home, you know, to our parents – my parents spoke it to one another" [M-14]. On the North Shore this change in home usage was accompanied by a change in public arenas. Gaelic was now used for quick greetings and comments, but not for extensive conversations. This change was noted by many informants, who variously attributed it to the growing numbers of non-Gaelic-speaking young, negative attitudes on the part of Gaelic speakers themselves, and a general view that "it [Gaelic] wasn't just the thing" [NS-23].

Data from current proficiency curves, scholars accounts, and retrospective accounts by informants, then, converge upon the 1930s and 1940s as the time when both Mabou and the North Shore experienced a rapid linguistic tip toward English monolingualism. We have seen that the two communities differ in many ways; yet despite differences in degree of isolation, length of settlement, religion, cultural/linguistic homogeneity, economic structure, the presence of a local English-monolingual elite, and contact with English-language schools, the two areas maintained Gaelic–English bilingualism until the same point in time, and then tipped toward English monolingualism. How can we account for this?

3.   Understanding the Cape Breton "tip"

A straightforward acculturative model linking language shift with pressure from a dominant English-monolingual society clearly would not suffice to explain the Cape Breton tip. There was no sudden intrusion upon either community at the time of the shift. Furthermore, if contact with the outside English-monolingual world were key, Mabou would have experienced a shift long before the North Shore. Not only did local "Mabouites" have ample opportunity during the nineteenth century to witness at close hand the superior status which English enjoyed in Nova Scotian schools and commerce, they also had a local English-monolingual elite in the United Empire Loyalists.

However, although we cannot make a simple correlation between external pressure or prestige values and language shift, there is no doubt that the difference in status between Gaelic and English played a role in shaping the interpretive filter through which Cape Breton Gaels understood their linguistic situation. As Dorian noted in the East Sutherland case, understanding the sociocultural background of language prestige and loyalty against which a sudden tip occurred is as critical to explaining the shift as is isolating one, or several, more immediate precipitating events. Rubin (1968), for example, looked at the official status and symbolic value accorded Spanish and Guarani in assessing the relationship between Paraguayan political structure and language maintenance.

Nova Scotia gave Gaelic official status in the schools with an 1841 bill which provided that: "[A]ny school wherein the ordinary instruction may be in the French, Gaelic, or German languages in any School District in this

Province shall be entitled to the like portion of the public money as any school wherein the ordinary instruction may be in the English language" (PANS Duplicate Bill and Amendments 1841 cap. 43). This provision was dropped in 1864 (Revised Statutes 1864 Title XVII Public Instruction). In the 1920s, in response to a petition drive in Cape Breton, Gaelic was again officially included on the Nova Scotian curriculum (see 1920 Petition, PANS). The Nova Scotian government at no time actively promoted Gaelic; there is no evidence of any systematic attempts to foster Gaelic-language schools or instruction. But at the same time, the government certainly did not openly discourage it. Gaelic was not legislated against; the official policy left open the possibility of Gaelic schools and media. This policy did not change during the 1930s.

On the other hand, it was clear that English was the language of the Nova Scotian government, from the laws printed by the Nova Scotian Assembly on through the tax, land petition, and census forms which the government used. Indeed, the first contact which many Scots immigrants had with Nova Scotian society was their meeting with an English-monolingual immigration officer, for whom they had to manufacture a patronymic consistent with the English system of naming (MacDonald 1959:3; Price and Price 1972, describe a similar situation in Saramaka). Schools were conducted in English. Men who served in World War I returned still more aware that outside of Cape Breton, English was Canada's dominant language.

Cape Breton Gaelic speakers, then, had long been conscious of the superior position which English held in official Nova Scotian life. This perception was reinforced by tourists and by native sons and daughters who returned to visit after emigrating to the United States or to central or western Canada. We can find negative assessments of Gaelic in the accounts of early tourists:

I have a reasonable amount of respect for a Highlandman in full costume; but for a sandy-haired, freckled, high-cheeked animal, in a round hat and breeches, that cannot utter a word of English, I have no sympathy. One fellow of this complexion, without a hat, trotted beside our coach for several miles, grunting forth his infernal Gaelic to John Ormond, with a hah! to every answer of the driver, that was really painful. . . . Now I have heard many languages in my time, and know how to appreciate the luxurious Greek, the stately Latin, the mellifluous Chinese, the epithetical Slavic, the soft Italian, the rich Castillian, the sprightly French, the sonorous German, and good old English, but candor compels me to say, that I do not think much of the Gaelic. It is not pleasing to the ear.

(Cozzens 1877, reprinted in Elliott 1956:70)

Other tourists were quite positive in their reactions to hearing Gaelic spoken, but the condescension inherent in their view of Gaelic as quaint or charming could hardly have escaped local residents (see Elliott 1971).[5]

Furthermore, Cape Breton residents began to develop, from an early time, a very specific theory about the relation between Gaelic and English.

From an early report of the Nova Scotian Superintendent of Education comes evidence of this folk theory – and possibly its origin:

> It may be proper to remark that in many sections the teacher has to labour under many disadvantages, . . . , and that circumstance is the perpetual contest which the teacher has to wage in conbating [*sic*] the peculiarities of idiom and pronunciation consequent on the prevalence of the Gaelic language . . . perhaps but few realize fully how great an obstacle it is to progress in the acquisition of a thorough English education in the county. The Gaelic-speaking population predominates.
>
> (Cited in Campbell and MacLean 1974:149)

This metalinguistic belief, that Gaelic speaking is an obstacle to learning correct English (and to the opportunity for advancement through education in general), is still prevalent today. During the critical period for language shift, Gaelic revivalists from nearby urban centers struggled in vain to combat the "one language theory", arguing for the "value" of speaking two languages (*Casket*, December 8, 1938: Gaelic College Special Publication 1943; *Cape Breton Post-Record*, March 15, 1939).

Informants today recall the influence of this "bilingual deficit" folk theory: "Parents thought teaching Gaelic would – 'twould sort of confuse the two languages in their minds" [M-14]. If the goal was to learn perfect, unmarked English with the accompanying cognitive benefits and increased possibilities for assimilation, parents must limit their children's exposure to Gaelic from the very beginning, "because when you start out and use Gaelic . . . [learning English is] really hard" [M-6].

A dramatic statement of the extent to which this belief was carried emerges from the following discussion with a man who never learned Gaelic, but who heard Gaelic at home because both of his parents were fluent Gaelic speakers:

Investigator: "Was it the Reverend Fraser that said that – that it would interfere with their English?"
NS-2: "Yea, he thought they should be speaking more English to the children in the homes, I was told that . . ."
Investigator: "Do you think that's true?"
NS-21: "It is, I know – one time, well when I went into the army . . . when he [the officer] was pretty near through [asking entrance questions], he said, 'What second language is bothering you?' "
NS-2: "He did? He knew darn well [everyone laughs]. Oh, you bet you can tell, that's the truth. A lot of people that I would talk English – speak English with, they'd say, 'Tell me, you can speak Gaelic, can you?' They could tell, yes, sure they could . . . that I was speaking – that I spoke Gaelic."
Investigator [to NS-21]: "Would you call Gaelic a second language of yours? I mean – that you spoke it that much that it would interfere with your English?"
NS-2: "No, he didn't speak to – you wouldn't say you did? [to NS-21] But like us, now, it does interfere."
NS-21: "I wasn't thinking it would but –"

NS-18: "No, but Gaelic is in your background, though, and –"
NS-21: "He noticed there was something there."
NS-2: "You bet he did."
NS-19: "Although . . . you didn't make a habit of speaking it, you – you know it in your mind."
NS-2: "It's there – up there, just the same, yes, listening to your parents talking and you had it up there, yea, that's true, I believe."

This is an extraordinary statement if we consider that NS-21's parents, like the parents of many in his generation, used Gaelic in the home only sparingly, for private communication and secrets. In an almost supernatural fashion, the background "noise" of a language he never spoke or understood entered his mind and affected his ability to speak English.[6] Just this slight degree of exposure was enough to leave his English permanently "marked".

Learning "unmarked" English did become the goal for many Cape Bretoners during the difficult Depression years, when ability to assimilate easily to the Canadian and US mainstream became increasingly important in local eyes.

Where before, the value of local in-group solidarity had counterbalanced the higher prestige of English monolingualism, now rural identity became a serious economic liability. Cape Breton had already been a depressed area; the 1930s brought severe economic hardship to the island. A fisherman recalls efforts by a Catholic priest to rescue Cape Bretoners: "He was after the bishop. 'Fellows down there are all going Communist, they're starving – why don't we do something for them?'" [Laben, in *Cape Breton's Magazine* 1977, 16:8]. The association of Gaelic with rural, "backward" areas took on a sharp economic focus. Attempts by young people to deny any knowledge of Gaelic were now also attempts to deny an image of themselves as poor or lower-class: "[If you spoke Gaelic] you were considered like . . . what they call today 'second-class' citizens" [M-7].

Along with the fact that local group identity, as a balance in favor of Gaelic use, was disappearing, came a change in attitude toward the possibility of upward mobility as the distance between economic core and peripheral areas was decreased by improved communications and transportation. Parents who wished to prepare their children for a modern world saw a necessary link between dropping Gaelic and upward mobility. And that link was provided by local beliefs about language, cognition, and social identity. Only through this interpretive filter did the events of the 1930s have any connection whatever with language. Language tip in Cape Breton resulted from an active decision on the part of rural Cape Bretoners, given their cultural–linguistic schema and reigning economic–political conditions, that they wished to "join the modern world" of mainstream Canada. The decision was a powerful rejection of any permanent identification of com-

munity children as members of a depressed economic periphery (Wallerstein 1976); in a sense, it was an effort to contest peripheralization.

4.   Creativity after the "tip"

The preceding section stressed that linguistic "tip" was not a mere reflex of
external pressures, but rather reflected Cape Bretoners' active interpretation of, and struggle with, changing circumstances. This section continues
that theme, noting that even after transmission of Gaelic ceased in Cape
Breton, Gaelic speakers continued to use their language in creative ways.
Indeed, the communicative force of a codeswitch to Gaelic today is all the
more potent because it is a marked rather than unmarked usage.

One could look at the reduced frequency of Gaelic use in Cape Breton
today as evidence of its unimportant and "vestigial" character. But this view
would not do justice to the critical pragmatic[7] functions which Gaelic use
fulfills today, nor would it take account of the continued importance of
Gaelic use within the community's linguistic ideology. The importance of a
language in the community's repertoire cannot be assessed by mere math-
ematical frequency of use; it is the entire cultural–linguistic framework
through which speakers actively interpret their linguistic experience which
gives relative weight and meaning to particular linguistic usages.

In public arenas in the two communities today, Gaelic is used sparingly.
The most common use is as a boundary marker. Conversations often begin
and end with a routine exchange of Gaelic greetings. Here use of the marked
code creatively indexes – indeed, creates – the edges of discourse.

Another boundary marked by Gaelic use is that between community
insiders and outsiders.[8] Thus, older community members switch to Gaelic in
order to convey secret or private information. For example, one woman
turned to her widowed sister while they were standing among a group of
friends in a public place, and asked her quietly *"Bheil airgead agad?"* ('Is
money at-you'/'Do you have money?'). Her sister assured her quickly that
she was okay ("Tha"/'Is'), and then they both rejoined the general English
conversation. The choice of Gaelic may also simply indicate a feeling of
closeness toward the person addressed, signaling as it does a shared history
as members of the community. Gaelic pet names or expressions are often
employed in addressing family members. In all of these cases, Gaelic speech
functions as an index of intimacy, creating an almost palpable boundary as it
closes strangers out of conversations. Perhaps the most intimate use of
Gaelic possible is in speech to oneself. A wonderful example of this was
provided by a woman who was in charge of a large church gathering. As she
walked among the people gathered there, I heard her say in a loud tone,
"Time to start". Then, turning quickly, she muttered *"Cait a' bheil a'
pheansail?"* ('Where's the pencil?'). After a brief look around, she turned

back to address the assembled women in English. Here the switch to Gaelic signaled a shift between addressing others and talking to herself.

At times the two boundary-marking functions of Gaelic coincide, as when the Gaelic greeting ritual is used as a test of Gaelic-speaking ability. I had an opportunity to observe this at close hand, because during my initial months in the community, informants would use the ritual exchange of greetings as an opportunity to test my mastery of Gaelic. When I could move beyond *"Ciamar a tha thu?"* ('How are you?') and standard phrases to unrehearsed and more complex sentences, it was generally agreed by those testing me that I now "had Gaelic". Nonverbal cues added to the sense that this was a test; as I replied to each question or remark, eyebrows would lift and nods of approval or murmurs would follow. A similar testing process is used with visiting relatives, visitors from Scotland, and children taking Gaelic classes. The assessment of ability through Gaelic greetings is a sensitive linguistic means of according insider status, at the same time as it establishes the boundary of the speech exchange itself.

Gaelic speakers also often codeswitch in order to convey strong emotion or humor. Thus informants will often respond to a shocking piece of news, or to the high point of a story with an exclaimed *"Dhia!"* or *"Thigherna!"* ('God!' or 'Lord!'). Strong agreement or assent is similarly often signaled in Gaelic (as, for example, when a woman nodded vigorously and said *"Mise cuideachd"* ('Me, too') in response to a comment in English).

In all of these cases community members use Gaelic creatively to highlight, emphasize, end, and begin speech. Simply by virtue of its reduced range, Gaelic packs a stronger sociolinguistic punch. And, by virtue of the history of association between community identity and minority language, speakers attach a strong affectual value to Gaelic which gives it emotional power. Finally, because only some community members now understand Gaelic, a codeswitch can function as a powerful rebuke, actually closing the conversation to some while including others. As Gaelic use ceases to serve as a regular medium for conveying semantico-referential information (see Silverstein 1976), it gains pragmatic force for expressing affect and creatively molding the speech situation.

5.   Conclusion

This chapter has emphasized the crucial role of a group's linguistic–cultural folk theories in filtering wide-scale social change. It is through this interpretive filter that speakers give local meaning to global economic and social changes, meaning which forms the critical background for language shift. I have also stressed that there is enormous creativity in this process. Speakers are actively struggling to create and control their social world through their act of interpretation; they are not merely yielding passively to wider social forces. This approach takes seriously the "active aspect of knowledge" discussed by Bourdieu:

> Those who suppose they are producing a materialist theory of knowledge when they make knowledge a passive recording and abandon the 'active aspect' of knowledge to idealism, as Marx complains in the Theses on Feuerbach, forget that all knowledge, and in particular all knowledge of the social world, is an act of construction implementing schemes of thought and expression, and that between conditions of existence and practices or representations there intervenes the structuring activity of the agents, who, far from reacting mechanically to mechanical stimulations, respond to the invitations or threats of a world whose meaning they have helped to produce.
>
> (1984:467)

Thus while one must certainly give weight to the "symbolic dominance" of English-monolingual core areas in analyzing Cape Bretons' language tip, the analysis would be completely inadequate if it did not also include the crucial role of local ideologies and interpretive struggles. Woolard (1985b) has similarly argued that although the notion of "cultural hegemony" may fruitfully be applied to sociolinguistic work on "status and solidarity", local community solidary linguistic values operate as a powerful counterweight to dominant ideologies. The Cape Breton case demonstrates that even where there is an apparent yielding to hegemonic values, there may also be resistance and creativity. Small-scale local creative acts of interpretation and of language choice are a form of cultural praxis through which local speakers respond to, but also effect, social change.

Notes

1. As W. Ross explains, "broadly speaking, in the eighteenth century people go from the Highlands; in the nineteenth they are sent" (1934:1). Whereas early emigrants took capital with them, later emigrants actually removed an economic liability from the area when they left. Predictably, the British at first attempted to discourage Scottish migration but then encouraged it, whereas the reverse was true of the Nova Scotian government (see MacDonald 1937:142, 144; Martell 1942:24, 26; Graham 1956:35; Cowan 1967:22, 27).
2. The only exceptions to this are young Gaelic teachers who either emigrated recently from Scotland, or went to Scotland to receive intensive training.
3. An alternative hypothesis might be that parents continued to socialize children in Gaelic, but that the children soon forgot it after participating in the primarily monolingual public life of their communities. This is not, however, supported by contemporaneous reports of social scientists or retrospective reports of informants.

   For the statistically minded, it may be convincing to see the results of a multiple regression, contrasting the effects of residence (Mabou or the North Shore) and age on Gaelic-speaking ability: the F-value for place of residence was 0.24, whereas for age it was 620.68, allowing us to conclude what is obvious without statistical support – that age is a good predictor of Gaelic-speaking ability, whereas place of residence (with all the accompanying social and economic differences) is not (Mertz 1982b:90).

4. My coding uses M to signify informants from Mabou, and NS for informants from the North Shore.

5. Certainly it did not escape my informants, several of whom commented to me wryly that American tourists often found "the Gaelic" quaint.

6. For a discussion of a similar (though less dramatic) US version of this crude "Whorfian" theory regarding the impact of language on mind, see Mertz (1982a).

7. By "pragmatic" function, I mean the way in which codeswitches to Gaelic index and create linguistic/social context (see Silverstein 1976).

8. See Mertz (1983) for a discussion of the different way in which Gaelic personal naming conventions perform dual boundary-marking functions.

8 Skewed performance and full performance in language obsolescence: The case of an Albanian variety

LUKAS D. TSITSIPIS

1.   Introduction

Studies in language obsolescence have broached significant directions of inquiry in the dynamics of language change. In scholars' efforts to circumscribe the field of language death research, the following major areas of findings seem to be the most conspicuous. (1) It is probable that language death does not differ in kind from other types of linguistic change, but in the speed with which structural changes occur and in the number of phenomena covered by the process (Dorian 1981; Schmidt 1985c). (2) In cases of contracting languages it is possible to end up with communities characterized by marked asymmetries in the development of pairs of skills such as phonology vs. grammar, passive vs. active competence, high vs. low or colloquial stylistic level, written vs. spoken discourse, which normally co-occur in a more balanced way in "healthy" mother-tongue situations (Dorian n.d.). (3) Language death studies raise crucial questions concerning the concept of the speech community, since the frequently appearing sociological category of imperfect speakers involves problems of successful participation in the various communicative events of the community (Dorian 1982a). (4) There is evidence to suggest that, despite certain similarities between language death and pidgins and creoles, the two processes differ crucially (Dorian 1981; Schmidt 1985a). (5) Significant structural restrictions in grammar have been convincingly correlated with reduction in speech genres which were once highly valued specimens of verbal art and competence (Hill 1978; Tsitsipis 1984). (6) Linguistic competence exists among fluent speakers in the ordinary sense of productivity, but the language has stopped being a source of continuous invention (Hymes 1984). (7) A very broad perspective encompassing other speech contexts in addition to linguistic attrition is proposed in the framework of functional explanations of syntactic complexity (Hill, this volume).[1]

In this chapter I want to examine some aspects of what I call terminal-speaker performance and compare it with fluent-speaker performance in the Arvanítika communities of modern Greece. I use for this purpose natural speech material as it was recorded from actual discourse and conversational interaction. In particular, I will suggest that we have more to learn about the linguistic situation in the context of a dying language if we explore things in the perspective provided by the ethnography of speaking and discourse analysis. I want first to introduce the reader to the ethnographic and sociolinguistic background of the communities.

1.1.   *The communicative situation and speakers' competence*

The Albanian speakers of Greece are bilingual in Modern Greek and the local variety of Albanian known as Arvanítika; the latter belongs to the southern or Tosk dialect of the language (for Albanian dialectology, see Gjinari 1970, 1976).[2] Arvanítika speakers are the descendants of settlers of Albanian ancestry who migrated to what is now Greece during the later period of the Byzantine empire, and lived in enclaved communities but not completely out of contact with the Greek-speaking populations (Tsitsipis 1981a). Relative geographical isolation, along with a socio-economically selfsufficient way of life, played a decisive role in the retention of the language for a period of almost five centuries.

The gradual emergence of the Modern Greek nation-state after the revolution against Ottoman rule (1821) signaled the beginning of minority-language status for Arvanítika. The use of Greek in education, government, and bureaucracy in general led to specific negative attitudes towards Arvanítika which over time were adopted by the speakers of the language too.

Early philological and linguistic students of the Arvanítika situation brought to light interesting information concerning the communities during part of the nineteenth century and the beginnings of the twentieth. From observations and collections by these scholars, we learn that Arvanítika served a wide variety of functions, and a whole range of speech genres were represented in this language (Meyer 1896; Furikēs 1932, 1933).

Comparing these earlier works with modern sociolinguistic findings (Kazazis 1976; Hamp 1978; Tsitsipis 1981a), we discover a progressive restriction in the language's functions. More specifically, at least until the beginnings of the socio-economic modernization of Greece between the 1940s and 1950s, Greek was primarily used for bureaucratic affairs and transactions at the national level, whereas Arvanítika served as the normal medium of communication in the intra-community spheres of interaction. An Arvanítika-dominant bilingualism was probably the rule, and the use of the Greek language in the community was stigmatized as revealing a "putting on airs" attitude, as elderly people still remember. Arvanítika was the language of cultural instruction and of children's introduction to the basic norms of the social order (see Tsitsipis 1984 for an account of verbal material introducing children to the complexities of the Arvanítika language based on narrative speech play).

Modern informants report on various kinds of discouragement concerning the use of the language, particularly in the school system and also in the army, where Arvanítika speakers serve as Greek citizens (Trudgill and Tzavaras 1977; Tsitsipis 1981a:90–176). In time, the attitudes governing the norms of what should constitute a proper language were adopted by Arvanítika speakers themselves, who thus went through a predictable process of *self-deprecation* (Hamp 1978). On many occasions and in natural speech contexts, older speakers frequently switch from praising Arvanítika as their mother tongue to suppressing its importance, shifting thus from a positive cultural stance to a pragmatic view that considers things Greek indispensable to progress, prosperity, and upward mobility (for a socio-linguistic elaboration of the concepts of *cultural stance* and *pragmatism* see Dorian 1982b; for an account of folklinguistic ideology through which Arvanítika people reveal their linguistic attitudes see Tsitsipis 1983b).

Sociolinguistic research conducted in two communities in southern Greece (Spata, a semi-urban locality with a prosperous economy, and Kiriaki, a rather isolated mountainous village) shows that people past their 50s on the average have a good command of the language and use it in various settings in their intra-community interaction. People of very old age are actually more comfortable with Arvanítika than with Greek. Furthermore, fluent Arvanítika speakers use both languages as symbolic resources for strategic interaction; that is, they switch codes situationally and metaphorically, and the manipulation of synonymous expressions serves the purpose of evaluation in narrative performances (Tsitsipis 1983a, 1988).

A particular sociolinguistic category of speakers emerges in the Arvanítika world that I call *terminal speakers*, very much resembling in their productive and receptive competence Dorian's semi-speakers in East Sutherland Gaelic (1981). Terminal speakers differ markedly from fluent members of the communities, because of their heavy lexical losses, loss or confusion of crucial phonological oppositions, simplification of grammatical paradigms through a tremendous amount of reduction in allomorphic variation, and communication basically through the use of formulaic expressions (Tsitsipis 1981a:55–6).[3]

The stage of Arvanítika speech terminality is reached either through a process of linguistic attrition of a previous, more advanced, competence in the language due to migratory movements and the negative attitude propagated by the older members of the communities, or through inadequate exposure and active discouragement of the very young people in particular. The age range of speech terminality varies according to the specific locality's degree of modernization. Thus, in the semi-urban center of Spata one can encounter terminal speakers who are as old as 40, whereas in Kiriaki village the same age range includes fluent speakers. In Kiriaki, people who are generally younger than 20 reveal symptoms of terminality.

The basic picture of communication that emerges from observation of the everyday interaction in the Arvanítika-speaking communities points to significant inter-generational differences. Members of the grandparental generation usually address younger people in Arvanítika and the latter answer in Greek. The functional shift in the use of the language is from a context- and topic-free but interlocutor-bound allocation (addressees must know the language) to a context-bound allocation of the Arvanítika speech resources as one moves from older fluent speakers to terminal ones. Terminal speakers use the language when forced to do so in order to clarify things for some older folks, on those restricted occasions when the interaction interests them, when they want either to test or to impress a foreigner (in my case the ethnographer), and when they consciously turn the language into an object of play and inquiry. This last aspect of terminal speech behavior deserves further discussion in the context of terminal performance and will be analyzed below.

2.   Discourse and performance

Sociolinguists have noted that inferences about the organization of means of speaking, their relation to the intended meanings in the interactional process, in communicative competence and discourse strategies can only be made by observing and recording speech production in real situations.

With regard to the above observations, Dorian (1982a:25–33) has pointed out that ESG semi-speakers should be considered as successful communicatively despite their skewed productive/receptive competence in the local variety of Gaelic, since they manage to react appropriately in the various speech events, even more so than the researcher herself who has a much better control of the structural resources of the language. As I have suggested elsewhere (Tsitsipis 1988), Dorian's observations apply also in the Arvanítika situation, but with some differences. These differences depend primarily on the kinds of speech genres performed in the two communities. Traditional storytellers are long gone for the Gaelic community in question, while competent narrators still perform in the Arvanítika-speaking areas, and it is in this domain of communicative competence that terminal speakers do *not* respond appropriately (see also Tsitsipis 1983a; it must be further noted here that in the more viable western Gaelic communities there are still traditional storytellers).

In the remainder of this chapter I will focus on both terminal and fluent speakers as they interact in natural conversation, and performance aspects of both speaker categories will be discussed. I will particularly suggest that terminal speakers, while capable of using some formulaic expressions and of minimally participating in the ongoing discourse, deviate from some of the rules of appropriate speaking. I will further provide evidence to the effect that for terminal speakers the Arvanítika language becomes an *object language*, attracting their attention very much in the way that this happens with foreign language learners. Finally, despite the terminal grammatical production of these people, their conscious attention to the linguistic, and specifically lexical, resources of Arvanítika becomes occasionally a source of creative behavior (see Gal, this volume). By contrast, fluent speakers perform in a distinctive manner in which figurative language predominates in natural conversations along with the proper control of phonology and grammar.

The speech segment to be examined here is part of a long conversation recorded in the community of Spata; participants were members belonging to both the terminal and the fluent category, as well as non-Arvanítika speakers who as affines of the local people become occasionally the addressees or themselves interject some Greek utterances.

3. The setting, natural conversation, and performance features

The conversation cited below, as well as many other instances of natural speech interaction, were recorded in summertime and in early evening outside one of the Spatan houses. In small communities in Greece, roads and back or front yards are common physical settings for talking activity. Another culturally appropriate setting for conversations is the coffee-house, also various central stores; but in these latter places chances to obtain a highly variable group of speakers are few in view of cultural norms that do not encourage the participation of female community members. A neighborhood site, therefore, becomes an ideal place for interaction, since it recruits a good mixture of speakers and variable audiences.

Arvanítika culture – Greek culture as well, for that matter – places much emphasis on speaking (for a similar case see discussion of Kuna ways of speaking in Sherzer 1983). This emphasis, of course, does not imply that there are no rules governing speech production as to the various components of verbal interaction. Despite the central role of speaking in the life of the local people, Arvanítika informants are not always capable of being explicit as to the features that comprise the portrait of a good speaker. However, competence in performing genres such as jokes is frequently singled out as the most significant aspect of a good speaker's ability, not features of grammar or other structural domains.

As to the times for speaking, early evening is quite significant for long conversations, since younger people have returned from their work and one can get the most variable participation. But in addition to this circumstantial reason, another factor, of a cultural nature, regulates speaking with regard to time. People of an economically productive age are not expected to engage in long and relaxed conversations during the productive hours of the day since they run the risk of being criticized for laziness. It is a common saying among both Greek- and Arvanítika-speaking people that X person is of a bad nature since he spends his time in the coffee-house all day long talking, or she goes around the neighborhood distracting other people with useless engagement in talk. In the evenings, on the contrary, no strict rules prevent people of all ages from participating in long talk exchanges. The following conversation has, therefore, been elicited in conditions natural for the emergence of the event.

Participants are old and middle-aged women and men, as well as younger women above their 40s, the investigator, and two terminal speakers who speak up in the conversation when discussion is already underway. The terminal speakers, who are both males around their 20s, function under optimum conditions for a natural participation in the event since the one is already familiar with the investigator, and the other – less well acquainted – has a bond with the ethnographer through a high school principal whose presence and work in the community has provided good ground for several discussions.

In the transcribed conversation, English translations are given and each turn at talk is numbered serially for later reference. Clarifying and explanatory comments are given in parentheses. The conversation takes up various subjects, from discussion about language to comments on the investigator's life and interests, on local affairs, moral views, and comparison of modern with earlier habits, customs, and behavior. Switches to Greek are given in italic and commented on when relevant to the argument developed. Since the conversation is especially long, some parts are not included where we judge that they do not contribute to the interpretation.[4]

In view of the informants' awareness of the investigator's interests they start out by talking about language:

1. *An old woman:* me djéljtë nëkë fljásëm moré; pljákat se cë jémi. 'We don't speak [Arvanítika] with the children; with old folks like ourselves.'

2. *Mrs Ksenu's mother:* me jirokomíotë! 'With the home for the aged!'

3. *Another old woman:* áma do conj térinë. 'When I find my counterpart [in speech].'

4. *A middle-aged woman:* pljákat rrínë enó e réa écur; háinë dhe dru ga búrrat. 'Old women were sitting in to prepare the meal [in those old days], whereas a younger woman was going around; [women] were being beaten by men.'

5. *An old woman:* háinë dru; jajá ímea hái dru ga búrri edhé . . . 'They

were beaten up; my grandmother was beaten up by her husband and . . .'

6. *Old Jannakis woman:* jánë grátë ató? dúan ató me kramanjóla. 'Are these [proper] women? they need to hang [they deserve the gallows].'

(In the preceding lines old women comment on modern morality of women who go out with more than one man.)

7. *Investigator:* atá vítra kózmi íku ga përdía. 'These [last] years people have gone away from God.'

8. *Another woman:* atá vítra e bënjënë érgha; naní jan tër kuvénde. 'Those years people were doing things; now there are only words.'

9. *All together:* fshéhura. 'Secretly.' (They state that morality was not so different in earlier times; people did the same things secretly.)

10. *The first old woman:* i zúre érotas. 'They were [women] led astray by love.'

11. *The second old woman:* zúre gazímë. 'Were led astray by happiness.'

12. *Mrs Ksenu's mother:* haré. 'Joy.'

13. *A woman:* (commenting on old Jannakis woman's brightness) íztë dríza ajó! 'She is a branch [bright] this one!'

14. *Investigator:* jikóneshin kózmi shum. 'People suffered a lot.'

15. *All together:* u, u, u: :h; shum, shum! 'u, u, u: :h; very, very much!' (strong agreement)

16. *Mrs Ksenu's mother:* ta katalavénis, jórjho, dhen da katalavénis? 'You understand it [i.e. Arvanítika], George, don't you?' (She addresses herself to a silent participant in the interaction, who is a monolingual Greek and an affinal relative in the community.)

17. *A middle-aged woman* (locally known as the "humoristic type"; hereinafter H.T.): *kséri ómos, dhen mborís na don koroidhépsis, na don vrísis Arvanítika.* 'He knows though, you cannot cheat on him, you cannot badmouth him in Arvanítika.'

18. *Old Jannakis woman:* andé chë púnë bënjën n' amerikjí? jo ti, kózmi andé. 'Over there in America what kinds of jobs people have? Not you, people there.' (She is now turning to the investigator's life.)

19. *Investigator:* tër chë bënjënë këtú. 'Everything people do here too.'

20. *Mrs Ksenu's mother:* edhé púnë të púnë alá djelj hriásën të kétë; áma të rrish dhe shúma vítëra pasadáj . . . 'Work is work but it is necessary [for people] to have children; when you sit [not having children] for many years then . . .'

21. *Old Jannakis woman:* eeem, ashtú isht; hriásën dhe engónja. 'Eeem, that's the way things are; and grandchildren are necessary.'

22. *Mrs Ksenu's mother:* ee! të mos kétë djeljt njeríu si kúchuro; pa djeljm vétëm nëk íshtë mírë; vásana káně dhe djéljtë, alá të mos késhë djelj pasandáj edhé mbljáke edhé bënë, ska njerí të jap nji potír uj; *katálaves?* 'Ee! not to have children the man [is] like a piece of wood; without children to be alone it is not a good thing; and children bring difficulties, but not to have children afterwards you grow old and you do, a man has nobody to give him a glass of water; did you understand?'

23. *H.T.:* rrói, u-mbljάk chë të bënj? '[A person] lived, grew old what can s/he do?'

24. *Middle-aged woman:* zërë atá peristérja; do bënesh njizé vítra. 'Catch these doves; you'll become twenty years old.'

25. *Mrs Ksenu's mother:* áma të zësh peristérja të shkónjë mési. 'If you catch doves your backpain will go away.'

26. *Middle-aged woman: kséris ti léne Arvanítika? áma tréksis na pjásis ta peristérja tha jínis íkoshi xronó kopéla* 'Do you know what they say in Arvanítika? If you run and catch the doves you'll become a twenty-year-old girl.'

27. *H.T.:* ató jáně tër kuvénde. 'All these are just words.'

(The discussion turns again to subjects of morality concerning the sensitive issue of sexual relations, and the next speaker comments):

28. *Old Jannakis woman:* pránë káshtës chë do spírtoa? mbërdha në káshtë? 'What's the purpose to put a match in the straws? Inside the straws?' (meaning that if the temptation is around people cannot resist it).

(After the conversation has progressed enough, terminal speakers start participating in it):

29. *Terminal speaker no. 1:* (addressing the investigator and asking a question of common concern in the Arvanítika communities): ti skrúanj Arvanít? 'Do you write the Arvanítika language?'

30. *Ms Jannakis' brother* (humoristically): ekshidár je ti? 'Are you 60 years old?'

31. *Terminal speaker no. 2:* këtú ístë mir, re. 'Here is good, man.'

32. *Old Jannakis woman:* këtú isht amerikjía áma isht prokomén njeríu. 'America is here if a person works hard.'

33. *Terminal speaker no. 2:* katú ístë mir, cë do bën? 'Here is good, what can I do?'

(Women engage in talk about a young person chasing small animals and birds for fun.)

34. *Terminal speaker no. 2:* si guc. guc ístë derk, kafs ístë jenikó. déljë, káljë. astú, péljë. 'Like a pig. "A pig" is a small pig, "animal" is general. A sheep, a horse. This way, a mare.'

(Continuation of conversation about greeting formulas and routines):

35. *Terminal speaker no. 2:* mírë hérdhe, mírë cóva 'You're welcome, well I found you.' (Other people laugh at a mistake that the speaker made and the investigator laughs, too, indicating that he got the point; for analysis of this point see discussion below.)

36. *Ms Jannakis* (addressing herself to the investigator): e zúre amésos. të shkonj ashtú mos e zúre, alá je asírmato. djálji bëri láthos, gólja . . . 'You got it at once. For it [the expression] to go away like that without being noticed by you [it is not possible], but you are a wireless [sharp minded]. The guy made a mistake, the mouth . . .'

37. *Terminal speaker no. 2:* cë të bës? 'What can you do?'

38. *Old Jannakis woman:* chë të bësh e chë të thúash? 'What are you to do and to say?'

(Discussion about various topics continues for a while, and speakers incorporate some information about animal names and other taxonomic domains.)

39. *Terminal speaker no. 2:* nji cíkë ver, djáthë, ulínë, búkë cíkë. axlázadhe ke? naní ístë paljofjáli. aí ci ístë fíkjë. do edhé u një. e urátënë të kesh. 'A little wine, cheese, olives, a little bread. Do you have a pear? Now it is a bad word. The one who is a fig. I want one myself. And may you have my wish [for a long life].'

Not every single line of the 39 turns at talk cited above will be analyzed here. The most significant discourse features which point to speakers' communicative competence will be taken up and focused upon. The limited participation of terminal speakers is the first thing that strikes the observer of this communicative event. The two terminal speakers who are participants in the event start talking relatively late, when the event has progressed a good deal. Certain features of their grammatical, phonological, and discursive structure set them apart from the other participants. The most prominent feature is perhaps terminal speakers' dependence on formulaic material and routines for their communication.

Starting with the examination of a later part of the conversation we notice that terminal speaker no. 2 – who produces more – uses a formula twice. This is the form *cë do bën* 'what can I do?' in turn 33 and *cë të bës* 'what can you do?' in turn 37. As a response to his second utterance the fluent speaker gives in turn 38 the more complete version of the formula *chë të bësh e chë të thúash?* 'what are you to do and to say?' with a strong exclamatory intonation, indirectly suggesting surprise at the young speaker's production at this point.

This particular expression is typically used either preceded or followed by segments of discourse which are unrelated in overt topic. It may be followed by a repetition of the very same expression by another speaker who thus echoes the first in normal speech. The major fluctuations that the formula reveals in fluent speakers' usage concern the grammatical number and person of the verb and the selection by the speaker of one verb *bënj* 'I do' or two verbs *bënj* and *thom* 'I do' and 'I say' to build the expression. Another important feature of the use of this formulaic unit is its position in the immediate discourse context. The formula appears either as a complete turn at talk, being thus the only verbal material offered by the speaker at this point, or as a concluding element attached to something the speaker has already said. When the second type of structure is the case, the fluent speaker generally separates the first nonformulaic part of her/his utterance from the second, formulaic part, with a short pause, and in progressing lowers the volume of the voice. Pitch also changes, taking a questioning coloration. This intonational structure is not attended to by the terminal speaker of our exemplifying conversation, as we will have the opportunity to find out below.

The formula is such that it can appropriately be uttered by middle-aged and elderly people and particularly women, and has the following meaning: 'There is almost nothing for us to do since life is hard and only God can make decisions concerning human beings.' It is a kind of fatalistic statement and hence its cultural appropriateness for the repertoire of older and female members of the community according to the local norms.

From the description above it becomes obvious that the formulaic expression under consideration allows discourse continuation, or marks the end of an exchange or a change in topic. Since the formula appears in the form of a rhetorical question – no specific or known answer can be provided – it would be interesting to see in future research how the formula and its repetition figure as an instance of an adjacency pair according to Schegloff and Sacks (1973). Fillmore (1976) has pointed to the significance of formulaic material, that is, ready-made or fixed expressions, for the carrying out of effective communication. Other scholars have elaborated on that in order to come to grips with situated discourse (Gumperz 1982), or to locate terminal-speaker communicative competence along a line of a proficiency continuum (Dorian 1982a). As is the case with all of communication, the use of verbal material is appropriate or inappropriate depending on the interplay among the various speech-event components such as participants, topic, rules of interpretation, key, and the like. Formulas are also expected to obey such rules and their examination helps us reach a better understanding of speakers' intent and discourse strategies, as well as locate the subtler aspects of their proficiency level.

First, as to the participants expected to use the formulas, we must note that young interactants are not habitually the ones to use this particular formula. If the speaker is male, as is the case here, the utterance becomes twice removed from appropriateness, since fatalism runs counter to the established image of male social status.

On various occasions during the fieldwork, testing of fluent speakers with formulaic expressions has generated results concerning appropriateness that reinforce the interpretation developed here. I have uttered the routine *të rrosh* 'may you live long' to older people while, by attending closely to the proper intonational pattern, trying not to contextualize it as humor. Fluent speakers have generally responded with the same exclamatory style that the speaker of our example used above in her reaction to the terminal speaker's utterance. The reaction to my utterance has been *ti të rrosh* 'you are the one to have a long life'. In speakers' responses the pronominal element *ti* 'you' is heavily – emphatically – stressed to convey the message that it is the addressor of the wish who should normally be the addressee. This particular formula has been exhaustively tested with my informants in the course of research for the status of the moribund grammatical mood of the optative in modern Arvanítika (Tsitsipis 1981b:378–83).

Having established that the terminal speaker of our example has used a formula against the community expectations as to which individuals are the appropriate ones to use it, we can now turn to some other aspects of his performance, matters of both linguistic and sociolinguistic competence. The syntactic structure of the formula requires use of the subjunctive with the complementizer *të* 'that, for/to' accompanied by the proper verb morphology. Terminal speaker no. 2 replaces in turn 33 the subjunctive complementizer with the future marker *do* 'shall, will' and retains the complementizer in turn 37. This fluctuation between the particles *të* and *do* (dialect variant *o* in some northern dialect varieties of Arvanítika) in constructions requiring the first is far from being an idiosyncratic feature of this particular speaker. Terminal speakers almost systematically use the future-marker *do* ~ *o* in place of the subordination marker in both translation tasks and in their limited natural speech production. This replacement obscures the distinction between the subjunctive mood and the future tense, the verb morphologies of which are identical. In terminal-speaker grammar, therefore, the two verb categories are indistinguishable (for a summary discussion of such problems, see Tsitsipis 1984). We must further note here that the particular formula under discussion requires the present tense subjunctive and not the future tense, since the subjunctive is semantically closer to the indeterminacy expressed by the fatalistic meaning of the formula as against the firm expectation expressed by the future.

One further problem in the terminal-speaker grammatical system is the morphology of the verb form *bën* in turn 33. This point also reflects a general trend in terminal grammar, i.e. wrong or morphologically invariant forms in which crucial grammatical distinctions are obscured. The ending /-n/ is inappropriate for both the future and the subjunctive for the 2nd and 3rd persons singular; also for the 1st person singular in all the three categories, i.e. present tense indicative, subjunctive, and future. If the speaker intended to express himself in the 1st person in any one of the three grammatical categories just mentioned, the form to be used should have been *bënj* not *bën*. If he intended to supply the 2nd or 3rd person, the introducing particle should constrain him to use the forms *bësh* or *bënj(ë)* respectively. I have chosen here to translate his utterance in the 1st person singular, basing my decision completely on intuitive grounds.

Finally, both utterances, 33 and 37 (by the same person), are rendered in terminal phonology. In both 33 and 37 the interrogative pronominal element *chë* 'what' is rendered as *cë*, and in 37 the verb ending is /-s/ rather than /-sh/. In the Arvanítika phonological system /c/, /ch/, /s/, and /sh/ are different phonemes. The difference becomes conspicuous if we compare the two terminal utterances with utterance no. 38 by the fluent speaker (for a discussion of Arvanítika phonology and the phonological inventory adapted from Haebler 1965:36–42 see Tsitsipis 1981a:182–91).

As to some significant aspects of discourse, the first occurrence of the formulaic expression in turn 33 is not separated from the first part by a short pause and the terminal speaker does not change pitch or volume as he progresses towards the closing of his statement. Thus the second, formulaic part of his utterance appears as the continuation of the first part (*katú ístë mir* 'here is fine', referring to Greece as against the United States), as if the formula completed the meaning of the other part in referential terms. The attachment, therefore, of this expression to another segment of his speech is mechanical and falls far short of a proper use of material of this sort according to normal rules of interaction and use.

The important notion that can explain this speaker's attempt to manipulate formulaic material of this kind is that of *key* as Hymes (1974:57) has developed it or *frame* as analyzed in seminal work by Goffman (1974). The terminal speaker of our case is trying at certain points to play the role of a fluent Arvanítika speaker by selecting fixed material which helps him foreground his communicative intent. His limited productive competence probably does not allow him to select from within the repertoire of fixed phrases formulas that would have been judged more appropriate for his age and his social identity. The speaker's choice presupposes some distance from the actual use of the language – to some extent a reality as far as speakers of limited productive competence are concerned. This distance allows the terminal speaker to introduce the frame of imitation in an otherwise unmarked conversation. In this case he tries, unsuccessfully, to imitate an Arvanítika speaker of full productive competence.

That this distance referred to above is indeed a prominent feature of terminal production becomes obvious in the treatment of lexicon by members of this speaker group. In all languages, speakers are often expected to focus consciously on lexical resources for various purposes such as speech-play, puns, codeswitching etc. There are, however, cases in which treatments of lexical material reveal a speaker's distance in pretty much the same way that foreign-language learners show lack of intimacy with the lexicons of the codes they are in the process of learning. In these latter cases it is not unusual for learners to express surprise at the shape of some words or to list items and expressions in order to exhibit their knowledge or to rehearse something they have learned. There would be nothing astonishing if speakers of a language interviewed by a linguist listed groups of words or lexical taxonomies, or switched from one lexical item to a synonymous one in the same or in another language for stylistic effect as part of their discourse competence (see below, discussion of fluent speech). There is something peculiar, however, about speakers who list lexical items in the process of a natural conversation without being tested for their knowledge by the investigator.

In several conversations and interviews that I carried out with terminal speakers in both communities I found an extra interest on their part in some lexical items that seemed to strike them as difficult to pronounce, or peculiar, and therefore worth remembering. Such an item, which terminal speakers have spent a tremendous amount of energy talking about and analyzing, is the common word *këmbëstrímbër* 'sprained leg'. Their reaction to this and similar lexical items suggests a metalinguistic focus as far as this group of speakers is concerned. This kind of talking *about* the Arvanítika language frequently takes precedence over the actual use of the language in natural interactions.

In turn 34 of the conversation cited above, terminal speaker no. 2 lists words he knows and, even more significantly, comments on the taxonomic status of the animal terms he mentions by stating that *kafs ístë jenikó* ['the term] animal is general [inclusive]'. The style of this delivery is monotonous, staccato, and with a color of slight hesitation as when somebody is trying to remember words that s/he is not actively familiar with. In turn 39 he repeats the same kind of lexical rehearsal, although in this second case there is more room for naturalness since a discussion about lexical domains has preceded his interjection. Nevertheless, the closing of his utterance culminates with the formula *urátënë të kesh* 'may you have my wish [for a long life]', which is completely inappropriate in the case of a young person addressing an older one. The formula – also tested by me in various contexts – is mechanically attached to the word list after a short pause, making the speaker's performance hardly recognizable as part of coherent discourse.

In addition to this distance from the normal Arvanítika linguistic communicative routines, revealed in terminal-speaker performance through the activation of the imitation frame and the word-listing, a third aspect of their communicative behavior should be mentioned here briefly. Terminal speakers occasionally exhibit some creativity in the manipulation of lexical resources when the situation calls for that. They build on their restricted lexical knowledge to introduce speech-play, particularly when they want to impress or test a foreigner who either claims that s/he knows the language or behaves in such a way as to trigger antagonistic reactions. (For a pun, with its source in the terminal speaker's confusion rather than in intended lexical manipulation, see further discussion of our conversation below.)

Turning now to fluent speech, we discover that one prominent feature of fluent-speaker performance is the appropriate and productive use of figurative language. Use of figurative expressions in natural speech presupposes in addition to a good knowledge of bilingual lexical resources a competence in properly judging discourse context, discourse topic, and participant relations. In this case we can say that the speaker is a highly skilled one. This observation translates speakers' intuitions about a good speaker, which, as stated earlier in this chapter, are not always very clear and straightforward.

We can roughly classify such figurative or metaphorical expressions as show up in our data into the following categories: simple metaphors, metaphorical utterances to other participants in the event which reveal an indexical or discourse-bound sense, and wise words or what may be called gnomic sayings that stand as commentaries on the realities of the world. Expressions of the above-cited conversation are listed below for readers' convenience and for further discussion.

no. 2. me jirokomíotë 'with the home for the aged!'
6. dúan ató me kramanjóla 'they must hang [literally: they need the gallows]'
13. ístë dríza ajó 'she is a branch [bright] this one'
22. ee të mos kétë (. . .) djeljt njeríu si kúchuro 'not to have children the man [is] like a piece of wood'
24. zérë atá peristérja; do bénesh njizé vítra 'catch these doves; you'll become twenty years old'
28. pránë káshtës chë do spírtoa? 'what's the purpose to put a match in the straws?'
36. alá je asírmato 'but you are a wireless [bright]'

Bauman (1977) in his extensive essay on performance includes *figurative language* as one among several communicative means that serve to key the performance frame. Performance in the sense that the concept is used in the ethnography of speaking means that assumptions of responsibility by a speaker to exhibit his/her communicative competence and to be evaluated for this (see Tsitsipis [1983a, 1988] for a discussion of those narrative devices that make performance possible in fluent-speaker narrations). Bauman considers figurative expressions important for performance-building because of their semantic density, foregroundedness, and the central role that expressive intensity and special communicative skill play (1977:17–18). One notable case in which the coinage and use of metaphorical *wise words* qualify as genuine performance in conversations is reported by Basso (1976).

In the context of the present discussion I would suggest that a careful examination of figurative language carries a multifaceted relevance for the exploration of aspects of discourse analysis and language obsolescence. First, the feature of foregroundedness that figures of speech contain lends convincingness to one's words; and convincingness is dependent upon the speech components of topic and participants jointly considered. Thus, the speaker in turn no. 2 summarizes in an excellent way the kinds of people she considers her expected interlocutors to be when she uses the Arvanítika language. The topic is *Arvanítika* and interlocutors are collectively referred to as 'the home for the aged'. Perhaps convincingness is more obvious in no. 6, which constitutes a general moral statement in which the speaker sets up an image of somebody being executed because of her immoral social conduct. She used the term 'gallows' to make the punishment resemble a real execution. The more sensitive to moral social issues a subject of discussion is, the more general and gnomic-sounding the expressed attitude is expected to be. Turn no. 6 therefore is a case of the gnomic type of figurative language, as against no. 2 above, which is a simple metaphor.

Second, figurative speech seems to be to some extent related to solidarity in small-group interaction where context-bound communication becomes predominant since many of the meaning elements of the expressions uttered are related to who speaks to whom and under what circumstances. Fluent speakers of the Arvanítika communities form a subgroup within their society, and particularly older women are members of rather closed networks of communication in which the use of Arvanítika prevails. (For a discussion of types of solidarity in obsolescence and in other kinds of communication situations, see Hill in this volume.) Turn no. 13 exhibits features of indexicality, since it is addressed to other participants in the event and refers to one of them. Figurative expressions of this sort presuppose a relationship the closeness of which can be tested publicly through direct comments of positive or critical content. Basso (1979:9) reports on the testing of a relationship through the exchange of mock insults in Western Apache culture. Comments of a personal character – even if their intended meaning is not negative – touch on sensitive aspects of somebody's personality, and it is more appropriate for participants in an event to direct them to people with whom there is an already established relationship.

In the same way we can interpret no. 36, addressed this time to the investigator reacting to a mistake made by the terminal speaker. The mistake consists in the substitution of *hérdhe* 'testicles' for *érdhe* 'come' in the greeting routine *mir érdhe* 'you are welcome'. Given the particular audience, the speaker did not shift from *érdhe* to *hérdhe* on purpose, as is the case with terminal speakers when they operate in other contexts. The shift is a genuine mistake and the other participants' willingness to allow a momentary reference to an obscene term rather than letting it go uncommented on says something about the kind of relationship that people have among themselves and with the ethnographer. Expressions such as the one in no. 36 presuppose some kind of intimacy that a two-year contact had helped to develop between the investigator and the local communities. The figure 'you are a wireless' that the investigator received because he indicated that he understood the mistake the terminal speaker made could be also taken as meaning 'you are sly' (in the sense of keeping one's antennas up to catch bits of information on matters that do not concern him). The successful use of the figure, therefore, depends heavily on discourse context and on the kind of relationship obtaining between the addressor and the addressee of the particular utterance.

No. 22 is a very common expression and is now used in a novel context – a sign of creativity – in order for the speaker to show the consequences of not having children (this kind of person resembles a piece of wood). The figure in no. 28 is a successful indirect comment on sexual morality, warning against allowing close encounters of unmarried young people in which case the feared outcome will become inevitable. The figure is offered in inter-rogative form. The habit of using wise words in the form of rhetorical questions is well established among fluent speakers. In this indirect speech act with the illocutionary force of warning, the form of question that has been selected by the speaker foregrounds the intended commentary on the crucial subject of morality. Repeated references at various points in the course of the conversation to matters of family, children, sexuality, and related subjects highlight the measure of importance attached to this cultural domain by elderly people, and as a consequence explain the use of figures of speech to emphasize their views.

Turns 4 and 12 indicate clearly this focus on morality (recall also figure no. 6). Finally, the expression in no. 24 foregrounds the contrast between old and young age as perceived by speakers whose experience in life makes them the proper spokesmen for the community's collective knowledge and experience. Selection of a wise saying to convey this information implies some sort of responsibility assumed by the participants at this point to reveal their competence in message elaboration and transmission. Furthermore, it is interesting to note that in the following turns, 25 and 26, fluent speakers undertake to elaborate on the meaning of the saying, first in Arvanítika (turn 25) and second in Greek (turn 26). The commentary provides the audience with additional clarification and serves as an attention-focusing discourse device.

Another aspect of fluent-speaker competence is the use of the bilingual lexical resources in a way that is relevant to discourse analysis. As extensive work on the problem of the retention and loss of Albanian vocabulary has shown, modern Arvanítika is suffering an intensive relexification in the direction of Greek which is comparable to the one described by Hill and Hill (1977) for modern Nahuatl. In Tsitsipis (1981a:198–312) various word classes are examined and comparative evidence from other dying languages is brought to bear on Arvanítika lexical dynamics. Earlier Arvanítika sources give support to the conclusion that the language has lost many lexical items and has not developed to its full potential the productivity of suffixes as compared with Albanian proper. Frequently enough, semantic differentiation problems arise in cases where the language does not have an abstract nominal suffixed form which could release a deverbative from part of its meaning, the latter thus becoming polysemous (Tsitsipis 1981b:378–83).[5]

A striking feature of natural speech is the alternation between Albanian and Greek words. This phenomenon covers even cases in which the Albanian items are part of terminal speakers' passive competence and of fluent speakers' active competence as suggested by a close examination of word lists. Despite, therefore, the relexifying tendency of modern Arvanítika, retention of indigenous vocabulary and frequent alternations between the lexical resources of the two codes are suggestive of certain discourse functions that need discussion in the context of the present chapter. One discourse device which consists of codeswitching between synonymous expressions and which serves as evaluation in narratives has been discussed in other works (Tsitsipis 1983a, 1988).

From the cited conversation, a similar but not identical instance of manipulation of bilingual resources emerges. In turns 10, 11, and 12 the same general meaning is expressed with three different words by three different speakers. The pattern is one of decreasing syntactic complexity. In no. 10 the sentence includes the verb, the noun, and a pronominal element, whereas in no. 11 the pronominal element is deleted and in no. 12 the verb meets the same fate. As the syntactic string becomes more elliptical, the loudness increases. What is happening here is that the syntactic framework is gradually discarded, leaving only the noun – different in each turn – as the variable. This increasingly elliptical syntactic frame is obviously the stable part, and this stability allows us to understand that the three filler-nouns which go into the frame are the same in some sense, since they can be substituted for one another in the same linguistic environment.

The above remarks, based on intuitive and observational grounds, require a more explicit formulation in order for the properties of the device used by the speakers to become clear. The key to the interpretation is to be found in the nouns used in this context. Although these are different

134 Lukas D. Tsitsipis

lexemes, it is clear that they are intended to be the same in a larger sense given the particular context. In no. 10, the Greek word sets up the frame for the interpretation of the other words too. *érotas* means specifically 'love with sexual desire' and not parental love, brotherly love, or general affection. The term is a loanword in Arvanítika, heard very frequently in otherwise unmarked conversations, but it appears here unadapted to the Arvanítika morphology. In no. 11, *gazímë* is an Albanian word very rarely heard today, and only among elderly people. In fact, this is one of the few instances in which I have heard the word uttered in a natural interaction. It covers the general meaning of 'joy, happiness'. But since the second speaker's voice volume increases to indicate agreement with the first speaker, we may infer that the word in no. 11 is semantically attracted by the word used in no. 10, and is, therefore, intended to express a more specific meaning, that is, 'happiness due to erotic love'. The same holds true for the word *haré* meaning 'joy' in no. 12. This term is a loanword in Arvanítika and is generally uttered by fluent speakers adapted to the proper Albanian morphology (*haré* and not *hará*). Given the status of the two Greek-in-origin words in the Arvanítika lexical repertoire, we should not consider the discourse segment under discussion as an instance of genuine codeswitching. Nevertheless, this portion of the conversation exhibits the properties of a creative manipulation of lexical resources from the two languages by the speakers, who thus manage to foreground an important message. It is in the sense of using this echoing device that we suggest that speakers here intend the "same meaning".

What we are dealing with in this discourse segment is a type of repetition of a basic meaning via different words. The repetition is obviously topic-related. Speakers who utter turns nos. 10, 11, and 12 by echoing each other conclude a portion of the conversation which has concentrated on the subject of morally sensitive behavior. The subject under discussion explains the ironical tone of speakers' voices when they utter their turns. The tone of voice helps us perceive the proper contextualization of the message. In speakers' conversational collaboration, surface syntactic material is gradu-ally peeled away from the central meaning, which thus becomes more prominent. In fact, the central point is doubly foregrounded, first by repetition, and second by the progressively more elliptical syntax that accompanies it.[6]

We can assume here that speakers' intent is to comment on moral behavior by conveying the message: "Women, unable to resist temptation, were attracted to love affairs; but we disapprove of this behavior." Gumperz (1982:94–5) has suggested that the violation of Grice's maxims can lead to chains of reasoning which help us to reinterpret what is said in such a way as to fit the situation. He then examines instances of codeswitching between synonymous passages which obviously violate the maxim of quantity, since the speakers repeat themselves, and this gives rise to situated interpretations. A similar case is the one examined here, with the difference, of course, that we are dealing with inter-speaker repetition rather than with the same person repeating her/his own words. Here, violation of quantity, along with the proper intonation and the syntactic pattern described above, make the transmission of the specific message possible. It is in such a discourse context that manipulation of bilingual lexical resources appears to be a useful communicative means called upon by fluent speakers.

4.   Conclusion

In this chapter, an analysis of terminal- and fluent-speaker performance as emerging from natural speech interaction has been presented. Given the restricted production of terminal speakers in the dying language, the rather limited data obtained from this sociolinguistic category of speakers can be profitably examined for the light they shed on both the linguistic and the sociolinguistic proficiency level in their weaker language. The emphasis in this chapter has been primarily on discourse structure and the various speakers' ability to manipulate creatively formulaic and lexical material as well as to produce contextually appropriate figurative speech. Thus, while fluent speakers manage to use skillfully the lexical resources of both languages in their repertoire by transforming their knowledge into discourse-coherent chunks of information which control simultaneously grammatical, phonological, and discursive structure, terminal speakers show, by comparison, a distance from the contracting language by using unprompted word-listing and inappropriate formulaic material, and this in ways that set them off from the normal and expected manners of speaking.

By using the discourse analysis and ethnography of speaking perspectives, we are thus able to locate subtle aspects of community members' communicative competence. By focusing attention on knowing how rather than simply on knowing what – to echo Hymes – we discover that even in the domain of lexicon, which is often the strongest element in the arsenal of terminal speakers of a dying language, they do not typically control the lexicon of their weaker language at a level which would permit them to manipulate discourse structure in as sophisticated a fashion as do fluent speakers.

Notes

This paper has greatly profited from comments, discussion, and thoughtful suggestions by Nancy Dorian. The author is the only one responsible for the remaining shortcomings.

1. We can also mention here the significant contribution of language death studies to a better understanding of the pragmatic functions of linguistic interaction. Thus, even after the language has suffered a serious erosion in the domains that are

related to its semantico-referential capacity, communicative creativity continues
to index important discourse aspects, and linguistic ideology remains a significant
force in keeping this creativity alive in the entire cultural–linguistic framework of
the community (see Mertz, this volume). In part, the present chapter addresses
similar issues.

2. The two major dialect divisions of Albanian are Geg, or northern dialect, and
   Tosk, or southern dialect. The basic ethnic-geographical area in the Balkans
   outside Albania proper that speaks the Geg dialect is Kosovë in Yugoslavia,
   whereas almost all the other outlying Albanian-speaking enclaves belong to the
   Tosk branch.

3. The reason that the label *terminal speaker* rather than Dorian's term *semi-speaker*
   has been selected is that Arvanítika imperfect speakers are somewhat closer to
   passive bilingualism than their Gaelic counterparts. Some of the asymmetries
   discovered by Dorian for East Sutherland Gaelic (ESG) semi-speakers do not
   apply to the same extent to the proficiency level of Arvanítika imperfect speakers.
   The latter's low proficiency in linguistic structure is matched by an inappropriate
   behavior in some of the communicative events in the Arvanítika language (for a
   discussion of semi-speakers see Dorian 1981:107–10; for the notion of sets of
   asymmetries see Dorian n.d.).

4. The conventions of the Albanian alphabet have been adopted in the transcription
   of the conversational text cited below. Some of the fundamental units of the
   Arvanítika phonological inventory adopted from Haebler (1965:36–42) and
   adapted to the communities from which my data comes are: /lj/, /kj/, /sh/, /ch/, /nj/
   for the palatal sounds, /ë/ for the schwa, /r/ and /rr/ for the flap and trill vibrants
   respectively, /x/ and /h/ for the velar and glottal fricatives respectively. Terminal
   speakers collapse the phonemic contrast /kj/ and /k/ in the stop series, confuse the
   schwa with /e/ (which form a minimal pair in fluent-speaker production), and are
   inconsistent in the pronunciation of /r/ and /rr/, also phonemically opposed. (For a
   more detailed discussion of the assignment of sounds to particular positions in
   terms of manner and place of articulation reflecting for Arvanítika the sprachbund effects due to the long contact with Greek, see Tsitsipis 1981a:183.)

5. Although we witness a gradual increase in the productivity of the abstract nouns
   with suffixes in modern Albanian, the deverbatives are retained since they are
   semantically specialized, expressing the process of an action, whereas the abstract
   suffixed forms denote the outcome (Byron 1976:110–11). In Arvanítika, the
   polysemy of the deverbative forms is obvious in instances such as the following: *të
   vráret të káfshavet* 'the slaughtering of the cattle' and *káfshat të vráret* 'the
   slaughtered cattle'. Informants have repeatedly commented on the difficulty they
   have in telling the meaning outside the syntactic context.

6. My discussion of this discourse device has profited from a thorough and extensive
   criticism by Nancy Dorian; some of the wording used derives from her suggestions. It must be noted that the phenomenon under consideration impinges upon
   the broader notion of repetition; various scholars have examined the significance
   of this notion for discourse. Differentiation between new information-introducing
   and grammatically determined repetition (Gleason 1968:47–8) and repetition of
   discourse chunks in codeswitched passages explained in terms of conversational
   implicature and culturally determined communicative intent (Gumperz 1982:94–5)
   are two out of many analyses of the phenomenon. In the ethnography of speaking

tradition, parallelistic repetition is viewed as revealing structural principles governing literary genre form (Sherzer 1977). There is no doubt that in narrative and conversational genres both, linguistic and cultural factors are expected to determine jointly the kind and the degree of repetition. The Arvanítika case of speakers' echoing one another carries some formal similarity to the pattern of *pragmatic dialog* studied by Urban (1986) in the context of ceremonial dialogic exchanges in South America. A pragmatic dialog is this special case of communication in which back-channel responses count as turns at speaking despite the fact that they do not contribute new semantic information. However, since Urban's analysis refers to a rather well established areal communicative feature with consequences for metacommunication, social action, and solidarity, one should be careful in generalizing his conclusions beyond a certain point.

9 On the social meaning of linguistic variability in language death situations: Variation in Newfoundland French

RUTH KING

1. Introduction

In the light of more than two decades of research in the Labovian frame-work, conducted mainly in urban speech communities, there exists a widespread belief that linguistic variability is most likely to appear when there is strong socio-economic stratification, or even that it only appears under these circumstances. This is the impression left, intentionally or not, by statements such as the following by D. Sankoff and Laberge (1978:239):

Though it is well known that the internal differentiation of spoken language is related to social class, the scientific study of this relationship poses a number of very different problems.

and by Labov (1966:111):

Variation in linguistic behavior does not in itself exert a powerful influence on social development, nor does it affect drastically the life chances of the individual; on the contrary, the shape of linguistic behavior changes rapidly as the speaker's social position changes.

Quantification of linguistic data according to linguistic environment and according to the speaker's social class is basic to the methodology of this branch of sociolinguistics. It is also an underlying assumption that variables involved in a linguistic change necessarily carry sociosymbolic meaning.

In the language death literature, it has been shown that variation may arise in languages undergoing attrition as a result of a language death process whereby simplified variants gradually replace more complex variants, especially in the speech of semi-speakers (see e.g. Dorian 1978c). Schmidt (1985a) also gives evidence for the creation of new, complex variants in dying Dyirbal. Contrary to the view expressed by, among others, Dressler and Wodak-Leodolter (1977) that language death is a type of

139

pidginization, I will argue here that linguistic variation may also be maintained in dying languages, in the absence of social differentiation, by fully fluent speakers of the language. It may be the case, however, that variation does not carry the weight of social meaning it does in healthier speech communities. These claims will be supported by evidence from a declining variety of Acadian French spoken in western Newfoundland, Canada.

2.   The speech community

A number of social characteristics have been found to be typical of language death situations, characteristics which are familiar to readers of Dorian's work on East Sutherland Gaelic, Gal's on Hungarian in Austria, etc. Also found in French Newfoundland, they include entrenchment of a high language in the education system with minimal or no use of the low language in the schools, restriction of the minority language to a limited set of domains, association of the high language with either social status and/or opportunities for socio-economic advancement, asymmetry between older and younger speakers' linguistic choices with younger speakers using the high language more, and diminished loyalty towards the minority language.[1]

2.1.   Settlement history

The variety of French spoken in the area of Newfoundland's Port-au-Port peninsula stands out clearly as a variety of Acadian (sharing features found in Nova Scotia, New Brunswick, and Prince Edward Island), while similarities with source dialects in Brittany and Normandy are also apparent. This area differs from other francophone areas of North America in that settlement was quite late, beginning in the mid-nineteenth century and ending only in the early years of the twentieth century. Settlers consisted of two distinct groups, French newly arrived from France and Acadians from Nova Scotia whose ancestors had been in North America for almost three hundred years before resettlement in Newfoundland. The politics of the late nineteenth century in Newfoundland resulted in these francophone settlers being geographically and culturally separate from anglophones for a number of decades, at least up until the 1930s, when improved means of communication and an influx of English settlers from other areas of Newfoundland significantly lessened their isolation. From that point on, French was a minority language in the Port-au-Port peninsula area of Newfoundland, as it has always been in Newfoundland as a whole.

With few exceptions, all essential services – schools, shops, the post office – have been provided to French Newfoundlanders uniquely in English, and virtually all persons of authority – doctors, magistrates, priests – have spoken only English. The absence of French from institutionalized settings, along with intermarriage of French and English people, has resulted in the failure of young people to learn French. Intermarriage typically results in childen being raised in English. French is spoken by people low in socio-economic status, i.e., by seasonal fishermen and their families. A language attitudes study (Clarke and King 1983b) employing an adaptation of the matched-guise technique found little status associated with Newfoundland French and French speakers having low feelings of group solidarity.

Whereas at the turn of the century the francophone population of the Port-au-Port peninsula area numbered approximately 2,000, today there are well under half that number. Newfoundland French is spoken in four villages – in one (Stephenville) there are no fluent French speakers left under the age of 50, in another (L'Anse-à-Canards) no fluent speakers under 20, and in the remaining two villages (Cap St-Georges and La Grand'Terre) the number of child francophones is few. Fewer than half-a-dozen French monolinguals remain, and they are octogenarians.

Most French Newfoundlanders have received little or no education in their mother tongue: only a very few French speakers are literate in French; many over the age of 60 cannot read or write either English or French. Older francophones tend to be French-dominant, those in their 40s and 50s more nearly balanced bilinguals, and those younger are English-dominant. All speakers, regardless of age, use English loanwords, since Newfoundland French has few native vocabulary items for twentieth-century inventions.

Despite improved local means of communication in the last two decades, the Port-au-Port peninsula area remains rural and isolated by urban standards. Cap St-Georges, the largest community on the peninsula itself, has a population of only 1,470, according to the 1981 Census. The total population of La Grand'Terre, L'Anse-à-Canards, and three neighboring villages numbers just over 1,000. Stephenville and environs has 10,095. However, it is one hour's drive by car from Stephenville to these communities; the last few miles to L'Anse-à-Canards and La Grand'Terre are over gravel roads. A mountain barrier separates Cap St-Georges from La Grand'Terre and L'Anse-à-Canards, making the drive from each to "the Cape" over three-quarters of an hour by car (though the distance is much shorter by boat). It is approximately 15 miles by poor gravel road from La Grand'Terre to L'Anse-à-Canards. The urban center for western New-foundland is Corner Brook, the only community on the west coast with a population greater than 30,000. It is three hours' drive from the peninsula villages to Corner Brook (two hours from Stephenville); many of my older informants have never been there, nor have they been to the equally distant port of departure for mainland Canada, Port-aux-Basques.

This area of Newfoundland is economically depressed and there is little occupational choice. The fishing industry, slowly dying, is the major source of employment. Many young French Newfoundlanders spend enough time in the urban industrial centers of mainland Canada – Halifax, Toronto, Calgary – to earn money to build their own houses at home in Newfoundland. Despite its hardships, theirs is a way of life they do not wish to leave permanently.

3.   Variation in Newfoundland French

French speakers who are unacquainted with Acadian typically find New-foundland French difficult to understand, largely due to morphological patterns quite distinct from those of Standard French.[2] The paradigm given below for the verb *parler* 'to speak' shows that (all) verbs have a 3rd person plural ending /ō/, as /i parlō/ 'they are speaking'. The paradigm also shows nonstandard (but distinctly Acadian) pronominal usage.

(1) *parler* 'to speak':

	Singular	Plural
1st person	ȝə parl	ȝə parlō
2nd person	ty parl	vu parle
3rd person m.	i parl	i parlō
f.	a parl	

As one becomes familiar with the dialect, one is struck by the wide range of variation which exists, some of which is linguistically conditioned, some of which is not. The sentences below give an example of linguistically condi-tioned syntactic variation in which the 3rd person plural agreement marker /ō/ is not usually present in relative clauses. In (2) *allont* contains the plural marker /ō/ while in (3) *va* is the singular form of the verb *aller*.

(2) Il allont à la côte à tous les matins
    'They go to the shore every morning'
(3) Y a des gars qui va pas à la côte
    'There are some guys who don't go to the shore'

The fact that two distinct varieties of French were spoken by the original settlers accounts for only a small amount of phonological variation in Newfoundland French (some speakers preserve Acadian *ouisme* – i.e., the realization [u] where standard French has [o] or [ɔ] in lexical items such as *chose* 'thing' and *connaître* 'to know') and for perhaps half-a-dozen lexical alternations. This finding is in keeping with those reported by Trudgill (1984a) for a number of speech communities where the effects of dialect mixing were found to be significantly reduced in three generations.

3.1.   Methodology

The local context made necessary an adaptation of the survey methodology common to urban variability studies in the investigation of grammatical variation in Newfoundland French. Unlike the samples used in most variability studies, the French Newfoundland sample was not stratified according to socio-economic class, since French Newfoundlanders display little or no variation in those factors typically employed in the construction of socio-economic indices, such as occupation, income, and housing. Education in English is strongly correlated with age (younger people are better educated than older people), whereas education in French is minimal or non-existent. The alternative method of categorizing speakers which has also been successfully implemented in urban contexts is the "linguistic marketplace" scale, which assesses the degree to which people have access to the standard or legitimized language in their area of work (see Sankoff and Laberge 1978). This approach is also inappropriate to the French Newfoundland context since there is no clear linguistic norm in either French or English, with the possible exception of "school English".

On the basis of longterm participant observation in L'Anse-à-Canards, Butler (1985) points out that in this small community, as in other face-to-face societies (see Frankenberg 1957:33ff), status is context-specific. For example, a person with high status in folk-narrative contexts might have low status in a discussion of carpentry. The combination of socially determined statuses (e.g. that of joketeller, musician, cook) makes up one's generally perceived status within the community. Subsequent work on language choice in L'Anse-à-Canards (King in press b) has shown that in small, rural communities such as these, investigation of such types of social roles and of individuals' social networks (based in large part on kinship) is revealing. However, since this first variability study concentrated on the speech of all four communities with significant French populations, these subtle relationships could not be investigated in detail.

A representative sample of speakers was chosen from each of the four francophone villages, consisting of older and younger speakers and of equal numbers of males and females. The final sample consisting of 68 speakers, somewhat under ten percent of the estimated total francophone population, was as follows:[3]

(4) *By age group*		*By sex*		*By locality*	
−50 years	30	F	34	Stephenville/Kippens	10
+60 years	38	M	34	La Grand'Terre	18
				Cap-St-Georges	20
				L'Anse-à-Canards/	20
				Maisons d'Hiver	

3.2. Variation in clitic-pronoun usage

Both free conversation and translation data were obtained for the study during fieldwork conducted during the summer of 1980. The dependent variables all concerned the use of clitic pronouns. Clitic pronouns were chosen since previous fieldwork had revealed a wide range of variation in their phonological realizations, in case marking, and in the syntax. French, unlike English, has both strong and clitic forms of subject and object personal pronouns as well as object clitics *y* (usually used to replace the preposition *à* followed by an inanimate NP) and *en* (usually used to replace the preposition *de* followed by an inanimate NP). Following Kayne (1975, etc.) we would argue that cliticization of object pronouns in French involves movement from argument positions following the verb to preverbal non-argument positions. In the case of cliticization of more than one object clitic in a single clause, their relative order is fixed in Standard French.

Newfoundland French exhibits variation in whether the object pronoun is cliticized or not (as in [5a] and [5b]), in the position clitics occupy (pronouns may be cliticized to the upper verb or to the lower verb in *faire*-infinitive constructions in Newfoundland French (as in [6a] and [6b]), and in their relative order (as in examples [7a] and [7b]), for an affirmative-imperative construction).

(5) a. Elle lui donne le livre
    b. A donne le livre à lui
       'She gives him the book'
(6) a. Ma mère m'en fait manger
    b. Ma mère me fait en manger
       'My mother makes me eat some'
(7) a. Donne-moi-les
    b. Donne-les-moi
       'Give them to me'

There is also variation in number and case marking in the 3rd person, with a tendency to generalize accusative and singular marking exhibited by younger speakers. While it is the case that younger speakers cliticize object pronouns less than older speakers, clitic movement is still an important grammatical rule in Newfoundland French. Only in one instance is there fairly strong evidence for the convergence of French and English systems – the use of *en* ('some') on the part of certain speakers who would appear to have reinterpreted it as a strong pronoun, in phrases such as *Ma mère me fait manger-z-en*.

Speakers of Newfoundland French themselves pay no attention to variation in clitic pronoun usage, with the exception of a few geographically scattered older speakers who volunteered that indicative constructions with postverbal *en* was the bad French of a limited group of young people, and at that of young people from another community.

Variation in clitic pronoun usage is to a certain extent dependent upon linguistic environment. Of the nonlinguistic variables in the study, variation is clearly related to the age of the speaker and the results may well indicate linguistic change in progress. However, it would appear to be change

Table 1. *Significant results according to age, sex, and locality (relative frequencies given as two-place decimals)*

Variables	Significant results
Phonological: *l* deletion (subject clitics)	Age (F = 4.32, df = 1, p <0.05)
	Younger speakers 0.44; Older speakers 0.25
	Age × Sex (F = 5.757, df. = 1, p <0.05)
en denasalization	Age (F = 13.383, df = 1, p <0.001)
	Younger speakers 0.24; Older speakers 0.12
en realized [ã]	Age (F = 63.522, df = 1, <0.001)
	Younger speakers 0.17; Older speakers 0.48
Grammatical: 1st and 2nd person object cliticization	
One-clitic constructions	Age (F = 6.836, df = 1, p <0.05)
	Younger speakers 0.82; Older speakers 0.99
Two-clitic constructions	Age (F = 26.682, df = 1, p <0.001)
	Younger speakers 0.56; Older speakers 0.65
3rd person object cliticization	
One-clitic constructions	Age (F = 3.617, df = 1, p = 0.06 not significant but trend/younger)
	La Grand'Terre speakers cliticized less often than all other speakers.

without the classic social motivation, since no particular social group stands out as linguistically different from other speakers, aside from the age distinction. The analysis of variance results given in Table 1 shows that sex of speaker and locality proved to be of minimal importance. That sex is unimportant here differs from the results of many studies done in speech communities in which the opportunities available to women are linked with their use of more prestigious variants. While the speech of older people is usually looked upon as good French, the local context is one in which speaking the minority language in any form is of little practical importance and in which there is no well-defined linguistic norm. The results with respect to the sex variable are understandable given the linguistic options available (see Nichols 1983).

3.3. Variation and language choice

Since the initial large-scale study, detailed study has been made of language use in one of the four francophone communities, the small village of L'Anse-à-Canards. Kinship patterns, work patterns, and the pattern of voluntary association have been found to play a significant role in language choice in L'Anse-à-Canards. Language choice appears to carry sociosymbolic meaning in much the same way as it does in the bilingual community of Oberwart, Austria, as reported by Susan Gal. The social network data, however, have not made it possible to isolate a particular social pattern which relates to grammatical variation within Newfoundland French (or with those cases of phonological variation investigated in the clitic pronoun study) although it has uncovered some idiosyncratic differences.

3.4.   Preliminary analysis of variation in agreement

Work-in-progress on variation in agreement marking has had similar results to the study of variation in clitic pronoun usage. In Newfoundland French, agreement may be marked on the verb (but not on the past participle, as it is in Standard French), on the adjective, and on the article. Examples (2) and (3) above show that the variable is sensitive to linguistic environment. The data have not yet been quantified, but comparison of tape transcripts for a number of speakers reveals some linguistic conditioning and some age-linked variation in agreement marking in line with what we have seen for clitic pronoun usage. In this case, we are fortunate to have results of a study of agreement in related varieties of French (Flikeid 1985) with which to compare Newfoundland French patterns. Nova Scotia Acadian is spoken in several villages throughout the province (one a source area for French Newfoundland settlement). French is a minority language in Nova Scotia as it is in Newfoundland, but it is not in such serious decline as Newfoundland French. In this more healthy context Flikeid has found variation in agreement marking to be significantly related to region, sex, age, and education. Preliminary analysis leads us to predict that when our results are submitted to statistical testing this will not turn out to be the case with agreement marking in Newfoundland French.

3.5.   Conclusions

We would argue, then, that a great deal of variation remains in Newfoundland French, despite its decline in status, restriction in contexts of usage, and loss of speakers. However, this variation does not appear to carry the social meaning one finds in healthier speech communities. Variation in Newfoundland French is not particularly salient to its speakers, the great majority of whom are illiterate in French. With respect to clitic pronoun usage, only indicative constructions with postverbal *en* (as in *Il achète-z-en* 'He buys some') would appear to be at all stigmatized. Discussion of fluency in French almost always focuses on the use of recent English borrowings vs. native French words. Phonological and grammatical variants figure minimally, if at all, as social markers.

It might be argued by some that the investigation of variation in Newfoundland French might not be expected to have uncovered socially meaningful variation, since it has concentrated heavily on nonphonological variation. Hudson (1980: 48) claims that one is not likely to find much syntactic variation at all in a language variety; he suggests that such variation is socially "suppressed". We would argue that while syntactic variation has not been widely studied in the past (most likely due to the considerable methodological difficulties involved), such variation is apparent in large linguistic corpora and, in those drawn from healthier speech communities, syntactic variation has been shown to be socially significant (see e.g. Shibamoto 1985 for Japanese). With respect to Newfoundland French, those phonological variables investigated (relating to the surface realization of certain clitics) have shown very similar social patterning (or lack thereof) to grammatical variables.

4. Comparison with other studies

How does variation in Newfoundland French compare with variation in other language death situations? Nancy Dorian's work on East Sutherland Gaelic is perhaps the best known and best documented study of language death. The social context in which Gaelic is spoken in East Sutherland, Scotland is very similar to the Newfoundland French context, as is the linguistic situation. Dorian has shown that the language death process is not characterized by complete breakdown of the grammatical system, but that a high degree of complexity is still apparent in East Sutherland Gaelic; she also shows that variation is maintained in East Sutherland Gaelic, in the absence of social differentiation, and that the variation is not linked to sex of the speaker.

The case of Hungarian in Oberwart, Austria, as reported by Susan Gal is also one of language shift. Residents of Oberwart were found regularly to use a range of styles in both the high language, German, and the low language, Hungarian. Gal states that community residents, to varying degrees, are aware of and actively control local and standard variants of a number of Hungarian linguistic variables. We might attribute these differences, in both linguistic awareness and linguistic usage, from the French Newfoundland case to the presence of Hungarian in institutionalized settings – the church and schools – in Oberwart, although less today than in the past. It is also the case that in Oberwart there is occupational choice, with factory work enjoying high status. This choice does not exist in more rural western Newfoundland. Younger people are said to be much less likely to approach Standard Hungarian than older speakers, so it may be that change is in the direction of the French Newfoundland and Gaelic East Sutherland patterns.

It might be argued that the sociolinguistic patterning found in East Sutherland and in French Newfoundland is a function of the rural (as opposed to urban) context, rather than to the fact that these are languages in decline. Most studies which have found definite social correlates of linguistic variation have been concentrated in urban centers of considerable social complexity. However, a number of recent studies conducted in healthy non-urban speech communities have revealed strong social conditioning in the absence of social stratification. For example, Clarke's (1985) work on variation in a dialect of Montagnais (an Algonquian language) spoken in the small bilingual community of Sheshatshui, Labrador, shows differentiation according to kinship group and according to sex. Smith and Johnson (1986) have found that certain linguistic variants, mainly lexical, serve as sociolinguistic markers in Kugu Nganhcara, an Aboriginal language spoken by a stable population of some 280–300 people in northern Queensland, Australia. Flikeid's work on related but healthier varieties of French, as we have seen, reveals linguistic variation to be more strongly related to social variables than is the case of Newfoundland French. These studies have all, like the Newfoundland French study, revealed wide-ranging linguistic variation.

We have argued that linguistic variation in Newfoundland French, though strongly correlated with age, does not carry the weight of social meaning which variation carries in healthy speech communities. Dorian's results for East Sutherland Gaelic support the claim that this may be a characteristic of declining speech communities. The notion of linguistic variation in declining speech communities which is not the result of language death is not overtly discussed in many studies of the phenomenon, probably because many fieldworkers have worked with very small samples in a single locale. More large-scale studies of non-urban speech communities, both healthy and declining, are clearly needed.

Notes

I am grateful to Gary Butler, Nancy Dorian, and Lesley Milroy for helpful suggestions on this chapter. An earlier version was presented at Sociolinguistics Symposium 6, University of Newcastle-upon-Tyne, April 1986.

1. As Fasold (1984:217) notes, it does not appear that any of these features, separately or together, are accurate predictors of language death, but they do tend to be associated with language death situations.
2. Up until the late 1970s, only fragmentary descriptions of Newfoundland French (written by nonlinguists) had appeared in print. For an overview of recent work, see King (in press b).
3. Only ten older informants were interviewed in Stephenville/Kippens since no younger informants could be found. In La Grand'Terre problems arose due to the surprisingly small number of older informants available. Only eight older informants could be interviewed. Kippens and Maisons d'Hiver adjoin Stephenville and L'Anse-à-Canards respectively and have virtually the same settlement patterns. No inter-community variation was found which could be attributed to geography.

10 The social functions of relativization in obsolescent and non-obsolescent languages

JANE H. HILL

1. Introduction

Reduction in the frequency of relative clauses in the usage of speakers in late stages of language death has been identified in languages of diverse genetic and typological affiliations: Cupeño and Luiseño (Hill 1973, 1978), Trinidad Bhojpuri (Durbin 1973), Tübatulabal (Voegelin and Voegelin 1977b), East Sutherland Gaelic (Dorian 1981, 1982b), and Dyirbal (Schmidt 1985c).[1] Relative clauses, along with other complex sentence phenomena, have also been reported as absent in pidgin languages, developing only upon creolization of a pidgin (Sankoff and Brown 1976). Low frequencies of complex sentences have been identified also in working-class (as opposed to middle-class) usage in British English (Bernstein 1972), American English (Wolfram 1969), and French (Lindenfeld 1972). Van den Broeck (1977) identified the phenomenon in some speech contexts for working-class varieties of Flemish. A low rate of relativization in oral, as opposed to written, language in Western languages has also been frequently noted (see Chafe 1982). Romaine (1981) found lower rates of relativization associated with more intimate, as opposed to more formal, written styles of Middle Scots. The identification of a similar pattern of change or differentiation in such a variety of contexts challenges us to develop a unified functional explanation. Such an explanation would be new support for a widely shared intuition that the processes of change in language death are differentiated from ordinary change processes primarily by their rapidity (Dorian 1981; Schmidt 1985c).

Benveniste (1971) called relative clauses "syntactic adjectives"; Foley (1980) has pointed out that they are the "most sentential" noun complements. Unlike adjectives, participles, and gerunds, relative clauses include tensed verbs. This property of relative clauses permits them to realize the same type of propositional content that can appear in a matrix sentence.

149

Hence, sentences with relative clauses can contain the highest informational density of any complex sentence type.

Amplification of propositional content can, of course, be accomplished simply by stringing together simple sentences. The difference between this strategy and the strategy of relativization lies primarily in the fact that relativization is "decontextualizing". In strings of simple sentences, topic continuity must be accomplished through ostensive deictic reference or through discourse-level conventions. In relativization, however, topic continuity is accomplished syntactically, either by equideletion or, in languages of the "pronominal argument" type (Jelinek 1984; Jelinek and Demers 1985) which do not exhibit argument deletion under identity, by a constraint against the presence in relative clauses of adjunct nominals which are co-indexed with the head of the clause. Kalmar (1985) has suggested that relativization of the type found in pronominal argument languages (his example is Eskimo) may be associated with the absence of literacy, but a variety of de-contextualizing (or, in the terms of Tannen 1982a, "literate") phenomena appear in them, such as the relativizing suffixes of Navajo, the special relativizing aspect markers of Cupeño, and the disambiguating case markers of Warlpiri.

2.   Low rates of relativization: solidarity, simplification, or stigma?

Brown and Gilman's (1960) power–solidarity framework suggests a functional account of the relationship between the informational density and decontextualization permitted by relativization and the social contexts in which it occurs. They observed that in European languages the same pronouns – the "pronouns of power" – were used for addressing "up" to a more powerful interlocutor, and for addressing across high social distance. Conversely, another set of pronouns – the "pronouns of solidarity" – were used for addressing "down", to a less powerful interlocutor, and for addressing across low social distance. The contexts of solidarity are prototypically contexts in which interlocutors share a great deal of information. Conversely, the contexts of high social distance are prototypically contexts in which little information is shared. Languages often encode social distance with metaphors of physical distance (as in 3rd person pronouns used with addressees, or the honorific prefix *on-* 'away' of Mexicano), which suggest not only lack of shared information, but lack of shared deictic context as well. Because of the high-information, decontextualizing properties of relativization, we would then expect higher frequencies of the strategy where interlocutors are not intimate, and lower frequencies where intimacy is assumed. Brown and Gilman's generalization suggests that the coding strategies which used high frequencies of relativization will be extended to contexts of "talking up", and strategies with low frequencies will be extended to "talking down". Under this general theory, I propose that the social feature which is shared in all the situations noted above where low rates of relativization have been noted – language death, pidginization, certain working-class registers, and face-to-face oral communication as opposed to written communication – is an assumption of low social distance and low power differential between interlocutors, with low relativization being an important aspect of the "audience design" (Bell 1984) which will index this assumption. I refer to this type of audience design as "solidarity coding".

I would suggest that solidarity coding exists in at least two forms, which I would term "defensive" and "cooperative". In defensive solidarity, the speaker uses a coding strategy of low informational specificity and high context dependency in order to exclude an interlocutor who does not in fact share the information or the context. In cooperative solidarity coding, the level of specificity is low precisely because interlocutors do share (or wish to appear to share) knowledge of information and of context. Defensive solidarity coding may be common in working-class usage in complex societies. An example is that described for working-class Flemish speakers speaking to a middle-class interviewer by Van den Broeck (1977, 1984). The normal rates of relativization which Van den Broeck found when these speakers conversed with peers suggest that cooperative solidarity strategies need not involve reduction of relativization (or perhaps that the strategy in play while Van den Broeck was observing did not emphasize solidarity). Many published findings about working-class usage based on interviews with middle-class researchers may turn out to be descriptions of defensive solidarity strategies

Solidarity coding of both types may be the most important usages in the substratum language in language shift. Cooperative solidarity coding is likely to dominate usage in a small, homogeneous community such as that described by Dorian (1981) for East Sutherland Gaelic. Cooperative solidarity coding deriving from the fact that the language is normally used between intimates may be amplified by the assignment to its registers of a general symbolic value of "intimacy". Gumperz (1982) emphasized that the substratum language often comes to stand for the "we", while the superstratum language symbolizes the "other", the "they". Defensive solidarity coding is likely where the community speaking the substratum language suffers economic oppression, or where its identity is stigmatized, as is very frequently the case in the language death context (Dressler 1982). While defensive and cooperative solidarity clearly differ in their social purpose, they can both be encoded by the low-information, high-context strategy of reduction in frequency of relativization.

Low relativization rates in usage in dying languages might, of course, have sources other than as an aspect of solidarity coding. Change in a substratum language in language shift may, for instance, be due to assimilation to the superstratum. Such an explanation is, however, inappropriate in the case of reduction in the frequency of relativization, since presumably usages in any superstratum language would have a normal frequency of relative clauses, and thus could not provide a model for a reduction in frequency in substratum usage.[2]

A second, more likely, hypothesis is that the decrease in the frequency of complex sentences in favor of simple sentences might be one aspect of a more general process of simplification taking place in a dying language, due to imperfect acquisition. Several authors have now shown that morphologically and phonologically marked constructions tend to become unstable in dying languages (Dressler 1972 and Dorian 1973 are the pioneering publications on this point). In many languages, relative clauses are a marked clause type. For instance, in English relative clauses do not exhibit the usual pronominal anaphora, but instead have special relative pronouns. In Cupeño the verbs in relative clauses are inflected differently for tense/aspect than the verbs in main clauses. Where a language permits relativization only high on the accessibility hierarchy, NPs must be promoted into a relativizable case; Schmidt (1985c) has shown that speakers of "young people's Dyirbal" find such constructions especially difficult. (Dorian [1986c] has pointed out, however, the necessity for caution in evaluating situations where poor speakers have difficulty with complex constructions. In East Sutherland Gaelic she found that even fluent speakers had difficulty with prepositional possessive relative clauses.) If relative clauses are a complex and marked clause type, they might be lost in a learning context where children acquiring a dying language are not exposed to adequate adult models. Such inadequate acquisition has also been suggested as one of the roots of the simplification processes associated with the formation of pidgins, particularly in recent work by Bickerton (1981, 1984a). However, while such a hypothesis about the reduction of relative clause frequency is attractive for dying languages and pidgins, it clearly is inappropriate in the case of the working-class varieties of major world languages, for presumably the processes of language acquisition in children are provided with normal input in these contexts. Also, of course, it does not account for the oral–written difference, style differences (as in Romaine's Middle Scots case), or for those cases of language shift where the relativization strategies in the subordinate language are extremely simple, as in Mexicano (Nahuatl), to be discussed below.

A third hypothesis is that the reduction in frequency of relative clauses is part of a general reduction in frequency of what Labov (1972a) has called "evaluation" – discourse material which answers the question, "What is the point?" Labov (1972a) has included relative clauses, along with adjectives and other attributive markers, in his discussion of the evaluative techniques which he calls "correlative". Since, as Dressler (1982) proposed, one of the reasons that languages die is that they become stigmatized through association with the stigmatized identity of their speakers, discourses uttered in a stigmatized substratum language might themselves acquire stigmatization, and be felt by their speakers to be relatively "pointless" and unworthy of evaluation compared to discourses in the superstratum language. We might, then, expect a reduction in relativization frequency to be part of a more widespread reduction in the rate of correlative evaluation, so that frequency of other correlative evaluators such as adjectives would also decline. Unlike the hypothesis of imperfect acquisition leading to simplification, the hypothesis that frequency of relativization will be reduced because evaluation in general is being reduced may be relevant to the case of working-class usage as well as to usage in language death. Working-class speakers of Western European languages with middle-class norms for "standard" usage are often quite sensitive about their speech. Since Labov has found that narratives by working-class speakers can be richly evaluated, the hypothesis should not be advanced to account for the working-class case without very careful qualification. Nonetheless, it is clearly attractive.

3.   Relativization in Cupeño and Mexicano

In this chapter, I will examine evidence from two Uto-Aztecan languages, Cupeño in Southern California and Mexicano (Nahuatl) of central Mexico, substratum languages in shifts to English and Spanish respectively. I will test the three hypotheses advanced above, that relativization rates are reduced due to (i) imperfect acquisition by speakers and consequent simplification, (ii) reduction of evaluation in a stigmatized language, and (iii) a speaker strategy of cooperative or defensive solidarity. Data from Cupeño do not support the first two hypotheses, and are inadequate to test the third, but data from Mexicano do support the third hypothesis, and also hint that there may be some support for the second.

Voegelin and Voegelin (1977b) presented evidence that loss of relativization in Tübatulabal, a Uto-Aztecan language of California, was the result of imperfect acquisition by the last generation of speakers. The usage of the last speakers of Cupeño, which is distantly related to Tübatulabal, would appear also to be an excellent candidate for an account in these terms, since the difference between relative clauses and main clauses in Cupeño is quite highly marked, and the morphological details of the different types of relativization are complex. The single example in (1) must suffice for the present discussion (a fuller treatment can be found in Hill and Nolasquez 1973; Jacobs 1975; Hill 1978).

(1) Mukut   pem-em   wen-t-im
    and then   they-3PL.AUX   lie-COMP.PRES-PL

    patish-pem-yax-we
    swell-they-NONVOLITIONAL-PRES.PL

    'And then the ones who are lying there are swollen up'

Here, the verb in the relative clause, *wentim* 'they are lying' is marked with a special suffix for present tense in complement clauses, *-(e)t*, and with a plural found with this suffix (and also on nouns), *-im*. This contrasts with the marking for the same tense/aspect and number on the matrix verb *patish-pemyaxwe* 'they are swollen up', which exhibits the present plural suffix *-we*, and is also marked for 3rd person plural subject by the suffix *-pem*.

While the Cupeño relativization markings are complex, Roscinda Nolasquez, a Cupeño speaker who exhibits a very low frequency of relativization in running speech (Hill 1973, 1978) appears to control the morphology of this clause type fully. She was the principal informant for Jacobs' (1975) study of relativization in the language. What we observe in Miss Nolasquez's speech is usage, not competence. Indeed, there is no evidence for disruption in her acquisition of Cupeño; Miss Nolasquez did not speak English until she was in her early teens.[3]

Data from Mexicano also fail to support the hypothesis of simplification due to inadequate acquisition, since in Mexicano, reduction in frequency of relativization is accompanied, diachronically speaking, by increasing complexity in the marking of the relative clause. Mexicano during the "Classical" period of the language (including texts collected through about 1580) exhibited a relative clause type typical of pronominal–argument languages, in which relativizing elements were simply adjoined to main elements without any morphological modification of the tensed relative-clause verbs, with no deletion under identity of arguments (although there was a prohibition on adjunct nominals identical to the head) and without relative pronouns (an account of the form of Mexicano relative clauses can be found in Hill and Hill 1980).

In modern Mexicano, a more "syntactic" type of relativization has appeared, almost certainly due to contact with Spanish (Hill and Hill 1980). In this new type, the most notable innovation is a set of relative pronouns. Speakers use relative clauses of the Spanish type alongside relative clauses of the Mexicano type. An example of the two types used in a single sentence is seen in (2):

(2) Pues,   cateh   persónahtin   āquin   cmatih
    well   there.are   person-PL   WHO-PROX   3SG OBJ-know-PL

    tlahtōzqueh,   persōnas   cpiah   ocachi   edād
    speak-IRR-FUT   person-PL   3SG OBJ-have-PL   more   age

    'Well, there are people who know how to speak, people who are older'

In the first relative clause a Mexicano indefinite noun *āquin* 'someone' is being used as a relative pronoun; it is a loan translation of Spanish *que*. The second relative clause lacks such a relativizer; the verb in this clause, *cpiah* 'they have it', is inflected in the same way as when it appears as a matrix clause verb (as are the verbs in the first relative clause).

Thus, while many modern speakers of Mexicano exhibit a very low frequency of relativization, this is accompanied not by grammatical simplification, but by increasing grammatical complexity, both in the larger number of options available for the formation of relative clauses, and in the innovation of a more marked clause type. In summary, in neither Cupeño nor Mexicano do we have evidence that reduction in frequency of relativization is the result of inadequate acquisition.

4.   The Cupeño evidence

The second major hypothesis is that relative clause frequency is reduced as part of an overall reduction in the rate of correlative evaluation in narrative discourse, perhaps due to stigmatization of the language. This hypothesis may be tested by comparing the rate of correlative evaluation in different speakers, who represent different stages either in real time (the case for our Cupeño data) or in apparent time (the Mexicano case). Relative clauses and adjectives are the two most important correlative evaluators. If the hypothesis of reduced evaluation is correct, then we should find that speakers are reducing adjective frequency as well a relative clause frequency, yielding an overall reduction in correlative evaluation.

In Cupeño, I counted relative clauses[4] and adjectives in a major text, the creation myth, which was recorded in 1920 by Paul-Louis Faye from an unknown speaker, and in 1962 from Roscinda Nolasquez. Both versions appear in Hill and Nolasquez (1973). The 1920 speaker used a far higher frequency of relativization than did Miss Nolasquez, as shown in Table 1. This difference replicates the finding on a larger group of texts reported in Hill (1973, 1978).

Miss Nolasquez's reduction in frequency of relativization does not appear to be part of a reduction in total correlative evaluation. This is seen when we examine the frequency of adjectives and relative clauses in the texts. When we compare the frequency of adjectives with the frequency of relative clauses in the two versions of the creation myth, we can see that there was a

Table 1. *Proportion of relative clauses to total T-unit[a] in the Cupeño creation myth*

T-unit	Rel. clause	Other	Total
1920 speaker	31	355	386
1962 speaker	9	353	362

Chi square = 10.97 $p < 0.01$

[a] T-units are units which include each matrix verb, and all clauses subordinate to it.

Table 2. *Proportion of adjectives to relative clauses in the Cupeño creation myth*

	Adjectives	Rel. clauses
1920 speaker	18	31
1962 speaker	26	9

Chi square = 11.59   p <0.001

Table 3. *Proportion of total correlative evaluation (adjectives and relative clauses) to total T-unit in the Cupeño ceation myth*

T-unit	Total evaluation	Other	Total
1920 speaker	49	337	386
1962 speaker	35	327	362

Chi square = 1.46 (NS)

change in the proportion of relative clauses compared to adjectives. Apparently, Miss Nolasquez compensated for her reduction in relativization frequency, keeping total correlative evaluation at the same level as that of the 1920 text by increasing her frequency of adjectives. This can be seen in Table 2 and Table 3. Table 2 shows that Miss Nolasquez used significantly more adjectives compared to relative clauses than the 1920 speaker; Table 3 shows that total correlative evaluation frequency is not significantly different between the two texts.

This evidence suggests that the reduction in relativization seen in Roscinda Nolasquez's speech is not part of an overall reduction in evaluation. Apparently she felt that the recitation of the creation myth, even in a language which was disappearing, still "had a point". Indeed, there is no evidence that she felt that discourses in Cupeño lacked value. To the contrary, Roscindo Nolasquez has been a leader in the movement to maintain the Cupeño language in her community.

5.   The Mexicano evidence

We have found that it is unlikely that reduction in relativization in the usage of Roscinda Nolasquez, one of the last speakers of Cupeño, is due either to imperfect acquisition or to reduction in total correlative evaluation. We cannot, however, test in Cupeño the hypothesis that reduction in relativization is an aspect of solidarity coding; the data are inadequate for such an investigation. For such a test we must turn to Mexicano, a Uto-Aztecan language spoken in central Mexico. The analysis presented here is conducted on narrative texts which were collected as part of a sociolinguistic survey of Mexicano-speaking communities in the region of the Malinche Volcano in the states of Tlaxcala and Puebla in Central Mexico (Hill and Hill 1986). The narratives include both traditional stories and accounts of personal experience.

It is first necessary to show that a process of reduction in frequency of relativization is indeed occurring in Malinche Mexicano.[5] In order to do this, I must briefly discuss two major types of Mexicano speakers which Kenneth Hill and I have identified in the course of work on the Malinche. We label them according to how they use the Mexicano honorific system, but they differ on many other indices (Hill and Hill 1986). *Narrow-honorific* speakers use honorific verbs in a relatively restricted range of environments compared to *broad-honorific* speakers. Narrow-honorific speakers are overwhelmingly factory workers, compared to broad-honorific speakers, who are overwhelmingly cultivators. Narrow-honorific speakers tend to be very purist about the Mexicano language. Most importantly for the present discussion, narrow-honorific speakers exhibit a sharp functional split between the two languages in their bilingual repertoire. They use Mexicano primarily as a conversational "solidarity code": by using Mexicano, instead of Spanish, they make a claim on important economic resources which are distributed through systems of reciprocity operating in the Malinche towns. Narrow-honorific speakers use Spanish primarily as a "power code", shifting into that language when they talk about "public" matters in a wide range of contexts.

In contrast to narrow-honorific speakers, broad-honorific speakers use honorific verbs across a full range of environments, and do not exhibit functional split of their bilingual repertoire into a language of solidarity and a language of power. Like the narrow-honorific speakers, they are bilingual in Spanish, but they use this language primarily outside their home communities. Within the communities, their power code is not Spanish, but a highly hispanicized Mexicano. A less hispanicized register functions as a solidarity code for these speakers. Narrow-honorific speakers are more advanced toward Spanish in the language shift ongoing in the Malinche region. This advance is apparently accompanied by a reduction in the frequency of relative clauses in their usage, compared to that of broad-honorific speakers. This reduction is significant for both male and female speakers (female speakers, who participate in the social organization of the Malinche in different roles from male speakers, show a number of differences from male usage [Hill 1987], and so are counted separately in this analysis). The frequencies are shown in Tables 4 and 5.

These differences in rate of relativization are not due to imperfect acquisition. The syntax of relativization indigenous to Mexicano is very simple: relative clauses are exactly like matrix clauses except that they cannot contain adjunct nominals identical to the adjunct nominal which

Table 4. *Proportion of relative clauses to total T-unit in Mexicano narrative texts (male speakers)*

T-unit	Rel. clause	Other	Total
Narrow-honorific speakers	42	546	588
Broad-honorific speakers	44	307	351

Chi square = 7.39   p <0.02

Table 5. *Proportion of relative clauses to total T-unit in Mexicano narrative texts (female speakers)*

T-Unit	Rel. clause	Other	Total
Narrow-honorific speakers	42	625	667
Broad-honorific speakers	28	201	229

Chi square = 9.17   p <0.02

represents the head NP of the clause. In addition, narrow-honorific speakers are not necessarily "worse" speakers of Mexicano than broad-honorific speakers. Some narrow-honorific speakers are superb speakers of Mexicano, and many are Mexicano-dominant bilinguals. Thus, their low frequency of use of relative clauses, compared to broad-honorific speakers, is not due to simplification of their Mexicano. Even very bad Mexicano speakers control the syntactic means to form relative clauses, because they can simply calque on Spanish models, as shown in example (2) above. Such calquing is entirely acceptable as "speaking *mexicano*" in the Malinche communities.

While reduction in relative clause frequency among narrow-honorific speakers is not related to imperfect acquisition, there is some evidence in support of the hypothesis that reduced relativization frequency is part of a general reduction in correlative evaluation, at least among male speakers. Narrow-honorific men are almost always wage workers who spend a good deal of time in non-Mexicano-speaking environments, and they are thoroughly exposed to the stigmatization of Indian identity, even though they are often the most insistent of all speakers about the value of Mexicano (broad-honorific women are the most likely to admit to negative attitudes about Mexicano [Hill and Hill 1986; Hill 1987]). In contrast, broad-honorific speakers are cultivators and members of their families who have comparatively less experience with the world outside their home communities, and may be less vulnerable to the effects of stigmatization (although no person who lives on the Malinche is in any way "isolated", since the region is highly accessible to major urban centers by excellent public transpor-

Table 6. *Proportion of adjectives and relative clauses in Mexicano narratives (male speakers)*

	Adjectives	Rel. clauses
Narrow-honorific speakers	44	42
Broad-honorific speakers	27	44

Chi square = 2.70 (NS)

Table 7. *Proportion of total correlative evaluation to total T-unit in Mexicano narratives (male speakers)*

T-unit	Total evaluation	Other	Total
Narrow-honorific speakers	86	502	588
Broad-honorific speakers	71	280	351

Chi square = 4.75   p <0.05

Table 8. *Proportion of adjectives and relative clauses in Mexicano narratives (female speakers)*

	Adjectives	Rel. clauses
Narrow-honorific speakers	50	42
Broad-honorific speakers	14	28

Chi square = 5.1   p <0.05

tation, and all members of the Malinche communities are frequent visitors to the cities).

The relationship between adjectives and relative clauses for male speakers is shown in Table 6. There has been no shift in evaluation strategy from relative clauses to adjectives by narrow-honorific men. However the figures for total correlative evaluation, shown in Table 7, show that there has been a slight but significant reduction in total correlative evaluation by these speakers.

The reduction in total correlative evaluation does not appear among narrow-honorific female speakers. In contrast to the men, these women are shifting their evaluation strategy in a pattern similar to that shown above for the Cupeño speaker, using significantly more adjectives in relation to relative clauses than their broad-honorific counterparts. This can be seen in Table 8. The high rate of adjectivalization is not the result of the use of more Spanish adjectives due to the more hispanicized speech of narrow-honorific

Table 9. *Proportion of total correlative evaluation to total T-unit in Mexicano narratives (female speakers)*

	Total evaluation	Other	Total
Narrow-honorific speakers	92	575	667
Broad-honorific speakers	42	187	229

Chi-square = 3.62 (NS)

women; narrow- and broad-honorific women use equal proportions of Spanish and Mexicano adjectives, with both favoring the latter.

Narrow-honorific women, unlike narrow-honorific men, are not significantly different from their broad-honorific counterparts in total correlative evaluation, as can be seen in Table 9.

In the case of Cupeño, we were able to rule out the conclusion that reduction in relative clause frequency is the result of disrupted acquisition or of reduced attention to evaluation. In the case of Mexicano, we are able also to test the third hypothesis, that relative clause frequency will be reduced in the solidarity-code register of a language, as opposed to the power-code register. I have noted above that many lines of investigation suggest that narrow-honorific speakers have a fairly strict functional split between the two languages in their repertoire, with Mexicano being the language of the solidarity code, and Spanish the language of the power code. We have already shown that their Mexicano usage shows a reduced frequency of relativization compared to the Mexicano of broad-honorific speakers. If the third hypothesis is correct, their Spanish should show an elevated frequency of relative clauses. In fact, this is precisely the result of an analysis of the Spanish usage of male speakers.

Since the interviews for the sociolinguistic survey of the Malinche communities were conducted in Mexicano, my sample of Spanish narrative usage is largely an accidental one. In some interviews, subjects switched into Spanish for fairly long stretches of text. I have also collected a few narrative texts and done some ethnographic interviewing in Spanish. The Spanish sample comes from all these sources, and represents the usage of three narrow-honorific men, two broad-honorific men, and two broad-honorific women. While the sample is small, the results of analysis of it are quite consistent with the hypothesis that rate of relativization is associated with coding strategy.

First, we find that narrow-honorific men use a significantly higher proportion of relative clauses in Spanish than do broad-honorific men. This pattern reverses the distribution for Mexicano usage, seen in Table 4. The pattern for Spanish is seen in Table 10.

Second, we find that when we compare Spanish to Mexicano usage,

Table 10. *Proportion of relative clauses to total T-unit in Spanish usage by male speakers*

T-unit	Rel. clause	Other	Total
Narrow-honorific speakers	25	50	75
Broad-honorific speakers	30	142	172

Chi square = 6.73   p <0.05

Table 11. *Proportion of relative clause to total T-unit for narrow-honorific male speakers in Spanish vs. Mexicano*

T-unit	Rel. clause	Other	Total
Narrow-honorific Spanish	25	50	75
Narrow-honorific Mexicano (narrative sample)	42	546	588

Chi square = 48.32   p <0.001

Table 12. *Proportion of relative clauses to total T-unit for broad-honorific male speakers in Spanish vs. Mexicano*

T-unit	Rel. clause	Other	Total
Broad-honorific Spanish	30	142	172
Broad-honorific Mexicano	44	307	351

Chi square = 1.90 (NS)

narrow-honorific men show a conspicuously higher rate of relativization in the former than in the latter. The figures for narrow-honorific men can be seen in Table 11. Table 11 shows a sharp reversal in relative clause frequency between the two languages, consistent with the hypothesis that Spanish for these speakers constitutes a power code, while Mexicano is primarily the language of solidarity coding.

In contrast to the findings for narrow-honorific men, when we examine the usage of broad-honorific men we do not find any significant differences in relativization in the two languages. Data on broad-honorific men are shown in Table 12. When relativization rates in both languages are compared for both groups of speakers, there is no significant difference, as is shown in Table 13.

I do not have sufficient data on narrow-honorific female speakers to determine whether or not they also exhibit high frequencies of relativization in Spanish. I do, however, have data on broad-honorific women, which

Table 13. *Relativization rates for both languages combined, narrow-honorific vs. broad-honorific male speakers*

T-unit	Rel. clause	Other	Total
Narrow-honorific men	67	596	663
Broad-honorific men	76	449	523

Chi square = 1.58 (NS)

Table 14. *Proportion of relative clauses to total T-unit for broad-honorific female speakers in Spanish vs. Mexicano*

T-unit	Rel. clause	Other	Total
Spanish (n = 2)	37	291	328
Mexicano (narrative sample)	28	201	229

Chi square = 0.23 (NS)

suggests that, like their male counterparts, they do not have any functional split between the two languages. These data are shown in Table 14.

In summary, in Mexicano-speaking communities, narrow-honorific men, who are precisely those speakers who can be shown, on independent grounds, to exhibit a distinct function split between a solidarity-coding Mexicano and a power-coding Spanish, exhibit an equally distinctive reversal of relative clause frequency. Their Spanish usage exhibits a high frequency of relativization compared to their Mexicano, and a high frequency of relativization compared to the Spanish usage of broad-honorific men. No broad-honorific speaker exhibits a comparable differentiation between the two languages. These findings are consistent with the hypothesis that rate of relativization is associated with the continuum of coding between solidarity and power.

6.   Conclusion

In conclusion, an examination of rates of relativization in two Uto-Aztecan languages, Cupeño and Mexicano, has failed to support hypotheses that reduced rates of relativization in substratum languages in language shift are always due to imperfect acquisition or to the failure of speakers to evaluate narrative in a stigmatized language, although the latter appears to be contributing to the reduction in rate of relativization in Mexicano discourse by narrow-honorific men. Data for Mexicano support the hypothesis that reduced rates of relativization in language death may be associated with the role of the substratum in solidarity coding. The variation in the language death situation is, then, parallel with coding variability in "normal" languages.

The Mexicano data are particularly interesting, because they show that there is no overall loss of stylistic options among these speakers. A full range of coding strategies is retained, but it is distributed across two languages instead of one. Another important feature of the Mexicano situation is that Mexicano is part of a syncretic system which has developed over several hundred years. Convergence between Mexicano and Spanish in the system allows speakers to shift back and forth between the two languages with little difficulty, so that a coding strategy using high relativization can be constituted in Mexicano, even by a poor speaker of the language, simply by calquing on Spanish syntax.

These results suggest that further exploration of the role of complex syntax in solidarity coding may enable us to better understand the relationship of change processes in language death to general processes of language change, and is likely to contribute importantly to our understanding of the functional foundations of language use.

Notes

Research on Cupeño was funded by the Survey of California Indian Languages and by the Penrose Fund of the American Philosophical Society. Research on Mexicano was supported by the National Endowment for the Humanities (NEH-RO-20495-74-572), the American Council of Learned Societies, the Phillips Fund of the American Philosophical Society, and by a sabbatical leave from Wayne State University.

1. It should be noted that reductions in the frequency of other complex sentence types have been reported from dying languages, both in the work cited above and in other work (for instance, the findings by Tsitsipis [1984] that gerunds and subjunctive subordination are disappearing in Arvanítika, an obsolescent variety of Albanian spoken in Greece). The present chapter deals only with relative clauses.

2. Dorian (pers. comm.) points out that influence on relativization rates by the superstratum language might occur in the kind of case described by Bloomfield (1927), of a speaker of Menomini who "spoke no language tolerably". Such a speaker, who might not control the relativization techniques of the superstratum language, might thereby conclude on the basis of this faulty model of the prestige code that relativization rates should be low. A similar situation might occur where the only variety of the superstratum accessible to members of the subordinate community is a "foreigner talk" variety.

3. Dorian (pers. comm.) points out that even where acquisition in childhood is uninterrupted, a speaker who has been unable to use a language regularly throughout adulthood may display language attrition. It is difficult to reconstruct with precision Miss Nolasquez's linguistic biography. She was in an English-speaking boarding school for two or three years during her teens, but lived

otherwise in communities where Cupeño and the closely-related Luiseño and Cahuilla were spoken. In 1962 Miss Nolasquez still spoke Cupeño fairly regularly with several other elderly people who also lived in the town of Pala. Miss Nolasquez died February 4 1987, in Pala, California, at the age of 94.

4. Strictly speaking, what is counted for the Cupeño creation myth is all subordinate clauses bearing sentential marking (with exceptions as noted below), since relative clauses are indistinguishable formally from other sentential complements. I have not counted sentential complements embedded under the verbs meaning 'to want' and 'to be possible'; these complement expressions were, in fact, used at a high frequency by Roscinda Nolasquez. But they are not notionally definable as relative clauses, although they use the same morphology.

5. Knab (1978) observed a reduction in frequency of relativization in Mexicano speech in the hinterlands of Cholula, on the other side of the Valley of Puebla from the Malinche region.

II
Focus on structure

11 Problems in obsolescence research: the Gros Ventres of Montana

ALLAN R. TAYLOR

Linguistic researchers who find themselves working with severely contracting speaker groups may begin with entirely different interests and objectives, yet very likely soon find themselves confronted by intriguing linguistic and sociolinguistic phenomena which turn up in the process of their investigations.

In theory, if the group is of sufficient size at the start of the investigation and the contraction of the linguistic community is gradual, there may be time and evidence enough to identify some of the phenomena early on and to observe their development. If the group is already small, its membership not entirely clearcut, and its further contraction rapid, then the researcher's observations are likely to be more tantalizing and suggestive than full and conclusive, and the fieldwork and research problems will be compounded. The latter is the case with many diminishing Native American languages, including the one reported on here.

In this chapter I will describe several different sociolinguistic and structural aspects of Gros Ventre[1] obsolescence. In passing, I will also refer to various problems which had to be confronted in the course of the research.

What I know about Gros Ventre obsolescence has been discovered largely by accident, and comes from random aberrant forms which have turned up in my fieldnotes, from remarks made by my informants about the speech of others, and from my own observations of life and personal relations on the reservation. I must admit, however, that some of what I claim rests on rather slim evidence, and may prove eventually to be erroneous or better explained in other ways. In other cases I believe that future research will bear out my present conjectures. I present the paper, therefore, as a preliminary statement on Gros Ventre obsolescence and a starting point for future research on the twilight of this Plains Algonquian language.

1.   Problems in group identification

The Gros Ventres Indians live on the Fort Belknap Indian Reservation in Blaine County, Montana. This is one of the northern tier of counties in the state; as such, the northern county line is also the international boundary between the United States and Canada. The northern boundary of the Reservation is the Milk River; the agency is located on the river, an artifact of the days when transportation in this part of the world was by boat. The nearest town off of the reservation is Harlem; the nearest large town is Havre, approximately 50 miles to the west.

Also living on the Fort Belknap Reservation is an Assiniboine-speaking tribe, one of several Assiniboine groups in Montana and the Canadian provinces of Alberta and Saskatchewan. The Assiniboines are a Siouan tribe whose language belongs to the Dakota branch of the Siouan family. The Fort Belknap Reservation is very close to the territories which both the Gros Ventres and the Assiniboines claimed before they were overwhelmed by Euroamericans around the middle of the nineteenth century.[2]

The language of the Gros Ventres is closely related to Arapaho, of which it has traditionally been considered a dialect.[3] Two of the four known Arapaho dialects are now extinct; the surviving dialects, Gros Ventre and Arapaho Proper, are themselves now obsolescent.

There are at the present time several hundred persons who are enrolled as Gros Ventres, but the designation can be largely meaningless today, since most persons on the reservation are of mixed descent. In addition to their Gros Ventre and Assiniboine ancestry, local people can also claim Euroamerican descent as well as some ancestry from such nearby Indian groups as Piegan, Cree, Chippewa, and Crow.

In order to be enrolled at the Fort Belknap Agency, an individual must be of at least one-quarter "tribal blood". This rule was adopted in 1968. This means that anyone who is at least one-quarter Gros Ventre, one-quarter Assiniboine, or one-eighth of each, can be enrolled under the Fort Belknap Agency. Where Gros Ventre and Assiniboine ancestry are equal, the individual (more properly, the individual's caretakers) designate one as the official affiliation. I do not know what basis, if any, is used for choice in the ambiguous cases. Quite likely the major influence is the psychological identity of the person who chooses. This probably depends to a great extent on persons in the kin group with whom the subject was most intimate: their affiliation would most likely be chosen. As of February 1986, there were 2,717 enrolled Gros Ventres and 1,997 enrolled Assiniboines.

Before the adoption of the blood quantum rule, especially in the early reservation period, persons not of Gros Ventre descent (especially French Crees) were enrolled as tribal members eligible to receive all benefits, such as allotment in severalty.[4] Reservation families of such foreign background are still regarded as not quite Gros Ventre, and their enrollment is still resented by some.

Residential patterns on the reservation are quite mixed, so that while many Gros Ventres live in the Hays community, and many Assiniboines live a short distance away in the Lodge Pole community, there are persons who identify with the other tribe in each of these communities. At the other (north) end of the reservation, around the agency, residence is completely mixed.[5]

All of the Fort Belknap people share a common reservation culture, which is a blend of historical Plains Indian and historical and contemporary Euroamerican elements. While most aspects of daily life on the reservation have been molded by more than a century of intense assimilative pressure from the American administration, they nevertheless do not lack indications of Indian identity, first and foremost of which is residence on a reservation. Uniquely Indian cultural traits are also abundant: "feeds" (traditional feasts) and "give-aways" (a public honoring ceremony, such as a naming, a memorial service for a dead person, or the return of a son or daughter from military service, when property such as blankets or quilts are given away) are frequent, and kinship networks are extensive and strong. Traditional Indian music[6] and dance are thriving, with several reservation groups, including one from Hays, the predominantly Gros Ventre settlement on the reservation. There is a well-attended annual powwow.[7] Several nearby reservations provide still other opportunities to engage in traditional Indian activities and to fraternize with other Indian people. This is especially true of the Rocky Boy Reservation, a traditional Cree reservation which is only a few miles away.

What establishes Gros Ventre (as opposed to Indian) identity is, I suspect, a vexed question. I did not question people in this respect, but I would guess that Gros Ventre identity is established, apart from official enrollment, by membership in a Gros Ventre kin group: an individual is whatever his prominent ancestors and present kin group are. What kin are recognized serves quite well to separate the two Fort Belknap groups, since their kinship systems and associated customs differ in important ways. The Assiniboine kinship system, for example, recognizes more categories than does the Gros Ventre, defined by parameters (e.g. gender of the reference) unknown in the Gros Ventre system

2. Problems in speaker identification and evaluation

When I began new fieldwork on Gros Ventre in 1980 I knew that it would be difficult to find persons with thorough knowledge of the language, since even in 1960 it was clear that few speakers were left. English only is spoken by the overwhelming majority of reservation residents, regardless of their ancestry, although the English of the oldest Native American residents shows strong traces from the tribal language, especially when the speaker knows the Indian language. My principal informant, for example, whose first language was Gros Ventre, speaks English with a strong Gros Ventre accent, although her understanding of English, and her fluency in the language, are excellent. Speakers who are not bilingual have several different kinds of English, depending on their backgrounds and identifications. This means that one can hear everything from US Standard English to an Indian creole, with the predominant variety being Montana rural nonstandard English.

Gros Ventre has not been any person's only, or even principal, language for at least forty years; for the community as a whole, this estimate of last principal use would have to be lengthened by an additional generation. Fewer than a dozen persons today retain relatively extensive knowledge of the language. Of those who claim to remember it, most admit that they could not express themselves fully in the language. The last person who was reputed to speak the language eloquently and correctly died in 1981; it is probably significant that his father was the last monolingual speaker of Gros Ventre. I never worked with this man, so I cannot corroborate the high reputation which he enjoyed locally as an accomplished speaker of Gros Ventre.

In the early 1960s I worked with several elderly men, each of whom was a fluent speaker of Gros Ventre. When I began the new fieldwork I had a list of persons regarded locally as good speakers, but no direct, personal knowledge of the competence of any of them. All of the persons were over 60 years of age, some well into their 80s. (Several of these people have since died.) By sampling the speaker pool one by one, I eventually discovered the best remaining speakers.[8]

Virtually all of my salvage work has been done with the half-dozen people whom I selected. Nevertheless, that even these people are not fully competent speakers is shown by their frequent gaps in knowledge, their hesitancy in many cases about the correctness of forms supplied by themselves or others, and by the fact that they occasionally produce competing or pseudoforms.[9]

Of all of these people, one woman has a control of the language which approaches that of the men I worked with earlier, and she has served as my principal informant in the dictionary research which I am doing. The others all have competence which ranges from fair to poor. I know of three or four others who are said to be speakers, but I have never worked with them, so I do not know the extent of their knowledge of Gros Ventre. One in particular would probably be a very good source of obsolescent Gros Ventre, since he told me that other speakers ridicule his efforts to speak the language. I have not yet been able to work with him, but I hope to eventually.

3.   **Problems arising from language attitudes accompanying functional restriction in language use**

Whether corrupt or not, knowledge of Gros Ventre is respected in the community, and prestige accrues to persons who possess some ability with the language, especially when it is accompanied by cultural knowledge which is perceived to be correct. Most persons who identify as Gros Ventre are also very interested in the language, and proud of its reputation as difficult. They love to point out to outsiders (and to Assiniboines) that Gros Ventre is the more difficult of the two languages – so difficult, in fact, that it "cannot be written", as can Assiniboine. Persons who have some knowledge of the language often talk about the language with each other; usually the conversation concerns how some particular thing was called in Gros Ventre, or how one would translate some English concept into Gros Ventre. If no one present can think of the proper Gros Ventre way of saying the item in question, someone usually promises to ask someone else who is believed to know. I was once present at such a session, and the discussion was lively. At that particular session there was a heavy emphasis on obsolete cultural concepts, and very few of the persons present could recall all of the associated words. Difficulty in recalling vocabulary is a function both of the age of speakers and of the fact that they now seldom think in the language. (I was often gratified by stumbling onto a term serendipitously which could not be obtained when I asked for it explicitly.)

The language seems to be used now mainly for demonstration or ritual purposes. For example, formal meetings (school committees, treaty committee, church activities, feasts) are opened by an invocation in Gros Ventre, usually by one particular, relatively well-educated man active in local affairs who is considered by most to be an authority on the Gros Ventre language. This man is also often asked to bestow Indian names on children at the annual summer powwow. These names, which must be given in a public ceremony, are by preference names which belonged to Gros Ventre persons when the tribe was still a functioning, independent entity. In the ceremonies which I have observed the name is given in Gros Ventre, together with its English translation. There is usually a short oration or prayer in Gros Ventre or English, and an explanation in English of why the name is a worthy one and why it is appropriate in the present case.

Such ceremonies are of great interest to the local people, as nearly as I can tell, because of the importance of possessing an authentic Indian name. I might add that the ceremonies are sometimes also a source of amusement to culturally or linguistically knowledgeable local people because of blunders made by people participating in the ceremonies – blunders which are presumed to be the result of ignorance of the language or of the relevant traditions. In one case that I know of, for example, the name chosen was a traditional woman's name, although the recipient child was male. This error seems to have escaped public notice; it was pointed out to me by an elderly full-blood, who mentioned it with a mixture of amusement and disgust.

Another example of the display of knowledge of Gros Ventre is in connection with the bilingual education project in the Hays-Lodgepole school. The bilingual teachers are to all intents actually monolingual speakers of English, reflecting the rather generous local definition of bilingual.[10] The linguistic content of the lessons comes from the teachers' aides, elders who *do* have knowledge of the language. The position of teacher's aide is a prestigious and well-paid one, and there is a great deal of vying for it and jealousy between the occupants and aspirants to the job. The role of the aide in this case is to supply Gros Ventre equivalents for specific English words. Usually the words refer to Indian culture in some way or to concept building (e.g. numbers), but some effort is spent also on teaching the children simplified versions of traditional Trickster narratives. Once practiced, these are recited at local school programs. Older persons who understand some of the language are immensely pleased when a child is able to say something which can be recognized.

I know of one additional use of Gros Ventre which is also an indication of the value which adheres in the community to knowledge of the language. This is getting together for the sole purpose of "visiting" in Gros Ventre. The person I mentioned above who is considered an authority on the language often does this. It keeps him in practice, and he learns new words and expressions from the persons he speaks with. My first informant in 1980 also did this a great deal. He had had a traditional upbringing on the reservation during the early years of this century, but had left the reservation as a young man in order to earn his livelihood. He settled in Butte, Montana, where he worked in the Anaconda copper mine. His wife was from Fort Belknap, but since she was a French Cree who did not speak Gros Ventre, he had few opportunities to practice the language, which he really regretted. After his retirement he often went back to the reservation to visit with other elderly persons who had better Gros Ventre than he did. He always took a tape-recorder with him and recorded the conversations, compiling in this way a kind of spoken lexicon, since he usually went equipped with a list in English of words for which he hoped to get Gros Ventre equivalents.

The older people, whether speakers or not, lament the imminent death of the language, and interest in my dictionary project has been rather high. There is a certain amount of skepticism also, since many do not believe that an outsider and non-Indian will be successful in writing their difficult language. Even when they are given a demonstration, they still remain doubtful; while they concede that I can read the terms back in a recognizable way, they fear that they themselves, or their children, will not be able to correctly pronounce words as I have transcribed them. Most feel that the best and only way to preserve a record of the language is to tape-record it.

This is essentially the approach which is being used in the bilingual project at the school.

While present-day Gros Ventres grieve for the loss of their language, it is nevertheless my impression that the previous generation anticipated the loss even more keenly. This may be because the present generation has grown up with the realization that the language is dying, but I believe that it is also because the Gros Ventre language has not been as much a part of their life as it was for earlier generations and that they do not link language and culture as closely as their ancestors did.

An interesting putative aspect of Gros Ventre obsolescence which I have reported on elsewhere[11] is the weakening of the traditional distinction between male and female pronunciation. The two slightly different phonologies are still recognized as characteristic of the two sexes, but they are at present unsupported by the traditional social roles of men and women. Words taught to children today may be in the form appropriate for the child's sex, but since women do not try to speak, or even claim to know, the male forms, and since most of the language aides in the school are female, most of the vocabulary given to children is in the female form. The consistent female usage of one of my elderly male informants, the retired miner, continues to puzzle me, for the gender-based difference must have been still quite strong during his childhood early in this century. Why he was allowed to grow up using female pronunciation is unknown to me, although I do not doubt that it is somehow connected with the accelerating cultural obsolescence of the early 1900s. It is probably significant that this man never gave any indication that he recognized that his speech was "unusual", and requests for evaluation of his usage from other speakers never once evoked any comment about his aberrant phonology. When his female pronunciation was then pointed out to these people, they acknowledged it, but still did not feel any need to comment on it.

Only once in my experience did a contemporary Gros Ventre speaker overtly acknowledge the existence of the two phonologies by codeswitching: one male informant began using female pronunciation at the beginning of our first work session. I stopped him immediately and asked him why he had done that. He replied that it was in order to make it easier for me. Whether this rested on an assumption that I was more familiar with female speech from long work with a female informant, or whether female speech was considered as more appropriate for children and cultural outsiders, I do not know.

4.   Structural problems in obsolescent languages

My chief interest in Gros Ventre obsolescence as a descriptive linguist has been in discovering which structures of the language have been affected, and the nature and direction of observable change.

The grammatical structure of Gros Ventre,[12] either viewed independently or in comparison with that of English, has a number of points where one would predict problems for the uncertain speaker. For some of these points I have actually recorded aberrant forms; for others, errors have not yet been found, although I expect eventually to encounter examples.

Noun morphology is rather complex in Algonquian languages. All nouns are inflected for gender and number, there being two of each. Animate nouns are also inflected for proximity (focus), and inanimate nouns for location. Some nouns are obligatorily inflected for possession, while the remainder have optional inflection for possession. Two different kinds of derivational morphology provide the two different kinds of stems. The derivation of compound stems is also complex, there being a special non-initial allomorph for many noun stems.

The other Gros Ventre grammatical category with complex morphology is verbs. The principal distinction in verbs is between those with one argument (intransitive) and those with two or more arguments (transitive). There are differences between these two categories, both in inflection and in the derivation of the stem. An additional complexity in Algonquian verbs is that modal notions, including negation and interrogation, as well as subordination, are expressed by different inflectional paradigms.

Most of the examples of what I believe to be obsolescence in the speech of semi-speakers I have worked with are the loss and/or replacement of structures, often through the operation of analogy. There are, nevertheless, several examples of phonological and syntactic change which also appear to be the result of obsolescence. In the remainder of this chapter I will give examples of the innovative morphology of several different Gros Ventre semi-speakers, including my principal informant. The errors in morphology which I have found all have to do with inflection and with incorrect stem derivation. Analogy, particularly paradigmatic leveling, has much to do with this, although the grammar and semantics of English also appear to be at work in some of the derivational errors.

In the following examples, the correct form of the example appears on the left, the incorrect on the right. The correctness of the left-hand form was established in a number of ways. In some cases, the form of the historical Algonquian prototype is known. In others, the correctness is presumed because of agreement on the form by more than one informant. Finally, violation of a well-known rule argues for the incorrectness of some of the forms on the right. Also given in some cases is an example of a paradigmatic form of the type presumed to have furnished the analogy for the incorrect form.

(1) *Correct form*   *Semi-speaker form*

        cʔíisikoh   'duck'   cʔíisikoh   'duck'

        cʔíisikóhoʔ 'ducks'   cʔíisikóuuh 'ducks'

	Compare:	ʔitétoh	'crane'
		ʔitétouuh	'cranes'
θéecʔi	'pine tree'	θéecʔi	'pine tree'
θéetoh	'pine trees'	θéeciih	'pine trees'
	Compare:	necʔi	'water'
		néciih	'waters'
		θéecííʔ	'pine tree'
		θéécíínoh	'pine trees'
	Compare:	ʔíiiʔ	'snow'
		ʔíiínoh	'snows'

In each of these cases, the wrong plural allomorph has been applied. The noun has been inflected in an appropriate paradigm, but all of the incorrect plural forms for 'pine tree' also include stem leveling toward the stem of the singular.

(2)	téʔyoonéh	'child'	téʔyoonóh	'child'
	téʔyoonóhoʔ	'children'	téʔyoonóhoʔ	'children'
	wóuʔúθeeʔ	'calf'	wóuʔúθeeʔ	'calf'
	wóuʔuθóónoh	'calves'	wóuʔuθéénoh	'calves'

In both of these cases, leveling has occurred between singular and plural stems. In the incorrect forms of 'child', the vowel of the diminutive suffix has been replaced in the singular by the vowel of the plural. The underlying form of the vowel is as in the correct singular form; in the correct plural, the surface vowel is the result of application of a vowel harmony rule. In the case of 'calf', a reverse analogy has taken place: the singular vowel of the medial suffix -θeeʔ-[13] has been extended into the plural, where the stem vowel should have harmonized with the vowel of the plural suffix, as in the correct forms of 'child'.

(3)	néekyékʔi	'my hand, arm'	néθeeʔ	'my arm'
	ʔíikyékʔi	'his hand, arm'	ʔíθeeʔ	'his arm'
		Compare:	binéesinéθeekʔi	'he has big arms'
			θoononéθeekʔi	'he has a stiff arm'

In (3) a correct medial noun suffix -θeeʔ- 'arm' has been inflected as if it were a dependent noun stem.[14] There *is* no dependent noun stem which has the unambiguous meaning 'arm': a single dependent stem means *either* 'hand' or 'arm'. The sharp English semantic distinction between 'hand' and 'arm' cannot be made lexically in Gros Ventre, so the bogus dependent noun stem created by the semi-speaker is probably the result of pressure from English semantic and lexical structure.

The same semi-speaker also created a dependent noun stem for 'face', -eeeθeʔ- (compare *néeeθʔe* 'my face'), a form rejected by all more competent speakers. The source for this creation is unknown; there is a medial noun stem of similar shape and meaning. The reason for the creation is again probably the structure of English: English has two morphemes, *face* and *eye*, which correspond to a single morpheme in Gros Ventre with both meanings.

(4) nesíiθeh   'my eye'   nebisíiθeh   'my eye'
         Compare: bisíiθeh   'someone's eye, an eye'

In (4) the semi-speaker has used a dependent noun stem already inflected for (indefinite) possession as a stem, adding a personal prefix before the personal prefix which is already present. English structure is again quite likely responsible here: any English noun can be marked for possession by the addition of a possessive adjective. Gros Ventre has no unmarked form for bodypart nouns: all take an obligatory possessive prefix. The indefinite possessed form of such nouns is as close to an unmarked form as is available.

(5) ʔibíiθékinoh   'his whiskers; whiskers'   bíiθéčinoh   'whiskers'

The mistake in (5) is an extremely subtle one. The stem is *-biiθ-eki-n-* 'hairy mouth'. Nouns which include a bodypart medial noun suffix (here -eki- 'mouth') are dependent, and require a possessive prefix, but the prefix cannot be that of an indefinite possessor. The form with the 3rd person prefix thus serves both as the marked form for the 3rd person, and as the analog for the unmarked form of English. The semi-speaker seems to have dropped the possessive prefix for the 3rd person possessor because the meaning seems too particular. Moreover, without the prefix, the noun resembles any nondependent noun stem containing the modifying element *-biis-*, *-biiθ-* 'hairy', compare *bíiθotóʔ* 'fur cap', *bíisnihʔootoh* 'monkey'. As in the previous cases, the semantically unmarked nouns of English seem to be behind the semi-speaker's aberrant use of the Gros Ventre dependent noun. The k: č correspondence reflects female pronunciation ([k]) vs. male pronunciation ([č]).

(6) nééhebyʔi   'my younger   nenééhebʔi   'my younger
                    sibling'   sibling'
     ʔééhebyʔi   'your—'
     ʔinóóhowʔo   'his, her —'

The correct dependent noun stem in (6) begins with a long vowel. In such cases, the vowel of the possessive prefix is elided in 1st and 2nd persons, but *not* in the 3rd person. The semi-speaker has again generalized the underlying form of the stem for the 3rd person (that is, without the vowel harmony caused by the the final vowel of the construction in the example). This permits him to eliminate the allomorphy of the personal prefix. Once again it seems that the 3rd person form comes closest to being unmarked for this speaker, and he generalizes its stem to the other persons. He has also reduced the complexity of the prefixal morphology.

Incorrect verbal morphology involves stem-final elements and such morphophonemic phenomena as vowel harmony and a peculiar Algonquian process called initial change:[15]

(7) nihbíícik?i   'he ate it'   nihbíícikíík?i   'he ate it'

The pseudo-transitive inanimate verb[16] in (7) was irregular even in Proto-Algonquian. In the incorrect form, the semi-speaker has added the productive pseudo-intransitive inanimate suffix -kii- (from Proto-Algonquian *-too-) to the historically correct stem to produce a "regular" pseudo-transitive form.

(8) niikonóón   'I am dreaming'   niikonéén   'I am dreaming'
        Compare: niikóneek?i   'he is dreaming'

The semi-speaker in (8) is using the underlying form of the stem, as seen in the correct 3rd person form, in the 1st person. This is incorrect because the final vowel of the stem should harmonize with the vowel of the suffix. (The suffix is -noo, 'I'.) Even when the suffix is truncated, as in the correct form here, the stem-final vowel should show harmony. Note that the 3rd person form again seems to have psychological prominence similar to that of the unmarked morpheme of English.

(9) yenééních   'there are four'   yeyééních   'there are four'
        Compare: yeen?i   'four'
                                    niis?i   'two'
                                    neníísích   'there are two'

This example in (9) demonstrates incorrect use of Algonquian initial change, which regularly appears in indicative verbal forms. The semi-speaker has apparently reanalyzed initial change as a kind of reduplication, an analysis which is plausible in some cases, cf. the forms for 'two' given above. The same semi-speaker who produced the incorrect form for 'there are four' also told me that the "prefix" of changed forms could be dropped. This is doubtful, since initial change is obligatory in verbal forms of this kind. Since initial change contributes no lexical meaning to the forms in which it appears (it marks finite verbal forms in the aorist tense), it seems that this semi-speaker regards it as unnecessary. He accordingly either drops it, or reinterprets it as reduplication, which *has* lexical meaning in Gros Ventre in many cases.

5.   Conclusion

As I noted at the beginning of this chapter, I do not feel that I have been able to devote enough field research to Gros Ventre language obsolescence to be able to speak with authority on the subject. Apart from the examples, which probably *are* the product of the dynamics of language death, much of what I have said may require further refinement. I hope to be able to do this before the language becomes definitively extinct sometime during my own lifetime.

Notes

1. The Gros Ventre self-designation is ʔoʔóóóniinénoh 'White Clay People'. The English name which they recognize and prefer is *Gros Ventre*. An additional name which appears in linguistic literature is *Atsina*. The Gros Ventre language belongs to the far-flung Algonquian linguistic family, represented on the Plains by Arapaho, of which Gros Ventre is a dialect, Blackfoot, Cheyenne, and some dialects of Cree and Ojibwa. The Algonquian Gros Ventres have sometimes been designated "Gros Ventres of the Prairie" to distinguish them from the Siouan Gros Ventres of the upper Missouri. The latter are often called Hidatsa or Minitaree. See Taylor (1983) for a discussion of the names by which the Algonquian Gros Ventre people have been known.
2. A good summary of what is known of the history of the Gros Ventres is given in Flannery (1953: chap. 1).
3. Kroeber (1916) is the classic description of the Arapaho dialects.
4. Allotment in severalty became official federal Indian policy in February of 1887 by the passage of the so-called Dawes Act. According to provisions of the act, every Indian head of family was to receive an allotment of reservation land which would eventually belong exclusively to him/her. The purpose of the act was twofold: to attempt to generate in individual Indians, by making them landowners, the same values as in White citizens, and to destroy the communal tribal way of life, eliminate the need for the reservation system, and to draw Native Americans into the Euroamerican mainstream as selfsupporting American citizens. The act and its subsequent execution were almost entirely unsuccessful, and it certainly caused far more harm than good for most Indians. (For example, 90 million acres of "surplus" reservation lands were removed from Tribal ownership and made available to Whites for settlement.) Nevertheless, the philosophical and legal basis for allotment was not officially repudiated until 1934, with the passage of the Indian Reorganization Act. A reader curious about the vast experiment in social engineering which US Indian policy has been can find much of interest – and much to regret – in Tyler (1973).
5. These residence patterns are reflected in the district representation on the Community Council. The Hays District elects four members, all of whom must be Gros Ventre, the Lodgepole District elects two members, both of whom must be Assiniboine. The River District elects two Gros Ventre members and four Assiniboine members, making a total of 12, six Gros Ventres and six Assiniboines.
6. This music differs so considerably in every way from Western music that there has been virtually no influence from the latter.
7. The term 'powwow' has several meanings in the western United States, all referring to a gathering of people. To Indians, the word designates a large, community-sponsored festival which features native dancing. Many people, both local and outside visitors, camp at the powwow grounds. The powwow is a time for renewing roots: native foods are prepared over open fires, guests are feasted, people sleep on the ground in tepees or tents, and everyone enjoys the crowds, the Indian dress, dancing, and music. Dance contests, sometimes with sizeable prizes, are an additional attraction. At Fort Belknap, the only thing

which mars the powwow (held in July) is the swarms of mosquitoes, which breed in the nearby Milk River.

8. My chief measure of linguistic competence in the preliminary screening was independent production by the person being evaluated of words which I had obtained in the early 1960s from known competent speakers. A second measure was the speaker's consistency in producing the same form at widely separated intervals. I also observed – and evaluated – the speaker's confidence when producing Gros Ventre items.

9. Dorian (1977b) terms such persons "semi-speakers". Dorian suggests three characteristics which she feels are typical of the speech of semi-speakers and which can be used to identify them: (i) They have few stylistic options, that is, they control only one or a few registers; (ii) Their usage contains relatively few marked forms; that is, many irregularities have been eliminated by processes of analogical leveling; (iii) They substitute analytic constructions for synthetic ones.

I would expand the third proposition to indicate that the speech of semi-speakers shows the unreplaced loss of some features, with the result that some things either cannot be expressed, or must be expressed in roundabout ways.

10. The generosity is at least partly administrative, and has to do with educational qualifications required for teacher certification. Stretching the definition seems to be justified, and to meet with local approval, since a bilingual education program would be impossible otherwise, and the cultural components of the program are considered to be very desirable.

11. For the details on male and female speech in Gros Ventre, see Flannery (1946) and Taylor (1982).

12. Bloomfield (1946) is the classic description of Algonquian morphology, and all subsequent Algonquianists have adopted terminology, if not always agreeing with his analysis. Although his "sketch" is difficult to read, anyone desirous of using descriptions of Algonquian languages must know it thoroughly. The definitions of grammatical terms used in this chapter come from Bloomfield's sketch.

13. Bloomfield gives no explicit definition of *medial* suffix in his sketch, but see his paragraphs 94–100. Medial suffixes are roots with concrete meaning which must follow another root, i.e., they can not be in initial position in a noun, or follow an inflectional prefix.

14. "Dependent nouns occur only in possessed form" (*Algonquian*, paragraph 32). Dependent nouns denote parts of the body, a few intimate possessions, and kin.

15. "A modification of the first vowel of the verb stem" (*Algonquian*, paragraph 45). Short vowels are lengthened, long vowels take a prefixed -ay- if the long vowel is initial, an inserted -ay- following the initial consonant when the vowel is not initial. Thus, an initial V becomes VV, an initial VV becomes ayVV, a CVV becomes CayVV. In Gros Ventre the element added to long vowels became -en- by normal sound change: (C)enVV.

16. "Pseudo-transitive verbs are intransitive verbs formed mostly with the suffixes -too, -htoo and take implied objects" (*Algonquian*, paragraph 27).

12 The structural consequences of language death

LYLE CAMPBELL and MARTHA C. MUNTZEL

1.   Introduction

In this chapter we are concerned with structural changes in obsolescing languages attributable to the language death process. On the basis of our experience with a number of dying languages we propose hypotheses about the characteristic structural developments within the languages concerned. These hypotheses can be confirmed, or contradicted and refined, as additional understanding of dying languages accumulates from the rapidly growing sources.

The languages of our experience upon which we base our observations are set forth below, presented with information on their geographic location, genetic affiliation, and number of speakers. Speakers' linguistic ability or structural knowledge of the obsolescing languages of this list varies greatly, and many communities exhibit a proficiency continuum ranging from fully competent speakers to individuals with very little knowledge at all. For purposes of exposition only, to give an idea of the kinds of speakers in each of the situations with which we worked, we characterize speakers roughly as *S* for "strong" or "(nearly) fully competent"; *I* for "imperfect", i.e. for reasonably fluent so-called "semi-speakers"; *W* "weak semi-speakers" with more restricted speaking competence (perhaps akin to Elmendorf's [1981] "last speakers"); and *R* for so-called "rememberers" who know only few words or isolated phrases ("word-inserters" may belong to this group: see Voegelin and Voegelin 1977b). Language communities with the full proficiency continuum from *S* to *W* and/or *R* are presented as *PC*.

American Finnish *PC*.   (Campbell 1980)

Cacaopera: El Salvador, Matagalpan branch of Misumalpan; 2 reasonably extensive *R*; extinct.   (Campbell 1975a and b)

Chiapanec: Chiapas, Mexico, Chiapanec-Mangue branch of Otomanguean; 3 *R* (one had memorized an entire religious text for recital on

ritual occasions: though he had no understanding of the constituents of the text).   (Campbell in press)

Chiapas dialects of Mam: Mamean branch, Mayan; data from several
locations in Chiapas representing two major dialects; Tuxtla Chico
1 *W*; *PC* in other villages; no young speakers. (Campbell in press)

Chicomuceltec: Chiapas, Mexico, Huastecan branch, Mayan; few *R*;
extinct.   (Campbell and Canger 1978; Campbell in press)

Jicaque dialects of Yoro: Honduras, Jicaque; few *S*/*I* (all elderly), few
W.   (Campbell and Oltrogge 1980)

Honduran Lencan: Honduras, Lencan; 1 *W*; now extinct.
                              (Campbell, Chapman and Dakin 1978)

Salvadoran Lenca: El Salvador, Lencan; 1 *S*; no *I*, *W*, few *R*; now
extinct.   (Campbell 1976a)

Ocuilteco: Central Mexico, Oto-Pamean branch of Otomanguean; ca.
400 speakers in four small towns; approximately 175 in Gustavo
Baz; *PC* (all over 45 years) (Muntzel 1982a and b, 1985, in press)

Pipil: El Salvador, Nahua branch of Uto-Aztecan; only few *S* (none
under 60), in several towns, very few *I*, very rare *W*; Comapa,
Guatemala: 1 *R*.   (Campbell 1985)

Southeastern Tzeltal: Chiapas, Mexico, Tzeltalan branch, Mayan;
only older *S* speakers (none under 55) in several towns, some
villages with *PC*.   (Campbell in press)

Chiquimulilla Xinca: Southeastern Guatemala, Xincan; 1 *S*, 3 *I*, 2 *W*;
now extinct.   (Field notes: Campbell)

Guazacapan Xinca: Southeastern Guatemala: Xincan; Weak *PC*, 1 *S*,
6 *I*.   (Field notes: Campbell)

Jumaytepeque Xinca: Southeastern Guatemala, Xincan; 5 reasonably
fluent *I*, 1 *W*.   (Campbell 1976a)

Yupiltepeque Xinca: Southeastern Guatemala, Xincan; extinct, 2 *R*
                                                           (Campbell 1976a)

2.   Kinds of language death situations

We begin by considering the different types of language death and their
linguistic characteristics.

"Sudden death". The case where a language abruptly disappears because
almost all of its speakers suddenly die or are killed (e.g. Tasmanian) leaves,

by definition, no obsolescing state to investigate structurally, and is therefore outside our examination.

"Radical death". "Radical language death" is like "sudden death" in that language loss is rapid and usually due to severe political repression, often with genocide, to the extent that speakers stop speaking the language out of selfdefense, a survival strategy. This is illustrated in our sample by the languages of El Salvador. In 1932, after a peasant uprising where the insurgents were thought to be "communist-inspired Indians", those identified as Indians by either dress or physical features were rounded up by Salvadoran soldiers and killed, 25,000 of them in an event called the *matanza* ('massacre'). Even three years later, radio broadcasts and newspapers were still calling for the total extermination of El Salvador's Indian people to prevent a repetition of the revolt (see Adams 1957; Anderson 1971; Marroquín 1975). Many simply stopped speaking their native languages to avoid being identified as Indians. The result was that Lenca and Cacaopera were abandoned and became extinct; Pipil was severely curtailed, with hardly any new speakers after 1932.

The situation in the early 1970s, when linguistic salvage work was being done, illustrated the process.

Cacaopera was, in effect, already extinct, though a few so-called rememberers could be found. Two of these produced a considerable corpus as rememberers go, one remembering forms from his grandfather, the other from his grandmother, who had raised him. Rememberers in this situation do not seem to differ much from those at the terminal stage of gradual death, save that the extent of their knowledge in the Cacaopera case was considerably larger (roughly five hundred words between the two best rememberers, as opposed to the handful perhaps more typical of others). So-called rememberers were never competent speakers, but are characterized by having learned and remembered isolated words and fixed phrases of the language, which in many cases may otherwise be extinct. Their renditions of these "remembered" forms rarely, if ever, contain phonetic material inconsistent with their native/dominant language, Spanish in these instances.

Salvadoran Lenca also had a few rememberers, though no one with more than a half-dozen or so items to offer. However, there was still one surviving once-fully-competent speaker. We believe that his language may typify the radical language death situation, and we hypothesize general features based on it. For such a speaker, once fluent but not having made active use of his or her language in many years, recall is bound to be limited (see Elmendorf's [1981] "former speakers", Dorian's [1982b] "formerly fluent"). Typically the phonology is intact, with few if any deviations from the former native model, but much of the lexicon is forgotten or only recalled after strained pondering, more frequent and salient vocabulary items being retained better than others. The grammar, as well, may be largely the same as the native model in its fully viable state, although actual production is characterized by fairly simple constructions and phrases, with reduced access to stylistic or pragmatic variants and complex sentences; such speakers are unable (at least initially) to produce a normal discourse. Situations which give rise to such a speaker may or may not produce so-called semi-speakers; in the case of Salvadoran Lenca, which we have treated as potentially typical of radical death, there are none (see also Elmendorf 1981). However, in the case of East Sutherland Gaelic there are a good number. Perhaps parallel to our "radical language death" situation is Dorian's (1982b:51–3) "exile", who, however, made some mistakes even though her phonology and morphology were intact. More examples of "exiles" and "radical language death" are needed to explore other characteristics which these situations may have in common.

This further exploration would seem to be all the more important in this case. Not only is Dorian's exile different, but Andersen makes an assumption quite at odds with ours; he expects erosion in general, seemingly including radical death cases, rather than the preservation of grammar which we expect in such cases:

> when . . . linguistic input and linguistic interaction become inadequate . . . to maintain . . . distinctions in that language, . . . there will be a hierarchy of linguistically marked distinctions ranging from early erosion of these distinctions to full maintenance . . .   (Andersen 1982:92)

Thus, more study is required to determine what is typical, if anything, of radical language death cases.

Pipil in El Salvador was spoken by a much larger and less acculturated number at the time of the *matanza*; nevertheless, it comes close to conforming to radical death in many instances. It has an age-based profiency continuum in some communities, but with very few representatives outside the older, more fully competent speakers (few in numbers and spread through a number of towns), with very few weaker semi-speakers. There are occasional rememberers in villages where the language is otherwise already extinct, one in Panchimalco, near San Salvador, and one in Comapa, in southeastern Guatemala.[1]

In effect, radical death can lack the age-gradation proficiency continuum more typical of gradual language death situations. Since for the most part the structure of the dying language may be intact, but production ability in it is atrophied for once-competent speakers, radical death situations, too, may be less relevant to our interest in the structural consequences for dying languages.

"Gradual death". Most cases in the literature on dying languages deal with

gradual death, the loss of a language due to gradual shift to the dominant language in language-contact situations. Such situations have an intermediate stage of bilingualism in which the dominant language comes to be employed by an ever increasing number of individuals in a growing number of contexts where the subordinate language was formerly used. This situation is characterized by a proficiency continuum determined principally by age (but also by attitude and other factors). Younger generations have greater proficiency in the dominant language and learn the obsolescing language imperfectly, if at all. Some terms employed in discussions of such language death situations are: imperfect learning, partial learning, restricted code, semi-speaker, last speaker, healthy speaker/preterminal speaker/ terminal speaker, better/worse terminal speakers, 'best' speakers/fluent speakers of single sentences/inserters of words/understanders, passive bilinguals, hybrid language, intermediate bilingualism, interlanguage, creolization in reverse, deacquisition, language decay, linguistic obsolescence, broken-down or eroded language, linguistic atrophy, language attrition, etc. Not accidentally, these different terms suggest different beliefs about and theoretical orientations toward the process of language death. We do not attempt to evaluate these general approaches, but rather limit ourselves to what we believe may be general characteristics of language death as perceived in our material.

"Bottom-to-top death". Another kind of language death in which the repertoire of stylistic registers suffers attrition from the bottom up has been dubbed the "latinate pattern"; here "the language is lost first in contexts of family intimacy and hangs on only in elevated ritual contexts" (Hill 1980). We have no pattern-perfect examples of this type; however, two come close. Our principal Chiapanec informant recalled a memorized Chiapanec religious text, called an *alabanza* ('hymn of praise'). It had been performed publicly on ritual occasions until recently, but was no longer presented because it required the interchange of two participants and the other fellow who had also memorized his part had recently died. Our informant did not know the meaning of the text in anything other than a very general way and he was unable to segment it into constituents, and in fact spoke no other Chiapanec, save a handful of isolated, "remembered" words (Campbell in press). Southeastern Tzeltal, very nearly extinct, with only a few older speakers in scattered villages, perhaps offers a better case. We recorded four prayers; one in particular, the *rezo tzeltal*, is quite important locally, since speakers of Tojolabal (a neighboring, healthy Mayan language) require this SE Tzeltal prayer in their own ceremonies and pilgrimages. This long prayer (45 minutes) employs typical Mayan ritual structure (paired couplets, much metaphor, etc.). Only four men, each a reasonably good semi-speaker, could recite the prayers, but they were unable to translate them in anything other than broad paraphrases; speakers from geographically isolated, but

completely viable Tzeltal dialects also had great difficulty in attempting to translate these, in part due to the dialect differences, but principally because the form of ritual language was no longer used by them. The SE Tzeltal situation is not completely parallel to Hill's "latinate" pattern, since it also offers a limited proficiency continuum more typical of other cases of gradual language death (Campbell in press).

Our concern here is with kinds of changes in the structure of languages that are in this process of being lost. Whereas some manifestations of change seem natural and likely to be widespread, others may be less so. We draw on our experience with this variety of dying languages to illustrate some of each sort.

3.   Change processes in dying languages

The most obvious prediction one can make about dying languages is that their structure is very likely to undergo a certain amount of change, and in all components at that: phonological, morphological, syntactic, semantic, and lexical. Nevertheless, it is much harder to predict the precise nature of the changes which may occur. We attempt to present examples of various sorts of change, giving preference to phonological examples only because they take up less space, though syntactic and other phenomena also illustrate many of these kinds of change and some examples are included.

3.1.   Predictable or expected changes

For phonology, Andersen (1982:95) proposes three hypotheses; they represent generalizations with which few would quarrel, given what has long been reported for language-contact situations: (1) the bilingual speaker of a threatened language (dying, for purposes of our discussion) will make fewer phonological distinctions in his or her use of the language than a fully competent (dominant or monolingual) speaker of the same language would. (2) However, he or she will preserve distinctions common to both his/her languages even while making fewer of the distinctions found only in the threatened language. (3) Distinctions with a functional load which is high (in terms of phonology and/or morphology) will survive longer in the speaker's use of his/her weaker language than distinctions which have a low functional load. The cases we have dealt with tend to support these generalizations, though the first is most obvious (see also Dorian 1977b:24).

For example, many Pipil speakers have lost contrastive vowel length, merging long vowels with short counterparts; the contrast is not found in Spanish, the dominant language. Chiltiupan Pipil in its moribund state has merged the affricate *ts* with the fricative *s* (Campbell 1985). Tuxtla Chico Mam, very nearly extinct, has merged the postvelar (uvular) *q* of viable Mam with velar *k* (Campbell in press), thus eliminating a contrast not found in dominant Spanish. Semi-speakers of American Finnish also often fail to produce the vowel length contrast, merging to short vowels; also they often reduce geminate consonants to nongeminates; and they produce a variety of substitutions for the front rounded vowels ranging from *yu* or *u* for /y/ ([ü]) to retroflexed schwas for /ö/ (Campbell 1980). These contrasts are missing from dominant English.

3.2. Changes of uncertain predictability

We have noted other kinds of structural changes which may or may not also be typical of dying languages; evidence from a much larger number of languages, distributed over more parts of the world, will probably be needed in order to determine how characteristic these may be of language death situations in general. The particular cases we discuss here are of interest precisely because of the open-question nature of their generalizability; we will suggest, where we feel there is some basis for it, the principles which we suspect may be involved.

Overgeneralization of unmarked features. There appears to be a tendency for marked forms to be replaced by less marked ones (see Campbell 1976c; Rankin 1978; Dressler 1981a). This observation is naturally related to Andersen's hypothesis (1) considered above, that bilingual speakers of a threatened language will make fewer phonological distinctions than will fully competent speakers. Reference to markedness, however, suggests some refinement of this hypothesis, potentially predicting that when distinctions are lost, it is the marked member of opposition which is lost. Thus, in the case of the Tuxtla Chico Mam merger of *q* with *k*, lost *q* is the marked member of the opposition, as is the lost vowel length in Pipil and American Finnish, short vowels being less marked.

Nevertheless, these two hypotheses are not necessarily completely compatible; the tendency to reduce markedness is not necessarily subsumed under Andersen's tendency to reduce oppositions not found in the dominant language. Loss of markedness may include some things not covered by Andersen's generalization. Thus, marked phenomena which do not involve contrasts, but rather subphonemic, allophonic variants, may also be covered by the latter hypothesis. For example, some moribund Pipil dialects have completely eliminated the marked noncontrastive voiceless variants of sonorants ([l̥, w̥, y̥]) which occur word-finally in viable Pipil, merging them with the unmarked voiced counterparts ([l, w, y]), which do not occur in final position in viable Pipil (see Campbell 1985). Moreover, the observation may also extend to nonphonological phenomena (see the Ocuilteco case below of failure to make the dual/plural contrast, with merger to unmarked plural).

The two hypotheses differ, however, not only in substance but in spirit.

That is, Andersen's generalization seems to suggest that it is something to do with the structure of the dominant language which lies behind loss of oppositions in the threatened language (i.e. an "external" motivation). The markedness proposal, while partially in sympathy with Andersen's view, suggests that it is another factor, namely the nature (marked or unmarked) of the linguistic phenomena in the structure of the dying language, which leads to loss (i.e. "internal" factors). Thus, in the case of Tuxtla Chico Mam, Andersen's approach seems to emphasize the lack of q in dominant Spanish as the causal factor in its loss through merger with k; the markedness view, on the other hand, suggests that the marked nature (unnaturalness, difficulty of pronunciation) of uvular q may contribute to its merger with unmarked k.

Some might be disturbed that the same case (e.g. merger of q with k) could be thought of as illustrating two separate and perhaps competing "hypotheses". This need not, however, be distressing. On the one hand, since the phenomenon under discussion seems to fit both hypotheses, it suggests that much greater work is required in this area in order to resolve any logical conflicts and to determine to what extent these different hypotheses may be valid or valuable. In our present state of knowledge, however, both are valuable as working hypotheses to be tested against further cases.

Another way out of the seeming conflict is to appeal to "multiple causation", a notion becoming increasingly more standard in other areas of historical linguistics. To illustrate, we consider an analogy. Suppose a list of potential causal factors in automobile accidents contains such varied things as excessive speed, bad road conditions, impaired driver (e.g. blurred vision, drunkenness, etc.), mechanical malfunctions, etc. Now suppose a car crashed against a tree, where it is dark, the road is icy, the driver is drunk, a tire blew out, and the driver was speeding. It can be presumed that any single factor may have been sufficient to cause the accident, but that it is also possible, even probable, that these factors combined, working in concert, contributing multiply to cause the wreck. So it is with linguistic change. Thus, in our example, the lack of the q vs. k contrast in dominant Spanish and the tendency to reduce markedness (q being marked) conceivably could have worked in concert, jointly leading to the loss in Tuxtla Chico Mam. Given multiple causation, we have the potential for reconciling the seeming difficulty of a single case exemplifying differing hypotheses. As will be obvious, some other examples discussed in this chapter also exemplify more than one hypothesis. We take these to be indications of either "multiple causation" or unsubstantiated hypotheses to be rectified in light of reports from other language death cases.

Overgeneralization of marked features. Marked forms may be used excessively. While there may often be a tendency to reduce or eliminate marked forms (as discussed above), the reverse also appears to be common. That is, things that are marked or "exotic" from the point of view of the dominant language may not be completely mastered by imperfect learners, and not knowing exactly where they belong, these speakers sometimes go hog-wild, as it were, employing the "exotic" version with great frequency in ways inappropriate for the healthy version of the same language. For example, Jumaytepeque Xinca has a complicated rule which glottalizes consonants in particular morphological environments; one Jumaytepeque speaker glottalized nearly every possible consonant, having failed to learn the rule, but using excessively the striking feature of glottalization. A few speakers of Guazacapan Xinca also used an excessive amount of otherwise inappropriate glottalization of consonants. Teotepeque Pipil in its moribund state has overemphasized voiceless *l*, employing it everywhere, not just word-finally as it was formerly (Campbell 1985).

These changes are internal to the structure of the obsolescent language in that they appear to have no direct analog in the dominant language. Hill (1980:4), without calling upon markedness, refers to such cases as "acts of creation". Thus, the overgeneralization of voiceless *l* in Teotepeque Pipil or the excessive glottalization in some Xinca speakers are "internal acts of creation" in that they appear to stem from imperfect learning of the moribund language and have nothing to do with Spanish.

Development of variability. Obligatory rules may come to apply optionally, fail to apply (i.e. be lost), or show substitutions. For example, American Finnish speakers sometimes fail to apply the consonant gradation rules. Thus, in Standard Finnish *t* gradates to *d* in closed syllables, e.g. *äiti* 'mother', *äidille* 'for mother': but frequently *äitille* is the form in American Finnish (Campbell 1980). In Ocuilteco, the native rule voicing stops after nasals fails to apply sometimes in the language of nonperfect speakers, producing free variations (e.g. *nd* alternating with *nt*; see Muntzel 1982a). In Cuisnahuat Pipil the formerly obligatory rule of final devoicing of sonorants (see above) has become optional, resulting in free variation between, for example, final [l] and [l̥]. (For similar claims about morphology, see below.)

Development of irregularity by extremes of regularization. There is sometimes failure to learn (i.e. imperfect learning of) rules by over-generalization and/or undergeneralization. For example, fully viable Pipil had a rule in which final sonorants (l, w, y) were devoiced word-finally (l̥, w̥, y̥); Teotepeque Pipil, however, has overgeneralized voiceless *l*, devoicing all *l*'s, not just final ones. In contrast, it has undergeneralized the portion of the rules dealing with *w* and *y*, not devoicing them anywhere, even in original final position. In effect, then, through overgeneralization (e.g. of [l̥]) and undergeneralization (of [w̥] and [y̥]), the rule of final devoicing of sonorants was lost. One speaker of Jumaytepeque Xinca illustrates a similar case. He failed to learn the rule of glottalization in various phonological and morphological environments and through overgeneralization (glottalizing all possible consonants) in his language the rule is lost. This phenomenon is connected to the overextensiion of marked ("exotic") features and to the tendency to reduce markedness, discussed above. The best way to view such cases and to test the validity of these partially overlapping proposals will depend on the findings from other language death situations.

Another example is the failure of consonant gradation to apply in American Finnish, which appears to reflect failure to learn the rule by undergeneralization. It might be noted that this case could fit Andersen's first generalization, since dominant English has no gradation rule. Again, then, we are faced with two alternatives, either of hypotheses yet to be tested properly or of multiple causation, as discussed above. Andersen's proposal, however, is not compatible with the overextension, for example, of voiceless *l* in Teotepeque Pipil, since local Spanish here has no voiceless *l* ([l̥]), finally or elsewhere.

"Acts of reception". Some changes in moribund languages may be "externally" motivated; that is, some structural changes in dying languages may be the result of influence from linguistic aspects of the dominant language, i.e. "acts of reception" (Hill 1980:4). A probable example is the change in Teotepeque Pipil of *š* to *r̃* under the external influence of sociolinguistic evaluation of these sounds in Spanish. The change is apparently motivated by the fact that in local Spanish, the dominant language, /r̃/ has a strongly stigmatized variant [š] (Campbell 1976c). The negative sociolinguistic evaluation of this variant in Spanish has apparently caused the native Pipil sound to shift to the Spanish prestige variant, producing an unnatural sound change, externally induced due to Spanish norms. Several grammatical changes in American Finnish can only be attributed to the external influence of English. Some examples follow.

The so-called "passive" in Finnish is an impersonal verb form which permits no overtly specified agent (as in the English *by* phrases), but American Finnish (AF) of non-first generation speakers now permits the agentive phrases, especially when the agent is a service organization such as church, funeral home, etc., employing the cases *-stA* 'from (within)' or *-ltA* 'from (without)' or the postposition *kautta* 'through'. Some examples are:

(1) häne-t   hauda-ttiin   kirko-sta
    he-ACC   bury-PAST.PASS   church-FROM
    'he was buried by the church'
(2) hautajaiset pide-ttiin   30 päivä heinäkuu-ta kirko-lta
    funeral   hold-PAST.PASS 30 day   July-PRT   church-FROM
    'the funeral was held the 30th day of July by the church'

(3) polttohautaus Lake Side kappeli-n kautta toimite-ttiin
    cremation Lake Side chapel-GEN through perform-
                                                PAST.PASS
'the cremation was performed by/through the Lake Side Chapel'
(See Eskola 1977:117–20)

In another example, Standard Finnish (SF) does not normally permit infinitival complements of nouns or adjectives to have subjects; however, AF has changed to be equivalent to English:

(4) tämä oli ensimmäinen kerta mei-lle men-nä tä-llä
    this was first time us-TO/FOR go-1.INF this-ON/BY
    laiva-lla Milwaukee-seen
    ship-ON/BY Milwaukee-INTO
'this was the first time for us to go on this ship to Milwaukee'

An equivalent SF form would be, e.g.:

(4') tämä oli ensimmäinen kerta, kun oli-mme matkusta-
                                                    neet
     this was first time, when had-WE travel-PAST.
                                                    PART
     tä-llä laiva-lla Milwaukee-seen
     this-ON ship-ON Milwaukee-INTO
(See Eskola 1977)

These changes appear to be due to the impact of English on the structure of the AF of imperfect speakers. They involve not loss of material from the threatened language, as in Andersen's phonology examples, but additions to AF grammar due to impact from English. (For details and several other examples, see Campbell 1980.)

4.   Changes outside phonology

4.1.   Morphological reduction

Language death may be accompanied by some degree of morphological reduction (in which we include the reduction of allomorphy and the leveling of paradigms). While we have several examples in our data, since this is reasonably well established (see Dorian 1977b; Andersen 1982:97), we present only two examples here. In Ocuilteco, imperfect speakers often leave out the dual and plural markers, as indicated in the following examples by the material in parentheses:

(5) kit-kwe-p-tyii   (-nkwe(-bi))
    FUT-1PL-EXCLUS-sing   (-DUAL(-EXCLUS))
'we (two, but not you) will sing'

(6) kit-kwe-p-tyɨɨ   (-hñə(-ɓi))
FUT-1PL-EXCLUS-sing   (-PL(-EXCLUS))
'we (all, but not you) will sing'

Our second example is from American Finnish. While Standard Finnish requires adjectives to agree in case (and number) with the nouns they modify, AF shows a tendency for case endings on adjectives to be lost, e.g.:

(7) sai-n   kirja-n   vanha   miehe-ltä
got-I   book-ACC   old   man-FROM
'I got the book from the old man'
Compare: SF:
sai-n kirja-n   vanha-lta   miehe-ltä
. . .   old-FROM   man-FROM

(8) vanha   miehe-n   hevonen   on   valkoinen
old   man-GEN   horse   is   white
'the old man's horse is white'
Compare SF:
vanha-n   miehe-n   hevonen on valkoinen
old-GEN   man-GEN   ...
(See Larmouth 1974; Eskola 1977.)

These examples appear to conform to Andersen's hypotheses concerning morphological reduction, in particular to:

A [semi-speaker] will exhibit a smaller number of morphologically-marked categories . . . than will a [fully competent speaker] of that language. Moreover, . . . the [semi-speaker] will tend to exhibit variability, the [fully competent speaker] categorical marking of that category.   (Andersen 1982:97)

(See also Dorian 1973, 1977a, 1983; Dressler 1981; Elmendorf 1981.)

4.2.   Syntactic reduction

Dying languages also exhibit modification of syntactic resources, a point well established in the language death literature (see Hill 1973, 1978; Andersen 1982). We consider only a few cases of several in our material.

In present-day Pipil the "future" suffixes of older texts are unused and almost unknown, replaced by periphrastic constructions, e.g.:

(9) ni-yu   ni-k-chiwa
I-go   I-it-do
'I'm going to do it'

The "future" suffixes of formerly viable Pipil, -s 'singular' and -s-ke-t 'plural', e.g. ni-panu-s 'I will pass', ti-panu-ske-t 'we will pass', now do not occur even in traditional texts, though they can still be elicited with difficulty from some speakers (Campbell 1985).

Another Pipil example is the once-productive passives (signaled by -lu,

-lw, and *-ua*); these are now found only in frozen verb forms. The only current equivalent is an impersonal construction formed of "3rd person plural" verbs (i.e. with the suffix *-t* '3rd person plural'), e.g.:

(10) yaha   ki-tahtan   se: konse:hoh   wan   ki-maka-ke-t
he   it-asked   an   advice   and   it-give-PRET-PL
'he asked for advice and then they gave it (to him)' = 'he asked for advice and was given it'

(11) k-ilwih-ke-t   ma: ki-ma:walti   chi:l
him-tell-PRET-PL   that   her-smear   chili
'They told him to anoint her (with) chili' = 'He was told to smear chili on her'

(12) nech-ilwih-ke-t   ka nu-siwa:-w   bru:hah
me-tell-PRET-PL   that my-wife-POSS   witch
'They told me that my wife [was a] witch' = 'I was told my wife is a witch'

Pipil has lost its original, morphological passives, but the 3rd person plural impersonal verb forms have come to function in context as agentless passives. Sentences (10)–(12), from a text about a supernatural being, have a specific discourse agent: it is the priest who gives the advice, tells him to smear chili on his wife, and tells him she is a witch, but the priest as agent is clear from the context and the impersonal is used to put other features in focus. This usage of 3rd person plural forms for impersonal utterances replaced the former passive constructions.

These two cases may well exemplify Andersen's hypotheses:

A [semi-speaker] will use a smaller number of syntactic devices . . . than a [fully competent speaker] of the same language.
The [semi-speaker] will preserve and overuse syntactic constructions that more transparently reflect the underlying semantic and syntactic relations.
Where there is more then one possible surface structure for a given underlying relation . . ., the [semi-speaker] will tend to collapse the different surface structures into one. (This will be evidenced by a smaller variety of surface structures for the [semi-speaker] as compared to a [fully competent speaker].)
(Andersen 1982:99)

If both the morphological and periphrastic "future" and "passive" constructions were once available, then Pipil in its moribund stage shows a "smaller number of syntactic devices", having eliminated the morphological constructions for the analytic, periphrastic ones. These periphrastic constructions have been "overused" – do they "more transparently reflect the underlying semantic and syntactic relations"? The different "surface structures" have "collapsed into one", periphrastic constructions winning at the expense of the morphological ones.

Not all examples, however, conform to or illustrate Andersen's hypotheses about syntactic reduction, as is seen in some examples from AF. The

SF so-called "second infinitive" is a gerundial form which permits no overtly specified subject. On the English model of appositive gerunds in -*ing*, AF now permits such subjects, even when they are not coreferential with the subject of the main clause:

(13) vainaja   syntyi   Duluthi-ssa, vanhemmat   oll-en Mr ja
                                                      Mrs Matt Salo
     deceased was born Duluth-IN,   parents   be-ING Mr and
                                                      Mrs Matt Salo
     'the deceased was born in Duluth, his parents being Mr and Mrs
     Matt Salo'

(14) entinen Hilda Paavola ja   Frank Andersen vihi-ttiin,
     former Hilda Paavola and Frank Andersen marry-PAST.PASS,
     pastori Mänttä vihki-en   heidät
     pastor Mänttä marry-ING them
     'the former Hilda Paavola and Frank Andersen were married,
     pastor Mänttä marrying them' (see Eskola 1977)

SF might employ e.g.

(15) vihki-en   heidät,   pastori   puhui hitaasti
     marry-ING   them   the. pastor spoke softly

Here *vihkien* can have no overt subject in the same clause; the AF extension to permit such subjects, as with *pastori Mänttä* in (14), is due to English influence, an "act of syntactic reception" (see Hill 1980:4), unlike Andersen's "reductions".

The final example involves AF word order. SF has relatively free (pragmatically determined) word order with respect to subject (S), verb (V), and object (O), but for some semi-speakers of AF it has become more rigidly SVO as case endings are being elided, mirroring English:

(16) AF: poika   syö   omena
          boy. NOM eats   apple   'the boy is eating
     SF: poika   syö   omena-a   an apple'
          boy. NOM eats   apple-PRT

(17) AF: mies   osti   talo   'the man bought
          man   bought house   the house'
     SF: mies   osti   talo-n
          man. NOM bought house-ACC

While loss of object cases is a kind of grammatical reduction, the compensating increase of rigid word order is an added aspect of AF grammar, conforming to the model of dominant English. (See Puromies 1966; Larmouth 1974:358; Vilkko 1974; Eskola 1977).

4.3. "Stylistic shrinkage"

Dying languages exhibit "stylistic shrinkage". This noncontroversial point
is also illustrated in our examples; only two Pipil speakers were found who
are proficient at telling tales with the traditional oral literary devices (e.g.
paired couplets; Campbell 1985). Certain options useful for discourse have
also been curtailed, for example, the original passives have been lost (see
note 1). Similarly, there may no longer be any Ocuilteco speakers competent in the formulaic ritual language employed in religious ceremonies
and marriage petitions; the last speaker competent in this style may well
have been our ritual-language informant, who died in the mid 1970s
(Muntzel 1979). (See also Hill 1973, 1978, 1980; Dorian 1980b.)

5.   Language death vs. other kinds of contact

It is worth drawing attention to the fact that in some cases it may be difficult
to distinguish some changes due to the language death process from the
consequences of other kinds of language contact. For example, in Pipil *wan*
'with' was originally a "relational noun" (structurally like a noun root,
bearing possessive pronominal prefixes), e.g. *nu-wan* 'with me', *mu-wan*
'with you', *i-wan* 'with him/her/it'. *Wan* (together with a few other relational
nouns) has lost the relational-noun requirement of occurring only with
possessive prefixes, thus becoming a preposition just as in Spanish, e.g.:

(18) nin   nemi   nu-chan   ti-se:n-nemi-t   *wan* se: nu-
                                                                amiguh
     here   I-am   my-house   we-together-are-PL   with a   my-
                                                                friend
     'here I am at my house, sitting together with my friend'
     (Formerly, . . . i-wan se: nu-amiguh [his-with a my-friend])

Similarly, *pal* 'in order to, so that', was a "relational noun", (*nu-pal* 'for
me, mine'), but now functions as a subordinate conjunction, which formerly
did not exist, similar to Spanish *para* 'in order to', e.g.:

(19) ni-mu-kets-ki   ni-k-tatia ti-t   *pal*   ni-mu-tutu:nia
     I-REFLEX-arise-PRET I-it-burn fire-ABSOL   so. that I-REFLEX-heat
     'I got up to light (the) fire in order to warm myself'

One might suspect that these Spanish-influenced structural mutations away
from relational nouns reflect the kind of change that would only take place in
Pipil's moribund state. However, completely parallel changes have taken
place in other completely viable Nahua dialects, Pipil's sister languages (see
Suárez 1977), showing the difficulty of distinguishing normal contact-
induced changes from changes due to the language death situation.
    For other proposals concerning general structural features of decaying

languages not discussed here, see, among others, Dorian (1980b, 1982b, 1983); Hill (1980); Dressler (1981); and Andersen (1982).

Notes

The research upon which this paper is based was supported in part by a grant from the National Science Foundation, No. BNS-8419143. We wish to thank Nancy Dorian for helpful comments on earlier versions of this paper.

Abbreviations employed in the examples cited are common ones; but note that here we use PRT for 'partitive' and PART for 'participle'.

1. In most of our cases "remembering" words of an otherwise extinct language seems to have no greater function than entertainment or mild amusement, and implies very little for one's identity. This appears to be the case with rememberers of Cacaopera, Chicomuceltec, Salvadoran Lenca, and Yupiltepeque Xinca. The most typical attitude in this area is quite negative toward indigenous languages; most are ashamed to speak an Indian language, while Spanish is held in esteem. This state of affairs no doubt has contributed to the obsolescence of these languages. The case is somewhat different in Pipil; that is, it suffers for the most part the same negative stigma as other languages, an attitude held particularly by its more fluent remaining speakers. At the same time, however, there was something of a reversal in the 1970s among non-Indian Salvadorans, many of whom came to lament their lost cultural heritage and began placing value on the Pipil past as a symbol of national pride, akin to Mexico's pride in its Aztec antecedents. In this situation, rememberers and terminal speakers received considerable prestige. The rememberers from Panchimalco and Comapa were revered in their villages as "real" Indians who spoke the now-vanishing language. The one surviving elderly woman rememberer in each of the two towns was held in esteem as a symbol of the Indian past; in both cases, the women attempted to fake or create words they did not know on our interview questionnaire, presumably in order to maintain their local status, which each seemed to enjoy, and perhaps to save face. We also encountered faking rememberers posing as full-fledged speakers in one other Pipil town and in one SE Tzeltal village. These two men seemed not to enjoy any particular status in their communities, but rather were apparently interested in payments we might make for informant services. The faked or created forms did not violate Spanish phonetics except in the case of the man in SE Tzeltal territory, who salted his forms with some glottalized consonants, apparently learned from growing up around Indian speakers without ever having learned more than a handful of real words.

13 On signs of health and death

ERIC P. HAMP

When a language, or reasonably isolated dialect, appears to be "on the way out" one might hope to find some traits or symptoms that would be interesting to watch. Nancy Dorian, in her numerous and seminal publications (1981 and refs. there cited), has in fact done just this in greater detail and with greater responsibility than anyone else. Over a goodly number of years I have collected data from living dialects for a number of purposes, often for more than one reason: in order to document a rare variety of a language for ultimate historical and comparative linguistic ends (e.g. North Geg Albanian or Vannetais Breton), to fill in the dialectology of a language (Tetovo Albanian, various sorts of Scottish Gaelic), to explore the manifestations of language contact and multilingualism (Prespa Albanian, Arvanìtika of younger speakers of Attica, Resia Slovene, Tiefencastel Romauntsch, Aromân / Koutsovlah, Mandrítsa Albanian), to verify the presence of a language (Màndres Albanian, Arbanasi Albanian at Zadar, various Albanian enclaves of Arbresh in southern Italy and Arvanìtika in Greece). I restrict the content of this chapter and the above mentions to dialects of Europe in order to give our discussion a degree of cultural and situational homogeneity, as well as to maximize the presentation of substance in a short space. In numerous such situations I have found myself observing societies with only vestigial groups of speakers or semi-speakers, and with predictably ultimate terminal heirs of the native language.

To make our topic manageable and to explore a consistent segment of linguistic structure, the ensuing observations will be restricted to phonology, including phonetics.

1. Two cases of shift

In more than a couple of parts of Greece I have encountered persons who could be induced to summon up faint memories of a handful of lexemes or to respond to bits of a test list by supplying Arvanìtika words in reply to Greek stimuli. In the west of the Peloponnesos in the mountains near Olympia there are toponyms that attest to the former presence of Arvanìtika; the toponyms of the area have been responsibly studied, and it has been stated

197

that Arvanìtika died out there by the turn of the century. A quarter of a century ago, after a careful search, I found an old man there who could give scattered responses to a test list in the form only of isolated lexemes, so that I was even able to classify this crucially valuable dialect by virtue of the incidence of a diagnostic vowel. Some of the man's vocables were seriously warped by interference from Greek or by simple mismemory apparently out of desuetude. Almost all his phonetics were purely local Eleian Greek; we will find this phenomenon to recur in further instances dealt with below. But the remarkable fact is that these fossil scraps of Arvanìtika contained the central vowel that the language possesses in addition to the Greek repertory. In such a case it seems scarcely possible to say whether the speaker was in his youth a terminal semi-speaker with a modest system contrastively charac-terized, distinct from the matrix dominant and successor language, or whether as an individual personality he was an apt phonetician and mimic within the normal range of variation found in samples of human groups (reflecting, say, a conscious recall of his grandparents' behavior). Suffice it to say that this last vestige was incompletely acculturated.

As a matter of fact, less remarkable than the presence of the telltale vowel mentioned above was the conservation of the Albanian and Arvanìtika consonantal contrast š : s in the expected words. From this and his non-Greek final obstruents I am inclined to class this last semi-speaker of Bášta, in Eleia, as a true terminal semi-speaker. On the other hand, in the nearby village of Mēliés (Olympiōn) I found two or three old men (depending on how you counted them) who could manage only some Arvanìtika numerals and a half-dozen everyday vocables and phrases. These were badly Hel-lenized and misremembered, and the best performer (aged 75) had a completely Greek phonology and only one groove-spirant series, as in Greek. These men had never been true terminal speakers; they had engaged in a kind of memorizing in their youth. But at this point let me emphasize that the old man from Bášta preserved some non-Greek features to the end.

In those same years I found a markedly different situation with several young university students whom I observed and who came from the villages of the main central valley of Attica east of Athens (from which the best known export wine is shipped). One, who came fom Liópesi (Paianía), heard and understood Arvanìtika from his grandmother, spoke very imper-fect and impoverished Arvanìtika, failed to answer many of my questions and probes, yet could supply much of the ordinary vocabulary, could form serviceable assertions, was very good-natured and obliging, and did not resent his "mistakes" (but always offered to check with grandma). In short, he showed signs of continuing as a limited semi-speaker, given the opportun-ity; I doubt that this actually ensued, considering the total social situation in post-World War II Greece. This young man possessed, among his other noticeable Hellenisms, but one series of groove-spirants. Yet his command of Arvanìtika, acculturated though it was, was vastly farther from death than that of the old man of Bášta.

It should be pointed out at this time that it is perfectly proper in each of the two cases mentioned to speak separately of "language death", and that the two cases may be treated independently, much as if they were, say, Cornish and Manx. Small as Greece is, the terrain is so rugged, the roads until 1950 so poor, the Arvanìtika enclaves so many and scattered, their language use socially so submerged (for a good century or so), the prestige of Greek and of Greek ethnicity so high, that the speech of more than a half-dozen Arvanìtika enclaves (to my own personal knowledge in situ) has come to the brink of death without any survival of direct knowledge or memory of their fellows. Thus the varieties of Eleia and Attica (and several other localities) may be safely treated as prima facie independent. Such is not the case simpliciter with Scottish Gaelic, participating as it does in a network of literacy, of highly esteemed inherited and ancient native literature, of supporting and even dissident religion, and of the urbanized and sophisticated trappings of the British Empire and its sequel. Death or survival of the Gaelic of the fishing communities of East Sutherland was surely relatively independent of the lobstering and farming culture of Kintyre (though not of the circulation of influential ministers, nor of the shipyards of Glasgow and the Clyde), but we must always be careful to sort out the parameters of contact between distillery workers of Jura in the southwest and of Speyside in the northeast.

We have seen in the two varieties of attenuated Albanian passed in review two contrastive sets of characteristics. The Eleian, surely as moribund a specimen as one can hope to find and study for its internal characteristics, retained some original Arvanìtika phonological traits. The youth from Attica, with the capacity to evade language death, seemed paradoxically to flirt with the erasure of some features that could be called the essence of an integral distinct Arvanìtika. This realization leads us to consider the question of language contact and convergence.

2. Contact and interference

The Arvanìtika dialects have been located in Greece, though perhaps not entirely in their exact present sites, a good three-quarters of a millennium. For much of that time they have pursued a vigorous separate life from Greek; indeed, until the organization and strengthening of the national Greek state in the nineteenth century, there was little outside the church – itself, however, a powerful force of cohesion – to impose the Greek language. Yet for some time, because of that symbiosis Arvanìtika has been getting somewhat more like Greek; e.g. 'be' and 'have', though uniquely suppletive and irregular, have developed the same defective morphology as we find in Greek. For the non-sonant consonants of Arvanìtika I have described (Hamp 1962:640–1) the development within a typological framework as set out below.

Many Tosk Albanian partial consonant systems are of the form:

(1) p   t   c   č   ǩ   k |
     b   d   ʒ   ž   ǵ   g |
     f   θ   s   š | h
... v   ð   z   ž | j

In these systems /h/ is usually realized as a voiceless vocoid phonetically (and in some dialects it then disappears) and /j/ is [i]. In the Albanian of Greece, where /γ/ has been borrowed with Greek loans and where inherited /hj/ falls in with /ç/ [ç] borrowed with Greek loans, the cadre is thereby enriched to the following form:

(2) p   t   c   č   ǩ   k
     b   d   ʒ   ž   ǵ   g
     f   θ   s   š   ç
     v   ð   z   ž   γ

/γ/ and /ç/ move into these positions by their phonetics and by the typology of the system too.

Then /j/ moves in to oppose /ç/, and takes on an articulation of a more fricative sort than it has in Albanian, and /h/ moves opposite /γ/, taking on a velar spirant articulation. Now we have:

(3) p   t   c   č   ǩ   k
     b   d   ʒ   ž   ǵ   g
     f   θ   s   š   ç   x
     v   ð   z   ž   j   γ

In other words, we say that /x/ turns out phonetically as it does because typologically it comes to oppose the new /γ/.

If I were writing that today I would probably speak in terms of a matrix of distinctive features; but the point of the argument is clear either way. In that same discussion I continued on the subject of Greek (p. 641):

One can judge from various aspects of the reactions of Greek speakers that they hear voiced stops and affricates in typical European languages as being nasal, because, for all Greek except acculturated varieties often heard in Athens, a voiced phone occurs either (i) automatically preceded by a nasal segment, or (ii) in free variation with nasal plus voiced stop segments, or (iii) selectively in complementation with nasal plus voiced segments. (I therefore analyze all forms of modern mainland Greek, with the exception of certain northern dialects where syncopies have occurred to occlude this, with nasal clusters composed of nasal plus stop. Thus Greek has only one series of stops, indifferent to voicing.)

Analyzed in the same framework, I saw at that time (Hamp 1961:101) the Greek consonants as:

(4) φ θ χ   χ′ ς(σ)
    β δ γ   γ′ ζ
    π τ κ   κ′ ϗ
    μ ν   ν′
       λ   λ′
       ϱ

We may rearrange the obstruents to compare optimally with the above arrays as follows:

(5) p t c ǩ k
    f θ s ç x
    v ð z j γ

With these facts in mind let us now frame a brief statement of the contact history of certain Arvanìtika consonants in the context of Greek. (It is worth noticing that ž was once vanishingly rare in Albanian.) Beginning with the distinctive features, common to all varieties of Albanian, of [voice] and [continuance] and six points of articulation, all intersections in the matrix have been filled in. This presents a topology similar to, but larger than, that of Greek. The faulty sample from the old man of Bášta shows clear traces of this; my materials lack only c, ȝ, ž̌, ž, ç, and γ. Of these, Greek loans would produce all but two, for I was deliberately trying to elicit inherited vocabulary.

The next stage in the contact history, essentially the modern intense Hellenization, eliminates one of the groove-spirant features (usually in favour of s, z, c) and binds up the phonetic voiced stop with nasality. This is of course what we find in the young man from Liópesi.

We can now make our findings explicit for these two cases, drawn from the same (related) set of dialects of the same language dying under highly similar conditions; perhaps an important difference lies in the fact that the mountains near Olympia have suffered depletion and lack of commerce from which (an invasive) proximity to Athens has rescued Liópesi – itself a mixed blessing for the health of Arvanìtika. It appears that the repair or disrepair of the phonology is not a sign of incipient death as such. Rather, it seems that convergence, or loss, in the phonology reflects the ongoing result of contact, the kind of phenomenon that characterizes a Sprachbund over centuries and millennia. Perhaps the result here is hastened, plausibly by virtue of decreasing numbers of speakers in a sharply curtailed network as the social conditions for language transfer and death set in. In this sense, what we see is simply more contact phenomena, under possibly unusual conditions. Paradoxically, this means that the more contact interference we see – within limits – the more adjustment, adaptation, longevity, and health we may expect! Let us go on now to exemplify this diversity in the face of death with more complex cases, instances where a richer material can be drawn upon.

However, the very richness of the data and the surrounding social conditions often makes incisive conclusions beyond the observational level difficult to reach at this stage: that is to say, we are often not readily able, especially in this short chapter, to specify precisely why one case shows noteworthy conservatism while another bears the marks of intense contact interference and diffusion. What we can say, on the available data, is that neither of these states is linked in a simple way to the process of language death.

3.   Survival

Let us first consider the situation of a conservatively preserved inherited phonology and phonetics (so far as we can infer the latter from the past) in a healthy surviving language. Icelandic would be close to an ideal example, but it might also be considered trivially so; it is not necessary to isolate a language with a forbidding sea to approximate this result. The valley of Gusinje (Albanian Gusî) in Crna Gora on the Albanian–Yugoslav border, with a population of ca. 7,000 Moslem Albanians, Roman Catholic Albanians, Moslem Slavs, Orthodox Slavs, and a handful of Roman Catholic Slavs is sealed off (under present political conditions) from Albania by a wall of high mountains, and furnishes a marvelous sociolinguistic microcosm. These Albanians live in close proximity to Slavs, they belong to a very small minority in Crna Gora (unlike the proportionality in Kosovo and Makedonija), and within the Moslem segment are able to enter into mixed marriages. There is no indication at present that this valley dialect is threatened with death, and we might say that in the case of a healthy language a conservative phonology is the expected thing. The thought always arises, however, that we really have no yardstick to determine when a linguistic community becomes too small to maintain itself indefinitely.

Furthermore, in the case of Gusî we have a single valley exposed to very powerful contacts with the entire mass of the extensive Serbo-Croatian language; in fact, the major part of the northern border of Albanian abutting Serbo-Croatian is remarkably sharp and clearcut in geography and in grammatical structure. When I term the Geg Albanian phonology of Gusî "conservative", this must be understood in a way that should be made clear. The phonology of Northern Geg has moved a considerable distance from that of Common Albanian; yet it is in some ways more retentive of old distinctive features (e.g. nasality with vowels, number and variety of diphthongs) than is Tosk. The important fact for us is that the changes undergone by Geg phonology have not been in the direction of contact accommodation to the neighboring language, and have not resulted in great loss of distinctions in forms. Conservatism, in this sense, admits considerable change in surface shape.

In phonology, Gusî contrasts abruptly with Serbo-Croatian by retaining its nasal vowels, its inherited diphthongs, its interdental spirants, to mention only some major features of contrast. The last named feature is, of course, shared with Greek to the south; but with the other two, Geg forms a curious island within the whole of the Balkans – an oddity from the point of view of language contact. Moreover, viewed diachronically and phonotactically, Gusî, as part of Northern Geg, has undergone severe vowel loss in unstressed syllables, with the resulting accumulation of consonant clusters; this is strongly counter to the Serbo-Croatian pattern. Finally, the sentence, prosodic, and intonational phonetics differ markedly in the two languages. We see here, then, a language traditionally insulated from its environment; this trait may perhaps be correlated with Albanian cultural attitudes toward its neighbors and the outside world. Yet if so, the correlation is a complex one.

We now note briefly in passing a partly similar case, the east Geg dialect of Tetovo (Tetovë), in Makedonija. This relatively conservative dialect is in no present danger of death; indeed its vitality is of some political concern to the Slavic Macedonians. On the other hand, the area from Tetovo to Debar (Dibrë) shows two sorts of innovations which are of interest to our present discussion. This area has undergone a striking diphthongization of older long vowels (somewhat like the English Great Vowel Shift), quite unlike the phonology of Makedonski; this is a case where older distinctions are conserved, but with new phonotactics, which do not find a simple contact correlation in the neighboring language. Now there is another innovation whereby much of Geg (including Gusî) shares a consonantal characteristic with the neighboring Slavic languages. In Northern Geg $k̂$ and $ĝ$ are articulated as affricates in exactly the same fashion as Serbo-Croatian $ć$ and $ʒ́$ (orthographic $đ$ or dj); in Dukagjin in northern Albania, the articulation shifts further to $ś$ and $ź$. In Kosovo these merge, in Albanian and in Serbo-Croatian, with $č$ and $ǯ$ (orthographic $dž$), and Makedonski has of these pairs only $č$ and $dž$; however, Makedonski possesses also $k̂$ and $ĝ$. Tetovo shows the following interference innovations: $*k̂ ĝ > *ć > ʒ́ > č ǯ$, and $*tj$ dj $> k̂ ĝ$, thereby exactly matching Makedonski in distinctive feature structure. If at any time language death were to occur in these two regions, we see that it would proceed on the basis of different degrees of acculturation.

This last train of reasoning may seem to be arguing from the vacuous case, but we must never underestimate the benign effects of contact or acculturation – the very characteristics that can easily be taken for malignant when death sets in. It may even be argued in a different vein that acculturation represents adaptation for survival.

There are some cases where survival is considered indeterminate in well informed circles, although it must be recognized that it is sometimes not easy to tell in such discussions at what level of language use survival will be considered adequate. I have heard at a symposium in Udine in September 1986 competent native scholars express dissatisfaction with the projected future of Romauntsch; nevertheless, one must say that the language has led a rather successful bilingual life during the twentieth century. On the other hand, from my studies of Surmeir at Tiefencastel I have been impressed by the degree to which this peripheral Romance variety has adapted its segmental sounds and phonotactics to the southernmost variety of German which it abuts.

4.   Survival with interference

We turn now briefly to pass in review a number of cases where a minority language is, or was recently, continuing in healthy repair in a state of stable bilingualism or in a multilingual Sprachbund situation. In these cases we find marked characteristics of acculturation in the phonology. Certainly the most remarkable case of this sort is Mandrìtsa, in southeasternmost Bulgaria, which I have discussed in this connection (Hamp 1970, 1978). Suffice it to say that among its phonological innovations Mandrìtsa, alone of all varieties of Albanian known to me, has merged its interdental spirants with the *s/z* set; it has also eliminated its diphthongs to conform phonotactically with Bulgarian, Turkish, and Greek. The various Arbresh enclaves of southern Italy have partially adapted their phonologies – and very much so their syllabic prosodics – to the adjacent Italian dialects; they are too diverse and too numerous to permit us a representative set of examples here. The Albanian of Prespa, in Makedonija on the periphery of the Albanian speech area, shows strong Makedonski interference: in this part of the Tosk spectrum all vowel length and the phoneme *h* have been lost, and the two *r*'s have merged.

   On the other hand, close by, the Aromân of southern Makedonija and the Pindos mountains in northern Greece have abandoned their Romanian diphthongs in two different directions (disyllables and new monophthongs) to accommodate to the Makedonski and Greek syllabic patterns. In the context of Greek and Makedonski, the display of Aromân (Vlah, Koutsovlah) obstruents appears as given in the schema (3) above. A classical Sprachbund result, with different mergers in different dialects.

5.   Death

We have now surveyed a number of cases which span the range from conservatism to acculturation and which are apparently not at present, nor in their recent history, threatened with imminent death. I feel confident of the data on which these observations are based since I have personally heard and studied these varieties over some considerable time in situ. We will turn now to consider in similar fashion a comparable range of cases which can be classified as in varying stages of language shift and death.

5.1.   *Without capitulation*

It is difficult to say today whether the dialects of the valley of Resia, a very removed and isolated form of Slovene in northeast Italy, will survive or not. After the usual results of urbanization, emigration, rapid highway communication, and the decline of local mountain economies, the discouraging earthquake of 1976 has left the valley (comprising six villages) with a population of under 2,000. Pride is high in this valley, and interest in local tradition is active; but there may be a limit in the critical mass which will pass the language on to the children – signs are already alarming. The characteristics of this remarkable form of Slavic have been known to the learned world in great detail ever since the pioneering work of Baudouin de Courtenay (1875). In short visits over the past ten years I have been studying this dialect (strictly speaking, the subdialect of Oseacco), originally with the intention of observing contact phenomena and aided by prior descriptive work. As it turns out, it has taken me so much time and effort merely to understand the complex phonological and morphological system of this dialect, and to grasp the inadequacies of earlier descriptive work, that I find myself obliged to prepare and present certain supplementary basic description, which I hope soon now to have in publishable form. My results will alter some of the statements of Baudouin de Courtenay, which have been strangely perpetuated for a century now; but for our present purposes the superb and perceptive work of genius that Baudouin has left us is not diminished or invalidated by my refinements.

Resia (and my favorite speaker and teacher of Oseacco, and numerous 30-year-old people of the valley) has an unusual phonology (and an astonishingly complex morphology, which must have been the source and goad and inspiration for Baudouin's theory of alternations) which is quite unlike anything in the neighboring contacts. The most famous property of Resian consists in the four distinctive vowels which Baudouin simply called "dark", but which I hear clearly as centralized, and which contrast very obviously with six nonsurprising peripheral vowels; the peripheral vowels are in the ranges [i e æ a o u], while the centralized (called by the Slovene scholars *zasopli* 'breathed') vary about [ï ə y ø]. The dialect also has a voiced *h* (which Baudouin and others have oddly missed) < Slavic *g*, which contrasts sharply with [x], the reflex of the Slavic sound often written with that Cyrillic and IPA shape. There is no sign of surrender of this areally unusual phonology in the face of death.

An even more resolute conservatism in the realm of phonology and phonetics in the face of death is to be seen in several parts of the Highlands of Scotland on the periphery of the Gaelic-speaking area. These also happen to contrast interestingly with the East Sutherland variety that has been studied so carefully by Nancy Dorian, which for whatever reason has reduced (even in the "healthiest" conservative speech of many people – now deceased –

raised in a time of widespread fluency and considerable monolingualism) a good number of phonological distinctions. With the exception of the northernmost dialects, Scottish Gaelic displays what is perhaps the most aberrant phonetic structure in Europe; for purposes of the present topic we shall leave the vowels and syllabic structure out of account and concentrate on the consonant system, though it may be of interest in passing to note that non-initial consonants always belong syllabically with the vowel that precedes them and not with the following vowel. Outside of the northernmost dialects, the entire consonant system is dominated by a fortis/lenis distinction, or dichotomy, and the obstruents show a negligible degree of voicing: with the stops, fortisness is accompanied by a prolonged aspiration, or velar or homorganic spirant (varying for geographic area), on the side of the consonant next to the stressed vowel. In South Argyll (see the map in Chapter 3) every stressed syllable not closed by a fortis consonant has its right-hand boundary marked by a glottal stop or constriction. The sonants of the language are completely integrated into this system.

The consonant system of Islay (still alive and well), in South Argyll, may be displayed as follows:

(6)   fortis

	t	č	ḱ	k	p	+
	d	ǰ	ǵ	g	b	−
h	s	š	ç	x	f	+
r			j	γ	v	−
					v̄	+
	n		n′			−
					m	
	N		N′			+
l	ł		l′			−
	L		L′			+

Now let us focus on West Kintyre, also in South Argyll. In all of Kintyre there cannot be more than a dozen or so local speakers left of any kind; the youngest must be over 60 or so, a couple are institutionalized, and there are three I know who have died since 1985. Recently there have been only two viable, totally local, speakers acceptable for purposes of the Scottish Gaelic Survey which except under marginal conditions accepts no semi-speakers; one, a beautifully clear and stylistically tasteful speaker, died early in 1985, and his cousin survives. This account, which I am writing up more fully elsewhere, comes from these two, both of Muasdale, halfway down the West Kintyre coast. The obstruents of Muasdale are the same (and much the same phonetically) as those of Islay, with the absence, so far as I know, of the fortis v̄. The laterals and nasals, however, are stupendous and unparalleled. There are six distinctive surface phonemes each for the laterals and the nasals, without counting *m*. These can be tabulated as follows; I give only the laterals as an example:

(7)

+velarized	{	+protruded	Ł	L̄
		−protruded	ł	
−velarized			l	
palatal			ʎ	ʎ̄
			−fortis	+fortis

It is hard to think of a European phonology more different from that of English. The question might be asked whether on such slender evidence from so few speakers these remarkable Muasdale features might not be really the products of idiosyncrasy in a couple of terminal speakers (who are by no means semi-speakers, but fully fluent). This can certainly not be the case, since attentive analysis shows that these subtle and highly specific distinctions find exact correlates in other distant Gaelic dialects and in the historical phonology of Old and Middle Irish; no unsophisticated native speaker could have invented and correctly distributed these refined phonetic discrimina, nor could they result from the loss of old rules that language decline or death seem to imply.

There can be no doubt that the dialect of Muasdale, and of Kintyre, is now at death's door; yet the phonology that we find in those last speakers is in many and important respects not only unimpaired, but conservative to a degree that tenaciously preserves archaic distinctions and features not paralleled elsewhere in our dossier in like richness and array. Moreover, the discourse and segmental phonetics of these last speakers is in every way appropriate to that section of the Gaidhealtachd. One may properly ask why it should be that such phonological conservation perseveres in such a case down to the very last speaker. It is worth remarking here that while the late George Thomson (born 1907) was a quiet, reflective, literate man with a natural feel for and curiosity about his language, he cultivated an easy, flowing delivery rich in vocabulary but free from pedantry; he was surprised to recognize for the first time in his life the distinctions in the laterals and nasals that I pointed out to him (after the fact, of course). His cousin is very different, an active, practical man, not at all bookish and somewhat impatient with the nuisance of a visiting grammarian. There is little inherently alike in these two personalities to furnish a substantial explanation for the observed conservatism; I can see here only a way of understanding how it is that George Thomson was an ideally clear and precise (yet relaxed) speaker whose every articulation I could watch and mimic, while his cousin is a convivial, tart, off-the-cuff speaker who takes a lot of strategy and watching to catch the rapid essentials. I am very grateful that I worked first with George Thomson.

The rapid decline of Scottish Gaelic in recent centuries has been written about on numerous occasions, and most recently Durkacz (1983:215–26) has briefly discussed some causes of decline. He stresses the degree and rapidity of surrender to English in Scotland (though Dorian [1981:51] points to the long period of cultural and psychological disfavor which paved the way for that surrender). We must also remember the extreme depopulation by emigration that Scottish Gaelic dialectology has suffered, and which makes it a special case among modern European languages. But perhaps this decline over the past few centuries carries a special pattern which paradoxically will furnish the key to our understanding of the phonological and phonetic conservatism observed among terminal speakers. We must recall here that as language death sets in with these speakers they and their community shift not to a worldwide English, nor to RP, nor to adjacent broad Scots, but to Highland English, whose phonetics carries a large number of the most distinctive traits of Gaelic phonetics. We may say, then, that in effecting language shift in the Highlands and Islands there is very little change or loss to be undergone in the phonology. That aspect has already been bridged in the opposite direction by the bilingualism of the recent past. The phonology of terminal Gaelic is, so to speak, protected by Highland English. The next question then is: what will become of Highland English? We might also ask whether the reclamation of territory by Gaelic might not be facilitated by Highland English.

5.2.   With accommodation

It is time now to remind ourselves of some cases showing strong acculturation which are surely marked for death by language shift. The Vannetais Breton of the Ploemel-Quiberon-Carnac region is certain to follow the fate of many varieties of coastal Breton, which are attacked by modern urbanization, tourism, and changes in values flowing in from the outside world; children have simply not been learning the local language. If a renaissance should somehow set in, it will bring with it a standardized book Vannetais, if not a broader and more distant Kerne-Leon-Treger (the norm of the other collective variety of Breton). This corner of Vannetais has remarkable phonological traits: extreme palatalization of velars, vowel shifts and diphthongization, loss of non-initial dental stops, change of final -*h* to pharyngealization of the preceding vowel, to mention only some arresting developments that render these dialects at first unintelligible to speakers of other dialects of their language. These changes are quite idiosyncratic developments over many recent generations that find no obvious correlation in contact interference. However, there are other characteristics going back many centuries that must be placed in relation to the adjacent French-speaking area: change of the original interdental spirants (to *z* and *h*), development of nasal vowels, realignment and conservation of front rounded vowels, development of *ẅ* from *w*, suppression of diphthongs, lack of word accent in favor of French-style phrasal contours, development of an *h*-aspiré rule – these will be sufficient to suggest the depth of the penetration. Yet all these marks of acculturation and change have been accomplished long before the phase heralding retreat and death set in.

I have described (Hamp 1965) the leading phonological features of Màndres in northern Greece, which was settled early in this century from Mandrìtsa, mentioned above. I visited Màndres again in 1982, and found that now only middle-aged and older men know that Albanian dialect; indeed, only a few of a large group I sat with had good control of more complex phrases and clauses, which were the object of my elicitation on that visit. From the phonological point of view, we may say confidently that the noteworthy acculturated traits that will die in Màndres were already acquired before their separation from Mandrìtsa.

The future does not look bright for Arbanasi (formerly Borgo Erizzo), at Zadar in Croatia on the Dalmatian coast (see Hamp 1972:1632), which was formed as a colony there a couple of centuries ago from near Lake Scutari. What was once, as recently as 1961, a small suburb outside Zadar is now engulfed by the city (by 1977) and seems unlikely to endure as an alloglot urban enclave. But already earlier in this century the phonological acculturation to Croatian was well advanced: merger of the two *r*'s, merger of the affricates as in Tetovo, merger of θ with *s* and $\eth$ with the solitary lateral left; Arbanasi has been adapting long before death.

We have already taken account above of the widespread phonological acculturation of Arvanìtika long before the advent of death in some of its detached areas, and surely in practically all of its extent before another generation of speakers live out their lives.

One last case has a particular interest because of its special circumstances and for its contrast with the Scottish Gaelic inspected in detail above. The island of St Kilda lies in the Atlantic approximately 50 miles off Harris, the latter together with Lewis forming the northernmost of the Outer Hebrides. From a population of a couple of hundred two centuries ago the total number of inhabitants had fallen to 36 in 1930, of which a half-dozen were still monoglot Gaelic speakers. Because the community was no longer socially viable, the St Kildians were removed at their own request to the main part of Scotland in August 1930. The remaining children were absorbed as Gaelic speakers in their new home. Of the original group there now survives two, only one of whom, aged 82, remains suitable for study (and a superb speaker and conversationalist he is!); we also know the precise fate of all the others, and three others have been studied over the past 35 years. There is no question of the purity of Lachlan MacDonald's dialect: he has lived apart from the others, is married to a non-Gaelic-speaking wife, has been employed outside the Gaidhealtachd, is not literate in Gaelic, and has an acute sense of his language while speaking with no pretension at all. The internal evidence of his usage is highly consistent. Yet for all that

Lachlan MacDonald has conserved, we find that the dialect of St Kilda had already undergone notable unique changes specific to that island: original palatal *r* had merged with *l*; the laterals (cf. Muasdale above) had been reduced to *l*, *l'*, and *w*; and the nasals stand at *m*, *n*, *n'*, and *ŋ*. This inventory greatly resembles that of Dorian's East Sutherland.

One sad day the St Kilda dialect will die, but with a diminished phonology intact with which it led a vigorous life.

14 Case usage among the Pennsylvania German sectarians and nonsectarians

MARION LOIS HUFFINES

For immigrant and minority languages in the United States, language death is an almost inevitable outcome of contact with American English. The promise of social and economic advancement proffered by mastery of English eventually overcomes the most fervent of language loyalty intentions. The number of social contexts in which speakers can use the minority language steadily declines. Without the support of continued immigration from the language homeland, the number of fluent interlocutors gradually decreases, and eventually no social context remains in which it is appropriate to speak the minority language. Pennsylvania German, although it has enjoyed a long history in America, is no exception to this general process.

Pennsylvania Germans settled in America during colonial times in farm communities across southeastern and central Pennsylvania. Secondary settlements arose later in Ohio, Indiana, Illinois, and the Virginias. While many of these communities have long ago completely and irrevocably assimilated into mainstream American society, some have maintained their peculiarly Pennsylvania German (PG) culture and language to the present time. Although all Pennsylvania Germans share many traits and values, the PG population is not one homogeneous group. It consists of many subgroups, each having a different relationship to the dominant society, and each speaking a variety of Pennsylvania German which fulfills different communicative and symbolic functions. The purpose of this study is to document linguistic change in such subgroups: Pennsylvania German, as it is dying in farm communities of nonsectarians, and as it is being maintained in farm communities of Amish and Mennonite sectarians.

1. Background

Within a community shifting from one language to another, proficiency in the receding language varies widely. Native speakers who continue to use the language with family members and friends exhibit full mastery; other bilinguals who use the language only in certain circumstances exhibit faulty grammar and large gaps in their lexicon. Nonfluent speakers by definition diverge from the language norms of fluent native speakers, but even young fluent speakers display linguistic norms which differ from those of older native speakers of a receding language (Dorian 1973, 1978c).

Studies have documented a number of linguistic consequences for receding languages: analogic leveling, use of analytic constructions in preference to synthetic grammatical forms, loss of grammatical categories and syntactic options, the loss of native vocabulary and extensive borrowing from the culturally dominant language, loss of stylistic options, and reduced phonological distinctions. These linguistic changes are typically found in the speech of younger and nonfluent speakers of dying languages. (See especially, Dorian 1973, 1981; Tsitsipis 1981a; Schmidt 1985c).

Case syncretism or case merger, long recognized as a common phenomenon in historical linguistics, characterizes terminal stages of receding languages. Case syncretism reduces morphological complexity and eradicates apparent irregularities in nominal paradigms. Younger fluent speakers and semi-speakers of East Sutherland Gaelic show weakened mastery of the dative case, and semi-speakers make little use of the vocative, resulting in some nominal declensions which consist of one invariant form in the speech of all but the older fluent speakers (Dorian 1977b, 1981, 1984). Terminal speakers of Arvanítika in Greece reduce meaningful morphological variation and lose case, gender, number, and definiteness distinctions (Tsitsipis 1981). Young speakers of Dyirbal generalize a single affix to mark several case functions or resort to the use of an English preposition and thereby avoid bound morphemes (Schmidt 1985c:61). The reduction of grammatically marked categories often results in compensating structures elsewhere in the language. Dorian (1981) reports the use of prepositional phrases by most fluent and nonfluent speakers for the moribund genitive case in East Sutherland Gaelic. Schmidt (1985c) describes allomorphic reduction and the loss of the ergative case accompanied by greater rigidity in word order for young people's Dyirbal.

Case syncretism is frequently found in American German language varieties, all of which are in various stages of decline. Only varieties spoken by separatist religious groups have the continued support of native speakers. Case syncretism in German typically involves the collapse of the nominative and accusative cases or the dative and the accusative cases. Such case merger in German need not result from contact with English. In many areas of northern Germany, including Berlin, speakers do not distinguish the accusative and dative cases, and in Rhenish areas the distinction between the nominative and accusative has been lost (Keller 1961). While the genitive exists in European Standard German, the genitive does not exist in spoken regional dialects. An alternative construction with the preposition *von* is general, but southern German and Swiss dialects use the dative construction described below for Pennsylvania German to express possession. Only fossilized remnants of the genitive case occur in either European or American German dialects.

Loss of the dative case is reported for several varieties of Texas German. Eikel (1949, 1967) finds that in New Braunfels (Texas) German the accusative case has replaced the dative in all its functions, especially among younger speakers. Similarly, Wilson (1960) describes the loss of the dative for the German spoken in Lee and Fayette counties. Gilbert (1987) and Salmons (1983a) report a loss of the dative in progress for Kendall and Gillespie counties: older speakers tend to retain the dative/accusative distinction; younger speakers do not. Salmons (1983b) finds no dative forms in the speech of his informants born after 1960.

For Wisconsin German, Eichoff (1971) makes no mention of dative loss, stating (p.52), "Wherever dialects are found, they faithfully continue the language of nineteenth-century Germany." Lewis (1973) specifically states that the dative has been preserved in Wisconsin German, but he reports a frequent failure to mark dative plural nouns.

Kehr (1979) identifies six areas in Virginia and West Virginia where German language varieties may be found. That the dative still exists in these varieties may be assumed in the absence of comments to the contrary. However, evidence from one sentence which Kehr cites to illustrate the six German varieties indicates that in three of the six areas speakers may not use dative forms. Two of those three areas are settled by separatist religious groups; in the third area the German language has almost disappeared, strong speakers coming from only one family. Pulte (1971) makes no mention of case syncretism for the same Virginia and West Virginia areas.

For Pennsylvania German, one notes the merger of the nominative and accusative cases for articles and adjectives to form a common case, a feature which Pennsylvania German shares with southeastern Rhine-Palatine dialects (Buffington and Barba 1965:141). The nominative/accusative distinction still exists for pronouns. Reports regarding the viability of the dative case vary considerably. Anderson and Martin (1976:78) report for the Pennsylvania German spoken among the Old Order Mennonites in Pennsylvania and Ontario a lack of the use of the dative case after certain prepositions and verbal expressions "which govern the dative in Standard German". Their investigation reveals that older informants and some preschool-age children use more datives. For the Pennsylvania German spoken by the Old Order Amish in Delaware, Enninger (1980:14) reports "a trend towards the neutralization of dative and accusative cases with pronouns" and "similar indications in the noun paradigms". Costello (1985) finds accusative as well as dative forms used as the object of agentive prepositional phrases following the passive, and he speculates that this is an incipient case merger. All published teaching grammars of Pennsylvania

German, even the most recent, carefully distinguish dative and accusative forms and functions (Frey 1942 [rpt.1981]; Druckenbrod 1981; Haag 1982), as do Buffington and Barba *A Pennsylvania German grammar* (1965), a standardization to which most scholars refer, and Reed (1948), a descriptive study based on fieldwork in Berks and Lehigh counties.[1] Older handbooks on Pennsylvania German also give no indication of variable usage of dative and accusative forms (Haldeman 1872; Learned 1889; Horne 1905).

2.   Procedures

2.1.   The sample

The following observations are based on interviews with 52 Pennsylvania Germans: 33 nonsectarians and 19 sectarians. Although both groups speak Pennsylvania German, there is almost no contact between sectarian and nonsectarian Pennsylvania Germans other than occasional business transactions. The groups know little about each other, and popular misconceptions prevail.

The nonsectarians. The nonsectarians were born and raised on farms in the Schwaben Creek Valley, the Mahantango Valley, or the Hegins Valley of lower Northumberland County, upper Dauphin County, and western Schuylkill County. The group of nonsectarians is classified into three groups:
  1. Native speakers of Pennsylvania German. The 13 native speakers of Pennsylvania German range in age from 35 to 75 years; all but four are 60+. All the informants over 60 had eight years of schooling and continue to live on the farms where they have spent most of their lives. All but the two youngest (35 and 47 years old) speak Pennsylvania German to their spouses and peers but English to their children. The two youngest informants have monolingual English-speaking spouses.
  2. First-in-the-family native English speakers. The nine Pennsylvania Germans in this group are the first in their respective families to speak English natively. They range in age from 32 to 54 years. All went through high school, and two graduated from college. All acquired Pennsylvania German in their preteen years by hearing it spoken by their parents to each other and older family members. Their parents spoke directly to them only in English. Members of this group generally use Pennsylvania German only when speaking to elderly members of the community for whom Pennsylvania German is the preferred language.
  3. Second- or later-in-the-family native English speakers. The 11 Pennsylvania Germans in this group are native speakers of English who are either the younger siblings or the oldest children of speakers in Group 1 or their linguistic cohort. They range in age from 22 to 65. They understand

Pennsylvania German without difficulty but seldom speak it. They learned what they know of Pennsylvania German from hearing it spoken in their childhood homes, but their parents always addressed them in English.

The sectarians. The PG sectarian sample consists of nine Amish and ten Mennonites, who live on farms in Union County. All except the youngest Mennonite (aged 24) were born and raised in Lancaster County; the youngest Mennonite was born in Union County four months after her parents settled there. All the sectarians speak Pennsylvania German natively. Most learned English in school, but some had learned English as preschoolers by waiting on customers at local farmers' markets or at roadside stands. All the sectarians are bilingual.

Of the Amish informants, eight are part of a conservative wing of the New Order Amish group consisting of 15 families in Union County. They range in age from 19 to 65. Their lifestyle is characterized by distinctive dress, education to the eighth grade, and horse and buggy transportation. Their homes have electricity and some modern conveniences, specifically a refrigerator, freezer, and washer. Church services are held in private homes. The hymns and Bible readings are in an archaic variety of Standard German, the sermons in Pennsylvania German. Some of the younger New Order Amish couples speak some English to their children before they enter school, and consequently more preschoolers can understand and speak English more fluently than their parents did at their age. The one Old Order Amish informant (age 32) in the sample lives across the Susquehanna River from Union County in Northumberland County. His home does not have electricity. The Old Order and the New Order Amish differ from each other in the interpretation of how to be separated "from the world".

Of the ten Mennonites in this sample, eight are Old Order Mennonites, also called Team Mennonites, and range in age from 24 to 51. Their lifestyle is similar to that of the Amish: distinctive dress, limited education, and horse and buggy transportation. Their church services are conducted in church buildings built for that purpose. Church readings are in an archaic variety of Standard German and the sermons in Pennsylvania German. Their homes have washers, refrigerators, and freezers. Two informants (both age 35) are members of a more modern Mennonite group. In that group only the women have obvious dress requirements; education is not limited, although they prefer private parochial schools to public ones. These two informants attended high school, and they drive cars.

2.2. The interview

The interviews were conducted in the informants' homes and lasted for about one-and-a-half hours. Each one consisted of three parts: free conversation, translation of English sentences into Pennsylvania German, and description of pictures. The interviewer spoke only English, and the informants responded in Pennsylvania German, a conversational pattern which is common in Pennsylvania German communities where the use of Pennsylvania German is declining (see Dorian 1981).

3.   Results

The dative case. Pennsylvania German as spoken by the oldest native speakers in the nonsectarian community investigated has three genders (masculine, feminine, and neuter), two numbers (singular and plural), and two cases (common and dative) in its noun system. As in Standard German, these categories are signaled by the form of the definite and indefinite articles and by the endings of possessive, demonstrative, and attributive adjectives. The common case fulfills the functions of the German nominative and accusative. The pronoun system has three cases: the nominative, accusative, and dative. Distinctively marked dative pronoun forms occur in the 1st, 2nd, and 3rd persons singular, and in the 3rd person plural. The interrogative personal pronoun also has two case forms, the common and the dative (see Table 1). There is no genitive case although relics of the genitive may be found in compound nouns (/kɪnskɪnd/'grandchild') and in adverbial forms expressing repeated time (/maryɛts/'mornings', /samšdags/ 'Saturdays'). A genitive -*s* is also used with proper nouns to express possessions.

The results in the rest of this section report dative case usage for each of

Table 1. *Pennsylvania German pronoun forms*†

	Nominative	Accusative	Dative
1sg.	ɪç	mɪç	mir/mər††
2sg.	du	dɪç	dir/dər
3sg. masc.	ar	in/ən	im/əm
3sg. fem.	si	si	irə,ir/rə
3sg. neut.	əs	əs	no forms elicited
1pl.	mir/mər	ʊns	ʊns
2pl.	dir/dər	aiç	aiç
3pl.	si	si	inə/nə
interrog.	var	var (vɛn)†††	vɛm

† All forms cited occur in the speech of nonsectarian native speakers.
†† Unstressed variants of pronoun forms follow the stressed forms given and are separated by a slash in the table.
††† The interrogative accusative pronoun form /vɛn/ occurs only once. The speaker who gives that form also uses /var/ in all other accusative functions. The sectarian speakers use /vɛr/ instead of /var/ for the interrogative nominative and accusative pronoun.

five groups of informants: N, nonsectarian native speakers; 1, first in the family to learn English natively; 2, second or later in the family to learn English natively; M, Mennonites; A, Amish. Results based on the translation task are reported separately from those of the picture descriptions and free conversation. Not all members of each group responded with comparable grammatical constructions to individual sentences in the translation task or to the pictures. In the tables that follow, scores reflect the number of times that informants responded with the form indicated. Informants' relative age is given where age is a factor in the distribution of dative forms. As will be seen below, age plays an important role in the occurrence of forms in the speech of the nonsectarians; age plays a marginal role in the distribution of forms in the speech of the sectarians.

Dative personal pronouns. In the translation task, 15 sentences are designed to elicit personal pronouns in dative functions. The nonsectarian native speakers respond with the most dative pronouns, a total of 83; of the 22 elicited accusative forms, 18 are given by the two youngest speakers in Group N. These two informants frequently diverge linguistically from the older native speakers, as will be noted below. First-native-English speakers respond with fewer dative pronoun forms. Second-native-English speakers have still fewer dative forms and more accusative forms; this group differs from the previous group in the number of faulty forms offered which are neither dative nor accusative. Of the sectarians, only the oldest Mennonite informant and the one Old Order Amish informant offer dative forms (see Table 2).

Table 2. *Case of personal pronouns in dative functions (number of responses in translation task)*

Group	Dative	Accusative	Other	Total
N	83	22	0	105
1	50	43	1	94
2	30	39	8	77
M	1	86	0	87
A	2	90	0	92

The free conversation and picture descriptions allow for the use of PG forms without overt reference to English. The free conversation and picture descriptions yield dative pronoun forms from nonsectarian speakers and the first-native-English speakers; only five dative forms occur in the speech of members in the other groups (see Table 3).

Possession. In Pennsylvania German the dative is used in conjunction with

Table 3. *Dative personal pronouns (number of responses on free conversation and picture descriptions)*

Group	1 sg.	2 sg.	3 masc. sg.	3 fem. sg.	3 pl.	Total
N	14	5	9	8	3	39
1	3	2	2	5	0	12
2	1	1	2†	0	0	4
M	0	1	0	0	0	1
A	0	0	0	0	0	0

†Other faulty forms given.

the possessive adjective to express possession. The possessor is expressed by the dative; the possessive adjective follows and agrees with the possessed, the noun it modifies; for example, /əm dadi sai bʊx/ 'daddy's book', /was dudšt du mɪt sɛləm man saim hut/ 'what are you doing with that man's hat'. The question form *whose* is rendered by the dative interrogative pronoun /vɛm/ followed by /sai/ which is followed by the possessed if it is stated. The question *Whose dog is that?* is rendered /vɛm sai hʊnd ɪs sɛl). The form /vɛm/ in this construction is invariant regardless of antecedent. If the possessed is left unstated, /sai/ functions as a pronoun and agrees grammatically with its antecedent; the question *Whose is that?* referring to /bʊx/ (neuter), is rendered /vɛm sains ɪs sɛl).

In the translation task, five sentences are designed to elicit expressions of possession. Nonsectarian native speakers respond most frequently with dative forms to express the possessor; for example, /maim grɛnpæp saini/ 'my grandfather's [sausage]'. The sectarians with one exception use the common case to express the possessor; for example, /mai grosdadi saini/. Nonsectarian English speakers show considerable variation. The second-native-English speakers resort most frequently to the English genitive -*s* and also produce faulty constructions lacking gender, number, and case agreement (see Table 4).

Informants use few possessive constructions during free conversation and picture descriptions, but the results parallel those obtained in the translation task. Among nonsectarian native speakers, only the two youngest speakers use the common case, and the group as a whole produces no errors. For first-native-English speakers dative usage recedes while common case usage increases. Second-native-English speakers demonstrate no mastery of the possession construction. Most of the forms produced by this group lack grammatical agreement or semantic appropriateness, and one speaker resorts twice to the English construction. The sectarians consistently use the common case to express possession. One Amish speaker uses the semantically inappropriate form, /sai/ 'his' for /ir/ 'her' (see Table 5.)

The question form /vɛm sai/ 'whose' seems best preserved of any possess-

Table 4. *Case of the possessor (number of responses on the translation task)*

Group	Dative	Common	−s	Other	Total
N	16	21	2	3	42
1	14	16	6	1	37
2	4	10	18	8	40
M	1	26	5	3	35
A	0	28	4	6	38

Table 5. *Case of the possessor (number of responses on free conversation and picture descriptions)*

Group	Dative	Common	−s	Other	Total
N	4	3	0	0	7
1	3	4	0	0	7
2	0	0	2	4	6
M	0	11	0	0	11
A	0	14	0	1	15

Table 6. *Case usage for 'whose' (number of responses on translation task)*

Group	vɛm sai	var/vɛr sai	Other	Total
N	9	0	0	9
1	5	1	1	7
2	5	0	4	9
M	2	5	0	7
A	1	6	0	7

ive construction. Two of the faulty forms given also mark common case /sai/ as dative /saim/; two delete /sai/ from the 'whose' construction while using the common case /var/. The sectarian variant of the common case /var/ is consistently /vɛr/ (see Table 6).

In two sentences the possessed also has a dative function; for example, /mir warə ɪn mainrə ænt irəm haus/ 'we were in my aunt's house'. For each of these two sentences, four nonsectarian native speakers and first-native-English speakers express that noun phrase in the dative. Other than the /vɛm sai/ construction, only one sectarian speaker uses a dative to express possession.

Prepositions. As in Standard German and according to the Buffington and Barba (1965) standardization, the PG dative is used to express the object of

Table 7. *Case usage with all dative prepositions (number of responses on translation task)*

Group	Dative	Common	Other	Total
N	127	99	5	231
1	71	74	24	169
2	27	81	41	149
M	3	175	8	186
A	2	172	4	178

Table 8. *Case usage with all dative prepositions (number of responses on free conversation and picture descriptions)*

Group	Dative	Common	Other	Total
N	331	132	6	469
1	142	126	35	303
2	95	123	24	242
M	40	346	0	386
A	14	303	3	320

two sets of prepositions. One set of prepositions always governs the dative; a second set governs the dative when the activity of the verb takes place within the spatial or temporal limits expressed by the prepositions; when the verbal activity crosses those limits, these prepositions govern the common case. Spoken Pennsylvania German presents a more complex picture than the above prescriptive rules suggest.

When one considers the total number of potentially marked forms (pronouns, articles, possessive adjectives) with dative prepositions, the nonsectarian native speakers produce dative forms most frequently, followed by the first-native-English speakers. The second-native-English speakers have a considerable number of forms which are neither the dative nor the common case. Many of these faulty forms lack grammatical agreement, especially in gender, and others are clearly aberrant constructions. With few exceptions, sectarians produce forms in the common case. These results obtain whether pronouns or noun phrases occur as objects of the prepositions (see Tables 7 and 8).

The nonsectarian groups diverge linguistically from each other more than the figures in Tables 7 and 8 suggest. The Buffington and Barba (1965) standardized grammar prescribes the feminine dative singular ending /-rə/ for possessive adjectives. In the interview data, these feminine forms are extremely rare. One nonsectarian native speaker uses /mainrə/ twice during the translation task; otherwise no other /-rə/ endings occur. The forms /sainə/ and /mainə/, rather than /sainrə/ and /mainrə/, appear to function as the feminine dative. Only occasionally are the common case forms /sai/ and /mai/ used. Certain phrases appear to be formulaic and are invariant. Two such phrases, /ɪn di šul/ 'in school' and /ɪn di mɪt/ 'in the middle', are particularly frequent. One statement occurring during free conversation suggests the formulaic nature of the feminine definite article /di/ with the noun /šul/: /wɛl di axt greds warə ɪn di em šulhaus/ 'well, the eight grades were in the one schoolhouse'. The form /em/, here a numeral used as an adjective, is marked for the dative case (and neuter at that, because /šul/ is compounded with neuter /haus/). The forms /sainə/ and /mainə/ and the formulaic expressions involving /šul/ and /mɪt/ account for most of the forms counted as "other" or "common case" in Tables 7 and 8 for Group N. Common case forms with dative prepositions not so accounted for are used only by the two youngest native speakers.

The first-native-English speakers use common case forms more frequently with prepositions governing the dative than do the nonsectarian native speakers, but this group differs from the latter in other ways. One of the oldest informants in this group uses /sainrə/ and /mainrə/ once each, but one of these two incorrectly modifies a plural. The /mainə/ and /sainə/ forms occur three times in the translation task and are used by the older members of this group. The aberrant form /ənə/ appears to function as the dative indefinite article for three members of this group and for one in particular. The form /ənə/ occurs with nouns of all genders, and accounts for over half of the total in the "other" category in the Tables 7 and 8. When compared to others in Group 1, the two youngest members of Group 1 (32 and 33 years old) make frequent errors in grammatical agreement and are especially weak in gender agreement.

The Pennsylvania German of the second-native-English speakers differs from that of the previous group in that it contains a larger number of aberrant forms and semantically inappropriate forms. Definite and indefinite articles, which normally carry case markings, are frequently omitted and the nouns occur in telegraphic-style strings. Such undifferentiated forms are not reflected in the tables above. Aberrant forms of the dative possessive adjectives include the frequent use of /main/ and /sain/; such forms in final /-n/ do not occur in Pennsylvania German. The forms /mainə/, /dainə/, and /sainə/ as well as dative forms /maim/, daim/, and /saim/ occur with all genders in no discernible pattern. Errors of grammatical agreement are frequent. Prepositions with contracted forms of the dative definite article (/tsʊm/, /ɪm/) occur as the prepositional form itself: /ɪm di šul/ 'in the school', /tsʊm di gans famɪlyə/ 'to the whole family'. When compared to all other groups, this group shows the least agreement on usage. Each individual's formulation of sentences in the translation task differs from all the others in the group on some dimension. Likewise, the formulations describing the pictures vary widely within the group.

The sectarians show a substantial amount of agreement in usage. Their use of the common case for dative functions far exceeds such usage among the nonsectarians. The dative forms that occur among the Mennonites are generally, though not always, found in the speech of the oldest members of that group. Some dative expressions seem to be fossilized; one informant uses /nax əm risɛs/ 'after recess' three times but has only one other occurrence of the dative definite article /əm/. The Amish group uses even fewer dative forms, several of which are given by the single Old Order Amish member of the group. In contrast to the nonsectarian native speakers, the sectarians have several errors in grammatical agreement involving gender. While these errors are relatively few when compared to those of the nonsectarian native English speakers, they are more frequent among the Amish than among the Mennonites. Aberrant forms such as those found in Group 2 do not occur in the speech of the sectarians.

4.   Discussion

The nonsectarian native speakers with few exceptions use dative forms to express dative functions. Except for the two youngest nonsectarian native speakers, almost all substitution of accusative pronouns and nouns in the common case is found in formulaic phrases. Faulty forms seem to be the formulation of a new feminine dative form which is used by most members of the group. The speech of the nonsectarian native speakers reflects a firmly established norm for PG dative usage. The two youngest nonsectarian native speakers diverge from that norm in ways which are consonant with the linguistic performance of the first-native-English speakers. Their use of PG also closely parallels the restricted use found in that group. Both have non-PG spouses and use Pennsylvania German with relatives only when unaccompanied by their spouses.

The first-in-the-family native English speakers use fewer datives and more accusative and common case forms to express dative functions than do the nonsectarian native speakers. Group 1 uses the feminine dative form established by the native speakers and the same formulaic phrases. The oldest members of the group occasionally use the more conservative forms of the native speaker group; the youngest members make frequent errors in grammatical agreement. The innovative form /ənə/ used by three members may be the attempt on the part of individuals to capture the dative, and except for one occurrence in Group 2, the form is restricted to use by members of Group 1.

The second-in-the-family native English speakers use still fewer datives and more accusative and common case forms to express dative functions. This Group 2 contrasts with all other groups by the large number of errors in agreement and of aberrant forms which are neither dative nor a correct formulation of accusative or common case forms. In addition, these speakers resort to other strategies in their effort to produce Pennsylvania

German. They delete articles and possessive adjectives which would normally mark grammatical agreement. They reformulate intended sentences in a seemingly extreme effort to maintain discourse in Pennsylvania German by using familiar constructions in sentences which *almost* say what they want to say. These reformulation efforts also result in repeated false starts and halting delivery. For the second-native-English speakers, dative forms are simply not available. Common case forms appear by default but so do others representing misfired attempts to produce Pennsylvania German. When compared to the discourse of the other groups, their sentences are simplified and approach a telegraphic-style mode of discourse punctuated by English and expressed in faulty PG grammar constructions. Particularly apparent in this group is the lack of unified usage or norm. Individuals often produce unique forms culled from their personal language acquisition history. Fossilized expressions come to function as forms, and memorized remnants serve as structural components. The norm established by the native speakers and aspired to by the first-native-English speakers has not been acquired by Group 2; the second-native-English speakers simply do not know the PG norm.

The sectarians use accusative and common case forms to express dative functions almost exclusively. The Mennonites produce some dative forms, most of which are fossilized remnants. Other dative forms were given by the oldest members of the Mennonite group. The Amish group uses even fewer dative forms than the Mennonites, and several of these were given by the Old Order Amish informant. It is clear from their uniform linguistic behavior that the sectarians have a firmly established norm. There is little linguistic variation among speakers. Their norm has adopted a one-case system for nouns and a two-case system for personal pronouns, and there is evidence for the possible future inclusion of the English genitive -*s* on nouns to express possession. The nominal system as a whole reflects an English model.

The sociolinguistic norm among sectarians requires discourse in Pennsylvania German unless sect members are in school or speaking with outsiders. While all community members are adept at codeswitching and easily switch from Pennsylvania German to English, that language behavior is not appropriate within the community. Pennsylvania German must meet all communicative needs within the sectarian community. The PG language resources are limited; it was cut off from its Germanic past at the time of settlement, and there is no productive relationship between Pennsylvania German and modern varieties of European or American German. Proficiency in Standard German is passive at best and usually limited to liturgical readings in archaic church German. The resources of language development beyond compounding and derivational processes must be derived from English. The relative lack of switching behavior has exposed the linguistic code to the influence of its English environment.

The sectarians are a separated people who maintain themselves within American society without being a part of it. Each sect interprets the degree of separation "from the world" for itself. The use of Pennsylvania German is part of that separated identity, but only one symbol among many of their separateness. The maintenance of Pennsylvania German among some of the Amish is becoming a debatable issue. For this Amish group, the use of Pennsylvania German in church is the paramount issue. Informants remark that to them it really does not matter if Pennsylvania German dies out, but that right now it is needed for participation in church. These informants clearly imply that if a communal decision were made to use English in church, then they would quickly switch to English for all other communicative functions. In this Amish community, most preschoolers know English, a marked departure from the previous generation. All informants state matter-of-factly that their Pennsylvania German contains a lot of English. English is part of their Pennsylvania German.

The Old Order Mennonites appear more committed to Pennsylvania German. All Old Order Mennonites reported speaking only Pennsylvania German to their children, who must "find their own way" in school. These informants express the view that those members who are dissatisfied with the use of Pennsylvania German are generally dissatisfied with other things. Those who give up Pennsylvania German also change in other areas of their lifestyle. The Old Order Mennonites seem to weight the symbolic value of Pennsylvania German more heavily than do the New Order Amish, and this is reflected to some extent in the conservative linguistic forms used by some members of the Mennonite group.

Each of the five groups has a different commitment to Pennsylvania German, a commitment which is ultimately tied to its communicative and symbolic uses. For the nonsectarians, native speakers use Pennsylvania German among themselves and with their linguistic peers, and they switch languages as is socially appropriate. The first-native-English speakers are part of the PG-speaking community. Pennsylvania German fulfills for them certain communicative functions, but these functions are limited. Here too the social environment requires that speakers use the appropriate language by switching. For the second-in-the-family native English speakers, Pennsylvania German generally serves no active communicative function. They cannot speak the language well enough to participate in PG conversations by speaking Pennsylvania German; they participate with their passive skills and by speaking English. Their attempts to use Pennsylvania German symbolize group membership. Informants relate instances of using Pennsylvania German "for fun" and to keep something hidden. Their faulty use of Pennsylvania German, though simplified to the point of telegraphic speech, serves them well in establishing their identity. Their efforts maintain enough Pennsylvania German for symbolic usage. Their language does not reflect strong tendencies of convergence to English (although they may resort to

English structures when their knowledge of PG forms fails them, as with the use of a possessive *-s*), but it does reflect abortive strategies at maintaining Pennsylvania German. Among the nonsectarians there is a sharp discontinuity in the transmission of Pennsylvania German: the present generation of native speakers chose to speak English to their children (see Huffines 1980). The PG norm was effectively removed from the acquisition potential for the next generation.

As Pennsylvania German dies out among the nonsectarians, one finds the loss of the PG norm reflected in faulty linguistic formulations, such as unsuccessful attempts to employ the dative case. Convergence to English is minimal. Attempts to converse in faulty Pennsylvania German on the part of nonfluent speakers result in a switch to English. The death of Pennsylvania German in nonsectarian communities is rapid once it begins and is complete across three generations, often across two. Among the sectarians, Pennsylvania German continues a forced existence where sociolinguistic norms prescribe its use but not its form. Convergence toward an English model is readily apparent.

The results reported in this study are not ones anticipated from a reading of previously published accounts of Pennsylvania German and its usage. Unexpected are the observations that the speech of the sectarians shows the most convergence to English, that some Mennonites are linguistically more conservative than some Amish, and that the speech of the nonsectarians is linguistically the most conservative of all groups and has the least amount of convergence to English. The distribution of speech forms among the nonsectarians varies by age and generation but correlates most closely with patterns of use: absolute age is less important than position within a linguistic cohort. Among the Amish and Mennonites, age has little bearing on the distribution of forms, and usage is uniform throughout sectarian communities. Evidence for the dative–accusative case merger appears in all age sectors of these sectarian speech communities. Previous studies of Pennsylvania German consider PG communities in isolation: individual Old Order communities (Anderson and Martin 1976, Enninger 1980) or individual nonsectarian communities (Dorian 1978a), often only considering the speech of fluent native speakers (Costello 1978, 1985) or variation across a broad geographical area (Reed 1948; Reed and Seifert 1954). This study documents linguistic variation within PG communities and compares the Pennsylvania German spoken in well-defined communities of sectarians with that spoken in a well-defined community of nonsectarians. By comparing Pennsylvania German across communities in which it functions differently, one ascertains that language death does not necessarily involve convergence to the dominant language in spite of lengthy contact, and that continued language contact may result in convergence in spite of considerable domain separation in patterns of use and without concomitant age correlations.

Note

1. Reference to the Buffington and Barba *A Pennsylvania German grammar* needs special comment because it has received so much attention by those who research Pennsylvania German. Buffington and Barba designed their text primarily as a teaching grammar and secondarily as a reference grammar for laypeople and scholars. They state specifically that they did not prepare it for the professional phonetician or philologist and that their endeavor has been "to establish a norm of usage, i.e., the kind of Pennsylvania German we should expect a literate person to use" (1965:vi). This study does not assume that the forms cited by Buffington and Barba have been attested in the spoken Pennsylvania German of any one community at a specific time.

15   Estonian among immigrants in Sweden

KATRIN MAANDI

1.   Introduction

The results of intensive language contact can have the effect of accelerating internally motivated changes in the system of the less-used language, and direct influence from the majority language will be difficult to resist. The changes in the minority language will, however, not be abrupt but will proceed step-by-step. In this chapter I will discuss the changes in the objective case-marking system in Estonian spoken as a minority language in Sweden. The Estonian objective case-marking system is much more complex than the Swedish one: this gives rise to the kind of development reported for another minority language under pressure, where "a system of morphological markers is confined primarily to a single high-frequency member of the word class concerned", and "competing structures that have the same semantic value, but different constraints, show movement toward a single favored structure" (Dorian 1983:161,160).

1.1.   Sweden as a multilingual and multicultural country

Sweden has been a multicultural country for a very long time with two indigenous minorities within its borders: the Finns in the Swedish part of the Torne Valley at the Finnish border, and the Lapps, who probably were the original population of northern Scandinavia. There has also been immigration to Sweden during several periods of Swedish history (e.g. Arnstberg and Ehn 1976; Wande 1984). Some ethnic groups have maintained their culture and ethnic identity while others have been absorbed into the Swedish majority.

Estonians, Latvians, and Lithuanians came to Sweden as refugees during World War II, mainly in 1944, in total approximately 35,000 people, and they were followed by labor-market immigration mainly in the 1960s and 1970s. The total number of foreign citizens and naturalized immigrants (all origins) residing in Sweden is today about 637,000 individuals, about 7.7 per

227

cent of the total Swedish population of approximately 8.3 millions (Widgren 1980).

1.2.   Estonians in Sweden

The Estonians came to Sweden as refugees at the end of World War II, an estimated number of 26,000 persons, thus forming the first large group of "modern" immigrants. This number decreased markedly around 1950, when several thousand Estonians emigrated to Canada. Within the first group the proportions with regard to age and sex differed from a normal society, the number of young males being disproportionately high; this led to a high rate of "mixed" marriages and a lower than normal proportion of Estonian-speaking children in the following generations born in Sweden. The present number of people born in Estonia or of Estonian heritage is about 35,000: 15,300 born in Estonia, about 14,000 belonging to the "second generation", and somewhat more than 6,000 belonging to the "third generation". Approximately one-third of the second generation has two Estonian-born parents.

1.3.   The Estonian minority in Sweden

The Estonian minority in Sweden has developed a pronounced infrastructure; there are more than 150 Estonian organizations in Sweden working in different spheres of the Estonian community. Since 1944, more than 1,000 books have been published in Estonian, Estonian daily or weekly newspapers have been in circulation, Estonian schools are still maintained in Stockholm and Gothenburg, and different types of education programs (e.g. afternoon schools, Saturday schools, special summer camps) have contributed to the language maintenance efforts. Along with these activities, numerous cultural and political organizations provide a wide range of settings where Estonian can be used in Sweden. From 1944 to the mid-60s, the immigrant policy in Sweden was one of assimilation, especially linguistically, and the minority groups were responsible themselves for any ethnic identity maintenance. Since 1968, however, the situation has changed: the ethnic minorities are supposed to have the same access to information, education, and culture as Swedes and the development and maintenance of skills in the home language is seen as an important part of this policy. In practical terms that means that minority language maintenance is supported within the normal schedule of Swedish schools, i.e., the home language is taught about two hours a week. If there is a sufficient number of children of the same linguistic background, classes in the minority language can be established; if not, the minority children of the same background form a part of the Swedish class and are given instruction in both their native language and Swedish. Mother tongue, history, and geography of their homelands are taught in the native language and in other subjects support and translations are offered, if needed. Contrary to the situation with many other immigrant groups, there is no concentration of Estonians in any area of (e.g.) Stockholm. If distances allow, children are sent to the Estonian school; otherwise the children participate in the home-language programs.

There are three generations of fully fluent speakers of Estonian available in Sweden, all fluent in Swedish as well. This offers an especially interesting contrast in the time-depth and the intensity of the language contact within the bilingual Estonian population in Sweden.

2.　　Language contact

Haugen (1953 [1969]) views bilingualism as a continuum of all degrees of accomplishment from the point where the speaker of one language can merely produce complete meaningful utterances in the other language up to the kind of skill that enables a person to pass as a native speaker in more than one linguistic environment. In studying the Estonian group in Sweden this broad concept is useful, since the older members have native control of Estonian but produce at least meaningful utterances in Swedish, while the younger generations pass as native Swedes but are still able to produce meaningful utterances in Estonian. It would also be accurate to say that in the Estonian–Swedish bilingual group all individuals have at least a minimum degree of all four basic language skills: speaking, understanding, reading, and writing. This reflects the fact that Estonians in Sweden have been a rather well-educated minority group of predominantly middle-class background. Linguistic changes have a strong chance of stabilizing themselves in a language contact situation if they attract no notice and therefore no resistance from speakers, especially in the early stages. Thus the bilingual context both initiates the language change process and promotes it. One source of change is borrowing of material from one language to another, which may in time lead to integration of the borrowed item into the recipient language. There are many obvious cases of borrowing from Swedish in Swedish-Estonian (SwE), on all levels of the language system and with greater or lesser degrees of integration. Some of the borrowing patterns of SwE are described in Roos (1980) and Raag (1982).

The alternate use of two languages in a discourse and even in a sentence may be considered as borrowing at an individual-speaker level, but not on the level of the community speech variety. Codeswitching is not identifiable by linguistic features alone. The occurrence of a borrowed item that shows a high degree of social integration, i.e. acceptance and use by community members, could be interpreted as an instance of a loanword, while one that shows a lower degree of social integration would be an instance of codeswitching (Hasselmo 1970). There are items frequently occurring in the SwE of younger speakers that can be regarded as integrated in their speech and more or less accepted as part of younger people's Estonian by older speakers who do not use the items themselves.

Language maintenance is often a characteristic of a bilingual community and a longterm collective result of language choice. Minority languages, whether maintaining themselves or giving way to a majority language, undergo interesting changes in their grammatical and phonological systems. It is relatively hard to find research that is focused on language maintenance and on distinctive forms preserved in the minority language grammar, since language shift has held more fascination for scholars. Language shift may ultimately lead to language death in the contact situation, but in the case of Estonian there will remain a native-speaker population in Estonia. Within Sweden, the contact situation would be unlikely to produce "terminal speakers" fully competent in Estonian; however there might be a gradual "death" due to extensive language contact. The Estonian population in Sweden is bilingual, the first generation (I) born in Estonia having become so as adults. The second generation (II) and the third generation (III) have been bilinguals from childhood on. Persons in group II are the children of adult bilinguals and parents of group III. The linguistic repertoire of the three generations differs, but awareness of differences in linguistic forms varies. Young speakers, childhood bilinguals, are often supposed to be responsible for introducing new forms into a language (Haugen 1953 [1969]).

Languages in contact provide, as noted above, dramatic instances of change in language structure and use. Within one generation, contact situations may lead to extensive rearrangement of language structure. In the case of a minority language, inadequate speaker control of grammatical distinctions leads to development of new paradigms and to new uses of lexical items. To the speaker of a minority language, structures and rules, as well as words, will be more easily mastered if opacity and/or ambiguity are/is eliminated. All levels of the language system can be changed or be inter-preted in a different way that seems clearer, or is more transparent, to the speaker. The increasing demands on communication in the minority language, arising from increasing technological and social complexity, give rise to problems and set conditions for their resolution in the minority language. This, combined with a diminishing lexicon and fewer domains for minority language use among its speakers, seems to be one of the main sources for the initiation of language change processes.

The opportunity to analyze the language of the three generations of Estonians in Sweden within a number of families may help determine which parts of a language system are particularly apt to change, and which parts are likely to be preserved, despite long language contact and diminishing functional use of the first (i.e. home) language. The permissible range of variation in usage, within the group in general and within different age groups, varies according to the degree of tolerance of the people using the language. New elements are continually entering a language and old elements drop out. But this process is not sudden; it takes place over time at a rate which is highly variable. The degree of stability can be modified by external factors such as speed of social change and intensity of language contact. There is a high tolerance for variation in the bilingual setting, and changes which in a monolingual setting would seem likely to take many generations may, under the impact of bilingualism, be realized in one generation.

3. Area of interest

When rules underlying an aspect of the grammar are not transparent, there is a potential source for reinterpretation, with more complex systems more likely to change than simpler ones. A case in point is the complex case-marking system of Estonian, in particular the system for object marking. In Standard Estonian, there are three separate cases which are used, each in specifiable conditions, to mark the direct object in a sentence. Below, we shall demonstate how these three cases converge into two, and, in the most extreme case, explicit object marking is confined to a single environment with fixed word order alone distinguishing object noun from subject noun in all other environments (see 4.4). This last outcome most nearly approaches the Swedish model, since in Swedish subject and object nouns are distinguished solely on the basis of word order.

3.1. The objective case markers

The object in Estonian is, unlike the English and Swedish object, usually recognizable by its form. Furthermore, the object in Estonian can take several forms: the so-called NOMINATIVE, GENITIVE and PARTITIVE cases. The general rule is that the "total" object, with the GENITIVE object marker, is used when *all* of the following *three* conditions are met: (i) the sentence is a positive statement; (ii) the action of the verb has been completed; and (iii) the action of the verb embraces the whole, total object. The "partial" object, in the PARTITIVE, is used when not all of the three conditions above are met. The NOMINATIVE is used for positive commands; this is the unmarked form of a noun equivalent to the root and as such indistinguishable from the subject. Thus the object in the NOMINATIVE case is the only SwE object form identical with the subject form of nouns (and is like all Swedish nouns in that respect). Examples of the three object case markers follow.

The NOMINATIVE is used in positive commands:

(1) *The imperative*
Pane   raamat   kinni
put-IMPERATIVE book-NOM shut
'Close the book!'

The "total" object is used when the object is quantitatively delimited and the verbal action is resultative.

(2) *The definite object, the completion of action*
Mina panin   raamatu   kinni
I   put-1SG-PAST book-GEN shut
'I closed the book'

The PARTITIVE is used when these conditions are not fulfilled and is also used in negated sentences:

(3) *The partial or indefinite object*
Mina nägin   raamatut
I   see-1SG-PAST book-PART
'I saw a book'

(4) *Uncompleted action*
Mina panin   raamatut   kinni
I   put-1SG-PAST book-PART shut
'I was closing the book'[1]

(5) *Negated sentences*
Mina ei   pannud[2]   raamatut   kinni
I   NEG put-PAST PARTICIP book-PART shut
'I didn't close the book'

There is relatively little change in the use of object-marking cases among Generations I and II, judging by selfreport (see Figure 1 on page 236), but the interest for this study in such change as does appear lies in a tendency to interchange GENITIVE and PARTITIVE, with some PARTITIVE where GENITIVE would be expected traditionally, and vice versa. There is a tendency in some Estonian dialects within Estonia itself towards a loss of the distinction between GENITIVE and PARTITIVE in certain word types, so that such a development in SwE need not be explained solely in terms of extensive contact with Swedish. On the other hand, changes in object marking among Generation III speakers of SwE are fairly dramatic, and since the GENITIVE vs. PARTITIVE distinction is either very limited or non-existent in the most extreme Generation III patterns (see Table 2 on page 238), it may be that the kind of change which appears in certain dialects of Estonian still in situ is "speeded up" by the relatively isolated situation of Estonian as a minority language. The fact that Swedish, the other tongue of all Generation III bilinguals, does not mark subject/object distinctions in nouns at all is obviously a potential factor in any such acceleration of change. All of these matters are discussed further below.

4. Methods, data, and results

4.1. The informants

Thirteen families, each including three generations of fully fluent Estonian speakers, were chosen for this study. The total number of bilingual subjects was 75: 24 in the first generation (ages 60–80), 26 in the second generation (ages 35–50), and 25 in the third generation (ages 10–20). The numbers are a result of the composition of each family; sometimes there is only one member from the first generation alive, in some cases the number of children in the third generation is uneven. The fact that the three-generational samples did not overlap made it possible to analyze the variety of Estonian spoken within distinct age groups, as well as to investigate the inter-generational transmission in the context of language maintenance. Each generation learns from native sources, e.g. the Estonian community in Sweden, and initially at least mainly from the parents. The influence from peer groups where Estonian schools are involved is of course notable, despite the fact that the children purely among themselves use almost exclusively Swedish. The impact of Swedish and the "innovations" in the language system are handed down to the next generation during the process of acquisition. All the subjects are interested in language maintenance and are well aware of the problems of language contact and, in groups I and II, of the language of their children, correcting the latter's linguistic forms if possible. The group of subjects was chosen from among committed main-tainers of Estonian in order to minimize the external effects of interference and transfer. Of course, many instances of influence will pass unnoticed, but to a lower degree than among less active and less conscious parents. A control group of five adults and five youngsters, relatively recent immigrants in Sweden, was used in order to compare SwE with the colloquial speech in Estonia today. The data from the oldest generation, I, was regarded as the intra-group norm, since it has served directly as input to the second generation, and directly and indirectly to the third generation.

4.2. The data

It would seem most natural, in studying the usage properties of the specific grammatical forms (the objective case markers, in this instance), to work with corpora of spontaneous bilingual discourse. This, however, was not feasible. A corpus of more or less formal (because recorded) speech was in fact obtained from each informant in order to measure degree of change by the frequency in use of the various objective case markers in the developing case system. Occurrence of an object in a sentence was expected to be very common, but proved to be relatively infrequent across all speakers. Accordingly, to gain a better reading of objective case-marking trends, a set of test sentences was constructed for presentation, consisting of an order-randomized series of sentences with conservatively correct object case markers as well as observed and hypothesized objective case markers of a deviant sort. The sentences were to be rated as to whether the subject would "say it that way": response 1, almost always; response 2, sometimes; response 3, never (but others would); or response 4, never (and others would not either). The results reported will show a complete range of degrees of acceptability, and will highlight any marked differences in acceptability which appear between generational groups.

The second part of the investigation was a videofilm used as an elicitation instrument. In the film, objects were taken from one location and transported to another place, e.g. a book was taken from a table and put into a bag, etc. (see Axelsson and Viberg 1985 for a full description of the test). The subjects were asked to tell what happened in the film, and the responses were recorded. Here the focus is on the use of case-marking of the "total, definite object and completed action", i.e. the use of the GENITIVE as an objective case marker, as variation in the use of this case marker is often observed and reported by proficient speakers.

As a third part of the study, subjects were asked to report how they spend their Christmas Eve. The theme turned out to be well chosen, in that the cultural and traditional background of the informants provided thematically similar stories. The use of the objective case markers, however, was surprisingly rare. This part of the test served to give information about the general language-use pattern of each subject.

The two elicited-response tasks and the free-production task were complemented by a questionnaire which was designed to probe linguistic background, language attitudes, self-estimated proficiency in all four basic skills in both Estonian and Swedish, and background variables such as education, number of siblings, contact with other languages, etc.

4.3.   The test design

A more specific description of the acceptability test may be useful. The test contains ninety sentences, divided according to the objective case markers which would be expected by the conservative norm, the NOMINATIVE, the GENITIVE, and the PARTITIVE (see 3.1). For each case, ten conservatively correct sentences were used: five sentences where the object was used in frequent everyday context (+), e.g. "Close the door!", "Have you done your homework?"; and five less usual contexts (−), "Burn the documents after having read them!", etc. For each of these ten sentences, two variants were presented in which the objective case marker was changed to one of the incorrect forms; this gives us a total of sixty sentences containing incorrect

Table 1. *Sets of Estonian sentences presented with traditionally correct object-marking cases (above dotted line) and traditionally incorrect object-marking cases (below dotted line) for the various syntactic structures requiring an object*

Nominative	Genitive	Partitive
NOM. (N/N):5(+),5(−)	GEN. (G/G):5(+),5(−)	PART. (P/P):5(+),5(−)
GEN. (G/N):5(+), 5(−)	PART. (P/G):5(+),5(−)	GEN. (G/P):5(+),5(−)
PART. (P/N):5(+),5(−)	NOM. (N/G):5(+),5(−)	NOM. (N/P):5(+),5(−)

case markers (Table 1), plus the thirty containing a case marker which is correct by conservative norms.

The entries above the dotted line in Table 1 represent the sentences in conformity with the conservative norm; those below the dotted line represent sentences which do not conform to the conservative norm. The sentences were randomized as to order of presentation (but with the order held constant across the entire sample of subjects); they were then recorded, spoken in a casual style by a native speaker of Estonian. Whenever a sentence was judged with response 3 or 4 ("never, but others would" and "never, and others wouldn't either"), the subjects were asked to give the correct form of the case marker. These answers were recorded.

4.4. The results and hypothesized changes in SwE

The results from the tests show how three generations of Estonian speakers in Sweden claim to use the objective case markers (Figure 1), and which forms they claim to have noticed being used by other speakers in the community (Figure 2).

The results reveal that all three generations are fully fluent speakers and as such are well aware of the conservative case-marking system. (They were chosen on the basis of fluency, after all.) There is, however, a clear tendency towards a "new" case marking. Despite the fact that all three generations claim to use N/N, G/G and P/P sentences most frequently, the number of such conservatively correct answers declines across generations.

With the N/N sentences the first generation had very few problems; they were all claimed in accordance with the conservative norm. The second generation claimed the conservative choice to a lesser degree, alternative choice being G/N more often than P/N. The third generation shows this pattern more strongly: N/N was still rated highest, with G/N as an attractive alternative. Within the third generation, P/N was claimed least often, but considerably more often than among the first and second generations, where

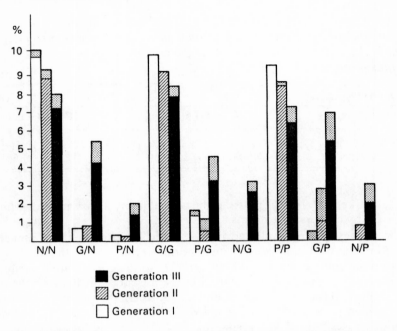

Figure 1. *Cross-generational acceptability of response 1 ("almost always"; blank, striped or solid areas) and response 2 ("sometimes"; dotted areas) to nominal object-marking*

it appears at an almost negligible level. Thus, in the less conservative groups II and (much more notably) III the GENITIVE is gaining in use at the expense of the NOMINATIVE.

Marking of the "total object" by the GENITIVE is still the norm of most speakers, judging by their usage claims. In Generation III, however, the sentences with the PARTITIVE and the NOMINATIVE instead of the GENITIVE (P/G and N/G) were rather frequently claimed too. This can be interpreted as restructuring of the borders between the rules governing the choice of case marker. In the context traditionally calling for the GENITIVE, the third generation in particular claims to be using the PARTITIVE and, to a somewhat lesser degree, the NOMINATIVE.

Finally, when the rules demand the PARTITIVE, groups I and II still seem to claim that they seldom if ever use any other case. In group III, by contrast, the choice seems to be between the conservative form and the GENITIVE, and, again to a lesser extent, the NOMINATIVE. The percentage of G/P seems surprisingly high, and thus not in support of the hypothesis that the NOMINATIVE will expand its use as case marker among the least conservative speakers. If one looks more closely at the sentences where use of the GENITIVE was claimed instead of the PARTITIVE, that is, (G/P) sentences, it becomes clear that nearly all these sentences were negated. Use of NOMINA-

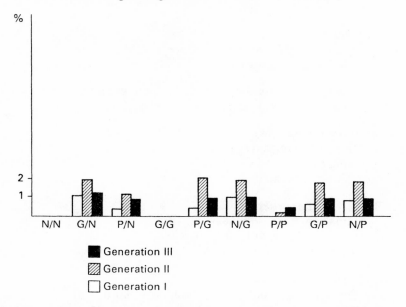

Figure 2. *Cross-generational acceptability of response 3 ("never, but others would") to nominal objecting-marking*

TIVE was claimed instead of the PARTITIVE (N/P) in the other non-conservative sentences. The conservative pattern was chosen by all members of the control group, thus indicating that there is no obvious change of this sort going on in colloquial speech in Estonia today.

The least conservative speakers in both II and III (still fully fluent speakers of Estonian) seem to have changed the original three-part case-marking system into two different types of two-part marking. This will be demonstrated by the following actual examples from the spontaneous speech from two of the informants from the third generation. The pattern they claim to use, according to the report-elicitation, shows the same tendency as their actual speech. Informant A claims to use the GENITIVE in the imperative sentences and the PARTITIVE in all other contexts:

(6a) *Incorrect use* (G/N)
Pane   ukse   kinni
put-IMPER- door-GEN shut
'Shut the door!'

(6b) *Incorrect use* (P/G)
Mina lugesin   raamatut läbi
I   read-1SG-PAST book-PART through
'I have read the book'

(6c) *Correct use* (P/P)
Poiss ei   ostnud   lennukit
boy   NEG buy-PAST PARTICIP plane-PART
'The boy didn't buy the plane'

Informant B seems to use the GENITIVE in the imperative sentences and Ø-marking (the NOMINATIVE) for all other direct objects:

(7a) *Incorrect use* (G/N)
Too   leiva   siia
bring-IMPER bread-GEN here
'Bring the bread'

(7b) *Incorrect use* (N/G)
Mina sôin   banaan   ära
I   eat-1SG-PAST banana-NOM up
'I have eaten the banana.'

(7c) *Incorrect use* (N/P)
Tema ei   pannud   raamat   kotti
he/she NEG put-PAST PARTICIP book-NOM bag-ILLATIVE
'she didn't put the book into the bag'

The least conservative speakers are included in Table 2, where the actual and claimed use of objective case marking of individuals from all three generations is summarized.

It is worth pointing out the role of the second generation as "monitors" in the immigrant community. Generation I seems to notice significantly less

Table 2. *Extremes of object-case-marking changes among the nonconservative speakers of Generations II and III, taking Generation I usage as the conservative norm*

Gen. I	NOMINATIVE	GENITIVE PARTITIVE	Stage I
Gens. II & III, less conservative speakers	NOMINATIVE; GENITIVE with Imper. only	PARTITIVE	Stage II
Gen. III, least conservative speakers	NOMINATIVE; GENITIVE with Imper. and Negated sentences	NOMINATIVE (i.e. Ø-marking)	Stage III

The curly braces indicate two traditional case markings, GEN and PART, being replaced by only one: PART among stage II speakers, and (unmarked) NOM among stage III speakers, with the limited exceptions indicated under NOM. Ed.

untraditional use of case markers, compared to Generation II, who in every instance notice most. Particularly striking is the fact that even Generation III, who presumably have the least knowledge and experience of conservative Estonian grammar, are more critical than Generation I. The belief that grandparents are very critical, always correcting "bad" grammar, doesn't seem to hold true here. The middle generation seems to be most aware of the incorrect forms, noticing mistakes more than their immigrant parents do and trying to combat them (Figure 2). This may reflect especially keen awareness of their Estonian-in-exile status (and with it the threat to their language) among the first foreign-born generation.

5. Summary and conclusions

The Estonian system of marking the direct object is much more complicated than the Swedish one and is therefore a possible area of change, especially as some Estonian dialects in Estonia itself already show loss of the distinction between the GENITIVE and the PARTITIVE as markers of the direct object. With such case-marker collapse in evidence even where Estonian is not in contact with Swedish, external factors alone are unlikely to be responsible for the ongoing changes in SwE; there must be some internal motivation for the change as well. With the added pressure of constant contact with Swedish, however, it is possible that the step-by-step reduction in case markings may eventually lead to a reliance solely on word order. Throughout the system of objective case marking, new forms show increased semantic transparency; there is a similar sort of movement toward greater transparency in SwE semantics, it seems, with verbs of motion expanding their range at the expense of verbs expressing change of state.[3] In the early stages of linguistic change, only forms tend to be involved while the system remains the same in terms of categories and oppositions: "conservative changes", according to Benveniste (1968). The speaker must be able to evaluate the distinctiveness of a given form, whether it serves as marker of one case only, of two, or of several. The GENITIVE serves as marker of two cases: the "true" GENITIVE (that is, the genitive as it is known in most Indo-European languages, a possessive marker) and the definite object. A useful definition of "norm" is given by Janson (1979): "A person's norm is the standard by which he judges the correctness of utterances." If "correctness" here is replaced by "acceptability", we might see, in the tests carried out, in which direction the norms of Estonian in Sweden will change, where marking of the direct object is concerned (and also in the semantic change discussed in note 3). It is also evident that age is the most important variable with respect to the usage of the objective case markers (as also with respect to the semantic change), and the innovations may well mark linguistic change in progress.

Notes

1. The distinction between completed and uncompleted action, expressed by the verbal structure in the English translations for examples (2) and (4), is expressed by the difference in nominal case markings in Estonian.
2. The PAST NEGATIVE is expressed by *ei* 'no/not' and the so-called "nud-PARTICIPLE".
3. While conservative Estonian provides two verbal possibilities for the expression of change of state, the irregular verbs *saama* 'to become, to receive' and *jääma* 'to become, to remain', each followed by TRANSLATIVE case marking, the irregular verb *minema* 'to go' can in some environments appear as an alternative to *jääma*. Thus, for example:

Lehid   läksid   kollaseks
leaf-PL   go-PAST   yellow-TRANSLATIVE
'The leaves turned yellow'

In the SwE of younger speakers, *minema* 'to go' shows a tendency to appear where the conservative norm would divide the semantic domain between *minema* and *jääma*, and another Estonian verb of motion, *tulema* 'to come' tends to appear where the conservative norm would call for *saama*. Swedish uses the verb *bli* 'to become' across the entire range of environments which would call for *saama*, *jääma* and *minema* and Swedish influence cannot therefore account for the two-way division of this semantic range in the SwE of younger speakers. Schematically:

Estonian		SwE	Swedish
saama	=	*tulema*	
'to become, receive'		'to come'	
jääma			*bli*
'to become, remain'		*minema*	'to become'
minema	=	'to go'	
'to go'			

The Estonian verbs *saama* and *jääma* without the TRANSLATIVE case marking do not express change of state, but rather 'to receive' and 'to remain' respectively; these will presumably come to be the only meanings of these verbs in the lexicon of the younger generations.

Although Swedish provides no model for the two-way *tulema/minema* restructuring, the possibility of using *bli* to express future tense in Swedish (by no means regularly marked since present-tense verbs can serve as the equivalent of English present and future) seems to be providing a model for incipient future marking in younger speakers' SwE, whereas traditional Estonian lacks any formal means of expressing future. Compare the following:

Swedish:

Det   kommer   att   bli   en   trevlig   konsert
it   come-PRES   to   become-INF   a   nice   concert
'It will be a nice concert'

SwE (actual example)

See   tuleb   et   olla   tore
this   come-3SG-PRES   that-SUBJUNCTION   be-COMPL INF nice
'This/that will be nice'

The SwE sentence is a direct translation of a perfectly acceptable Swedish sentence (*Det kommer att bli trevligt*) and is used only by the most imperfect young speakers.

Expansion of the meaning of verbs of motion can be found in the development of several languages and is not rare in pidgin and creole languages. The SwE instance and the possible semantic features involved are discussed further in Maandi (n.d.).

16   The incipient obsolescence of polysynthesis: Cayuga in Ontario and Oklahoma

MARIANNE MITHUN

Cayuga, an Iroquoian language, was originally spoken in what is now New York State. When first encountered by Europeans, the Cayuga lived in villages around Cayuga Lake, surrounded by the other related Five Nations Iroquois. To the west were the Seneca, to the east the Onondaga, beyond them the Oneida, and finally, the Mohawk. Due to a series of unfortunate events, Cayuga speakers now live in two distantly separated communities, one in Ontario and the other in Oklahoma. While the language is still very much alive in Ontario, it is receding in Oklahoma, as fewer and fewer speakers use it on rarer and rarer occasions. Not surprisingly, the Cayuga spoken in Oklahoma has begun to differ in subtle ways from that spoken in Ontario.

1.   Historical background

The Cayuga had occupied the same land for centuries before the American Revolution. When war erupted, they were drawn into battle on the side of the British, and in 1779 an American expedition destroyed their villages. This led to their dispersal. Some Cayugas remained with their land, but others went to live with Senecas at Buffalo Creek, and still others went with other Iroquoians to Ontario to form the Six Nations Reserve. By the end of the Revolution, only about 130 Cayugas remained at Cayuga Lake, 350 were with the Seneca at Buffalo Creek, and 382 were at Six Nations. (For a detailed discussion of the history of the Cayuga, see Sturtevant 1978; White, Englebrecht and Tooker 1978.)

In the years following the war, the Cayuga remaining at Cayuga Lake sold most of their land. Some then followed their relatives to Six Nations. Others went to live in Seneca communities at Buffalo Creek, Tonawanda, Cattaraugus, and Allegany. A number of others joined other New York Iroquois and moved to the Lower Sandusky River in Ohio, where the entire group became known as the "Sandusky Senecas". During the early nineteenth century, Cayugas continued to emigrate from Buffalo Creek to Sandusky. By 1829, 322 Iroquois were counted at Sandusky, 157 of them Cayuga.

Following President Jackson's Removal Bill in 1830, the Sandusky group sold their Ohio land and began to move west again, eventually settling in northeastern Oklahoma. Throughout the remainder of the nineteenth century, Iroquois immigrants from New York and Ontario continued to join them. The original "Sandusky Senecas", along with these later immigrants, became the ancestors of the "Seneca" or "Seneca-Cayuga" who reside in northeastern Oklahoma today.

The Cayuga language was to experience different fates in the areas where it was spoken in New York, Ontario, and Oklahoma. The Seneca, Cayuga, Onondaga, Oneida, and Mohawk languages are mutually unintelligible, but they are sufficiently closely related that speakers of one can learn others with relative ease. In New York, the Cayuga language exerted a significant influence on Seneca and, in turn, on Onondaga. A loss of original Proto-Iroquoian *r in certain contexts in Cayuga was imitated and generalized in both Seneca and Onondaga, so that by the end of the eighteenth century, neither Seneca nor Onondaga had any /r/ at all (Mithun 1980). The Cayuga language was not to prevail in New York, however, even though there were still 183 Cayugas living in New York State in 1980, 153 in the Seneca community at Cattaraugus (Buffalo Creek had been sold). Seneca is still spoken in all of the Seneca communities, but Cayuga has not been spoken in any of them for as long as anyone can remember.

In Ontario, by contrast, there are now more speakers of Cayuga than of any other Iroquoian language. Although children are no longer learning the language as a mother tongue, approximately 375 adults speak Cayuga. It is used both in daily conversation and ceremonially.

In Oklahoma, Cayuga is now the only Northern Iroquoian language spoken, but it is used by few individuals and only rarely. As early as 1912, Barbeau reported (see Sturtevant 1978) that only one family still spoke Seneca, and all others spoke either Cayuga or English. By 1962, Seneca was no longer spoken at all. Cayuga "was hardly used except in ritual contexts and had only 11 fluent speakers and 12 others with some competence, the youngest speaker having been born in 1918" (ibid.: 543). By 1980, perhaps a half-dozen speakers remained, and several of these have passed away since that time. Although the Oklahoma speakers consider themselves "Seneca", their language is pure Cayuga, with little observable influence from the other Iroquoian languages. For the most part, they have had little occasion to speak the language for a long time. They meet primarily on ceremonial occasions, and have tended to use Cayuga primarily in ceremonial speeches, seldom in conversation.

2.   Discourse and syntax

The Iroquois have always enjoyed a reputation for eloquence. The earliest European descriptions of the New World include commentaries on the rhetorical skills of the Iroquois, and the tradition has continued to this day in all communities. Skillful use of language is discussed, appreciated, and cultivated by speakers in all contexts, not only in formal oratory, but also in informal narrative and conversation. All of the languages are rich in stylistic devices, and speakers take great pleasure in exploiting them.

It is difficult to measure and compare a quality as individual as rhetorical skill. One fact might suggest some loss of stylistic elasticity in Oklahoma Cayuga. In both Ontario and Oklahoma, traditional ceremonial speeches are given in Cayuga. In Ontario, the ceremonies last for days. Each morning, everyone gathers in the Longhouse for hour after hour of magnificent formal oratory. A single speaker performs, aided only occasionally by a prompter seated behind him. The speeches follow well established structures and contain traditional rhetorical devices, but they are not memorized. In Oklahoma, the oratory typically lasts only a day or so. Of course, their brevity is probably due not just to a loss of rhetorical skill, but also to the smaller pool of speakers who remember the traditions and who understand the speeches.

Unfortunately, it was not possible to record long stretches of connected discourse from the Oklahoma speakers. Conversations between Oklahoma speakers and an Ontario speaker, however, have provided an opportunity to compare a number of features of the two Cayuga dialects. The Ontario speaker, Reginald Henry, uses Cayuga in daily conversation and performs the traditional speeches in the Longhouse. He is a skillful speaker, keenly sensitive to subtle intricacies of his language, and he was quite interested in comparing Oklahoma and Ontario Cayuga. Probably the best speaker remaining in Oklahoma was born in 1888. When interviewed in Cayuga, she often replied in English, although she was quite capable of good Cayuga. Her preference for English was clearly a matter of relative facility and habit rather than prestige, since good control of Cayuga is all the more highly valued in this community as it disappears. She enjoyed speaking the language, but felt that Mr Henry's Ontario Cayuga was the correct version and that she might be making mistakes.

The style and syntax of this Oklahoma speaker's conversation appeared to be essentially unaffected by English. In Cayuga, word order is not syntactically determined (SVO, SOV, etc.). Since the roles of core arguments are expressed by verbal prefixes, word order need not reiterate them. Instead, constituents are ordered according to pragmatic considerations: their relative importance within the discourse. The most significant element of a clause appears first, followed by increasingly predictable or incidental information (Mithun 1987). This speaker consistently ordered constituents accordingly, with no loss in stylistic elasticity. Since the newsworthy-first ordering of Cayuga usually contrasts with the typical theme–rheme order of English, it is clear that word order in Oklahoma has remained largely uninfluenced by English.

(1) Tkai?ní: hatí:?as
N-loud-STATIVE M.PL.AG-shoot-HABITUAL
'Their shooting is loud'

(2) Tkaná:taę   akatekhǫ́nyane:?
CISLOCATIVE-N-town-lie-STATIVE FACTUAL-1.SG.AG-dine-DISLOCATIVE
to town   I am going to dine
hate:tsę́?ts   ęyá:kwe:?
M.SG.AG-cure-HABITUAL FUT-1-PL.EXCL.AG-go-PUNCTUAL
doctor   we all will go
'I am going to town with the doctor to eat'

(Note the pronominal expression of the plural agent of the last clause, typical of languages of this type, rendered in English by a prepositional phrase. Transcription conventions are as follows. Vowels followed by a colon are long, those accompanied by an acute accent are stressed, those with a Polish hook are nasalized, those with a subscript circle are voiceless, and those with a superscript ? are glottalized. Nasalization may co-occur with any of the other features. Glosses separated by periods indicate semantic components that do not correspond to separate morphemes in Cayuga. The sequence -k-, for example, glossed 1.SG.AG., is the 1st person singular agent pronominal prefix ('I'), but it consists of a single, unsegmentable morpheme.)

Because of their rich morphology, Iroquoian languages exhibit somewhat less grammaticized syntactic complexity than languages like English. All verbs are finite, and clauses are backgrounded or foregrounded by means of discourse particles and ordering. The conversation of this Oklahoma speaker seemed to show approximately the same degree of syntactic complexity as that of a typical Ontario speaker.

(3) Wahé?tshų: aka:tkę̨   nę̨ hne:?   thú:ha wąshę̨:
just.only   FAC.1.SG-get.up now CONTRASTIVE there-DIM ten
niyahwihstá:?eh
PARTITIVE.N-metal-strike-STATIVE
'I just now got up and here it is almost ten o'clock'

Nę̨h ki? akekhwętá?ǫh   ne? ki? ne:? katshe:nę́?
now just 1.SG.PAT-food-finish-STATIVE the just it.is N-stock
(ę)kęnǫte:khǫ́:ni?
(FUT)-1.SG.AG-feed-PUNCTUAL
'Now that I have finished eating, I will feed my stock'

3.   Lexicon

Usually the first differences noticed by speakers hearing another dialect of their language are in vocabulary. As might be expected, Ontario and Oklahoma Cayuga are distinguished by neologisms created since their separation. For 'tomato', for example, Ontario speakers use *ohyákhahǫˀ* 'it-fruit-divides', or 'fruit in sections'. Oklahoma speakers use *kǫˀnyaˀ*, which refers to the ring in a bull's nose in Ontario. For 'railroad track', Ontario speakers use *kǫnyǫˀǫhšráˀkęsǫˀ* 'along the iron'. Oklahoma speakers use *kàtrehtaya:nu:wéˀ uha:te*, 'it-drags-fast road', or 'train road'.

The word for 'automobile' is interesting. Ontario speakers, like other Northern Iroquoians, use *kàtréhtaˀ* 'it is used to drag'. Oklahoma speakers use *kakǫ́owanęˀs* 'it has big eyes'. The literal meaning is the same as that of the Shawnee word (Ives Goddard, pers. comm.). This is no accident. Early in the nineteenth century, a group of Shawnees and Senecas known collectively as the "Mixed Band" also occupied a reservation in Ohio. They migrated west at the same time as the Sandusky Senecas and both groups eventually settled on the same Oklahoma reservation, the Mixed Band in the north, and the Sandusky Senecas in the south.

Surprisingly few words in Oklahoma Cayuga show any Seneca influence. One may be the term for 'nose'. The root *-kǫt-* is the basic term for 'nose' in both Oklahoma Cayuga and Seneca. This root refers to the 'bridge of the nose' in Ontario Cayuga. The Ontario root for 'nose' is cognate to those in other more distant Northern Iroquoian languages like Tuscarora, so the Oklahoma shift seems to represent an innovation.

A number of recent neologisms are the same in Ontario and Oklahoma Cayuga, such as *k'atrehtaya:nú:weˀ* 'train' ('it drags fast') *katsíˀnǫtas* 'monkey' ('it eats lice') *kǫthá:haˀ* 'radio, television' ('it talks'), and *shako:yé:nas* 'policeman' ('he arrests/grabs them'). Since these words generally match their counterparts in the other Northern Iroquoian languages, it appears that they were brought into Oklahoma by the later immigrants and visitors from Ontario, whose language has probably always enjoyed special prestige in Oklahoma.

Some neologisms created in Ontario apparently never had counterparts in Oklahoma. Ontario and Oklahoma Cayuga share the original terms for 'black', 'white', 'red', 'green', 'yellow', and 'blue'. A term for 'pink' has been created in both communities, but from different descriptions. The Ontario term is *otkwęhtsìa:kę́:t* ('it-red-white.is') 'light red'. The Oklahoma term is *tkwęhtsíˀá:ˀah* (red-DIMINUTIVE) 'a little red', 'sort of red', 'reddish'. The Ontario word for 'brown', based on the noun 'dirt', was understood in Oklahoma as 'purple'. The Ontario term for 'gray' is an innovation based on the noun 'ash', but there is no counterpart in Oklahoma. (Both dialects retain an older term for 'gray-haired'.) Neither has a special term for 'orange'.

Lexical loss in Oklahoma Cayuga shows a predictable pattern. Words for objects no longer discussed have been forgotten, such as 'moose', 'beaver', 'mink', and 'weasel'. Some specific terms seem to be disappearing before more general ones. The Ontario speaker remarked that he would be more likely to say (4a), for 'Come on in the house', where an Oklahoma speaker said (4b).

(4)a. Ontario: Kanǫhskǫ́:   tatsǫh!
                      N-house-in   CISLOCATIVE-2.SG.AG-enter

(4)b. Oklahoma: Kanǫhskǫ́:   tá:seʔ
                      N-house-in   CISLOCATIVE-2.SAG.AG-go

When asked for a word for 'thigh', the best Oklahoma speaker supplied the term for 'leg'. Although she knew 'foot', she could not come up with 'ankle' or 'toes'. For 'hip', she suggested 'buttocks'. She knew 'eyes', but had never heard the Ontario word for 'eyebrow'. She knew 'face' but not 'cheeks'.

4.   Morphology

Cayuga morphology is not only complex, it is also highly productive, and good speakers manipulate it extensively for stylistic purposes. If a particular element of meaning is in focus, it is usually expressed by a separate word: a particle, noun, or verb. If it merely provides background information, it may be expressed by a bound morpheme within the verb. A separate particle and a verbal affix may cooccur. A speaker wishing to emphasize that an event occurred *again*, might use a separate particle meaning 'again' as well as a repetitive verbal prefix something like English *re-*. If the repetition is not the main point of the clause, or if it is established information, the prefix alone is sufficient. Good speakers can pack a considerable amount of background information into verbs by means of affixation.

Productivity is probably one of the first aspects of morphology to be receding in Oklahoma Cayuga. The best Oklahoma speaker could use all of the affixes, but on occasion, she would hesitate to combine several within a single word. When there were few other prepronominal prefixes, she used the repetitive prefix *s-* with the particle *é:ʔ* 'again', as an Ontario speaker would.

(5)a. aǫtatiʔtanyúʔuh   'she beat her up'
   b. saǫtatiʔtanyúʔ é:ʔ   'she beat her up again'

When more prepronominal prefixes were present, she relied on the separate particle alone to carry the meaning 'again'. An Ontario speaker would have simply combined prefixes in that context.

(6) Ontario: tǫsasatkahaté:nih
                    DUALIC-REPETITIVE-2.SG-SEMI.REFLEXIVE-turn.around
                    'turn back around, re-turn'

Oklahoma: teskạa:té:ni   é:ʔ
          DUALIC-2.SG.AG-SEMI.REFLEXIVE-turn.around again
          'turn around again'

At other times, the Oklahoma speaker did use expressions containing multiple prepronominal prefixes. These may have been somewhat more familiar combinations.

(7) Ka:oʔ   n̓åtọtesá:tih
    toward   PARTITIVE-DUALIC/CISLOCATIVE-2SG.PAT-throw
    'Throw it back here'

The reluctance to combine morphemes within single words extends to noun incorporation. In all of the Northern Iroquoian languages, verbs may incorporate noun stems referring to their patients. Incorporation can be used for several purposes. It often functions as a word-formation device, creating unitary lexical items to represent unitary concepts. Many of the resulting verbs normally function as predicates, like -*khwẹtaʔ* 'finish eating' ('meal-finish'), -*atekhọni* 'eat' ('self-meal-make'). Many others have been coined to function as nominals, especially in response to the introduction of so many new objects requiring names over the past several centuries. Terms formed in this way include *kaọtanéhkwih* 'horse' ('it-log-haul-s') and *kayáʔtakrahs* 'goat' ('it-body-stink-s'). Such words are not formed anew each time a speaker uses them, of course. The majority are learned and remembered as lexical units in both Ontario and Oklahoma.

Incorporation can also be used as a stylistic device in discourse, as a means of backgrounding established or incidental information. When an important entity is first introduced into discourse, or is in focus, it usually appears as a separate noun. Once its identity has been established, it is usually referred to only pronominally or by an incorporated noun. A characteristic of especially admired speakers is the profusion of incorporation in their speech for stylistic effect.

Some noun–verb combinations are used very often, while others may be quite rare. The best Oklahoma Cayuga speaker used combinations that would be familiar as frequently recurring units. For 'she has a big house/her house is big', she used nearly the same word as the Ontario speaker would have chosen. Having a big house is a frequently occurring conceptual unit, in which neither the house nor its size is in focus. (She did omit the patient pronominal prefix for 'her'.)

(8) Ontario: konọhsowá:neh
               F.SG.PAT-house-large. STATIVE
    Oklahoma: kanọhsuwá:nẹh
               N-house-large.STATIVE

The Oklahoma speaker used rarer combinations less often, if at all. Where she used a simplex verb with a separate noun, as below, the Ontario speaker noted that he would have used a verb with incorporated noun. (As before, she did not specify the possessor of the onion.)

(9) Ontario: kǫ́nǫhsowá:nęh
        ko-ʔnǫhs-owanę
        F.SG.PAT-onion-large.STATIVE
        'she has a big onion'

    Oklahoma: kuwa:nę́   ʔnǫ́hsaʔ
        k-uwane   ʔnǫhs-aʔ
        N-big.STATIVE   onion-NOMINAL.SUFFIX
        'the onion is big'

Morphophonemic alternations, which can be quite complex in Cayuga, are essentially the same in both dialects. The shape of the stem for 'leg' originally -*hsin*-, has been remodeled to -*ahsin*-, probably by analogy to -*ahsiʔt*- 'foot'. The difference has always been neutralized in some forms, like *ohsí:naʔ* 'a leg' and *ohsíʔtaʔ* 'a foot'. In other forms, original differences have been leveled in Oklahoma. Compare Ontario, *kǫsíhàkeh* 'on its leg' and *wǫsíʔtàkeh* 'on its foot', with Oklahoma *wǫsíhàkeh* 'on its leg' and *wǫsíʔtàkeh* 'on its foot'. It is interesting that such a frequent word could be subject to remodeling.

5.   Phonology

Most phonological distinctions and processes have remained the same in Ontario and Oklahoma. One Oklahoma vowel shift is particularly salient to Ontario speakers: **o* appears as a lax, fronted, barely rounded [ʉ] in all contexts. It is actually quite close to the Oklahoma Cayuga speakers' pronunciation of the vowel in English *too*.

(10) Ontario: [othó:weʔ] 'cold'
    Oklahoma: [ʉthʉ́:weʔ]

It could be hypothesized that the Oklahoma vowel is simply the result of contamination from English. This seems extremely unlikely, given the intact state of the rest of the phonology. All other vowels, including nasalized, creaky, and voiceless ones, have remained just as in Ontario. Furthermore, there is nothing articulatorily complex about the vowel [o] that should cause instability.

Better hypotheses come from historical considerations. The Huron, who occupied what is now Ontario until the mid-seventeenth century, were linguistically related to the Five Nations Iroquois, but they constituted an opposing political unit. Although the Huron language is no longer spoken, records left by seventeenth- and eighteenth-century French missionaries show several interesting phonetic alternations present in the language at that time. In particular, the pronunciation of the sound corresponding to original Proto-Iroquoian **o* was sometimes [o], and sometimes [u].

When they were defeated by the Five Nations Iroquois in 1649, the surviving Huron scattered in several directions. Many went eastward toward Quebec City. A number of others settled among the Iroquois in New York State, including the Cayuga. Interestingly, some modern Ontario dialects of Cayuga show some of the same alternations recorded in seventeenth-century Huron. In particular, **o* sometimes appears as [u] in certain contexts adjacent to *n*, *y*, and *ʔ*, as in *oná:ʔno:/oná:ʔnu*: 'it is cold', *oyó:tshaʔ/oyú:tshaʔ/uyú:tshaʔ* 'jaw', or *onó:ʔtshaʔ/onú:ʔtshaʔ* 'tooth'. This [o]/[u] alternation may have originated with the early Huron refugees (Mithun 1985), then remained unchanged in Ontario, but been generalized to [u] in Oklahoma.

There is another possible explanation behind the Oklahoma [ʉ]. Some of the defeated Huron banded together with remnants of neighboring tribes and fled westward toward Detroit, where they became known as the Wyandot. They eventually moved into northwestern Oklahoma, not far from the area occupied by the Oklahoma Seneca-Cayuga today. Although Wyandot is no longer spoken, we have excellent documentation of the language in narratives and notes transcribed by Marius Barbeau in the early part of this century (Barbeau 1960). From these it is clear that **o* was pronounced [u] in all contexts in Wyandot. It may thus have been the Wyandots who generalized the [o]/[u] alternation to [u], then passed it on to the Oklahoma Cayuga. In any case, it is unlikely that the Oklahoma [ʉ] is merely a mark of English influence or obsolescence.

Patterns of stress and length are relatively complex in Cayuga, depending upon interactions between syllable count from both ends of the word and syllable structure. Phrase-medial words have ultimate stress, but in phrase-final words, stress placement is essentially as follows. (The examples are from Oklahoma Cayuga.)

(a) If the penultimate syllable of a word is even-numbered (counting from the left), it is stressed: *ką̄sáʔkeh* 'on its lips', 'mouth'.
(b) If the penultimate syllable is odd-numbered and open, it is still usually stressed: *hǭ:ka:k* 'goose'.
(c) If the penultimate syllable is odd-numbered and contains the vowel /a/, stress moves to the antepenult: *kekǭtakǫ:* 'in my nose'.
(d) If the penultimate syllable is odd-numbered and closed, stress moves to the antepenult: *(e)shúwektha ʔ* 'cover, lid'.
(e) If stress would otherwise fall on the second of two adjacent vowels, it moves leftward to the first: *tsiʔáoyę:* 'spider'.

For the most part, these patterns have remained the same in both dialects. Several Oklahoma words hint at incipient generalizations in the stress rules, however. The word 'in my eye', for example, is pronounced *kekáhakǫ:* in Ontario in accordance with (c) above: the penultimate syllable *-ka-* is odd-numbered and contains /a/, so stress moves leftward to the antepenult. In Oklahoma, it is pronounced *kekahá:kǫ:.* The penultimate syllable is treated like any other open syllable, despite the /a/. The word for 'cat', originally borrowed into the North Iroquoian languages from Dutch, shows the same innovation. In the north, this has remained *takú:ʔs.* In Oklahoma, it is now *tá:kuʔs.* Numerous other words, like 'in my nose' cited above, indicate that the generalization is not systematic, however.

When asked what she called 'eyebrows', the best Oklahoma speaker supplied *kekahéhtǫ:t,* a word interpreted by the Ontario speaker as 'my eyelashes'. In Ontario, this term is pronounced *kekáhehtǫ:t,* in accordance with (d) above: the penultimate syllable *-heh-* is odd-numbered and closed, so stress moves leftward to the antepenult. The Oklahoma speaker treated the penult here as if it were even or open, and stress remained penultimate. In another word based on the same root, *kekáhàkeh* '(on) my eyes', she did shift the stress to the antepenult. Many other words in her speech, like that for 'lid' above, confirm that the generalization is not systematic.

Perhaps the most interesting aspect of Cayuga phonology is a phenomenon usually referred to as "laryngeal metathesis", actually a process of feature spreading. It operates as follows: if an odd-numbered syllable is closed with a laryngeal (*h* or *ʔ*), features of the laryngeal are spread leftward over the entire syllable, and the laryngeal itself is usually no longer audible as a separate segment.

When an odd-numbered syllable would otherwise be closed by *h*, the voicelessness moves leftward and the entire syllable is devoiced. In (11) below, the syllable *-truh-* is pronounced [druh] when even-numbered, but [trụ] when odd-numbered. (Oral stops are automatically voiced throughout the language before other voiced segments. Voicelessness on sonorants is indicated by small circles under the letters.)

> **(11)** hę na trụ é: ktha^ʔ   'they use it to gather together'
>   1 2 *3* 4 5
>   (term used for the Longhouse)
> Compare: tsa trú he ktha^ʔ   'you two use it to gather'
>   1 *2* 3 4
> (Word elicited for comparison: *ts-=* 'You two')

When an odd-numbered syllable is closed by glottal stop, the glottalization moves leftward and the entire syllable is laryngealized. In (12), the syllable *-niʔ-* is pronounced as [niʔ] when even-numbered, but as [ñì] when odd-numbered. (Apostrophes above sonorants indicate glottalization.)

> **(12)** sa thrǫ́ ñì ta^ʔ   'your clothes'
>   1 2 *3* 4

Compare: (a) ka   thrǫ́ ní? ta? 'my clothes'
            1   2   3   **4** 5

Laryngeal metathesis is very much alive in Oklahoma, but it differs in two ways from the Ontario version. First, it appears to be optional in Oklahoma, often simply failing to operate. In the Oklahoma versions of (13a and b), devoicing failed to take place, a common occurrence. Compare the shapes of italicized syllables.

(13)a. Underlying: keh soh ta? ke   'on my hand'
                     1   2   3   4
      Ontario: kę̊ sóh tå̊ keh
                   1   2   3   4
      Oklahoma: keh súh tå̊ keh
                    1   2   3   4
  b. Underlying: tę hat   'he will dance'
                  1   2
      Ontario: tę̊ a:t
                  1   2
      Oklahoma: tę ha:t
                  1   2

In the Oklahoma versions of (c) and (d), glottalization failed to spread.

  c. Underlying: ka? no   wa? ke   'on its back'
                  1   2   3   4
      Ontario: kå nó   ẘå keh
                  1   2   *3*   4
      Oklahoma: ka? nú   wa? keh
                  1   2   *3*   4
  d. Underlying: a   ta? ti?   thra? 'cane'
                  1   2   3   4
      Ontario: a   tá? ti   thra?
                  1   2   *3*   4
      Oklahoma: tá? ti? thra?
                     2   *3*   4

Note that in the Oklahoma version of (13a) 'on my hand', devoicing did not spread but laryngealization did. In fact, the same word may be pronounced sometimes with devoicing, sometimes without.

  (14) Underlying: keh sa? ka hę:t 'my mouth' ('my lips have a hole')
                  1   2   3 4
      Ontario: kę̊ sá? ką ę:t
                  1   2   *3* 4
      Oklahoma: kę̊ sá? ką ę:t / keh sá? ką ę:t
                  1   2   *3* 4   *1*   2   *3* 4

(No doublets occurred in the Oklahoma corpus showing the optionality of glottal spreading for a single word, but this may simply be an accident of the data.)

In Ontario, the laryngeal metathesis is context sensitive: it does not occur in syllables beginning with vowels or laryngeals, nor word-finally. In Oklahoma, the process has been generalized to all but word-final syllables. It appears in vowel-initial syllables as often as in other odd-numbered syllables. (Vowel-initial syllables occur only word-initially.)

(15) a. Ontario: ahsǫ́h   'still'
         Oklahoma: ǫsųh
     b. Ontario: ohká:eʔ   'squash'
         Oklahoma: ǫká:eʔ

It also appears in laryngeal-initial syllables as often as in other odd-numbered syllables, whether the laryngeal is *h* or *ʔ*.

(16) a. Ontario: khehso:t   'my grandmother'
         Oklahoma: kęsu:t
     b. Ontario: onę́hohkwaʔ   'lyed hominy'
         Oklahoma: nę́hųkwaʔ
     c. Ontario: kekáhaʔkeh   'on my eye'
         Oklahoma: kekáhą̊keh
     d. Ontario: ketsyęʔohtáʔke '(on) my fingernail'
         Oklahoma: ketyséʔǫtaʔ   'my fingernail'

The general retention of the complex stress and metathesis patterns, which depend on syllable count from the beginning of words, is especially impressive in light of another innovation. In Cayuga, the neuter pronominal prefix *o-* is often dropped by both Ontario and Oklahoma speakers in certain color and animal names:

(17) a. (o)nráhtą̀:ʔ   'green'
     b. (o)thahyó:nih 'wolf'

In both dialects, stress placement and metathesis still operate as if the missing syllables were present. In the term for 'green', for example, the syllable *-nrah-* would be unstressed and voiceless if it were initial, and *-taʔ-* would not undergo metathesis if it were actually the second syllable.

Oklahoma Cayuga has extended this deletion process. The neuter prefix *o-* is usually dropped from most nouns and stative verbs.

(18) a. Ontario: osáheʔtaʔ   'beans'
         Oklahoma: sáheʔtaʔ
     b. Ontario: ohyuʔthí:yeht   'it is sharp'
         Oklahoma: (h)yuʔthí:yeht

No irrecoverable information is lost with a systematic dropping of the pronoun. The loss is not restricted to the pronoun in Oklahoma, however. Words like those in (19) are typical.

(19) a. Ontario: owitrá:tha?   'butter'
          Oklahoma: trá:tha?
  b. Ontario: sate:khǫ́:nih   'eat!'
          Oklahoma: te:khǫ́:nih

The loss is phonologically rather than morphologically conditioned. In (19a), the initial *o-* is the neuter pronominal prefix, but *wi-* is part of the root. In (19b), the original initial *s-* is the 2nd person singular pronominal prefix, and *-a-* is the beginning of the semireflexive *-ate-*. No matter how many syllables are deleted, however, stress and metathesis continue to reflect the original syllable count.

6.   Acquisition and deacquisition

It has sometimes been suggested that obsolescing languages resemble child language. Those aspects of a language that are the most complex tend to be acquired last and lost first. Unfortunately, moribund languages are usually just the ones that are not being learned by children, so it is difficult to compare the first and last stages of the same language. This is the case with Cayuga. It has been possible, however, to observe some children learning Mohawk as a first language (Mithun forthcoming). Their early Mohawk is both similar to, and different from, the Cayuga spoken in Oklahoma, in interesting ways.

In Mohawk, as in Cayuga, constituents are ordered according to their relative importance to the discourse. Ordering principles are consistently intact in both child Mohawk and Oklahoma Cayuga. As soon as Mohawk children use sentences of more than one word, they order the words appropriately. Similarly, Oklahoma Cayuga speakers have not lost their pragmatically conditioned order.

As Annette Schmidt (1985c) has pointed out, children acquiring a language and adults losing one do differ in a fundamental way. The language of young children is constrained not only by structural parameters, but also by their cognitive development. Speakers of receding languages undergo no parallel shrinking of cognitive capacities: they simply use a different language for their purposes. This difference is reflected in the two Iroquoian languages. Children learning Mohawk develop syntactic complexity relatively slowly, using few clauses per utterance for a considerable period as they acquire morphology. Oklahoma Cayuga speakers apparently continue to use sentences of approximately normal complexity, even after their command of productive morphology has begun to weaken.

The morphology of the Mohawk children and the Oklahoma adults show striking parallels. Both the children and the adults tend to avoid long combinations of morphemes, even in cases where they control each affix individually. They substitute separate particles for crucial morphemes, and simply do not mention less important ones. The same principles characterize the use of incorporation. Both the children and adults use verbs with incorporated nouns, but they tend to use only those combinations that they would have heard often as lexical items and learned and remembered as units. There seems to be relatively little creative use of the morphology in the strictest sense for word formation, nor is there manipulation of alternative morphological structures for stylistic purposes.

Unfortunately, Mohawk does not share some of the most intriguing phonological characteristics of Cayuga, in particular, the complex stress assignment and metathesis patterns. Child Mohawk does share one interesting phonological feature with Oklahoma Cayuga. For the first few years that children learn Mohawk, there are strong limitations on how many syllables they utter at once. Children begin by pronouncing only the stressed syllable of each word, usually the penultimate or antepenultimate syllable. This coincides sufficiently often with a part of the stem so that some communication is possible. As they progress, they add post-tonic syllables until their renditions of words consist of the stressed syllable plus all following ones. Once this is mastered, they begin to move leftward, so that utterances consist of the final three syllables of words, then the final four syllables, etc. It is at about this point that their words begin to include pronominal prefixes and they discover morphological structure. Limitations on the number of syllables pronounced per word still persist for a certain length of time, although a few well-known words are pronounced in their entirety. This tendency to omit syllables from the beginnings of words is reminiscent of the truncation of words in Oklahoma Cayuga described above.

7.   Conclusion

It is not clear to what extent circumstances have interfered with the Oklahoma speakers' initial acquisition of Cayuga. It may be that those interviewed learned the language relatively well as children. Their language does now differ in subtle ways from that spoken in Ontario, particularly in the areas of morphology and phonology.

Many differences between Ontario and Oklahoma Cayuga are probably due to the sorts of natural processes of change that occur in all languages. The raising of *o to [u], the remodeling of the root for 'leg' by analogy to 'foot', and the regularization of stress assignment and metathesis contexts, are probably in this category. It is interesting that these last innovations have begun with relatively common, established words. This suggests that the stress and metathesis patterns are not necessarily mere diachronic relics passed on with lexical items, but, rather, that they have had a certain synchronic reality, at least at some point.

Certain other differences distinguishing Oklahoma Cayuga could be interpreted as reductions, such as the shrinking of the lexical inventory and the truncation of words. Some of the creative devices formerly used to expand the system may be less exploited by these speakers. The elaborate word-formation processes for the creation of new lexical items are undoubtedly used less often now. The stylistic choices afforded speakers by such a productive morphology, with its rich inventory of affixes as well as noun incorporation, are probably also less exploited by Oklahoma speakers than they once were.

In the end, however, what is most striking about the Oklahoma speakers is not the minor ways in which they differ from Ontario speakers; it is, instead, their nearly complete retention of an amazingly complex morphological and phonological system, under such limited opportunities to use it.

17 Urban and non-urban Egyptian Nubian: Is there a reduction in language skill?

ALEYA ROUCHDY

In Old Nubia, that is, before the 1964 resettlement (see Chapter 6), the Nubian language was resistant to Arabic interference because it was an undisputed language in a remote place. Women and children were mostly monolingual Nubian speakers. Men in general spoke both Nubian and Arabic due to the fact that they had to travel to cities such as Cairo and Alexandria looking for wage labor. However, there is a noticeable difference in the trend of migration after the resettlement of 1964. Labor migration to big cities is not as high as it was prior to resettlement, due to the availability of job opportunities in New Nubia.

Nubians can be found as well-entrenched and well-assimilated urbanized groups in cities, and on the other hand as non-urbanized groups living in Southern Egypt in small villages. Groups in several types of locations were chosen for this study. The first group was drawn from isolated villages, where Nubian inhabitants must take a bus to go to the nearest city. The second group was drawn from villages near Aswan, where Nubians can walk or cross the river by boat to that city. The third and final group was drawn from the cities of Aswan, Cairo, and Alexandria, where Nubian men work, but still maintain a home in their Nubian village in Southern Egypt. The different locations were chosen because they give a representative sample of urban, quasi-urban, and non-urban Nubian speakers.

In the new community created after the resettlement of 1964, the Egyptian Nubians came into closer contact with non-Nubian Egyptians. Nubian, an East Sudanic language, came into contact with a dominant Semitic language, Arabic.

Nubian is not a written language. It is not Egypt's official language, nor is it the language of any religion. It is not taught in schools and is spoken only by a minority of the Egyptian population. Moreover, with the resettlement the shift in demographic patterns brought Nubians into closer contact with each other as well as with non-Nubians. Distance was no longer a barrier.

The Nubians were not as isolated as before. In both groups, the Fadicca and the Matoki, a very few speakers understand each other's dialect, and in order to communicate, the speakers of the different dialects use Arabic.

"Where a language shift is taking place, . . . so that a new language is gradually replacing the original language of a community, without the extinction of a people, it is common to find speakers of quite different ability among the residual population which still speaks the older tongue" (Dorian 1981:114). In order to examine the situation of Nubian in Egypt, in 1979 I conducted interviews with 110 Nubians drawn from both dialect groups. Speakers include both males and females ranging from ages 14 to 75. The speakers were given an oral list containing fifty Arabic items and asked to supply the Nubian equivalent in the singular and in the plural. They were also given 63 sentences to translate from Arabic into the specific dialects; 29 of these were intended to examine the syntactic structure, more specifically the word order. In addition to the formal interviews, some Nubian stories and informal conversation by the same individuals were recorded. This was mainly designed to reveal the amount of borrowing and interference in the subject's performance in a less formal situation, and to reveal situations where the Nubian language is used. A lexicon was extracted from the material collected and was checked and reviewed by competent bilinguals.

Based on the material collected, I have categorized my speaker-sample into the following groups (see Figure 1):

1. *Monolinguals who speak Arabic only*. They were born in big cities and their families did not maintain a strong link with their home town. They do not speak Nubian and are not interested in learning it.

2. *Monolinguals who speak Nubian only*. They are older women, 60 years of age and above. They live in villages or moved later in life to live in a city with their children. They have never attended school. This group is linguistically the most conservative in maintaining the Nubian language. However, during my last visit (winter 1986) a new linguistic development was observed among this conservative group of Nubians. The elderly women spoke Arabic and were able to participate in our conversation, which was conducted in Arabic. This group is in the process of becoming bilingual and will in the future be categorized as such. Thus in the future there will be no monolingual Nubian speakers, because the few remaining elderly will have learned some Arabic.

3. *Bilinguals consisting of:*
a. fully competent bilinguals who speak both a Nubian dialect and Arabic. This is a small group that consists of middle-aged urban Nubians. They have a government position in the cities of Cairo or Alexandria, a job which requires fluency in Arabic. Their Nubian has been maintained due to the fact that they keep a close contact with their families in non-urban areas; and
b. noncompetent as bilinguals. These include:

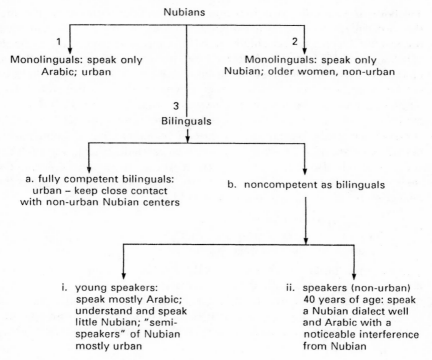

Figure1. *Nubians*

i. speakers, mostly young, who speak Arabic, and understand and speak little Nubian. They live in an urban area. Arabic is their dominant language.[1]

ii. adult bilinguals, 40 years old and above, who speak a Nubian dialect fluently and Arabic with a "foreign accent".

It is group 3, consisting of urban/non-urban fully competent and noncompetent bilinguals that is of interest in this chapter.

Linguistically, every Nubian bilingual speaker passes through a stage of "asymmetry" (cf. Dorian 1981:155), where his/her skills are unbalanced. This phenomenon occurs whether the speaker is acquiring a second language (group 3b, ii), or is in the process of losing the mother tongue (group 3b, i) due to the preponderance of a dominant language. In both cases the speaker's receptive skill in the language is greater than his/her productive skill. How does this asymmetry affect the language production of the bilingual Nubians? Dorian maintains that the "semi-speakers" show certain similarities to other reductive language systems, such as that of child language or a pidgin language. Vocabulary is restricted, morphological inflection is generalized or lost, and some transformations are missing. Paradoxically, however, there is also a retention of complexity. Among East Sutherland Gaelic semi-speakers word order is unchanged, for example (Dorian 1981:155). In the Nubian case, however, there is an apparent change in the word order of urban bilingual Nubians, one that might be related to the word order of colloquial Egyptian (see also Rouchdy 1980). The accepted word order for both Fadicca and Matoki is an SOV order, with an alternative order OSV. For instance in Matoki, the sentence 'the man is carrying the basket' would be *id karadji indjikagi*, that is 'man basket carried' or *karadji id indjikagi*, 'basket man carried'. Changes to an SVO order, which is also the order of Egyptian Arabic, were noticed during the interviews conducted in the city of Cairo. The sentence 'the man put the basket on his big head' was given in Matoki as:

id	kujursu	sabati	ur-dul	dogor
S	V	DO	IO-ADJ	PREP
man	put	basket	head-big	on

The word for 'basket' here, *sabat-i*, is the Arabic word *sabat* 'basket'. The above sentence was accepted by speakers belonging to group 3b, i, the "semi-speakers" who live in urban centers. The competent bilinguals (group 3a) rejected any sentence with an SVO order as being non-Nubian.

In urban Fadicca the same sentence was always given in the order SOV or OSV never as SVO:

idi	sabati	urtān	dabun	doro	okkiro
man	basket	head	big	on	carried

In the Kom Ombo area, referred to as New Nubia, a strict SOV order was always maintained in both dialects, Fadicca and Matoki.

Another disturbance in the word order found in the speech of noncompetent bilinguals (group 3b, i), is that of the phrase (noun + numeral). The correct Nubian phrase (noun + numeral) was often affected by the Arabic phrase structure (numeral + noun). For instance, in Fadicca the sentence 'yesterday I carried 23 baskets' was given as:

aywi	arow	toskun	sabati	sokka-kāgis
I-yesterday	twenty	three	baskets	carried-along

'I yesterday carried with me 23 baskets'

with *arow toskun sabati* for 'twenty-three baskets' instead of conservative *sabati arow toskun* (noun + numeral). If, however, the numeral itself is borrowed from Arabic (which is the case most of the time, among both urban and non-urban Nubians) the structure is definitely Arabic. The Nubian word order does not interfere, e.g. Fadicca:

ay	wili	talāta	wi	išrīn	sabati	sokka kāgis
I	yesterday	three	and	twenty	baskets	carried-along

talāta wi išrīn being 'twenty-three' in Arabic. The same phenomenon occurs among the Matoki speakers. Thus, in the above example, speakers' lexical substitution of Arabic numerals for Nubian numerals is also accompanied by structural interference. Arabic is thus the "model" pattern for these speakers in such a numerical construction.

Changes in word order were always rejected as being ungrammatical by competent bilinguals (group 3a). This rejection leads to the issue of whether competent bilinguals and semi-speakers have different judgement and perception about mixed language. The semi-speakers (group 3b, i) did not think of the above-mentioned word order deviance as being a grammatical deviance. This linguistic incompetence is reflected in their defective speech production. What is more critical is that these speakers' receptiveness to correct Nubian structure is equally defective. They accept an SVO word order for the Nubian sentence. However, they have a strong productive and receptive control of the Arabic language, which leads to their "skewed performance" in Nubian. Thus, this type of bilingual speaker encounters two types of asymmetry, and inter- and intra-language asymmetry. The inter-language asymmetry is a stage where the receptiveness of the speaker/listener exceeds the linguistic production; we find, therefore, that "while most of the ESG semi-speakers *produce* a Gaelic with very evident deficiencies, their *receptive* control of the language is outstanding" (Dorian 1981:155). Both competent and noncompetent bilinguals go through a stage of asymmetry relative to the societally dominant language. The intra-language asymmetry however, is a stage that only the semi-speaker encounters. It is a type of asymmetry in the speaker's receptive skills in two different languages. It is a case where the receptive skills in the second language (Arabic) are greater than the receptive skills in the first language (Nubian). When the Nubian semi-speaker's linguistic performance exhibits the latter type of asymmetry, his/her language competence in the first language (Nubian) is threatened.

Phonological and morphological interference from Nubian into Arabic was observed mostly in the speech of noncompetent adult bilinguals (group 3b, ii). It results in what is commonly referred to conventionally by both Nubian and Arabic Egyptian speakers as a "foreign accent" in Arabic. Although "foreign accent" is properly used for phonological interference alone, Egyptians in this case refer to any interference, phonological and/or morphological, as a "foreign accent". An example would be the case of a 50-year-old Nubian musician and singer who was born in Old Nubia (i.e., before the resettlement) and lived there until he was 25 years old. Later he settled in Cairo. He sings and speaks Matoki fluently. He also speaks Arabic but transfers Nubian rules into Arabic. For example, when addressing me, he said in Arabic *ha'ulak* instead of *ha'ulik* for 'I'll tell you', and *šuf* instead of *šūfi* for the feminine imperative 'look'. He changed /ħ/ > /h/ since the Nubian phonological system lacks the voiced and voiceless pharyngeals.

Thus, he substituted a native Nubian phoneme for an Arabic phoneme. Moreover, the feminine object pronouns were replaced by the masculine counterparts, e.g. /-ik/ > /-ak/ and /-i/ > /-Ø/. This is consistently repeated in the speech of group 3b, ii, since in Nubian there is no gender differentiation.

The suffixes -*a* and -*ma*, in Fadicca and Matoki respectively, represent the copula in a sentence with predicate nominative. The Fadicca speakers of group 3b, ii, never fail to add this suffix to the borrowed Arabic adjectives, while the Matoki speakers belonging to the same proficiency group are inconsistent in their performance:

	Arabic	*Fadicca*	*Matoki*
'stubborn'	⁹anīd (masc. sg.)	anīd-a	⁹anīd ~ anīd-ma
	⁹anīda (fem. sg.)		
'weak'	da⁹īf (masc. sg.)	daīf-a	da⁹īf ~ da⁹īf-ma
	da⁹īfa (fem. sg.)		

The voiced pharyngeal is lost in the above examples of Fadicca. The addition of the Nubian suffix -*a* to the borrowed Arabic lexical item is translated into Nubian as the copula in the sentence, 'he/she is stubborn'. In Arabic, the suffix -*a* when added to an adjective marks it as feminine: ⁹*anīda* means 'stubborn' (feminine). Whenever a Fadicca speaker uses such a pattern, he/she is applying the Nubian morphological rule to the Arabic lexical item. Arab speakers in Egypt, who do not know that the Nubian language lacks gender differentiation, and do not know the meaning of the suffix -*a*, always wonder why Nubians never address the appropriate sex properly, and ridicule them. This pattern in Nubian handling of borrowing is due to the existence of morphemes which are phonologically homophonous but semantically quite distinct. It creates predictable deviation in the Arabic performance of the Fadicca speakers and gives rise to a linguistic stereotype of Nubian rendering of Arabic among Egyptian Arabs: when imitating Nubian speakers, Arabs introduce incorrect gender-markers of this type. This is done chiefly by Arab actors and singers in films and plays when they take the role of a Nubian.

In Matoki this similarity of sound does not exist; the copula is marked by the suffix -*ma*. A speaker of Matoki will refer to a stubborn male as ⁹*anīd* which is the same as in Arabic, or as ⁹*anīdma* to Nubianize the borrowed Arabic item. A non-Nubian Egyptian typically concludes that Matoki know better Arabic than the Fadicca, even though the Matoki version may show a suffix, since that suffix can not be mistaken for a gender confusion.

The above example of phonological and morphological interference results in an imperfect performance of Arabic. In Nubian, among group 3b speakers, morphological inflection is not reduced as in the case of some reports of semi-speakers, nor is Arabic morphology borrowed. Nubian morphology is supplied, which in some cases leads to ambiguous structures, as in the case of pluralization:

Arabic		Matoki	
kitab (sg.)	'book'	kitab (sg.)	'book'
kitab-i (sg.)	'my book'	kitab-i (sg.)	'my book'
kutub (pl.)	'books'	kutub-i (pl.)	'books'
kutub-i (pl.)	'my books'	kutub-i (pl.)	'my books'

Here the noun *kitab* 'book', an Arabic borrowing in Nubian, is pluralized by Matoki speakers by using two plural markers, one Arabic (*kutub*) and one Nubian (*kutub-i*) (= the Arabic plural *plus* the Nubian plural). According to the rules of the Matoki plural, it should be *kitab-i*. But the form *kitab-i* in Arabic means 'my book'; the Arabic suffix *-i* marks the possessive 1st person singular. The bilingual Nubian speakers, being influenced by Arabic, feel that *kitab-i* (singular Arabic form + plural Nubian suffix) does not adequately express plurality in Nubian, since *kitab-i* can also represent the Arabic singular noun with borrowed Arabic 1st person singular possessive element. To avoid this ambiguity the speakers use a double plural: the Nubian plural suffix *-i* is added to the Arabic plural form *kutub*. The Nubian form *kutub-i* 'books' incorporating the marked Arabic plural and the homophonous Arabic possessive and Nubian plural *-i*, sounds "more plural" to Nubian speakers than the correct Nubian form *kitab-i* 'books'. This linguistic *Gefühl* among the Nubian speakers results in an ambiguous structure, since the hearer has no way of being sure whether the form *kutub-i* is intended to mean just 'books' or 'my books'

The situation of language contact, Arabic/Nubian, leads to two different manifestations of reduction in linguistic skills within the group categorized as noncompetent bilinguals (3b, i and ii). The first group (3b, i) consists of urban speakers with strongly asymmetrical productive and receptive skills. The maintenance of the Nubian language is threatened within this group. In the case of group 3b, ii, however, we encounter a situation of language change. Nubian, among these speakers, has remained a viable language in spite of a large number of Arabic words and usages. However, the infrequent use of Nubian is causing some changes in the language which can not be attributed directly to influence from Arabic. The reduced use of Nubian, actively and passively, results in a generalization in the application of grammatical rules. An example would be the deviation in the Nubian plural formation of nouns among the Fadicca and Matoki speakers. The plural traditionally is formed by adding a suffix to the singular noun. The form of the suffix is conditioned by the immediately preceding sound. Some of the bilingual speakers, competent as well as noncompetent, generalized by using one plural suffix for a majority of nouns given to them. For example, the suffix *-ku-*, *-gu* was used more often among the Fadicca speakers, and the suffix *-chi* among the Matoki speakers. For example:

Fadicca		Correct plural	Generalized plural
agar	'place'	agar-i	agar-ku ~ agar-gu
tu	'stomach'	tu-wi	tu-gu

Matoki		*Correct plural*	*Generalized plural*
kulu	'stone'	kul-wi	kulu-chi
ulug	'ear'	ulg-i	ulgi-chi

When more than one plural occurs in relatively rapid succession, the plural formation of the first noun is especially likely to be generalized to succeeding nouns. Thus if the speaker begins with a noun ending with the plural suffix *-i*, this same suffix is applied to the next noun, regardless of the conservative grammatical rules for plural formation.

The formation of the plural was *the* linguistic rule that bilingual Nubians disagreed about. During the interviews, there were many arguments among the Nubians as to what the correct plural form should be. Generalization was apparent in the speech of both competent and noncompetent bilinguals. However, the competent bilinguals (3a) and the imperfect bilinguals of group 3b, ii, whenever provided with the correct form of the plural, would suddenly remember it and would apply it to the nouns that have a similar pattern. Moreover, they insisted on correcting their earlier plural forms if they had been wrong. Noncompetent bilinguals (group 3b, i) remained consistently unable to provide the correct form.

The generalization of the plural is not attributed directly to influence from Arabic, but is the product of decreased opportunities in the use of the Nubian language. Similarly "steadily decreasing use of Gaelic might be invoked to explain the amount of change [found in East Sutherland Gaelic], and clearly it is a major factor in the differences between semi-speakers' grammar and fluent-speakers' grammar [as opposed to differences found among fluent speakers themselves]" (Dorian 1981:153). In the case of a minority language vs. a dominant language, the phenomenon "language contact" cannot really be considered a separate issue from that of "decreasing usage". The decreased use of Nubian is indeed due to the dominance of the Arabic language. Thus, whether the influence is directly or indirectly manifested, the presence of extensive language contact is to be considered first in explaining either the viability of Nubian or the linguistic reduction in the display of language skills among the speakers of Nubian. Second, the Nubian attitude toward their language is a determining factor as to their willingness in the future to speak Nubian or alternatively to opt for Arabic. This attitude will play a major role in the persistence of the Nubian language or the linguistic tip in favor of Arabic (see Chapter 6 of this volume).

Notes

The research reported in this chapter was supported by grants from the American Research Center in Egypt and the Social Science Research Council (1979), and again by the American Research Center in Egypt in 1984.
1. Dorian's term "semi-speakers" can be used to refer to this group of speakers (Dorian 1981:155).

18 Some lexical and morphological changes in Warlpiri

EDITH L. BAVIN

1. Introduction

The first point I would like to stress in this chapter is that Warlpiri is not yet a dying language. The positive attitudes of the Warlpiri people towards their language and way of life encourage language maintenance. However, the young people are attracted by aspects of the non-Aboriginal way of life. The adoption of new ways, together with exposure to the English language, have led to changes in the language. There are many changes taking place quite rapidly, particularly in the language of the young people. Given statements that are frequently made in the Australian context, statements to the effect that all Aboriginal languages will soon have died out, it is worthwhile to point out some of the changes in progress that we have observed in the speech of the people in the community, particularly in that of the children. The data I will use in the paper have been collected as part of a longterm project on the children's acquisition of Warlpiri as a first language.

In this chapter I will discuss two major aspects of the changes in progress. One is the borrowing of lexical items from English; these borrowings are for both new and existing concepts, and what is of particular interest is the replacement of traditional words with English borrowings as well as the assimilation of the loanwords into the Warlpiri system. It is not unusual to find lexical borrowings when two languages are in contact. Dorian (1986c:259), for example, states that English words have been readily taken into East Sutherland Gaelic and adapted to the Gaelic grammar and morphophonology. The second area of change is in the pronominal system. Reduction of morphological complexity is a factor that has been discussed in the literature on language shift and language death. For example, Dorian (1978c) discusses the reduction of morphological complexity in East Sutherland Gaelic, although pointing out that some complexity does remain. Schmidt (1985a) discusses the reduction of morphological complexity in young people's Dyirbal, although she also illustrates that there has been some creation of new affixes as well as some resistance to simplification. The changes in the Warlpiri pronominal system show not only innovations in the

267

forms used, but also a reduction in the number of oppositions. Before giving details about the changes, I will give an overview of the Aboriginal language situation in Australia today, and then outline aspects of the social situation in Yuendumu, the Warlpiri community from which our data are collected.

When the Europeans first settled in Australia, there were over two hundred Aboriginal languages spoken. The exact number is debatable, depending partly on how the languages and dialects are defined (Dixon 1980; Blake 1981; Yallop 1982; Black 1983). Over the years, as more of the land was settled by Europeans, many Aboriginal tribes were taken from their traditional lands and placed into government settlements, sometimes with several tribes mixed together. Many of the children were taken away from their parents. In more recent years, Aboriginal groups have been fighting for both land rights and language rights. Some groups have had their traditional lands restored. In the center of Australia there has been an increased interest in moving away from larger settlements and, for the Warlpiri people, a number of outstations have been established recently. Over the past ten years the Northern Territory government has organized bilingual programs in some Aboriginal community schools, although recently there have been threats to cut some of the programs because of the costs involved in administering them in remote areas.

According to Dixon (1980:18) over fifty of the languages spoken when the Europeans settled have already died out, a hundred are on the way, and for only about fifty are the children speaking the language. But this situation has been changing rapidly and there are now already fewer than fifty languages that are spoken by children. Many of the languages are dying out rapidly. For example, in her recent study, Schmidt (1985b:128), claims that no individual under 15 years of age could speak either traditional or a radically changed form of Dyirbal. Evans (1986:1) writes that only 38 years ago, Kaiadilt people only knew their own language, but now no one under 27 years has any active knowledge of the language at all, and no one under 44 could be described as fluent. In the most recent surveys that I know about, Black (1983) lists only 11 languages (or dialects) with 1,000 or more speakers, while Yallop (1982:30) lists only five languages with over 1,000 speakers. The languages given in both lists are all located in the center and north of Australia (including islands) and they include two creoles: Kriol and Torres Strait (Cape York) Creole. The creoles have the largest number of speakers, 15,000 or more for Kriol and an estimated 15,000 for Torres Strait Creole.

The rapid disappearance of Aboriginal languages is a cause for concern among many Aboriginal groups. A recent workshop on language maintenance (Canberra, May 1986), the establishment of a language maintenance newsletter, requests from communities for linguists to come and write down the language, and requests for Aboriginal schools or bilingual education programs are all signs of the concern. Clearly the major factor in the loss of the languages is the contact with European culture. It is not just contact with the English language that has resulted in language change or language shift, but rather the adaptation of the traditional lifestyles to more Western ways, as well as the difference in status between the Aboriginal languages and English in the Australian context. It is important to recognize that language contact itself is not a sufficient cause for language death. For example, there are ten languages spoken in Maningrida and there is a great deal of multilingualism (Dixon 1980:94).

Yuendumu is a remote settlement 300 kilometers from Alice Springs. Most of the Aboriginal residents live in camps rather than houses. The community had only radio telephone contact with outside communities until late 1987 when television reception and a telephone service were introduced via satellite. The community has about 800 Warlpiri residents as well as about 65 non-Aboriginal English-speaking residents. Few of the Warlpiri people in Yuendumu are fluent in English. Warlpiri is the first language of the community, with English as a foreign language for the Aboriginal people. Although English is the major language of instruction in the school after the first four years, the school only goes through primary grades.[1] After that, any Warlpiri child must move into a residential secondary school in Alice Springs, a school at which English is the language of instruction. Children attend from the surrounding Aboriginal communities (and Warlpiri is one of many languages represented). But few people from Yuendumu have completed secondary education. Even if the children start to attend the school in Alice Springs, they become homesick and move back to the community.

Outside the school, there is very little functional need for English in the community. The shop is selfservice, so English is not required; money can just be exchanged. The Warlpiri people who use English are those who have contact with English-speaking people mainly in the school (teaching assistants and literacy workers), in the clinic, in service encounters (such as motor vehicle maintenance) and in administering the community. In the school, the children use Warlpiri to each other in the classroom and in the school grounds. So in Yuendumu there has not been an overwhelming functional decline in the use of Warlpiri as there has been for other languages in other places, for example, for East Sutherland Gaelic (Dorian 1978c), Arvanítika (Tsitsipis 1984) and Newfoundland French (King, this volume).

We have not been aware of extensive codeswitching (the alternate use of English and Warlpiri), although there is some when Warlpiri people are talking to each other. Two main contexts for codeswitching seem to be outside the community administrative (council) office and on the basketball courts. My colleague has observed that some males employed by the council use a style of speech with codeswitching when gathered outside the office before starting work in the morning and after lunch, as well as during the tea break (*smokoe*).

McConvell (1985) has noted that people often use codeswitching to mark humor; and in Yuendumu there is sometimes joking associated with the codeswitching. On the basketball courts, English numbers are used for scoring and this, plus words for actions associated with the game, seems to facilitate codeswitching.

2.   Lexical borrowings

Many words have been borrowed from English into Warlpiri. Some have been readily assimilated into the language, although we do hear variations in the pronunciations of some loanwords. For example, the pronunciation of the borrowed item *swim* varies from a close approximation of the English word to [juwimi]. However, we have no evidence that the children use Warlpiri vs. English pronunciation in different registers; when we have noted variation in the pronunciation of one word by the same speaker, it seems to be free variation, although further research may reveal some relationship between context and pronunciation. English pronunciations for newly borrowed words are generally restricted to the speakers who have a fairly good knowledge of English, so they will be aware of the English origin. Haugen (1972:87) claims that a bilingual speaker will introduce a new loanword "in a phonetic form as near that of the model language as he can" but a monolingual will substitute elements from his own language in producing the new word. This claim seems to be supported by our data. A number of old people in Yuendumu are monolingual and others speak very little English. The oldest lady in Yuendumu (about 90) told about her life experiences; the passage included the following items: *mijirnirri, nanukutu, rajini,* and *mija* for 'missionary', 'goat (nanny goat)', 'rations', and 'mister' (*Junga Yimi* 1983:21). Although these items are taken from a written account, they would represent the pronunciation used by the old lady. The words illustrate some of the new concepts that the old lady was exposed to in her first contacts with White people early this century. Generally, English loanwords show "interference" from the Warlpiri phonology. Most of this represents underdifferentiation of phonemes, and phoneme substitution (Weinreich 1966). For example, /p,b,f,v/ will be treated as /p/.

Loanwords from English include placenames and personal names as well as words for new concepts, so are mainly cultural borrowings. Selected examples of loanwords are listed in (1). Note that these are given with forms that reflect assimilation to the Warlpiri phonological system. However, there is variation in how loanwords are pronounced, and this point will be discussed later. The examples in (1) are taken from tapes of children playing and telling narratives; the children are aged between 3 and 14 years.

(1)	truck	[turaki]	blanket	[pilaŋkiti]	cool drink	[kul tiriŋki]
	lunch	[lanji]	naked	[nayikiti]	bus	[paji]

side	[jayidi]	married	[marriti]	light	[layiti]
bicycle	[pajikirli]	battery	[patiriya]	wire	[waya]
picture	[pija]	video	[pitiyu]	town	[tawunu]
school	[kuurlu]	chicken	[jukujuku]		

(from the Australian use of *chook* for 'chicken')

Note that the words show assimilation to the Warlpiri phonological system:[2] the words begin with a consonant and end with a vowel; in addition, the words contain no fricatives, nor any non-Warlpiri clusters such as stop followed by liquid as in the English words *truck* and *blanket*. In the pronunciation given for *cool drink*, the first syllable ends with [l], a possible final sound for a CVC syllable, and the second syllable starts with [t]. When English words beginning with *h* are borrowed, it is common to hear a vowel-initial pronunciation, as in [apiji] for *half each* and [ayiti] for *hide*, particularly from the children, but when a vowel-initial word is borrowed, *y* is usually added, producing words such as *yinjayiti* for *inside*.

The vowel added to a borrowed word with a final consonant is generally [i], although [u] is added following stems with [u]; for borrowed words that end with vowels, the added vowel is generally the closest in sound to the English. Note that Warlpiri has only three short vowels [i, u, a] and three long [ii, uu, aa]. Although Warlpiri words end in vowels, in fast speech it is usual for the final syllable to lose its syllabicity. For example, the dative form for 'woman' is *karntaku*, but the pronunciation for fast speech is [karntak]. It's not surprising, then, that speakers do not always add a final vowel to borrowed English words. For example, we have heard children use the word [tak] for both English *dog* and *duck*. The amount of phonological assimilation necessary for a new loanword is related to its shape. If an English word follows the phonotactic constraints for Warlpiri, and only includes Warlpiri sounds, the form will be readily adopted. For example *kangkaru* [kaŋgaru] from English *kangaroo* does not include foreign sound elements. When a word like *frog* is borrowed, however, the Warlpiri speaker will substitute [p] for *f*, and will break up the unacceptable consonant cluster *fr*. So the pronunciation becomes [paraki]. Note that there is no phonemic distinction between voiced and voiceless stops in Warlpiri. Following a nasal, the stop will be voiced; otherwise the pronunciation will vary between a voiced and voiceless version.

A distinction that is often drawn in the literature on loanwords is that between interference and assimilation. For example, in discussing the language behavior of bilinguals, Mackey (1970:195) draws a distinction between interference and integration. He characterizes interference as "the use of elements of one language or dialect while speaking or writing another", and integration as "the incorporation into one language or dialect of elements from another". However, Poplack and Sankoff (1984) point out the difficulties in determining when foreign words become integrated into a language. They take the position that there is a gradual transition as borrowed words become linguistically and sociologically integrated into the system. They argue (p. 103) that there is not one criterion that can be used to characterize loanwords; instead, a number of factors are useful. These factors are: the frequency of use of an item in the community, displacement of an indigenous term, morphophonemic and/or syntactic integration, and acceptability by native speakers.

An examination of English loanwords in Welland French shows that not all items are integrated to the same extent. In their discussion of phonological integration of loanwords in Welland French, Mougeon and Beniak (this volume) document the use of [h] in the pronunciation of the word *hockey*. The young bilinguals who are fluent in English show high or categorical retention of the *h*. In addition, the *h*-pronunciation is spreading to younger speakers who are dominant in French. These findings indicate that the French-dominant speakers are conforming to a new norm that is being established. Fluent bilinguals play a major role as instigators of lexical borrowings, and the forms the bilinguals use serve as a model for others. Another example to illustrate that integration is not a straightforward matter is taken from Melbourne Russian. Kouzmin cited in Clyne (1982:98) noted that for established and integrated Russian loanwords, some speakers produced the unintegrated English forms. Presumably, the bilingual speaker who has knowledge about the origin of loanwords uses this knowledge for prestige or other reasons.

When we consider the English loanwords in Warlpiri, we see that most of them are words for concepts that are not traditional. For example, words that relate to buildings, clothes, sport, food available for purchase (as opposed to food gathered or hunted in the bush), domestic animals, technology and schooling are borrowed from English, along with the concepts they represent. This cultural borrowing reflects the changes in the traditional lifestyle of the Warlpiri people, changes resulting from contact with non-Aboriginal society. The frequency with which the words are used in the community relates to the importance of the concept for the group as well as for the individual speakers. Words that were borrowed at the time of the earliest contacts are well established in the language. For example, *puluku* 'cow' from English *bullock* is a Warlpiri word as is *makiti* 'gun' from English *musket*, although this word is being replaced with *rayipuli* 'rifle' (because rifles are the weapons that the men now buy).

The new words are readily integrated into the morphosyntax of the language – see examples (14–17) below. For example, a noun loanword will carry case marking and number marking as would a traditional Warlpiri word. Loanwords used as verbs are compounded, following a productive word-formation principle in Warlpiri. Borrowed words used as intransitive verbs in Warlpiri are compounded with the inchoative verb *jarrimi*, as in the following example:

(2) Wirriya-wirriya-lu jalpi juwimi-jarrija . . . . .
boy-boy-3PL SUBJ self swim-intr(PAST) . . . . .
'Boys were swimming on their own' [N,12.7][3]

When words are borrowed from English and used as transitive verbs in Warlpiri they precede the verb *mani* 'to have, hold'. Romaine (1985) reports a similar compounding process for verbs in Panjabi; an English loanword is compounded with a Panjabi verb to give a new verb. In the following Warlpiri example, the imperative form of *mani*, namely *manta*, is used.[4]

(3) Holda-manta n(y)ampu (ny)ampu mardaka
hold-TRANS this this hold(IMP)
'Hold this one, hold it' [J, 3.0]

We have heard English participles used as nominals with Warlpiri case affixes as in (4), but note example (5) in which *swimming* does not have a case marker.

(4) Nganimpa-rnalu yanu swimming-kirra
We(PL EX)-1PL EX SUBJ go (PAST) swimming-ALLATIVE
'We went swimming' [N,10]

(5) Swimming-rnalu yanu
swimming-1PL EX SUBJ go (PAST)
'We went swimming' [N,10.2]

When adjectives are borrowed from English, they are affixed with *one* which is pronounced [wan] or [wani]. In Warlpiri there is no justification for a syntactic category adjective. Any "adjective" is a nominal in that it can form a noun phrase on its own. It can also function as a modifier to another nominal (as can other nominals). So in sentence (6), *wiri* is translated as 'the big one', but in (7) as 'big':

(6) Nyangu-rna wiri.
saw-1SG big
'I saw the big one'

(7) Nyangu-rna marlu wiri
saw-1SG kangaroo big
'I saw the big kangaroo'[5]

The addition of *wani* to borrowed English adjectives marks them as nominals. The use of *one* following an adjective is also a feature of Aboriginal English. Kaldor and Malcolm (1982:87) report that in Aboriginal English in Western Australia, if there are several adjectives modifying a noun, one usually precedes the noun and the others follow; those that follow have the affix *one*. In Warlpiri, any borrowed adjective has *wani* attached, regardless of its position in the sentence, so it is assimilated into the system, which distinguishes nouns and verbs but not adjectives. Warlpiri nominals (such as *wiri* 'big' and *wita* 'small') do not have *wani* attached. A *wani*-suffixed word can have other Warlpiri affixes attached (case and number markers).

When the loanwords are written down, the school literacy workers (who assist in the preparation of materials for the school) will generally attempt to write them in standard Warlpiri orthography. However, there are instances when this does not happen. Note the following examples from *Junga Yimi*, a community publication which comes out several times each year. The words *ribbon* and *Land Council* are written with English orthography in (8). In (9), *ribbon, can,* and *flour* are written in Warlpiri orthography.

(8) a. Kajili wina-jarrimi, kapijana yirrarni malikikiji *ribbon* waninjawana
   'Winners will get a ribbon around their neck' (1984a:12)

   b. . . . manu *Land Council*-wardingkipatu yungulujana wangkami
   . . .
   '. . . and people from the Land Council gave the news' (1984a:18)

(9) a. Ngulajana yungu *ripinilki* winakuju
   'The winners were given a ribbon' (1984b:14)

   b. Ngula kalu mani *kartaku* manu *parlawu* manu jara
   'They are holding the can (pan), flour and fat' (1984b:20)

How the word is written will depend on how literate, in Warlpiri and English, the writer is. Since there is a place to check the written form of English words (a dictionary) but not the written form of recent loanwords in Warlpiri, a person who is not confident in Warlpiri literacy may not attempt to represent the loanword in Warlpiri orthography. Although there is a longterm dictionary project coordinated by Ken Hale and Mary Laughren, the words they are documenting are traditional words.

As soon as a concept is introduced into the community, the word that represents that concept is accepted. However, some loanwords are being used even though a word already exists in the language. For most of these items, the time depth is too short to indicate whether the old word will be replaced entirely by the new, or whether it will take on a different meaning, as happened with the words *beef, veal, mutton,* and *pork* which were borrowed from Norman French into English. They are used in English in reference to the meat, not the animal; the already existing Anglo-Saxon words (*ox, sheep* etc.) are used to refer to the animals themselves. Functional shifts have been recorded in other contact situations. For example, in Melbourne Italian *foresta* is restricted to 'forest' in the European sense; the Australian bush is referred to as *bosca*. The word *fattoria* has been restricted to 'factory' now that the loanword *farm* has been adopted for 'farm' (Clyne 1982:97).

A number of loanwords are being used in the community, particularly by the small children, even when there are existing words in Warlpiri. A few are given in (10).

(10) **a.** boomerang   for *karli*
        kangaroo   for *marlu* and *wawirri*
        dingo   for *warnapari*
        tea   for *nalija*
        horse   for *nantuwu*
        no   for *lawa*
        and   for *manu*
        night   for *munga*
    b. play-jarrimi for *manyu-karrimi*
        pipi-kirlangu for *parraja*

It is of interest that *kangaroo*, *boomerang*, and *dingo* are words that have been borrowed into English from other Aboriginal languages. Blake (1981:95) notes that the form *kanguroo* was recorded in 1770 in Cook's journal; the word comes from the Guugu-Yimidhirr language. According to the same author the earliest record of *boomerang* was in 1827 and *dingo* was recorded in 1793 (1981:88,92). The origin of *nalija* 'tea' and *nantuwu* 'horse' is unclear. The words have no other meanings in Warlpiri. According to Blake (p.31), the word for 'horse' in many Aboriginal languages is *yaraman* with a meaning 'long-toothed one'; it seems to have spread from a language in the southeast of Australia. *Parraja* is still a commonly used word; in fact, many children below 5 years often overgeneralize and refer to all oval shapes in *parraja*. (The *parraja* is oval, carved from lightweight wood and painted. A baby sleeps on it, wrapped in blankets, and the mother carries the *parraja* on her hip.) The alternative word consists of [pipi] from English *baby* together with a productive possessive suffix, *kirlangu*, used with nouns.

In a number of texts, we have noted both the English and the Warlpiri words alternating, sometimes side-by-side, as in (11). This was produced by a boy of 12;5 as the third sentence in a narrative spoken to a friend. The two boys were left alone with a tape-recorder running, and they spent the time telling each other stories. Although they knew the tape-recorder was on, they were relaxed. We have found that when adults are present at taping sessions, there is often a great deal of prompting. Children over 4 years are encouraged to be independent, and are used to being in peer groups. From the taping session from which this example was taken, a number of narratives collected were later judged to be good stories by adults.

(11) Manu-lpa-rnalu   *yuparli,*   *bush banana, yuparli*
      get(PAST)-CONT-1PL SUBJ bush-banana bush-banana bush-banana
      'We got bush bananas'

There is some hesitation as the boy produces the sentence. The hesitation appears in an otherwise fluent text with no other English borrowings. The use of both a Warlpiri and English word could be treated as an example of codeswitching at the lexical level, and may reflect the fact that people do not rely on bush-bananas as a source of food as much as they did traditionally. So the boy may be unsure if *yuparli* is the right Warlpiri word.[6]

Another example, from a 12-year-old girl, shows a similar alternation between a Warlpiri and an English word for an equivalent concept ('drunk'):

(12) Kulkurru-lpa, yeh, *pama*-kurlu. *Drungki*-patu-rlu yampija
    middle-CONT   yeh alcohol-with drunk-few-ERG   leave (PAST)
    kulkurru road-rla Alice Springs-janka
    middle   road-LOC Alice Springs-from
    'In the middle. Yes, drunk. Some drunks left it in the middle of the road from Alice Springs'

There is no hesitancy from this speaker (she is, in fact, quite emphatic about the situation), but she uses the Warlpiri construction for 'drunk' alongside the English; so the English is used for emphasis. Another example, from a male of 18, is taken from a story; the boy is telling a story he remembered being told as a young boy. He uses the traditional word *jara* and the loanword *pata* for 'fat':

(13) Warluraji-lpa   yulpa-ngku   mapurnu   jukanyanu-rlu
    initiated-boy-CONT red-ochre-INST paint(PAST) brother-in-law-ERG
    warnirri-rla   jayiti. *Pata*-ngku-lpa mapurnu   jukanyanu-rlu
    water hole-LOC side   fat-INS-CONT   paint(PAST) brother-in-law-ERG
    warluraji. Wali, waniyarra-rlu-lpa,   waniyarra-rlu
    boy   well water snake-ERG-CONT water snake-ERG
    parnti-nyangu *jara*
    smell(PAST)   fat
    'His brother-in-law was painting the initiated boy with red ochre beside a waterhole. He was painting the boy with fat. Well, a water snake smelled the fat'

The story continues with one other instance of *jara* for 'fat'. We have other texts in which there is an alternation between the English-origin and Warlpiri words and certainly for some speakers, hesitancy is associated with this style. For others, this does not appear to be so – see also example (18). It may be that the young people sometimes use English-origin words for emphasis – see also example (21). Romaine (1985:23) states that one of the most common discourse functions of codeswitching is to repeat the same thing in both languages. So the use of both English-origin and Warlpiri words side-by-side in the texts we have may just reflect a discourse style, and any hesitancy may merely reflect uncertainty in how to proceed with the story, rather than uncertainty with linguistic forms. What is clear is that the lexical borrowings are used in all contexts, even when the topic is a traditional story.

As noted above, some English-origin words seem to be replacing the Warlpiri equivalents. Warlpiri, like other Aboriginal languages, has a history of word replacement: when a Warlpiri person dies, the name of that person together with words that resemble the name become taboo. Either the word *Kumunjayi* replaces the taboo word, or a new name/word is adopted. One source for a new word is a neighboring language, including English. However, the examples cited do not represent replacements for taboo words. The Warlpiri words are still in use by many of the Warlpiri people although the children often seem more familiar with the English equivalents. We have spoken with children aged 4 to 6 years who do not use *warnapari* for 'dingo', *karli* for 'boomerang' or *marlu* for 'kangaroo', preferring instead the non-Warlpiri forms for which English is the immediate source.

We also find that children of this age are not familiar with traditional words for hunting weapons, words such as *pikirri* 'spear thrower', and *kurdiji* 'shield', although *kurlarda* 'spear' is still well known. Although people no longer rely on spears for hunting, using instead rifles if possible, the *kurlarda* still has a function in ceremonies, and is also used in traditional law; legs are still speared for certain offences. The *pikirri* is not generally used now.

One reason for the use of English loanwords in place of traditional words in the speech of young children may be the incorporation of these words into a speech style that is used by adults and older children when addressing young children. The speech style ('Warlpiri Baby Talk') is used mainly when directly addressing a child of about 1–3½ years. The register is characterized mainly by phonological variation: alveolars are replaced by palatals and palatals are replaced by alveolars; initial consonants are sometimes dropped. In addition to the phonological variation, there is also a small specialized vocabulary. (See Laughren 1984 for a description of the register.) We have noted that young mothers are now incorporating a few English words into the Baby Talk.[7] Some of these are animal names; for example, we have heard *horse* and *horsey*, and *kangaroo*, and *moo* for 'cow'. When English words are used in addressing a young child, we have noted [s] being retained in the pronunciations (e.g. in *star* and *horse*). It will be of interest to see whether the baby-register loanwords will be retained by the children as they grow older, and if so whether the *s*-pronunciations will also be retained, functioning as a marker of borrowed words.

As stated earlier, English words are assimilated into the morphosyntax of Warlpiri. They can take focus markers, case markers and other morphology. A few examples follow (note that borrowed words are italicized):

(14) Ngaju-ku ngaju *pulapi*-lki
me-DAT   me   a lot-now
'There's a lot for me now' [N,4.8]
(*pulapi* is from English *full up*.)

(15) Nyangka *tiriji*-kirli, ngaju-nyangu
look(IMP) dress with me-POSS
'Look mine's with a dress' [N,4]
(from English *dress*)

(16) Kapu-lu   ngunami *marriti*
FUT-3PL SUBJ lie   married
'They will be married' [N,4.8]

(17) *Pulapi*-lki nganta yinjiki-kirlangu
lot-now it seems Ursula-POSS
'It seems Ursula's got a lot' [N,4.8]

A longer text is given below. The narrative from a female aged 12;8 contains a number of items borrowed from English. The girl is speaking with her half-sister about a hunting trip, a usual weekend activity. The girls are the same age and are alone, being taped under the same conditions as described for (11).

(18) Yanu-rnalu   Warlura-kurra.   Nyangu-rnalu
go(PAST)-1PL EX SUBJ Warlura-ALLATIVE see (PAST);1PL EX SUBJ
duck-wati *pulapi* an   wirriya-wirriya-lu *jaslpi juwimi*-jarrija
duck-PL   a lot   and boy-boy-3PL SUBJ self   swim-INT(PAST)
an karnta-karnta   *jalpi*. *Ducks*-lpa-rnalu   luwarnu
and woman-woman self   Ducks-CONT-1PL EX SUBJ shoot(PAST)
panu-jarlu. Ngula-jangka-rnalu yanu   *lunchi*-kirra   *an*
many-very after that -1PL EX SUBJ go(PAST) lunch-ALLATIVE and
nyangu-rnalu   Tyian ngunanja-kurra.
see(PAST)-1PL EX SUBJ Diyon sleep(INF)-OBCON
'We went to Warlura dam. We saw a lot of ducks and boys swimming on their own and girls on their own. We shot a lot of ducks. After that, we went to lunch and saw Diyon sleeping.'

The text continues about going to a disco and seeing movies. It is striking because of the number of different plural forms used. Traditionally some human nouns are reduplicated to show plural number, as with *wirriya-wirriya* and *karnta-karnta* in the text. Other plural markers for nouns are *panu* 'many' and *patu* 'few'. In the text, however, we see the use of the innovation *wati* for plural. The origin of this is uncertain, since *wati* means 'man', but it is used by all the young Warlpiri speakers as a plural suffix on nouns, even humans. It may be used on analogy with *pala* (from English

fella) which is suffixed to English numbers (e.g. *nine-pala* for 'nine') We also
see in the text the traditional word for 'many' *panu* as well as the English
plural *-s* on *ducks*. Even though the passage has so much borrowing, it does
show a complex Warlpiri construction in the use of *ngunanja-kurra*, which is
an embedded clause. The *kurra* shows that the subject of the infinitive is the
same referent as the object of the matrix verb.

We have collected a number of texts from this girl, and we have observed
her in family situations in Yuendumu and away, as well as in the school
setting. She can and does use complex morphology which includes case
markers, focus markers, compound verbs, infinitive constructions, and
modal particles. What seems to mark different styles for her, and other
young people, is not how many English loanwords are included but how
much is said, as well as the rate of speaking, and the pitch. As with the
women in the community, a deep pitch is used for annoyance and anger. In a
more formal situation, the girl is often shy and hesitant and her utterances
are short. With friends, when speaking about familiar things, her utterances
are longer and so there is more opportunity for discourse-linking morphology as well as for elaboration in content.

Items that occur frequently in young people's Warlpiri are *and* and *well* as
well as the English negatives *no* and *not*.[8] Warlpiri has the words *lawa* 'no',
wangu 'without' and *kalu* 'not', but now English [na] or [nati] are commonly
used. In addition, children are using them to form a new Warlpiri construction – a negative imperative. In traditional Warlpiri, an infinitive verb
followed by *wangu* is used for this function, but in example (19), from a 4-
year-old, [nati] followed by the imperative verb forms a negative imperative
for the child, who is warning a friend. The construction appears to be
influenced by the English negative imperative which is formed with a
negative and imperative verb form, although English also uses the auxiliary
do for which Warlpiri has no equivalent. Notice in (21) the use of both
Warlpiri and English negative words, perhaps for emphasis.

(19) Nati wangkaya kaji   ka-ngku   purda-nyanyi
     not talk(IMP)   might AUX-2SG OBJ hear
     'Don't talk; she might hear you'

(20) Nati kangka
     not carry(IMP)
     'Don't take it' [N,4.11]

(21) Na nyangka lawa
     no look(IMP) no
     'Don't look' [N, 4.8]

Another word that is occurring frequently in the children's speech
appears to be a recent innovation. The word *yini* from English *any* (or *any*

way) is used by the small children with a negative connotation; so there has been a semantic shift. The adults we have worked with unanimously interpret the word as a negative in the children's speech. We elicited the form *yini* from a male in his 30s and the word was used in the English sense of 'any', although also as a tag with the sense 'is that really true'. Notice the following short dialog between two 3-year-old children:

(22) M: *Yini* Nungarrayi 'It's not Nungarrayi'
      J: Japangardi nganta 'It seems to be Japangardi'

The word *reckon* has also undergone some semantic shift. Compounded with *wangu*, it is used in the sense 'definitely, without doubt'. Another word borrowed from English is *inside: yinjayiti*. In Warlpiri, the concepts of 'inside' and 'under' can be expressed with the same word *kaninjarni*; the children use *yinjayiti* to mean both 'inside' and 'under'. That is, the Warlpiri concept 'covered' has been retained.

3.   **Changes in the pronominal system**

One of the domains in which we have noted most variation in the speech community is the pronominal system. Warlpiri has independent pronouns for 1st and 2nd persons singular, dual, and plural. For the 1st person, there is also a distinction between inclusive (of hearer) and exclusive (of hearer) for the dual and plural forms. In addition, there is a series of cross-reference clitics which appear in second position in the clause, either attached to an auxiliary base (marking imperfective aspect or future tense) or attached to the end of the first element in the clause, whatever that element may be. There are distinct forms for subject and object with the dative object taking precedence over the absolutive (Hale 1982). There are 21 clitic forms in the traditional system, as illustrated in Table 1. Note that it is not easy to segment these forms into distinct morphemes for person, number, and inclusion.

From the data we have collected we see that some of the traditional distinctions are being lost, and some of the forms being used show innovation. An example of one of the widespread innovations is given below. In Warlpiri, the ergative case marker has four allomorphs: *ngki, ngku, rli, rlu*. The first two of these forms are used on two-syllable words and the other two on longer words. The vowel used depends on the preceding stem vowel. In traditional Warlpiri (Hale 1973), the case markers are attached to a long form of the 1st and 2nd person singular independent pronouns. This means that *rli/rlu* are the allomorphs for ergative on these pronouns. However, the young children use the *rli/rlu* forms but on a short form of the pronoun, so creating another exception (to the few already in the language) for the rule about which allomorph to use:

Table 1. *The traditional Warlpiri pronominal forms (as described by Hale, 1973)*

	Singular	Dual	Plural
1st person			
Independent pronouns	1. ngaju	4. ngajarra	7. nganimpa
Subject clitics	2. rna	5. rlijarra	8. rna-lu (*exclusive*)
Object clitics	3. ju	6. jarrangku	9. nganpa
Independent pronouns		10. ngali(jarra)	13. ngalipa
Subject clitics		11. rli	14. rlipa (*inclusive*)
Object clitics		12. ngali(ngki)	15. ngalpa
2nd person			
Independent pronouns	16. nyuntu	19. nyumpala	22. nyurrula
Subject clitics	17. n(pa)	20. n(pa)-pala	23. nku-lu
Object clitics	18. ngku	21. ngku-pala	24. nyarra
3rd person			
Subject clitics	25. Ø	27. pala	29. lu
Object clitics	26. Ø/rla (*dative*)	28. palangu	30. jana

(23) Wal nyuntu wiyi ngaju-rlu
      well you   first me-ERG
      'Well, you [take it] first, then me' [N, 7.7]

The adult would use the form: *ngajulu-rlu-lku* 'me-ERG-then'.

This example is cited because it caused our helper (an adult female) to remark that the children do say *ngaju-rlu* for 'I-ERG'. In other words, adults are aware of this (and other differences) between the traditional adult system and the forms produced by young people.

It is clear that the complex system is changing. The results of a survey of Warlpiri speakers ranging in age from 9 to 60 indicate that for the 1st person pronominal forms, all speakers interviewed over the age of 37 retained five distinct forms for independent pronouns, five distinct forms for subject clitics, and five distinct forms for object clitics. No person younger than 17 did. Table 2 summarizes the percentages of responses given in the survey for the dual and plural categories for 1st person. (The singular forms did not show variation from the traditional system.)

The 166 people surveyed were from four age groups: group 1 (37 people), aged 9–16 years; group 2 (45 people), aged 17–24; group 3 (45 people), aged 25–33; and group 4 (44 people), all over 33. Males and females were fairly evenly represented. The forms were collected using pictures to create a hunting story, and questions were asked of the interviewee (see Bavin and Shopen 1987 for details).

The findings of the survey indicate that in the 1st person forms, the number of distinctions is being reduced. Specifically, there is a merger

Table 2. *Percentage of "traditional" forms by age groups*

		Groups			
		1	2	3	4
1st person					
Dual	*Exclusive*				
	Ind. Pro.	77.3	93.3	100.0	100.0
	Subj. Cl.	18.2	53.3	87.5	100.0
	Obj. Cl.	0	35.5	85.0	100.0
Plural	*Exclusive*				
	Ind. Pro.	79.5	93.3	100.0	100.0
	Subj. Cl.	100.0	95.6	100.0	100.0
	Obj. Cl.	29.5	60.0	92.5	100.0
Dual	*Inclusive*				
	Ind. Pro.	43.2	53.3	72.5	97.3
	Subj. Cl.	45.5	53.3	82.5	100.0
	Obj. Cl.	43.2	48.9	75.0	100.0
Plural	*Inclusive*				
	Ind. Pro.	40.9	62.2	75.0	94.6
	Subj. Cl.	50.0	64.4	82.5	100.0
	Obj. Cl.	68.2	46.7	70.0	100.0
2nd person					
Dual					
	Ind. Pro.	9.1	13.0	36.8	70.0
	Subj. Cl.	27.3	73.9	78.9	100.0
	Obj. Cl.	54.5	87.0	100.0	100.0
Plural					
	Ind. Pro.	18.2	82.6	100.0	100.0
	Subj. Cl.	0	17.4	68.4	95.0
	Obj. Cl.	68.2	100.0	100.0	100.0

between the inclusive and exclusive categories. This is reflected also in the texts we have; it is unusual to find an inclusive plural object form used as clitic with an exclusive referent. For the independent pronouns, the traditional exclusive dual form (*ngajarra*) was used in the survey for the inclusive dual function by 52.3 percent of group 1, 44.4 percent of group 2, 27.5 percent of group 3, and nobody in group 4. The traditional exclusive plural form (*nganimpa*) was used for the inclusive plural function by 59.1 percent of group 1, 31.1 percent of group 2, 20 percent of group 3, and nobody in group 4. For the subject clitics, a similar age gradation can be seen in the merger between inclusive and exclusive. For the inclusive plural function, the traditional exclusive plural form (*rnalu*) was used by 45.5 percent of group 1, 33.3 percent of group 2 and 17.5 percent of group 3. For the object clitics for 1st person, the traditional inclusive plural form (*ngalpa*) was used by 52.3 percent of group 1 and 22.2 percent of group 2 for the exclusive plural function. The inclusive dual (*ngalingki*) was used for the exclusive dual function by 29.5 percent of group 1 and 11.1 percent of group 2. The

Table 3. *Forms frequently used by young Warlpiri speakers*

	Singular	Dual	Plural
1st person			
Ind. Pro.	ngaju	ngajarra	nganimpa
Subj.	rna	rnapala	rnalu
Obj.	ju	ngalingki/ngalpa	ngalpa
2nd person			
Ind. Pro.	nyuntu	nyuntujarra	nyunturra
Subj.	npa	npapala	npalu
Obj.	ngku	ngkupala	nyarra
3rd person			
Subj.	—	pala	lu
Obj.	—/rla (*dative*)	pala/palangu	jana

inclusive plural form from the traditional system (*ngalpa*) was used for both inclusive dual and exclusive dual functions showing also a plural–dual merger. From group 1, 31.8 percent used the inclusive plural form for the exclusive dual function and 38.6 percent used it – for the inclusive dual function. From group 2, 6.7 percent used it for the exclusive dual and 15.5 percent for the inclusive dual functions, while only one person in group 3 used it – for the inclusive dual; in group 4 there were no instances of *ngalpa* being used for other functions.

As well as these mergers in the 1st person, the survey indicated that *rna-pala* has been extended in use by the young people. It was noted as an alternative for the exclusive dual subject clitic by Laughren (1977). However, we found that 61.4 percent of group 1 used the form as did 24.4 percent of group 2 and 7.5 percent of group 3. In addition, 34.1 percent of group 1 used it for the inclusive dual function, as did 8.9 percent of group 2 and 5 percent of group 3. The form is semantically transparent with *rna* marking person and *pala* number. Both forms are used elsewhere in the pronominal paradigms. Table 3 summarizes the most frequently used forms for group 1 (9–16 years).

In the 2nd person paradigm, the changes from the traditional system are mainly in the form of innovations. The pronouns *nyuntu-jarra* and *nyuntu-rra* are both easily segmentable into morphemes for person and number: *nyuntu* is the singular form for 2nd person and *jarra* and *rra* are used in the grammar to mark dual and plural respectively. Another change noted for 2nd person forms is the leveling of allomorphy for the 2nd person subject clitic. Traditionally, the two allomorphs are *n* and *npa*; in the survey, 50 percent of the speakers from group 1 used *npa* in a context in which the older speakers use the allomorph *n*. So there are a number of changes in the complex pronominal system, changes that are clearly age-graded.[9] There are both innovations and neutralizations. There is a great deal of variation in the forms used but this variation does not have social correlates. Rather it reflects a move towards more semantic transparency in the pronominal forms as well as a move towards reducing the number of oppositions in the system. As the young people receive so much language input from peers as well as from people a few generations older, it is likely that the changes will continue.

4.   Conclusion

In other Warlpiri speech communities there has been language shift. For example, Jane Simpson reports (pers. comm.) that in Tennant Creek the Warlpiri children answer their Warlpiri-speaking parents in English. In Lajamanu, another Warlpiri settlement, English is used much more than in Yuendumu. In our one trip to the community, we noticed that the children were not as familiar with the case-marking system as the children at Yuendumu. We also heard a lot of codeswitching. The community hopes that the introduction of a Warlpiri program in the school will help the children retain Warlpiri as their language, although people in the community feel, as do people in Yuendumu, that the children should also know English.

In Yuendumu, the people express strong loyalty to their language, and the bilingual school program is certainly helping to establish Warlpiri as a legitimate language for education. A major problem exists in the limited amount of materials available for use in the school. Attempts have been made, and are being made, at language engineering; for example, Ken Hale initiated using the word *rdaka* 'hand' as the word for 'five', the word *wirlki* 'a curved boomerang' as the word for 'seven' and the word *milpa* 'eyes' as the word for 'eight'. Other concepts have been named using Warlpiri morphology to coin new expressions. However, language engineering requires not only the coining of new expressions, but also the acceptance of them by the speech community. The Warlpiri teaching staff are working with linguists to prepare a book for teaching mathematics; however, it is taking a while for fluent speakers to find the best way to express concepts such as 'addition', 'equals', and 'multiplication'. Often the coined terms are lengthier than the equivalent English words. Once the terms are agreed upon, they will be taught in the school, but they will not necessarily be adopted. One lady involved with preparing a Warlpiri script for a training video (to teach people about road law) wanted to retain the English *sixty* rather than use the coined expression which was much longer; others would probably support this view.

Tsitsipis (1983a), mentions that the traditional contexts for the emergence of narrative genres has eroded in the Arvanítika community. We have not yet documented the amount of storytelling that does take place in the different camps in Yuendumu, but we have been told that the young children do not sit around the camp fires at night to listen to stories as much as they used to. After an overnight camping trip for two of the school grades, one of the Warlpiri ladies was pleased that the children had a chance to hear the old people telling stories. There seems to be some pride when a young adult tells us that his/her father (or someone else) was the source of a particular story. In addition, people in the community are aware of who the good storytellers are, so storytelling is a valued skill. Now, however, there is a place where children can go in the evenings to listen to music, and the adults are often busy with cardgames so, according to our helpers, the children no longer have the same exposure to traditional stories. When we have more details, it will be of interest to see if there is a strong correlation between the linguistic skills of the children and their exposure to storytelling. Our impressions are that there may be.

The changes in the pronominal system discussed in this chapter cannot be attributed just to contact with English. English does not have an inclusive–exclusive distinction, nor a dual number, and if these categories are lost in Warlpiri, a motivating factor could be the absence of them in English. However, other changes are going on, and these reflect a move towards semantic transparency, which is generally internally motivated change.

We have not yet analyzed adequately the frequency of borrowed words either by different speakers or by the same speakers in different texts. Our impressions are that the children of school age use more than their parents. Many times when we have been transcribing tapes, our helpers have remarked about the way the young children speak. They point out overgeneralizations of the types noted for other children acquiring their first language (for example, in case forms); they also point out innovations in Warlpiri, innovations such as the use of the negative imperative and *yini*, as well as lexical borrowings. The attitudes expressed by our helpers indicate that the frequent use of English words is not considered to be good Warlpiri.

Notes

The research is funded by the Australian Research Grants Scheme and the Australian Institute of Aboriginal Studies. The project is carried out with the support of the community and with much help from the children. Until July 1987 Tim Shopen assisted me in this project.
1. The children start preschool when they are four and then move to Transition, a class in which Warlpiri literacy skills are introduced. In grades 1 and 2 literacy skills in Warlpiri are taught, and English literacy skills are then introduced.
2. The standard orthography for Warlpiri (which has been in use for 11 years) is based on the phonemic distinctions. The digraph *ng* is used to represent the velar nasal, and other digraphs are used to represent retroflex sounds (e.g. *rl* and *rt*).
3. The reference indicates the sex and age of the speaker; N indicates a female and J a male. Female skin names in Warlpiri begin with N and male skin names begin

with J. There are eight subsections (skin groups); each one has a male and female name. Marriage choices depend on which subsection a person belongs to; a person's skin name depends on those of his parents.

4. Note that the parts of words in brackets were not articulated; dropping of initial consonants is a feature of the Warlpiri Baby Talk, but it is variable, as is the substitution of alveolars for palatals. This is discussed later in the paper. The child used two pronunciations in this example.

5. Note that the Warlpiri has varied word order, so these two sentences could have alternate word orders; they could also include the subject pronoun *ngajulu-rlu* 'I-ERGATIVE'. The only restriction on the word order is that the cross-reference marker *rna*, which shows that the subject is 1st person singular be in second position in the clause.

6. The children are not just influenced by our presence, since they use these English-origin words in natural speech with their friends when we are not present. We have made a point of speaking only Warlpiri to the young children. Since we started working in the community in 1982, any child of 4 years and under has been born since we started our work, and so is quite familiar with our presence in the community.

7. Warlpiri is not unique in incorporating English words into its baby talk; Dixon (1980:84) reports from Leeding that Anindilyakwa, an Aboriginal language of the northeast, also uses some English words in this register.

8. *Well* is used at the beginning of sentences in connected discourse. It seems to be used in place of *ngula jangka* 'and then, after that' for some speakers, but we have no counts on how frequent this item is or whether its use is conditioned by any factors. The speaker of example (13) uses it frequently, no matter what the content of the narrative.

9. King (1984b) found age-related change in progress in a study of clitic pronoun usage in Newfoundland French; she found a greater usage of strong pronouns than object clitics.

19 Language contraction and linguistic change: The case of Welland French

RAYMOND MOUGEON and EDOUARD BENIAK

1. Community profile

1.1. French settlement

The city of Welland, Ontario is located in the heart of the Niagara Peninsula close to the famous falls of the same name. The story of its French community is that of practically all communities of the French-Canadian diaspora.[1] The exodus of French Canadians beyond the borders of the province of Quebec (the principal stronghold of the French language in North America) was essentially touched off by rural overpopulation, forcing many to leave their old settled parishes in search of manual work in the developing urban industrial centers of Ontario to the west and New England to the south. Although the initial migration of French Canadians from Quebec to Ontario dates back to the early nineteenth century, the origins of Welland's French-speaking minority are more recent, since they can only be traced back to the turn of this century. Welland's industries (chiefly textile mills, iron and steel factories, and rubber plants) were spurred by the outbreak of World War I, creating many new, well-paid jobs which were to attract, by 1919, around forty French-Canadian families from Quebec. These families may be considered the historical kernel of the French-speaking community of Welland.[2] They settled in the eastern half of the city where the industrial plants were located, an area which was soon to be known as "Frenchtown". By the end of the 1940s, however, social mobility had brought about some residential dispersion.

As an industrial center, Welland was hit hard by the great Depression, which saw the departure of numerous francophone families. Still, by 1931 the number of residents of French ethnic origin had increased to 911 out of 10,709 (8.5 percent), confirming the existence of an influx of French Canadians after the turn of the century. With the rekindling of industrial activity triggered by the outbreak of World War II, a major wave of French-Canadian immigration to Welland (again primarily from Quebec) began which was to last throughout the wartime period and continue into the economic boom of the '50s. There was at the same time significant immigration from European countries (mostly Italians, Hungarians, and various Slavic peoples), just as there had been during the industrial labor shortage occasioned by World War I. Thus, by 1961 the size of the community had increased considerably, the number of French mother tongue (FMT) individuals standing at 5,976 or 16.6 percent of the city's population.[3] Although French-Canadian immigration to Welland had by then ceased, the tailend of the postwar "baby boom" saw the FMT population continue to climb to 7,590 in 1971, more than holding its own at 17.1 percent of the local population. Today, according to the 1981 Census of Canada, Welland is a multi-ethnic city of close to 45,000 people with an anglophone majority of 65 percent, francophones forming the largest linguistic minority (15.5 percent), ahead of Italians (7 percent), Hungarians (3 percent), and several Slavic minorities (Ukrainians, Poles, Slovaks, etc.). In sum, in spite of notable growth over the last seventy years or so, francophones are and always have been in the minority locally.

1.2.   The French Catholic church

As devout Catholics, the first French-Canadian families to settle in Welland had no alternative but to attend the English parish. This affiliation was soon judged unsatisfactory because of the language difference. The budding French community was quick to found a parish of its own, ministered by a French-Canadian priest from Quebec, who became the community spokesperson, especially when it came to voicing the educational concerns of his parishioners (see further).

Although the French Catholic parish was initially founded to serve the religious needs of basically unilingual francophones, over the years it has had to adapt to the growing proportion of parishioners who have become fully proficient in English (for some at the expense of their French) and have married anglophones. As a result, the current parish priest has had to take on a bilingual assistant to handle the various requests for religious ceremonies in English or in both languages (funerals, baptisms, masses, weddings, etc.). The assistant priest offered the following comments on the response of the Church to requests for bilingual weddings due to the rise of exogamy: "Somebody has got to do them [the mixed marriages], you see. If we say no then they [the parishioners] go away and don't come back. But now we marry them in English and they come back to have the kids baptized and maybe then send the kids to the French schools."

The above is indicative of the fact that the Church has been reduced to a passive role in defending the French language. It can no longer afford to militate actively and overtly in favor of French as it once did, for fear of turning away its (anglicized) faithful. Religion and language, once inseparable, have had to be dissociated, a common evolution within linguistic minorities in North America (Fishman, Nahirni, Hofman and Hayden 1966; Haugen, this volume).

1.3. French language education

Upon arriving in Welland, the first French-Canadian families were forced to send their children to the English public (i.e. nondenominational) schools for lack of French language schools or even English separate (i.e. Catholic) schools. The parish priest's official request that the French students be taught in their language was refused by the Ontario Ministry of Education on the grounds that it was contrary to Regulation XVII, a 1912 act of the Legislature proclaiming English as the sole language of instruction in the province's elementary schools. Following the abrogation of Regulation XVII in 1927, permission was granted by the Minister of Education to teach one hour of French a day. French students were grouped into "bilingual" classes, a situation which remained unchanged until the 1960s, when the number of bilingual classes was sufficient to justify their groupings into entirely bilingual schools, that is, schools not shared with the anglophone majority. Although in theory the amount of French instruction was still legally limited to the daily one-hour French period, in practice other subjects were also taught in French. In other words, the bilingual schools already functioned to some extent as French language schools and foreshadowed the new legislation which was to be introduced in 1968. That year the Ontario government finally legalized French as a language of instruction in the province's primary and secondary public school system. Previously there were no public French-language high schools for the French student to attend following the primary level. As a result, the French-Canadian minority in Ontario had established a few private high schools in major urban communities like Ottawa and Sudbury. Only the wealthiest could afford to send their children to these private institutions. Most French students in Welland simply either did not attend the English language high schools or dropped out after grade 10. Thus unlike previous francophones growing up in Welland, today's young French people can be schooled entirely in French from kindergarten to the end of high school. A similar development has taken place in most of Ontario's francophone communities.

Welland francophones are divided as to whether the language of instruction in the city's French-language schools should be French only or both French and English. Overall, 46.5 percent of the respondents to Mougeon's (1977a) survey expressed the desire that their children receive a bilingual education. More were in favor of bilingual education in high school (59 percent) than in primary school (32 percent). Most supportive of the concept of bilingual schooling are the working-class parents, who have obtained from the school authorities a partial bilingualization of the curriculum, that is, the availability of instruction in English or French for those subject matters which they see as important for the socio-economic improvement of their children (technical, scientific, and commercial subjects) and which were originally taught only in French. Working-class parents often point out that when they arrived in Welland they experienced the frustrations of insufficient bilingualism (especially at work). Even today there are proportionally fewer fluent bilinguals among the working-class adults than among the professional (Mougeon 1977a). Their fight to partly bilingualize the curriculum may therefore be motivated by a desire to spare their children the same experience. In fact, many of the working-class parents have openly come out in support of a return to the pre-1968 system of bilingual schools. As one of the more radical working-class parents put it:

We have to remember that if our children want to become, say, a lawyer and have to learn the terms in French, it'll make it twice as hard for them when they go to an English university. It's pretty bad when a grade 7 student cannot describe the parts of a flower in English because she only learned them in French. I refuse to let my children get stuck like this. At this point I'm planning to send my children to an English high school unless our system changes to a fully bilingual school.

Schneiderman (1975) has perceptively pointed out that the professional class has a greater stake in French language maintenance in Welland, as the livelihood of many of its members (e.g. French language educators, the administrators of the French-Canadian Credit Union) consists in or involves providing services to the French-speaking minority. This may explain why the professional-class parents tend to place a higher value on the acquisition of fluency in French by their children than the working-class parents, who by and large do not and cannot use French at work (see further).

The professional-class parents are also particularly sensitive to the crucial role that the French language schools have come to play in connection with French language maintenance in Welland given the inroads that English has made in francophone households (see further). According to them, French children have more than ample opportunities to learn English outside the school and so allowing English too much place in the curriculum would defeat the purpose of French-language schooling. But as we have seen, the working-class parents were successful in partially bilingualizing the curriculum. To somewhat counterbalance this, the professional-class parents have in turn succeeded in delaying the teaching of English language arts until the latest permissible grade level (grade 3).

Ironically, while the parents are divided as to the role of the school (promotion of bilingualism vs. maintenance of French), the students overwhelmingly use English for peer-group communication on the school premises (corridors, playground, and classrooms). They will even try to use English with school personnel if they can get away with it. The president of the French high school's Student Council testifies to this: "In elementary school the teachers force the students to speak French but here at Confédération [the French high school] there is no restriction so we speak English, it's easier. I myself am more fluent in English."

It is apparent that the French-language schools have not escaped penetration by the majority language in spite of the fact that they were precisely established to play what has proven to be an increasingly important role in the maintenance of French. That the French-language schools have become a focal point of class conflict is not unique to Welland, however, since in other Franco-Ontarian communities similar class-related divisions in parental attitudes toward French language schooling have been observed, as has widespread use of English by the students on the school premises (Mougeon and Heller 1986).

1.4.   The home

The home does not seem to have fared any better than the Church and the schools in resisting the intrusion of English. One teacher at the local French high school explained that "Those [students] who speak French with their parents have probably not been here long (four or five years). Those who were born here, unless they have parents who have insisted on French at home, don't speak French at home anymore." The first category of home language maintainers (the recent arrivals) cannot be very important since significant French-Canadian immigration to Welland dried up at the end of the 1950s. As to the second category (the locally born), one would think that they are more likely to be the children of professional than of working-class parents, given the more favorable attitudes of the former toward French language maintenance. Yet this doesn't seem to be the case, since Mougeon and Hébrard (1975) failed to detect any significant differences between working-class and professional-class parents' frequency of use of French with their children. That the attitudinal differences between the classes do not translate into differences in home language use is probably due to the poorer English language skills of the working class (see above).

The principal of the French high school echoed the teacher's opinion while expressing dismay at the failure to secure French language maintenance via domain separation (English at work/French at home): "I don't want the students graduating from Confédération to be weak in English, because they'll have to live in Ontario. But one can work in English and at home continue to speak French . . . yet there are many who speak English at home to their children."

Last but not least, exogamy is another phenomenon detracting from French language maintenance at home (see next section). One who has firsthand knowledge of the very poor or nil French language skills of the offspring of mixed marriages is the kindergarten teacher at one of the primary French schools: "Most of the students who either don't understand French at all or who don't speak it very much come from families where one of the parents is English but sometimes also from families where both parents are French but speak English at home."

1.5.   The workplace

Control of the local economy rests in the hands of the anglophone majority. This means that English is the language of the workplace, especially in the industrial sector, which still employs 69 percent of active francophones in Welland (Mougeon 1977a). Although francophones may make up between 20 and 25 percent of workers in a plant, French is given no special status; English remains the only language of communication on the job (signs and memos are written in English, foremen's instructions are given in English, etc.). Only when older French workers manage to form a crew do they speak in French together. Some stores and small businesses are owned and operated by francophones, but because their clientele is far from being exclusively French-speaking, the owners see no reason to promote the use of French in their establishments and consequently they as well as their francophone staff use English most of the time. It is only in those institutions controlled by francophones and serving exclusively their needs (e.g. the French language schools, the Credit Union, most sociocultural organizations) that francophones can work in French.

1.6.   French media and other public institutions

Welland is without a French language daily (there is only an English language one). Up until recently there were no French TV or radio stations broadcasting in the area. However, there was no lack of English TV or radio stations broadcasting either locally or from across the border. Thus when it finally became possible (late 1970s) to pick up French TV and radio programs from the French CBC (the national television network) and the French programs of TVO (the provincial educational channel), the local francophones had already well established English viewing and listening habits. Thus by and large French language TV and radio programs have not had much of an impact on the francophone population and especially on the younger generation who find the contents of the programs unappealing and the type (the high variety) of French used on them difficult to understand as most of the programs emanate from Quebec or even Europe.

We touch here on a common problem in linguistic minority settings where a nonstandard variety of a standardized language is spoken and where the difference between the two varieties is sizeable, a situation which does little to promote minority language maintenance (see Dorian 1987). The problem is not as acute in Ontario's French language schools (the key institution for the promotion of French), as these schools are staffed by Franco-Ontarians who use a standardized variety of French which is less divergent from the local vernacular than the French used in the media. Furthermore, a communicative approach to the teaching of French recognizing the authenticity of Ontarian French is now gaining acceptance in the schools. In this respect Franco-Ontarians are much better off than most other French-Canadian minorities (cf. Chapter 9, this volume).

While French-language services have become increasingly available in local public institutions (e.g. branches of the Banque Canadienne Nationale, the post office, some federal government offices), francophones usually do not avail themselves of them, as one person who ought to know (the manager of the local unemployment insurance office) confirmed:

> Generally speaking at the office bilingual services are relatively little used by francophones. It is hard to explain this; perhaps it is because most French people are bilingual and up until recently they were not used to receiving services in French. They had to speak English in order to survive. In other words, there isn't much demand for bilingual services.

2. Bilingualism and shift

The above community profile has shown that after having successfully set up a number of important institutions for the maintenance of French (e.g. schools, church, sociocultural organizations), Welland francophones are now in a stage where these institutions are undergoing English language penetration to varying degrees. In other words, there is now little compartmentalization of English and French, a fact which ties in well with the existence of widespread bilingualism and shift in the community, two phenomena which we will now attempt to gauge more accurately.

Societal bilingualism is frequently mentioned as a prerequisite for language shift (Fasold 1984:216–17) and it is indeed difficult to imagine a linguistic group adopting a new language without going through a phase of bilingualism. This precondition would certainly seem to hold, since according to the most recent Census of Canada (1981) an estimated 87 percent of Welland's FMT population could conduct a conversation in either one of the nation's two official languages, French or English.[4] Yet this high average would seem to hide the fact that the current rate of bilingualism is higher still, as illustrated by Figure 1.

The adult portion of the graph suggests that the rate of bilingualism has increased over the past four decades or so, reaching a peak of 96 percent with today's young adults (25–34) who can be taken as reference group to evaluate the current rate of bilingualism. Doubtless the lower ratios of bilinguals among the older adults are due to the relative recency of the last

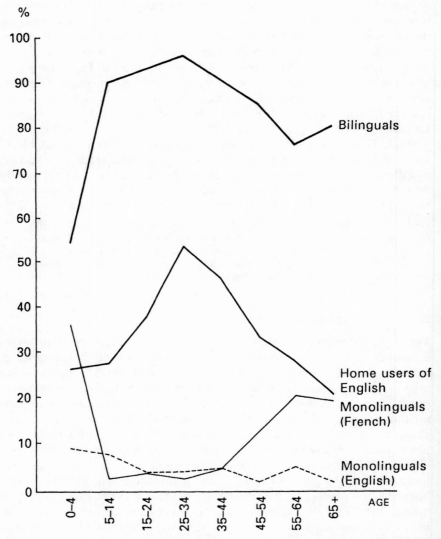

Figure 1. *Rates of bilingualism, monolingualism, and home language shift for Welland FMT respondents*
Source: *1981 Census of Canada*
Tables SPC81B15 and SPC81B16

wave of French-Canadian immigration to Welland, a consequence of which is that many of the older adults were neither born nor raised locally and thus encountered English only relatively late in life.[5] As Figure 1 shows, some got by without ever learning to speak English.

As Fasold (1984:215) has warned, age grading can be a confounding factor when interpreting one-time survey results like those in Figure 1. If the adult portion of the graph depicts a real increase in societal bilingualism over the last forty years or so, by contrast the portion of the graph corresponding to the under-25 age groups provides an illustration of age grading in the acquisition of bilingualism. The much lower ratio of bilinguals in the youngest age group (0–4) merely reflects the fact that many of these infants and young children (36 percent to be exact) are still monolingual in French, in all likelihood for want of exposure to English at home. As these young monolinguals grow older and come into contact with English in the wider community, most if not all will become bilingual, a development which is prefigured by the linguistic abilities of the FMT speakers belonging to the immediately older age group (5–14), 90 percent of which is bilingual.

It remains nonetheless the case that bilingualism appears to be somewhat on the wane among the under-25 respondents. The dotted line in Figure 1 shows why: 9 percent of the 0–4-year-olds and 7 percent of the 5–14-year-olds have in effect lost the ability to converse in their mother tongue, French. Castonguay (1984: note 1) talks of "profound assimilation" when referring to such cases of precocious loss of the ability to speak one's mother tongue.[6] Since the wider community will provide few opportunities to make up for the failure to acquire French at home, these youngsters are unlikely to reacquire French later in life (though some of these currently assimilated youngsters may eventually recover productive skills in French if they attend a French language school).

Ability to speak French does not mean that the language is actually still used by the respondent. Here is where the census question on home language[7] takes on all of its importance. By comparing the respondent's mother tongue (the language s/he habitually used at home when a child) and the language s/he is now currently using at home, we are in a position to calculate in a straightforward manner a rate of home language shift, following the example of Castonguay (1979).

Figure 1 graphs the rate of home language shift by age group. It can be seen that as many as 54 percent of today's francophone adults who are of prime child-rearing age (25–44) use English as their domestic language. It comes as no surprise, then, that significant proportions of the 0–24-year-olds (the replacement generation) no longer speak French at home. Their lower home language shift rates in comparison to the parent generation are probably to be attributed to the fact that language choice in the home is parentally imposed. As shown by Mougeon, Brent-Palmer, Bélanger and Cichocki (1982), Franco-Ontarian parents speak French less often to each other than they do to their children (an indication that they are concerned about transmitting French to their offspring although they themselves are setting a "bad example") and the children respond by speaking French to their parents about as often as they are spoken to in French by their parents. This behavior is quite unlike the situation which obtains in the case of threatened languages and may be attributed to the fact that at least some Franco-Ontarian parents perceive French as a useful language to know not only in Ontario but in Canada in general. The tremendous popularity of French immersion programs among English Canadians is perhaps the best proof of the instrumental value of French in Canada.

It is not exactly clear what parental answers to the census question on the home language use of their children correspond to: an average? an assessment mostly focused on those situations of communication where parents are involved? In any case, had the home language question been more precise and for instance required of the family head that s/he indicate what language the child speaks in situations where parental pressure is not as high (as when the child is interacting with his/her siblings), it is expected that the rates of shift to English would have been considerably higher for the 0–24-year-olds (see Mougeon and Canale's 1978 survey of French elementary school children in Welland for supporting evidence).

The much lower home language shift rates for the adults aged 45+ are at first glance rather puzzling. After all, the ratio of bilinguals among the 45+ adults is consistently high (never lower than 77 percent). A likely explanation for this discrepancy is suggested by the age distribution of the random variable *degrees of bilingualism* in the stratified sample of speakers described in note 5. An important majority (75 percent) of the older speakers (55+) are French-dominant. Conversely, the majority (52 percent) of the younger adults (20–34) are English-dominant bilinguals, hence more likely to give up the use of French, their weaker language, at home. It would seem, therefore, that because it is too imprecise (i.e. does not take into account differences in degree of bilingualism), the Canadian census definition of bilingualism does not allow for a reliable correlation of bilingualism with language shift. Thus the claim of Lieberson (1970) and other students of language maintenance and shift (e.g. Fasold 1984) that bilingualism does not necessarily entail shift underscores the methodological problems posed by the oftentimes crude nature of census-based measures of bilingualism (see de Vries 1985).

An intertwining but perhaps more important cause of home language shift among francophones is to be seen in the rising incidence of linguistically mixed marriages (a francophone married to an anglophone). Figure 2 provides a graphic illustration of the evolution of the ratio of mixed to nonmixed marriages celebrated in the French Catholic parish between 1930 and 1975.[8]

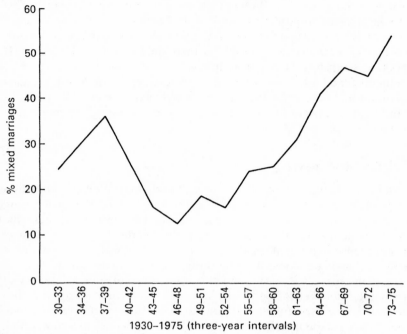

Figure 2. *Evolution of linguistically mixed marriages between 1930 and 1975*

The graph indicates that Welland francophones tended very early toward exogamy since the rate was already 24 percent for the period 1930–3 and rose to 36 percent by 1939. The 1930s were a period of demographic stability after the initial influx of immigrants during World War I. After 1939 we note a sharp decrease in the rate of exogamy, bottoming out around 1946–8 and more or less stagnating until 1954. This corresponds almost exactly to the period of the second wave of French-Canadian immigration to Welland. Thus it looks as if the inflow of new speakers from Quebec brought about a decrease in the proportion of mixed marriages between 1939 and 1954. By 1955, mixed marriages started to increase in proportion again, reaching a peak of 55 percent in 1975. In short, the francophone population has tended toward exogamy almost from its implantation in Welland but the rate of exogamy has fluctuated, progressing during times of demographic stability, receding during times of rapid demographic growth due to immigration (see Mougeon 1977b).

For the Welland francophone, linguistic exogamy quite likely means that English will be the language of the home, given the lower utilitarian value of French vs. English locally and provincially and the fact that Welland anglophones are massively unilingual (according to the 1981 Census of

Canada only 5.4 percent of Welland's EMT population is bilingual). This prediction receives confirming support from Castonguay's (1979) study of French–English mixed couples in Ontario, which revealed that 90.1 percent of the French partners use English as their habitual home language. It follows that English is the language that is handed down to the children of heterolinguistic couples, not French.[9] The augmentation of mixed marriages therefore bodes ill for the longterm survival of French in Welland, as does the tendency toward home language shift even among the children of homolinguistic couples.[10]

3.   Linguistic aspects

The previous sections have served to establish that Welland French is "contracting", so to speak, not only in the strict sense that it is losing speakers (we saw that the community is not renewing itself adequately due chiefly to a high rate of exogamy), but also in the linguistically more interesting sense that fluent speakers are a declining lot, English-dominant bilingualism having become the rule rather than the exception among the younger generation.[11] It is precisely the appearance of such a category of less than fluent speakers of a minority language that is (or at least should be) of interest to linguists, for they typify language shift, and even more so, death.[12] What are the linguistic correlates of lack of fluency in a contracting or dying language? We will seek to answer this question as concerns specifically the English-dominant adolescents in our sample (see note 5). The 14–19-year-olds were all students at the local French high school and the offspring of nonmixed couples who still used French at home. Yet in spite of this, some of the students evaluated themselves as being English-dominant, a self-evaluation which ties in with the more or less pronounced disuse of French at home reported by the English-dominant adolescents. Thus it is clear that we are not investigating as extreme a case of English-dominant bilingualism as is exemplified by the new "breed" of speakers mentioned earlier (see note 9).

Most of the recent sociolinguistic research investigating the linguistic consequences of minority language restriction has not followed a traditional contrastivist approach but rather an intra-lingual one which has brought to light the existence of two major kinds of internal change occurring in contracting/dying languages: simplification and style reduction. The phenomenon of structural simplification has been investigated, notably by Karttunen (1977), Giacalone Ramat (1979), Mougeon and Beniak (1981), Trudgill (1983), but perhaps most extensively by Dorian (1981) in her work on the dying Gaelic of East Sutherland, Scotland (see also the other papers in this section). What the above researchers have established is that insufficient exposure to and use of a minority language brings about an increase in regularity in that language. For example, in our research on the spoken French of Franco-Ontarian high school students living in Hawkesbury, Cornwall, North Bay and Pembroke, we discovered that the English-dominant bilinguals tended to level the 3rd person singular/plural verb distinctions by generalizing the unmarked 3rd person singular verb forms to 3rd person plural contexts (e.g. *ils savent* > *ils sait*; *ils veulent* > *ils veut*; etc.), the end result of which would be loss of the marked 3rd person plural verb forms (see Mougeon and Beniak 1981).

If simplification is the result of disuse of a minority language, style reduction is the consequence of its *functional* restriction and usually involves the decline of stylistic options which are tied to those societal domains where use of the minority language is excluded. The "classic" case of style reduction is one where formal stylistic options are reduced as minority language use gradually becomes confined to informal situations (e.g. the home). For instance, in a Hungarian-speaking enclave in Austria, Gal (1984) observed a narrowing of the phonological style of young Hungarian/German bilinguals whose use of Hungarian was confined to the home. Similar examples of formal style reduction have been reported by among others Hill and Hill (1977), Giacalone Ramat (1979), and Dorian (1985). However, there are particular circumstances in which reduction can also apply to the informal register of a minority language, as when use of the minority language is chiefly restricted to a formal setting for some speakers (e.g. the school domain). We have studied the linguistic effects of the tendency to relegate minority language learning and use to the school context in previous research in other Franco-Ontarian settings. Each time we found the informal variants under study (nonstandard prepositional usages) to meet the same fate in the speech of the English-dominant adolescents: loss (Beniak and Mougeon 1984; Mougeon, Beniak and Valois 1985b).

3.1. Simplification and style reduction

The determinative pronoun system of Welland French displays a great deal of allomorphic variation, as can be seen in Table 1.[13] It is composed of no fewer than 16 forms when only four would suffice to mark the different possible combinations of gender (excluding neuter) and number! Each one of the four variables is actualized by a standard variant: *celui* (masc. sg.; see example 1a below), *celle* (fem. sg.), *ceux* (masc. pl.), *celles* (fem. pl.)[14] and by several nonstandard variants (marked with an asterisk) which may be subdivided into five categories: (i) the nominalized forms, i.e. forms preceded by an article: *le celui* (masc. sg.), *la celle* (fem. sg.; see example 1b), *les ceux* (masc. pl.), *les celles* (fem. pl.); (ii) the neutralized forms, i.e. forms which are the product of a generalization of the feminine form *celle(s)* to masculine contexts; *celle* (masc. sg.; see example 1c); (iii) the simultaneously nominalized and neutralized forms: *le celle* (masc. sg.; see

Table 1. *Determinative pronoun system of Welland French†*

Variables	Variants	N	%††
Masculine singular	celui	34	57
	*le celle	13	22
	*celui-ci/là	9	15
	*celle	3	5
	*le celui	1	2
Feminine singular	celle	20	59
	*la celle	10	29
	*celle-là	4	12
Masculine plural	ceux	123	74
	*les ceux	14	8
	*les celles	13	8
	*ceux-là	11	7
	*ceusses	5	3
Feminine plural	celles	8	62
	*les celles	4	31
	*celles-là	1	8

†The speaker sample for the determinative pronoun study (see Mougeon, Beniak, & Bélanger 1982) was augmented by a group of 6–13-year-olds at the lower reaches of the age continuum. These younger speakers were also students enrolled in a French language school.

††The columns may not add up to 100 percent, due to rounding.

example 1d) and *les celles* (masc. pl.); (iv) the demonstrative forms, i.e. the extension of deictic pronouns to determinative contexts: *celui-ci/là* (masc. sg.), *celle-là* (fem. sg.), *ceux-là* (masc. pl.; see example 1e), *celles-là* (fem. pl.); and (v) the masculine plural form *ceusses*, an archaic pronunciation of *ceux* (see example 1f).

(1) a. C'était *celui* [le garçon] que j'trustais le plus dans 'a gang
   'He was the one [the boy] I trusted most in the gang'

   b. *La celle* [la voiture] qu'on chauffe est un peu grosse
   'The one [the car] we drive is a bit big'

   c. Heu . . . l'mien heu . . . *celle* [mon garçon] de 14 ans, j'ai encore contrôle sur lui
   'Uh . . . mine uh . . . the one [my son] who is 14, I still have control over him'

   d. Mon français i' fait ben dur . . . *le celle* de mon mari est aussi pire
   'My French is really pitiful . . . that of my husband is just as bad'

   e. Les vieux de mon âge, là, *ceux-là* qui sont arrivés à mon âge
   'The old people of my age, the ones/those who came [here] at my age'

f. *Ceusses* [les prêtres] qui veulent se marier, j'serais pas contre ça
'The ones/those [the priests] who want to marry, I wouldn't be
against it'

Behind the variability depicted in Table 1 lies orderly heterogeneity
reflecting both the social stratification of the French-speaking community of
Welland (the nonstandard variants are typical features of working-class
speech) and the alternative structurings of the system of determinative
pronouns that emerged in earlier stages of the language's history and have
survived to this day in nonstandard varieties of French (both regional and
popular) on both sides of the Atlantic. The speech of the old working-class
French-dominant adults can be taken to represent what vernacular Welland
French was like at the beginning of French settlement in Welland, i.e. before
the rise of bilingualism and language shift in the community. The system of
determinative pronouns which these speakers exhibit is indeed still quite
similar to that which has been recently reported for popular Québécois
French (see Fournier 1981). Now let us look at the system as it is used by the
young working-class adolescents who are most likely to experience informal
style reduction, that is the English-dominant bilinguals. Informal style
reduction was found to operate as concerns the archaic form *ceusses* and the
demonstrative variants, since both were absent in their speech. However,
informal style reduction failed to extend to the nominalized forms, especially those also involving generalization of *celle(s)* to masculine contexts. The
young English-dominant working-class speakers used them about as
frequently as did the old French-dominant working-class speakers.

Mougeon, Beniak, and Bélanger (1982) sought to explain this apparently
aborted reduction of the nominalized forms not as the result of an unexpected and hard to explain retention of vernacular traits (given the loss of
ceusses and the demonstrative variants) but rather as the result of the
fossilization of the product of two interrelated processes of simplification
triggered by the incomplete language acquisition histories of the English-
dominant speakers. Both nominalization and extension of *celle(s)* to masculine contexts are ways of optimizing the system of determinative pronouns.
Nominalization has the effect of formalizing the noun-like status of determinative pronouns, a characteristic which many other pronouns already have
(e.g. possessive pronouns: *le mien, la sienne*, etc.; some relative pronouns:
lequel, laquelle, etc; some indefinite pronouns: *les uns, les autres*, etc.).
Generalization of *celle(s)* to masculine contexts represents a case of analogical leveling since *celle(s)* already occupies two of the four determinative
contexts and so is a logical choice for extension to all contexts, especially if
the gender distinction is kept via article preposing (the most popular
solution according to the data displayed in Table 1). Evidence in support of
the developmental origin of these processes of simplification can be found in

the acquisition literature. It has been reported that native children exposed to the standard article-less determinative pronouns nonetheless nominalize them in the early stages of acquisition. The first author has made similar observations as concerns the speech of his own daughter. Although generalization of *celle(s)* to masculine contexts has apparently not been reported in the acquisition literature, it is probably safe to assume that it is a feature of child language as well.[15] Furthermore, the nominalized forms were also present in the speech of the French-dominant 6–13-year-olds of professional-class backgrounds who presumably were only exposed to the standard determinative forms. That the article forms linger until puberty suggests that the standard system of determinative pronouns takes some time before it is mastered even by those professional-class children who have not suffered from reduced exposure to French. This makes the persistence of the nominalized forms into adolescence all the more understandable as concerns the English-dominant working-class speakers. Nor is it surprising that the nominalized forms surfaced in the speech of the professional-class English-dominant adolescents, since they too have experienced minority language restriction.

We must now consider the role, if any, that English language influence may have had in the development and fossilization of the nominalized forms in the speech of the young English-dominant speakers. This question is not just rhetorical, since in English one series of determinative pronouns takes the definite article: *the one, the ones* (see glosses of examples 1a–f). One has to rule out the possibility that interference is behind the actual formation of the nominalized forms in the speech of the English-dominant adolescents since, as has been amply demonstrated, these forms are certainly not lacking in the way of internal structural motivation. Viewed differently, the fact that the English language also features nominalized determinative pronouns is further indication of the noun-like status of these pronouns and of the logic of article preposing, at least as far as Indo-European languages are concerned. However, it is quite possible that English may be exerting a more subtle influence by favoring, through positive reinforcement, the fossilization of the nominalized forms in the speech of the English-dominant adolescents. This view of things is entirely consistent with Silva-Corvalán's (1986:6) recent account of the different causes of "convergence":

Transfer leads to, but is not the single cause of, *convergence*, defined as the achievement of structural similarity in a given aspect of the grammar of two or more languages assumed to be different at the onset of contact. Indeed, convergence may result as well from internally motivated changes in one of the languages, most likely accelerated by contact, rather than as a consequence of direct interlingual influence.

We can probably expect apparent exceptions to the principle of informal style reduction whenever innovations coinciding with nonstandard features already extant in the vernacular form of a minority language (one showing at least a partial reversal of the classical home/school domain division) can be produced via processes of structural simplification.[16]

3.2. Lexical borrowing

Poplack and Sankoff (1984) pointed out that the phenomenon of lexical borrowing has been the object of numerous linguistically oriented studies but has received little attention from sociolinguists. According to these authors (p.105), this has meant among other things that basic assumptions about "The role of bilingual versus monolingual, or older versus younger speakers, in introducing and propagating loanwords has never been empirically investigated or established."

The study of the social distribution of English loanwords in Welland French requires a distinction to be made between those loanwords that were already present in the speech of the original Québécois settlers (i.e. integrated in the French they spoke) and those that have been borrowed following immigration. Given that French–English contact in Quebec dates back to the British conquest of 1760 but only to the turn of the century in Welland, the number of post-immigration loanwords, as would be expected, is small in comparison to the number of pre-immigration loanwords. Thus only 57 (or 20 percent) of the 281 different loanword types encountered in the speech corpus are peculiar to the local variety of French; the remainder are all attested in dictionaries or lexicographic works on Québécois French.

The pre-immigration loanwords can be subdivided into two categories. The first consists of loanwords which have been imported into Québécois French for lack of native lexical equivalents. These loanwords designate entities which were once (or are still) typical of the English-speaking world (e.g. *bacon, (blue) jeans, cowboy, football, gallon, hamburger, hockey*, etc.). Most of these culturally motivated loanwords are also found in European French and hence may be said to constitute a class of "international" loanwords. They are considered part of accepted usage. The second category consists of loanwords which have a native variant, which either already existed when the English word was first borrowed or came into use after the fact. They were borrowed due to the former dominance of English in certain key sectors of Quebec society such as industry, commerce, etc. (e.g. *truck*, variant of *camion*; *factory*, variant of *usine*; *plugger* < *to plug*, variant of *brancher*, etc.). Most of these loanwords are considered nonstandard. The second category of pre-immigration loanwords also includes some which cannot be so easily associated with specific domains of Quebec society where English had a dominant position, or with any specific societal domain for that matter. They correspond to basic and common entities or concepts for which there was no lack of viable native equivalents.

Examples of such loanwords are *smart* (variant of *intelligent*), *anyway* (variant of *en tout cas*), *badluck* (variant of *malchance*), etc. Because they alternate with common French equivalents, loanwords of this latter type strike one as being on the "gratuitous" side. They constitute a telling illustration of the fact that among French Quebeckers there has long been a non-negligible number of proficient bilinguals. (See Scotton and Okeju 1973 on the link between widespread individual bilingualism and the emergence of gratuitous borrowings in contact languages.) The gratuitous pre-immigration loanwords are typical features of vernacular Québécois French.

The post-immigration loanwords continue the pre-immigration pattern of borrowing English words as variants of native ones. Thus most of the post-immigration loanwords have a French equivalent and again include some that were borrowed due to the dominance of English in certain societal domains (e.g. *fridge*, variant of *réfrigérateur*; *movie*, variant of *film*; *high school*, variant of *école secondaire*, etc.) but a greater number that cannot be associated with specific societal domains (e.g. *but*, variant of *mais*; *so*, variant of *ça fait que*; *dumb*, variant of *stupide*, etc.). The post-immigration loanwords underscore the fact that after it took root in Welland, French came into contact with English in domains which had remained under French control in Quebec such as education, entertainment, etc. The preponderance of gratuitous loanwords in the post-immigration category ties in well with the rapid and widespread rise of bilingualism among Welland francophones which was documented in the previous sections.

Given the nonstandard status of most of the pre-immigration loanwords possessing a French variant, it will come as no surprise that they were used proportionally more often by the working-class speakers (2.9 tokens per 1,000 words) than by the professional-class speakers (1.2 tokens per 1,000 words). It stands to reason that the professional-class speakers, concerned as they are about preserving (the integrity of) the French language in Welland, would make lesser use of *English-origin* vernacular features, especially if they are "unnecessary" additions to the native lexical stock. The pre-immigration loanwords with French variants were used most frequently by the old working-class French-dominant adults (3.5 tokens per 1,000 words). These findings suggest a picture which is reminiscent of the one which obtained for the determinative pronouns, in that these latter speakers, who best exemplify pre-immigration vernacular Québécois French, once more lead in nonstandard usage. It is therefore pertinent to ask again what fate these pre-immigration loanwords have met in the speech of the English-dominant working-class adolescents. Judging by the results obtained (1.9 tokens per 1,000 words) it seems that there has been a decline in the use of these English-origin vernacular features and therefore that they too are the object of informal style reduction. That informal style reduction is not more pronounced is not surprising since, as we have just seen, not all of these loanwords are avoided by the professional-class speakers.

Turning to the post-immigration borrowings, they were found to be used far more frequently by the adolescents (2.5 tokens per 1,000 words) than by the adults (the highest rate for the adult speakers being 0.6 tokens per 1,000 words). Furthermore, among the young speakers it was the balanced bilinguals who were by far the prime users of post-immigration loanwords (3.7 tokens per 1,000 words), the French-dominant bilinguals having a score of 1.1 tokens per 1,000 words and the English-dominant bilinguals a score of 0.4 tokens per 1,000 words. These findings suggest that post-immigration borrowings are a recent development in the local speech and that they are strongly correlated with balanced bilingualism. This is perhaps only the second time (see Mougeon and Beniak 1987 on the use of loanword *so*) that the role of fluent bilinguals as instigators of lexical borrowings has been empirically established (see Poplack and Sankoff's assertion quoted above). This does not mean that the speech of the English-dominant adolescents is void of English-origin lexical items or that they do not actively borrow from English. They certainly make use of international loanwords and of what Poplack and Sankoff (1984) refer to as "nonce" or idiosyncratic borrowings. In other words, the English-dominant adolescents use loanwords that are part of the standard language or resort to borrowing as a communicative strategy to fill lexical gaps.

A more specific aspect of lexical borrowing from English which has engaged our attention has to do with a recent controversy surrounding the phonological assimilation of loanwords. A traditional view among students of lexical borrowing is that loanword assimilation to the phonology of the recipient language is apt to vary according to the speaker's degree of bilingualism. Whereas it is within the capacity of a fluent bilingual to preserve the original donor-language phonology of a loanword, less fluent bilinguals and monolinguals are more likely to assimilate the loanword to the phonology of their native language. It is probably with the work of Haugen (1953 [1969]) that the thesis of variable phonological integration of loanwords is most closely associated. He found the phenomenon to be quite commonplace among immigrant groups in the United States. In fact, he even found that bilinguals could "touch up" the form of older nativized loanwords to bring them more in line with donor-language phonology.

The traditional position has been questioned by Poplack and Sankoff (1984). They believe that phonological vacillation is merely a transitory phenomenon occurring at the beginning of a loanword's incorporation into the host language, ultimately under a single, fixed guise. According to these authors, "once a term is accepted into the speech community, and adapted into a particular phonological form, it is that form which is transmitted across generations in much the same way as monolingual neologisms". They provided empirical support for their view in an experimental study of the phonological integration of English loanwords in New York City Puerto Rican Spanish.

Table 2. */h/-retention rate in* 'hockey'

Aget	Degrees of bilingualism		
	French-dominant	Balanced	English-dominant
14–34	71% (N=17)††	100% (N=7)	95% (N=19)
35+	11% (N=18)	78% (N=9)	100% (N=11)

†Reduced to two groups due to limited number of tokens.
††The N's in the parentheses indicate the number of tokens of the word *hockey*.

Hockey was one of several loanwords in our list which proved well suited for the purpose of re-examining the issue of phonological integration: it was frequent enough, featured a clearcut English-like (/h/ sounded) vs. French-like pronunciation (/h/ not sounded) and predated immigration to Welland (first attested in a lexicographic work on Québécois French published in 1909). According to Picard and Nicol (1982), /h/ is always deleted in English loanwords in Québécois French. Extrapolating backwards in time we may therefore suppose that the pre-immigration pronunciation of *hockey* was /h/-less. /h/-retention was examined as a function of age and degree of bilingualism. The results are presented in Table 2.

Table 2 provides clear-cut evidence of the phonological denativization that a well-established loanword may undergo as a minority language community becomes bilingual and experiences shift over successive generations. We see that the older French-dominant bilinguals' pronunciation of *hockey* is still quite close to the pronunciation which was prevalent during the pre-immigration period. In contrast, the bilinguals who are fluent in English, whether young or old, show very high or categorical retention of /h/. It could be that fluent bilinguals, as proposed by Haugen, have an enhanced awareness of the foreign origin of the loanword and possess the necessary skills to render it according to donor-language phonology. Another explanation, also borrowed from Haugen's account of denativization of old integrated loanwords, is that some speakers may have actually "reborrowed" *hockey* rather than "touched up" the phonological form of the old integrated word, an explanation which is not unreasonable given the dominant position of English in the sports domain.

Not only has denativization reached very high proportions as concerns the balanced and English-dominant bilinguals but it is also obviously spreading to the younger French-dominant bilinguals, who sounded the /h/ no less than 71 percent of the time. The changing composition of the French-speaking community of Welland over the years and its attendant consequences on the "direction of linguistic pressure within the community" (Haugen 1953 [1969]: 370–1) could be responsible for this dramatic increase in /h/-pronunciation. The relative strength of the balanced and English-dominant bilinguals has increased steadily to the point where they now represent the dominant linguistic group in the community (see above). It could be, then, that the younger French-dominant bilinguals are conforming to the dominant pronunciation of *hockey* in Welland French today.

The results for *hockey* (and other variably integrated loanwords which were examined in Mougeon, Beniak and Valois 1984) speak conclusively in favor of the traditional view of loanword phonology. Yet there were others which were always pronounced according to French phonology, although they could display internal allophonic variation (e.g. Engl. *factory* > Fr. [faktRi] or [faktri]). These loanwords behave exactly in the manner predicted by Poplack and Sankoff and underline the fact that the existence of levels of bilingualism within a speech community does not mean that all loanwords will exhibit variably integrated forms correlated with these levels. A goal of our future research on borrowing in Welland French is to try to determine what it is about certain English loanwords that fosters variable phonological integration and what it is about others that prevents it. It is already clear from the example presented above that the answer is not as simple as Poplack and Sankoff's belief that only incipient loanwords are able to show variable phonological integration.

4.   Conclusion

No one will express surprise at the fact that Welland francophones are shifting to English, given the conspiracy of causes pushing in the direction of shift: minority status, urban industrial setting, cessation of immigration, societal bilingualism, exogamy, etc. The high rate of exogamy is especially indicative of the lack of attachment of Welland francophones to their ethnic and cultural origins. Socioeconomic betterment is what matters most for the mainly working-class community, and that means knowing English above all. Now while language shift has reached advanced levels, many francophone parents have availed themselves of the opportunity of sending their children to the local French language schools with the result that for many children the responsibility of French language transmission tends to be transferred from parents to educators. This study has attempted to determine the linguistic consequences of this sociological development by focusing on the spoken French of the English-dominant adolescents. Such a focus is justified on the ground that these speakers are becoming a sociological reality to be reckoned with. The progression of linguistic assimilation among Ontario's francophone minority means that an ever increasing number of young Franco-Ontarians are learning the bulk of their French at school. The focus is further justified because of the unusualness of the phenomenon of school-inculcation of a minority language. That is not to say, however, that such school-based learning of minority languages will not become more commonplace, at least in Europe if not elsewhere, a possibility which Bourhis (1984) links to the adoption of the European Convention of the Rights of Man guaranteeing minorities the right to instruction in their own language. As sociolinguistic research on these minorities proceeds, it should prove interesting to see whether the linguistic effects identified in this study and which we have also attested in the speech of adolescents in other Franco-Ontarian minority communities – informal style reduction, morphological simplification, nonparticipation in borrowing processes observable in the wider community, denativization of loanword phonology – are also observable.[17] These linguistic developments suggest that minority language schooling on its own or as the primary setting for language learning and use is not sufficient to produce full-fledged speakers (all the more if, as in Welland, the curriculum is partly bilingualized). We think it unlikely – and the case of Irish would seem to justify our skepticism – that these nonfluent speakers will contribute to the maintenance of French in Ontario. It seems unrealistic indeed to expect them to transmit French, their weaker language, to their offspring. However, since this question has not been researched our skepticism remains guarded.

Finally, let us consider the bearing that the findings of this study have on some of the research questions proposed by the editor of this volume as guidelines for the contributors.

Are there constraints operating to reduce the language skills of minority language speakers? Two constraints identified in this study are type and quantity of minority language exposure and use. The first constraint – the tendency to relegate minority language learning to the formal setting of the school – has the effect of producing speakers who, to borrow a term from Dorian (1985), display an "asymmetry" in their command of the registers since they are losing the linguistic resources to style-shift in the direction of the informal registers. The second constraint – insufficient exposure to and use of the minority language, be it the high or low variety – has the effect of producing speakers who display obvious signs of incomplete mastery of the morphology of the minority language. Note, however, that the level of morphological simplification that such restricted linguistic input brings about is not very drastic when compared with the kind of morphological simplification French-based creoles display. For example, Chaudenson (1986:99) reports that the determinative pronoun system of Réunion Creole has been reduced to the unique form *sa* < French neuter *ça*. In fact the output of the simplification process (article + pronoun) is not even more advanced than an alternative structuring of the determinative pronoun system that had already developed diachronically in monolingual lower-class speech.[18] We can cite here Dorian's (1978c:608) vivid metaphor of East Sutherland Gaelic "dying with its morphological boots on". The metaphor – the allusion to language death aside – aptly applies to the system of determinative pronouns in Welland French as there is no wholesale breakdown of its morphology in English-dominant speech.

Is variability typically higher in terminal/contracting speech communities than in "healthy" ones? Minority language contraction certainly triggers linguistic developments that simply do not arise in monolingual settings, such as morphological simplification due to insufficient linguistic input, gratuitous borrowings, nonce or idiosyncratic borrowings, phonological denativization of loanwords, interference-based innovations, etc. On the other hand, reduction of the less formal registers amounts to *loss* of linguistic variability. The answer to the above question would therefore appear to be a qualified yes.

Does variability carry the freight of social meaning in terminal/contracting speech communities that it does in (monolingual) urban communities where it has been most intensively studied? We saw that Welland francophones form a socially differentiated small urban community in which bilingualism is widespread and comes in varying degrees. If variability continues to be the vehicle of social meaning for the speakers who remain fluent in the minority language, no matter how small their group has become, it ceases to perform that function as far as the English-dominant speakers are concerned. This is because all of the processes operating in the French speech of the English-dominant adolescents cut across the social classes and thus have the effect of neutralizing sociolectal differences. Informal style reduction causes the French speech of the working-class English-dominant adolescents to become like that of the professional class. Conversely, simplification processes whose output coincides with vernacular features makes the French speech of the English-dominant adolescents of professional-class background more like that of working-class speakers. Finally, innovations due to simplification or to interference and nonce or idiosyncratic borrowings are once again not social class markers or indicators in English-dominant speech but simply tell-tale signs of imperfect mastery of the minority language.

Notes

We would like to take this opportunity of thanking the Social Sciences and Humanities Research Council of Canada for its financial support of the Welland sociolinguistic research project.
1. The sociohistorical material presented here is drawn mainly from the following sources: Poulin (1969), Schneiderman (1975), Trudel (1982), Mougeon and Heller (1986). The demographic statistics come from the decennial censuses of Canada.
2. Prior to World War I there were just a few isolated French Canadians living in Welland. In 1871 there were only 18 persons of French ethnic origin out of a total population of 1,110 (1.6 percent). In 1901 the numbers were only slightly greater: 67 out of 1,863 (3.6 percent). In comparison, anglophone presence in the present-day area of Welland dates back to the period of the American Revolution, when Loyalists fleeing the United States came to settle in Canada (late eighteenth century).

3. The 1951 census was the first to include a question on mother tongue, which refers to the first language learned and still understood by an individual. An unfortunate shortcoming of this definition is that, as Castonguay (1981:7) has indicated, an individual may no longer be able to speak his or her mother tongue, hence the interest of the official languages question (see further). In spite of its imprecision, the concept of mother tongue provides a more accurate criterion for estimating the current size of a language group than does ethnic origin, which refers to the linguistic group to which the respondent or his paternal ancestor belonged upon arriving on the continent and thus may hide considerable "ancestral shift" (de Vries 1985:361). Henceforth we will only provide population statistics based on mother tongue.

4. The 1981 census marks the first time that statistics on official language by mother tongue were available in the public domain for the city of Welland. The official languages question, relying as it does on self-assessment, is admittedly a rather crude measure of oral comprehension and production skills in French and English, all the more as it fails to distinguish degrees of bilingualism (e.g. English-dominant, balanced, French-dominant) whose importance will become clear later. Be that as it may, the official languages question may be said to provide statistics on unilingual vs. at least functionally bilingual individuals.

5. We may mention in the way of confirming evidence that in a sample of 68 FMT speakers stratified according to age, sex and social class (but in which degree of bilingualism, place of birth and age of arrival were random variables), none of the speakers belonging to the 14–19 age group and only one of the speakers belonging to the 20–34 age group had not grown up in Welland whereas more than a third of those in the 35–54 age group and almost three-quarters of those in the 55+ age group had arrived in Welland after the age of 19 (Beniak, Mougeon and Valois 1985:68–71).

6. In theory, the observed mother tongue loss among the 0–14-year-olds is not attributable to parental failure to transmit French to their children, since the latter were declared by their parents to be of FMT. In practice, however, one may suspect the parents of having made only a token effort to pass on the language to their children. In fact, given the definition of mother tongue (see note 3), it is conceivable that the children in question never had more than passive knowledge of French. However, it will be simpler to assume that these children once could speak the language but have since lost the capacity to do so.

7. Home language refers to the specific language spoken at home by the respondent at the time of the census. If more than one language was spoken, the language spoken most often was to be reported. Canadian demographers (e.g. Castonguay 1979; Lachapelle and Henripin 1980) are agreed that the most direct measure of language shift available from the censuses is the calculation of the number of individuals who report one language as their mother tongue but who use another as the home language. Such a measure only became available with the 1971 census as previous censuses did not include a home language question.

8. The rates of exogamy are actually greater than those graphed in Figure 2 since some mixed marriages are also celebrated in the English parishes. The French parish priest is advised of all such English-parish mixed marriages although exact statistics do not seem to have been kept.

9. Somewhat surprisingly, Mougeon's (1977a) survey revealed that not far from

half the linguistically mixed couples who had school-age children chose to send them to French language schools. Evidence was provided earlier (see community profile) that there are also nonmixed couples who have shifted to English at home who enroll their children in French language schools. What this means is that for a growing number of parents in Welland (and other Franco-Ontarian minorities for that matter) inter-generational transmission of French is left almost entirely to the school. The offspring of these parents represent a new "breed" of speakers that have learned the bulk of their French at school and mostly confine their use of French to that formal setting.

10. It may be inferred from the results presented earlier in Figure 1 that home language shift is taking place in endogamous French couples as well. We saw that no fewer than 27 percent and as many as 38 percent of the 0–14-year-olds no longer speak French at home in spite of being born of what must be taken to be FMT parents (otherwise they would not have been declared as FMT individuals). Incidentally, this bears out the testimony of the French kindergarten teacher cited earlier.

11. For the first time in its history, Welland's FMT population decreased in terms of relative weight from 17.1 percent in 1971 to 15.5 percent in 1981. During that ten-year span the community actually had a negative growth rate (−8 percent), contracting by a total of 645 speakers. It appears as though the decade 1971–81 represented a watershed and that now the full impact of home language shift is making itself felt, whereas in the past it was mitigated by such factors as the arrival of new francophones from Quebec and a high birth rate.

12. The difference is one of degree; in situations of impending language death there are no fluent speakers of the dying language left at all among the younger replacement generation (Dorian 1981; King 1984a; Mertz, this volume).

13. By *determinative pronouns* we mean demonstrative pronouns used in a determinative fashion (see Quirk, Greenbaum, Leech and Svartvik 1972:217–18). The label *demonstrative* is misleading when the idea of deixis is obliterated as it is in determinative pronouns (e.g. *ceux qui parlent bien* 'those who speak well').

14. It may be noted that the standard system gets by with just three forms given the phonetic identity [sɛl] of feminine singular *celle* and feminine plural *celles*. Thus the feminine forms do not mark number as do the masculine forms *celui* and *ceux*.

15. In fact, children may well have been historically responsible for creating and introducing nominalized forms in adult language (see Mougeon, Beniak and Valois 1986 for an examination of the possible link between child language and linguistic change). Be that as it may, the important point to be made here is that the French child's spontaneous creation of nominalized forms during acquisition underscores the fact that the internal tendency of the determinative pronoun system to evolve nominalized forms in diachrony is still extant in synchrony.

16. The fact that the nominalized forms produced by the English-dominant adolescents are not true vernacular features raises the question of how they are sociostylistically perceived and used by these speakers. As we have already seen, the nominalized forms don't function as social indicators in the speech of the English-dominant adolescents since they are spread across the social classes. One can hypothesize furthermore that, unlike the French-dominant working-class speakers, the English-dominant adolescents (whatever their social back-

ground) are less aware of the informal stylistic value of the nominalized forms and therefore may be unable to use them appropriately to style-shift. Assuming this view of things is correct, then in a sense the English-dominant adolescents, in addition to experiencing strict style reduction via the loss of vernacular features like *ceusses* and the demonstrative variants, would experience a weaker form of style reduction involving loss of ability to style-shift, in spite of having at their disposal the forms which would allow them to do so.

While the process of simplification studied here (i.e. nominalization of determinative pronouns) was found to produce an output coinciding with vernacular forms and thus to blur the role of simplification as a source of innovation, in other studies we have looked at processes of simplification which were unambiguous in that they produced entirely innovative outputs, i.e. forms with no counterpart in the local vernacular (see e.g. Mougeon and Beniak 1981; Mougeon 1982).

17. Marilyn Martin-Jones (pers. comm) reports that speakers comparable to the English-dominant bilinguals examined here (i.e. speakers who have poor command of the casual vernacular style because of school-based learning of the minority language) are present within the Welsh-speaking community and that the "schoolish" Welsh they speak has not gone unnoticed in the community, witness the fact that it has actually been given a special name!

18. This structural coincidence constitutes evidence which supports Chaudenson's theory of change as linguistically determined by "auto-regulatory" processes that are liberated under certain sociolinguistic conditions such as the two investigated here: minimal prescriptive monitoring in lower-class milieus and restricted exposure to and use of a contracting language.

20 Lexical innovation and loss: The use and value of restricted Hungarian

SUSAN GAL

1. Introduction

This chapter considers the Hungarian lexicon of Hungarian–German bilingual speakers in an Austrian community that has been shifting away from Hungarian for about forty years. I will use evidence about the formation and use of verbs in order to address the following questions: Which word-formation devices or patterns are retained and which are lost by those speakers who use Hungarian only in a narrow range of contexts? What accounts for the fact that, despite diminishing social function for the language, narrow-users are in one sense *more* innovative than broad-users in several kinds of word formation?

Among documented cases of community-wide language loss there is considerable variation in the rapidity of loss and in the extent of discontinuity between generations or social groups of speakers. When, as in the present case, the shift takes more than one generation and occurs through a restriction in the social functions of the obsolescent language, it raises theoretical questions about the relationship of language use to linguistic structure (Hymes 1974). The explanation for documented linguistic differences between those who use a language in a wide range of contexts and those who do not has most often been sought in the early and continuing effects of those very differences in range of use. According to this hypothesis, the decreasing use of the obsolescent language by adults, and its increasing functional specialization, lead to the incomplete acquisition of the language by children. We can thus understand the frequent loss of linguistic structures that are not available at all for input to children. This may occur because the structure is limited to genres, styles, or registers which are no longer performed at all, or because the obsolescent language is no longer used in speech events which require that style or register (e.g. Hill 1973; Dressler and Wodak-Leodolter 1977; Tsitsipis 1984; Mougeon, Beniak and Valois 1985a). But this hypothesis does not explain differential

313

retention among structures which are *not* strictly compartmentalized and so occur in many styles of speech. Such cases are better handled by another version of the hypothesis which argues that complex linguistic structures that are acquired late in childhood will be lost since this is the very time when children in many communities stop fully using the obsolescent language (Voegelin and Voegelin 1977b). This set of arguments centering on children's experience also suggests probable loss for structures which are infrequent in the speech of fluent speakers and thus less available for acquisition, or whose complexity may require consistent and copious input, as well as continued use (e.g. Hill 1983a; Dorian 1986c). But for these arguments to apply without tautology, it is important to have supporting evidence (e.g. from psycholinguistics) that will enable us to classify a form as linguistically complex on independent grounds, or document that it is the type of structure that is infrequent or acquired late, before we attribute the loss of it by semi-speakers to incomplete acquisition.

With respect to the lexicon, the notion of incomplete acquisition can easily be used to explain loss of lexical inventory, one of the most commonly reported observations about language death. Loss of productivity is a closely related lexical phenomenon also observed to occur during language obsolescence. For example, in an important paper on the Breton lexicon, Dressler shows that "terminal" speakers (some as young as 15) have no productivity in word formation, and along with the oldest and quite fluent speakers, they show an "inability to construct neologisms" (1977:84–5).

Yet when we consider such data in the light of recent evidence about acquisition of the lexicon, a puzzle emerges. Developmental psycholinguists have been demonstrating that even the very young child has a formidable capacity to invent new words in the course of acquiring language, and this ability continues into adulthood (e.g. Clark and Clark 1979; Clark 1982). One writer alludes to "the child's wizardry" in constructing the lexicon with apparently minimal input (Carey 1978:265). In this body of research, the lexical creativity of speakers appears too robust to be completely destroyed by limited access to the language. We are left with the puzzle of why young Breton speakers fail to show the innovativeness typical of acquisition. Moreover, the results of my own investigation of lexical processes in a restricted language seem to provide a challenge both to the view that speakers are indomitably innovative, and to the view that language death eliminates innovation. Using a different methodology from Dressler's, I found evidence of lexical innovation, along with considerable loss of productivity, among young speakers during language shift.

In order to make sense of these apparently contradictory findings, we need a framework broader than the hypothesis of incomplete acquisition. It is necessary to explain not only the structural locus of change – why one particular kind of device remains productive while another does not – but also the social motivation for the simultaneous occurrence of innovation and loss. In many cases of gradual shift the abandonment of one language in favor of another is linked to the symbolic values constructed for the language by minority speakers responding to their position in a political–economic system. These same symbolic constructions, I suggest, mediate not only language choice, but also internal change in the lexicon. As Hill (1983a) has astutely argued, the nature of change during obsolescence depends in part on the local cultural definition of a language's purpose in social life. Indeed, such symbolic constructions may work against cognitive or acquisitional pressures, or may themselves have contradictory effects on the resulting linguistic change. In sum, while the range of contexts in which speakers acquire the language is surely important, it is only one of a set of factors, including symbolic constructions and independently measured cognitive and acquisitional capacities, whose effects must be considered in understanding linguistic change during language shift.

In what follows I will first describe the political–economic and symbolic terrain of language choice in the community, including the scholarly writing *about* that choice; then discuss some of the differences between the lexicons of speakers who contrast in age, social identity, and use of Hungarian. The focus will be on the nature of the verb formation devices apparent in the taped conversations of two groups. Finally, I will return to the question of how symbolic factors affect the creativity of speakers.

2.   Writing about language death

For Oberwart [Felsőőr], the Austrian town whose Hungarian–German bilingual population forms the subject of this chapter, scholars have been heralding the corruption and demise of Hungarian, and warning of its "endangered existence" at least since 1942 (Imre 1942:3, 1971; most recently Gal 1979); and of the corruption and "loss" of the local Hungarian dialect since the turn of the century (Varga 1903). Yet, some of today's speakers are teenagers and the local dialect is primarily the form they know. Repeated reports of the language's imminent disappearance from the community reflect not only actual longterm changes in the linguistic usage of Oberwart's speakers – who have indeed been using a changing Hungarian and in fewer and fewer social situations – but also the scholarly and literary traditions of the reporters.

Announcing the extinction of cultures, languages, and dialects at the moment they are first described by outsiders has been a rhetorical construct central to Western ethnography, as Clifford has recently noted (1986). In a parallel way, looking for the "best speakers" who will provide evidence of the most "unadulterated" form of the language, has been common practice in anthropological linguistics, as Dorian (1981:3) has argued. It is also a characteristic thread in European dialectology and national folklore, the sources of much early evidence about language death. Practitioners in these disciplines looked to the countryside for archaic, unchanging and therefore authentic cultural elements to use in defining national cultures and buttressing nationalism. They lamented changes, which they saw as corruptions. All of these scholarly enterprises are within the Western literary tradition of the "pastoral", a rhetorical convention which continually looks back, often nostalgically and for moral guidance, to a lost but supposedly more pristine, rural, homogeneous, and authentic past (Williams 1973b).

Current studies of language obsolescence often take the past as their standard, usually in the form of the oldest speakers. This is due in part to the logic and constraints of research; but the pastoral convention also plays a part. To be sure, investigating the link between the structure and function of linguistic forms requires comparison of speakers with contrasting sociolinguistic practices, and in contracting speech communities age is often the best index to significant sociolinguistic differences. Indeed, some studies of language loss have opposed the pastoral convention, at least implicitly, by claiming theoretical interest for the varying and substantially changing present as against an ideal, only partly reconstructable past. Yet the pastoral convention continues to have an effect. This is apparent in the metaphor of language "death" itself, and in the attention focused on the loss of structures and the inadequacy of speakers. Contrary processes of innovation are only rarely noticed and less well studied. It is true that there are scattered and intriguing references in the literature on language death to the emergence of new forms amidst linguistic losses (e.g. Schmidt 1985a); and some studies of codeswitching and bilingual discourse have documented pragmatically novel versions of both the old and the new languages (e.g. Hill and Hill 1980; Gumperz 1982). Yet such sociolinguistic inventions are most often reported outside the rubric of language obsolescence and their linkage to processes of shift is not discussed. Perhaps, reflexive consciousness about the pervasive effects of the pastoral tradition can provide us with the analytic distance to confront this discursive convention more explicitly and pointedly. While documenting the extensive inventory of losses during language shift, we can make visible the simultaneous but contradictory tendencies toward invention of new social and linguistic forms, within the same historical process.

3.   The value of Hungarian

Located in Austria, very near the border with Hungary, and with a current bilingual population of about 2,000 out of approximately 6,000, Oberwart has been a Hungarian speech-island surrounded by German-speaking villages for about four hundred years. Both German and Hungarian are in daily use in the Hungarian section of town.

Elsewhere I have described in detail the prosperity and industrialization following World War II that pulled Oberwarters out of agriculture and pushed them into wage labor or service work, often supplemented by farming (Gal 1979). In addition to these economic transformations, political changes in the region were instrumental in setting the stage for language shift. With the withdrawal of Allied occupation forces, ties to Hungary in the east were severed; the border was virtually closed to traffic in labor, goods, and even visitors until the late 1960s. In the educational system German became the only language of instruction by the mid-1950s, and the local political and administrative machinery was increasingly controlled not by Hungarian-speaking natives of Oberwart but by German-speaking migrants. A widespread fear of Hungarian collectivization and nationalization accompanied the local awareness, throughout the 1960s and 1970s, of the substantially higher standard of living in Austria than in Hungary.

The current pattern of language attitudes in bilingual Oberwart can be summarized briefly as the widespread and familiar one in which a language of solidarity (Hungarian), identified with the past, with peasant agriculture, with the town's minority population and labeled economically "useless", is in symbolic contrast with a language of power (German) which is admired, associated with the state, with the prestige of education, and with the ability to provide material success in the form of mobility out of agriculture into wage labor and skilled occupations. The contrast is reinforced by the hostility expressed locally by many German monolinguals toward the use of Hungarian, and their denigration of Hungarian accents. It was during the extended postwar boom that this symbolic alignment emerged.

The evidence for the newer symbolic pattern comes from the explicit statements of speakers, when discussing other speakers' reasons for using or not using the languages. In addition, the local interpretations of conversational codeswitching hinge on this juxtaposition of "low, in-group" with "high, out-group" codes, to produce, for example, inferences of interpersonal authority on the one hand and intimacy and trust on the other. Finally, many young speakers retain the phonological variants which signal formality and social status in Hungarian, but they fail to use these to mark differences either in context or in identity (Gal 1984). This too can be interpreted as a symbolic coding of Hungarian as a language of solidarity, making distinctions of formality inappropriate within it.

All of these economic, political, and symbolic factors militate against the use of Hungarian by speakers born after World War II, most of whom were educated in German and are employed outside of agriculture. But, although a restriction in the contexts of use for Hungarian is incontrovertibly occurring, there are weaker but continuing pressures, exercised by the older generations on the younger, and by peasant networks on their members, for choice of Hungarian in the neighborhood (see Gal 1979:131–52). As Hungarian has become a language of solidarity, failure to use it locally has become costly: ridicule and accusations of social pretension are frequently the sanctions for those who reject Hungarian. And this can have material consequences. Conformity to the social and linguistic norms of local networks helps assure the support of these networks in mutual aid, labor exchange, and the transactions of the informal economy. All of these gain added importance in times of unemployment and economic stagnation, such as the late 1970s and early 1980s.

These practices are perhaps best understood as a form of oppositional culture that is created in response to the dominant culture, yet resistant to it (Williams 1980). Although the use of the minority language is selfdefeating from the point of view of the dominant ideology, it is an active gesture asserting the countervalue of solidarity that the language expresses locally. As Woolard (1985a) has convincingly argued, it constitutes a resistance – partial and implicit – to the authority of the state-supported dominant language and to the hegemonic ideology of individual mobility that it symbolizes.

The tension between the authority of German and opposition to it is inscribed in patterns of codeswitching and, as I suggest below, in simultaneous loss and innovation within Hungarian. Many young people register their internal experience of this tension by claiming they will respond in whatever language their interlocutor uses. And it is also voiced in subtler aspects of discourse, such as the unintended irony in the comment of a railroad worker in his 30s who, at a family gathering, insisted *in Hungarian* to all who would listen, that in Oberwart only the peasants speak Hungarian.

4.   The speakers

The social groups to be compared below are most conveniently labeled by age, and as the broad historical context outlined above would indicate, age in this case is also a rough but adequate surrogate for the social distinctions of occupation, social network and for contrasts in patterns of choice between Hungarian and German.[1]

Those in the oldest group, (60+, Group A) are uniformly peasant agriculturalists, now retired. They use Hungarian to everyone but German monolinguals and, on rare occasions, their own grandchildren. Most speakers in this group learned German when they were sent as domestics or farmhands to German villages at the age of 12–15. Those between 40 and 59 (Group B), all from agricultural families, are a more varied group. Most are workers, full- or part-time, unskilled or semiskilled. But these are "peasant-workers" who, with their families, also operate limited farms; two are entrepreneurs. They use Hungarian with all bilinguals except their own children. However, the spouses of some of these speakers, and many workmates, colleagues and friends, are monolingual German speakers. These middle-generation speakers also learned German in their early teens, at school, or later at work. The youngest group (Group C, in most cases the children and grandchildren of the speakers in the other two groups) includes speakers aged 20–39, who are most aptly called "narrow-users" of Hungarian. Their occupations differ, especially with respect to education and income, but their friendship networks cross-cut such differences: unemployed domestic worker, factory worker, sales and delivery, hairdresser, several secretaries, bank teller, high-school teacher, certified public accountant. For most of these speakers, Hungarian was the first language but German was the language of school, which they entered at the age of 5 or 6. They use Hungarian in the narrowest range of contexts, only to their grandparents' generation, or rarely with parents. Thus they have no Hungarian-speaking peer-group.[2]

5.   Overview of the lexicon

As a basis for comparing the Hungarian lexicon and word-formation devices used by the three groups of speakers, I selected 45 minutes of tape-recorded conversation for each of 36 speakers (ten in Group A, ten in Group B and 16 in Group C) and examined the verbs occurring in that segment. The rich derivational morphology of Hungarian provides considerable room for variation among groups. The conversations were unarranged, occurred during household occasions such as dinner or evening visiting and, to assure that they would be in Hungarian, most often included older family members or neighbors. Occasionally I asked speakers to tape themselves during such conversations.

While this kind of speech sample is relatively uncontrolled in comparison to translation or elicited judgements of acceptability, it has some compensating advantages, especially in shifting communities where norms are flexible or problematic and many speakers are linguistically selfconscious. Judgements and translations are metalinguistic tasks which may be unfamiliar, especially for narrow-users; their performance on such tasks may not directly tap their everyday linguistic abilities. Thus, intuition and passive knowledge of words are neglected here in favor of active usage. The compensating advantage of conversational speech samples is that speakers can be observed operating in the customary social contexts of word use, as they react to the usual interactional pressures and incentives for expressiveness. The transcripts give access to the context-dependent innovations of narrow-users in a way that explicit judgement would not.

5.1.

An indirect but simple measure of the relative breadth of speakers' active lexicons is the type/token ratio, here applied to verbs. If the type/token ratio is relatively high, then many different verbs are used and most are not repeated or only rarely repeated in the course of talk; if the type/token ratio

Table 1. *Type/token ratios for three groups of speakers*

	Group A	Group B	Group C
Type/token ratio	0.52	0.47	0.31
Total tokens	444	431	504
	N=10	N=10	N=16

is low then the relative number of different verbs is low and each verb is used and re-used many times, indicating a more restricted active lexicon.

The finite verb in Hungarian consists of a base which can be followed by one or more derivational (formative) suffixes, followed by either a tense or mood marker and finally a personal ending. The stem may also be compounded and, in one form of compounding, may be preceded by a separable "preverb". Some scholars analyze these preverbs as restricted adverbs or separable verbal prefixes. All compound stems, preverb + verb compounds, and verbs formed from nouns, adjectives, and other verbs by means of suffixation were counted as separate verb types. This follows the distinction in Hungarian grammar between *képzők* or formative affixes which form new words by addition of nonrelational semantic material and *ragok* or flectional suffixes which form new words by the addition of material relating the root to other parts of the sentence (Tompa 1970). The only *képző* not counted as a separate verb type was the "potential" *hat/het* 'can, may, is capable', which functions more as a modal auxiliary (see Benkő and Imre 1972:152).[3]

Table 1 shows the type/token ratios for each of the three groups. The difference between Groups A and C is large enough to make statistical tests of significance unnecessary. The youngest speakers (C) have a ratio that is about a third less than the oldest group (A), with no overlap between their ranges. The difference between Groups A and B is significant ($p = > 0.05$ on a two-tailed t-test). Thus there is a gradual decrease in the active lexicon and a corresponding increase in the re-use of particular verbs as we look across groups. This is striking, since in psychological testing the size of vocabulary for adults is ordinarily correlated with education and general intelligence, not with age (Matarazzo 1972). Yet here the youngest speakers with the smaller lexicons have more education – some as many as nine years more – than their elders.[4]

5.2.

But such a rough measure only opens the question of what differences in the speakers' lexicons produce these quantitative results. One source of difference may well be the productivity of word-formation devices. An initial indicator of possible productivity in a word-formation pattern is the frequency with which word types in that pattern occur in the transcripts. However, frequency counts run the risk of conflating rote-learned lexical

Table 2. *Average frequency for five word-formation devices*

Word-formation device	Group A	Group C	C as a % of A
1. Denominal and deadjectival causative -*ít*	1.4	0.5	35
2. Deverbal causative -*ít*	2.8	1.3	46
3. Deverbal causative -*tet/tat*	2.2	1.1	50
4. Preverb + verb	103	72	70
5. General verbalizer -*ol*	12.1	8.6	71
	N=10	N=16	

items with those produced on the basis of linguistic analysis and knowledge of word-formation devices. Thus frequency is always supplemented here with other, stronger kinds of evidence.[5]

Table 2 shows the average number of times each of five word-formation patterns occurred in the tapes of the broad-users in Group A and the narrow-users in Group C. Because non-occurrence is also an important datum, such a direct comparison gives more information than one based on percentage figures that are relative to total number of types produced. And since young speakers produced a significantly larger number of tokens overall, their considerably lower number of types cannot be due simply to differences in the size of the speech sample. As in the type/token ratios, the figures for Group B consistently fell between those for Groups A and C. Thus the focus here will be on the contrasts between Groups A and C, which provide the strongest axis of comparison.

In Table 2, the word-formation devices are entered in order of decreasing difference between groups. Those in which the young narrow-users differed most from their elders are listed first (and numbered accordingly), those in which their frequencies approached the frequencies of Group A are listed last. To make these figures easier to interpret, the third column shows the performance of Group C as a percentage of Group A's frequency. Although some of the numbers in Table 2 are small, suggesting that larger samples should be used for the study of some word-formation patterns, the relative frequencies are revealing. The differences between groups in the first three word-formation devices are so great and their ranges so disparate that no statistical tests are needed to demonstrate their significance. Nevertheless, there is a trend in which the difference between groups decreases as one reads down the page, with the young speakers more closely approximating the more productive older speakers on the last two patterns. In fact, on the final device the young speakers produced 71 percent of the types that their elders produced, and a two-tailed t-test showed that this is *not* a statistically significant difference.

A brief description of these word-formation patterns will provide the background for further comparisons. The root types of Hungarian are divided into phonological classes on the basis of their mutations during suffixation and their participation in other morphophonological processes, including vowel harmony. All form classes may be grouped into the same root types and combine selectively with formatives that have different semantic or aspectual qualities. The word-formation patterns discussed here are characterized by the standard sources as highly "productive" in the standard language, although the criteria for this are not always clear. They are certainly productive for older speakers of the relatively divergent Oberwart variety, in the sense that at least some older speakers have coined nonce neologisms based on these devices.

Pattern 1. Causative verbs are formed from adjectives and nouns with the suffix *-ít-*. The root is most often from the largest class of Hungarian roots, those that do not vary in shape, but this formative also combines with roots which undergo a rule of internal vowel deletion in which the final vowel or the vowel preceding the final consonant is deleted when suffixes are added: *rövid/rövidít* 'short/shorten' and *piszok/piszkít* 'dirt/make dirty, soil'.

Pattern 2. This deverbal causative is formed with the suffix *-ít-* and a verb root from the unvarying class. The root is either a separately occurring verb, *áll/állít* 'stand/place, make stand up' or is the transitive counterpart, with causative force, of intransitive verbs ending in *ul/ül, od(ik)/ed(ik)öd(ik)*, and a few others. In this latter case there is no separately functioning verb but rather pairs formed on the same bound verbal root which may also occur with other formatives: *indul* (intr.)/*indít* (trans.) 'a thing starts up/make something start up' but no verb **ind*. Other examples include *tanul/tanít* 'learn,study/teach, make learn', *fordul/fordít* 'turn/make turn'.

Pattern 3. The suffix *tat* (or *tet*, depending on vowel harmony) and *at/et*, add a causative meaning to virtually all verb roots that have no semantic constraints against causativization, and no suppletive causatives. The choice between *tat/tet* and *at/et* is phonologically constrained: except where otherwise specified by the lexicon, *at/et* is the productive suffix for verbs ending in consonant + *t*, and with monosyllabic verbs other than those ending in vowel + *t*. Hetzron (1976) shows that in its semantics this causative differs from the others listed above. For *tat/tet* the causee, that is the entity caused to do something, must be a performer, an instruction giver, and not just an executor. Examples include: *csinál/csináltat* 'make/have (something) made', *ír/irat* 'write/have someone write'.

Pattern 4. The preverb and verb combination, already mentioned above, forms a compound verb which phonologically may take any of the suffixes that the simple root is eligible for. The prefix is separated from the root in many syntactic constructions so that the compound nature of the verb is clear. There is a limited number of adverbial expressions which combine as preverbs (about thirty), six of which occur only as preverbs. The meaning of these verbal compounds is often transparently combinatorial, with the adverbial prefix indicating some directionality of the action, either concretely or in metaphorical, abstract terms: *fel+áll* (up+stand) 'stand up'; *ellen+áll* (against+stand) 'resist'. But in other preverbal compounds the adverbial element affects the aspectual interpretation of the verb: perfective in the case of *beszél/meg+beszél* 'talk/discuss, talk over', coding the result of action in *vág/szét+vág* 'cut/cut apart, in two'.

Pattern 5. The suffix *-ol* (the vowel changes in accordance with vowel harmony) is a denominal and deadjectival verbalizer. It is among the oldest and currently one of the most productive derivational suffixes in Standard Hungarian. It operates on unvarying roots and also those with internal vowel deletion; it forms verbs out of numerous semantic relations including instrument: *kalapács/kalapácsol* 'hammer/to hammer'; location: *vásár/ vásárol* 'market/to shop'; result: *dal/dalol* 'song/sing'.

5.3.

For the three causatives (Patterns 1, 2, 3) there are a number of indications that the formatives are not productive for the young speakers in Group C. With only two verbs as exceptions, the *tat* causatives in the speech of Group C were the extremely frequent and irregular forms *etet* 'feed' and *ültet* 'plant', essential for any conversation about farming and animal husbandry. Stronger evidence about the lack of productivity of these forms is provided by numerous examples of discourse contexts where one of the causatives is required semantically but does not appear. Instead, the causative meaning is expressed syntactically or periphrastically (on a model from German) or left implicit. The broad-users in Group A never employed these unconventional expressions of causation.

In Standard Hungarian as well as the local Oberwart variety, the person made to do the action in the *-tat* causative is in the accusative or, more rarely, and with subtly different meaning, in the instrumental. In the examples from the young speakers in Group C, however, the noncausative form of the verb is used and causation is expressed by marking the causee with the dative–genitive.

(1) Neki   buta   szokása volt,   de *le*   tudtam neki
    he-DAT stupid habit   PAST COPULA, but down+   could-I he DAT
    szokni
    get out of the habit
    'He had a stupid habit but I got him out of it'
    Conventionally: *leszoktat*

(2) Játszottunk és   *tanult*   nekem
    (we) played and (he) *learned* me-DAT
    'We played and he *taught* me (things)'
    Conventionally: *tánit*

In other examples from young speakers, a periphrastic causative, modeled on the German factitive expression with *lassen* + infinitive, is used instead of the similarly factitive/causative *tat*. (*Lassen* German 'permit, cause or have done' is translated with Hungarian *hagy* 'permit, let'.)

(3) *Ki*   hagyta   *venni*   a   gyereket
     out+ [she]permitted *take*-INF the child-ACC
     'She had them take out the child' (referring to an abortion)
     Conventionally: *ki/elvetet*

(4) *Ő* maga   hagyta   a   székeket *rajzolni*
     he himself permitted the chairs-ACC *draw*-INF
     'He had the chairs *designed* himself'
     Conventionally: *(meg)rajzoltat*

Finally, speakers in Group C often use the noncausative version of the verb and the causative meaning, although clear from the context, is not indicated morphologically:

(5) És akkoriba át*fordultam* magam
     'And in those days I *turned* myself [around]'
     Conventionally: *fordít*

(6) Jobb ha nyáron születik a gyerek, nem kell úgy *felkészülni* (a gyereket)
     'It is better if the child is born in the summer, it is not necessary to *dress* [it] *up* so (dress the child)'
     Conventionally: fel*készít*

(7) *Ki* akarják őket *éhezni*
     'They want to *starve* them out'
     Conventionally: *kiéheztet*

(8) Éjjel *levetkőzöm* (a gyereket)
     'At night I *undress* (the child)'
     Conventionally: *levetkőztet*

A final indication that most young speakers have lost the conventional use of these formatives is the appearance of these forms in their speech when no causative meaning is intended:

(9) Ő már sokszor meg*hívatta*
     'He *had* them *invited* already many times'
     (clear from context that he himself invited them)

(10) A kocsit lassan *betolattam*
     'I *had* the car *pushed in* slowly'
     (point of the whole story was that he pushed it himself)

Although the German periphrastic factitive clearly serves as a model for the paraphrases above, systematic pressure from German cannot alone account for the loss of productivity of the Hungarian forms. In fact, German has several morphophonological processes for deriving causatives (Lederer 1969), one of which, though not very widespread, is somewhat parallel to the Hungarian deadjectival causative: German *rein/reinigen* 'clean/cleanse, to clean' = Hungarian *tiszta/tisztít*. An alternative hypothesis worth considering is that, lacking a productive causative form, speakers employ a lexical strategy of recruiting the forms they do know: noncausatives, dative constructions, calques on German forms.

In the light of the "incomplete acquisition" framework it is interesting that these causatives are not limited to any style, genre, or speech register. Nor are they structures which appear very late in child speech. Studies of monolingual Hungarian acquisition – and recall that most speakers of Group C were Hungarian monolinguals in the early years – show the appearance of *-tat-* and *-ít-* causatives in neologisms by children as young as 2 years, although it is perhaps significant that errors with causatives are documented even in the seventh year (MacWhinney 1974:364–5). Alternatively, the framework also draws attention to the frequency of these forms in the everyday speech that would constitute input to young speakers. A similar focus on frequency is suggested by Dressler (1977) and Clark and Berman (1984). The latter show that for monolinguals the differential frequency of word-formation devices in the speech of adults affects the order of acquisition of those devices by children, with high-frequency patterns acquired first. Notice that in the data presented here, the three devices which are not productively used by the young speakers (Patterns 1, 2, 3) are strikingly less frequent in the usage of the *older* speakers than the devices (Patterns 4, 5) which, as I argue below, young people use innovatively.

6. Innovations

In the final two word-formation processes of Table 2, the narrow-users come considerably closer to the frequencies of their elders. In fact, for the last pattern there is no statistical difference between the two groups. More importantly, the transcripts of conversations show these forms not only to be relatively frequent but also highly productive for young speakers. With these word-formation processes they form neologisms that do not appear in the speech of their elders. Other studies have shown that lexical innovations, sometimes analyzed as "errors" because they are non-normative, are widespread among monolingual adults (Downing 1977; Clark and Clark 1979). They not only provide evidence of lexical creativity but also strong indications of what speakers actively but implicitly know and expect others to know about word formation. Clark (1982) argues that both children and adults use innovations when they lack a word for the meaning they want to express. Such lexical gaps may be due to momentary difficulties in remembering a word, or there may be no word conventionally used to express that meaning in the community. In the case of narrow-users of Hungarian, often the conventional Hungarian word exists in the community but the speakers do not know it.

In the transcripts I have examined, speakers of all ages use innovative words. These are words which use the word-formation patterns of the language, are interpretable from context, but do not appear in standard or dialect dictionaries, are not in common use in Oberwart, and are not familiar to Hungarian speakers I have consulted from various regions of Hungary. But the narrow-users invented far more such words than the other groups. Here I would like to describe their innovations, suggest some very general reasons for the productivity of these particular devices, and in the last section raise the issue of why – given the much more obvious loss of productivity documented above, and the general devaluation of the language described in section 3 – these young speakers bother to create new forms in Hungarian.

The reason for productivity in the denominal verbalizer *-ol* is relatively straightforward. Imre (1971) has noted that historically most German verbal borrowings entered the dialect as *-ol* verbs. This continues today, so that the increased use of *-ol* verbs reflects the increased frequency of verbal borrowing among the narrow-users. Compared to the broad-users, four times as many of their *-ol* verbs are nonconventional, often with a German source. On the one hand, this signals the familiar phenomenon of vocabulary loss in the obsolescent language. On the other hand, within the perspective of this chapter, it is worth highlighting the retention and even increased productivity of this device.

Preverbal compounding (Pattern 4) provides another site for innovations. Among the word-formation devices examined in this chapter, this is the one that, on a number of quite general grounds and according to several divergent theoretical frameworks, should be the most preferred and therefore productive, the most "natural" and the easiest for children to analyze and use. In contrast to all the other verb-formation devices, it is based on independently occurring words and prefixation, rather than bound suffixes; the compounds are mostly semantically transparent; none of the roots is changed in phonological shape. What is perhaps most striking, and illustrated by Group A, is the fact that these kinds of compounds are extraordinarily common in the everyday speech of the community. (See Aronoff 1976; Cutler 1980; Dressler 1981b; Clark and Berman 1984, for discussions of these criteria.) What is more, a similar though far from identical system of separable verbal prefixes with adverbial import exists in German.

As an indication of productivity it would be interesting to know whether, for any verb root, young speakers combine it with as many preverbs as their elders. If they do, then the lower frequency of such compounds among young speakers is due to a dearth of root verbs in their vocabularies and *not* to an inability to analyze the compounds and form either conventional or unconventional words. Dividing the number of root verb types that have preverbs by the total number of preverb + root verb types gives such a measure. The young narrow-users of Group C (0.69) are almost identical on this measure to the older broad-users in A (0.71) as well as to the middle group. Thus it is not their combinatorial ability that is different, but their repertoire of verb roots.

But the strongest evidence for productivity is the coining of new compounds. These occur with great frequency. The partial parallel between the German and Hungarian verbal prefix systems is actually a complex relationship. Any single German verbal prefix has several elements of meaning which, depending on the particular compound and its denotation, can be translated by a number of Hungarian preverbs. While some German and Hungarian verbal prefixes have rough semantic and aspectual correspondences, these are always in a many-to-many relationship. Thus, while the existence of the two systems invites mirror translations, this is by no means a simple or automatic task. Speakers must analyze whatever they know about both systems in order to come up with a parallel that is suited to the occasion. Young Oberwarters often coin Hungarian preverb compounds based on German models, but here I will concentrate on the equally numerous cases in which the innovations are not based on German. It is these innovations that most clearly demonstrate the lexical creativity of narrow-users in Hungarian. Such innovations are usually comprehensible in context but noticeable in transcripts because they are unidiomatic; some other compound is the conventional expression. Those forms that young speakers invent which, unbeknownst to them, happen to match the conventions are, of course, undetectable. Examples of unconventional innovation include:

Neologism	*Conventional*
(11) Azok olyan nagy fejek voltak, nem tudod *meggondolni*	
'They were such big shots, you can't *imagine*'	
meggondol	elképzel
PERF + think	away + picture
(12) A pénz amibe került, az is *összejátszott* hogy nem akartam menni	
'The money it cost also *contributed* to my not wanting to go'	
összejátszik	belejátszik
together + play	into + play
(13) *Összecsináltuk* a listat	
'We *made up* the list'	
összecsinál	összeállít, megcsinál
together + make	together + set up, PERF + make

(14) Az első nap elkapott és *lemondott*
'On the first day she caught me and *bawled* me *out*'

lemond	lehord
down + say	down + carry, drag

(15) Én mindent *dobok utána*
'I *throw* everything at him'

utánadob	nekivág
after + throw	at him + cast

(16) Az erdőt *letüzelték*, aztan leégett
'They *set fire* to the wood and it burned down'

letüzel	felgyújt
down + heat, fire	up + light, ignite

(17) (In answer to the question: how did she die?)
Lejárták
'They *ran* her *over*'

lejár	elüt
down + run (of vehicle)	away + hit

(18) Akarják *lehozni* hogy melyik csinálta
'They want to *find out/show* which one did it'

lehoz	kihoz, kitalál
down + bring	out + bring, out + find

(19) Mikor a könyvet *megolvastuk* akkor visszaadtuk
'After we *read over* the book we gave it back'

megolvas	elolvas
PERF + read	away + read

(20) Csak azt *veszik el*
'They *hire* only him'

elvesz	felvesz
away + take	up + take

With the exception of *összejátszik* and *letüzel*, each of the neologisms above has a conventional meaning: *meggondol* 'think over', *lemond* 'refuse', *lejár* 'visit or go down customarily', *lehoz* 'bring down', *megolvas* 'count', and so on. (The young speakers express these meanings with other conventional terms: for instance, for 'count' they use the *ol* denominal *számol*, for 'visit or go down' they allow *lejár* synonymously, or *lemegy* 'down + go'.) The usual processes of suppletion and blocking fail to operate for the narrow-users. Thus they re-invent conventional words and use them in unconventional ways.

This kind of innovation is apparent not only in the formation of verbs but across the lexicon. In the examples below, the nouns are formed on unconventional roots or the match between suffix and root is not conventional, but the suffixes, e.g. *-ás*, *-ság*, are the Hungarian nominalizers, and reduplication a common word-formation device. Here there is no question of German influence.

Neologism	Conventional	Gloss
esküvés	esküvő	wedding
akadék	akadály	obstacle
dolgozás	munka	work
nagyság	többség	majority
nagyüzletes	nagykereskedö	wholesaler
önkigyilkolás	öngyilkosság	suicide
hímes-hámos	? hímes = many-colored	variegated, diverse

In these examples the speakers demonstrate their ability to analyze and construct words. What is missing is the active correction exercised by others and the implicit pressure of a peer group to conform to norms of usage. Recall that unlike the other groups examined here, these speakers have no age-mates with whom they use Hungarian. There is also no ideology of linguistic purity among the older generations; for instance, popular German borrowings, and even nonce borrowings, are used and accepted as normal by speakers of all ages. Somewhat ironically then, the local network pressures which encourage young speakers to use Hungarian some of the time, thereby maintaining the language, lead to the creation of innovations which make the young speakers' dialect more obviously divergent and illegitimate when they (rather rarely) attempt to use it on tourist trips to Hungary.

7.   Conclusions

In one sense the evidence provided here resolves the apparent paradox between the psycholinguists' characterization of children as "word makers" and the image of speakers during language shift as nonproductive and unable to coin new words. In the spontaneous Hungarian speech of narrow-users, lexical innovations abound. This provides evidence both for speakers' knowledge of certain word-formation devices and for the presence of interactional incentive to fill lexical gaps in order to communicate. The word-formation devices narrow-users use productively are structurally distinguishable from the ones they have lost in a number of quite general ways that may have implications for ease of acquisition. Most strikingly, those devices which appear with highest frequency in the speech of the broad-users are precisely the ones which narrow-users employ innovatively.

However, the understanding of simultaneous innovation and loss as documented here will also require a broad social perspective. For it appears that while the innovations of narrow-users are made possible by the structural features of certain word-formation patterns, the innovations are evoked, in concrete social contexts, in numbers otherwise unusual for the community, exactly because of the losses elsewhere in the lexicons of these speakers. Narrow-users must rely on innovations where broad-users have well established conventional items. The basis of this contradiction becomes clearer if we switch the focus from acquisition of Hungarian and linguistic factors to the symbolic constructions of the two languages.

Both innovation and loss are the consequences of a social opposition: the pressures to abandon Hungarian and the simultaneous forces of solidarity that resist the authority of German. More concretely, in the midst of diminishing use and input from Hungarian, young speakers must nevertheless use that language to communicate effectively on some occasions. These social occasions provide the interactional demand for lexical innovations in the face of lexical losses. It is therefore significant that most of the evidence in this chapter consists not of judgements or translations, but of speech samples from just such occasions: interactions between young speakers and several older members of their kin and neighborhood networks.

Thus linguistic creativity during language shift is linked both to cognitive, acquisitional factors that hinge on patterns of use, and to the symbolic significance that speakers create for their languages in response to a political–economic context. More broadly this suggests that we should examine the linguistic changes occurring during language shift not only through the metaphor of death and decay that the "pastoral" tradition provides, but also through an image of conflict and competition between differing forces – cognitive, interactional, symbolic – whose effects on the details of linguistic practice are sometimes contradictory.

Notes

This chapter is based on fieldwork conducted between 1974 and 1983 and was supported by grants from the National Science Foundation (BNS 80–50889) and the Rutgers Research Council. While writing this chapter I was a Fellow of The American Council of Learned Societies, funded by the National Endowment for the Humanities and the Ford Foundation. This support is gratefully acknowledged. I would also like to thank Attila Dobó for his help in transcribing and discussing these tapes, along with Susan Crane, Nancy Dorian, and Michael Moffatt who provided valuable suggestions and critical reading of the manuscript.

1. Although the sample of speakers to be discussed here is not representative in the statistical sense, the social location of the speakers in each group does reflect the general pattern of that age group in the bilingual neighborhood. There are ten speakers in Group A, ten in Group B, and 16 in Group C, with comparable numbers of men and women in each group. Since the recordings to be discussed below were made in 1979 and 1981, the ages of speakers in 1981 were used as the basis for placing them into age categories.

2. Here I use the term "narrow-user" to characterize the youngest generation,

rather than Dorian's important notion of the "semi-speaker". One difference is in the direction of inquiry. The speaker's linguistic production, recognized as aberrant by both community and the investigator, is the basis for the "semi-speaker" category. The social and sociolinguistic experiences and characteristics of such speakers can then be explored for factors that would explain their speech patterns. In contrast, by constructing a category of "narrow-users" I start by drawing together certain social and symbolic practices along with patterns of language use and then inquire whether these have had any unified linguistic effect on those who engage in them.

However, as Dorian (pers. comm.) has pointed out, there may well be another, and more substantive difference between narrow-users and semi-speakers. The narrow-users whose speech I am describing were each able to provide approximately 45 minutes of their own stories, life experiences, jokes, opinions, and general conversation within the context of other people's talk. Although they do not usually speak that much Hungarian, when provided with the appropriate context they evidently can. Dorian's own description of semi-speakers indicates considerably less conversational production than this, apparently even under the most auspicious circumstances. It may well be that "semi-speaker" and "narrow-user" describe communities and speakers at quite different levels of linguistic contraction.

3. For these counts the copula, the auxiliary *tud* 'know, can', and the verb *mond* 'say' were omitted. The uses of the copula and *tud* deserve separate treatment; the frequencies of *tud* and *mond* were idiosyncratically affected by the ubiquity, for some speakers in each group, of the conventional hesitation markers *tudod* 'you know' and *hogyan mondjam* 'how should I say it'. For the sake of simplicity, standard Hungarian orthography is used both for the examples cited and material quoted from tapes.

4. In 1979 I became acquainted with a young speaker who had an exceptional interest in the Hungarian language, buying and reading books in Hungarian, seeking out Hungarian migrants and visiting Hungary frequently. After a concerted search I was able to locate just five other speakers with similarly strong personal or professional interest in the Hungarian language. This is clearly a very minor pattern in Oberwart, but interesting for the contrast it provides. The speakers included the teacher of the elementary school's weekly Hungarian class; a young woman who was being courted by a man she had met on a tourist trip to Hungary; and some of the young officers of the Hungarian Calvinist church. The way these speakers used Hungarian within the neighborhood matched the patterns of their age-mates in Group C. However, their evaluations and symbolic constructions of Hungarian were quite different. Interestingly, the type/token ratio of this group of five was virtually identical (0.46) to that of the *middle* generation, suggesting again that generation alone, and even everyday use, are not the only important social factors controlling lexical phenomena.

5. As Aronoff (1976), Romaine (1983), Clark and Berman (1984), among others from varied theoretical perspectives, have noted, the problem of how to measure productivity in studies of word formation is a controversial conceptual issue. Arguments have been marshalled for and against a number of measures including dictionary lists (which are similar in some ways to frequency counts in communities that have no dictionaries), speaker intuitions, speaker errors in free environments, experimental errors, and spontaneous neologisms.

III
Invited commentaries

Discussion from the perspectives of child language and aphasia; of historical linguistics; of social process; of pidgins, creoles and immigrant languages; and of second language acquisition

21 Some people who don't talk right: Universal and particular in child language, aphasia, and language obsolescence

LISE MENN

Linguistics lacks a term more felicitous than "normal" for language in its optimal state of knowledge and use, i.e., language as it is commanded by native (mono- or multilingual) speakers in full possession of adult intelligence, social skills, language processing abilities, etc. But we need a way to refer to this unmarked case, one which does not invite the kind of confusion between the state of the speaker and the state of his/her language abilities which arises from the use of the term "normal" language. I propose to call this optimal state "full" language: this is to be distinguished from the abstract notion of "ideal" language, since "full" language is intended to denote a normal range of lects and modalities; thus it is not homogeneous within or across speakers, nor devoid of metaphor, archaism, or the like.

The label "full" encodes our sense that language which has been learned and/or deployed under various less-than-optimal circumstances is simpler and poorer than "full" language. In the first section of this discussion chapter, I offer some comments on the notion of "simplicity" as it applies to child language and aphasic language, comparing it with the kinds of simplification in the contracted manifestations of language reported in the present volume. This volume in fact demonstrates that a rich set of dimensions of variation, rather than a unidimensional (implicational) simplicity hierarchy, will be required for the characterization of potential universals in the case of language contraction. In particular, we have seen that degrees and differing circumstances of original acquisition and conditions of subsequent use/disuse appear to have important effects on the patterns of the contracted language, as already suggested by Dorian (1982c).

In the second section of this chapter, I therefore go on to show how consideration of the conditions under which a contracted language has been acquired can provide a framework for understanding many of the observed patterns of language contraction which escape markedness-based notions of simplification.

In a short final section, starting from a psycholinguistic view of some syntactic deficits in aphasia, I make some further suggestions about the kinds of comprehension and production deficits that might be expected in speakers who have little practice in the use of a language and who find its grammar and vocabulary difficult to retrieve.

1.   Hierarchical description of distance from "full" language in child language and aphasia

Linguistics has a tradition (virtually personified, for most of us, by Roman Jakobson) of searching for strong language universals, i.e. variables which will define a hierarchy that can characterize degrees of "simplicity" regardless of the particular circumstances which have caused the simplification. The fullest statements of linguistic hierarchies are proposed markedness hierarchies such as the phonological feature hierarchy found in *Kindersprache* (Jakobson 1941 [1968]) and in Jakobson and Halle's *Fundamentals* (1956). (This tradition is continued in much recent work on second language acquisition, e.g. in the volume *Markedness*, edited by Eckman, Moravscik and Wirth [1986].) How is the hierarchy approach to "simplification" holding out in the areas of child language and aphasia? Is it still viable there?

Opinions of course differ, but it can be shown that the Jakobson phonological hierarchy has serious inadequacies. Rhetoric to the contrary, Jakobson's claims are actually quite weak and correspondingly difficult to falsify, as Kiparsky taught me long ago. This is partly because the hierarchy does not deal with certain very common phonemes, notably the glides, and partly because it is stated in terms of implicational relations among phonemic *oppositions* rather than among phonemes (as most restatements have it), or among phones. Jakobson does not claim, for example, that children will acquire [b] and [d] before learning to produce [g], or that children will acquire stops and fricatives before affricates; what he says is that a phonemic distinction between two anterior consonantal phonemes will be acquired before a phonemic distinction between an anterior and a posterior phoneme, and that the phonemic distinction between stop and fricative will be acquired before the distinction between fricative and affricate.[1]

Cases that do in fact violate some aspects of the Jakobson hierarchy have now been found (Menn 1976 [1979]); on the other hand, it fits many children quite well, as far as it goes. Thus, it does reflect some of the probabilities (across languages and children) of the incidence of phonemic contrast. More to the point, however, is the fact that many of the interesting phenomena of simplification in child phonology cannot in any way be reduced to acquisition of distinctive phonemic oppositions; obviously, children are also engaged in mastering phonetics, and this was not a topic addressed by Jakobson at all.[2]

In aphasic phonology, the predictive value of a phonological hierarchy is even more limited, because aphasic errors within the individual patient are much less systematic and more probabilistic than children's rules/processes. (Here as elsewhere, the behavior of those who have once had a skill differs from the behavior of those who have never attained it.) It appears to be true that particular patients with dysfluent aphasias never manage certain difficult phones or clusters – [θ] and [ð], unsurprisingly, are unattainable for many aphasics with problems of articulatory control, and [t], [d] are used instead. However, two-way errors, e.g. substitutions both of [t] for [k] and of [k] for [t] in the same patient, are the rule, and in general, all that we can find is a tendency for such substitutions to have a bias favoring the phonologically less marked member (Blumstein 1973; Nespoulous *et al.* 1984; Menn 1986).

The most reliable phonological generalizations, both in child language and in aphasia, appear to be those based not on (any version of) the phonological hierarchy itself, but rather on the more concrete statements which correspond to much of it, that is, statements based on aerodynamic reasoning about mechanisms of sound production, and on claims such as "double articulations ought to be harder to control than single ones". A certain number of results remain less than fully rationalized, to be sure – I don't think we know *exactly* why rounding is more stable for back vowels than for front ones, or why velar closure is commoner than uvular – but I have seen no argument in favor of regarding these as phonological matters rather than as matters of articulatory control. And there are certainly ways in which an abstract phonological approach fails to predict phenomena which are perfectly transparent to a more concrete way of thinking: if we move to the area of deaf speech, we find persistent difficulties with the control of nasalization, although nasality is among the most widespread of distinctive features. Here the hierarchy has to be set aside in favor of a straightforward explanation: when there is no auditory feedback (due to deafness) and the articulator is not visible, the learner is left with only sensory feedback, which each of us knows from experience to be quite minimal from the velum. Of course a defender of the phonological hierarchy has every right to say that its applicability depends on the presence of a normal perceptual and articulatory apparatus – but surely this is the point: the hierarchy actually explains nothing that a more concrete approach cannot do as well or better.

Moving into morphology and syntax: In aphasia, there are some current attempts (e.g. LaPointe 1985) to treat the morphological errors of certain dysfluent aphasic patients in terms of a markedness hierarchy, since they show clear tendencies to substitute nominative case forms for other cases and infinitives for finite verb forms in many languages. However, there are problems with this approach; for example, where the infinitive is not the basic form used in naming the action denoted by the verb, e.g. Finnish, it is not used as a "default" form (Lorch 1985; Menn and Obler in press).[3] Again, the errors are probabilistic (e.g. in German, French, or Italian, a given patient may both substitute masculine for feminine forms and feminine for masculine). There is much work to be done in mapping out biases in patients' errors across languages; semantic and morphosyntactic factors both appear to be involved, and these would be expected to interact differently in different languages.

But in aphasia, Jakobson himself recognized that the principal syndromes could not be described in terms of a single hierarchy. As is well known, he invoked two dimensions, the syntagmatic and paradigmatic axes, to deal with the disparate syndromes of the dysfluent and fluent speakers. Dysfluent patients, who omit function words (and have articulatory problems) were described as having disruption of sequential operations; this very Markovian explanation of syntactic problems may well prove partly translatable into more contemporary models of output processing. Fluent patients, on the other hand, were described as having difficulty selecting among the alternatives offered by semantic and morphological paradigms, and therefore making the semantic and morphological substitution errors which are so conspicuous in their speech. In the light of data which have become available in more recent years, this description, while valid, can now be seen as much too limited; all aphasics having a sufficient degree of general impairment are subject to output errors of substitution as well as omission (Heeschen 1985; Kolk, van Grunsven and Keyser 1985). Indeed many of us now think that a cross-linguistically valid description of dysfluent aphasia requires us to regard so-called "omission of inflectional endings" as substitution of zero-marked forms for, e.g., plural and possessive nouns and tensed verbs, because this phenomenon appears to be found only in languages which, like English, have widespread use of zero marking (Menn and Obler in press). (Zero-marked forms have not been found as substitutions for overtly marked forms in languages where zero marking occurs but is very restricted, as in e.g. Italian or Icelandic, where "zero" only signals the 2nd person singular imperative.)

Classification of aphasic syndromes (Albert *et al.* 1981) is actually much more detailed than the above dysfluent/fluent dichotomy, and takes comprehension impairments as well as production impairments into account. Indeed, for some researchers (Caramazza and Berndt 1985) the classical syndromes have all but fallen apart in the face of accumulating data on individual variation within syndromes. But similarities between children and aphasic patients (of all types) are to be found in a few domains, and the nature of these similarities is worth examining for the light they can throw on language contraction in general.

The major similarities are limitation of vocabulary, limited use of all types of grammatical subordination and, at least in dysfluent patients, reduction in the use of many grammatical morphemes. (Grammatical morphemes whose deployment does not require much syntactic computation, such as extra-clausal coordinating conjunctions and sentence-final particles, seem to be unimpaired; Menn and Obler in press). De Villiers (1974) has shown for English that the best-preserved grammatical morphemes in aphasic patients are not necessarily those acquired earliest, but it is important to go behind this finding; current cross-linguistic work suggests that the factors which govern the order of acquisition have to do with the cognitive accessibility of the notion being encoded by the functor, the complexity with which the ambient language happens to do that encoding, and the child's opportunity to hear the functor in a particular use (Slobin 1985a). At present, it is still quite possible to choose not to believe in the existence of any irreducibly linguistic acquisition hierarchy, even though one must certainly acknowledge the presence of an immense cognitive "language-making capacity" focused on and probably specialized for language acquisition – see Slobin (1985a, b).

A major difference between aphasics and children which must be emphasized is the near-absence of morphophonemically overregularized forms in aphasic speech. As is well known, children, after initial stages of rote learning of a grammatical morpheme, extract the pattern and generalize it; if there are allomorphies to be mastered, the child errs on these by over-extending one allomorph (not always the most frequent one; Slobin 1973; MacWhinney 1978; Slobin 1985a, b). Only in cases where the allomorphy arises from a pervasive and transparent (and/or phonetically "natural"?) rule of the language, such as Turkish vowel harmony or English devoicing of the "Z" (plural, possessive, 3rd person singular, cliticized auxiliaries) and "D" (past tense) morphemes do we appear to find error-free acquisition of allomorphy. On the other hand, recent extensive cross-linguistic comparison of nonfluent aphasics (and extensive English-language data on fluent aphasics) supports the conclusion that allomorph-choice errors are extremely rare (about four allomorph-choice errors documented as compared to many hundreds of errors in morpheme choice). Thus, it appears that aphasics are drawing (incorrectly) on paradigms which they have already learned, and choosing the wrong forms, while children are still learning the irregularities of those paradigms.

In the lexical domain, there appears to be somewhat more similarity among all groups of limited speakers. Speakers who have diminished access to a word for a given concept and speakers who have never acquired the word are similar in their efforts to communicate by the use of circumlocutions, coinages, and the use of not-quite-adequate related words. Here, furthermore, limited speakers are not essentially different from "full" speakers trying to express a new concept or one for which the correct word escaped them, except that they probably will lack some of the devices that the language offers (e.g. for word formation). However, limited speakers will generally be inferior, in the precision and vividness of their creations, to "full" speakers who want a more striking way to say something – the poet, the preacher, or the aphorist, as described in this volume by Tsitsipis.

2.   General patterns and particular circumstances of language acquisition

At this point, let us see what can be gained by applying currently accepted generalizations about first language acquisition to the various particular circumstances under which people become limited speakers of a language. With respect to any pattern or rule of a language, we may distinguish four broad levels of acquisition: (0) ignorance, (1) rote or formulaic knowledge, (2) pre-conventional or overgenerative knowledge (the level at which overgeneralizations are produced), and (3) full conventionalized knowledge.

To expand somewhat: The overregulations of level 2 (e.g. paradigmatic leveling of various types, *bring-ed* or *bring, brang, brung*) and, more generally, the tendency to use locutions of maximal semantic transparency have long been understood as characteristics of an intermediate stage of language acquisition which are pruned back to/towards the norm principally through sufficient exposure to counterexamples and/or examples of alternative options. These tendencies are not associated with any one age or stage, or even specifically with language learning (mutatis mutandis), but are clearly the result of the way cognition works. They are evident at the earliest stages of language use and continue in effect for each of us in the regions near the frontiers of our knowledge.

Less generally recognized is level 1, at which we find the countervailing tendency to rely on unanalyzed (rote) forms, or on formulaic utterances. Formulaic utterances are commonly referred to as "unanalyzed", but this may not always be the case – many an idiom, complex lexical item, or minor syntactic pattern is at least partially analyzable; what's critical here is that it is not synthesizable, that is, not productive for its users (Peters 1980, 1986). Clearly, for a given construction, this represents a state of knowledge more primitive than the levels 2 and 3 at which a construction can be synthesized by the speaker. We tend to be able to see level 1 performance most clearly in second language acquisition, where communication pressure on the older language learner probably throws it into sharper relief (Hakuta 1974; Wong-Fillmore 1979). Reliance on formulaic utterances for conversational turns, whether executed correctly by the more skilled semi-speaker (Dorian 1982c etc.) or bungled by the less skilled speaker (perhaps only a "rememberer"; Tsitispis, this volume) again is a pattern of a speaker at the limits of his/her knowledge – and again, any of us will exhibit this pattern when pushed to those limits, say in a dialect or in a genre of rhetoric which we do not fully command. As a further illustration: Gal's paper in this volume convincingly explains the causative verb-formation patterns used by young limited Hungarian speakers from bilingual homes in terms of what I would call level 2 (overproductive) knowledge of the commonest of these patterns and level 1 (formulaic) knowledge of the less common ones.

I think that the general procedure will be evident from these examples: in each case, one must ask what of the contracted language has the learner been exposed to and how much of it, and what level of knowledge of each structure is likely to be associated with that kind of exposure, given what else is known about acquisition of that specific language.

Using the terms of Campbell and Muntzel (this volume): when circumstances of input have been restricted and appear to be the major determinant of the behavior of a particular speaker of a contracted language, then principles which describe the behavior of language learners should apply. So here we look to the operating principles originally formulated by Slobin (1973) and now refined by him and his colleagues through 15 years of cross-linguistic research (Slobin 1985b). Regularity, frequency, perceptual saliency, and redundancy all contribute to the discoverability of the form–meaning correspondences of a language; the reader who is unfamiliar with this research area is enjoined to read at least Slobin (1985a).

Let us review some of the sets of input circumstances that have been described in this volume, now, and then look briefly at what this claim entails. We have as input variables the language being acquired in the home, or as the language of instruction at elementary or secondary school, or as a language of ritual/religion, or as a language taught in supplementary schooling, or as a language needed in the workplace, or as the language of one's spouse. A great variety of combinations of the above (and other circumstances, no doubt) may be found in the history of a given person, and within any one of them there often appears to be gradation. For example, as we have seen, under "language of home", the home may be effectively monolingual in the minority language (at least as far as speech directed to/heard by the child is concerned) or it may have varying degrees of bilingualism either within or across individuals.

Now the framework can be used to organize what we already know, and hopefully to make new predictions which can be tested. Has the learner encountered the language in question through heavy exposure to ritual language and little else? Then probably a great many of the constructions used by that register will be at level 1, but almost nothing will be at level 2 unless a few constructions are both very common and exemplified by a sufficient variety of types. Or, for another example: Did the learner hear the contracted language in the home until about age 4, and then have virtually no further exposure to it? Then we expect, of course, that the formal register will be absent, and that the constructions that are of minimal frequency in household discourse (e.g. probably many types of embedding) will be absent (level 0) or at level 1. And we expect that the vocabulary will be restricted to the domestic domain – a domain that, conversely, will be impoverished for those who have never used their contracted language in a home.

This framework seems to be what is required to handle the similarities and differences that Dorian (1982b:56) found between her one "formerly fluent adult" speaker of East Sutherland Gaelic and her several imperfect speakers who had never reached that stage, although additional information about acquisition would be required to test its correctness. Both groups of speakers showed loss of vocabulary and overregularization of grammatical morphemes, but the formerly-fluent speaker did not show any tendency to make synthetic structures analytic, as the other imperfect speakers did. According to our definitions, the overregularized structures are at level 2 of acquisition for both groups. However, the structures which have been made analytic (circumlocutory) are either at level 0 (ignorance) or level 1 (formulaic, subject unable to go beyond rote-learned forms) for the speakers who were never fluent, while they are at level 2 or 3 for the formerly-fluent speaker. Clearly, for this to make sense, it should be the case that in communities where children are still acquiring Gaelic as a native language, the structures which Dorian found to be generally overregularized are acquired earlier than the structures which she found to be intact only in her formerly-fluent speaker. (If this hypothesis should prove to be false, my chapter will have to be drastically revised in the next edition. . . .)

I also suggest that there may be some particular morphological consequences of exposure which is effectively terminated in childhood: consider the following. Overgeneralization by nonfull adult speakers of verb stems in complex paradigms tends to take the 3rd person singular indicative as the base form, which linguists then want to label "unmarked". It is not hard to rationalize this: the frequency of the 3rd person singular indicative is high and its marking is correspondingly the most redundant, narrative being a major communicative mode for adults. But for the very young child, narrative plays a minor role, and in many (most?) families, 2nd person singular imperatives (directed to the child and his/her siblings) probably are more frequent and more decodable by the child than the 3rd person singular indicative. Indeed, 2nd person singular imperatives tend to be learned early (Stephany 1986; Weist 1986). This may be further facilitated by the fact that they also usually bear zero or minimal markings across languages – a useful property for a modality which is used unceremoniously to elicit prompt action. Thus, for the limited speaker whose exposure to a language underwent a sharp curtailment after early family use, we might expect the 2nd person singular imperative to be a better preserved form than the "unmarked" 3rd person singular indicative, and perhaps to be the one used as the basis for any overregularized verb paradigm. Dorian, in fact, has some data from East Sutherland Gaelic which might be interpreted as being in accord with this prediction (pers. comm.).

As a caveat to the approach I have been describing, it must be said that there may be major differences between monolingual first language acquisition and acquisition of language in a contact setting. But the child in the monolingual setting at any time after the onset of speech has a system of her own, and is adapting the adult system to her own even as she is adapting hers to it. (Thus we have child phonology "rules" and so on, which are inherently the same kind of thing as loanword adaptation rules.) Consider again the child in what appears to be one of the commonest configurations of the above exposure variables, one who spends say the first four or so years in a relatively monolingual minority-language home environment, and learns the dominant language in the streets and at school. What is salient to the child in the new language? The Slobin operating principles, referred to above, are basic cognitive variables; the only thing about them that can reasonably be said to be specific to language learning is that humans may well be better at responding to these variables in the context of learning language than in the context of learning anything else. Therefore, we expect these variables to have the same effect in language contact acquisition settings as in monolingual acquisition settings, except for the probable extra boosts given to calques and to morphemes which happen to have a high degree of phonetic and semantic resemblance across the languages in question (diamorphs).

It is, in fact, startling to see the specificity with which these principles may be operating across immensely differing circumstances: Bavin (this volume) reports that Warlpiri-speaking children (of English–Warlpiri bilingual parents, surrounded by an English-speaking community) form negative imperatives with initial *not* followed by a Warlpiri verb (and possibly the Warlpiri negative morpheme). This pattern is not found in adult English of any variety to my knowledge, but it is very common as an early intermediate stage in monolingual English-acquiring children. Bavin also reports the negative polarity word *any* as a negative morpheme in her Warlpiri child subjects, and this can equally be found in young English-monolingual children. Both *not* and *any* rank rather high in saliency for a creature that operates on Slobin principles: both are typically stressed, and *any* is frequently found in sentence-final position in speech addressed to children and/or produced by their slightly older peers (*Do you want any? I don't have any*).

Another caveat, which echoes a point made in Dorian 1982c (and see also Fillmore, Kempler and Wang 1979): Individual variation in language acquisition styles is one of those frustrating facts of life – individuals show preferences for one syllable type rather than another, or strategies contrasted as "analytic" vs. "holistic" (Peters 1977) or "expressive" vs.

"referential" (Nelson 1973), or dissociations between phonological and syntactic abilities, and probably many others waiting to be found. Expectations can be contravened startlingly – for one child acquiring English, [ð] was first found only after nasalized vowels and in clusters following nasals or dental stops (Moskowitz 1970). Some of the same strategic or temperamental factors may underlie the similar dissociations across component linguistic skills noted by Hamp (this volume) – dissociations between individuals in their relative command of the phonology, morphology, and syntax of the contracting language. While some of these might be accounted for by the fine texture of the individual's history of exposure to the contracting language, there is probably an irreducible core of sheer individuality.

I will bring up just one more acquisition problem, which was originally drawn to my attention by Susan Philips: the interpretation of age grading. In looking at the language of younger speakers in language contraction situations, if we see them looking more like speakers of the dominant language than older speakers do, can we judge that the contracted language is going to move in that direction? Not conclusively, for just as children go through overgeneralization and then retraction (apparently to the point of near match of frequency of choice of options in appropriate contexts), they also go through age-marked style changes that they may later reject as their self-image changes. Interruption/curtailment of exposure to adult models may lead to absence of an attempt to match the prior generation's usage, but in many cases the younger speakers probably have at least an idea of how adults are supposed to sound, just as they know approximately how adults are supposed to dress.

3.   Psycholinguistic consideration of the effects of limited interaction opportunities: Processing load, production, and comprehension

This section is much shorter and more tentative than the preceding ones, because in neurolinguistics we are still far from being able to disentangle what may be fairly specific effects of particular brain lesions from the more general ones that I would describe as reduction in available language processing capacity. Nevertheless, some features of aphasic language, at present, seem best to be described in the latter terms. One of these is difficulty (presently documented only for dysfluent patients) in both the comprehension and production of embedded structures.

Goodglass *et al.* (1979) showed that English-speaking agrammatic patients comprehended two conjoined sentences better than a sentence conveying the same information with one main clause and one embedded clause; the agrammatic narratives in the Menn and Obler cross-linguistic study (in press) showed almost no embedded clauses and a dearth of attributive adjectives (excluding determiners), but no corresponding lack of predicate adjectives. This can be interpreted as a matter of a limited pushdown store (Yngve 1960); patients find it difficult to interrupt one structure in order to work on lexical retrieval or on building another structure, and then to go back to the "outer" structure again.

If this is true, then one might expect reduction in subordinate clauses and attributive adjective use (outside of formulaic expressions) among speakers who actually do know how to deploy these structures but whose interaction opportunities have been limited – speakers who are just plain "rusty" and are having to expend a great deal of energy on retrieving words and putting sentences together. Even comprehension of these structures might be impaired – but judgements of grammaticality should be relatively spared, since the processing load is lighter in that task, at least when there is no time pressure. Here, however, as pointed out by Dorian (1982c), the effects of talking to oneself (and reading) will have to be taken into account in evaluating a given speaker's "interaction" opportunities.

Rather than waiting for further results from neurolinguistics, research on potential psycholinguistic explanations for effects of reduced interaction opportunities (and the way in which these might interact with reduced knowledge of a language) should turn to laboratory psycholinguistics for an estimate of what structures in a given language ought to be most vulnerable to a competing cognitive load; according to the reasoning that I have been using in this section, these should be the ones most impaired for the rusty speaker, and it would be interesting to find out if this is really the case.

Notes

With thanks to William Bright for his editorial suggestions, most of which were accepted with varying degrees of gratitude.

1. A typical case that evades the predictions (Menn 1973): A child acquiring English who had [t] and [tš] in contrast, but no [š], was not a counterexample because she did not have an affricate–fricative contrast; furthermore, even if she had had the [s]/[tš] contrast before acquiring [t], it can be argued that for English, the stop/affricate contrast is nondistinctive, affrication being redundantly conditioned by palatal position of articulation.
2. The (quite possibly apocryphal) story is told that Jakobson was approached after a lecture by a member of the audience who timidly asked: "Professor Jakobson, according to your theory, a child's first word should be 'pa', but my child's first word was 'goo'. How is this possible?" Jakobson responded, in his *very* imitable accent: "Phawnyetyically 'goo', phawnyimyically 'pa'."
3. In English, the *-ing* form is found in dysfluent aphasic speech almost as frequently as the zero-marked form; hence the "naming the action" formulation used here.

22 Language obsolescence and language history: Matters of linearity, leveling, loss, and the like

HENRY M. HOENIGSWALD

Thinking about language death confronts the historical linguist constantly with awkward questions concerning his fundamental concepts. All the contributors to this collection are up against these questions whether or not they say so explicitly and, for that matter, whether or not they call themselves historians. In what follows we shall discuss a few of the more explicit comments.

There was at one time a set of preconceptions into which the subject would have fitted only too well: the framework of growth and decay and ultimate death, or of evolution and ultimate extinction. Those ideas are no longer virulent. Their latency, however, is another matter. Living individuals and living species with their rather well defined physical boundaries may have proved poor sources of metaphor; but metaphor of the kind that makes a language into a corporeal object of *some* sort will always be with us, and so, along with its blessings, will be its pitfalls.

In retrospect – that is, to the historian – what is obsolescence? Aside from instances where speakers are killed off ("extremely rare in eastern Africa" says Dimmendaal [this volume] in one of his many intriguing asides) or, under some kind of pressure, abandon their language with a will, obsolescence occurs when a population shifts from one language to another, in ways which are open to observation (as regards the present) and to surmise (as regards the past; Campbell and Muntzel, Dimmendaal). Usually, therefore, language death is preceded by bilingualism, though, of course, bilingualism does not always presage language death. English could have died in the Middle Ages but didn't. In some ways, perhaps harmless ones, our use of metaphor is a little uncertain here. It doesn't seem to be common usage to say that French "died in England" when the same French (or was it "the same"?) survived in France; but once we call it Anglo-Norman we do not hesitate. Under what conditions could it make a difference to the individuals living through the shift – be it a concerted one

347

affecting a compact population, or a shift due to dispersal (Silesian German is no doubt going to be extinct as a sequel to the post-World War II exodus) – if somewhere in the world their language happens to live on?

A second point is more disturbing. The recognition of language death depends on our ability to distinguish clearly between two things. One is the learning *of* another language, perhaps with substratum effects and with "need-filling" borrowings from the former, now "dead" language; "in the recent shift from Elmolo to Samburu the original Elmolo lexicon pertaining to lake bio-nomenclature and fishing largely survived unscathed", says Dimmendaal (quoting Heine 1982). The other is the near-total borrowing of vocabulary, syntax and what not, from another language (with a retained core indicating survival). So long as the differences between the two languages are gross, the distinction seems feasible and meaningful. But what about dialects? Which do we believe or expect: that dialect death is an unspectacular, endemic, everyday occurrence, taking place pervasively and beneath the threshold of awareness; or, contrariwise, that there can be no such thing as dialect death by definition? Or does it matter? It is probably no accident that none of the papers assembled here deals with such a situation however remotely,[1] not even by way of remembering that European standby, the Rise of the Standard Language.

More than anything else, we would like to be able to tell when change merely happens to affect a language which will in the end also become extinct, and when, on the other hand, the link between impending extinction and change is a necessary one – and that not so much because as historical linguists we are interested in maintenance and obsolescence as because we are interested in the properties of what is either maintained or lost. Nobody, it appears, has ever seriously said that some changes will make a language unfit for survival, though absence of change, or failure to adapt, was on occasion so charged in the heyday of speculative pseudo-Darwinian writing.[2] Nowadays we are certainly content to blame the extinction of a language on the forces of general history first, and only then to consider the possible linguistic consequences.[3] We ask to what extent languages made obsolescent by circumstances typically take on diagnostic characteristics.

One particular observation is easy, but it is marginal. Languages about to disappear are sometimes said to suffer *style reduction* (see also Campbell and Muntzel's chapter). This is only to be expected whenever during the period of bilingualism a particular style – that is, speech on particular kinds of occasion – is left to the other language. Mougeon and Beniak mention specifically that if in their Ontarian French "simplification" is a mark of overall disuse, style reduction is one of functional disuse or restriction, the "decline of options which are tied to those societal domains where use of the minority language is excluded". It is fitting here to point to King's study of the situation in Newfoundland where it seems to be the absence of internal social differentiation among the fully fluent speakers of Acadian French which enables them to maintain linguistic variation, much as in Dorian's East Sutherland Gaelic. The relevance of this to style reduction emerges when we read (emphasis supplied) that "a great deal of variation remains in Newfoundland French, despite its decline in status, *restriction in contexts of usage*, and loss of speakers". This adds depth to the concept of style reduction as it interacts with the other variables.

Another claim which has been made is that while change during obsolescence may not, in a given instance, differ much from change in general, it takes place more rapidly. Hill's bare mention of this (p. 149) is a little tantalizing since her data (Nahuatl, known from the classical, sixteenth-century period onward – the author seems to be sure that there is a straight line of descent, a rare phenomenon in attested history) might have allowed something like measuring the rate of change directly; the other contributors must or do rely on occasional reconstruction by the use of "apparent time" or age grading (with its limitations in depth) or by the "comparative" method (with its limitations of scope). This is slippery ground.[4] According to Maandi, case markers are "collapsing" "even where Estonian is not in contact with Swedish"; such contact merely "speeds it up". Cayuga provides Mithun with an enviable laboratory case: what had apparently been a fairly homogeneous speech community was forcibly split apart and survives in two widely separated locations where things have "begun to differ in subtle ways". The language is "very much alive in Ontario" (although we do learn that "children are no longer learning the language as a mother tongue"), while in Oklahoma "fewer and fewer speakers use it on rarer and rarer occasions". Productivity in the matter of affixes and noun incorporation is receding in Oklahoma. There is, then, an impression that alterations are more in evidence on the Oklahoma side (p. 257). Though the author warns emphatically against rash conclusions, there is more here than just an echo of Dorian's tentative statement on East Sutherland Gaelic (1981:151–2; 154; I am not aware that Dorian's call for a control through comparison with the rate of change in a largely unwritten language within a stable bilingual community was ever taken up).

"Simplification" ranks high among the putative characteristics of dying languages. This could be a case in point, since simplification is also one of the principles that have been alleged to explain ordinary linguistic change. But, as philosophers well know, and as linguists have learned, simplicity is not simple. As we look for concrete argument we notice, not without relief, that there is some complexity to the claim. The contexts in which simplification is most often pleaded are, in fact, quite diverse. It would be best to follow some of our authors and distinguish what can be labeled a version of the substratum theory in reverse (distinctions not known to the superstratum are given up; hence a form of "convergence") from simplification per se (as a facet of "autonomous change") such as is sometimes reported for pidginization. The former, with examples both from the so-called higher levels (semantics, syntax, inflectional and derivational morphology) and from phonology, is obviously of a piece with "healthy" history. It may be otherwise with the latter. But it seems that the very characteristics of the former (relative) variety, are definable in ways which stand up to critique just a little better than the latter (absolute) one. Bavin, for example, reports a number of developments in Warlpiri, some of which are very ordinary consequences of contact, such as loanwords. She also reports morphological simplifications, but these are of two kinds. Some, e.g. the loss of categories that are not English (the dual, or the inclusive/exclusive distinction in the pronominal dual and plural) can be put down to "influence", but others constitute, as it were, simplification in the pure state: the innovated forms are characterized as "easily segmentable", less diversified allomorphically ("leveled") and hence (?) more "transparent" semantically. This is perhaps not far removed from Itkonen's proposed universal (1982), put forward, be it noted, precisely as a universal of change and not of evanescence. Maandi believes that semantic transparency is increased and complexity lessened in Swedish Estonian (for the direct object "case"); importance is attached to a future tense that is said to be marked. In Mithun's obsolescent Oklahoma Cayuga (see above) there is some allomorphic leveling, certain stress and metathesis patterns have been "generalized", and there is an impression of "reduction" in sound and in morphology, though we are warned not to be rash on this score. Huffines makes it clear (à propos of Pennsylvania German) that we are largely dealing with ordinary – not morbid – processes, and she stresses that would-be simplification is typically compensated from other quarters: for example, analyticity by word order complications.

Let us for a moment concentrate on allomorphic leveling. It is taken for granted that such *Ausgleich* is the essence, or an important part of the essence, of all analogic change. It must be said, first of all, that appearances favor such a view. It must further be suspected that it has its foundation deep in the design of language. That foundation is, however, also curiously restricted. Imagine a language like Standard German or Russian in which the voicing contrast in stops and fricatives is neutralized at the end of "words" etc. in favor of (unmarked?) voicelessness, with resulting paradigms of the type (Germ.) *Volk: Volkes* vs. *Erfolg* [k]: *Erfolges* [g]. To begin at the speculative end, it takes a really massive belief in the unique adequacy of "autonomous" phonology (or rather: alphabetization) to find ultimate truth in the greater notational simplicity of *Volk*. If, for one or another of the many reasons one could think of, the *k/g* paradigms were better entrenched (more frequent or what not) than the *k/k* paradigms, the exposure factor (on which allomorphic simplification tends to be blamed in the case of semi-speakers and other bilinguals) could be expected to favor them; if they are equally well entrenched, how can we ever know the odds? The historical record points the same lesson. Umlaut is an allomorphic alternation, which, going back to a secondary split due to a merger (of front vowel with Ø, etc.) *in the conditioning environment* does not entail neutralization. In some German nouns it receded (*Aal*, pl. *Äle* 'eel[s]' is now *Aal*, pl. *Aale*, like *Wirt:Wirte* 'host[s]', while in others it spread (*Hals:Halse* > *Hälse* 'neck[s]', like *Gast:Gäste* 'guest[s]')[5] – whether with equal ease or not who can say? There is certainly nothing unfamiliar about such situations. To search for special overriding factors merely to save the maxim of allomorphic simplification would be ad hoc and selfdefeating. Kuryłowicz' first law of analogic innovation, which gives an edge to doubly characterized forms in paradigms (like Germ. *Bäume* 'trees', with vowel alternant *and* suffix) is sometimes quoted with approval by scholars who will be quite strong on leveling, too, though the two principles tend in opposite directions. The fact is that these principles once again furnish classifications rather than, by themselves, causal explanation. Which road the language takes depends, we say, on the prevailing (or on some aimed-for) typology – a statement the dimness of which is excused only by our difficulties with the sociolinguistic underpinnings of directionality, areal and chronological.

The chapter by Campbell and Muntzel goes to the (historical) center of things and therefore prompts special scrutiny. The coverage of material is impressive, and so is the frankness with which the authors propose what they call hypotheses, to be confirmed, refined, or contradicted. It is regrettable that the generalizations offered (like those contained in Hamp's similarly broad paper) are so strongly weighted on the phonological side, since there is no good reason to feel that the "levels" simply repeat one another. The first three hypotheses, taken from Andersen (1982), are to the effect that (1) "the bilingual speaker of a threatened . . . language will make fewer phonological distinctions . . . than a fully competent . . . speaker . . . would"; (2) "distinctions common to both . . . [competing] languages" will be preserved; and (3) distinctions with a high functional load will survive longer (p. 186). There is a promising "for example" here, but evidence is offered only for the second. Despite the assurance that "few would quarrel" with any of them, considering the notorious difficulties that attach to the notion of functional load, the third one is, but also remains, intriguing. Next comes "overgeneralization of unmarked features". In Tuxtla Chico Mam, the distinction between *k* and *q* is given up, under hypothesis (1), in favor of *k*, since *q* "is" the marked member of the opposition[6] – assuming, clearly, that there can be unquestioning agreement on this kind of proposition (just so, long vowels in Pipil and in Finnish are said to "be" marked). It is valuable to be reminded (p. 188) that this is an up-to-date version of the venerable distinction between "internal" and "external" causes of change, although a more complete reminder would not gloss over the suspicion of circularity on the "internal" side. However that may be, the authors do not convince us that dying languages are not merely changing languages in this respect. We are told, however, that "multiple causation" is available to resolve a seeming conflict (among "hypotheses"; p. 188); of course, it always is. But then, "while there may often be a tendency to reduce . . . marked forms . . . the reverse also appears to be common", and we end up with descriptions of hyperforms ("Teotepeque Pipil in its moribund state has over-emphasized voiceless *l*, employing it everywhere, not just word-finally as it was formerly" – another internally motivated development). "[O]bligatory rules may come to apply optionally", and "there is sometimes failure to learn . . . rules by overgeneralization and/or under-generalization". "Some changes in moribund languages may be externally motivated" by "influence from linguistic aspects of the dominant language". The passive in American Finnish appears to be due to the impact of English because it involves addition, not reduction of devices (p. 190). "Language death may be accompanied by . . . morphological reduction (in which we include the reduction of allomorphy and the leveling of paradigms." "Not all examples, however, conform to or illustrate Andersen's hypotheses about syntactic reduction. . . . On the English model of appositive gerunds in *-ing*, A[merican] F[innish] now permits [overtly specified] . . . subjects, even when . . . not coreferential with the subject of the main clause." Finally, the central point finds very restrained acknowledgement: ". . . in *some* cases it may be difficult to distinguish *some* changes *due to* the language death process [emphasis supplied] from the consequences of other kinds of language contact". "Completely parallel changes" – parallel, that is, to a syntactic innovation in Pipil – "have taken place in other completely viable Nahua dialects . . . showing the difficulty of distinguishing normal contact-induced change from changes due to the language death situation." Precisely.

It has been necessary to quote so fully from the Campbell and Muntzel paper because of its methodological ambitions. Evidently, what the authors attempt here are not hypotheses in anything like a strict sense, and one notes with some satisfaction that the word is enclosed in quotation marks once (perhaps in implied criticism of Andersen?). What we do find instead, beyond valuable observations, are classifications by definition, with defining properties chosen "arbitrarily", that is, in this case, most commendably borrowed from all kinds of existing work and existing speculation: hence, internal/external, reductive/additive, marked/unmarked, natural/unnatural (for an example see p. 191), etc. – not to mention certain sociolinguistic (as distinct from linguistic) parameters such as Dorian's "semi-speaker". This is an old story in linguistics; to this day the profession is, after all, reluctant to entertain the possibility that the neogrammarians' regularity concept was neither an empirical finding nor a so-called postulate, but was definitional in nature. Yet this is what would seem to emerge, not from their methodological pronouncements, but from their practice; as often as not, they proceed as though they were saying: "'regular', i.e. *phonologically statable*, replacements may also be called 'sound-changes'".[7] What gives us pause in the case of Campbell and Muntzel is their need to admit each of two opposites as generalizations ("such-and-such is the case, but the contrary case also occurs commonly"). This casts a pall over their selection of defining properties which no amount of hypothesis-testing can dispel.

Hamp, "On signs of health and death", is also concerned about how to discriminate between changing and dying language. Convergence in a sprachbund is pronounced normal. In a sense and within limits, the more contact interference we see, the more adjustment, adaptation, and longevity we might expect (p. 201; see also p. 350 above). Just so, Huffines has found (this volume) that there is a great deal of convergence in the speech of the stably bilingual Mennonites and Amish of Pennsylvania while the unstable nonsectarian speakers are showing little convergence but losing their German in rather short order now.[8] Language death may overtake highly conservative forms, as can be seen from the case of Hamp's West Kintyre Gaelic. One of the most provocative remarks is made in passing: speakers shift "not to a worldwide English, nor to RP, nor to adjacent broad Scots, but to Highland English, whose phonetics carries a large number of the most distinctive traits of Gaelic phonetics . . . there is very little change or loss to be undergone"! And the sentence which follows is fraught with more meaning than is apparent: "The next question then is: what will become of Highland English?" This is one of the very few moves toward raising, at least indirectly, the problem of deadly *dialect* conflict (see above).

Obsolescence itself is a sociolinguistic matter and not a specifically linguistic one. Demise can be predicted, it seems, only at the terminal stage, where it is obvious, what with a last speaker surviving in California or on some Dalmatian island. Occasionally there is a report of a surprising stability or reversal (Hamp, this volume). The clearest lessons to be learned from the study of language obsolescence are also sociolinguistic ones; they have to do with style reduction and with the semi-speaker. Linguistic questions do arise constantly, however. For this historical linguists could not be more grateful, embarrassed though they find themselves as they face their own generalizations which are sometimes more honored in the programmatic formulation than in the execution. A straightforward question with regard to the rate of change per time unit reminds them of the feebleness of their efforts to find a meaningful measure (other than lexicostatistic vocabulary loss). If overwhelming allomorph loss – leveling – should really prove to be a general characteristic of obsolescent languages, regardless of type, this would teach us something specific about language death: this because we have seen (pp. 350–1 above) that in ordinary nonmorbid history leveling is more constrained typologically (i.e. less of a universal) than is sometimes thought. It is quite possible that more investigation of obsolescence will also present us with counterexamples. Interference from the neighbors, including the neighbor who will take over, can be observed in many languages that are on the way out, but it is of course just as well known from contact situations that are nonthreatening and viable. On the other hand, just as the more easily recognizable symptoms of interference may be absent in ordinary histories, so, as we have now learned, they can be strikingly absent in morbid ones.

Notes

1. There is a hint in Hamp's paper; see the last but one paragraph below.
2. "[T]he North American Indian tribes . . . are unfitted for historical life because of their endlessly complicated . . . languages, bristling with overabundant forms; they can only undergo retrogression, even extinction" says Schleicher (1983:82), calling into question, it seems, not only the survival of the language but that of the speakers themselves.
3. Dimmendaal speaks of "the erroneous conclusion that economic transformations provide the decisive incentives in . . . language shift" and argues in what follows for a picture that is more complex, using the spread of Maa as an example.
4. See Dorian (1986b:559–60), with special application to Arvanítika. Roughly speaking, the ideal direct lines of descent are available not from the record but from "comparative" reconstruction with its harvest of necessarily schematic proto-languages.
5. Wright (1907:169).
6. However, since q is also not Spanish, two tendencies could have worked "in concert"; pp. 188.
7. This is at the basis of the orthodox anathema on sporadicity, which is manifestly not a matter of existential fact subject to confirmation or disconfirmation, but one of "making sense", i.e. of noncontradictoriness. The choice of the criterion, phonologial statability – "sound-change insofar as it goes forward mechanically", as Karl Brugmann had it (Osthoff and Brugmann 1878:200 [of the reprinting]; Jankowsky 1972;125) – is arbitrary only in an abstract formal sense; in terms of sociolinguistic and of general history it has proved to be eminently interpretable. See, however, Labov (1981).
8. I am obliged to Nancy Dorian for pointing out to me the special importance of this observation.

23 Language convergence and language death as social processes

KATHRYN A. WOOLARD

1. Linguistic conservatism and language maintenance

An intriguing question that echoes through many of the studies in this volume is whether there is a relationship between linguistic conservatism or corruption and language maintenance or death. The relationship between persistence of form and persistence of use can be phrased and questioned in two directions. The functional linguist asks whether, when we know that a language has undergone contraction in number of speakers or domains of use, we can predict certain types of changes in linguistic structure as a consequence. The editor of this volume has led in formulating and investigating that question (e.g. Dorian 1981, 1986c), and articles in the second section of this volume in particular bring important evidence to bear on the issue.

A different ordering of the variables gives rise to a different question, one of considerable interest to those readers concerned with the social, political, and social-psychological processes of language maintenance and shift, those of us still struggling to understand how the battery of factors that seem to overwhelm minority languages combine to produce their effects, or occasionally are turned back. The question is raised and confronted most directly in Eric Hamp's linguistically erudite review of phonological change in dying languages, but it is a question that is fundamentally about the social processes underlying language change and language loss. That question is whether, when we find interference or convergence phenomena in the structure of a language in contact with others, we should necessarily see these as signs that shift is in progress and loss impending. What we are asking in this formulation is whether the social conditions, processes, and activities that affect a language's form are the same as the social processes that encourage or discourage that language's continued use.

The issue is not only of theoretical interest to social scientists studying the causes of language change and language shift, but also of considerable practical concern to amateur and professional language defenders interested in protecting or fomenting particular minority languages. Should language

355

loyalists or planners read change phenomena as either direct threats or indicators of threat to the continued existence of their language, and take some kind of action accordingly?

Dorian has given us the term "tip" for the situation in which a demographically stable language experiences a sudden change that leads rapidly to loss. "Tip" is of course the concern of defenders of such lively but dominated languages as Catalan (Woolard 1989). Could this apparently vigorous language with a stable demographic base, yet still politically precarious, suddenly overturn and sink into a sea of Spanish like the Herald of Free Enterprise into the English channel?[1] Can certain kinds of changes in linguistic structures be taken as harbingers of impending language shift; in the disease metaphor, are there linguistic symptoms of an infirmity that is quietly killing the linguistic corpus?

Disease metaphors and the pastoralist vision discussed by Gal in this volume offer an affirmative answer to this question, linking structural change, viewed as decay, with impending death. In the evaluations of Hungarian that Gal cites, "corruption" and "demise" are not so much twin threats as the same threat. Hungarian scholars are far from alone or unusual in making such an estimation; commentators on numerous minority languages over time have offered similar evaluations and thus similar prognostications linking interference to eventual loss.[2]

In the present collection, the case of Norwegian in America might support the view that contact interference is a precursor to minority language loss. Haugen tells us that the Norwegian used by immigrants represented a first step toward acculturation since it was heavily interlarded with lexical borrowings from English, including what Mougeon and Beniak (this volume) call "gratuitous" loanwords, replacing vocabulary items already present in Norwegian. The "innumerable Low German loans in Norwegian" cited by Haugen clearly indicate that "from loans to loss" cannot be generalized as an inviolable rule even in the case history of this one language. But from the vantage point of hindsight, Haugen finds that in the Norwegian–American instance, "a 'drift' toward English was apparent from the start, preceding the ultimate 'shift'".

While the "loans to loss" model is quite widely held, especially among non-linguists, it is not clear what the mechanism is that would relate language convergence to language shift. A social-psychological mechanism is suggested, however, in Haugen's reporting of the Norwegian case. Extensive borrowing, particularly gratuitous borrowing, can be taken to indicate an openness to English influence, perhaps even an eagerness for assimilation to the English language and the cultural practices it encodes. If early generations with little opportunity for contact and thus occasion for borrowing show such accomplishment in that direction, then later generations with increased opportunity for contact can be expected to accomplish in the same spirit a fairly complete language shift. The idea here is not that linguistic interference is a cause of language shift, but only an indicator of it; shift is a quantitative extension of borrowing. In this model, the same social motivations and processes underlie both. Certainly, those of us working with minority languages do frequently find it to be the case that loyalists motivated to maintain the use of a language are often also highly conservative monitors of the form of that language. At least when language defense is a conscious process, the will for maintenance and for purity do seem to have the same roots; whether this also holds for less selfconscious processes is not entirely clear.

There are circumstances under which we might expect that linguistic interference or convergence is not only an indicator but also an additional cause of language shift. This might be the case in the politically motivated process that Heinz Kloss (1967) refers to as "dialectalization", as exemplified in the treatment of Gallego and Catalan in Spain in the early Franco period, and more thoroughly and effectively in the treatment of the so-called "patois" of southern France. If enough structural similarity obtains or can be created between a dominant and a minority language, that similarity may be used to convince speakers of the minority variety that theirs is a corrupted, substandard dialect, and that the dominant language is the standard variety toward which they should shift. (This insidious logic of dialectalization and shift is of course often evident in decreolization processes.) In this model, we note that dialectalization is a political and social-psychological process as well as a linguistic one. Convergence of two languages alone is not an adequate impetus for the abandonment of one; rather, it provides a material base which is then interpreted and evaluated by interested parties as a motivation for language shift.

Although we can sketch, as I've done above, at least two possible rationales for the suggested link between structural interference and language loss, such a link is by no means empirically confirmed by all the contributions to this volume. Hamp argues that there is no direct relationship between language purity and language death or maintenance, at least where phonological conservatism is concerned. He even goes so far as to suggest that the more contact interference seen " – within limits – the more . . . longevity and health we may expect". (It is of course just what those limits might be that is a main concern here, and it may be that Haugen has found them.) Hamp suggests that linguistic acculturation may in fact represent adaptation for survival. The position he develops calls to mind the seminal work on convergence by Gumperz and Wilson (1971); they found that morpho-syntactic convergence toward a single grammar over centuries in an Indian community's multilingual repertoire coexisted with, perhaps even enabled, the continued maintenance of three nominally distinct codes, identified by their distinctive lexicons.

One strong proposition, that linguistic conservatism is a sufficient condition for, or predictor of, language maintenance, can be dismissed quickly on the evidence offered by various authors in this volume. Situations where language loss is well advanced offer no insight into conditions for maintenance, but several studies of nearly extinct languages do tell us that purity and conservatism are no guarantee of endurance. Mithun finds in a nearly extinct Oklahoma Cayuga an almost complete retention of a complex morphological and phonological system. Hamp also shows for the Scottish Gaelic of Muasdale (West Kintyre) that a language variety can go to its grave with its phonological boots on.[3] While the processes that allow the maintenance of a conservative form are still somewhat mystifying, they clearly are not necessarily the same processes that will lead to longterm survival among a community of speakers.

The hypothesis suggested by Hamp is that the two kinds of processes may actually be in opposition, with flexibility viewed as adaptive and conservatism as maladaptive. A number of contributors here offer evidence of long-continued language maintenance after interference phenomena have been integrated into a minority language system. For example, although Watson claims that having to speak English often adversely affects the Irish morphology and phonology of fluent conservative elders, he also notes that English loanwords have existed for the last century in some dialects that are still very vigorous. Several researchers have been able to address our present question even more directly, having the opportunity to compare the vitality of more and less conservative varieties of the same language (or, working in the opposite direction, the conservatism of more or less vigorous varieties). In almost all of these cases, the more convergent speech varieties have indeed been found to be livelier than related conservative forms, in accord with Hamp's hypothesis.

For Arvanítika, Hamp himself finds a "moribund specimen", Eleian, retaining original phonological traits, while an Attican youth showing capability of continued use had lost essential distinctive phonological features. Huffines finds that nonsectarian Pennsylvanian German speakers, among whom the language is on the brink of death, are more conservative in case morphology than sectarian speakers, among whom the language has a lively continued existence. In Welland French, Mougeon and Beniak find that English-dominant bilinguals, i.e. the more advanced in shift away from French, use fewer English-based loanwords when speaking French than do balanced bilinguals (although French-dominant bilinguals also use fewer loans than these balanced bilinguals).

While it is not the focus of her article for this volume, Hill also cites evidence that can be brought to bear on this question of the relation between language convergence and shift. Hill and Hill have found that "narrow-honorific speakers" of Malinche Mexicano, generally factory workers, tend to be very purist about the Mexicano language, and are sometimes "superb speakers of Mexicano". Yet these purists are more advanced toward Spanish in the language shift ongoing in the Malinche region than are the cultivators in the "broad-honorific speaker" category. The narrow-honorific speakers use Spanish as well as Mexicano for in-group purposes, while the cultivators, who are less advanced in the path of language shift to Spanish, use a highly hispanicized version of Mexicano for power functions within the community.

Is there a generalizable phenomenon relating convergence and maintenance here, one that perhaps could lead us to insight into the causes of change or continuity? While we may not yet have sufficient information to develop a coherent model, reorganizing the evidence and in some cases reorienting our metaphorical and thus theoretical perspective as Gal suggests may help us sketch the outlines of such a model. When we deal with linguistic data as aggregate data, detached from the speakers and instances of speaking, we often anthropomorphize languages as the principal actors of the sociolinguistic drama. This leads to forceful and often powerfully suggestive generalizations cast in agentivizing metaphors: "languages that are flexible and can adapt may survive longer", or "the more powerful language drives out the weaker". If we rephrase findings in terms of what *people* are doing – how they are speaking and what they are accomplishing or trying to accomplish when they are speaking that way, as Mertz has argued in her contribution – we may find ourselves open to new insights about why such linguistic phenomena occur.

All of the groups of speakers in the cases studied here are of course at least bilingual (although this is a fact so basic that occasionally it disappears from view as we talk about the process of language death). There are two salient principles by which speakers allocate their resources in a bilingual repertoire. The repertoire may be divided according to interlocutor, and/or it may be divided according to topic and context. In the first case, speakers use one language when speaking with a particular individual, and the other language will not enter into that relationship. In the second case, a speaker may use both languages at different times (or within the same speech exchange) with the same interlocutor, depending on topic, context, and function.

Tsitsipis notes that in his Albanian case, the progress of language shift is from a context-free, interlocutor-bound allocation of Arvanítika speech resources to a context-bound allocation. It is noteworthy that in one of the most successful cases of minority language maintenance in Europe, Catalan, the interlocutor principle is primary in determining conversational language choice (Woolard 1987). Tsitsipis' observation also fits with Gal's (1979) identification of conversational codeswitching, or bilingual relationships between individuals, as symptoms of the progressive advance of language shift. In Hill's case, the progress is in the same direction. Broad-honorific speakers do not exhibit a functional split of their bilingual repertoire, but use Spanish primarily with interlocutors outside their home communities. Narrow-honorific speakers, farther along in language shift according to the author, exhibit a sharp functional split between the two languages, using both in different contexts within the community. Huffines' sectarians also show the pattern of an interlocutor principle for splitting of the bilingual repertoire, and extensive language maintenance concurrent with substantial structural interference.

In all of these cases, codeswitching between the two languages would not be found among the less-shifted but more structurally cavalier sectors of the population, while it could conceivably be appropriate among the possibly more purist sectors more advanced in language shift. This schema sounds like a familiar echo of Fishman's (1967) generalization about diglossia, strict domain compartmentalization, and language maintenance. But in the findings of Tsitsipis and of Hill, those who strictly compartmentalize their repertoire by function or context are those who are in fact more affected by shift. It is when not just functions, but *personal relationships* order the bilingual repertoire and mandate the use of a particular language that we find evidence of more resistance to language shift in the cases mentioned here.[4]

Both Huffines and Gal suggest the social mechanisms that might create the paradoxical constellation of relatively high structural interference with relatively high maintenance rates, and lower interference with lower retention. Gal claims that the *same* local network pressures that maintain the language by requiring young speakers to use Hungarian lead to the creation of morphological and lexical innovations which make the young speakers' dialect more divergent. Similarly, Huffines points out that the sociolinguistic norm in the sectarian community requires discourse in Pennsylvania German to meet all communicative needs within the community. Codeswitching is not appropriate within the community. Thus if a speaker has difficulty finding words or forms in the minority language, switching to the other language is not a legitimate solution.

Huffines argues that this "lack of switching behavior has exposed the linguistic code to the influence of its English environment"; codeswitching is here seen as a safety valve that allows social purposes to be accomplished while conserving the integrity of the minority code from depredations of less proficient speakers. In the nonswitching situation, forms that are used may be erroneous or innovative, but they will be offered and taken as constituents of the minority, in-group code. Since there is little other fresh linguistic input available, English is often likely to provide the basis for such errors and innovations, which over time may be incorporated into the in-group code.

In both of these cases, the constellation of language maintenance and structural innovation derives not just from the social demands for use of the in-group language embodied in specific personal relationships, but from a tolerant linguistic ideology on the part of the proficient interlocutor. Like Huffines' Amish and Hill's broad-honorific speakers, Gal's older generations have no ideology of linguistic purity, only an ideology of solidarity that demands use of the minority code within the group. The pairing is not given by nature; one can imagine a tyrannical grandfather or a martinet aunt who demand both use of a particular variety and that the speaker get it right, perhaps pedantically correcting errors. (One can also imagine a young speaker avoiding those conditions of talk whenever possible. Annette Schmidt [1985c] in fact reports that older Dyirbal speakers constantly correct less proficient young speakers, but these latter can and do resort to Jambun English to avoid this merciless correction.) This raises a question of the social and sociolinguistic functions of purist ideologies, and it is of interest to consider whether there are certain stages in processes of language contact and shift at which such ideologies are more likely to arise; I will return briefly to that question in a later section.

Once we look at the suggested correlation of structural convergence to code maintenance with *speakers* as our center of interest, and consider speakers' performances as social strategies and solutions to social demands, Hamp's insight about language adaptation and survival takes on a different significance. It is probably not the case that the more "flexible" languages have been better able to survive, as the somewhat Darwinian formulation would incline us to believe. While there may be a correlation between linguistic adaptation and higher frequency of use, the adaptation does not seem to be a causal condition of this survival. If anything, Gal and Huffines suggest the causal relation is the reverse. Those social situations which enforce language survival create demands that lead to innovation and adaptation of forms. It is not the survival of the fittest that we see reflected in the coincidence of convergence and maintenance, but the declared fitting-ness of the survivors; forms that are in use under these social circumstances come to be regarded as fitting and acceptable, whatever their source.

I have drawn together here into a rather broad sketch the insights and evidence of several of the contributors. In bringing out certain questions and distinctions, this sketch overlooks several other important distinctions that may highlight conflicting findings and may render this incipient generaliza-tion about language maintenance and convergent change inappropriate. For example, we must of course consider the part of the linguistic system in which interference phenomena appear. The drift that preceded shift in American Norwegian involved extensive lexical borrowing, and especially borrowing of the "gratuitous" kind. Hamp's contrary suggestion, that adaptation accompanies survival, refers to phonological phenomena, and Huffines' correlations concern case morphology. Careful examination of whether these phenomena coincide may lead us to reconsider any generalization. It is interesting to note, for example, that Haugen's Ameri-can Norwegian speakers tolerated considerable lexical borrowing and considered their language distinct as long as the phonological and syntactic systems remained distinct; their toleration of borrowing gave way to shift.

Gumperz and Wilson (1971), in contrast, found toleration of extensive syntactic convergence in their Indian village, as long as the lexicons remained distinct; there the separate languages seemed to lead a stable and continuing existence. It may well be that certain types of convergent change are indicative of threat to language survival while others are not, and further comparison of change across subsystems may revise this most tentative model.

2.   Creative and receptive change: Symbolic resistance and capitulation?

Closely related to the question of linguistic change and language maintenance is the issue of linguistic change as a symbol of social or political resistance. In this collection, Campbell and Muntzel invoke Hill's stimulating contrast of "acts of creation" and "acts of reception" in language change. Acts of creation are changes considered "internal to the structure of the obsolescent language in that they appear to have no direct analog in the dominant language", while "acts of reception" are externally motivated, the result of influence from linguistic aspects of the dominant language. Campbell and Muntzel classify excessive glottalization in Xinca speakers as an internal act of creation because it stems from imperfect learning of the moribund language and "has nothing to do with Spanish". In contrast, a sound shift in Pipil away from a segment that is a stigmatized variant in Spanish is seen as an "unnatural sound change, externally induced due to Spanish norms".

These concepts of receptive and creative change are very useful in that they capture an important linguistic contrast between sources of innovation. However, as compared to such alternative possible labels as "convergent" and "divergent", for example, they seem also to be highly evaluative terms. Under the influence perhaps of this evaluative connotation, it is tempting to read the linguistic contrast as symbolic of significant differences in social processes as well, with receptive change symbolizing capitulation to intruding dominant forces and creative change symbolizing resistance or rejection of foreign hegemony (see Woolard 1985b). I would, however, like to explore ways in which the two kinds of change might be more similar than they appear at first glance.[5]

From the point of view of speakers' activities, both creative and receptive change are equally creative or uncreative, in that they take a given variant, evaluate it (as "good" or "bad" speech, or as either "appropriate" or "inappropriate" to the variety), and overgeneralize that evaluation. We should ask how the "receptive" change triggered in the Pipil case by the similarity between a valid native form and a stigmatized Spanish form differs from the language-internal process of hypercorrection that has led in English, for example, to the construction *For John and I*. In both situations, the stigmatization of a form is overgeneralized to other parts of a linguistic system (if we consider a bilingual repertoire a single system), where it was not originally stigmatized. While our differentiation of two systems in the bilingual's repertoire is not necessarily artificial, it is not entirely clear that either the psychological or the social processes involved in such over-generalization of stigma and resultant avoidance of a form are very different in the bilingual and monolingual cases.

More significantly, we can question whether "acts of creation" are indeed internally motivated, "having nothing to do with Spanish" in the Xinca example. Rouchdy (this volume) points out that "in the case of a minority language *versus* a dominant language, the phenomenon 'language contact' cannot really be considered as a separate issue" (emphasis mine) from internal sources of change. While that point can be debated, it is relevant here. Campbell and Muntzel explicitly recognize that the forms with which speakers go "hog-wild" are those that are marked or "exotic" from the point of view of the dominant language. So excessive glottalization in Xinca has everything to do with Spanish; sounds are overgeneralized precisely because they do not appear in Spanish, as Campbell and Muntzel have made clear in their excellent examples.

In both the receptive and the creative changes seen in these examples, the dominant code is the reference point which shapes the change in the minority language, whether the direction of that change is toward or away from the dominant variety. For that reason, the terms "convergent" and "divergent" might be preferable, rather than "receptive/creative" or "externally/internally motivated". Both convergent and divergent changes are responses to a kind of folk "contrastive analysis", and both deform language systematically in response to the contact situation.

In divergent change, the deformation is a kind of Batesonian complementary schismogenesis (Bateson 1972), a progressive differentiation of two entities through the systematic stressing of distinctive traits in interaction, resulting in a distortion of character. If we take them to be apparent acts of cultural resistance, divergent linguistic changes are a wedding of what Williams (1973a) distinguishes as residual and emergent forms of opposi-tional culture: traditional, pre-contact characteristics of the language are elaborated to the point that a different linguistic form emerges. The paradoxical symbolism of such selfdistorting resistance is similar to that which Richard Fox (1985) finds in the cultural forms of Ghandian socialism in India. Fox identifies the British influences that led to the selection and projection of certain images of Indian culture as the essence of Indianness, in service of the independence movement. In the oppositional act of creative or divergent change just as in receptive or convergent change, the indi-genous system is *reshaped through the eyes of the dominant system*.[6] This is one sense in which Bourdieu is quite right when he comments that all linguistic varieties are virtually always subject to the logic and standards of the dominant language (Bourdieu 1982; see Woolard 1985a for a discussion of the issue which is more critical of Bourdieu's point). However, the possibility of truly "autonomous" change (Dorian, pers. comm.), neither convergent nor divergent but simply on a skew line with the dominant language, has been documented by many of the researchers represented here, and must not be overlooked (see Dorian 1981, as well as several of the examples given in Campbell and Muntzel's chapter).[7]

In language change as in cultural conflict or personality development, it may be tempting to see the result of schismogenesis as somehow natural, revealing the "true" essence of the entity involved. But it does not seem to me that either convergent ("receptive") or divergent ("creative") change should be viewed as more natural than the other, since for both the first impetus comes from outside immediate linguistic practice, and for both the process is similar to internal processes of hypercorrective change. Certainly one does not want to deny the possible significance of the difference in the direction of change, but when we look closely at this kind of act of resistance from the point of view of speakers and interlocutors rather than *languages* in conflict, it is not entirely clear what the significance is, or against whom such resistance is directed.

In sociolinguistic variation within a single language, when change accentuates the distinctiveness of a speech community from others who are moving into its territory, we can interpret it as an emphatic gesture of in-group identification and solidarity. This is the case, for example, with vowel centralization discovered among young islanders on Martha's Vineyard by Labov (1965). In that example, we can interpret the accentuation and extension of local dialect features as distinguishing island-identified speakers from other speakers, summer people and tourists. The divergent change is a sociolinguistic commentary on the relations of islanders and outsiders.

However, when we get similar processes of creative internal change in bilingual situations, it is less clear what the sociolinguistic commentary is. When we think of the process with the languages as our focus, creative change seems directed toward keeping the languages apart, holding back the influence of the dominant language, and thus of the speakers or culture of the dominant language. But if we focus on speakers and their interlocutors, this interpretation clouds. In most situations of language obsolescence, it is extremely unlikely that divergent change is directed toward distinguishing in-group from out-group. Since members of the dominant speech community do not usually learn the minority language, more or less divergence in its forms will not make that language a more powerful barrier against the dominant. Divergent change in the minority code cannot be used to mark social distance in exchanges with members of the dominant group, because these are unlikely to occur in the minority code. Divergent or creative change, then, to the extent that it is a symbolic act, must be an act of differentiation internal to the minority speech community. What from a macrosociolinguistic perspective looks like a coalescence of minority group solidarity in the face of linguistic intrusion, from a microsociolinguistic, interaction-focused perspective may be seen as the development of symbolic capital (Bourdieu 1977) for internal power struggles in an incipiently differentiated community. And it may well be the more socially and economically assimilated sectors of the minority population who control and deploy this symbolic capital of minority language purity (see Hill 1985). To better understand the social meaning of divergent and convergent linguistic changes, and their connection to language shift, it will be important (although difficult) to trace the relative timing and social distribution of these kinds of changes as well as their relation to the emergence of purist ideologies.

3. Conclusion

There is a wealth of evidence in this volume that is suggestive of a causal relation, or at least a correlation, between language maintenance and linguistic convergence. In this most tentative of attempts to account for the intriguing constellations we find of linguistic conservatism and language death or linguistic adaptation and language maintenance, I have suggested we best begin by anchoring our generalizations in speakers' activities. Human actors rather than personified languages are the active agents in the processes we wish to explain, and as Gal points out, the metaphors we use affect the theories we build.

In calling for a focus on actors and speakers I am not, I hope, calling for reductionist explanations of linguistic and social phenomena. Rejection of mechanistic theories in favor of theories of human practice in no way implies that we should reduce the significance of actions to the conscious and deliberate intentions of their authors (Bourdieu 1977:73). But in order for functionalist linguistics to avoid the trap of autonomous motivation and agentless action that has proved so deadly to functionalist social theory, it is necessary to keep speakers central in our thinking and in our metaphorical formulations.

Notes

1. If my rhetorical invocation of a maritime tragedy that took the lives of so many unsuspecting holiday travelers seems too callous, I apologize to the reader. The image of a sudden tip and sinking of the apparently stable channel ferry in the early spring of 1987 is a powerful image for me of Dorian's metaphor of language "tip"; that the ship should have been named the "Herald of Free Enterprise" and that it should have sunk while attempting to cross the English Channel are

bitter ironies that make the metaphor only too apt for many cases of language obsolescence.

2. In part the answer to this question depends, of course, on the definition of "loss". As Hamp points out in his chapter, there is not always agreement about what level of language use will constitute adequate "survival", especially in discussion between native scholars and outsiders. For many language loyalists, a substantially changed variety of the mother tongue might simply not count as the same language, regardless of what speakers of the changed variety think, and it might be counted as lost or dead. So in the case Haugen reports, American Norwegian seems barely to have counted as Norwegian in the view of visitors raised in the mother country, but from the point of view of the local speech community and from that of the researcher, the Americanized Norwegian was indeed their Norwegian, and its continued use until the 1940s constituted language maintenance. It is for this sense of maintenance that we are questioning the relationship to structural change; to adopt the view that substantial change actually constitutes loss is to form a tautology, and leaves us with no question to ask.

3. My evocation here of Dorian's characterization of East Sutherland Gaelic as dying "with its morphological boots on" (Dorian 1978c) reveals one of the many problems in knowing what should be counted as a sample of a dying language. Dorian (pers. comm.) points out that the East Sutherland Gaelic she characterizes in that memorable phrase is that of semi-speakers, while Hamp's West Kintyre informants are the last *fluent* speakers of a language "at death's door", as Hamp puts it. In assessing comparatively the structural concomitants of language death, it is of course important to attend not only to the status of the community of speakers (aging, shrinking numerically, lacking younger generations of speakers, etc.), but to the position of the individual speaker within that community. Campbell and Muntzel's contribution to this volume offers a particularly lucid review of the possible types of both community and speaker situations.

4. Rather than contradicting Fishman's observation, this reading of the importance of monolingual personal relationships in determining language maintenance may simply be a step in restoring some of the complexity originally intended in the concept of "domain". Fishman has observed (pers. comm.) that the term was never meant as a synonym for physical or topical context, although it has been interpreted critically as such; as initially developed, interlocutor was an integral component of the domain concept.

5. The following discussion is in no way meant as a critique of Hill's original contrast between "acts of creation" and "acts of reception"; since I am writing from the field, I have not had an opportunity to consult the work in which she develops those terms, and so proceed with apologies to her. My comments are based more on possible interpretations and connotations of the distinction which have occurred to me and may occur to others; my position in fact owes much to insights developed in other writings by Hill, cited here.

6. In her review of Scollon and Scollon's characterization of American Indian communicative styles, Jane Hill (1983b) has noted previously the importance of this schismogenic interaction with the dominant group in creating the communicative patterns we may take to be most essentially characteristic of a given minority group.

7. Additionally, as Dorian points out (pers. comm.), languages being the compli-

cated structures that they are, the "logic and standards" of the dominant language will have several dimensions, which could point toward multiple possibilities for change in any given case. When we have classified a change as convergent/divergent (or receptive/creative), we have not done with explaining it.

24 Pidgins, creoles, immigrant and dying languages

SUZANNE ROMAINE

In dealing with the similarities and differences between dying languages, pidgins, creoles, and immigrant languages, I will concentrate my remarks on two areas: the nature of the sociolinguistic context which gives rise to these varieties of language, and structural factors common to these cases. Finally, I will draw some conclusions about the implications of the study of these languages for linguistic theory and suggest some directions for further research.

In attempting to sketch a sociolinguistic profile of the context in which pidgins, creoles, dying, and immigrant languages emerge, the most general factor that can be mentioned is that of language contact. Seuren (1984:209) says that whatever is universal in creoles is also characteristic of contact languages of any kind that get turned into native languages. Even leaving aside the question of how much nativization owes to universals, at the moment there is not enough systematic descriptive and theoretical work in language contact to draw up a typology of parameters from the relevant cases. This collection is a particularly useful beginning.

I will not single out immigrant languages as a special case because immigrant languages may of course be as healthy as varieties of these languages spoken elsewhere. Typically, however, for a variety of political and social reasons, which many of the contributors here discuss in detail, they aren't. The fact that healthier varieties of these languages exist elsewhere for comparison is in many ways a methodological advantage. Another, on occasion, is the existence of a range of communities using a restricted variety for different purposes (see, for example, Huffines on Pennsylvania German, Mithun on Cayuga, also Hamp 1978 and this volume). This allows us at least some purchase on the question of which social factors in a contact setting have greater impact. Another advantage is the availability of a pidgin or creole variety with a superstrate which is the same as the restricted variety. For example, what is the status of French-based creoles by comparison with immigrant varieties of French? It is no accident that many of the pidgin and creole languages of the world have

European language bases. The very expansion in the political power of these language communities which led to the pidginization and creolization of their languages in a variety of colonial settings is a sign, if indeed a somewhat unpleasant one, of their former health.

However, there are parts of the world where the languages of former colonial powers (such as German, French, and Spanish) are undergoing attrition as minority languages. These afford the most direct comparisons with pidgins and creoles of a related base. In some cases a language may exist in pidginized or creolized form, in several immigrant varieties with differing degrees of vitality, as well as in its full form with social and regional variation. Spanish, French and Arabic are such cases. Although French is represented here (see King, also Mougeon and Beniak), it is unfortunate that Spanish and Arabic aren't.

1.   Sociolinguistic factors in language contact

It is important to point out at this stage that it would be misguided to compare dying languages with pidgins and creoles without at first attempting to delimit these phenomena in more precise linguistic and social terms (see Aitchison 1983 for a discussion of problems in making sweeping comparisons between child language, pidgins, and creoles).

Defining pidgins and creoles is easier said than done (see section 3 below on defining language death). Although all scholars agree that there is a group of languages called pidgins and creoles, one of the biggest disputes at present is how they are to be defined, and whether, for example, a pidgin history is a prerequisite for a creole. Pidgins can be recognized as a special or limiting case of reduction in form resulting from restriction in use, but their complexity will range from relatively rudimentary (e.g. Chinook Jargon) to fairly complex (e.g. Tok Pisin). Creolization can occur at any stage in the developmental continuum from jargon to expanded pidgin.

This means, among other things, that purely formal criteria cannot serve to distinguish a pidgin from a creole. Definitions such as those proposed by Bickerton (1981) and others ignore the fact that pidgins and creoles are developing systems which may overlap in terms of structural complexity reached at any point in their life cycle depending on their functions. Mühlhäusler (1979) has shown how in the case of Tok Pisin, an expanding pidgin currently undergoing creolization in Papua New Guinea, structural expansion is concomitant with functional spread.

Now that we begin to have a substantial body of case studies of language death it may be possible to identify stages in the life cycle of dying languages which are marked by differing degrees of social and structural contraction (section 3 below). One reason why researchers may fail to identify similarities among dying languages is that they are comparing entities which are not at comparable stages of development.

I will turn now more specifically to some social similarities among dying languages, pidgins, and creoles. The authors here cite a range of contributory social factors which accompany language death. These appear, for the most part, to be consequent on basic inequalities which may exist between the users of languages with differing prestige, utility, and recognized legitimacy in situations of contact. Many of these same features accompany colonization and have led to pidginization in some cases and/or to language death (see e.g. Sankoff 1980a). Among these features are: encroaching diglossia (cf. Dimmendaal), failure of children to acquire the mother tongue, schooling in a second language, resettlement, dispersion and intermarriage (see Bradley). In other words, the value of these language varieties on what Sankoff and Laberge (1978) call the "linguistic marketplace" is low.

Nevertheless, studies of all these varieties are of central importance because they challenge the status which a number of notions, such as competence, native speaker, speech community, etc., have occupied in linguistic theory and/or sociolinguistics. Linguists have given a special place to the native speaker as the most reliable source for data which provide input to linguistic theories (see e.g. Chomsky 1965). It was of course Dorian (1977b) who first brought to light in a systematic way the problem of semi-speakers and their somewhat less than ideal competence and who discussed the methodological implications of their existence for the study of language death. Studies of language contact such as those of Dorian (1981) and Silva-Corvalán (1986) have shown that a proficiency continuum may develop between two languages in contact, which resembles in some respects a creole continuum. Individuals can be located at various points along it depending on their level of dominance and/or proficiency in one or other of the languages.

In cases where languages are dying or undergoing functional restriction, difficulties arise in determining basic matters such as who is a speaker of the language or a member of the community which speaks a particular language. Watson, for instance, notes that it is not clear to outsiders or even to the oldest members of Irish and Scottish Gaelic-speaking communities who can speak the language and who cannot. The youngest speakers may not always be aware of the full extent of their linguistic abilities.

Pidgins have often been defined as "nobody's first language" (see e.g. Todd 1974). Expanded pidgins such as Tok Pisin and West African Pidgin English, however, may show a range of uses equivalent to those which a native speaker of a nonpidgin language might command. Both these languages have viable creole communities while continuing to serve as second languages for most of their speakers. In such a situation a speaker's dominant language may not be the first acquired. Mafeni (1971:112), for example, writes of his own language skills: "I have the feeling I speak Pidgin more fluently than any other Nigerian language which I know and use.

Although my mother tongue is Isako, Yoruba seems to be the dominant substrate in my variety of Pidgin." Failure to distinguish between qualitatively different stages in the development of languages which have been given the label "pidgin" can rise to the kind of misleading view put forward by Labov about competence. Labov (1970/77) claims that full competence in a pidgin grammar is still less than competence in one's native grammar. For some like Mafeni, a pidgin grammar *is* a native grammar.

A related problem is that of the speech community (see Labov 1980 on the question of whether there is a creole speech community, and Dorian 1982a). Usually definitions of the speech community make reference to shared norms of use and evaluation. However, these matters are problematic enough even for healthy speech communities (see e.g. the papers in Romaine 1982b), let alone the "communities" in which dying languages, pidgins, and creoles are spoken. A common theoretical concern which needs to be addressed by researchers is the referential and stylistic adequacy of these languages (see e.g. Rickford 1986) for certain discourse functions and semantic domains.

The kind of stylistic shrinkage noted by Campbell and Muntzel, Taylor, and Mithun is a clear example of a linguistic change which is functionally motivated. I found Hill's chapter one of the most interesting because it addresses the decline in one particular structure from a functional perspective. She ties together under the notion of solidarity encoding factors such as intimacy and low power differential between interlocutors and treats the linguistic consequences of these.

In general, the pattern is for formal stylistic options to be reduced, as discussed by Hill (1973). Mougeon and Beniak, however, have documented shrinkage at the informal end of the stylistic continuum as a result of the confinement of the use of the minority language to formal settings, such as school. The same is true of some minority languages in Britain, where the main institution of transmission is religious school. Expanding pidgins show an increase in stylistic range. An interesting question is whether children or adults contribute more to these changes.

Bavin found that children were introducing changes into the pronominal system of Warlpiri. It may be that in a community of expanded-pidgin or dying-language speakers the innovations of children have a better chance of catching on than in "normal" communities. It is interesting that Bavin found that mothers were introducing some English animal names into Warlpiri Baby-Talk register since I found that one area in which there was increasing anglicization in young children's Tok Pisin was in the semantic domain of animal terms (see Romaine 1988:4.4).

In normal communities the expectation is that adults act as brakes on the innovations produced by children so that analogical and other deviant forms like *foots* get corrected and do not persist. In the case of dying and pidgin languages it may be that children have greater scope to act as norm-makers due to the fact that a great deal of variability exists among the adult community. Mougeon and Beniak cite evidence to support the developmental origin of some of the processes of simplification in Ontarian French. Simplified forms can persist in the speech of children in English-dominant homes presumably because there is little corrective pressure or model.

One of the changes which I have been documenting in young children's creolized Tok Pisin is the use of short forms as the result of the introduction of rules of morphophonemic condensation. Among the short forms in use are the following: *laus* [<*long haus* 'at home'], *disa/disla* [<*dispela-* 'the/ this'], and *blol* [<*bilong ol-* 'theirs'] (see Romaine and Wright 1987). The more basic a pidgin is, the more likely it is that its speakers will rely on strategies which maximize naturalness of encoding and decoding. It is only in a community of fluent second and first language speakers that rules which greatly enhance rate of production will have a chance of acceptance. While these rules simplify output at one level, and make it easier for the speaker to articulate at a faster rate and increase stylistic flexibility, they complicate the decoding process and increase the likelihood of comprehension difficulties. One effect of the introduction of allegro speech styles is an increase in depth of the phonological component, so that surface forms become derivable by rule from underlying form.

The term *simplification* figures prominently in discussions of pidgins and creoles and dying languages. However, it has to be used with caution. Hymes (1971:72), for example, distinguishes between what is simple for the speaker in terms of production and what is simple for the hearer in terms of perception. Corder (1975) distinguishes structurally-simple codes, e.g. foreigner talk, from the simplified use of a complex code, e.g. caretakers' speech to babies.

There has of course been a great deal of discussion among creolists about the significance of creolization, i.e. the presence of native speakers in bringing about the changes that accompany expansion. G. Sankoff and Laberge (1973) observe that the presence of native speakers of a language does not necessarily create sudden and dramatic changes in a language, but their presence may be one factor in influencing its direction. In the case of shortened forms in Tok Pisin, it may be true that a certain amount of this reduction is part of the normal tendency at this stage in children's acquisition, which accelerates this part of the expansion phase of the language as a whole. If so, then over time, we would expect that as children got older, more short forms would expand in conformity with the norms of adult speech in general.

Other methodological consequences follow from the functional restriction of speaker and community repertoires. Since loss of variability often accompanies restriction, a problem for both the historical linguist and the sociolinguist is how to reconstruct prior stages with possibly richer morphophonemic alternation and variability differentiated according to a number of social parameters, such as style, ethnicity, age, sex, etc. – for example, in Gros Ventre the demise of male forms of speaking and the survival of the female forms (Taylor). Often only age-graded variability remains. A number of the contributors support Dorian's findings for East Sutherland Gaelic; namely, variability is often unaccompanied by stratification along the familiar social dimensions of class, style, sex, etc. (see further in section 2 below).

Another common factor is the affective value ascribed to these languages. Watson's anecdote of an elderly woman traveler ready to place her trust in and accompany anyone who spoke Gaelic finds parallels in other places. In many creole-speaking communities, like Haiti, the creole is the language of truth and solidarity. To speak French is synonymous with duplicity and falsehood; to talk creole is to talk straight (see Rickford and Traugott 1985 for a discussion of attitudes).

Kuter says that the negative and positive attitudes attached by Bretons to French and Breton are the key variable in the transmission of these languages. She identifies a number of differing symbolic values which are attached to the two languages, e.g. political, social, cultural, and economic. Watson notes the importance attached to speaking what community members regard as the "right Gaelic" and the incredulity with which he was met as a researcher wanting to learn what members often regarded as an inferior and incorrect way of speaking (see also Rouchdy). I have encountered the same reaction in both pidgin-speaking and immigrant-language communities. In Papua New Guinea, for example, people were surprised that I was interested in children's acquisition of Tok Pisin rather than English, since it is knowledge of English which is desirable and prestigious. There are many who still regard Tok Pisin as a corrupted form of English. In Britain, while working in the Panjabi-speaking community I encountered the attitude that Panjabi which was mixed with English was not "real" or "pure" Panjabi (see Chana and Romaine 1984). There is an almost inherent conflict here between the desire to adopt English loanwords as prestige markers and their condemnation as foreign elements destroying the purity of the borrowing language.

Relexification is often an impending threat to the maintenance of the structural integrity of the minority language (see e.g. Tsitsipis, Bavin, also Mougeon and Beniak). This may be true for many creoles, such as Tok Pisin. It is a sign of increasing metalinguistic awareness that many speakers of Tok Pisin are now beginning to recognize different varieties of the language and to stigmatize those (particularly urban ones) that are heavily anglicized (see Romaine 1986 for a discussion of language mixing and judgements of language purism).

This highlights the problem too of notions like shared competence or shared grammar and lexicon throughout a community (see Tsitsipis) whose productive and receptive skills vary enormously. Maandi's chapter shows how sensitivity to correctness may in fact increase over subsequent generations (cf. however, Schmidt 1985c). Rouchdy, however, found an asymmetry between assessments of grammatical deviance and speakers' productive norms. These differences may again reflect differences in developmental stages.

The importance of religion and home as domains emerges in a number of the chapters as a decisive factor either in language maintenance or in fostering linguistic differences. Haugen, for example, notes how the Norwegian language and a strong degree of religious cohesion were instruments of union and a barrier against rival English-speaking Protestant sects (see also Huffines on differences between sectarian and nonsectarian German). Missionaries are often important standardizing forces for pidgin languages: different policies in Papua New Guinea, for example, have led to differences in the lexicon of Tok Pisin.

Mougeon and Beniak address the problem of shift in home use and the failure of the francophone community to renew itself due to a high rate of exogamy. Many researchers of immigrant languages have identified the inter-generational shift to the new language in the domain of the home as decisive for language shift and death. Family cohesion and traditional values of respect for elders etc. are also cited by Haugen as factors promoting the retention of Norwegian (see also Mertz on the effect of Gaelic-speaking grandparents in Cape Breton homes). This is also true in other immigrant communities, such as the Panjabi-speaking one in Britain. Parents fear that children's inability to speak the home language will prevent communication with the older generation. It can be a potential embarrassment when older relatives visit.

The role of the school as a factor in creating a negative identity for the minority language is mentioned by Kuter and by Haugen. The idea that retention of an immigrant language, or a pidgin, e.g. in countries like Papua New Guinea, where the official medium of education is English, interferes with the acquisition of the dominant language is well documented (e.g. Mertz). Efforts made by educators to eradicate the use of the minority language are often seen by the communities themselves as well intentioned. Many parents of Southeast Asian origin in Britain have been led to believe that bilingualism is inherently problematic and confusing for their children.

2.   Structural consequences of language contact

Among the linguistic effects common to situations of language contact are the following: convergence, loss of morphological and syntactic complexity, and an overall increase in semantic transparency. Dressler and Wodak-Leodolter (1977) were among the first to suggest an analogy between language death and pidginization, while Trudgill (1978) drew parallels between language death and creolization in referring to the former as a kind of "creolization in reverse". The problem here hinges again on the appropriate stages of development at which to make such comparisons. A main source of developments in creolization is the grammaticalization of distinctions and the movement from a more pragmatic to a more syntactic mode of communication. In language death the reverse is true.

The distinction between pragmatic and syntactic modes of communication is drawn by Givón (1979b). The process of syntacticization involves a move away from a more transparent iconic mode of communication to a more abstract and less obviously iconic one. Givón claims that this process is a pervasive fact of language change, language ontogeny, and language evolution.

A number of linguists have tried to explain the similarities which pidginized speech varieties show in the expression of grammatical categories and syntactic relationships by appealing to more general principles of linguistic organization motivated by specialization to the referential function. One such principle is that of paradigmatic univocity, as defined, for example, by Hjelmslev (1938:285). This refers to cases in which there is a stable relationship between form and meaning. It has been variously formulated and applied to first language acquisition (see e.g. Slobin's [1973] *Operating Principles*), second language acquisition (see e.g. Andersen's [1984a] *One-to-One Principle*), and/or creolization (see Naro's [1978:340–1] *factorization principle* and Seuren and Wekker's [1986] *semantic transparency*).

A preference for analytical, as opposed to synthetic, syntax is a hallmark of both pidgins and dying languages. Among other things, this means that languages which have a greater degree of morphological and syntactic complexity are the most interesting ones to investigate. Case syncretism and reduction of polysynthesis (see Mithun) are consequences of the trend towards a more analytical structure.

Concomitant with their tendency to eliminate allomorphy, pidgins often display a fixed and invariable word order. In Haiman's (1985:162) terms they avoid *allotaxy*, i.e. the use of different word orders to signal the expression of the same grammatical relationships. For example, in Standard German different word orders are required in main and subordinate clauses. Rabaul Creole German, however, has SVO word order in both (see also Stammler 1922–3 on the immigrant German spoken in Estonia). Other pidgins such as Pidgin Fijian and Chinook Jargon show a tendency towards SVO order, which cannot be attributed to transfer. Standard Fijian has a preference for VSO. Similarly, Thomason (1983a:844) says that SVO is not a statistically dominant word order pattern in any of the Indian languages spoken in the northwest. The basic word order is VSO.

Givón (1979) has claimed that SVO is the most common word order in pidgins because it is the easiest to process. In languages in which subjects precede objects, the possibility of confusion between the two is reduced.

The invariable nature of pidgin word order leads to a greater isomorphism between form and meaning. Because young pidgins are weakly grammaticalized, they depend heavily on context for their interpretation. Markey (1982) cites SVO word order as a defining characteristic of creoles too. He notes (1982:179) that SVO is the typical order for analytical languages, and that contact situations appear to precipitate a change towards this ordering pattern. Hymes (1971:73) has observed that these tendencies toward invariance in form and reliance on SVO word order have in common that they minimize the knowledge a speaker must have and the speed with which he must decode.

Unlike many pidgins and creoles, dying languages do not on the whole show a tendency to uniformity of word order. Moreover, there are pidgins and creoles which do not show SVO word order, e.g. Hiri Motu, an indigenous pidgin of Papua New Guinea, which is OSV. Trader Navajo, like Navajo is VSO, and Eskimo Trade Jargon is SOV. Mithun (this volume) found that the pragmatic basis of Cayuga word order remained intact. Dorian (1981:155) reports that even semi-speakers of East Sutherland Gaelic retained word order. Rouchdy, however, found an apparent change in the word order of urban Nubian bilinguals from verb-final to SVO, possibly under the influence of colloquial Egyptian Arabic (see also Maandi). In this case it is unclear whether to attribute the Egyptian development to convergence or a general tendency towards the use of a pragmatically unmarked strategy. Changes in word order were, however, rejected by competent bilinguals.

Many of the structural economies that result from language death arise by dint of analogy (see e.g. Taylor). An interesting question is the extent to which on-going changes in dying languages can be attributed to internal independent development or influence from the dominant languages. Bavin, for example, says that semantic transparency is an internally motivated change. Rouchdy observes that the phenomenon of language contact cannot be separated from the issue of decreasing usage. A similar question plagues pidgin and creole studies: namely, the extent to which developments follow internal universals which operate independently of substratum or superstratum influence. A related question is the extent to which normal contact-induced change can be distinguished from changes due to the language death situation. Huffines, for example, notes that the absence of some case distinctions is well within the bounds of regional variation in German, but it also characterizes immigrant varieties of German in the United States. Silva-Corvalán (1986) claims that convergence may result from internally motivated changes in one of the languages in contact as well as from transfer.

Another issue of relevance is that of the role of universals vs. transfer or substratum at particular stages. Dorian (1981), for example, says that most of the changes which are on-going in East Sutherland Gaelic cannot be explained as interference from English. Similarly, Silva-Corvalán attaches more significance to universals than transfer. She observes, however, that transfer may play a role once certain forms have been lost. At this stage, and under pressure to communicate a particular message, bilinguals make use of the forms available to them in the recessive language, but tend to distribute them according to the syntactic and semantic rules of the dominant language. It may be possible to isolate a single factor. It may also be that the more divergent the structures in the two languages are, the less likely transfer is.

The hypotheses proposed by Campbell and Muntzel are a useful starting point for examining some of the phonological similarities between pidgins and creoles and dying languages. They claim (following Andersen 1982:95) that the bilingual will make fewer phonological distinctions than a monolingual, but preserve features common to both languages, especially those with a greater functional load. Bender (1987) has proposed that constraints on phonological inventories and phonotactics may be part of a set of pan-creole features (see also Johnson 1974 on morpheme structure rules). Hall (1966) and others have commented on the small size or reduction of pidgin phonological inventories when compared to their lexifier or substratum languages. The same has been noted in connection with the number of phonological contrasts (see also Mithun for constraints on syllable structure in Oklahoma Cayuga and child Mohawk). A number of marked sounds in the lexifier language tend to be represented by a single phoneme in the pidgin. Thus, in Fanagalo as used by speakers of non-Bantu languages, the clicks are replaced by /k/. In Fanagalo words tend to be bisyllabic, whereas in Zulu they tend to be trisyllabic (see Heine 1979).

Pronunciation has often been singled out as the area where substratum influence can be felt most strongly. While many have noted the tendency for marked forms to be replaced by unmarked ones, it is evident that the phonologies of stabilized pidgins do not simply represent the lowest common denominator of the languages involved. However, whether or not these generalities in surface phonological structure are due to substratum influence or universal natural phonological processes, there are some difficult exceptions to explain (see e.g. Hamp, this volume). For example, although consonant clusters do not occur in Tahitian, they do in Pitcairnese, which stabilized from the contact between Tahitians and the mutineers from the Bounty on Pitcairn and Norfolk Islands (see Ross and Moverley 1964).

Campbell and Muntzel also note the overgeneralization of marked features in ways inappropriate for healthy varieties of the language. A well-known case from an immigrant language is the survival and overuse of retroflexion by second generation Indian speakers (see e.g. Trinidadian vs. South African Bhojpuri; on the latter variety, see Mesthrie 1985). Hill and Hill (1980) refer to use of features in this way as acts of creation. New linguistic forms within an old language can be interpreted as the creation of a new code of solidarity. I think they may be in many cases acts of creation of a social identity (e.g. in the sense of Le Page and Tabouret-Keller 1985). This shows the importance of the symbolic factors discussed in section 1 above in affecting the creativity of speakers (see also Gal). It illustrates too that social factors may constrain the operation of linguistic tendencies towards unmarking, but there is no warrant for supposing that pidgins, creoles, and dying languages are special in this regard.

One of the important differences identified by Dorian (1983) between pidgins and dying languages is the retention of a considerable amount of morphological complexity by the latter (see also Mithun, also Mougeon and Beniak). Moreover, as noted earlier, both dying languages and pidgins may have a considerable amount of variation in the absence of social correlates (see e.g. King, Bavin). As pointed out by Mougeon and Beniak, the reduction of register range entails a loss in variability. The same would apply for pidgins, which at least in their early stages of development, do not have stylistic options. Thus, the kind of variability found in some pidgins and dying languages does not appear to be functionally motivated. Particularly in the case of young pidgins, it appears to be largely idiosyncratic and tied to native language background. Campbell and Muntzel cite the development of optional rules from obligatory ones as a feature of language death, as in the failure of American Finnish speakers to apply the consonant gradation rules.

This might be one sense in which the term *degrammaticalization* can be used.[1] Pidgins undergoing expansion or creolization show the reverse process, in that a major portion of the changes they undergo serve to grammaticalize distinctions that were only variably marked, if indeed marked at all. Independent words become grammaticalized and begin to exhibit allomorphy. Reduced forms become crystallized and obligatory. They are then reinforced by independent words, giving rise to agreement systems (see the discussion of the cliticization of the subject pronoun *he* in Tok Pisin by Sankoff 1977).

It is by no means clear that all of the kinds of changes which typically accompany the expansion or creolization of a pidgin involve an increase in complexity. Similarly, not all changes in dying languages result in its loss. Some of the former lead to stylistic flexibility without apparently increasing the referential power of the grammar, e.g. the short forms in Tok Pisin. This is mirrored by a similar tendency in dying languages towards the elimination of forms with the same meaning, which amounts to a reduction in stylistic options.

Gal identifies lexical contraction as a factor affecting productivity. Lack of base forms to apply word-formation rules to, rather than lack of knowledge of the rules themselves, is at the root of the observation made by many that there is a loss of productivity of morphological processes in language death. Those word-formation rules which appear with the highest frequency in the speech of those with a broad range of use of Hungarian are the ones that less frequent users employ innovatively. Pidgins typically lack word-formation rules, but acquire them as part of the expansion phase (see Mühlhäusler 1979).

A number of researchers have noted that the kinds of changes which take place in language death are just ordinary changes speeded up. A similar point has been made in connection with the evolutionary pace of creoles. Some such as Markey (1982:173) estimate that thirty years in the life cycle of a creole might well be equivalent to three centuries in the life cycle of a non-creole.

3.   Some theoretical implications for further research

Language contact is a sufficient cause neither for death nor for pidginization and/or creolization. None of the factors mentioned here, separately or together, is an absolute predictor of language death, but they do tend to accompany situations in which languages are dying. If it's of any consolation to the specialist in language death, creolists have failed to identify anything unique in the social context which gives rise to creolization (see e.g. Romaine 1984b). Hymes (1971:5) has remarked that pidginization and creolization represent the extreme to which social factors can go in shaping the transmission and use of language. However, there does not seem to be a common set of socio-historical factors which give rise to creoles.

The concern to identify characteristic features of language death is of interest not only to linguists. When speaking to members of minority communities in Britain, I have frequently been asked whether, for example, languages like Panjabi are dying or will die in subsequent generations. The notion of death carries a stigma (see e.g. Bavin's opening assertion that Warlpiri is not yet a dying language). Community members often want to ask linguists if certain patterns of language use like codeswitching are signs of incipient death.

Dorian's interpretation of the biological metaphor of death relies on external criteria; namely, a language dies when it no longer has any speakers. For various reasons, such as the existence of semi-speakers etc., the actual endpoint may in practice be impossible to delimit. Pidgins and creoles too may die. When the social circumstances which bring a pidgin into being as a useful vehicle for trade cease, as in the case of Russenorsk, the language is no longer used.

This raises many questions. Is there any sense in which a coherent notion of death can be defined in linguistic terms? That is, is there a point beyond which a system cannot change without its structural integrity being undermined to such an extent that it ceases to be a continuation of the "same" system? This question has been addressed by those studying pidgins and creoles (see e.g. Hall 1966:116). For example, the term *decreolization* is generally used to refer to a process of change which results in a merger of the creole with its superstratum language. Alternatively, as in the case of Berbice Dutch, it may be relexified and its lexical origins obscured. Some linguists have also argued that Black English in the United States represents a case where extensive and nearly complete decreolization has obscured creole origins. Not enough is known about the life cycles of creoles (see DeCamp 1971:349; Romaine 1987:ch.5).

Researchers of language death could profit from catastrophe theory models (see Thom 1975). There has been until recently a general reluctance among linguists to treat language mixing and borrowing as systematic, rule-governed phenomena. The relative contribution of catastrophic vs. ordinary evolutive change in pidginization, creolization, and language death needs to be examined.

There do not seem to be any clear criteria for determining how much mixture there must be in any given case of language contact before deciding that we are dealing with a case of pidginization or creolization as distinct from the effects of borrowing and interference. In connection with a case of language contact persisting over several centuries in the Indian village of Kupwar, involving unrelated languages, Gumperz and Wilson (1971:151;165) note that it "can result in such far-reaching changes that the affected language assumes a different structural type". There seems to be no reason therefore to draw an a priori distinction among pidginization, creolization, and other diffusion processes; the difference may be merely one of degree. "The Kupwar varieties have processes of reduction and convergence suggestive of pidginization and creolization. To say that the varieties have in fact undergone these processes would of course be misleading, if creolization is defined as requiring a pidgin as its starting point. We have no evidence of a pidgin-stage in the history of the village, or reason to suspect one." They conclude that the present state of the languages is creole-like, in that grammatical structure and lexical shape have different sources. However, they are unlike pidgins in that Kupwar varieties seem to have undergone "re-syntactification" rather than relexification. The latter is thought to be a major process in pidginization.

Some have used the term *creole* to refer to the process of adaptation which has led to the convergence of influence from two different input languages. (Others, like Whinnom [1971], reserve the term *creole* for cases where two or more substratum languages are involved.) Remnants of this kind of convergence include the fact that many forms can be assigned competing etymologies. In Tok Pisin, for example, some attribute the origin of the word *bel* 'stomach, belly, seat of emotions' to English, but in Tolai, the most important substratum language involved in Tok Pisin's development, there is a word *bala* meaning 'stomach, seat of emotions'.

It would be wrong to attach too much importance to the process of creolization as the unique source of universal grammar. Even Bickerton

(1984b:148) has recently noted that studies of language contact can provide support for the bioprogram hypothesis. Some bioprogram features may emerge when languages undergo extreme forms of change such as from SOV to SVO word order. The fact that bioprogram-like features surface in other contact situations, which are qualitatively different from those which produce creoles, but give rise, nonetheless, to some of the same features as creolization, is evidence that the bioprogram does not self-destruct, as claimed in Bickerton (1981). The convergence in Kupwar discussed earlier is such a case.

More work needs to be done on language in general with a view to testing bioprogram predictions in core areas of grammar. One could ask, for instance, why it is that all natural languages do not gradually evolve towards creoles? Why aren't they gradually modified by the children of each new generation into a form that is closer to creoles? Bickerton would argue that the presence of a target would override the influence of the bioprogram. Some of the similarities which exist between dying languages and creoles may be due at least partially, as suggested above, to the relaxing of norms (cf. however, Schmidt 1985c).

An exemplary study done by Silva-Corvalán (1986a) looked specifically at changes which were taking place in the verb morphology used to mark tense, mood and aspect in the speech of Spanish–English bilinguals in Los Angeles. She found a progressive simplification and loss of verbal morphemes marking tense, mood, and aspect. She was able to establish a series of eight implicationally ordered stages in this progressive simplification. What is of particular relevance for the discussion here is her argument that these stages conformed to a predictable trend to develop a least-grammaticalized system. There are five separate systems which represent a steady move towards a less grammaticalized system, which relies heavily on context.

Among the first distinctions to be lost are in the area of modality, e.g. the subjunctive and conditional (see also Trudgill 1978 on Arvanítika). The last distinction to disappear is the past with present relevance, or the present perfect. This category overlaps with Bickerton's [anterior], one of the basic distinctions encoded in the bioprogram, and thus alleged to be present in true creoles. Its pervasiveness might be taken as an indication of its basicness. However, this basicness could also be the result of biological universals or more general principles of markedness, such as those discussed, for example by Muysken (1981a) for tense, mood and aspect systems. His hierarchy too would predict the loss of more marked tense forms like the future and past perfect, if we assume that contact involves a progressive unmarking. Silva-Corvalán, however, suggests that the pattern of change for the preterite and the imperfect may be an indication that the location of matter in time, i.e. tense, is more crucial than signaling, at least morphologically, certain aspectual distinctions. This would not appear to follow predictions made by Bickerton and others about the primacy of aspect over tense.

More work should address the question of whether the features which are closest to the bioprogram are the last to be lost (see Jakobson 1972:60 on the principle of irreversible solidarity, which predicts that the dissolution of the linguistic sound system in aphasia is an exact mirror-image of the phonological development in child language). The notion of markedness will, however, like that of simplification, have to be clarified, and some attention will need to be given to the relationship between the two.

It is evident that a number of the processes observed in pidginization, creolization, and the historical development of languages appear to have their own seemingly internally-targeted trajectories (see e.g. Slobin 1977 for a discussion of some of the parallels). Implicational patterns of loss such as those identified by Silva-Corvalán will be particularly important in testing predictions about universal stages of development. There are a number of phenomena in first and second language acquisition and creolization which appear to be governed by implicational hierarchies, e.g. relativization (see Romaine 1984a), and number marking (see Mühlhäusler 1981). These features will provide useful points of comparison.

Notes

1. This is not in the sense in which, e.g. Kuryłowicz (1975), would have used it to refer to cases in which a derivational category grammaticalizes to an inflectional category, which then lexicalizes or degrammaticalizes to a derivational category.

25 The "up" and "down" staircase in secondary language development

ROGER W. ANDERSEN

The primary objective of second language acquisition (SLA) research is to uncover the principles which govern the process by which someone moves from no knowledge of a second language through various intermediate "stages" towards near-native control of the second language. This book provides an opportunity to view some of these principles from a different vantage point as well as an opportunity possibly to provide some new insights into the process of language obsolescence.

The standard view of second language acquisition (by immigrants and their children)[1] makes it seem as if the chronologically first-acquired language will always be totally native and "successful" and any subsequent languages will be nonnative and often unsuccessfully acquired. The cases discussed in this volume show how one-sided the standard view of SLA is: SLA often proceeds the way it does because of inadequate access to and interaction with the people who speak and use the "second" language as their primary, fully-developed native language, not just because it is not the native ("first") language of the learner. Immigrants typically have restricted access to the situations where they can successfully acquire the language of the country to which they have immigrated. Second- and third-generation speakers of a contracting or dying language are similarly limited in their access to the type of linguistic input and interaction that is necessary for them to become or remain competent speakers of their ancestral language. From this perspective, languages being partially acquired and dying languages seem very similar. My purpose in this commentary is to suggest why they are so similar.

I argue in the following pages that many of the linguistic consequences of language contraction and death discussed in the chapters in this book are consistent with two major principles of second language development and that this similarity between second language acquisition ("growth") and language obsolescence ("erosion", "contraction", "reduction", etc.) is not accidental: Expanding and shrinking linguistic repertoires are both constrained by the same cognitive processes which govern language acquisition and use in general. The first principle I will discuss, the *One-to-One*

Principle, applies to both first and second language acquisition, whereas the second principle, the *Transfer to Somewhere Principle*, is uniquely a principle of *second* language development.

Language contraction is typically a phenomenon of second language development in that the weaker, contracting language is almost always a secondary language for the speaker, even though it may be the speaker's original mother tongue (being the "first" acquired and the family language). It is for this reason that it is important to view language contraction from a second language perspective.[2] And adding language contraction to the set of linguistic phenomena to be accounted for by second language acquisition theory puts important demands on the validity of proposed principles of second language development.

1.   Simplification and transfer

Language contraction, almost by definition, seems to involve reduction to fewer forms, fewer oppositions. The contributors to this book refer to such types of reduction as loss of case markers (e.g. Maandi, on Estonian in Sweden; Huffines, on Pennsylvania German) and agreement markers (e.g. Campbell and Muntzel, dual and plural in Ocuilteco; Bavin, in loss of an inclusive–exclusive distinction in Walpiri; Mougeon and Beniak, in loss of the 3rd person plural inflection in Welland French). Such reduction is frequently attributed to some sort of process of "simplification" or the influence of another language (usually the language of the larger community or nation) or some combined influence of both. The two processes of simplification and transfer seem to account for a majority of the linguistic consequences of language contraction and death discussed in the chapters of this book. I will discuss these two processes within the context of recent SLA research. More specifically, I will claim that "simplification" is the surface result of a process whereby each linguistic form is uniquely linked to one and only one intended meaning (or function) and that language transfer (or interference) operates only in conjunction with this and related cognitive operating principles. Both principles (the One-to-One Principle and the Transfer to Somewhere Principle) follow naturally from inherent cognitive processing constraints in the acquisition and use of natural languages.

2.   Principles of language acquisition

2.1.   *Cognitive processing of linguistic input*

It is clear from such studies as Brown (1973) and Peters (1977, 1983, 1985) for first language acquisition and Hakuta (1974, 1976), Huang and Hatch (1978), and Wong-Fillmore (1976, 1979) for second language acquisition that both first and second language learners are fully capable of perceiving and extracting meaningful segments of language from the input directed to them. Such a capacity for perceiving, analyzing, storing and somehow organizing in memory meaningful bits and pieces of language without any formal instruction must be an important prerequisite for any language learning. Slobin (1985a) incorporates Peters' (1985) principles for perceiving, storing and tagging such segments of speech into his revised group of forty *Operating Principles* for first language acquisition. He restates Peters' eight basic principles as the first eight of his forty, since they are prerequisites to all the others. Four examples of these initial operating principles are (Slobin 1985a:1251–2):

ATTENTION PRINCIPLES:
  SOUNDS: Store any perceptually salient stretches of speech.
  STRESS: Pay attention to stressed syllables in extracted speech units. Store such syllables separately and also in relation to the units with which they occur.

STORAGE PRINCIPLES:
  FREQUENCY: Keep track of the frequency of occurrence of every unit and pattern that you store.
  UNITS: Determine whether a newly extracted stretch of speech seems to be the same as or different from anything you have already stored. If it is different, store it separately; if it is the same, take note of this sameness by increasing its frequency count by one.

In addition to perceiving and storing such segments, the learner must impose some organization on them within his memory, so that they can be retrieved rapidly and accurately and integrated into the stream of speech during production (as well as utilized during comprehension).[3]

The psycholinguistic constraints on speech perception and production are well known (see, for example, Clark and Clark 1977). Within a psycholinguistic framework, Clahsen (1984) draws on three language processing constraints to explain the order of acquisition of a number of word order and negative placement rules in German by non-instructed immigrant workers in West Germany. He concludes that the first interlanguage[4] structures to emerge are those which conform to these constraints. The next structures to emerge in a subsequent stage violate one but conform to the other two constraints, followed by structures which violate two and finally all three constraints. He thus argues that delay in acquisition of certain word order permutations is a consequence of these processing constraints: it takes time for the learner to override these constraints and acquire the mechanism for doing so.

2.2.   Principles of second language acquisition

I will now turn to the major area of this chapter: the cognitive operating principles that govern the path the learner takes in developing linguistic competence in a second language. During the past several years I have been influenced considerably by the first-language acquisition work of Dan Slobin in this area (Slobin 1973, 1977, 1982, 1985a, b). I will proceed to discuss two potential operating principles for second language acquisition which I believe are consistent with the psycholinguistic processing framework I have just touched on. Just how many such principles are needed to begin to account for empirical evidence within the field of second language acquisition is a difficult question to answer. For native language acquisition, Slobin has increased his initial seven operating principles (Slobin 1973) to forty (Slobin 1985a). The two principles that I discuss here have evolved primarily out of my own research on the acquisition of Spanish and English as second languages, as well as my understanding of related research on other languages.

The One-to-One Principle

This principle (hereafter the 1:1 Principle) states that "an interlanguage system should be constructed in such a way that an intended underlying meaning is expressed with one clear invariant surface form (or construction)" (Andersen 1984a:79). The motivation for such a principle is probably the processing constraints discussed earlier. In fact, the earliest constructions to emerge in German as a second language, following Clahsen's (1984) three processing constraints, conform to the 1:1 Principle. His speakers initially maintained a subject-verb-object word order, even though native German requires verb-subject order in certain contexts, clause-final placement of nonfinite verb forms, and final placement of finite verb forms in subordinate clauses.

Native French and Spanish require clitic objects to be placed preverbally, but in early stages of SLA of these languages learners maintain the canonical postverbal position, which conforms to the 1:1 Principle, since full NPs and pronouns alike are placed in the same postverbal position (see Zobl 1980; Andersen 1983b). In placement of a negator, native English, German, and Swedish each has language-specific rules which are hard to acquire. For each of these languages learners initially choose the simplest solution, which conforms to the 1:1 Principle: place the negator directly before the entity to be negated (the verb or predicate, for propositional negation; see Andersen 1984a:81-2 for further details).

Articles in German and Spanish (and many other languages) encode, in addition to specificity of the referent, gender, number, and, for German, case. Learners, however, initially disregard all but specificity as the relevant meaning to encode (Gilbert 1983; Andersen 1984b; Pfaff 1987a; see also

Huebner 1983, 1985). Personal pronouns similarly encode a number of features in native languages like English, German, and Spanish. In second-language Spanish, there is a strong tendency to disregard case marking and use the same form (usually a stressed form) for subject, direct and indirect object, and possessives (Andersen 1983b).

Finally, a number of first and second language acquisition studies (summarized in Andersen, 1986a, b) suggest that learners first use past-reference verbal morphology according to whether the event is punctual (i.e. one simple completed act of limited duration). In first and second language acquisition of English, past morphology (especially strong past) is first attached to punctual verbs (Antinucci and Miller 1976; Bloom, Lifter and Hafitz 1980; see Andersen 1986a, b for discussion of SLA). In Spanish, there are two past forms: preterit and imperfect. The preterit is the first form to be used (Simões and Stoel-Gammon 1979; Andersen 1986a,b; Jacobsen 1986). The preterit form is initially restricted to punctual events and, when the imperfect form begins to emerge, it is restricted to states. Both of these cases conform to the 1:1 Principle.[5]

The Transfer to Somewhere Principle
The Transfer to Somewhere Principle (hereafter, the TTS Principle) states that:

A grammatical form or structure will occur consistently and to a significant extent in the interlanguage as a result of transfer if and only if (1) natural and acquisitional principles are consistent with the L1 structure or (2) there already exists within the L2 input the potential for (mis-)generalization from the input to produce the same form or structure. Furthermore, in such transfer preference is given in the resulting interlanguage to *free, invariant,* functionally *simple* morphemes which are congruent with the L1 and L2 (or there is congruence between the L1 and natural acquisitional processes) and [to] . . . morphemes [which] occur *frequently* in the L1 and/or the L2.   (Andersen 1986b:182)

I will provide only one example here, since I have discussed this principle in detail elsewhere (Andersen 1983a; earlier versions in Andersen 1979a, 1980, and 1982).

Zobl (1980) has pointed out that while English speakers will place object pronouns postverbally in their French interlanguage, following English word order but violating French rules, French learners of English do not follow French rules for placement of object pronouns in their English. The explanation for this follows the TTS Principle: both French and English require postverbal placement of full NPs, which provides a model for postverbal placement of pronouns, which happens to match English but violate French rules. Thus, English speakers have a model in the input to transfer to: postverbal placement of full NP objects in French. But French speakers have no such native English model to cause them to transfer their preverbal placement of clitics to English. A similar finding pertains to the acquisition of Spanish by English speakers (Andersen 1983b). The Spanish data, however, reveal that the TTS Principle (or any equivalent transfer principle) operates in conjunction with other operating principles (such as the Principle of Formal Determinism; see Andersen forthcoming).

3.   Language contraction and death

Here I will discuss cases of simplification and language transfer from several of the chapters in this book which, I believe, conform to the 1:1 Principle and the TTS Principle.

Rouchdy makes frequent reference to assumed (and plausible) influence from Nubian in Nubian speakers' Arabic, most notably with regard to lack of gender distinctions and in regularization of plural markers. In one case of generalization of plural formation in Nubian, however, Rouchdy attributes the change to "decreased opportunities in the use of the Nubian language" (p. 266), not to influence from Arabic. However, in all three of these cases (masculine used in place of feminine and regularization of plural markers in Arabic and generalization of one plural marker in Nubian where normally Nubian uses two different plural suffixes) the 1:1 Principle can also account for the result, without any reference to language transfer. If language transfer is involved, then it is clearly transfer that follows the TTS Principle.

In King's discussion of variation in the verb paradigm, pronoun form, and placement of the French clitics *y* and *en*, only sporadic mention is made of the sources of the various changes from the French norm. Her concern seems mainly whether she can find sociolinguistic correlates for the variation. The features she discusses, however, are all consistent with change in the direction of the 1:1 Principle and, where one would argue for an influence from English, such an influence follows the TTS Principle.

The reduction of the verb paradigm (p. 142) such that 1st and 3rd plural have the same ending is in the direction of one form for one meaning. Although King does not discuss the pronominal forms in any detail, there is also an apparent collapse from distinct singular and plural forms for 1st and 3rd person to no number distinction in the pronoun forms; the inflection alone carries the meaning of plural. Such an efficient system whereby number is conveyed only once (on the verb inflection) is in the predictable direction of one form per meaning. Mougeon and Beniak also mention a sort of simplification in the verb paradigm for English-dominant bilinguals: the 3rd person singular verb forms tend to be generalized to 3rd person plural contexts (e.g. *ils savent* > *ils sait; ils veulent* > *ils veut*; p. 299).

At least one of the cases of placement of clitic pronouns mentioned by King follows both the 1:1 Principle and the TTS Principle:

a. Elle lui donne le livre
b. A donne le livre à lui
    'She gives him the book'

The position of *lui* in (a) (the Standard French norm) is unique to clitics, whereas the stressed position in (b) is also the usual position for full noun phrases (such as *au garçon*). It has been argued in Zobl (1980) and Andersen (1983b) that similar constructions in the second language French and Spanish of English speakers are "possible" not simply because it is the English position of such pronouns, but because it is the usual position for full NPs in French and Spanish (and English). To prefer to place pronouns in the same position as the full NP they refer to is a 1:1 Principle solution and any transfer argument is consistent with the TTS Principle, since independent operation of the 1:1 Principle provides the "somewhere" for transfer to take place.

A similar argument can be made for the example King gives of *Ma mère me fait manger-z-en* 'My mother makes me eat some'. The position of *z-en*, while definitely odd for French[6] not only matches the English position for 'some' but also the French position for the full NP.

Campbell and Muntzel discuss a variety of linguistic consequences of language contraction and death. Although most of their observations deal with phonology, I will restrict my comments to their discussion of morphology and syntax.[7] They discuss loss of agreement markers: dual and plural markers in Ocuilteco and case endings on Finnish adjectives (pp. 191–2). When viewed from the perspective of the 1:1 Principle, these are more than simply another case of morphological reduction: agreement markers are redundant and the 1:1 Principle dictates a preference for one and only one encoding of a particular meaning in a proposition. Agreement markers are therefore an especially logical type of reduction.

Campbell and Muntzel provide examples of two cases of what they argue are "additions to AF [American Finnish] grammar due to impact from English". These are the (1) addition of agentive phrases to passives, and (2) permitting infinitival complements of nouns or adjectives to have subjects (p. 191).[8] Their point is that not all changes consist of *reductions* as my 1982 predictions suggested. This is correct. While such "additions" do not fit the 1982 predictions completely, they do conform to the 1:1 Principle and the TTS Principle: an underlying meaning is given surface expression and this seems to reflect the English equivalent construction. Their discussion of the more rigid word order of American Finnish as an "addition" rather than a reduction is also covered by the two principles under discussion here: with loss of certain case markers rigid word order permits a clear 1:1 mapping of meaning onto form. Since it seems to match English rigid word order, this also conforms to the TTS Principle.

The study by Marion Lois Huffines on Pennsylvania German provides evidence of the elimination of the inflectional category "dative" in the German of those groups who depart from the Pennsylvania German norm. What is maintained is a two-category system for pronouns (common and accusative) and a one-category system for nouns (i.e. no explicit morphological distinctions for case). These reductions can easily be interpreted as evidence for the operation of the 1:1 Principle. Under conditions of limited input on which to base a complex case system, the cognitively simpler solution is to rely on word order, explicit prepositions by themselves (without the accompanying dative inflection), and simply general pragmatic and discourse-based information to convey the meaning encoded in dative case endings in the native nonsectarian norm.

It is worth noting that a nominative case/accusative case distinction is maintained in the pronominal system of sectarian speakers, while dative case is eliminated (or significantly reduced). In a study of the German of Turkish adolescents in West Germany who were relatively fluent in German, their second language, Pfaff (1987b) finds that a nominative/accusative distinction is maintained (although not categorically and not by all the subjects) even when the more arbitrary gender marking is not. Her argument, which supports the 1:1 Principle, is that case marking is semantically based (distinguishing agents from patients) whereas grammatical gender marking on determiners[9] is not.

Maandi argues that the loss of case distinctions and greater reliance on rigid word order that she finds in Estonian as spoken in Sweden, while apparently a result of contact with Swedish, is not simply a case of convergence between the two grammatical systems. She argues that the tendency for these changes was already there independently in Estonian and that contact with Swedish has simply accelerated this change.[10] The changes themselves follow the 1:1 Principle and the influence from Swedish conforms to the TTS Principle.

Bavin's interpretation of the changes she found to be taking place in the pronoun system in the Warlpiri of younger speakers is fully consistent with the 1:1 Principle:

> There is a great deal of variation in the forms used but this variation does not have social correlates. Rather it reflects a move towards more semantic transparency in the pronominal forms as well as a move towards reducing the number of oppositions in the system.   (pp. 283–4)

That is, the changes that Bavin reports obey a preference for one form per meaning as well as a preference for fewer meanings to be encoded (due to the loss of the exclusive/inclusive distinction).

However, Bavin also seems to be making an argument along the lines of the TTS Principle:

> The changes in the pronominal system discussed in this chapter cannot be attributed just to contact with English. English does not have an inclusive/exclusive distinction, nor a dual number, and if these categories are lost in Warlpiri, a motivating factor could be the absence of them in English. However, other changes are going on, and these reflect a move towards semantic transparency, which is generally internally motivated change.   (p. 285)

The differences between Bavin's Tables 1 (the traditional pronoun system) and 3 (the form most frequently used by the youngest group) on the surface seem to be few. However, a simple change in number of forms is misleading. Part of the change is the result of a loss of the exclusive/inclusive distinction, which makes the paradigm more uniform. The morpheme -*lu* then becomes an exceptionless marker of plural for subject clitics, -*pala* becomes the most general marker for dual number for clitics (exceptionless for subjects and almost exceptionless for objects), and -*jarra* becomes the exceptionless marker of dual number for independent pronouns. In both the clitic and full pronoun systems, person and number have become independent in the Warlpiri of the younger speakers. These changes clearly follow the 1:1 Principle.[11] As Bavin argues, these changes are internally motivated and are not necessarily due to the influence of English. However, since English *is* the language Warlpiri is in contact with, the fact that English lacks an exclusive/inclusive distinction could be seen as contributing to the loss of this distinction in the younger speakers' Warlpiri. But this would mean that the dual number would also be lost. Since it is not (and, in fact, is more explicitly encoded, following the 1:1 Principle), transfer alone cannot explain these changes.

4.   Conclusion

It is common in a number of areas of linguistic inquiry to appeal to "simplification" and "interference" (from the dominant language in a language contact situation) to explain linguistic phenomena.[12] It is probably equally common for others to argue against appealing to "interference" or, perhaps less often, "simplification". Both of these trends are evident in the chapters in this volume. I have tried to argue for a substitute for "simplification" in the guise of the One-to-One Principle, partly because it covers other cases that cannot be called "simplification" even though the mechanism seems to be the same. In addition, I have argued for a more constrained view of "interference" or transfer of features from another (usually dominant) language. I have tried to show that interpreting the various cases reported in this book in terms of these two principles in no way weakens the authors' arguments and actually strengthens most of them. Since the One-to-One Principle and the Transfer to Somewhere Principle evolved out of research in a different discipline, the relevance of these principles to the cases of language contraction and death in this volume appears to validate the principles and also shows that the linguistic consequences of language contraction and death are not simply "oddities" of little relevance to "normal" language bahavior, but linguistic phenomena which can be seen in other areas of language acquisition, use, and disuse as well.

Notes

1. My focus on SLA is on natural uninstructed acquisition.
2. Dorian (1983) makes clear several important differences between semi-speakers and immigrant SL learners, including the observation that semi-speakers retain a well developed receptive competence in spite of their limited productive ability, whereas this is generally not the case with SLA by immigrants.
3. Lenneberg (1967:89–120) has shown how the brain is capable of incredible coordination and planning of speech on all linguistic levels in order to access the information stored in memory and integrate it rapidly in linear order in speech production.
4. "Interlanguage" refers to the learner's linguistic system.
5. See Silva-Corvalán (1986) for related discussion of loss of tense–aspect categories in Spanish–English bilinguals.
6. Note that King does mention that this form and position are stigmatized in the community.
7. I should note in passing that their discussion of limitations in my earlier predictions concerning phonological reductions in language attrition (Andersen 1982) are quite valid (p. 187). They are rightfully critical of my overemphasis on phonological differences between the dominant and the retreating language, whereas a more logical hypothesis is that, in conjunction with such language transfer prediction, linguistic markedness should be given a more important role. This interpretation is fully consistent with both the 1:1 Principle and the TTS Principle.
8. They discuss a similar case (p. 191) involving Finnish gerundial forms which permit subjects in American Finnish but not Standard Finnish.
9. See also Gilbert (1983).
10. See Silva-Corvalán (1986) for a similar position with regard to changes in Spanish in contact with English.
11. Interestingly enough, the object clitics have not undergone these changes and are still synthetic (person and number are fused into a single morpheme) and irregular (all 1st person object forms are suppletive, as is the plural 2nd person form).
12. Such areas certainly include most represented in this volume, e.g. historical linguistics, language contact, second language acquisition, pidgin and creole studies, language contraction and death.

Bibliography

Adams, R. N. 1957. *Cultural surveys of Panama, Nicaragua, Guatemala, El Salvador, and Honduras*. Detroit:Plain Ethridge.

Adams, W. Y. 1977. *Nubia, corridor to Africa*. Princeton:Princeton University Press.

Aitchison, J. 1983. Pidgins, creoles and child language. *Working Papers of the London Psycholinguistics Research Group* 5:5–16.

Alatis, J. E. (ed.) 1968. *Contrastive linguistics and its pedagogical implications*. Washington, DC:Georgetown University Press.

   (ed.) 1970. *Bilingualism and language contact*. Washington, DC:Georgetown University Press.

   (ed.) 1978. *International dimensions of bilingual education*. Washington, DC:Georgetown University Press.

Albert, M. L., Goodglass, H., Helm, N. A., Rubens, A. B. & Alexander, M. P. 1981. *Clinical aspects of dysphasia*. Wien:Springer Verlag.

Allardt, E. 1984. What constitutes a language minority? *Journal of Multilingual and Multicultural Developments* 5(3 & 4):195–205.

Amyot, M. (ed.) 1984. *Actes du Congrès language et société au Québec*. Quebec City:Editeur official du Québec.

Andersen, R. W. 1979a. The relationship between first language transfer and second language overgeneralization:Data from the English of Spanish speakers. In Andersen 1979b.

   (ed.) 1979b. *The acquisition and use of Spanish and English as first and second languages*. Washington, DC:Teachers of English to Speakers of Other Languages.

   1980. Creolization as the acquisition of a second language as a first language. In Valdman & Highfield 1980.

   1982. Determining the linguistic attributes of language attrition. In Lambert & Freed 1982.

   (ed.) 1983a. *Pidginization and creolization as language acquisition*. Rowley, MA:Newbury House.

   1983b. Transfer to somewhere. In Gass & Selinker 1983.

   1984a. The One to One Principle of interlanguage construction. *Language Learning* 34:77–95.

   1984b. What's gender good for, anyway? In Andersen 1984c.

   (ed.) 1984c. *Second languages:A cross-linguistic perspective*. Cambridge, MA:Newbury House.

   1986a. El desarrollo de la morfología verbal en el español como segundo idioma. In Meisel 1986.

   1986b. Interpreting data:Second language acquisition of verbal aspect. MS.

Forthcoming. Models, processes, principles, and strategies:Second language acquisition in and out of the classroom. In VanPatten & Lee forthcoming.

Anderson, S. & Kiparsky, P. (eds.) 1973. *A Festschrift for Morris Halle.* New York:Holt, Rinehart & Winston.

Anderson, K. O. & Martin, W. 1976. Language loyalty among the Pennsylvania Germans. A status report on Old Order Mennonites in Pennsylvania and Ontario. In E. A. Albrecht & J. A. Burzle (eds.) *Germanica–Americana.* Lawrence, KS:University of Kansas.

Anderson T. 1971. *Matanza.* Lincoln:University of Nebraska Press.

Anonymous. 1979. Le Bac en breton reçu. *Ouest France* 10 juillet.

Anonymous. 1985a. Langues régionales – M. Chevènement:une langue doit ouvrir des perspectives. *Ouest France* 19 juin.

Anonymous. 1985b. Langues régionales – l'UDB répond à J.P. Chevènement. *Ouest France* 22–23 juin.

Anonymous. 1986. Le Conseil des langues et cultures régionales installés par le Premier ministre. *Le Bretagne à Paris* 31 janvier.

Antinucci, F. & Miller, R. 1976. How children talk about what happened. *Journal of Child Language* 3:169–89.

Antoine, G. 1975. Faut-il décentraliser le français? *Le Figaro* 17 décembre.

Arkell, A. J. 1961. *A history of the Sudan from the earliest times to 1821.* 2nd edn. London:University of London.

Arnstberg, K.-O., & Ehn, B. 1976. *Etniska minoriteter i Sverige förr och nu.* Lund:Liber Läromedel.

Aronoff, M. 1976. *Word-formation in generative grammar.* Cambridge, MA:MIT Press.

Aronson, H. I. & Darden, B. J. (eds.) 1981. *Folio slavica:Studies in Balkan lingustics to honor E. P. Hamp on his sixtieth birthday.* Columbus:Slavica Publishers.

Ash, S. (ed.) In press. *Proceedings of NWAVE-13.* San Diego:Harcourt, Brace, Jovanovich.

Axelsson, M. & Viberg, Å. 1985. *Inlärning av species och lexical struktur. En undersökning med introdutionstest. SUM-rapport 2.* Stockholm:Stockholms universitet, Institutionen för linguistik.

Badr, M. 1955. *Study in Nubian language.* Cairo:dar misr liltiba a.

Baldi, P. (ed.) 1984. *Papers from the XIIth Linguistic Symposium on Romance Languages.* Amsterdam:Benjamins.

Barbeau, M. 1960. Huron-Wyandot traditional narratives in translations and native texts. *Anthropological Series 47, National Museum of Canada Bulletin 165.* Ottawa.

Basso, K. H. 1976. 'Wise words' of the Western Apache:Metaphor and semantic theory. In Basso & Selby 1976.

    1979. *Portraits of the Whiteman:Linguistic play and cultural symbols among the Western Apache.* Cambridge:Cambridge University Press.

    & Selby, H. A. (eds.) 1976. *Meaning in anthropology.* Albuquerque:University of New Mexico Press.

Bateson, G. 1972. *Steps to an ecology of mind.* New York:Ballantine.

Baudouin de Courtenay, J. 1875. *Opyt fonetiki rez'janskix govorov.* Varšava-Peterburg.

Bauman, R. (ed.) 1977. *Verbal art as performance.* Rowley, MA:Newbury House.

Bavin, E. & Shopen, T. 1985. Warlpiri and English:Languages in contact. In Clyne 1985.

1987. Innovations and neutralizations in the Warlpiri pronominal system. *Journal of Linguistics* 23:149–75.

Beckett, C. (ed.) 1967. *Fealsúnacht Aodha Mhic Dhomhnaill.* Dublin:An Clóchomhar.

Bell, A. 1984. Language style as audience design. *Language in Society* 13:145–204.

Bender, M. L. (ed.) 1976. *The non-Semitic languages of Ethiopia.* East Lansing:African Studies Center, Michigan State University.

1977. The Surma language group:A preliminary report. *Studies in African Linguistics Supplement* 7:11–21.

1987. Some possible African creoles: A pilot study. In Gilbert 1987.

Bender, Bowen, J. D., Cooper, R. L. & Ferguson, C. A. (eds.) 1976. *Language in Ethiopia.* London:Oxford University Press.

Beniak, E. & Mougeon, R. 1984. Possessive *à* and *de* in informal Ontarian French:A longstanding case of linguistic variation. In Baldi 1984.

Beniak, E., Mougeon, R. & Valois, D. 1985. *Contact des langues et changement linguistique:étude sociolinguistique du français parlé à Welland (Ontario).* Quebec City:International Center for Research on Bilingualism.

Benkő, L. & Imre, S. 1972. *The Hungarian language.* The Hague:Mouton.

Benveniste, E. 1968. Mutations of linguistic categories. In W. Lehman and Y. Malkiel (eds.), *Directions for historical linguistics.* Austin:University of Texas Press.

1971. The relative clause, a problem in general syntax. In *Problems in general linguistics, a collection of Benveniste's papers.* Coral Gables, FL:University of Miami Press.

Bernstein, B. 1972. *Class, codes, and control,* vol. I. New York:Shocken Books.

Bernstein, R. 1985. France speaks up for regional languages. *New York Times* August 19:Sec. 4, 6E.

Bickerton, D. 1981. *Roots of language.* Ann Arbor:Karoma.

1984a. The language bioprogram hypothesis. *Behavioral and Brain Sciences* 7:173–221.

1984b. The language bioprogram hypothesis and second language acquisition. In Rutherford 1984.

Black, P. 1983. *Aboriginal languages of the Northern Territory.* Batchelor, Northern Territory:School of Australian Linguistics.

Blake, B. 1981. *Australian Aboriginal languages.* Sydney:Angus & Robertson.

Blegen, T. C. 1931, 1940. *Norwegian migration to America.* 2 vols. Northfield, MN:The Norwegian–American Historical Association.

Bloom, L., Lifter, K. & Hafitz, J. 1980. Semantics of verbs and the development of verb inflection in child language. *Language* 56:386–412.

Bloomfield, L. 1927. Literate and illiterate speech. *American Speech* 2:432–9.

1946. Algonquian. In Osgood 1946.

Blount, B. G. & Sanches, M. (eds.) 1977. *Sociocultural dimensions of language change.* New York:Academic Press.

Blumstein, S. E. 1973. *A phonological investigation of aphasic speech.* The Hague:Mouton.

Bothne, T. 1898. *Kort Udsigt over det lutherske Kirkearbeide blandt Normændene i Amerika.* Chicago:Publisher unknown.

Bourdieu, P. 1977. *Outline of a theory of practice.* Cambridge:Cambridge University Press.

1982. *Ce que parler veut dire.* Paris:Fayard.

1984. *Distinction:A social critique of the judgement of taste.* Cambridge, MA:Harvard University Press.
Bourhis, R. Y. 1984. Introduction: Language policies in multilingual settings. In R. Y. Bourhis (ed.) *Conflict and language planning in Quebec.* Clevedon, England:Multilingual Matters Ltd.
Bradley, D. 1978. Identity, dialect and sound change in mBisu and ʔùgɔ̃ŋ. *Working Papers in Linguistics,* University of Melbourne 4:37–46.
1981. Majority–minority linguistic interfaces in Thailand. *Working Papers in Linguistics,* University of Melbourne 7:79–86.
(ed.) 1985a. *Language policy, language planning and sociolinguistics in South-East Asia.* Pacific Linguistics A–67. Canberra:Australian National University.
1985b. Traditional minorities and language education in Thailand. In Bradley 1985a.
1986. Phonological convergence in a minority language:Ugong in Thailand. Chicago Linguistic Society presession on Southeast Asia as a linguistic area. MS.
1988. Tone alternations in Ugong (Thailand). In J. Hartman & G. Compton (eds.), *Papers to honor William J. Gedney on his sixth cycle.* De Kalb, IL:Center for Southeast Asian Studies, Northern Illinois University.
Brekilien, Y. (ed.) 1982. *La Bretagne.* Paris:Les Editions d'Organisation.
Brekle, W. & Kastovsky, D. (eds.) 1977. *Perspektiven der Wortbildungsforschung.* Bonn:Bouvier Verlag Herbert Grundmann.
Brown, R. 1973. *A first language,* Cambridge, MA: Harvard University Press.
& Gilman, A. 1960. The pronouns of power and solidarity. In Sebeok 1960.
Bruford, A. 1969. *Gaelic folk-tales and medieval romances.* Dublin:Folklore Council of Ireland.
Buffington, A. F. and Barba, P. A. 1954 (rev. 1965). *A Pennsylvania German grammar.* Allentown, PA:Schlechter.
Butler, G. R. 1985. Supernatural folk belief expression in a French–Newfoundland community:A study of expressive form, communicative process, and social function in L'Anse-à-Canards. Ph.D. dissertation, Memorial University of Newfoundland.
Byron, J. L. 1976. *Selection among alternates in languages standardization:The case of Albanian.* Paris:Mouton.
Calvet, L. J. 1973. Le colonisation linguistique en France. *Les Temps Moderns* 324–325–326:74–89.
Campbell, D. & MacLean, R. A. 1974. *Beyond the Atlantic roar:Nova Scotian Scots.* Toronto:McClelland & Stewart.
Campbell, J. L. 1948. Scottish Gaelic in Canada. *An Gaidheal* 43:128–36.
Campbell, L. 1975a. El estado actual y la afinidad genética de la lengua indigena de Cacaopera. *Le Universidad* (refista de la Universidad de El Salvador) 1975:45–54 (January–February).
1975b. Cacaopera. *Anthropological Linguistics* 17(4):146–53.
1976a. The linguistic prehistory of the southern Mesoamerican periphery. *Fronteras de Mesoamerica,* 14a Mesa Redonda, vol. 1. Mexico: Sociedad Mexicana de Antropologia.
1976b. The last Lenca. *International Journal of American Linguistics* 42:73–8.
1976c. Language contact and sound change. In Christie 1976.
1980. Towards new perspectives on American Finnish. In Paunonen & Suojanen 1980.

1985. *The Pipil language of El Salvador*. Berlin:Mouton.
In press. *The linguistics of southeastern Chiapas*. Provo:New World
Archaeological Foundation.
& Canger, U. 1978. Chicomuceltec's last throes. *International Journal of
American Linguistics* 44:228–30.
& Oltrogge, D. 1980. Proto-Tol (Jicaque). *International Journal of American
Linguistics* 46:205–23.
, Chapman, A. & Dakin, K. 1978. Honduran Lenca. *International Journal of
American Linguistics* 44:330–2.
Cape Breton Post-Record. 1939. Sydney:March 15.
Caramazza, A. & Berndt, S. R. 1985. A multicomponent deficit view of
agrammatic Broca's aphasia. In Kean 1985.
Carey, S. 1978. The child as a word learner. In Halle, Bresnan & Miller 1978.
Casket. 1938. Antigonish:December 8 issue.
Castile, G. P. & Kushner, G. (eds.) 1981. *Persistent peoples:Cultural enclaves in
perspective*. Tucson:The University of Arizona Press.
Castonguay, C. 1979. Exogamie et anglicisation chez les minorités canadiennes-
françaises. *Canadian Review of Sociology and Anthropology* 16:21–31.
1981. *Exogamie et anglicisation dans les régions de Montréal, Hull, Ottawa, et
Sudbury*. Quebec City:International Center for Research on Bilingualism.
1984. Le dilemme démolinguistique du Québec. In Amyot 1984.
Cazaboni, B. (ed.) 1978. *Langue maternelle, langue première de communication?*
Sudbury:Institut franco-ontarien, Laurentian University.
Chafe, W. 1982. Integration and involvement in speaking, writing, and oral
literature. In Tannen 1982b.
Chana, U. K. & Romaine, S. 1984. Evaluative reactions to Panjabi/English
code-switching. *Journal of Multilingual and Multicultural Development*
5:447–73.
Chaudenson, R. 1986. Français marginaux, français zéro et créolisation.
Unpublished research report, Université de Provence at Aix-en-Provence.
Chomsky, N. 1965. *Aspects of the theory of syntax*. Cambridge, MA:MIT Press.
Chrislock, C. H. 1981. *Ethnicity challenged:The upper Midwest Norwegian–
American experience in World War I*. Northfield, MN:The Norwegian–
American Historical Association.
Christie, W. W. Jr (ed.) 1976. *Current progress on historical linguistics:
Proceedings of the Second International Conference on Historical Linguistics*.
Amsterdam:North-Holland.
Clahsen, H. 1984. The acquisition of German word order:A test case for
cognitive approaches to L2 development. In Andersen 1984c.
Clark, E. V. 1982. The young word maker: A case study of innovation in the
child's lexicon. In Wanner & Gleitman 1982.
& Berman, R. 1984. Structure and use in the acquisition of word-formation.
Language 60:542–90.
& Clark, H. H. 1979. When nouns surface as verbs. *Language* 55:767–811.
Clark, H. H. & Clark, E. V. 1977. *Psychology and language:An introduction to
psycholinguistics*. New York:Harcourt, Brace, Jovanovich.
Clarke, S. 1985. Social correlates of linguistic variation in Sheshatshiu
Montagnais. Paper presented at the 19th Algonquian Conference, McGill
University (Montreal).
& King, R. (eds.) 1983a. *Papers from the Sixth Annual Meeting of the Atlantic
Provinces Linguistic Association*. St John's:Memorial University of
Newfoundland.

& King, R. 1983b. Speech stereotyping in French Newfoundland:An investigation of language attitudes on the Port-au-Port peninsula. In Clarke & King 1983a.

Clifford, J. 1986. On ethnographic allegory. In Clifford & Marcus 1986.

& Marcus, G. E. (eds.) 1986. *Writing culture:The poetics and politics of ethnography*. Berkeley:University of California.

Clyne, M. 1982. *Multilingual Australia*. Melbourne:River Seine Publications.

(ed.) 1985. *Australia, meeting place of languages*. Pacific Linguistic Series C–92. Canberra:Pacific Linguistics.

Cooper, R. L. (ed.) 1982. *Language spread:Studies in diffusion and social change*. Bloomington:Indiana University Press.

Corder, S. P. 1975. Simple codes and the source of the second language learner's initial heuristic hypothesis. In Corder & Roulet 1975.

& Roulet, E. (eds.) 1975. *Linguistic approaches in applied linguistics*. Paris:Didier.

Corum, C., Smith-Stark, T. C. & Weiser, A. (eds.) 1973. *You take the high node and I'll take the low node:Papers from the Comparative Syntax Festival*. Chicago:Chicago Linguistic Society.

Costello, J. R. 1978. Syntactic change and second language acquisition:the case for Pennsylvania German. *Linguistics* 213:29–50.

1985. Pennsylvania German and English:languages in contact. In H. Kloss (ed.) *Deutsch als Muttersprache in den vereinigten Staaten, Teil II*. Wiesbaden:Franz Steiner.

Cowan, H. 1967. *British emigration to North America*. Toronto:Toronto University Press.

Croix, A. 1981. *La Bretagne aux 16e et 17e siècles:la vie – la mort – la foi*. Paris:Maloine S. A. Editeur.

Cutler, A. 1980. Productivity in word-formation. *Chicago Linguistic Society* 16:45–51.

Danaher, K. 1972. *The year in Ireland*. Cork:Mercier Press.

DeCamp, D. 1971. Towards a generative analysis of a post-creole continuum. In Hymes 1971.

& Hancock, I. (eds.) 1974. *Pidgins and creoles*. Washington, DC:Georgetown University Press.

Delargy, J. H. 1945. The Gaelic story-teller with some notes on Gaelic folktales. *Proceedings of the British Academy* 31:177–221.

Deniel, A. 1976. *Le Mouvement breton 1919–1945*. Paris:François Maspero.

Denison, N. 1981. Conservation and adaptation in a plurilingual context. In Meid & Heller 1981.

Deprez, K. (ed.) 1984. *Sociolinguistics in the Low Countries*. Amsterdam:Benjamins.

de Villiers, J. 1974. Quantitative aspects of agrammatism in aphasia. *Cortex* 10:36–54.

de Vries, J. 1985. Some methodological aspects of self-report questions on language and ethnicity. *Journal of Multilingual and Multicultural Development* 6:347–68.

Dil, A. S. (ed.) 1972. *The ecology of language*. Palo-Alto:Stanford University Press.

Dimmendaal, G. J. 1982. Contacts between Eastern Nilotic and Surma groups:Linguistic evidence. In Mack & Robertshaw 1982.

1983a. Tenet (Surma):ein Fall partiellen Sprachwechsels. In Vossen & Claudi 1983.

1983b. *The Turkana language*. Dordrecht:Foris.

Forthcoming. *Language contraction and reductive processes in Kore.* In
   M. Brenzinger (ed.) *Language death: Factual and theoretical explorations.*
   Berlin:de Gruyter.
Dittmar, N. & Schlieben-Lange, B. (eds.) 1982. *Die Soziolinguistik in
   romanischsprachigen Ländern.* Tübingen:Gunter Narr Verlag.
Dixon, R. M. W. 1980. *The languages of Australia.* Cambridge:Cambridge
   University Press.
Donaldson, T. 1985. From speaking Ngiyambaa to speaking English. *Aboriginal
   History* 9:126–46.
Dorian, N. C. 1970. A substitute name system in the Scottish Highlands.
   American Anthropologist 72:303–19.
   1973. Grammatical change in a dying dialect. *Language* 49:413–38.
   1977a. A hierarchy of morphophonemic decay in Scottish Gaelic language
   death: The differential failure of lenition. *Word* 28:96–109. [This issue of
   Word is officially dated 1972. However, this contribution was written well
   after that date and the issue was actually published in 1977.]
   1977b. The problem of the semi-speaker in language death. *International
   Journal of the Sociology of Language* 12:23–32.
   1978a. The dying dialect and the role of the schools:East Sutherland Gaelic
   and Pennsylvania Dutch. In Alatis 1978.
   1978b. *East Sutherland Gaelic.* Dublin:Dublin Institute for Advanced Studies.
   1978c. The fate of morphological complexity in language death:Evidence from
   East Sutherland Gaelic. *Language* 54:590–609.
   1980a. Linguistic lag as an ethnic marker. *Language in Society* 9:33–41.
   1980b. Maintenance and loss of same-meaning structures in language death.
   Word 31:39–45.
   1981. *Language death:The life cycle of a Scottish Gaelic dialect.*
   Philadelphia:University of Pennsylvania Press.
   1982a. Defining the speech community in terms of its working margins. In
   Romaine 1982b.
   1982b. Language loss and maintenance in language contact situations. In
   Lambert & Freed 1982.
   1982c. Linguistic models and language death evidence. In Obler & Menn
   1982.
   1983. Natural second language acquisition from the perspective of the study of
   language death. In Andersen 1983a.
   1984. Declensional regularity as a possible factor in paradigm stability. *Journal
   of Historical Linguistics and Philology* 1:15–30.
   1985. Radical asymmetries in the skills of speakers of obsolescent languages.
   Invited paper presented at the Centre for Franco-Ontarian Studies, The
   Ontario Institute for Studies in Education, Toronto, May 1.
   1986a. Abrupt transmission failure in obsolescing languages: How sudden the
   "tip" to the dominant language in communities and families? In Nikiforidu
   et al. 1986.
   1986b. Gathering language data in terminal speech communities. In Fishman
   et al. 1986.
   1986c. Making do with less:Some surprises along the language death
   proficiency continuum. *Applied Psycholinguistics* 7:257–76.
   1987. The value of language maintenance efforts that are unlikely to succeed.
   International Journal of the Sociology of Language 68:57–67.
   n.d. The asymmetries of obsolescence. MS.
Downing, P. 1977. On the creation and use of English compound nouns.
   Language 53:810–42.

Dressler, W. U. 1972. On the phonology of language death. *Papers from the Eighth Regional Meeting of the Chicago Linguistic Society.* Chicago:Chicago Linguistic Society.
1977. Wortbildung bei Sprachverfall. In Brekle & Kastovsky 1977.
1981a. Language shift and language death – a protean challenge for the linguist. *Folia Linguistica* 15:5–27.
1981b. On word-formation in natural morphology. *Wiener Linguistische Gazette* 26:3–13.
1982. Acceleration, retardation, and reversal in language decay? In Cooper 1982.
& Wodak-Leodolter, R. 1977. Language preservation and language death in Brittany. *International Journal of the Sociology of Language* 12:33–44.
Driberg, J. H. 1932. Lotuxo dialects. *American Anthropologist* 34:601–9.
Druckenbrod, R. 1981. *Mir lanne Deitsch:A guide for learning the skills of reading, writing, and speaking Pennsylvania German.* Allentown, PA:private printing.
Dunn, C. 1953. *Highland settler.* Toronto:University of Toronto Press.
Durbin, M. 1973. Formal changes in Trinidad Hindi as a result of language adaptation. *American Anthropologist* 75:1290–304.
Durkacz, V. E. 1983. *The decline of the Celtic languages.* Edinburgh:John Donald.
Eagleson, R., Kaldor, S. & Malcolm, I. G. (eds.) 1982. *English and the Aboriginal child.* Canberra:Curriculum Development Centre.
Ebneter, T. 1983. *Romanisch und Deutsch am Hinterrhein/GR.* Zürich:Verlag des Phonogrammarchivs der Universität.
Eckman, F. R., Moravscik, E. A. & Wirth, J. R. (eds.) 1986. *Markedness.* New York:Plenum Press.
Ehret, C. & Nurse, D. 1981. The Taita Cushites. *Sprache und Geschichte in Afrika* 3:125–68.
Eichoff, J. 1971. German in Wisconsin. In Gilbert 1971.
Eikel, F. 1949. The use of cases in New Braunfels German. *American Speech* 24:278–81.
1966–7. The New Braunfels German dialect. *American Speech* 41:5–16, 254–60; 42:83–104.
Elegoet, F. 1971–2. *La domination linguistique en Bretagne.* Mémoire de Maîtrise du Sociologie, Université de Paris X, Nanterre.
1978. *Nous ne savions que le breton et il fallait parler français – mémoires d'un paysan du Léon.* La Baule:Editions Breizh hor Bro.
Elliott, S. 1956. A pretty piece of prejudice. *Journal of Education* Series 5, 6(1).
1971. A nineteenth-century tourist in Cape Breton, Part II. *Journal of Education* 20(4).
Elmendorf, W. W. 1981. Last speakers and language change:Two Californian cases. *Anthropological Linguistics* 23(1):36–49.
Enninger, W. 1980. Syntactic convergence in a stable triglossia plus trilingualism situation in Kent County, Delaware. In Nelde 1980.
Eskola, P. 1977. Englannin kielen lainavaikutus amerikansuomalaisen sanomalehden kansankirieiden keileen. Unpublished Pro gradututkielma. Helsinki:Castrenianum, Helsinki University.
Evans, N. 1986. Language shift among the Kaiadilt. MS.
Fahim, H. M. 1983. *The Egyptian Nubian, resettlement and years of coping.* Salt Lake City:University of Utah Press.

Falc'hun, F. 1969. Essay on the lingual minority of Basse-Bretagne. In Holmstad & Lade 1969.

Fasold, R. 1984. *The sociolinguistics of society*. Oxford:Blackwell.

Fennell, D. 1981. Can a shrinking linguistic minority be saved? In Haugen, McClure & Thomson 1981.

Ferguson, C. A. & Slobin, D. I. (eds.) 1973. *Studies of child language development*. New York:Holt, Rinehart & Winston.

Fernea, R. 1979. Traditions and change in Egyptian Nubia. *Africa in antiquity. Meroitica* 5:41–9.

Fillmore, C. J. 1976. The need for frame semantics in linguistics. In *Statistical Methods of Linguistics*. Stockholm:Skriptor.

, Kempler, D. & Wang, W. S-Y. (eds.) 1979. *Individual differences in language ability and language behavior*. New York:Academic Press.

Fishman, J. A. 1967. Bilingualism with and without diglossia; diglossia with and without bilingualism. *Journal of Social Issues* 23:29–38.

(ed.) 1971a. *Advances in the sociology of language*, vol. 1, The Hague: Mouton.

1971b. The sociology of language:An interdisciplinary social science approach to language in society. In Fishman 1971a.

(ed.) 1972. *Advances in the sociology of language,* vol. 2. The Hague:Mouton.

1977. Language and ethnicity. In Giles 1977.

, Nahirny, V., Hofman, J. & Hayden, R. (eds.) 1966. *Language loyalty in the United States*. The Hague:Mouton.

, Tabouret-Keller, A., Clyne, M., Krishnamurti, Bh. & Abdulaziz, M. (eds.) 1986. *The Fergusonian impact*, vol 2. *Sociolinguistics and the sociology of language*. Berlin:Mouton de Gruyter.

Flannery, R. 1946. Men's and women's speech in Gros Ventre. *International Journal of American Linguistics* 12:133–5.

1953. *The Gros Ventres of Montana:Part I, Social life*. Washington, DC:Catholic University of America.

Fletcher, P. & Garman, M. 1968. *Language acquisition*, 2nd edn. Cambridge:Cambridge University Press.

Fleuriot, L. 1981. L'histoire des Bretons explique leur identité. *Breizh* 265:6–8.

Flikeid, K. 1985. L'accord dans les propositions relatives:Le cas d'un parler acadien. Paper presented at the annual meeting of the Canadian Linguistics Association, Université de Montréal.

Foley, W. A. 1980. Toward a universal typology of the noun phrase. *Studies in Language* 4:171–99.

Fournier, R. 1981. Les démonstratifs . . . et ça continue. *Montreal Working Papers in Linguistics* 17:43–56.

Fox, R. G. 1985. Ghandian socialism as belief and practice:Revolutionary resistance in the world system. Paper presented at the annual meetings of the American Ethnological Society, Toronto.

Frankenberg, R. 1957. *Village on the border*. London:Cohen & West.

Frey, J. W. 1942 [rpt. 1981] *A simple grammar of Pennsylvania German*. Reissued with a new preface by C. R. Beam. Lancaster, PA:Brookshire Publications.

Furikēs, P. A. 1932. Ē en Attikē Ellēnoalvanikē dialektos. *Athēnā* 44:28–76.

1933. Ē en Attikē Ellēnoalvanikē dialektos. *Athēnā* 45:49–181.

Gaelic College Special Publication. 1943. *The Canadian-American Gael*, vol. 1.

Gal, S. 1976. Language change and its social determinants in a bilingual community. Ph.D. dissertation. University of California, Berkeley.

404   *Investigating obsolescence*

1978. Peasant men can't get wives:Language change and sex roles in a bilingual community. *Language in Society* 7(1):1–16.
1979. *Language shift:Social determinants of linguistic change in bilingual Austria.* New York:Academic Press.
1984. Phonological style in bilingualism:The interaction of structure and use. In Schiffrin 1984.
Gardin, B., Marcellesi, J-B. & GRECO, Rouen (eds.) 1980. *Sociolinguistique: Approches, theories, pratiques,* tome 1. Paris:Presses Universitaires de France.
Gardner, R. C. & Lambert, W. F. 1972. *Attitudes and motivation in second language learning.* Rowley, MA:Newbury House Publishers.
Gass, S. & Selinker, L. (eds.) 1983. *Language transfer in language learning.* Cambridge, MA:Newbury House/Harper & Row.
Giacalone Ramat, A. 1979. Language function and language change in minority languages. *Journal of Italian Linguistics* 4:141–62.
Giacomo, M. 1975. Le politique à propos des langues régionales:Cadre historique. *Langue française* 25:12–28.
Gilbert, G. G. 1965. Dative versus accusative in the dialects of central Texas. *Zeitschrift für Mundartforschung* 32:288–96.
 (ed.) 1971. *The German language in America.* Austin:University of Texas Press.
1983. Transfer in second language acquisition. In Andersen 1983a.
 (ed.) 1987. *Pidgin and creole languages. Essays in memory of John Reinecke.* Honolulu:University of Hawaii Press.
Giles, H. (ed.) 1977. *Language, ethnicity and intergroup relations.* New York:Academic Press.
, Bourhis, R. Y. & Taylor, T. M. 1977. Towards a theory of language in ethnic group relations. In Giles 1977.
Giordan, H. 1982. *Démocratie culturelle et droit à la différence – rapport présenté à Jack Lang, Ministre de la Culture.* Paris:La Documentation Française.
Givón, T. (ed.) 1979a. *Discourse and syntax,* vol. 12. *Syntax and semantics.* New York:Academic Press.
1979b. From discourse to syntax:Grammar as a processing strategy. In Givón 1979a.
Gjinari, J. 1970. *Dialectologjia Shqiptare.* Prishtinë:Enti i Teksteve dhe i Mjeteve i Krahinës Socialiste Autonome të Kosovës.
1976. La structure dialectale de l'Albanais et son rapport avec l' histoire du peuple. *Studia Albanica* 2:151–71.
Gleason, H. A. 1968. Contrastive analysis in discourse structure. In Alatis 1968.
Goffman, E. 1974. *Frame analysis:An essay on the organization of experience.* New York:Harper Colophon Books.
Goodenough, W. 1956. Residence rules. *Southwestern Journal of Anthropology* 12:22–37.
Goodglass, H., Blumstein, S. E., Gleason, J. B., Green, E., Hyde, M. E. & Statlender, S. 1979. The effects of syntactic encoding on sentence comprehension in aphasia. *Brain and Language* 7:201–9.
Graham, I. C. 1956. *Colonists from Scotland:Emigration to North America 1707–1783.* Ithaca:Cornell University Press.
Greenbaum, S. (ed.) 1985. *The English language today.* Oxford:Pergamon.
Greenberg, J. H. 1948. The classification of African languages. *American Anthropologist* 50:24–30.
1963a. *The languages of Africa.* The Hague:Mouton.
1963b. The Mogogodo, a forgotten Cushitic people. *Journal of African Languages* 2:29–43.

1965. Urbanization and migration in West Africa. In Kuper 1965.

1966. *Languages of Africa*. 2nd edn. The Hague:Mouton.

Greene, D. 1966. *The Irish language*. Dublin:Cultural Relations Committee of Ireland.

Gumperz, J. J. 1982. *Discourse strategies*. Cambridge:Cambridge University Press.

& Wilson, R. 1971. Convergence and creolization: A case from the Indo-Aryan/Dravidian border in India. In Hymes 1971.

Gwegen, J. 1975. *La langue bretonne face à ses oppresseurs*. Quimper:Nature et Bretagne.

Haag, E. C. 1982. *A Pennsylvania German reader and grammar*. University Park, PA:The Pennsylvania State University Press.

Haebler, C. 1965. *Grammatik der Albanischen Mundart von Salamis*. Wiesbaden:Otto Harrassawitz.

Haiman, J. 1985. *Natural syntax. Iconicity and erosion*. Cambridge:Cambridge University Press.

Hakuta, K. 1974. Prefabricated patterns and the emergence of structure in second language acquisition. *Language Learning* 24:289–97.

1976. A case study of a Japanese child learning English as a second language. *Language Learning* 26:321–51.

Haldeman, S. S. 1872. *Pennsylvania Dutch:A dialect of south German with an infusion of English*. London:Trübner.

Hale, K. 1973. Person marking in Warlpiri. In Anderson & Kiparsky 1973.

1982. Some essential features of Warlpiri verbal clauses. In Swartz 1982.

Hall, R. A. 1966. *Pidgin and creole languages*. Ithaca:Cornell University Press.

Halle, M., Bresnan, J. & Miller, G. A. (eds.) 1978. *Linguistic theory and psychological reality*. Cambridge, MA:MIT Press.

Hamid, S. A. 1973. *al nuba al qidida*. Alexandria:Al hiy'a al masriya algama lilkitab.

Hamp, E. P. 1961. To rēma en tēi sēmerinēi omiloumene Hēllenikēi glóssēi. *Athēnā* 65:101–28.

1962. The interconnection of sound production, perception, and phonemic typology. *Proceedings of the Fourth International Congress of Phonetic Sciences*. Helsinki.

1965. The Albanian dialect of Màndres. *Die Sprache* 11:137–54.

1970. The diphthongs of Mandrica. *Linguistique Balkanique* 14(2):21–5.

1972. Albanian. In Sebeok 1972.

1978. Problems of multilingualism in small linguistic communities. In Alatis 1978.

1979. The North European word for 'apple'. *Zeitschrift für Celtische Philologie* 37:158–66.

Hancock, I. (ed.) 1979. *Readings in creole studies*. Ghent:E. Story-Scientia.

Hasselmo, N. 1970. *Americasvenska*. Stockhom:University of Stockholm.

Hatch, E. (ed.) 1978. *Second language acquisition:A book of readings*. Cambridge, MA:Newbury House Publishers.

Haugen, E. 1953 [rpt. 1969]. *The Norwegian language in America:A study in bilingual behavior*. Philadelphia:University of Pennsylvania Press/ Bloomington:Indiana University Press.

1972. The analysis of linguistic borrowing. In Dil 1972.

1974. The ecology of language. *The Linguistic Reporter,* Supplement 25:19–26.

, McClure, J. D. & Thomson, D. S. (eds.) 1981. *Minority languages today*. Edinburgh:Edinburgh University Press.

Heeschen, C. 1985. Agrammatism vs. paragrammatism:A fictitious opposition. In Kean 1985.

Heine, B. 1970. *Status and use of African lingua francas*. München:Weltforum Verlag.

1973. Vokabulare ostafrikanischer Restsprachen, teil 2:Sogoo und Omotik. *Afrika und Uebersee* 57:38–49.

1976a. *The Kuliak languages of eastern Uganda*. Nairobi:East African Publishing House.

1976b. *A typology of African languages based on the order of meaningful elements*. Berlin:Dietrich Reimer.

1979. Some linguistic characteristics of African-based pidgins. In Hancock 1979.

1980. *The non-Bantu languages of Kenya*. Berlin:Dietrich Reimer.

1982. Traditional fishing in the Rift Valley of Kenya:A linguistic survey. *Sprache und Geschichte in Afrika* 4:7–40.

& Vossen, R. 1975. Zur Stellung der Ongamo-Sprache (Kilimandscharo). *Afrika und Uebersee* 59:81–105.

& Vossen, R. 1980. The Kore of Lamu:A contribution to Maa dialectology. *Afrika und Uebersee* 62:272–88.

Hélias, P.-J. 1975. *Le Cheval d'orgueil – mémoires d'un Breton du pays bigouden*. Paris:Libraire Plon.

Henry, C. 1979. Extinction de parole? *Autrement* 19:15–22.

Hetzron, R. 1976. On the Hungarian causative verb and its syntax. In Shibatani 1976.

Hill, J. H. 1973. Subordinate clause density and language function. In Corum, Smith-Stark & Weiser 1973.

1978. Language death, language contact, and language function. In McCormack & Wurm 1978.

1980. Language death in Uto-Aztecan. Paper for the Conference on Uto-Aztecan Linguistics, Albuquerque. MS.

1983a. Language death in Uto-Aztecan. *International Journal of American Linguistics* 49:258–76.

1983b. Review of Scollon & Scollon, *Narrative, literacy, and face in interethnic communication*. *American Anthropologist* 85:484.

1985. The grammar of consciousness and the consciousness of grammar, *American Ethnologist* 12:725–37.

1987. Women's speech in modern Mexicano. In Philips, Steele & Tanz 1987.

& Hill, K. C. 1977. Language death and relexification in Tlaxcalan Nahuatl. *International Journal of the Sociology of Language* 12:55–69.

& Hill, K. C. 1980. Mixed grammar, purist grammar and language attitudes in modern Nahuatl. *Language in Society* 9:321–48.

& Hill, K. C. 1981. Variation in relative clause construction in modern Nahuatl. In Karttunen 1981.

& Hill, K. C. 1986. *Speaking Mexicano*. Tucson:University of Arizona Press.

& Nolasquez, R. 1973. *Mulu'wetam:The first people*. Banning, CA:Malki Museum Press.

Hillelson, S. 1930. Nubian origins. *Sudan Notes and Records* 13 (1):137–48.

Hjelmslev, L. 1938. Relations de parenté dans les langues creoles. *Revue des Etudes Indo-Européennes* 1:271–86.

Hohenthal, W. D. & McCorkle, T. 1955. The problem of aboriginal persistence. *Southwestern Journal of Anthropology* 11:288–300.

Holmstad, E. & Lade, J. (eds.) 1969. *Lingual minorities in Europe*. Oslo:Det Norskle Samlaget.

Horne, A. R. 1905. *Horne's Pennsylvania German manual,* 3rd edn. Allentown, PA:T. K. Horne.

Hornung, M. 1972. *Wörterbuch der deutschen Sprachinselmundart von Pladen/ Sappada in Karnien (Italien)* Vienna:Studien zu österr.-bair. Dialektkunde, Nr. 6.

1977. Strukturen deutsch-romanischer toponomastischer Lehnbeziehungen im oberitalienischen Sprachinselbereich. *Onoma* 22(1–2):463–731.

Huang, J. & Hatch, E. 1978. A Chinese child's acquisition of English. In Hatch 1978.

Hudson, R. A. 1980. *Sociolinguistics.* Cambridge:Cambridge University Press.

Huebner, T. 1983. *A longitudinal analysis of the acquisition of English.* Ann Arbor, MI:Karoma Publishers.

1985. System and variablity in interlanguage syntax. *Language Learning* 35:141–63.

Huffines, M. L. 1980. Pennsylvania German:Maintenance and shift. *International Journal of the Sociology of Language* 25:43–57.

Hymes, D. 1964. Introduction:Toward ethnographies of communication. *American Anthropologist* 66 (6):1–34.

(ed.) 1971. *Pidginization and creolization of languages.* Cambridge:Cambridge University Press.

1974. *Foundations in sociolinguistics:An ethnographic approach.* Philadelphia:University of Pennsylvania Press.

1984. *Vers la compétence de communication.* Paris:Hatier-Credif.

Imre, S. 1942. Az e hangok állapota a felsőőri nép nyelvében [The e sounds in the dialect of Felsőőr]. *Magyar Nyelv* 2:115–29.

1971. A felsőőri nyelvjárás [The dialect of Felsőőr]. *Nyelvtudomanyi értekezések,* no. 72. Budapest:Akadémiai Kiadó.

Itkonen, E. 1982. Short-term and long-term teleology in linguistic change. In Maher, Bombard & Koerner 1982.

Jackson, K. H. 1951. Common Gaelic:The evolution of the Gaelic languages. *Proceedings of the British Academy* 37:71–97.

Jacobs, A. H. 1965. The traditional political organization of the pastoral Masai. Ph.D. dissertation, Oxford University.

Jacobs, R. 1975. *Syntactic change: A Cupan (Uto-Aztecan) case study.* Berkeley:University of California.

Jacobsen, T. 1986. ¿Aspecto antes que tiempo? Una mirada a la adquisición temprana del español. In Meisel 1986.

Jakobson, R. 1941 (trans. 1968). *Child language, aphasia, and phonological universals.* Trans. by A. R. Keiler, from *Kindersprache, aphasie, und allgemeine lautgesetze.* The Hague:Mouton.

1972. *Child language, aphasia and phonological universals.* The Hague: Mouton.

& Halle, M. 1956. *Fundamentals of language.* The Hague:Mouton.

Janko, A. 1978. Die deutsche Sprachinsel Gottschee (Kočevje). *Michigan Germanic Studies* 4(1):85–100.

Jankowsky, K. R. 1972. *The neogrammarians* The Hague:Mouton.

Janson, K. 1913. *Hvad jeg har oplevet.* Oslo, Norway:publisher not known.

Janson, T. 1979. Capacity and norm. *Papers from the Institute of Linguistics* 37. Stockholm:University of Stockholm.

Jelinek, E. 1984. Empty categories, case, and configurationality. *Natural Language and Linguistic Theory* 2:39–76.

& Demers, R. 1985. Constraints on arguments in Lummi. *20th International*

Conference on Salish and Related Languages. Vancouver, August 15–17, 1985.

Johnson, M. C. 1974. Two morpheme structure rules in an English proto-creole. In DeCamp & Hancock 1974.

Junga Yimi. 1983. vol. 4, no. 2. Warlpiri Literacy Production Centre Inc.

1984a. Vol. 4, no. 5. Warlpiri Literacy Production Centre Inc.

1984b. Vol. 5, no 1. Warlpiri Literacy Production Centre Inc.

Kaldor, S. & Malcolm, I. G. 1982. Aboriginal English in country and remote areas:A western Australian perspective. In Eagleson, Kaldor & Malcolm 1982.

Kalmar, I. 1985. Are there really no primitive languages? In Olson, Torrance & Hilyard 1985.

Karttunen, F. 1977. Finnish in America:A case study in monogenerational language change. In Blount & Sanches 1977.

(ed.) 1981. Nahuatl studies in memory of Fernando Horcasitas. *Texas Linguistic Forum*. 18:89–104.

Kayne, R. 1975. *French syntax*. Cambridge, MA:MIT Press.

Kazazis, K. 1976. Greek and Arvanítika in Corinthia. In Naylor 1976.

Kean, M. L. (ed.) 1985. *Agrammatism*. London:Academic Press.

Kehr, K. 1979. "Deutsche" Dialekte in Virginia und West Virginia (USA). *Zeitschrift für Dialektologie und Linguistik* 46:289–319.

Keineg, P. 1973. Littérature bretonne. *Présence francophone* 6:139–41.

Keller, R. E. 1961. *German dialects*. Manchester:Manchester University Press.

Kerr, A. F. G. 1927. Two Lawa vocabularies. *Journal of the Siam Society* 21 (1):53–63.

King, R. 1984a. Linguistic variation and language contact:A study of French spoken in four Newfoundland communities. In Warkentyne 1984.

1984b. Variation and change in a bilingual speech community:Clitic pronoun usage in Newfoundland French NWAVE-13.

In press a. Variation and change in a bilingual speech community:Clitic-pronoun usage in Newfoundland French. In Ash in press.

In press b. Newfoundland French:An overview. In Mougeon in press.

Kloss, H. 1967. Bilingualism and nationalism. *Journal of Social Issues* 23:39–47.

Knab, T. 1978. Language death in the Valley of Puebla: A socio-geographic approach. MS.

Koenig, E. L. 1980. Ethnicity:The key variable in a case study of language maintenance and language shift. *Ethnicity* 7:1–14.

Koerner, K. (ed.) 1983. *Linguistics and evolutionary theory*. Amsterdam:Benjamins.

Kolk, H. H. J., van Grunsven, M. J. F. & Keyser, A. 1985. On parallelism between production and comprehension in agrammatism. In Kean 1985.

Kranzmayer, E. 1925. *Laut- und Flexionslehre der deutschen zimbrischen Mundart*. (Publ. 1980; M. Hornung, ed.) Vienna:Verlag des Verbandes der wissenschaftlichen Gesellschaften Österreichs.

Kreidler, C. W. (ed.) 1965. *Report of the sixteenth annual Round Table Meeting on Linguistics and Language Studies*. Washington, DC:Georgetown University Press.

Kroeber, A. L. 1916. The Arapaho dialects. *University of California Publications in American Archaeology and Ethnology* 12:71–138.

Kull, R. & Raiet, E. 1976. *Oige Keelsus Sônaraamat*. Tallinn:Valgus.

Kuper, H. (ed.) 1965. *Urbanism, migration, and language*. Berkeley:University of California Press.

Kurath, H. 1939. *Handbook of the linguistic geography of New England.* Providence:Brown University.

Kuryłowicz, J. 1975. The evolution of grammatical categories. In *Esquisses linguistiques II.* München:Fink.

Kuter, L. 1984. Life histories and the creation of new ways of doing sociology – a review essay. *Comparative Studies in Society and History* 26(2):345–51.

1985. Labeling people:Who are the Bretons? *Anthropological Quarterly* 58(1):13–29.

1987. How many people speak Breton today? *Bro Nevez* 24–25:3–4.

Laben, J. 1977. Remarks in "Father Jimmy Tompkins of Reserve Mines". In R. Caplan (ed.) *Cape Breton's Magazine,* 16:8.

Labov, W. 1965. On the mechanism of linguistic change. In Kreidler 1965.

1966. *The social stratification of English in New York City.* Washington, DC:Center for Applied Linguistics.

1970/77. On the adequacy of natural languages:The development of tense. *Linguistic Agency University of Trier Paper* No. 23. Series B.

1972a. *Language in the inner city.* Philadelphia:University of Pennsylvania Press.

1972b. *Sociolinguistic patterns.* Philadelphia:University of Pennsylvania Press.

1980. Is there a creole speech community? In Valdman & Highfield 1980.

1981. Resolving the neogrammarian controversy. *Language* 57:267–308.

Lachapelle, R. & Henripin, J. 1980. *La situation démolinguistique au Canada:Evolution passée et prospective.* Montreal:The Institute for Research on Public Policy.

Lamb, S. 1964. Linguistic diversification and extinction in North America. *XXXV Congreso Internacional de Americanistas, Mexico.*

Lambert, R. D. & Freed, B. F. (eds.) 1982. *The loss of language skills.* Rowley, MA:Newbury House Publishers.

Lamphear, J. 1976. *The traditional history of the Jie of Uganda.* Oxford:Clarendon Press.

Lantolf, J. P. & Stone, J. B. (eds.) 1981. *Current research in Romance languages.* Bloomington, IN:Indiana University Linguistics Club.

LaPointe, S. 1985. A theory of verb form use in the speech of agrammatic aphasics. *Brain and Language* 24:100–55.

Larmouth, D. 1974. Differential interference in American Finnish cases. *Language* 50:356–66.

Laughren, M. 1977. Pronouns in Warlpiri and the category of number. MS.

1984. Warlpiri Baby Talk. *Australian Journal of Linguistics* 4(1):73–88.

Le Du, J. 1980. Sociolinguistique et diglossie:Le cas du Breton. In Gardin, Marcellesi & GRECO 1980.

Le Lannou, M. 1978. *La Bretagne et les Bretons.* Paris:Presses Universitaires de France.

Le Menn, G. 1975. Le Breton et son enseignement. *Langue française* 25:71–83.

1985. Une "Bibliothèque bleue" en langue bretonne. *Annales de Bretagne et des Pays de l'Ouest* 92(3):299–40.

Le Nail, B. 1985. La création littéraire et l'édition en langue bretonne aujourd'hui. *Bibliothèques publiques et langues régionales.* Paris:Ministère de la Culture, Direction du Livre et de la Lecture.

Le Page, R. B. & Tabouret-Keller, A. 1985. *Acts of identity.* Cambridge:Cambridge University Press.

Learned, M. D. 1889. *The Pennsylvania German dialect.* Baltimore:Isaac Friedenwald.

Lederer, H. 1969. *Reference grammar of the German language.* New York:Scribner.

Lenneberg, E. H. 1967. *Biological foundations of language.* New York:John Wiley & Sons.

Lepsius, R. 1880. *Nubische Grammatik mit einer Einleitung ueber die Voelker und Sprachen Afrikas.* Berlin:W. Hertz.

Leslau, W. 1952. The influence of Sidamo on the Ethiopic language of Gurage. *Language* 28:63–81.

Levesque, M. 1982. Etude sociolinguistique. In Brekilien 1982.

Lewis, B. A. 1973. Swiss German in Wisconsin:The impact of English. *American Speech* 48:211–28.

Lichem, K. & Simon, J. (eds.) 1980. *Schuchardt-Symposium 1977 in Graz.* Vienna:Österreichische Akademie der Wissenschaften.

Lieberson, S. 1970. *Language and ethnic relations in Canada.* New York:John Wiley & Sons.

Lindenfeld, J. 1972. The social conditioning of syntactic variation in French. In Fishman 1972.

Lorch, M. P. 1985. A cross-linguistic study of verb inflection in agrammatism. Ph.D. dissertation, Boston University.

Lorenz, K. 1970. The enmity between generations and its probable causes. *Studium Generale* 23:963–97.

Lovoll, O. S. (ed.) 1977. *Cultural pluralism and assimilation.* Northfield, MN:The Norwegian–American Historical Association.

1984. *The promise of America:A history of the Norwegian–American people.* Minneapolis:The University of Minnesota Press and the Norwegian–American Historical Association.

Lucas, L. W. 1979. *Grammar of Ros Goill Irish, Co. Donegal.* Belfast:Institute of Irish Studies, the Queen's University of Belfast.

Lühr, R. 1979. Das Wort 'und' im Westgermanischen. *Münchener Studien zur Sprachwissenschaft* 24:117–54.

Maandi, K. n.d. Language change: Estonian in Sweden. MS.

Mabou Pioneer Committee. 1977. *Mabou Pioneer II.* Port Hawkesbury:Mabou Pioneer Committee.

Mac Cana, P. 1970. *Celtic mythology.* London:Hamlyn.

Mac Grianna, S. 1969. *An druma mór.* Dublin:Stationery Office.

Mac 'Ill-Fhialain, A. 1972. *Saoghal an treabhaiche.* Uppsala:Almqvist & Wiksells.

MacBain, A. 1894. The Gaelic of Badenoch. *Transactions of the Gaelic Society of Inverness* 18:79–86.

MacDonald, A. & Macdonald, A. 1924. *The poems of Alexander MacDonald.* Inverness:Northern Counties Newspaper and Printing and Publishing Company Ltd.

MacDonald, A. D. n.d. *Mabou pioneers.* Private printing.

MacDonald, C. S. 1959. *Early highland emigration to Nova Scotia and Prince Edward Island 1770–1853.* Collections of the Nova Scotia Historical Society 23.

MacDonald, D. F. 1937. Scotland's shifting population 1770–1850. Glasgow:Glasgow University Press.

MacDougall, J. L. 1976. *History of Inverness County.* Ontario:MIKA Publishing Company.

MacGaffey, W. 1961. The history of Negro migrations in the Sudan. *Journal of Anthropology* 17:178–97.

Mack, J. & Robertshaw, P. T. (eds.) 1982. *Culture history in the Southern Sudan:Archaeology, linguistics, and ethnohistory.* Nairobi:British Institute in Eastern Africa.

Mackey, W. F. 1970. Interference, integration and the synchronic fallacy. In Alatis 1970.

MacKinnon, J. 1903. Na gaedheil an Ceap Breatunn. In C. W. Vernon (ed.) *Cape Breton, Canada.* Toronto:Nation Publishing Co.

MacKinnon, K. 1977. *Language, education and social processes in a Gaelic community.* London:Routledge & Kegan Paul.

1984. Scottish Gaelic and English in the Highlands. In Trudgill 1984b.

Macleod, D. J. (Gaelic adviser) 1979. *Can Seo.* London:British Broadcasting Corporation.

Macnamara, J. (ed.) 1977. *Language learning and thought.* New York:Academic Press.

MacNeill, M. 1962. *The festival of Lughnasa.* Oxford:Oxford University Press.

MacWhinney, B. 1974. How Hungarian children learn to speak. Ph.D. dissertation. University Microfilms.

1978. *The acquisition of morphology.* Chicago:University of Chicago.

Mafeni, B. 1971. Nigerian Pidgin. In Spencer 1971.

Maher, J. P., Bombard, A. R. & Koerner, E. F. K. (eds.) 1982. *Papers from the Third International Conference on Historical Linguistics.* Amsterdam:Benjamins.

Mannion, J. J. 1977a. Settlers and traders in western Newfoundland. In Mannion 1977b.

(ed.) 1977b. *The peopling of Newfoundland:Essays in historical geography.* Toronto:University of Toronto Press.

Markey, T. L. 1982. Afrikaans:Creole or non-creole? *Zeitschrift für Dialektologie und Linguistik* 49:169–207.

Marroquín, A. D. 1975. El problema indígena en El Salvador. *America Latina* 35.4:747–71.

Martell, J. S. 1942. *Immigration to, and emigration from, Nova Scotia 1815–1838.* Halifax:Public Archives of Nova Scotia.

Matarazzo, J. 1972. *Wechsler's measurement and appraisal of adult intelligence,* 5th edn. Baltimore:Williams & Wilkins.

Mayer, R. 1971. Zur Phonetik des Cimbro. *Linguistische Berichte* 11:48–54.

McConvell, P. 1985. Domains and code switching among bilingual Aborigines. In Clyne 1985.

(ed.) Forthcoming. *Language shift in Aboriginal Australia.*

McCormack, W. C. & Wurm, S. A. (eds.) 1978. *Approaches to language:Anthropological issues.* The Hague:Mouton.

Meid, W. 1975. Zimbrisch *kartak* "Gefälligkeit, Liebesdienst". *Grazer linguistische Studien* 2:138–42.

& Heller, K. 1979. *Italienische Interferenzen in der lautlichen Struktur des Zimbrischen.* Vienna:Spies.

& Heller, K. (eds.) 1981. *Sprachkontakt als Ursache von Veränderungen der Sprache- und Bewusstseinsstruktur.* Innsbruck:Innsbrucker Beiträge zur Sprachwissenschaft.

Meinhof, C. 1912. *Die Sprachen der Hamiten.* Hamburg:L. & R. Friedrichsen.

Meisel, J. M. (ed.) 1986. *Adquisición de lenguaje. Aquisição da linguagem.* Frankfurt/M.:Vervuert.

Menn, L. 1973. A note on the acquisition of affricates and fricatives. *Stanford Papers and Reports on Child Language Development* 6:87–96.

1976 [1979]. Pattern, control, and contrast in beginning speech. Ph.D. dissertation, University of Illinois at Champaign-Urbana. (Distributed 1979 by Indiana University Linguistics Club.)

1986. Language acquisition, aphasia, and phonotactic universals. In Eckman, Moravscik & Wirth.

& Obler, L. K. In press. *Agrammatic aphasia:A cross-language narrative sourcebook.* Amsterdam:Benjamins.

Mertz, E. 1982a. Language and mind:A Whorfian folk theory in United States language law. *Working Papers in Sociolinguistics* 93:1–21.

1982b. "No burden to carry": Cape Breton pragmatics and metapragmatics. Ph.D. dissertation, Duke University.

1983. A Cape Breton system of personal names:Pragmatic and semantic change. *Semiotica* 44–1/2:55–74.

Mesthrie, R. 1985. A history of the Bhojpuri (or 'Hindi') language in South Africa. Ph.D. dissertation, University of Cape Town, South Africa.

Meyer, G. 1896. *Albanesische studien V:Beiträge zur kenntniss der in Griechenland gesprochenen Albanesischen mundarten.* Wien:Wiener Akademie Sitzungsberichte.

Mithun, M. 1980. Northern Iroquoian dating strategies. *Man in the Northeast* 131–46.

1985. Untangling the Huron and the Iroquois. *International Journal of American Linguistics* 51:504–7.

1987. Is basic word order universal? In Tomlin 1987.

Forthcoming. The acquisition of polysynthesis. *Journal of Child Language.*

Morvannou, F. 1980. *Le breton, la jeunesse d'une vielle langue.* Paris:Presses Populaires de Bretagne.

Moskowitz, A. I. 1970. The two-year-old stage in the acquisition of English phonology. *Language* 46:426–41. Reprinted in Ferguson & Slobin 1973.

Mougeon, R. 1977a. *Enquête sociolinguistique.* Welland:Conseil régional de l'Association canadienne-française de l'Ontario.

1977b. French language replacement and mixed marriages:The case of the francophone minority of Welland, Ontario. *Anthropological Linguistics* 19:368–77.

1982. Paramètres extralinguistiques de la variabilité morphologique en français ontarien. In Dittmar & Schlieben-Lange 1982.

(ed.) In press. *Recherches sociolinguistiques sur le français parlé hors Québec.* Quebec City:University of Quebec Press.

& Beniak, E. 1981. Leveling of the 3sg./pl. verb distinctions in Ontarian French. In Lantolf & Stone 1981.

& Beniak, E. 1987. The extralinguistic correlates of core lexical borrowing. In K. M. Denning, S. Inkelas, F. C. McNair-Knox & J. R. Rickford (eds.) *Variation in language:NWAVE-XV at Stanford.* Stanford:Dept. of Linguistics.

& Canale, M. 1978. Maintien du français par les jeunes élèves franco-ontariens de Welland. In Cazaboni 1978.

& Hébrard, P. 1975. Aspects de l'assimilation linguistique dans une communauté francophone de l'Ontario. *Working Papers on Bilingualism* 5:1–38.

& Heller, M. 1986. The social and historical context of minority French language education in Ontario. *Journal of Multilingual and Multicultural Development* 7:219–27.

, Beniak, E. & Bélanger, M. 1982. Morphologie et évolution des pronoms determinatifs dans le français parlé à Welland (Ontario). *Canadian Journal of Linguistics* 27:1–22.

, Beniak, E. & Valois, D. 1984. Variation in the phonological integration of loanwords in a bilingual speech community. Paper presented at NWAVE XIII, Philadelphia, Oct. 25–27.

, Beniak, E. & Valois, D. 1985a. Issues in the study of language contact:Evidence from Ontarian French. MS.

, Beniak, E. & Valois, D. 1985b. A sociolinguistic study of language contact, shift and change. *Linguistics* 23:455–87.

, Beniak, E. & Valois, D. 1986. Is child language a possible source of linguistic variation? In D. Sankoff (ed.) *Diversity and diachrony.* Amsterdam/Philadelphia:Benjamins.

, Valois, D. & Beniak, E. 1983. Is child language a possible source of linguistic variation? Paper presented at NWAVE XII, Montreal, Oct. 27–29.

, Brent-Palmer, C., Bélanger, M. & Cichocki, W. (eds.) 1982. *Le français parlé en situation minoritaire,* vol. 1. Quebec City:International Center for Research on Bilingualism.

Mühlhäusler, P. 1979. *Growth and structure of the lexicon in New Guinea Pidgin.* Pacific Linguistics C-52. Canberra:Australian National University.

1981. The development of the category of number in Tok Pisin. In Muyksen 1981b.

Muldrow, W. 1976. Languages of the Maji area. In Bender *et al.* 1976.

Muntzel, M. C. 1979. Language death. MA dissertation, Department of Anthropology, SUNY Albany.

1980. La desaparición de lenguas como consecüencia del contacto lingüístico. *XNI Mesa Redonda,* vol. 1. Mexico:Sociedad Mexicana de Antropología.

1982a. *La aplicación de un modelo generativo a la fonología del tlahuica (ocuilteco).* Colección Científica, 118. Mexico:Secretaria de Educación Pública, Instituto Nacional de Antropología e Historia.

1982b. Problems of language loss for the descriptive linguist. Paper presented at the Symposium, Features of Indigenous Languages, Mexico. MS.

1985. Spanish loanwords in Ocuiltec. *International Journal of American Linguistics* 51:515–18.

In press. La contribución del español a la perdida de lenguas mesoamericanas. *Actas del Iº Congreso Internacional sobre el Español de América.* Rio Piedras:Puerto Rico.

Murphy, G. 1955. *Ossianic lore and romantic tales of mediaeval Ireland.* Dublin:Cultural Relations Committee of Ireland.

Muysken, P. 1981a. Creole tense/mood/aspect systems:The unmarked case. In Muysken 1981b.

(ed.) 1981b. *Generative studies on creole languages.* Dordrecht:Foris.

& Smith, N. (eds.) 1986. *Universals vs. substrata in creole genesis.* Amsterdam:Benjamins.

Naro, A. J. 1978. A study on the origins of pidginization. *Language* 54:314–47.

Naylor, K. E. (ed.) 1976. *Balkanistika:Occasional papers in Southeast European Studies* 3.

Nelde, P. H. (ed.) 1980. *Sprachkontakt und Sprachkonflikt.* Zeitschrift für Dialektologie und Linguistik, Beiheft 32. Wiesbaden:Franz Steiner.

Nelson, K. E. 1973. *Structure and strategy in learning to talk.* Chicago:University of Chicago Press.

Nespoulous, J. L., Joanette, I., Beland, R., Caplan, D. & Lecours, A. R. 1984.

Phonological disturbances in aphasia:Is there a "markedness effect" in aphasic phonemic errors? In Rose 1984.

Newman, P. 1970. Linguistic relationship, language shifting and historical inference. *Afrika und Uebersee* 53:217–23.

Nichols, P. O. 1983. Linguistic options and choices for Black women in the rural south. In Thorne, Kramarae & Henley 1983.

Nicolas, M. 1982. *Histoire du mouvement breton.* Paris:Editions Syros.

Nikiforidu, V., Van Clay, M., Niepokuj, M. & Feder, D. (eds.) 1986. *Proceedings of the Twelfth Annual Meeting of the Berkeley Linguistics Society.* Berkeley, CA:Berkeley Linguistics Society.

Ó Canainn, T. 1978. *Traditional music in Ireland.* London:Routledge & Kegan Paul.

Ó Catháin, S. 1985. *Uair an chloid cois teallaigh/An hour by the hearth.* Dublin:Folklore Council of Ireland.

Ó Cuív, B. (ed.) 1969. *A view of the Irish language.* Dublin:Stationery Office.

Ó hEochaidh, S. 1965. Seanchas iascaireachta agus farraige. *Bealoideas* 33:1–96. 1966. An seanchas beo. *Feasta* 19(3):7–12.

    , Ní Néill, M. & Ó Catháin, S. 1977. *Sí-scéalta as Tír Chonaill/Fairy-legends from Donegal.* Dublin:Folklore Council of Ireland.

Ó Murchú, M. 1985. *The Irish language.* Dublin:Department of Foreign Affairs and Bord na Gaeilge.

O'Rahilly, T. F. 1913. Irish scholars in Dublin in the early eighteenth century. *Gadelica* 1:156–262.

    1921. *Dánfhocail/Irish epigrams in verse.* Dublin:Talbot Press.

    1932 [1972]. *Irish dialects past and present.* Dublin:Dublin Institute for Advanced Studies. [1972 is repr. of 1932 with fuller index by B. O. Cuív.]

Obler, L. & Menn, L. (eds.) 1982. *Exceptional language and linguistic theory.* New York:Academic Press.

Olson, D. R., Torrance, N. & Hilyard, A. (eds.) 1985. *Literacy, language, and learning.* Cambridge:Cambridge University Press.

Osgood, C. (ed.) 1946. *Linguistic structures of native America.* Viking Fund Publications in Anthropology, Number Six.

Osthoff, H. & Brugmann, K. 1878. *Morphologische Untersuchungen auf dem Gebiete der indogermanischen Sprachen*, 1. Teil. [Repr. in H. H. Christmann (ed.) *Sprachwisssenschaft des 19. Jahrhunderts.* Darmstadt:Wissenschaftliche Buchgesellschaft.]

Paunonen, H. & Suojanen, M. (eds.) 1980. *Central problems of bilingualism.* Turku, Finland:Sluomen Kielen Seura.

Person, Y. 1973. Impérialisme linguistique et colonialisme. *Les Temps Moderns* 324–325–326:90–118.

Peters, A. M. 1977. Language learning strategies:Does the whole equal the sum of the parts? *Language* 53:560–73.

    1983. *The units of language acquisition.* Cambridge:Cambridge University Press.

    1985. Language segmentation:Operating principles for the perception and analysis of language. In Slobin 1985b.

    1986. Early syntax. In Fletcher & Garman 1986.

Pfaff, C. (ed.) 1987a. *First and second language acquisition processes.* Cambridge, MA:Newbury House/Harper & Row.

    1987b. Functional approaches to interlanguage. In Pfaff 1987a.

Philips, S., Steele, S. & Tanz, C. (eds.) 1987. *Language, gender, and sex in comparative perspective.* Cambridge:Cambridge University Press.

Picard, M. & Nicol, J. 1982. *Loanwords and concrete phonology*. Bloomington:Indiana University Linguistics Club.
Piriou, Y. B. 1971. *Défense de cracher par terre et de parler breton*. Paris:P. J. Oswold.
Poplack, S. & Sankoff, D. 1984. Borrowing:The synchrony of integration. *Linguistics* 22:99–135.
Poulin, G. 1969. *Paroisse du Sacré-Coeur 1919–1969*. Welland:Les Artisans.
Price, R. & Price, S. 1972. Saramaka onomastics:An Afro-American naming system. *Ethnology* 11(4):341–67.
Public Archives of Nova Scotia. 1920. Assembly Petitions:Education IV–21 [RG Series P, Vol. 79, 1920].
    1941. Duplicate Bills and Amendments.
Pulte, W. J. 1971. German in Virginia and West Virginia. In Gilbert 1971.
Puromies, M. 1966. Amiericansuomen englantilaisperäusestä sanastosta ja sen muodostumistavoista. Ph.D. dissertation, Helsinki:Castrenianum, Helsinki University.
Quirk, R., Greenbaum, S., Leech, G. & Svartvik, J. 1972. *A grammar of contemporary English*. London:Longman.
Raag, R. 1982. *Lexical characteristics in Swedish Estonian*. Upsala:University of Upsala.
Rankin, R. 1978. The unmarking of Quapaw phonology:A study in language death. *Kansas Working Papers in Linguistics* 3:45–52.
Reece, J. E. 1977. *The Bretons against France*. Chapel Hill:University of North Carolina Press.
Reed, C. E. 1948. A survey of Pennsylvania German morphology. *Modern Language Quarterly*, 9:322–42.
    & Seifert, L. W. 1954. *A linguistic atlas of Pennsylvania German*. Marburg:private printing.
Reinisch, L. 1911. Die sprachliche stellung des Nuba. *Schriften der Sprachen*, vol. 3. Wien:Komission der Akademie der Wissenchaften in Wien.
Richebuono, J. 1980. Von der einstigen zur heutigen Ausdehnung des ladinischen Sprachraumes. *Ladinia* 4:219–41.
Rickford, J. 1986. 'Me Tarzan, you Jane!' Adequacy, expressiveness and the creole speaker. *Journal of Linguistics* 22:281–311.
    & Traugott, E. C. 1985. Symbol of powerlessness and degeneracy, or symbol of solidarity and truth? Paradoxical attitudes towards pidgins and creoles. In Greenbaum 1985.
Rølvaag, O. E. 1922. *Omkring Fædrearven*. Northfield, MN:St Olaf College.
    1927. *Giants in the earth:A saga of the prairie*. New York & London:Harper & brothers.
Romaine, S. 1981. Syntactic complexity, relativization and stylistic levels in Middle Scots. *Folio Linguistica Historica* 2:56–77.
    1982a. *Socio-historical linguistics*. Cambridge:Cambridge University Press.
    (ed.) 1982b. *Sociolinguistic variation in speech communities*. London:Edward Arnold.
    1983. On the productivity of word-formation rules and limits of variability in the lexicon. *Australian Journal of Linguistics* 3:177–200.
    1984a. Relative clauses in child language, pidgins and creoles. *Australian Journal of Linguistics* 4:237–81.
    1984b. Review of E. Woolford and W. Washabaugh (eds.) *The social context of creolization*. *Linguistics* 22:137–40.
    1985. The notion of government as a constraint on language mixing:Some

evidence from the code-mixed compound verb in Panjabi. Keynote paper presented at the Australian Linguistics Society Annual Meeting, Brisbane.
1986. Sprachmischung und Purismus:Sprich mir nicht von Mischmasch. *Lili* 62:92–107.
1988. *Pidgin and creole languages*. London:Longman.
& Wright, F. 1987. A short note on short forms in Tok Pisin. *Journal of Pidgin and Creole Studies* 2(1):63–7.
Romero Curtin, P. 1985. Generations of strangers:The Kore of Lamu. *International Journal of African Historical Studies* 18:455–72.
Roos, A. 1980. *Morfologiska tendenser vid språklig interferens med estniska som bas*. Upsala:University of Upsala.
Rose, F. C. (ed.) 1984. *Advances in aphasia 42:Progress in aphasiology*. London:Raven Press.
Ross, A. S. C. & Moverley, A. W. 1964. *The Pitcairnese language*. London:Deutsch.
Ross, W. C. A. 1934. Highland emigration. *Scottish Geographical Magazine*, May issue:155–66.
Rottland, F. 1982. *Die südnilotischen Sprachen:Beschreibung, Vergleichung und Rekonstruktion*. Berlin:Dietrich Reimer.
& Okoth Okombo, D. 1986. The Suba of Kenya:A case of growing ethnicity with receding language competence. *Afrikanistische Arbeitspapiere* 7:115–26.
Rouchdy, A. 1980. Languages in contact:Arabic–Nubian. *Anthropological Linguistics* 22:334–44.
Rubin, J. 1968. *National bilingualism in Paraguay*. The Hague:Mouton.
Rutherford, W. E. (ed.) 1984. *Language universals and second language acquisition*. Amsterdam:Benjamins.
Salmons, J. C. 1983a. Issues in Texas German language maintenance and shift. *Monatshefte* 75:187–96.
1983b. Language variety and language change among Texas Germans. Paper delivered at the Modern Language Association Convention, New York.
Sankoff, D. (ed.) 1978. *Linguistic variation:Models and methods*. New York:Academic Press.
& Laberge, S. 1978. The linguistic market and the statistical explanation of variability. In Sankoff 1978.
Sankoff, G. 1977. Variability and explanation in language and culture:Cliticization in New Guinea Tok Pisin. In Saville-Troike 1977.
1980a. Political power and linguistic inequality in Papua New Guinea. In Sankoff 1980b.
1980b. *The social life of language*. Philadelphia:University of Pennsylvania Press.
& Brown, P. 1976. The origins of syntax in discourse. *Language* 52:631–66.
& Laberge, S. 1973. On the acquisition of native speakers by a language. *Kivung* 6:32–47.
Saville-Troike, M. (ed.) 1977. *Linguistics and anthropology*. Washington DC:Georgetown University Press.
Schegloff, E. & Sacks, H. 1973. Opening up closings. *Semiotica* 8:289–327.
Schiffrin, D. (ed.) 1984. *Meaning, form and use in context:Linguistic applications*. Washington, DC:Georgetown University Press.
Schleicher, A. 1983 [original 1865]. On the significance of language for the natural history of man. In Koerner 1983.
Schmidt, A. 1985a. The fate of ergativity in dying Dyirbal. *Language* 61:378–96.
1985b. Speech variation and social networks in dying Dyirbal. In Clyne 1985.

1985c. *Young people's Dyirbal:An example of language death from Australia.* Cambridge:Cambridge University Press.
Schneiderman, E. I. 1975. Attitudinal determinants of the linguistic behavior of French–English bilinguals in Welland, Ontario. Ph.D. dissertation, SUNY at Buffalo.
Schuchardt, H. 1884. *Slawo-deutsches und Slawo-italienisches.* Graz:Leuschner & Lubensky.
Scollon, R. & Scollon, S. 1979. *Linguistic convergence:An ethnography of speaking at Fort Chipewyan, Alberta.* New York:Academic Press.
Scotton, C. M. & Okeju, J. 1973. Neighbors and lexical borrowings. *Language* 49:871–89.
Sebeok, T. A. (ed.) 1960. *Style in language.* Cambridge, MA:The Technology Press.
(ed.) 1972. *Current trends in linguistics.* Vol. 9:*Linguistics in Western Europe.* The Hague/Paris:Mouton.
Semmingsen, I. 1978. *Norway to America:A history of the immigration.* (Trans. by E. Haugen.) Minneapolis:University of Minnesota Press.
Seuren, P. A. M. 1984. The bioprogram hypothesis:Facts and fancy. *The Behavioral and Brain Sciences* 7:208–9.
& Wekker, H. 1986. Semantic transparency as a factor in creole genesis. In Muysken & Smith 1986.
Sherzer, J. F. 1977. Cuna Ikala:Literature in San Blas. In Bauman 1977.
1983. *Kuna ways of speaking:An ethnographic perspective.* Austin:University of Texas Press.
Shibamoto, J. 1985. *Japanese women's language.* New York:Academic Press.
Shibatani, M. (ed.) 1976. *The grammar of causative constructions.* New York:Academic Press.
Silva-Corvalán, C. 1986a. Tense-mood-aspect across the Spanish–English bilingual continuum. MS, University of Southern California.
1986b. Bilingualism and language change. *Language* 62:587–608.
Silverstein, M. 1976. Shifters, linguistic categories and cultural description. In Basso & Selby 1976.
Simões, M., Perroni, C. & Stoel-Gammon, C. 1979. The acquisition of inflections in Portuguese:A study of the development of person markers on verbs. *Journal of Child Language* 6:53–67.
Simon, P. 1979. Aspects de l'ethnicité bretonne. *Pluriel* 19:23–43.
Slobin, D. I. 1973. Cognitive prerequisites for the development of grammar. In Ferguson & Slobin 1973.
1977. Language change in childhood and history. In Macnamara 1977.
1982. Universal and particular in the acquisition of language. In Wanner & Gleitman 1982.
1985a. Crosslinguistic evidence for the language-making capacity. In Slobin 1985b, vol. 2.
(ed.) 1985b. *The cross-linguistic study of language acquisition.* 2 vols. Hillsdale, NJ:Lawrence Erlbaum Associates.
Smith, I. & Johnson, S. 1986. Sociolinguistic patterns in an unstratified society:The patrilects of Kugu Nganhcara. *Journal of the Atlantic Provinces Linguistic Association (JAPLA)* 8:29–43.
Sorskiva, M. 1982. Infinitiivijärjestelmän muutoksia lasten Kielessä. *Virittäjä* 86:377–91.
Spagnolo, L. M. 1933. *Bari grammar.* Verona:Missioni Africane.
Spencer, J. (ed.) 1971. *The English language in West Africa.* London:Longman.

418   *Investigating obsolescence*

Spicer, E. H. 1980. *The Yaquis:A cultural history*. Tucson:The University of Arizona Press.
Stammler, W. 1922–23. Das 'Halbdeutsch' der Esten. *Zeitschrift für deutsche Mundarten* 17:160–72.
Statutes of Nova Scotia. 1841. Cap. 43, sec. 14.
    1864. Revised Statutes, Title XVII Public Instruction.
Stauder, J. 1971. *The Majangir:Ecology and society of the southwest Ethiopian people*. Cambridge:Cambridge University Press.
Stephany, U. 1986. Modality. In Fletcher & Garman 1986.
Sturtevant, W. C. 1978. Oklahoma Seneca-Cayuga. In Trigger 1978.
Suárez, J. 1977. La influencia del espanol en la estructura gramatical del nahuatl. *Anuaria de Letras* 15:115–64. (Centro de Lingüistica Hispanica, Universidad Nacional Autonoma de Mexico).
Swadesh, M. 1948. Sociologic notes on obsolescent languages. *International Journal of American Linguistics* 14:226–35.
Swartz, S. (ed.) 1982. *Papers in Warlpiri grammar*. Work Papers of SIL [Summer Institute of Linguistics], Series A, 6.
Tabouret-Keller, A. 1972. A contribution to the sociological study of language maintenance and language shift. In Fishman 1972.
Tannen, D. 1982a. Oral and literate strategies in spoken and written narratives. *Language* 58:1–21.
    (ed.) 1982b. *Spoken and written language*. Norwood, NJ: Ablex Publishing Co.
Tauli, V. 1966. *Structural tendencies in Uralic languages*. The Hague:Mouton.
Taylor, A. R. 1982. 'Male' and 'female' speech in Gros Ventre. *Anthropological Linguistics* 24:301–7.
    1983. The many names of the White Clay People. *International Journal of American Linguistics* 49:429–34.
    Forthcoming. Language obscolescence, shift, and death in native American communities. *International Journal of the Sociology of Language*.
Thom, R. 1975. *Structural stability and morphogenesis:An outline of a general theory of models*. (Trans. by D. Fowler.) Reading, MA:W.A: Benjamins.
Thomason, S. G. 1983a. Chinook Jargon in a real and historical context. *Language* 59:820–71.
    1983b. Genetic relationship and the case of Ma'a (Mbugu). *Studies in African Linguistics* 14:195–231.
Thomson, D. S. (ed.) 1976. *Gáidhlig ann an Albainn/Gaelic in Scotland*. Glasgow:Gairm.
    (ed.) 1983. *A companion to Gaelic studies*. Oxford:Blackwell.
Thorne, B., Kramarae, C. & Henley, N. (eds.) 1983. *Language, gender and society*. Rowley, MA:Newbury House Publishers.
Timm, L. A. 1980. Bilingualism, diglossia and language shift in Brittany. *International Journal of the Sociology of Language* 25:29–41.
    1982. Language treatment in Brittany. *Language Planning Newsletter* 8(3):1–6.
Todd, L. 1974. *Pidgins and creoles*. London:Routledge & Kegan Paul.
Tomlin, R. (ed.) 1987. *Coherence and grounding in discourse*. Amsterdam:Benjamins.
Tompa, J. (ed.) 1970. *A mai magyar nyelv rendszere* [*The structure of modern Hungarian*]. Budapest:Akadémiai Kiadó.
Tornay, S. 1978. L'enige des Murle de l'Omo. *L'Ethnographie* 76:57–75.
Trigger, B. G. 1965. *History and settlement in Lower Nubia*. New Haven:Yale University Press.

1976. *Nubia under the pharaohs.* London:Thames & Hudson.
(ed.) 1978. *Handbook of North American Indians:Northeast.* Washington, DC:Smithsonian Institution.
Trudel, C. 1982. *Welland.* Ottawa:Centre franco-ontarien de ressources pédagogiques.
Trudgill, P. 1978. Creolization in reverse. *Transactions of the Philological Society* 1976–7:32–50.
1983. *On dialect.* Oxford:Basil Blackwell.
1984a. Contact and mixture in colonial English dialects. Paper presented at the NWAVE-13 conference, University of Pennsylvania (Philadelphia).
(ed.) 1984b. *Language in the British Isles.* Cambridge:Cambridge University Press.
& Tzavaras, G. 1977. Why Albanian Greeks are not Albanians:Language shift in Attica and Biotia. In Giles 1977.
Tsitsipis, L. D. 1981a. Language change and language death in Albanian speech communities in Greece:A sociolinguistic study. Ph.D. dissertation, University of Wisconsin, Madison.
1981b. Arvanítika language change in speech communities in Greece. In Aronson & Darden 1981.
1983a. Narrative performance in a dying language:Evidence from Albanian in Greece. *Word* 34:25–36.
1983b. Language shift among the Albanian speakers of Greece. *Anthropological Linguistics* 25:288–308.
1984. Functional restriction and grammatical reduction in Albanian language in Greece. *Zeitschrift für Balkanologie*, 20:122–31.
1988. Language shift and narrative performance:on the structure and function of Arvanítika narratives. *Language in Society* 17(1):61–86.
Turton, D. & Bender, M. L. 1976. Mursi. In Bender 1976.
Tyler, S. 1973. *A history of Indian policy.* Washington:U.S. Government Printing Office.
Unseth, P. 1985. Report on the Majang. MS.
Urban, G. 1986. Ceremonial dialogues in South America. *American Anthropologist* 88:371–86.
Valdman, A. & Highfield, A. (eds.) 1980. *Theoretical orientations in creole studies.* New York:Academic Press.
Van den Broeck, J. 1977. Class differences in syntactic complexity in the Flemish town of Maaseik. *Language in Society* 6:149–82.
1984. Why do some people speak in a more complicated way than others? In Deprez 1984.
VanPatten, B. & Lee, J. R. (eds.) Forthcoming. *SLA-FLL:On the relationship between second language acquisition and foreign language learning.*
Varga, I. 1903. A Felsőőrvidek nepe es nyelve [The people and language of Felsőőr and vicinity]. *Nyelveszeti Fuzetek* 9.
Vilkko, M.-L. 1974. Englantilainen lainavaikutus amerikansuomalaisen sanomalehden ilmoitusten kieleen. Ph.D dissertation, Castrenianum, Helsinki University.
Voegelin, C. F. & Voegelin, F. M. 1977a. *Classification and index of the world's languages.* New York:Elsevier.
1977b. Is Tübatulabal de-acquisition relevant to theories of language acquisition? *International Journal of American Linguistics* 43:333–6.
Vossen, R. 1980. Grundzüge der Territorialgeschichte der Maa-sprechenden Bevölkerung Ostafrikas. *Paideuma* 26:93–121.

1982. *The eastern Nilotes: Linguistic and historical reconstructions.* Berlin:Dietrich Reimer.

& Claudi, U. (eds.) 1983. *Sprache, Geschichte und Kultur in Afrika.* Hamburg:Helmut Buske.

Wagner, H. 1958. *Linguistic atlas and survey of Irish dialects.* Dublin:Dublin Institute for Advanced Studies.

Wall, M. 1969. The decline of the Irish language. In Ó Cuív 1969.

Wallerstein, I. 1976. *The modern world-system,* vol. 1. New York:Academic Press.

Wande, E. 1984. Two Finnish minorities in Sweden. *Journal of Multilingual and Multicultural Development* 5:3–4.

Wanner, E. & Gleitman, L. (eds.) 1982. *Language acquisition:The state of the art.* New York:Cambridge University Press.

Warkentyne, H. (ed.) 1984. *Papers from the Fifth International Conference on Methods in Dialectology.* Victoria, BC:University of Victoria.

Watson, S. 1983. Loan-words and initial mutations in a Gaelic dialect. *Scottish Gaelic Studies* 14(1):100–13.

1986. The sounds of Easter Ross Gaelic:Historical development. *Scottish Gaelic Studies* 14(2):51–93.

Wayland, E. J. 1931. Preliminary studies of the tribes of Karamoja. *Journal of the Royal Anthropological Institute* 61:187–230.

Weber, E. 1976. *Peasants into Frenchmen:The modernization of rural France 1870–1914.* Palo Alto CA:Stanford University Press.

Weber, M. 1958. *The Protestant ethic and the spirit of capitalism.* (Trans. by T. Parsons.) New York:Charles Scribner's Sons.

Weinreich, U. 1966. *Languages in contact.* The Hague:Mouton.

Weist, R. M. 1986. Tense and aspect. In Fletcher & Garman 1986.

Westermann, D. 1911. *Die Sudansprachen.* Hamburg:L. & R. Friederichsen.

Whinnom, K. 1971. Linguistic hybridization and the 'special case' of pidgins and creoles. In Hymes 1971.

White, M. E., Englebrecht, W. E. & Tooker, E. 1978. Cayuga. In Trigger 1978.

Widgren, J. 1980. *Invandrar politik.* Lund:Liber Läromedel.

Williams, R. 1973a. Base and superstructure in Marxist cultural theory. *New Left Review* 87:3–16.

1973b. *The country and the city.* New York:Oxford University Press.

1980. Base and superstructure in Marxist cultural theory. In *Problems in materialism and culture:Selected essays.* London:Verso.

Wilson, J. 1960. The Texas German of Lee and Fayette Counties. *Rice University Studies* 47:83–98.

Winter, J. Ch. 1979. Language shift among the Aasáx, a hunter–gatherer tribe in Tanzania. *Sprache und Geschichte in Afrika* 1:175–204.

Withers, C. W. J. 1985. *Gaelic in Scotland 1689–1981.* Edinburgh:John Donald.

Wolfram, W. 1969. *A sociolinguistic description of Detroit negro speech.* Washington, DC:Center for Applied Linguistics.

Wong-Fillmore, L. 1976. The second time around:Cognitive and social strategies in second language acquisition. Ph.D. dissertation, Stanford University.

1979. Individual differences in language ability and language behavior. In Fillmore, Kempler, & Wang 1979.

Woolard, K. 1985a. Language variation and cultural hegemony:Toward an integration of sociolinguistic and social theory. *American Ethnologist* 12:738–48.

1985b. Status and solidarity in sociolinguistic theory. Paper delivered at the American Ethnological Society Meetings, Toronto, Canada.

1987. Codeswitching and comedy in Catalonia. *Papers in Pragmatics* 1.
1989. *Double talk: Bilingualism and the politics of ethnicity in Catalonia.* Palo Alto:Stanford University Press.
Wright, J. 1907. *Historical German grammar.* Oxford:The Oxford University Press.
Yallop, C. 1982. *Australian Aboriginal languages.* London:Deutsch.
Yngve, V. H. 1960. A model and an hypothesis for language structure. *Proceedings of the American Philosophical Society* 104:444–66. Also reprinted as no. 101, Bobbs-Merrill Reprint Series in Language and Linguistics.
Zobl, H. 1980. The formal and developmental selectivity of L1 influence on L2 acquisition. *Language Learning* 30:43–57.

Index of languages

Entries for language families are in capital letters; entries for branches of language families are italicized. In the case of language-family branches with many sub-branches, only some of which are explicitly identified in a given chapter, placement of a sub-branch division may be supplied parenthetically. Proto-languages and ancestral forms of modern languages are given separate entries, likewise supranational standard languages; hence separate entries for (e.g.) Proto-Iroquoian, Common Albanian, Anglo-Saxon, Classical Arabic.

General index

In keeping with the purpose stated in the Preface and Introduction, namely furthering cross-communication among the scholars and students of various fields and subfields for which the subject of language obsolescence has actual or potential interest, this general index is cast in a form designed in the hope of meeting a variety of needs. Ideally it should be possible for the reader who wishes to trace the interconnection between the decline of venerable subsistence modes or traditional occupations and the loss of an ethnic language or dialect to pursue that interest as easily as another reader might pursue the fate of marked vs. unmarked linguistic features during language obsolescence. A user's guide to the index follows.

Main entries are in the form of nouns, for the most part; an adjective deriving from a particular noun then appears as an indented subentry beneath it: thus *dominance* is a main entry, *dominant* a subentry. Count nouns as main entries appear by and large in plural form, the plural taken to subsume the singular of the same noun. Where nominal forms with -*s* have specialized meanings, especially in linguistic connections (e.g. *communications* vs. *communication*, *conjunctions* vs. *conjunction*), separate main entries appear for each meaning.

In cases where modifiers which precede a noun and modifiers which follow it are both entered, preceding modifiers always appear first. The entries with following modifier then appear indented, to indicate the change in modification structure (and ordering), as in the following example:

> nouns, . . .; abstract, . . .; relational, . . .;
>> subject, . . .
> noun classes, . . .; stem, . . .; system, . . .

Main entries which cluster around a single root all forms of which have approximately the same importance to the volume's themes are grouped serially, set off from each other by commas, if the page references are not too numerous: thus a subsistence mode which takes its importance from association with rural as opposed to urban lifeways appears in the clustered serial entry-form *farmers, farming, farms*.

In multiword subentries (also occasionally main entries), semantically close words each of which occurs with the same modifier or each of which has the same general thematic significance appear separated by slashes: thus *ancestral language/speech/tongue*.

Parenthesized material following an entry represents grouping by general theme rather than by actual word(s). Under *distinctions* the entry (*phonological*) includes references to phonological distinctions of both phonetic and phonemic sorts. In contrast, the unparenthesized entry *distinctions* which appears to the right of *phonological* (subentry to *phonology*) refers to occurrences of the phrase *phonological distinctions* in the text, while a separate occurrence of *distinctions* under the *phonemic* subentry to *phoneme* accounts for instances of *phonemic distinctions*. Unparenthesized multiword entries usually appear in full form on the pages listed; the chief exceptions are entries in which *language* is the first word: *language use*, for example, includes many instances of the type: *the [instructional] use of [language name]*, or *[language name] is no longer in [regular] use*.

Placename entries are chiefly by country, and provinces, regions, states, etc., appear as subentries; islands, however, are given entries of their own, free-standing or under the country of which they are part, in recognition of the often distinct and discrete linguistic and

426

cultural features which they display as relatively closed communities. Compass-point distinctions (eastern, southern, etc.) are given only where an entire continent is in question: see the entry for *Africa*.

Bold face numbers represent chapters or chapter sections which include the subject of the entry in their title.

restricted language/variety, 314, 369;
restricted Hungarian, **313–31**
restructuring 30, 236, 240
re-syntactification, 381
retention: (linguistic and cultural features),
25, 133, 254, 257, 262, 272, 301, 306,
314, 326, 358, 379; *see also* language/
dialect retention
revival: (ethnicity), 97; *see also* language
revival, religion
revolution, 76–7, 87, 118, 243, 309
rhetoric, 341
rhetorical conventions, 316; devices/skills,
245
roads, roadways, 7, 35–6, 40, 76, 121, 141
rote learning, 339; *see also* knowledge
rote(-learned) forms/items, 320, 340, 342
ritual, 27, 99, 114, 171, 182, 185, 244;
language, 186, 195, 341
roots (gr.), 179, 195, 231, 247, 252, 255,
320–3, 326–8
rules, 56, 121, 126–8, 144, 174–5, 189–90,
207, 220, 230–1, 236, 251, 263–6, 280,
322, 337, 339–40, 343, 352, 356, 373,
378–81, 387–9; obligatory, 189, 379;
optional, 379; *see also* morphology,
semantics, substitutions, syntax
rural: areas, 79, 112, 141; communities, 80,
143; context, 147; districts, 52; dwellers,
79, 96; language, 84; life, 53, 79;
overpopulation, 287; settlements, 62,
70, 73; society, 79, 82; speakers, 70, 84;
see also identity
rusty speaker, 345

salvage work, 170, 183
saliency, 341, 343
Scandinavia, 227
schooling, 61, 105, 214, 272, 291, 308, 341;
see also bilingualism
schools: (availability/presence), 33–5, 37, 94,
97–8, 104–5, 260, 268–9; (superordinate
language used), 39, 49, 62, 67, 73, 77,
80–1, 100, 108–9, 143, 147, 163, 215,
223–4, 269, 289, 318, 341, 343, 375;
(contracting/obsolescing language
limited or excluded), 68, 77–8, 80, 83,
88–9, 101, 119, 140, 223, 259, 269, 289;
(contracting/obsolescing language
provided for in the curriculum or taught
in ethnic school), 51, 62, 67, 71, 85–6,
88, 99, 110, 114, 172–3, 228–9, 233, 268,
284–5, 288–93, 295–6, 307, 311, 331,
341, 372; (domain), 291, 299, 303,
307–8, 311–12, 327; *see also* religion
language of school, 319
schoolteachers: *see* teachers
Scotland, 7, 41–2, 44–7, 49, 51, 53–4, 58,

114–15, 147, 205–9, 298; Argyll, 206–8;
Outer Hebrides, 47, 58, 209; Ross-shire,
44, 48, 53, 56; St Kilda, 209–10;
Sutherland, 103, 109, 199, 205, 210, 298;
Western Isles, 44, 105
second language, 19, 38, 84–5, 111, 261, 263,
371, 385–6, 388, 391–2
second-language speakers, 33, 38; *see also*
acquisition, language learning
segments, 58, 121, 126, 128, 134, 200, 252,
362, 387
self-assessment, 310
self-evaluation, 298
self-definition/ -identification, 9, 41
self-image, 95, 344
self-report, 232
semantics, 174, 239, 322, 350
semantic component, 246; constraints,
322; differentiation, 133; domains, 372;
factors, 338; features, 241; material,
320; paradigms, 338; range, 240;
relations, 193, 323; resemblance, 343;
rules, 378; shift, 280; structures, 175;
value, 227
semi-speakers, 5, 35, 37–8, 40, 56, 98, 106,
119–20, 136, 139, 174–7, 179, 181,
184–5, 187, 192–4, 197, 206–7, 212,
261–4, 266, 314, 331, 340, 350, 352–3,
366, 371, 377, 380, 394; former, 38;
limited, 198; terminal, 198; weak, 181,
184
sentences, 150, 203, 229, 241, 263, 274, 286,
320, 339, 343–5; complex,114, 149–50,
152, 163, 184, 255; conjoined, 344;
matrix, 149; negated, 232, 237; simple,
150, 152; test, 215–23, 234–8, 260, 262,
264
separatism, 78
separatists: religious, 211–26
settlement: (location/creation), 3, 18, 62, 68,
70, 73, 140–1, 148, 211, 268–9, 284;
(size), 18, 141, 268; (time depth), 64,
105, 109, 140, 223, **287–8**, 301
settlers, 104, 118, 140, 142, 303
sex: (as a variable), 143, 145–7, 310, 374; (in
form selection), 173, 264
shrinkage, shrinking (lg.), **195**, 255, 257, 372
shrinking language, 4–5, 41
simplicity, 335, 349–50
simplification, 6, 56, 119, **150–3**, 154, 158,
267, 298, **299–303**, 308–9, 312, 335–6,
348–51, 373, 382–3, **386**, 390, 393; *see
also* grammar, morphology
singular, 175, 260, 280–1, 283, 390
skills, **8**, 70, 117, 131, 228, 234, 306, 337;
language, 8, 229, 260, **259–66**, 292, 308,
371; linguistic, 55, 265, 285, 344;
literacy, 285; passive, 224; productive/

writing, 8, 70, 88, 172, 229, 271; *see also* religion

written communication, 151; form, 47, 274; language, 56, 149, 259; *see also* tradition

young people's/speakers' dialect/version (or proper name of a language), 2, 152, 212, 230, 267, 329, 360, 393

young speakers, 126, 182, 212, 230, 241, 261, 305, 314, 317, 321, 323–31, 360–1; younger, 52, 55, 140, 143–5, 197, 212–13, 229, 240, 272, 300, 303, 320, 344, 392–3; youngest, 42, 69, 206, 217–18, 144, 320, 371

Yugoslavia, 136; Croatia, 209; Makedonija, 202–4

Printed in the United Kingdom
by Lightning Source UK Ltd.
9768300001B/142-147